POULENC

BOOKS BY GRAHAM JOHNSON

Franz Schubert: The Complete Songs, translations of song texts
by Richard Wigmore

Gabriel Fauré: The Songs and Their Poets, translations of song
texts by Richard Stokes

Britten: Voice and Piano

A French Song Companion, with Richard Stokes

*The Songmakers' Almanac: Twenty Years of Song Recitals
in London*

The Spanish Song Companion, with Jacqueline Cockburn and
Richard Stokes

POULENC

THE LIFE IN THE SONGS

GRAHAM JOHNSON

Translations of the song texts by Jeremy Sams

LIVERIGHT PUBLISHING CORPORATION
A Division of
W. W. Norton & Company
Independent Publishers Since 1923
New York   London

The publisher would like to acknowledge the generous support of
Guildhall School of Music & Drama, London.

For information about permission to reproduce selections from this book,
write to Permissions, Liveright Publishing Corporation, a division of
W. W. Norton & Company, Inc., 500 Fifth Avenue, New York, NY 10110

For information about special discounts for bulk purchases, please contact
W. W. Norton Special Sales at specialsales@wwnorton.com or 800-233-4830

Manufacturing by LSC Communications, Harrisonburg
Book design by Helen Berinsky
Production manager: Anna Oler

Library of Congress Cataloging-in-Publication Data

Names: Johnson, Graham, 1950– author. | Sams, Jeremy, translator.
Title: Poulenc : the life in the songs / Graham Johnson ;
translations of the song texts by Jeremy Sams.
Description: First edition. | New York : Liveright Publishing Corporation, 2020. |
Includes bibliographical references and index.
Identifiers: LCCN 2020010683 | ISBN 9781631495236 (hardcover) |
ISBN 9781631495243 (epub)
Subjects: LCSH: Poulenc, Francis, 1899–1963. | Composers—France—Biography.
Classification: LCC ML410.P787 J65 2020 | DDC 782.42168092 [B]—dc23
LC record available at https://lccn.loc.gov/2020010683

Liveright Publishing Corporation, 500 Fifth Avenue, New York, N.Y. 10110
www.wwnorton.com

W. W. Norton & Company Ltd., 15 Carlisle Street, London W1D 3BS

1 2 3 4 5 6 7 8 9 0

For Flott, the recital partner of a lifetime

Dame Felicity Lott at the window of the music room of Le Grand
Coteau, Noizay.

In Paris they all said "How Francis would have loved you,
Composed for you his newest mélodie,
Your voice and style adorable in Poulenc!"
While your pianist dreamed that he
Might learn the secret of the absent master's touch
And magically accompany.

Contents

∘ III ∘

◦ V ◦

∘ VI ∘

Preface

OF POULENC'S GENIUS, AND OF HIS IMPORTANCE IN FRENCH MUSIC, THERE CAN now be little doubt. It has been more than half a century since his death, and the passing of time has done little to diminish his reputation; indeed, the opposite is true. On the day of his unexpected demise, 30 January 1963, it could not be stated with any certainty that his compositions would endure. Cultural values were changing with dizzying speed in a new age of science, with a British prime minister promising that the future lay in "the white heat of technology." The Cuban missile crisis had recently threatened universal destruction, the Soviet Union had launched a man into space, and it seemed as if the arts were destined, or doomed, to rocket into the same trajectory. The serialists of the "Domaine musicale" and Darmstadt, Pierre Boulez and Karlheinz Stockhausen and their disciples, were convinced that the future of music was theirs for the taking, and that the public would soon be weaned from a diet of compositions by insignificant tonal dabblers. At the times of their passing, both Poulenc and Benjamin Britten (they died thirteen years apart, at almost the same age) had faced up to the prospect of being more or less forgotten.

And yet both composers are now acknowledged as among the twentieth century's most significant masters of vocal music—solo, choral, and operatic—quite apart from their achievements in instrumental spheres. Poulenc was always content to measure his success and status in national rather than international terms: Parisian opinion counted most, and French song, not German, English, or American, was what really mattered to him. Just as Hugo Wolf in Vienna (caring not at all what Gabriel Fauré or Claude Debussy might be doing) opined that no one had written songs like his since Franz Schubert and Robert Schumann, Poulenc (far too diplomatic to boast openly but more direct with friends) was no shrinking violet when it came to his own private estimation of where his mélodies stood in the world: "*In the field of song I fear no one, and being the best* ["la primauté"] *is always very pleasant.*"[1] Posterity has come to agree with him, more or less: his songs feature on singers' programs throughout the world, while those of most of his contemporaries (the other members of Les Six, for example) appear only occasionally and modestly.

But while it is true that Poulenc's songs are everywhere loved and enjoyed, one cannot always assume that they are taken seriously. It might be fair to say that some of his music is loved for the wrong reasons, even if treated affectionately and indulgently. To amuse and delight was not his only aim. What it cost Poulenc to create his life's work has always been underestimated, as has the almost Proustian manner in which he drew on his visual memories and pricked up his avid, pickpocketing ears to create a synthesis of his own past and present—a brand of nostalgia so much his own that "nostalgia" seems inadequate, not creative and forward-looking enough, just as that word is thoroughly unequal to defining Proust's searches for lost time. Perhaps we are now at a sufficient distance from Poulenc's era to understand how truly extraordinary his music is, a one-off. In fact, we should be very grateful that he had a composing career at all; it needed propitious circumstances and great personal determination and bravery, effrontery even, for such a fragile and unusual talent to thrive.

It was similarly touch and go whether Schumann, initially known as a pianist and critic, would become a composer. I regard this great German Romantic as one of Poulenc's spiritual antecedents, not least in terms of a mysterious affinity with poets: Schumann's with Heinrich Heine and Joseph von Eichendorff and Poulenc's with Apollinaire and Paul Éluard. Schumann's route to the making of music was spectacularly different from that of his musical forebears: he was inspired by verbal and literary allusions, his piano music of the late 1830s freshly woven from the prose of Jean Paul and E. T. A. Hoffmann. We also hear his homage to composers as widely different as Frédéric Chopin and J. S. Bach—Chopin (and later Brahms) receiving open-hearted and generous compliments.[2]

The pathway of Poulenc, pianist and potential dilettante, was strangely similar to that of Schumann. During a remarkable period of musical diversity in the aftermath of the First World War, young Francis became a composer by dint of translating and conjuring his memories and impressions into musical forms of unlikely potency. When vocal lines and Apollinaire poems were added to the mix, the results were even more powerful. His visual take on the world was a vital part of this process, but his memories were also associated with the music he had heard, music of every kind. His assimilations of the work of other composers (the best of whom he acknowledged in a generously Schumann-like manner) are love-borrowings, and thus nostalgic by their very nature, rather than plagiarism. Poulenc invented an allusive category of imitation-cum-originality hitherto unknown in music, which is, somewhat paradoxically, definitively inimitable—as several would-be Poulenc imitators have found out to their cost.

I now see Poulenc (and who he is as a musician) differently from when I first took to the airwaves of BBC Radio 3 in 1977 to present, with Elaine Padmore, a

series of thirteen substantial programs encompassing all of Poulenc's songs, entitled *Journal de mes mélodies*. One of my principal sources of information was the
Correspondance, gathered together by Hélène de Wendel and published in 1967.
In it there was hardly the sounding of a problematic note: all was "luxe, calme,"
and a very respectable kind of "volupté"—with mention of neither homosexuality nor emotional crises. An almost complete discretion was maintained by
the composer's great baritone Pierre Bernac, still alive and teaching at the time,
who had taught me in master classes and journeyed to London to record with
me *L'Histoire de Babar, le petit éléphant.*[3] As part of the BBC series, I interviewed
Bernac, who knew everything about the darker side of Poulenc's nature but was
prepared to divulge very little, even years after the composer's death. The only
thing he mentioned, in private conversation, was his fear for Poulenc's safety
when he insisted on going out in the middle of the night (when the duo were on
tour) to look for sexual adventure, leaving his wallet in the safekeeping of his
singer colleague.

The composer's homosexuality had long been assumed from the absence of a
Mme Poulenc. Students of Les Six can easily read about those formidable wives
Nora Auric and Madeleine Milhaud; the great singer Claire Croiza had a child by
Honegger, who later married the pianist Andrée Vaurabourg; Germaine Tailleferre married a cartoonist (whom she later divorced); and even the elusive Louis
Durey was married. Poulenc, whose music has proved to be the most enduring, was the exception. Long before I met Bernac, the critic Felix Aprahamian (a
friend of Poulenc's, and useful to his cause in London) assured me that the singer
had never been the composer's lover. In fact, Bernac and Poulenc addressed each
other as "vous" to the end of their association. Like many people, I had earlier
assumed a Pears-Britten romantic equivalence in their duo relationship. I also
learned that "Francis" had a long relationship with one Raymond Destouches
(the dedicatee, I knew, of a beautiful piano piece, *Mélancolie*), who had lived in
Noizay. This seemed like insider information at the time (Raymond was never
mentioned on any of the occasions when, some years later, I was a house guest of
the composer's niece). Aprahamian could not resist adding that on account of the
composer's friendship with this former taxi driver, Poulenc was known in malicious Parisian circles as "La Princesse de Thun et Taxis." Destouches remained
something of a legendary figure because no one outside the inner circle even
knew what he looked like. I am grateful to Benoît Seringe for lifting what seems
to have been an unofficial family embargo on the iconography (such as it is) of
Poulenc's three important lovers in time to be included in this book.

At the time I presented the BBC's series, the composer's own narrative voice
was behind much if not all the information that was to hand—and, of course,
how enchanted I was by *him,* not just his music. In fact, I wanted to slightly
change the words that conclude Poulenc's own book on Emmanuel Chabrier

("*Cher Chabrier, comme on vous aime!*") and proclaim to the rooftops, "Dear Poulenc, how we love you!" What was there not to love? He was funny, gay in every sense; he was generous (both in financial terms, and in his admiration of the music of others); he was humble and open and relaxed, and disarmingly frank and uncomplicated (in comparison with the "difficult" Britten, for example); he was rich but not ostentatiously so; he tended to laziness (a very human quality) but seemed to compose music like falling off a log; he loved his food and wine; he was religious without being dogmatic; he had been an important figure in the Resistance (one took it for granted, I don't know why, that his sympathies were somewhat to the left, if not earnestly so); he was unfailingly charming to all who knew him—and nobody who wrote such tuneful songs, inflected with populist chanson and working-class nostalgia, could ever be called a snob; he was the quintessential Parisian, friend of the great poets and a natural member of the glamorous artistic elite. Above all, he had written all that adorable, heavenly music, and if those adjectives applied to the music, why should they not also have applied to its creator?

Much of the above paragraph (though certainly not all) I now consider to be inaccurate or simply not true. The essay that closes this book is intended to be something of a corrective to my rose-tinted evaluations in those early days. It is important for me to say, however, that a deepening awareness of the complications of the composer's life has not dimmed my affection for the man, or my love for his music. After all, why should the lieder giants—Schubert, Schumann, and Wolf—have the monopoly on tragedy and illness triumphantly surmounted? Is it a subconscious and unreasonable requirement we English speakers have of the French that they should amuse us more, and disturb us less, than the Germans?

This is no conventional biography, but rather a study of the songs that aims to place these important works within a biographical context without shying away from the facts that have emerged in the last few decades. And the songs form a biography in themselves. They show us almost everything about the man, and studying them gives us more information about Poulenc and his times than would be revealed by any study of his piano and chamber music, his religious music, or even his operas. It is in his songs, and understanding how they fit into his life—his real life, not the legendary construct that once so diverted me and led me astray (me and thousands of others)—that we are able to discover Francis Poulenc heart and soul.

1. Kerbastic (nicknamed "Kerker"), the summer home in Guildel, Brittany, of Jean and Marie-Blanche, the Comte and Comtesse de Polignac.
2. Le Tremblay, the place name designating the eighteenth-century Château Omonville in Normandy (thirty kilometers from Evreux), country residence of the Manceaux family.
3. Nogent-sur-Marne, small town on the banks of the river Marne and home of Poulenc's maternal grandparents.
4. Noizay, near Tours (Loire Valley), where Poulenc bought a large and comfortable home, Le Grand Coteau, in 1927.
5. Autun and Anost, small towns in the Morvan, Burgundy, and near the home of Poulenc's former nurse, where the composer frequently holidayed.
6. Lyon, the home of Suzanne Latarjet, married to the choral conductor André Latarjet and sister of Raymonde Linossier.
7. Brive-la-Gaillarde, in Corrèze, a place of refuge for the Poulenc family in June 1940, and the home of the composer's friend Marthe Bosredon.
8. Rocamadour, the famous shrine of the Black Virgin built into rock face of the Causses du Quercy. A visit here in 1936 led to Poulenc's reconversion to Catholicism.
9-10-11. Poulenc enjoyed his first international success in Monte Carlo in 1924, with his ballet Les Biches, and from the late 1950s was a regular guest at the Hôtel Majestic in Cannes. From 1958 he lived periodically in Bagnols-en-Forêt with Louis Gautier.

∘ I ∘

Francis Poulenc, aged eight, on the steps of his grandparents' mansion in Nogent-sur-Marne.

Outline of a Musical Life:

1855–1919

Quoted words in *italics* are those of Poulenc himself, throughout.

1855

Birth of Francis Poulenc's father, Émile Poulenc (d. 1917). *"My father came originally from Aveyron. He was, together with my two uncles, at the head of a very old chemical products firm which eventually became Rhône-Poulenc."*[1]

1862

Birth of FP's uncle and godfather Marcel Royer, nicknamed "Papoum" (d. 1945).

1865

Birth of FP's mother, Jenny Royer (d. 1915). *"My mother, of purely Parisian descent (since the beginning of the nineteenth century her family had only intermarried with Parisians), came from a line of cabinet-makers, bronze workers and tapestry weavers."*[2]

1885

(18 March) Marriage of FP's parents at the church of Saint-Denys-du-Saint-Sacrement, rue de Turenne, in the Marais district of Paris.

1887

Birth of FP's sister Jeanne Élise Marguerite, in Nogent-sur-Marne (d. 1974).

1888

Birth of FP's brother Louis Étienne (d. 1891). Another child was stillborn in May 1892.

1897

(25 March) Birth of Raymonde Linossier in Lyon. She would be a close friend of Poulenc from his childhood. "He never forgot the girl who enchanted his youth and adolescence, and who was the person who introduced him to literature," above all contemporary literature.[3]

1899

(7 January) Birth of Francis Jean Marcel Poulenc, "*in the very heart of Paris, a few yards away from the Madeleine*"—at 2, rue de Cambacérès, renamed place des Saussaies in 1901.[4]

"*I was born a few meters away from the Élysées Palace, when Félix Faure was president. Like Gilberte Swann I played in the Champs-Élysées,[5] and that was where I spent all my early childhood. On my mother's side I came from a family that was pure Parisian, which is rare in Paris. In marrying my father, who came from Aveyron, my mother went against a kind of family rule.*"[6]

"*The Madeleine district is the city of my birth, and Le Marais my village. And then a little farther away, continuing to the east of Paris, there is also my 'country': dear Nogent-sur-Marne where I spent my entire childhood.*"[7]

(12 January) Birth of the future singer Pierre Bernac (Pierre Bertin) in Paris.[8]

1904 (aged 5)

FP begins to learn the piano from his mother.

The very young Poulenc, seemingly already interested in literary pursuits, c. 1903–4.

1905 (aged 6)

FP's nurse ("Nounou," to whom he is devoted) is Marie-Françoise Lauxière (née Pastour, 1860–1931), a native of the Morvan, a region the composer would later visit on working holidays.

(9 December) The French law on the separation of church and state ("Laïcité") is enacted, ending government funding of religious groups and reinforcing the essentially secular nature of the French state. The appointment of a nonpracticing Catholic, the composer Gabriel Fauré, as director of the Paris Conservatoire is a sign of a new era.

1906 (aged 7)

(13 July) In one of the greatest and most complex of all French political scandals, Captain Alfred Dreyfus, a Jewish army officer falsely accused of treason in 1894, is finally exonerated and reinstated into the army.

1907 (aged 8)

"The Manifesto of modern art," Pablo Picasso's 1907 *Les Demoiselles d'Avignon*, "ties together ancient and modern references, popular, Parisian, Iberian, African, and opens up a new world. This great painting remained completely misunderstood in its own time."[9]

FP takes piano lessons from Mlle Melon, teaching assistant of pianist Cécile Boutet de Monvel, niece and pupil of composer César Franck. He practices every evening for an hour, and any spare time during the day is spent sight-reading at the piano. His favorite work is Mozart's *Fantasy in C Minor*.

FP hears Claude Debussy's *Danse sacrée et profane* played by a harpist and is fascinated by the "out-of-tune" ninths.

At a student concert in which his sister takes part, FP hears Gabriel Fauré accompany his own songs. "*When my sister, who studied with* [Jeanne] *Raunay and* [Claire] *Croiza, sang Schumann, Schubert, Debussy, perfectly accompanied by my mother, I went to the piano and closed my eyes with happiness. When Fauré's turn came I said 'Not Fauré!'*"[10]

By now FP is familiar with the work of such great stage personalities as Sarah Bernhardt, Gabrielle Réjane, and Eva Lavallière.

During a stay in Vichy, FP hears a phonograph for the first time. The sound of the first disc, the *Marche Lorraine* of Louis Ganne (1862–1923), terrifies him, but he is won over by the sound of the voice in a chanson with words risqué enough to embarrass his mother.[11]

"*My mother played the piano exquisitely. In those times the ladies of the bourgeoisie didn't have the almost professional technique they have nowadays, but my mother with her impeccable musicality and ravishing touch cast a spell over my childhood. Her favorite composers were Mozart, Chopin, Schubert, and Schumann."*[12]

1909 (aged 10)

"I was brought up on the knees of the tenor Édouard Clément and by the time I was ten, Carmen, La Bohème *and* Manon *held no secrets for me."*[13]

The precocious FP learns how to play bridge; he is later to play the game regularly with Sergei Prokofiev and with Darius Milhaud.

"At the age of ten I knew [Stéphane] Mallarmé's 'Apparition' by heart, and for several months I dreamt of becoming a great actor. The classical matinées at the Comédie-Française had turned my head. . . . I have to confess that the occasion of being confirmed by Monsignor Amette at the end of the same year had inclined me toward a cardinal's purple."[14]

1910 (aged 11)

"The following winter, I had, if I may so put it, found my vocation and decided to become a singer. . . . At that period heaven had blessed me with a nice voice. . . . in my childish mezzo I spent my time sight-reading songs by Schumann, Fauré, Duparc and Debussy."[15]

At the beginning of this decade, the Poulenc family's chemical firm, employing more than 500 workers, with 11 pharmacists, 5 civil engineers, and 19 chemists, transfers its factories from Ivry to Vitry-sur-Seine.[16]

The young FP, exiled from Paris and staying in Fontainebleau during a disastrous flood when the Seine overflowed its banks, discovers Franz Schubert's song cycle *Winterreise* (*Le Voyage d'hiver*). He plays the whole score through *"from magic moment to magic moment,"* thoroughly absorbed.

FP's first piano piece, *En Barque*, dates from this period.[17]

1911 (aged 12)

On holiday in Bagnères-de-Luchon and Biarritz in August, FP hears a performance of Giacomo Puccini's *Tosca*, and some weeks later one of Georges Bizet's *Carmen*. Both operas make an impression, especially *Carmen*, of which Poulenc—already a partisan of contemporary music—writes: *"It's not modern, no dissonances, but it doesn't matter."*

1912 (aged 13)

At a recital given by piano pupils of Mlle Boutet de Montvel, Poulenc admires a young girl he had seen walking near the Champs-Élysées a few years earlier, the beautiful Marguerite di Pietro—the future Marie-Blanche de Polignac (1897–1958), daughter of couturier Jeanne Lanvin.[18]

FP hears Claude Debussy accompany soprano Maggie Teyte at the Théâtre Marigny in the first book of his *Fêtes galantes*.[19] Later, in a clothing store, he surreptitiously touches the lining of Debussy's hat, left on a chair while the great composer was making a phone call: "*I was blushing with pleasure, shame and timidity.*"[20]

FP discovers the music of Modest Musorgsky.[21] He begins to accompany his sister's voice lessons with the mezzo-soprano Claire Croiza (1882–1946), much preferring Debussy's *Ariettes oubliées* to Fauré's *La Bonne Chanson*.

Apart from regular parentally approved visits to the Opéra and Opéra-Comique, FP, with the complicity of the family cook, begins secretly to visit Le Petit Casino, a music hall on the boulevard de Montmartre; La Scala and L'Eldorado in the insalubrious boulevard de Strasbourg; and the Folies Bergère. (See "The Sexual Milieu of Francis Poulenc," p. 194.)

FP begins to read contemporary poetry, including works by Guillaume Apollinaire: "*From as early as 1912 I was fascinated by everything of his I read.*"[22]

1913 (aged 14)

Thanks to his Uncle "Papoum," FP is present at one of the first performances of Stravinsky's *The Rite of Spring*.

"*I have to say I was quite good at getting through the notes ('getting through' is the only phrase to describe my lack of piano technique at the time). That's how I was able, in 1913 at the age of 14, to enjoy Debussy, Ravel and Stravinsky.*"[23]

1914 (aged 15)

On the recommendation of his mother's pianist friend Geneviève Sienkiewicz (1878–1971), who will remain a lifelong friend, FP begins piano lessons with the Catalan pianist Ricardo Viñes (1875–1943). "*That meeting with Viñes was paramount in my life: I owe him everything . . . my fledgling efforts in composition and everything I know about the piano.*"[24] Lessons with Viñes will continue until 1917.

At a listening booth in the Maison Pathé, FP hears a recording of pianist Édouard Risler playing *Idylle* from the *Dix Pièces pittoresques* of Emmanuel Chabrier, a *coup de foudre* prompting lifelong veneration: Chabrier "*caused tenderness and joy to enter into French music.*"[25]

(3 August) Germany declares war on France. The First Battle of the Marne halts the German advance on Paris (4–13 September).

(14 December) Birth of Brigitte Manceaux (d. 1963), FP's elder niece (his sister Jeanne's daughter) and from her late teens a close confidante of the composer, often assuming the role of unofficial private secretary.

1915 (aged 16)

FP meets Darius Milhaud (1892–1974) and attends an all-Milhaud concert in Paris in May. The two will become close friends after Milhaud returns in late 1918 from a sojourn in Brazil with ambassador and poet Paul Claudel.

(2 June) Jenny Poulenc, FP's mother, dies. No contemporary reaction on FP's part to this unexpected early death survives.

At the end of the year FP sends out a questionnaire to famous composers asking for their opinions of César Franck and his music. He receives replies from Debussy, Vincent D'Indy, Guy Ropartz, Albert Roussel, Erik Satie, and Camille Saint-Saëns.

1916 (aged 17)

FP passes the first part of his *baccalauréat* (he never completes the second) and is rewarded by his father with a camera; the Poulenc firm is closely associated with the manufacture of chemicals used in photography.

FP composes more piano pieces, *Processional pour la crémation d'un mandarin* and *Préludes*, which he will later destroy.

(21 February) The Battle of Verdun begins. While fighting at the front, the poet Guillaume Apollinaire receives a serious head wound (17 March).

Through Ricardo Viñes, FP meets composer Georges Auric (1899–1983), living at the time in a small room in Montmartre with an out-of-tune piano laden with scores of every kind—the initiation of the first of FP's great friendships with a musical contemporary. Later Viñes will furnish introductions to such key figures in his life as Jean Cocteau, Manuel de Falla, harpsichordist Wanda Landowska, and pianist Marcelle Meyer.

FP is taken by his childhood friend Raymonde Linossier to visit the bookshop of Adrienne Monnier, La Maison des Amis des Livres (at 7, rue de l'Odéon), where he will later meet poets Paul Éluard, André Breton, and Louis Aragon.[26]

(July–November) More than 65,000 French lives are lost in the Battle of the Somme.

When FP sees Igor Stravinsky in a music shop, "*I thought that God had entered the room.*"[27]

1917 (aged 18)

Through Ricardo Viñes, FP meets Erik Satie (1866–1925), a composer he comes to consider an alternative guru to Debussy and Stravinsky.

(March) FP plays to Maurice Ravel, who is critical and bad-tempered.[28]

(Spring) **Rapsodie nègre FP3** (Kangourou), composed in Paris.

(6 April) The United States enters the Great War in Europe.

(5 May) FP hears the first performance of Debussy's Violin Sonata, played by Gaston Poulet accompanied by the composer.

More composers come into FP's circle. He meets Arthur Honegger (1892–1955) at the home of the mezzo-soprano Jane Bathori, on the boulevard Pereire; there, André Caplet (1878–1925) conducts a choral ensemble, in which composer Charles Koechlin and Ricardo Viñes sing the bass line. (FP, who also sang, remembered being chided by Honegger for solfège mistakes.) He also meets two future members of Les Six, Louis Durey (1888–1979) and Germaine Tailleferre (1892–1983).

(18 May) FP attends the first performance at the Théâtre du Châtelet of *Parade*, a "ballet réaliste" with music by Erik Satie and décor by Picasso.

Raymond Radiguet (1903–1923), a precocious writer, takes FP to meet the poet Max Jacob (see p. 375) in Jacob's lodgings in Montmartre.

(24 June) FP attends the first performance of Apollinaire's surrealistic play *Les Mamelles de Tirésias*, at the Théâtre René Maubel in Montmartre. He had possibly met Apollinaire earlier at the home of Valentine Hugo (1887–1968).[29] It is more certain that he hears the poet give a reading at Monnier's bookshop.

(15 July) FP's father, Émile Poulenc, dies. As with his mother, there is no surviving documentary reaction from the son to this loss. Poulenc, technically an orphan who has not yet attained his majority, is placed under the

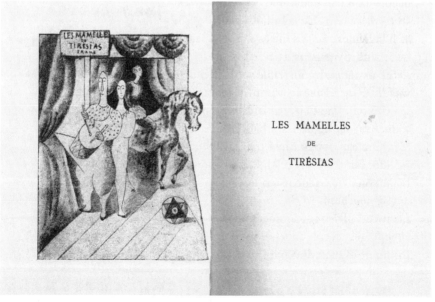

Title page of Apollinaire's "Drame surréaliste" Les Mamelles de Tirésias *(1918), with frontispiece by Serge Férat (1881–1958).*

care of a "curateur" at 3, rue de Saint-Simon. He then moves in with with his sister and brother-in-law, André Manceaux (1883–1967), at 76, rue de Monceau. When the Manceaux move to 83, rue de Monceau in 1919, FP occupies a bachelor flat ("garçonnière") above what had been the stables.

Through his friend Emmanuel Faÿ, FP meets the patron of music and art Comte Étienne de Beaumont (1883–1956).

(26 September) FP, in search of a composition teacher, has an explosive encounter with the conductor Paul Vidal (1863–1931), who all but throws the young composer out on reading through the score of *Rapsodie nègre* and noticing its dedication to Erik Satie.[30]

Satie, delighted with the Vidal fiasco, takes Poulenc under his wing as a member of "Les Nouveaux Jeunes," a group of composers that includes Auric, Louis Durey, Honegger, and Satie as patron. *"The orchestration of* Parade *and the transparency of* Socrate *were the two influences that enabled us to turn our backs on the spells of Debussy and Ravel exactly when it was imperative to do so."*[31]

(11 December) First public performance of **Rapsodie nègre FP3**, at the Théâtre du Vieux-Colombier, Paris—at a matinee billed as Musique d'Avant-Garde that includes works by Satie, Stravinsky, Auric, and Durey among others.

1918 (aged 19)

(18 January) FP's military service begins, and will end almost exactly three years later. He is initially sent to Vincennes, 6.5 kilometers from Paris, and given a job as a driver. *"I didn't know the countryside until I was 18, when I joined the army."*[32]

(March) *Le Coq et l'arlequin,* a tract on music and aesthetics by Jean Cocteau, is published.

(23 March–7 August) Paris is bombarded by German artillery.

FP encounters the poet Paul Éluard at Adrienne Monnier's bookshop.[33] He meets Manuel de Falla at the home of Ricardo Viñes.

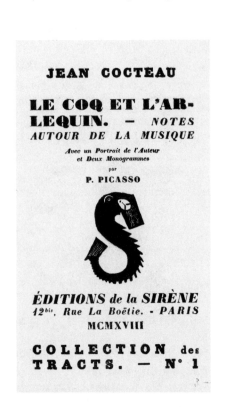

JEAN COCTEAU

LE COQ ET L'AR-
LEQUIN. — NOTES
AUTOUR DE LA MUSIQUE

*Avec un Portrait de l'Auteur
et Deux Monogrammes*

par
P. PICASSO

ÉDITIONS de la SIRÈNE
12bis, Rue La Boëtie. - PARIS
MCMXVIII

COLLECTION des
TRACTS. — N° 1

Title page of Cocteau's manifesto Le Coq et l'arlequin *(1918), with a monogram by Picasso.*

FP collaborates for the first time with Jean Cocteau (see p. 15).

(Late August) FP is briefly assigned to the 63rd Régiment d'Artillerie in the Val d'Oise, not far from Paris. He is imprisoned for a week for having slept in Paris without permission and is reassigned to the 66th regiment at Saint-Martin-sur-le-Pré, 165 kilometers from his home city. In December another reassignment places him closer to Paris. Despite being fortunate enough never to have experienced the horrors of the Front, Poulenc still complains: "*I am truly beginning to feel the stupid and strict discipline of the army.*"[34]

(Autumn) *Toréador* **FP11** (Cocteau), composed in Paris.

Violinist Hélène Jourdan-Morhange (1892–1961) takes FP to the home of Jean de Polignac in Neuilly, where he finally meets Marguerite di Pietro, who will eventually marry Jean. As Marie-Blanche, Comtesse de Polignac, this gifted pianist and singer will become one of FP's closest friends and supporters, and the dedicatee of fourteen songs.

(3 October) Birth of Rosine Manceaux (later Mme Jean Seringe, d. 2017), FP's younger niece. Following the sudden death of her sister Brigitte in 1963, Rosine will inherit Poulenc's house in Noizay, manage his "droit moral," and head Les Amis de Francis Poulenc for fifty years following her uncle's death.

(1 November) Erik Satie resigns in high dudgeon from "Les Nouveaux Jeunes."

(9 November) Apollinaire, weakened by long-term complications from his war wound, succumbs to the Spanish flu and dies.

(11 November) The first armistice between France and Germany is signed at Compiègne, ending the Great War. France regains control of Alsace-Lorraine.

FP continues with his military duties: "*Truly the countryside is something frightful for young persons, especially in circumstances such as those in which I find myself.*"[35]

1919 (aged 20)

(January) Adrienne Monnier sends Poulenc a reissue of Apollinaire's *Le Bestiaire*, featuring woodcuts by Raoul Dufy.

(Mid-January) FP is assigned to the Défense Contre Avions (DCA) at Pont-sur-Seine, twenty kilometers from Paris.

(21 March) Erik Satie accompanies Suzanne Balguerie (1888–1973) in a performance of his *Socrate*, Part I, at Monnier's bookshop.

(April) FP meets Sergei Diaghilev at the home of the pianist and arts patron Misia Sert and plays him *Rapsodie nègre*. The connection between impresario and composer is immediately warm.

(April–May) *Le Bestiaire* **FP15a** (Apollinaire), composed in Pont-sur-Seine.

For the first private performance of *Le Bestiaire*, FP accompanies soprano

Suzanne Rivière, who is soon to work under her married name, Suzanne Peignot (1895–1993).

(April–June) *Cocardes* **FP16** (Cocteau), composed in Pont-sur-Seine.

(8 June) First public performance of *Le Bestiaire* **FP15a**, at the gallery
L'Effort Moderne, Paris. The concert is a "Matinée poétique" in memory of
Apollinaire. Jeanne Borel is accompanied by FP.

(28 June) The Treaty of Versailles (with unrealistically punitive terms for
Germany, and disastrous long-term consequences) is signed in the Hall of
Mirrors at Versailles, just outside Paris.

(July) FP obtains a desk job at the War Office in Paris, remaining there
until he is released from military service in January 1921.

On the recommendation of Diaghilev and Stravinsky, the firm of J & W
Chester in London begins to publish FP's instrumental music. With support
from director Otto Marius Kling and poet Georges Jean-Aubry, editor of the
influential house magazine *The Chesterian*, FP begins to build a reputation
in Britain. Through Jean-Aubry, FP wins the friendship and encouragement
of Albert Roussel—a composer whose music is not to his taste, but whom he
likes and respects.

At the home of René Chalupt, an amateur poet set by Satie and Roussel,
FP once again encounters Milhaud (recently returned from Brazil) and performs *Le Bestiaire* for him. They become fast friends.

(12 September) FP boldly invites Diaghilev to dinner at 83, rue de Monceau.

(October) An advertisement appears in *The Chesterian* announcing the
publication of four new works by Poulenc: *Trois Mouvements perpétuels*,
the Piano Sonata for Four Hands, the Sonata for Two Clarinets, and *Rapsodie nègre*. Poulenc himself provided a blurb, as if he were a critic evaluating a
young composer's work. He writes of his music as a reaction against "*Impressionist snow*," and acknowledges the influence of Satie and a "*tendency to get
away from mere harmony, not by the obvious device of orthodox counterpoint,
but by what the composer styles as 'polytony.'*" The new solo piano pieces are "*a
new step toward simplicity. . . . The music of Francis Poulenc may be likened in
some ways to the art of Picasso; there is no perspective, as it were, and no elaborate detail. But it must not be surmised from this that he is a 'cubist' or 'futurist'
composer; he is too refined an artist and too great an individual to be dismissed
with one of these vaguely comprehensive labels.*"

By the end of 1919, Cocteau's share of the artistic limelight seems to be
ever-increasing, and the composers of Les Nouveaux Jeunes appear to be in
the forefront of the musical avant-garde, although Satie himself was no longer directly involved. In January 1920 a critic would propose a new collective
name (like the Russian "Five") for the group, a name that became an enduring
means of labeling an exciting and volatile chapter in French musical history.

Songs for a New Century

Mélopée d'automne (for piano), preceded by a quotation from Paul Verlaine's "En sourdine": "Calmes dans le demi-jour" (unpublished), 14 March 1913[36]

Viens! (Victor Hugo, voice and piano), probably a wedding present for Jeanne and André Manceaux (unpublished), 2 June 1913[37]

FP1   *Processional pour la crémation d'un mandarin* (piano, destroyed by the composer), 1914

FP2   *Préludes* (piano, destroyed), 1916

o   o   o

[Brackets below a song's or song cycle's title give names of dedicatee(s) (*italic*) and publisher.]

FP3   **Rapsodie nègre** (third movement)
         Composed in Paris, spring 1917 (revised 1933)
         [*Erik Satie*; Chester]
         Literary source: *Les Poésies de Makoko Kangourou*, ed. Marcel Prouille (another pseudonym of the author, Marcel Ormoy, 1891–1934) and Charles Moulié (Paris: Dorbon Aîné, 1910). The bracketed information below is printed as pseudo-scholastic footnotes in the original publication, as is the supposed date, 11 January 1892.
         A minor; $\frac{1}{2}$ [*sic*]; *Lent et monotone* $\quarternote = 69$

Honoloulou [written by Makoko Kangourou in his mother tongue]
Honoloulou, poti lama! [Honoloulou is the name of Kangourou's girlfriend]
Honoloulou, Honoloulou,
Kati moko, mosi bolou
Ratakou sira, polama!

Watakousi, motimasou,
Etchepango ectehpanga,
Kaka nounou nounouranga,
lolo, luluma, tamasou.

Pata tabo, ananalou,
Mandès, Golas, Gbêles i Krous. [names of Liberian tribes]
Bananalou ityo Kouskous,
Poti lama, Honoloulou!

Poulenc claimed to have discovered Kangourou's book of poems in a stall along the banks of the Seine. The five-movement work (Prélude, Ronde, Honoloulou—Intermède vocal, Pastorale, Final), dedicated to Erik Satic, is scored for piano, two violins, viola, cello, flute, and clarinet; the third movement is for voice and piano alone, which qualifies this strange piece for inclusion here. It was, as Poulenc explained, "*a reflection of the taste for African art that had flourished since 1912 under the impetus of Apollinaire.*" Just before its first performance, "*the baritone [named Feiner] threw in the towel saying it was all too stupid and he didn't want to be taken for a fool. . . . I had to sing this interlude myself, partially obscured by a huge music stand. As I had already been mobilized one can imagine the unexpected effect of this soldier bawling in pseudo-Malagasy.*"[38]

The music for the sung movement is in a repetitive style that would today be labeled minimalist: a cell of descending eighth notes (B, A, G-sharp, F-sharp) is heard nineteen times in all (the words to be sung *sans nuances*), the iterations slightly different in rhythm and duration but never straying from the same four notes, an inadvertent prophecy of the exotic linguistics and musical stasis in some of Messiaen's music from decades later. We hear the future Poulenc in the music's inventive audacity rather than in any command of melody, harmony, or form.

∘ ∘ ∘

FP4 Scherzo for Two Pianos (*Zèbre*) (lost or destroyed), 1917
FP5 *Trois Pastorales* (piano), autumn 1917
FP6 *Poèmes sénégalais* (voice and string quartet); no trace of the songs has been found, and the origin of the texts is unknown.
FP7 Sonata for Two Clarinets, spring 1918
FP8 Sonata for Piano Four Hands, June 1918
FP9 *Prélude percussion* (to precede the ballet *Le Jongleur*), October 1918
FP10 *Le Jongleur*, orchestrated by January 1919

∘ ∘ ∘

FP11 *Toréador* (*Chanson hispano-italienne*)
　　Composed in Paris, autumn 1918 (revised 1932)
　　[*Pierre Bertin*; Deiss]
　　Literary source: Jean Cocteau (1889–1963), letter to the composer, 13
　　September 1918
　　D major; $\frac{3}{8}$; *Allant* ♩. = 92

<table>
<tr><td>

1
Pépita reine de Venise
Quand tu vas sous ton mirador
Tous les gondoliers se dissent
Prends garde toréador!

2
Sur ton cœur personne ne règne
Dans le grand palais ou tu dors
Et près de toi la vieille duègne
Guette le toréador.

3
Toréador brave des braves
Lorsque sur la place Saint-Marc
Le taureau en fureur qui bave
Tombe tué par ton poignard

4
Ce n'est pas l'orgueil qui caresse
Ton cœur sous la baouta d'or
Car pour une jeune déesse
Tu brûles toréador.

Refrain
Belle Espagno o le
Dans ta gondo o le
Tu caraco o les
Carmencita!
Sous ta manti i lle
Œil qui pét i lle
Bouche qui bri i lle
C'est Pépita a a

5
C'est demain (jour de Saint Escure)
Qu'aura lieu le combat à mort
Le canal est pléin de voitures
Fêtant le toréador.

</td><td>

1
Pepita, queen of Venice
When you go out onto your balcony
All the gondoliers are thinking
"Beware . . . Toreador!"

2
Nobody is master of your heart
In the grand palazzo where you sleep
And nearby the old duenna
Keeps an eye out for the Toreador.

3
Toreador, bravest of the brave
When on the Piazza San Marco
The angry slavering bull
Falls slain by your blade

4
It's not pride which fires
Your heart, beneath your gilded cape
No, it is for a young goddess
That you are burning, Toreador.

Refrain
Lovely Spanish lady
In your gondola
Preening yourself
Carmencita!
Beneath your mantilla
Sparkling eye
Shimmering mouth
That's Pepita.

5
Tomorrow (St. Escurio's day)
Is the day of the fight to the death
The Grand Canal is full of carriages
All celebrating the Toreador!

</td></tr>
</table>

6

De Venise plus d'une belle	More than one Venetian beauty

De Venise plus d'une belle
Palpite pour savoir ton sort
Mais tu méprises leurs dentelles
Tu souffres toréador.

7

Car ne voyant pas apparaître
(caché derrière un oranger)
Pépita seule à sa fenêtre
Tu médites de te venger,

8

Sous ton caftan passe ta dague

La jalousie au cœur te mord
Et seul avec le bruit des vagues
Tu pleures toréador

Refrain

9

Que de cavaliers! Que de monde!
Remplit l'arène jusqu'au bord
On vient de cent lieues à la ronde

T'acclamer toréador!

10

C'est fait il entre dans l'arène
Avec plus de flegme qu'un lord.
Mais il peut avancer à peine
Le pauvre toréador.

11

Il ne reste à son rêve morne
Que de mourir sous tous les yeux
En sentant pénétrer des cornes
Dans son triste front soucieux

12

Car Pépita se montre assise
Offrant son regard et son corps
Au plus vieux doge de Venise
Et rit du toréador.

Refrain

6

More than one Venetian beauty
Trembles to know your fate
But you scorn their lace finery
You're suffering, Toreador.

7

For since you cannot see
(concealed behind an orange tree)
Pepita, alone at her window,
You are plotting revenge.

8

Under your caftan you've slipped a
    dagger
Jealousy gnaws at your heart
And all alone, to the lap of the waves
You're weeping, Toreador.

Refrain

9

So many horsemen! So many people!
Filling the bullring to bursting
People come from a hundred miles
    around
To cheer you, Toreador!

10

We're off! He enters the ring
With more cool than a lord
But he can hardly walk
The poor Toreador.

11

All that's left of his gloomy dream
Is to die in front of everyone
And to feel the bull's horns
Gore his sad furrowed brow

12

For there is Pepita, sitting
And offering her gaze and her body
To the oldest Doge in Venice
And laughing at the Toreador.

Refrain

Poulenc's main preoccupation between fall 1918 and spring 1919 (when he was on nonactive military duty) was attempting to write a ballet, music-hall style, entitled *Le Jongleur* (he sometimes referred to it as *Jongleurs*). This was to be performed for a Jean Cocteau–inspired "Séance–Music Hall" at the Théâtre du Vieux-Colombier, an event for which *Toréador* was also destined. Plans for Cocteau's Séance–Music Hall collapsed, and *Le Jongleur,* clearly a disappointment to Poulenc, was quickly withdrawn; the score has long since disappeared.

But *Toréador* survived. It was not quite his first Cocteau piece—that honor belongs to *Zèbre* FP4, a lost scherzo for two pianos from the summer of 1917, inspired by Cocteau's poem of the same name. Poulenc received the poem for *Toréador* from Cocteau himself,[39] together with the instruction to show it to no one else (the poet clearly felt he could better control his musical collaborators if they were kept in the dark about what the others were doing). Cocteau wanted his lyric composed in the style of "Bobino," the famous music hall in Montparnasse belonging to the Pathé Brothers, and featuring such variety artists as Mistinguett, an extremely glamorous female singer-entertainer much admired by the young Poulenc. Shamelessly micromanaging, Cocteau urged Poulenc not to make the song sound too much like Chabrier, but rather "bien <u>mais</u> moche" (good but trashy), fin-

ishing with "rapid quarter notes" (he was no schooled musician). He also insisted that the final syllables of words like "Venise" ("Veni-*se*") should be emphasized.[40] Early in 1919 Poulenc assured the poet that versions of *Toréador* for voice and piano and for voice and instruments were with the copyist[41]—the only time we hear of an instrumental accompaniment, the score for which (if it existed) has since disappeared. At the later urging of painter Jacques-Émile Blanche, the chanson (clearly no mélodie) was eventually published in 1932 by Deiss. Cocteau's cover design shows the toreador's costume decorated with the poet's "rapid quarter notes" (rapidly drawn perhaps), as are the head and hooves of the bull.

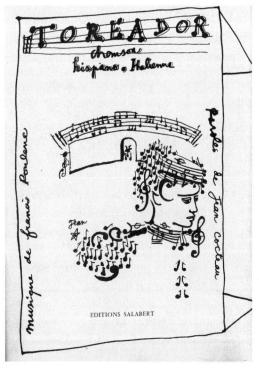

The cover of Toréador *FP11, first published in 1933, lithograph by Cocteau.*

The song is a strictly strophic creation and, as Cocteau demanded, conceived in the manner of popular hits of the time. The story concerns Pépita, so-called queen of Venice, for whom a toreador conceives an unrequited passion. In a zany montage anticipating Monty Python by four decades, the bullring is transported to Venice's Piazza San Marco, gondoliers become Spanish galleons, and the oldest doge in the city enjoys Pépita's favors—whimsical nonsense that nods to the surrealists, but was hated by them for not taking surrealism seriously enough. Much later, during the broadcast of one of his fifteen conversations with Claude Rostand (1953–54), Poulenc described his madcap creation as a "*Hispano-Italian ditty . . . which lampoons the geography of the café-concert songs of the time, in which a Japanese girl would go to the bad in Peking, and Sappho would fire questions at the Sphinx.*"[42]

There is no record of a first public performance, but it was often performed by the composer (in his nasal singing voice) in the company of other members of Les Six or at gatherings of friends. "*Bernac maintains that I sing this song, forgive me, like nobody else,*" he later wrote. "*It is enough to say that the voice does not matter for this interpretation of this musical pleasantry, and that the 'oins oins' coming from my nose, which is not Grecian, are sufficient to amuse the people for whom it is destined.*"[43] *Toréador* became a kind of theme song for the young composer. He performed it during the same 1950s broadcast with Rostand, accompanying himself—his sole radio appearance as a singer.

∘   ∘   ∘

FP12 Sonata for Violin and Piano (first version, destroyed), October 1918

FP13 Sonata for Piano, Violin, and Violoncello (lost or destroyed), October 1918

FP14 *Trois Mouvements perpétuels* (piano), December 1918

∘   ∘   ∘

FP15a ***Le Bestiaire, ou Cortège d'Orphée*** (*The Bestiary, or Procession of Orpheus*)
Composed in Pont-sur-Seine, April–May 1919 (with the exception of vi, which Poulenc later claimed to have composed in February)[44]
[*Louis Durey*; Éditions de la Sirène]
Literary source: Guillaume Apollinaire (1880–1918), a reissued edition (1918) of *Le Bestiaire, ou Cortège d'Orphée*, woodcut illustrations by Raoul Dufy (Paris: Deplanche, Éditeur d'Art, 1911). The pages of this edition are unnumbered; within the anthology, the relevant poems are positioned as follows: (i) 10, (ii) 4, (iii) 17, (iv) 19, (v) 22, (vi) 23.

(i)   *Le Dromadaire*
(ii) *La Chèvre du Thibet*

(iii) *La Sauterelle*

(iv) *Le Dauphin*

(v) *L'Écrevisse*

(vi) *La Carpe*

Apollinaire was an enthusiastic, if not wealthy, bibliophile. Subjects of his eclectic reading included magic, theosophy, religion, and medieval history, and he was well aware of the exquisitely illuminated bestiaries of the Middle Ages. Eighteen of his eventual thirty animal quatrains were published under the title *La Marchande des quatre saisons, ou Le Bestiaire mondain* in a June 1908 review called *La Phalange*. Always interested in enterprises where writers and artists or musicians pooled their talents, the poet promised readers of *La Phalange* an illustrated edition of the poems, hoping to col-

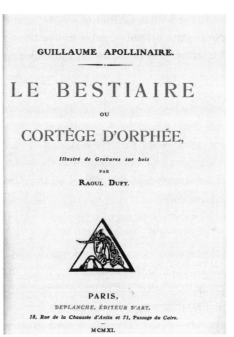

GUILLAUME APOLLINAIRE.

LE BESTIAIRE

ou

CORTÈGE D'ORPHÉE,

Illustré de Gravures sur bois

PAR

RAOUL DUFY.

PARIS,

DEPLANCHE, ÉDITEUR D'ART,

18, Rue de la Chaussée d'Antin et 71, Passage du Caire.

MCMXI.

Apollinaire's Le Bestiaire, *title page of the first edition (1911), with illustrations by Raoul Dufy.*

laborate with his friend Picasso (who had made some experimental woodcuts of animals). But Picasso, ever elusive, was impossible to pin down, and the poet persuaded Raoul Dufy to provide the woodcuts, the first of that artist's many illustrations.

Adopting the motto "J'émerveille" (I astonish), Apollinaire chose Orpheus as his authorial voice—an important figure in his creative life. In 1912 he would establish a school of painting (with Robert Delaunay, Fernand Léger, Francis Picabia, and Marcel Duchamp) known as Orphism, fauvism crossed with cubism. "At the dawn of Modernism," writes Michael Schmidt, "it was appropriate that the singer who enchanted the beasts with his lyre and charmed the trees to gather round him in attentive groves should guard the door of Apollinaire's *Bestiary*. Orpheus helps the French poet to tame his animals in epigrams that contain but do not confine them."[45] Apollinaire allowed this ancient and powerful persona to appear in poems 1, 13, 18, and 24 of the overall sequence, lyrics that Poulenc ignored for his musical purposes.

Le Bestiaire, ou Cortège d'Orphée, published by Deplanche in March 1911 in a handsome large-format edition, was a commercial disaster for Apollinaire and Dufy. Of the 120 printed copies of the poems, barely 50 were sold. In 1918 bookseller Adrienne Monnier (1892–1955) sent Poulenc a packet of books that included a later edition of the same work (in the intervening seven years the poet's reputation had grown enormously). Poulenc, who was stationed at Pont-sur-Seine, had heard the poet give a reading at Monnier's bookshop and fallen in love with this allusive charivari of animals: "*A crucial fact: I heard the sound of his voice. I think that's an essential point for a composer who doesn't want to betray a poet. The timbre of Apollinaire's voice, like that of his work as a whole, was both melancholy and cheerful. What he said was sometimes tinged with irony, but never with the deadpan humor of someone like Jules Renard. . . . what always struck me with him was the melancholy of his smile.*"[46] (Poulenc said that this memory was the reason all his Apollinaire settings had a mood of tender melancholy.[47])

Twelve songs were composed mainly in April and May 1919, "*on an old piano in a house in the provinces.*"[48] Poulenc was deeply aware that Apollinaire had died in November of the previous year, and the idea of a *tombeau* may have been in his mind. Though these songs are always heard today with their piano accompaniment, they were originally conceived for voice with two violins, viola, flute, clarinet, and bassoon. At the first performance of the instrumentally accompanied version—in the presence of such great surrealist poets as André Breton, Blaise Cendrars, and Pierre Reverdy—the order of songs was *La Tortue, La Chèvre du Thibet, Le Serpent, Le Dromadaire, Le Dauphin, La Sauterelle, La Mouche, L'Écrevisse, La Carpe, La Puce, La Colombe, Le Bœuf.* Of these, *La Tortue, La Mouche,* and *Le Bœuf* have vanished without a trace.

Having set twelve poems to music, Poulenc reduced the number to six on the advice of Georges Auric, whom he came to regard as a perspicacious judge of his music. Whether or not Auric played any part in deciding the order of the published songs, it is a sequence that has triumphantly stood the test of time. On learning that Louis Durey (fellow member of Les Six) was working at the same time on setting the entire collection, Poulenc rather gallantly dedicated his own set to Durey, who was by no means a close friend. The cycle was first published in 1920 by Les Éditions de la Sirène, a firm Poulenc later roundly blamed for not printing an instrumental version, and losing an accurate copy of the orchestration.[49] It is perhaps on account of this chaotic beginning, when it was well-nigh impossible to obtain a correct score and parts from the publishers, that the instrumental version is seldom heard.

In September 1921 Poulenc received a letter from Apollinaire's former mistress Marie Laurencin, who by this time had become an intimate friend:

> Mon petit garçon,
> Am I going to surprise you! This letter is from an admirer. Since my return I have been humming your Bestiaire as best I can and you have no idea, Francis Poulenc, how well you have conveyed both the nostalgia

and the singsong quality of those admirable quatrains. And what I find so moving is that you would think you were hearing the voice of Guillaume Apollinaire himself reciting those very lines. Work hard and be good.

Your elder and your friend, Marie Laurencin[50]

The cycle quickly became famous with singers with a taste for the unusual and modern. On 11 February 1922, at the Salle Gaveau, Maria Olenina-d'Alheim, a great pioneer of the songs of Musorgsky, performed *Le Bestiaire* in a program consecrated to animals.[51] Poulenc later named Claire Croiza, Marya Freund (who sang it *"as gravely as a song of Schubert"*),[52] and Pierre Bernac as the most distinguished of its interpreters.

The tender seriousness of the poet's voice is very much in tune with Poulenc's almost unnervingly simple style. The composer is amusing, chic, naughty, and self-consciously modern; he may be an artistic snob, but he is clearly already a young man able to conjure real magic from the most slender of musical means.

(i) *Le Dromadaire* (*The Dromedary*)

No key signature (E minor/major); $\frac{2}{4}$; *Très rythmé, Pesant* ♩= 76

Avec ses quatre dromadaires	With his four dromedaries
Don Pedro d'Alfaroubeira	Don Pedro d'Alfaroubeira
Courut le monde et l'admira.	Roamed round the world and admired it.
Il fit ce que je voudrais faire	He did exactly what I'd do
Si j'avais quatre dromadaires.	If I had four dromedaries too.

A less than nimble falling quintuplet in the left-hand accompaniment brilliantly suggests a dour fleet of haunch-rolling dromedaries galumphing through the sands of the world. According to the source of Apollinaire's story (the sixteenth-century Portuguese explorer Gomez de Santistevan), the journey takes three years and four months (via Norway and Babylon), but Poulenc keeps the song mercifully short and to the point. *Le Dromadaire* is a minor relation of Schubert's *Die Forelle* (*The Trout*), where a simple piano figuration drawn from nature becomes a memorable motif for a song's accompaniment. The melody of the interlude is a slow-motion variation of the opening of the *Farandole* from Bizet's *L'Arlésienne*, while the tiny postlude, whoopla in deadpan manner, betrays Poulenc's delight in the solemn scenario. The composer-accompanist always made a slight *ralentando* at the end, and used a touch of pedal here, despite his instructions to do neither. Bernac draws attention to the poem's relationship with the "unappeased longing for great departures" expressed in the final song of Fauré's cycle *L'Horizon chimérique*.[53]

(ii)   *La Chèvre du Thibet* (*The Tibetan Goat*)
No key signature (G minor); $\frac{4}{4}$; *Très modéré* ♩ = 72

Les poils de cette chèvre et même	The fleece of this goat and even
Ceux d'or pour qui prit tant de peine	The Golden Fleece which Jason strove so hard for
Jason, ne valent rien aux prix	Are worth nothing
Des cheveux dont je suis épris.	Compared to the hair I'm smitten with.

In this love song in disguise (and even if much of the music is tinged by the minor key), Bernac always insisted on a smile in both voice and eyes at the end. The piano interlude in bars 4–5 skips smoothly across the bar lines, its goat-like clamberings with cheeky *acciaccature* in both hands rendered suave by the pedal. In the closing cadence Poulenc shows that he already knows how to write music of genuine tenderness.

(iii)   *La Sauterelle* (*The Grasshopper*)
Modal; $\frac{4}{4}$; *Lent* ♩ = 66

Voici la fine sauterelle	Here's the little grasshopper
La nourriture de Saint Jean	Which nourished John the Baptist
Puissent mes vers être comme elle	I'd like my verses to be like that
Le régal des meilleures gens.	A special treat for the elite.

The grasshopper of the wilderness, ennobled by its culinary link with the insect-consuming John the Baptist, is a perfect match for the mock-snobbism of Apollinaire. In his notes to the original edition, Apollinaire quotes St. Mark 1:6, about St. John eating wild honey and locusts ("locustas et mel silvestre edebat"). His self-parodying fastidiousness regarding the social niveau of his readers is perfectly captured by Poulenc's heady, oscillating tones at the end of the song. The composer seldom set a baritone more of a challenge in head voice than in these two bars, right on the "break" between registers. Even so, the tempo should be imperturbable.

(iv)   *Le Dauphin* (*The Dolphin*)
No key signature (A major); $\frac{4}{4}$; *Animé* ♩ = 136 (corrected by Bernac to 120)[54]

Dauphins, vous jouez dans la mer	Dolphins, you play in the briny
Mais le flot est toujours amer	But the sea is always bitter
Parfois, ma joie éclate-t-elle?	I may sometimes burst with joy
La vie est encore cruelle.	But life is still cruel.

"Les flots amers" is a frequent romantic characterization of the ocean: "the bitter tides," or perhaps "the cruel sea." J. S.

The dolphin gambols joyfully in the sea, a creature clever and good-natured enough to be a stand-in for the composer, who made something of a splash with this cycle. Poulenc may not yet be *roi de la mélodie française* (Fauré and Ravel are still alive), but with this little cycle he unexpectedly proves himself heir-presumptive—the dauphin, in fact.

(v)   *L'Écrevisse (The Crayfish)*
       No key signature (A-flat minor); $\frac{4}{4}$; *Assez vif* ♩ = 96 (corrected by Bernac
       to between 76 and 88)

Incertitude, ô mes délices	Uncertainty, oh my delights,
Vous et moi nous nous en allons	You and I progress
Comme s'en vont les écrevisses	Like crayfish do
À reculons, à reculons.	Backwards. Backwards.

This music paints to perfection the forward-sideways-backward movement of a crayfish, now a rising motif in the treble clef, now a descending one in the bass as the pianist's right hand crosses over the left. The use of *portato* in the voice for "À reculons" is an early sign of the composer's feeling for vocal sensuousness (as is also the setting of "mélancolie" at the close of the next song).

(vi)   *La Carpe (The Carp)*
        No key signature (A-flat minor); $\frac{4}{4}$; *Très triste—Très lent* ♩ = 58 (cor-
        rected by Bernac to 54)

Dans vos viviers, dans vos étangs,	In your pools, in your ponds,
Carpes, que vous vivez longtemps!	Carp, you live so long!
Est-ce que la mort vous oublie,	Has death forgotten you,
Poissons de la mélancolie.	Fish of Melancholy?

La Carpe is, in some ways, the masterpiece of the set although (or perhaps because) so little happens. The sadness of these large fish moving sluggishly in the pond's depths, their movement giving rise only to tiny ripples on the surface, is caught in a single page of such atmosphere that, once heard, is never forgotten.

In his *Journal* the composer makes a point of denying any connection between this song and the famous Étang aux Carpes (Lake of Carp) at Fontainebleau. Instead, he linked it with wartime memories of an army officer: "La Carpe *found*

LA CARPE.

Dans vos viviers, dans vos étangs,
Carpes, que vous vivez longtemps !
Est-ce que la mort vous oublie,
Poissons de la mélancolie.

La Carpe, *woodcut by Raoul Dufy for Apollinaire's poem from* Le Bestiaire.

its visual counterpart in a melancholy pond where, in melancholy fashion, my melancholy captain used to fish, and one evening in February 1919 I set to music that 'poisson de la mélancholie.'"[55] As is common with Poulenc, whose anecdotes often contradict each other in date and detail, he elsewhere gave a different version, claiming to have composed *La Carpe* in a dining-car during a journey between Longueville and Paris.[56] But he composed in such fits and starts, regularly taking work with him on the train, that both stories may well be true.

FP15b ***Deux Mélodies inédites du "Bestiaire"*** (*Two Unpublished Songs from "Le Bestiaire"*)

> Literary source: Guillaume Apollinaire (1880–1918), *Le Bestiaire, ou Cortège d'Orphée*, woodcut illustrations by Raoul Dufy (Paris: Deplanche, Éditeur d'Art, 1911). Numbers refer to the poems' position in the anthology: (i) 5, (ii) 26.

As noted above, Poulenc set six further *Bestiaire* poems in 1919 before Auric advised him to cut the cycle down to six: of these, *Le Bœuf*, *La Mouche*, and *La Tortue* have disappeared. *La Puce* was reworked in 1960 as a tribute to Raoul Dufy (see p. 455), and *La Souris*, not one of the original twelve, was newly set in 1956. By 1992 *Le Serpent* and *La Colombe*, copied out for a friend and dating from 1944, had been acquired by the Bibliothèque Nationale. In the absence of an extant autograph of the cycle, it is unclear whether those two songs had been revised since 1919.

(i) *Le Serpent* (*The Serpent*)
    Très vite

Tu t'acharnes sur la beauté	You latch on to beauty
Et quelles femmes ont été	And what women have been
Victimes de ta cruauté!	Victims of your cruelty!
Ève, Euridyce, Cléopâtre;	Eve, Euridice, Cleopatra
J'en connais encore trois ou quatre.	I know three or four others.

(ii)   *La Colombe (The Dove)*
          Très lent

Colombe, l'amour et l'esprit	Dove, the love and spirit
Qui engendrâtes Jésus-Christ,	That begat Jesus Christ,
Comme vous j'aime une Marie.	Like you I love a Mary.
Qu'avec elle je me marie.	Whom I mean to marry.

Le Serpent is cast as a mock-seductive cancan in Satie's cabaret style; the chromatic vocal line of *La Colombe* is woven around a static and strangely hypnotic accompaniment that evokes the cooing of doves. "Marie" is the poet's beloved, painter Marie Laurencin, whom he never married. Poulenc was probably wise to cut from his original cycle a song requiring singers to intone "Jésus-Christ" in a somewhat facetious context, thereby probably lessening the number of its performances.

BIOGRAPHICAL INTERLUDE: GUILLAUME APOLLINAIRE

THE APOLLINAIRE SONGS: *Le Bestiaire* FP15a/b (1919); *Trois Poèmes de Louise Lalanne* FP57/ii (1931); *Quatre Poèmes de Guillaume Apollinaire* FP58 (1931); *Deux Poèmes de Guillaume Apollinaire* FP94 (1938); *La Grenouillère* FP96 (1938); *Bleuet* FP102 (1939); *Banalités* FP107 (1940); *Montparnasse* and *Hyde Park* FP127 (1945); *Le Pont* and *Un poème* FP131 (1946); *Calligrammes* FP140 (1948); *Rosemonde* FP158 (1954); *La Souris* FP162 (1956); *La Puce* (1960). Poulenc also set two further poems as part of the unaccompanied *Sept Chansons* FP81, and turned the 1917 play *Les Mamelles de Tirésias* into an opera (FP125).

○   ○   ○

Both Poulenc and Apollinaire loved Paris, the City of Light. The composer was born with a silver spoon in his mouth on the Right Bank, while the impoverished Apollinaire, Parisian only by adoption, was a Left Bank garret dweller. They were also both enthusiasts of modernity, when anything could be the subject of poetry—trains and trams, planes, posters, modern architecture, electricity, machines, cannon and shrapnel, any picturesque curiosity, any unexpected or outlandish juxtaposition. Such earthy eclecticism suited Poulenc, the musical magpie, to a T; he gobbled up composers from Monteverdi to Malipiero, just as Apollinaire revered poets from Villon to Verlaine, recycling them to his purpose. Both artists were masters of the audaciously allusive. Apollinaire was in addition the most lubricious and anti-puritan of poets (relishing his "bad boy"

Apollinaire in the studio of Picasso, c. 1910.

status) and also the most intrinsically musical (a lover of popular song as much as of medieval virelais, and even, according to Georges Auric, of Schubert) and the creative link between composer and poet seems almost inevitable. In Apollinaire's poetry there is a simplicity of emotion beneath the outré sophistication, an unashamed elegiac lyricism that inspired some of Poulenc's greatest music, similarly avant-garde on the outside and utterly accessible on the inside—and/or the other way around. Side by side with his passion for the here and now, Apollinaire sang of lost paradise, the tragedy of "never again," the intimate and melancholy music of the star-crossed in love, the unlikely hero with his face turned expectantly toward the future. In some ways he was Poulenc's literary alter-ego: "*I have found in his poetry a rhythm corresponding exactly to the rhythm of my music.*"[57]

"Guillaume Apollinaire" was the pseudonym of Wilhelm Apollinaris de Kostrowitsky, born in Rome on 26 August 1880, the first of two illegitimate sons of Angelica de Kostrowitsky, a down-at-heel yet formidable noblewoman of Polish-Russian stock,[58] and Francesco Flugi d'Aspermont, a feckless Italian playboy-aristocrat. Until the age of seven, young Wilhelm spoke only Polish and Italian. In 1885 the abandoned

Angelica moved to France with her children, and Guillaume (as he became) went to school in Cannes and Nice; like Poulenc some twenty years later, he did not bother to finish his *baccalauréat*. Apollinaire's disrupted childhood, with its polyglot background, may have been responsible both for the upheavals he later effected in French literature and for the cosmopolitan charm with which they were accomplished. (Because he was naturalized only in 1916, the greatest French poet of the early twentieth century was a citizen of France for just the last thirty-two months of his life.) At the age of seventeen he was already as interested in anarchism as in the prevailing orthodoxy of symbolism—indeed, he was destined to become the liquidator of symbolism. A Debussy song to an Apollinaire text thus seems an impossible proposition, although the two men died in the same year.

After a year of Bohemian living in Monaco, Guillaume moved to Paris with his family in 1899—a city he idealized (see *Montparnasse* FP127/i). Excluded from the literary establishment, he faced the daily challenge of escaping poverty by working as an odd-jobs man of the printed word, putting together anthologies, penning articles for other writers, and proving himself a master pornographer admired not only for his salacious imagination but for his style and wit. Paris became a base for travel on a shoestring. He and his brother Albert (passing themselves off as Russian nobility) lived for a while near Liège, where they learned the local dialect, explored the Walloon countryside (*Banalités* FP107/iii), and engaged in amatory adventures. More in earnest was Guillaume's futile courtship of Linda Molina in 1901 (*Carte postale* FP58/ii). Striking it lucky that same year with the Vicomtesse de Milhau, who needed a tutor for her daughter, Apollinaire was whisked off to Germany and discovered the Rhineland. At the same time, he initiated a frustrating relationship with the family's English governess, Annie Playden, that was to drag on for three years. Early in 1902 the poet traveled to Cologne during the Carnaval (a later trip to Strasbourg at Carnaval time would inspire the poem set as *1904* FP58/iv), then went on to visit Berlin, Dresden, Prague, Vienna, and Munich.

Apollinaire's fortunes improved somewhat in 1903, when a job was found for him in a Paris bank. He made trips to London (*Hyde Park* FP127/ii), in the vain hope of persuading Annie to elope with him, and Holland (*Rosemonde* FP158), where he pursued further amatory adventures. At this time he began to meet important people in artistic circles: writers Max Jacob, André Salmon, and Alfred Jarry, and painters Picasso and André Derain (the latter illustrated his first book, *L'Enchanteur pourrissant*, in 1909). By 1907 Apollinaire had left his mother's apartment and moved into his own lodgings in Montmartre, where he frequented the louche bars and "Bateau-Lavoir," the nickname for the insalubrious building where avant-garde artists, mainly painters (including Picasso), had taken up residence. Apollinaire's profound knowledge of modern painting and his book *Les Peintres cubistes* (1913) have their origin here. In 1908 Picasso introduced him to the painter Marie Laurencin, with whom he had a passionate and stormy affair (*Trois Poèmes de Louise Lalanne* FP57). Marie terminated the liaison four years later on account of his jealousy and incorrigible infidelities; nevertheless, there remained an emotional link between them, reflected in *Calligrammes* FP140/v. Although Apollinaire's poetry implies, disingenuously, that women habitually mistreated him, his perpetually roving eye was largely to blame for the failure of his relationships.

In 1911, the year he published *Le Bestiaire,* Apollinaire spent some days in prison, bizarrely suspected of being mixed up in the theft of Leonardo's *Mona Lisa* from the Louvre (he was known to associate with a person who had stolen other artifacts from the museum); as a Russian national, through his mother, he risked deportation. This low point was followed, however, by increasing literary success, although it was lost on nobody that the poet kept questionable company and was ready to sweep aside the accepted way of doing things. At the same time, he sincerely professed himself a dyed-in-the-wool Parisian and patriotic Frenchman precisely because he was neither Parisian nor French; like an Indian-born writer bemoaning the end of the British aristocracy, he reveled in a nostalgia for a *vieille* France that another side of his nature sought to modernize by any and every means.

Apollinaire's most famous poetry collection, *Alcools,* was published in 1913. On the outbreak of war in 1914, he volunteered immediately but, as a Russian citizen, encountered a barrier of red tape. In Nice in September of that year, he met Louise de Coligny-Chatillon ("Lou"), who resisted his romantic advances. He then successfully enlisted in the 38th infantry regiment at Nîmes (*Calligrammes* FP140/vi); by December "Lou" had capitulated to the poet in uniform, and the couple spent an idyllic week together (*Calligrammes* FP140/iii). On a train journey to Nice-Nîmes in January 1915, Apollinaire met the young Madeleine Pagès, to whom he became engaged; his frustration at having to spend time away from Madeleine because of war duties inspired *L'Espionne* (*Calligrammes* FP140/i). The following Easter he was sent to the front at Champagne, and by November he had been promoted to sub-lieutenant in the 96th regiment and had experienced the horror of the trenches.

On 17 March 1916, Apollinaire suffered a head wound from shrapnel at Berry-au-Bac and underwent sub-cranial surgery and a lengthy convalescence. By September his collection of stories *Le Poète assassiné* had been published, and the thirty-six-year-old poet had become the idol of a group of younger men who espoused the literary avant-garde—André Breton, Tristan Tzara, Pierre Reverdy, and Jean Cocteau. He wrote the program note for the Cocteau-Satie ballet *Parade* in 1917, and shortly afterward his play *Les Mamelles de Tirésias* was performed, the work for which he first formulated the label "surrealist"; in 1946 Poulenc would turn it into an *opéra-bouffe*. While recuperating from a lung infection, Apollinaire met Jacqueline Kolb, who soon became

Apollinaire sustained a head injury in the trenches during the First World War.

his wife (the relationship with Madeleine Pagès having petered out)—much later Poulenc became Jacqueline's friend and dedicated *Calligrammes* FP140/iii to her.

The poet, weakened by his illnesses, died of Spanish flu on 9 November 1918. Poulenc later spoke about the sound of Apollinaire's voice reading his own poetry at Adrienne Monnier's bookshop in the rue de l'Odéon ("*the timbre . . . was both melancholic and cheerful at the same time*"), though he no doubt exaggerated how many times (a dozen, he later claimed) he had actually met the poet, if he actually met him at all.[59] The Apollinaire songs, like the Schumann-Heine settings (a similarly powerful conjunction of two very different geniuses, seemingly made for each other), came about as the result of reverence for an older living poet (Schumann met Heine when the composer was eighteen). In both cases, fleeting personal contact glamorized youthful admiration for groundbreaking poetry and turned it into hero worship. In Poulenc's case, friendship with Marie Laurencin and Jacqueline Apollinaire, women the poet had loved, became an additional spur to his musical creativity. "*I've learned so much about him,*" he marveled, "*it's as if I'd known him.*"[60]

FP16 ***Cocardes, Chansons populaires sur des poèmes de Jean Cocteau***
(Cockades, Popular Songs on Poems of Jean Cocteau)
    Composed in Pont-sur-Seine, April–June 1919 (revised 1939)
    [*Georges Auric*; Éditions de la Sirène]
    Literary source: Jean Cocteau (1889–1963), *Poésies 1917–1920* (Paris: Éditions de la Sirène, 1920), "Cocardes (Petites Pièces plaisantes)," p. 84

    (i) *Miel de Narbonne*
    (ii) *Bonne d'enfant*
    (iii) *Enfant de troupe*

When Cocteau's planned "Séance–Music Hall" failed to materialize in 1919, he was determined to create another "Séance," this time dubbing it a "Spectacle-Concert." Thanks to financial support from Comte Étienne de Beaumont, this event took place on 21 February 1920 at the Théâtre des Champs-Élysées. The concert was billed as a postwar fundraiser for military hospitals and was supported by the Noailles family, who were later to play a significant role as Poulenc's patrons. Georges Auric judged Cocteau to be a supremely able organizer for this novel combination of theater, opera, ballet, and circus—a kind of junior Diaghilev.[61] Unlike ordinary concerts, this one boasted décor by Raoul Dufy, with masks and costumes, and the Fratellini family clowns from the Cirque Médrano. Poulenc's *Cocardes* was not the only premiere of the evening; there were also first performances of Auric's fox trot *Adieu New York*, Milhaud's ballet *Le Bœuf sur le toit*, and Satie's *Trois Petites Pièces montées* (a second "Spectacle-Concert" was to be consecrated to Satie's music).

    If the format of the evening was a shock, it was also less revolutionary than it seemed to be. Such a compilation of popular performing arts was more or less posh music hall, with a Dada twist. Charles B. Cochran in London, for example, included wrestling and Houdini in his famed musical revues; unconcerned with cultural chic, Cochran would have been happy with Cocteau's clowns but nonplussed by Poulenc's music. In his speech before the show began, Cocteau explained that "the *Cocardes* are fake folk-songs, just like our fake circus and *trompe-l'œil* theater. We have wanted to draw on neglected Parisian sources just as Russian musicians draw on popular Russian sources."[62] This first performance featured the original instrumental accompaniment (violin, cornet in B-flat, trombone, bass drum, triangle, cymbal), and the singer was Alexander Koubitzky, a habitué of Milhaud's circle, whose Russian accent reportedly added to the music's charm.

    This tiny cycle is an evocative time capsule of popular culture during the immediate postwar period—Poulenc described it to the Belgian musicologist Paul Collaer as *"about Paris above all"*[63]—when everything was fast changing and modernizing. The title "Cockades" is emblematic of the tricolor fervor of the French Revolution. Old institutions like music halls had taken on a new chic; entertainments like the Médrano circus, suddenly invested with glamour, were visited by both accustomed voluptuaries and earnest, self-conscious aesthetes— "slumming" became all the rage and something of a relief for those who had previously visited low-life Parisian haunts only with the utmost discretion. Poulenc's Uncle Papoum was one of those well-off members of the upper middle class who for years had liked nothing better than to frequent the temples of working-class entertainment, and introduce his nephew to their forbidden pleasures.

Poulenc makes a highly subjective list in his *Journal* of the things that are evoked in *Cocardes*—"*like views you have to look at in a pen holder.*" Recalling crime stories and newsreels from his adolescence, he includes the Bonnot gang, notorious anarchists from 1912, and "Marseilles 1918"—perhaps on account of the victory parades of the Allied troops on that city's streets. It seems certain that in later years Poulenc linked historical events with personal allusions and somersaults of childhood memory. This stream-of-consciousness approach is also at the heart of the poetry. Poulenc stresses that the essential thing is to believe in the words, which "*fly like a bird from one branch to another.*" The end of one word is often the beginning of the next, which Cocteau highlighted in red ink in the copy he sent to Poulenc—"Carnot, *Joffre*" leading to "*J'offre,*" "Un bonjour de Gust*ave*" juxtaposed to "*Ave* Maria," "piano méca*nique*" morphing into "*Nick* Carter," and so on; and, for that matter, the title *Miel de Narbonne* followed by *Bonne d'enfant*. The poet also underlined the first and last syllable in each poem to show that they matched: "Use, muse," and so on.

Also in his *Journal*, Poulenc classes *Cocardes* "*among my Nogent works, with the smell of frites, the accordion, Piver perfume. In a word, all that I loved at that age, and that I still love. Why not?*"[64] How typical of Poulenc (and the bane of his biographers): something is labeled utterly Parisian on one day and utterly *nogentais* the next—and they are not quite the same thing. As it happens, however, the best description of life among the young artists of this period, and their enduring affection for *Cocardes*, is entirely Parisian. It comes from a rather unexpected source: the autobiography of Darius Milhaud (1952):

> We were not all composers, for our numbers also included performers: Marcelle Meyer, Juliette Meerovitch, Andrée Vaurabourg, the Russian singer Koubitzky; and painters: Marie Laurencin, Irène Lagut, Jean Hugo's fiancée Valentine Gross, Guy Pierre Fauconnet; and writers: Lucien Daudet, Raymond Radiguet, a young poet who was brought to us by Cocteau. After dinner [in the rue Blanche], lured by the steam-driven roundabouts, the mysterious booths . . . the shooting galleries, the games of chance, the menageries, the din of the mechanical organs with their perforated rolls seeming to grind out simultaneously and implacably

all the blaring tunes from the music halls and revues, we would visit the Fair of Montmartre, or occasionally the Cirque Médrano, to see the Fratellinis in their sketches, so steeped in poetry and imagination that they were worthy of the Commedia dell'arte. We finished up the evening at my house. The poets would read their poems, and we would play our latest compositions. Some of them, such as Auric's *Adieu New York*, Poulenc's *Cocardes* and my *Bœuf sur le toit* were continually being played. We even used to insist on Poulenc playing *Cocardes* every Saturday evening: he did so most readily. Out of these meetings, in which a spirit of carefree gaiety reigned, many a fruitful collaboration was to be born.[65]

JOURNAL
DE MES MÉLODIES
FRANCIS POULENC
GRASSET

The cover of the first privately printed edition of Poulenc's Journal de mes mélodies *(1964). The portrait is by Roger de la Fresnaye.*

One of the artists not mentioned here but nevertheless a part of the circle was Roger de la Fresnaye (1885–1925), well known for his fetching cubist watercolors, sometimes linked to themes taken from the war. He also made a pencil drawing of Poulenc that decades later appeared on the cover of the first edition of the *Journal de mes mélodies*.

Although Poulenc said nothing about de la Fresnaye in 1919, by the early fifties he had come to associate the artist's work with the spirit of *Cocardes*.[66] This link with a specific artist, although someone largely forgotten, is a fascinating precursor of Poulenc's cycle *Le Travail du peintre* FP161. A performance of *Cocardes*, illustrated by projected images of de la Fresnaye's watercolors, would make an unusual prelude to a similar performance of the larger cycle.

(i)   *Miel de Narbonne (Honey from Narbonne)*
        D major; frequent changes of time signature ($\frac{4}{8}$, $\frac{5}{4}$, $\frac{4}{4}$) as well as tempo
        (*Très vite, Subito très lent, Très modéré, Très calme*)

Use ton cœur Les clowns fleurissent	Wear out your heart. The clowns
du crottin d'or	flourish on golden manure
Dormir Un coup d'orteils on vole.	Sleep! A toe-kick: we fly.

Volez-vous jouer avec moa	You wanna play with me
Moabite dame de la croix-bleue Caravane.	Moabite, lady of the blue cross. Caravan.
Vanille Poivre Confitures de tamarin.	Vanilla, Pepper, Tamarind Jam.
Marin cou le pompon moustaches mandoline.	Sailor, neck, pompom, moustache, mandoline.
Linoléum en trompe-l'œil Merci.	Trompe-l'oeil linoleum. Thanks.
CINÉMA nouvelle muse	CINEMA, new muse.

This fragmentary song, with all its sudden changes, is a veritable patchwork quilt of allusions to yesterday's century. An invitation to play ("Voulez-vous jouer avec moi?"), charmingly rendered by Cocteau into child's dialect, is the key of the cycle. The musical phrases that connect the seemingly arbitrary images of caravan, vanilla, pepper, and tamarind jam are the first genuine expression of human (rather than animal) nostalgia in Poulenc's songs—moments of luxurious repose that alternate with mock fanfares and winsome coquetry. The final bar ("Cinéma, nouvelle muse") bears some relationship to the 1931 *Avant le cinéma* FP58/iii. Young artists like Cocteau (who was to play an important role in the history of French cinema) were beginning to think of film as something artistic in its own right rather than merely a bizarrely modern entertainment.

(ii)   *Bonne d'enfant (Children's Nursemaid)*
        C major; $\frac{4}{8}$; *Andante* ♪ = 88

Técla notre âge d'or Pipe Carnot Joffre	Técla: our golden age. Pipe, Carnot, Joffre
J'offre à toute personne ayant des névralgies	I offer to anyone suffering from neuralgia . . .
Girafe Noce *un bonjour de Gustave*	Giraffe. Wedding. *Good morning from Gustave.*
Ave Maria de Gounod Rosière	Gounod's Ave Maria, rosy cheeked virgin,
Air de Mayol Touring-Club Phonographe.	Tune by Mayol, Touring Club, Phonograph.
Affiche crime en couleurs Piano mécanique	Poster, "Crime in Full Color." Mechanical piano.
Nick Carter C'est du joli	Nick Carter; It's gorgeous!
Liberté Égalité Fraternité	Liberty, Equality, Fraternity

This is a disingenuous Mozartian pastiche (via neoclassical Stravinsky), with many contemporary allusions. It is only when reading Apollinaire side by side with Cocteau that one realizes how subtle was Apollinaire's ability to synthesize the past and the present, and how much more of a pop artist was Cocteau, an Andy Warhol *avant la lettre*. The allusions come thick and fast. Técla is the name of a Parisian jeweler, famous for cultured pearls and costume jewelry; the implication here is that the "âge d'or" is also not the real thing. Marie-François Carnot and Joseph Joffre, respectively a president (assassinated in 1894) and a revered marshal of France, would seem to have numbered among the heroes of Cocteau's parents' generation. The poet throws some light on this in a 1918 letter to his mother, in which he describes a dance hall close to Bordeaux whose walls are decorated with portraits of Carnot and Joffre, along with paper flowers and reproductions of Renoir; he sees in this kitsch a Picasso-like incongruity.[67] Félix Mayol (1872–1941), a famously camp music-hall star, was well known for singing a cheery and suggestive chanson entitled *Viens, Poupoule!*—which gave Poulenc a self-employed nickname for life. The Touring Club of France, founded in 1890, was a social organization for bicycle enthusiasts. Fictional detective Nick Carter first surfaced in America in 1886 and then went around the world in translation; the serialized film *Nick Carter, le roi des détectives* (with Pierre Bressol in the title role) was released in 1908. "Liberté, Égalité, Fraternité," the three words ending this ditty, are a reminder that Cocteau's postwar intention in writing these poems—"*poèmes tricolores de Cocteau*," as Poulenc later referred to them—was partly patriotic.

(iii)   *Enfant de troupe* (*Child of the Troupe*)
        C major; ¢; *Vite* ♩ = 108, frequent changes of tempo

Morceau pour piston seul polka	Piece for solo cornet, polka
Caramels mous bonbons acidulés pastilles de menthe	Soft toffees, acid-drops, mint pastilles
ENTRACTE L'odeur en sabots	ENTRACTE The smell in clogs
Beau gibier de satin tué par le tambour	Lovely satin gamebird killed by the drum
Hambourg bock sirop de framboise	Hamburg bock beer, raspberry syrup
Oiseleur de ses propres mains	Birdcatcher with his own hands
Intermède uniforme bleu	Intermission, blue uniform
Le trapèze encense la mort	The trapeze praises death to the skies

Here is an enchanting, if rather disjointed, circus scene—perhaps at the Foire du Trône funfair, not far from Nogent—replete with popular culture references. Ushers with trays of refreshments tout their wares during the interval. In a letter to Cocteau, Poulenc boasts of having found a phrase of great gentleness for "uniforme bleu,"[68] with a vocal line that rises in heady, almost erotic admiration. As in all these songs, Cocteau's imagery links war and patriotism: soldiers on leave wearing blue uniforms enjoy the circus, and the term "enfant de troupe" could refer equally to an apprentice acrobat or a young military cadet—both trained to face sudden death. Risking one's life for either country or art is a cause for jubilation. The most powerful moment in the song is at Figure 6 in the score, four bars suspended in time, where a trapeze artist crosses from one side to the other of the high wire, the singer teetering at the top of the stave. The orchestra raucously strikes up at the successful conclusion of the stunt, a perfect parody of the kind of music, empty and purely gestural, to be heard under the big top.

◦   ◦   ◦

FP17 *Valse,* No. 5 of *L'Album des Six* (piano or orchestra), July 1919
FP18 *Quadrille* for piano, four hands, November 1919

° II °

Poulenc in soldier's uniform, 1919.

Outline of a Musical Life:
1920–1929

1920 (aged 21)

(16 and 23 January) In the newspaper *Comœdia,* the critic Henri Collet names Darius Milhaud, Louis Durey, Georges Auric, Arthur Honegger, Germaine Tailleferre, and Poulenc "Les Six," to the group's delight.

(21 February) First public performance of **Cocardes FP16**, at the Théâtre des Champs-Élysées, Paris. The instrumentally accompanied version is sung by Alexander (Sacha) Koubitzky.

FP is invited to Misia Sert's apartment to hear Ravel play through his *La Valse* for Diaghilev, in the presence of Stravinsky. The Russian impresario dismisses the work as a mere "portrait of a ballet," after which Ravel quietly and calmly leaves the room—for FP "*a lesson of a lifetime in modesty.*"[1]

(27 March) At the home of Valentine Hugo, FP—assuming the role of "La belle Poulenka" and accompanied by Jean Cocteau at the piano—dances a ballet-cum-striptease for his friends entitled "Visions de beauté," at one point prancing around in the nude seemingly without embarrassment.[2]

(15 May) Stravinsky's *Pulcinella* is given its premiere at the Opéra.

FP pays a summer visit to Albert Roussel ("*truly charming and so clair-voyant, what a difference from Maurice R*") and his wife at Vastérival, their home near Dieppe.[3] He also spends some days with the painter Jacques-Émile Blanche (1861–1942) in the same vicinity, and sits for a portrait.

(7 December) Raymonde Linossier is admitted to the Paris bar, and will work at the law courts until 1926. Earlier in the year her "novel" *Bibi-la-Bibiste,* although only seventeen lines long, was welcomed by Ezra Pound in *The Little Review.*

1921 (aged 22)

Pianist and composer Jean Wiéner, describing an evening at the bar called Gaya in the rue Boissy-d'Anglais, provides a portrait of the new decade in Paris:

At one table, André Gide, Marc Allégret and a lady. To their side, Diaghilev, Kochno, Picasso and Misia Sert. A little farther away, Mlle Mistinguett, Volterra and Maurice Chevalier. Against the wall Satie, René Clair, his wife, and [Jane] Bathori. Then I noticed Picabia debating with Paul Poiret and Tzara.... Cocteau and Radiguet are saying hello to every table. They embrace Anna de Noailles, whom Lucien Daudet, just having entered, joins.... Léon-Paul Fargue is all alone, standing in front of the door... Fernand Léger gets up and comes to ask us to play *Saint Louis Blues*.... Artur Rubinstein will come this evening after his concert. We can already be sure he will ask me to relinquish my place and that he will play Mazurkas by Chopin for the beautiful ladies accompanying him.... While waiting, Cocteau has come to sit down in front of his drums, and, with his sleeves rolled up, he strikes the cymbal a small blow with his stick from time to time, and right on cue to accompany us in *Old-Fashioned Love*, which Poulenc listens to religiously, leaning on the piano.... I did not see Ravel enter, but he is there with Hélène Jourdan-Morhange... they are looking for Misia's table.[4]

(21 January) FP is demobilized from military service after three years, and goes to the south of France to visit writer Lucien Daudet (1878–1946) and artist Roger de la Fresnaye, who makes several pencil drawings of him.

(Early March) *"Today I depart for Rome... very moved to leave FRANCE for the first time in my life."*[5] Poulenc, traveling with Milhaud, meets composers Alfredo Casella, Mario Labroca, Francesco Malipiero, and Vittorio Rieti during his weeks in Rome, and breakfasts with painter André Derain.

(19 June) First performance of *Les Mariés de la Tour Eiffel* FP23, a collaborative ballet of Les Six, with a libretto by Jean Cocteau. This is the third of Cocteau's experiments in ballet, the others being Satie's *Parade* and Milhaud's *Le Bœuf sur le toit*. Aaron Copland, newly arrived from America to study with Nadia Boulanger, is in the audience.

(November) FP begins his period of tutelage with composer Charles Koechlin (1867–1950). He receives lessons on Mondays and Thursdays until July 1922, and will then continue to see Koechlin on and off until March 1925—seventy hours of tuition in all.

1922 (aged 23)

(Early January) FP meets a younger composer from Bordeaux, Henri Sauguet (1901–1989), having corresponded with him since 1920. Sauguet is to become a lifelong friend and ally.

(Late January–early February) Milhaud and FP, together with the soprano Marya Freund (1876–1966), visit Vienna. They give a concert, all three performing, at the Musikverein on 7 February (*Mouvements perpétuels, Le Bestiaire*). For several days in a row they are received by Alma Mahler (still only in her early forties), and they meet Arnold Schoenberg, Alban Berg, Anton Webern, Egon Wellesz, and Hugo von Hofmannsthal. FP is uneasy with Schoenberg and finds that his study, hung with Expressionist paintings, feels like a laboratory; he is attracted to Berg's lyricism and Webern's purity of sonority.

(Spring) When Béla Bartók visits Paris, FP invites him to lunch with Satie and Auric. "*Satie and Bartók looked at each other as a Martian would look at an inhabitant of the moon.*"[6]

(15 May) Poulenc sits next to Ravel at the French premiere of Prokofiev's Third Piano Concerto. By the middle of this year he is content to follow the pathways indicated by this work and Stravinsky's *Mavra*, claiming to be finished with atonality and polytonality. "*After eighteen months of uncertainty, I have found my true path.*"[7]

(7–10 August) FP visits Salzburg (its music festival had been established in 1920) as Marya Freund's accompanist, giving the world premiere of Falla's *Seven Popular Songs*. He once again encounters Webern, who inscribes a copy of his Quartet Op. 5. Poulenc detects little interest in Salzburg for the music of Stravinsky, Satie, Auric, or Prokofiev; Paul Hindemith, on the other hand, is much in fashion.

After returning from Salzburg and visiting his sister, FP is a guest of Virginie Liénard (1845–1935) at La Lezardière, her home in Nazelles, in the Touraine. "Tante Liénard," as he calls her, is a prodigious fan of modern music, and Stravinsky in particular. We may guess that she has become something of a mother figure for Poulenc. He will spend part of the summer with this beloved friend every year between 1922 and 1927, and will also often stay in her apartment in Cannes.

(22 October) Benito Mussolini forms a government in Italy.

1923 (aged 24)

(January) FP studies the scores of Charles Gounod's operas as part of his task of providing recitatives, at Diaghilev's request (or command), for performances of Gounod's *La Colombe* in Monte Carlo, planned for the beginning of 1924: "*All the arts, from 1910 to 1930, were more or less tributaries of the Ballets Russes, with music seeming to benefit the most from Diaghilev's prophetic impulsion.*"[8]

FP begins composing *Les Biches* FP36, a ballet for Diaghilev.

(March or early April) FP becomes ill with hepatitis. As a result, he is unable to play the fourth piano part in Stravinsky's *Les Noces* on 13 June, as planned—although he does attend the concert, and goes on to play that part more than fifty times during his career. He also applauds Roussel's *Padmâvatî* at the Opéra.

(June) Erik Satie gathers around him a group of composers (Henri Sauguet, Maxime Jacob, Roger Désormière, and Henri Cliquet-Pleyel) that he names "L'École d'Arcueil" (Arcueil was the suburb, south of Paris, where Satie lived), but the group does not survive his death in 1925.

(Late June) FP works on the orchestration of *Les Biches* at his grandparents' home in Nogent-sur-Marne.

(25 June) FP re-encounters harpsichordist Wanda Landowska (1879–1959) at a performance of Falla's *El Retablo de maese pedro,* at the home of Princesse Edmond de Polignac (née Winnaretta Singer), matchless patron of Chabrier, Fauré, Stravinsky, and many others. He will later count his meeting with Landowska—as well as those with Viñes, Jane Bathori, Bernac, and Éluard—as one of the most important of his life.

(August) FP plays the score of *Les Biches* to Diaghilev, who is pleased with its progress. In the next month he seeks advice about the ballet from Charles Koechlin and Sauguet, and plays the score again to Diaghilev in October.

(4 November) FP, accompanied by his friend Auric, arrives in Monte Carlo to work on both *Les Biches* and Gounod's *La Colombe*, rubbing shoulders with Picasso, Georges Braque, and British musicologist Edwin Evans.

(8 November) Adolf Hitler stages a Putsch in Munich in an attempt by the Nazis to overthrow the elected government of Germany.

(12 December) Twenty-year-old poet and writer Raymond Radiguet dies of typhoid fever. FP's friend and colleague Jean Cocteau is inconsolable.

1924 (aged 25)

(1 January) In Monte Carlo, Gounod's *La Colombe*, with recitatives by Poulenc (FP35) and décor by Juan Gris, is given its first performance. *Les Biches* receives its highly successful first performance with the Ballets Russes on the 6th. The premiere of Auric's *Les Fâcheux* takes place three days later.

(21 January) The death of Lenin in Russia clears the way for the ascent of Stalin and the purging of his rivals.

Satie, furious about the friendship between Poulenc, Cocteau, and the critic Louis Laloy (1874–1944), leaves Monte Carlo, where he feels he is being ignored. In *Paris-Journal* (15 February), Satie refers to *Les Biches* and *Les Fâcheux* as "lots of syrupy things" and "buckets of musical lemonade." Later, when Auric and Poulenc send Satie in jest a child's rattle decorated with a beard (which seemed to resemble the older composer), the rupture is complete. Of Les Six, only Milhaud maintains contact with Satie. Possibly the break with Poulenc and Cocteau is also to do with Satie's disapproval of homosexuality and opium—a drug supplied to Cocteau by Laloy.[9]

(12 May) Max Jacob writes a long poem to FP that includes the lines "I have learned of your great success in Monte Carlo / because entire newspapers are filled with your name. / More than of Deputies, Francis, they speak of you / from the banks of the Ganges to the Phlegethon."[10]

(26 May) *Les Biches* is performed at the Théâtre des Champs-Élysées.

After spending a holiday in Vichy playing golf and dancing, FP returns to the Touraine to work on his *Marches militaires* FP30 for piano and orchestra (a work that never sees the light of day), the suite *Napoli* FP40 for piano, the Trio for Oboe, Bassoon, and Piano FP43, and settings of Pierre de Ronsard.

1925 (aged 26)

(December 1924–January 1925) **Poèmes de Ronsard FP38**, composed in Amboise.

(6–27 March) Poulenc has his last seven lessons with Charles Koechlin.

(10 March) First public performance of **Poèmes de Ronsard FP38**, at the Salle des Agriculteurs, Paris. Suzanne Peignot is accompanied by FP. Theirs is a guest appearance in a concert given by pianist Marcelle Meyer.

(4 May) Darius Milhaud marries Madeleine Milhaud (his cousin) at the synagogue in Aix-en-Provence.

(25 May) *Les Biches* is given its first performance in London, at the Coliseum.

During the summer, FP attends a revival of *Les Biches* in Monte Carlo. He spends two weeks with the painter Russell Greeley and his partner, Count François de Gouy d'Arcy, at their estate (Clavary) north of Cannes. Another guest is the Welsh writer and artist Nina Hamnett (1890–1956), who teaches Poulenc some sailors' shanties.[11] At Clavary, Poulenc is already busy working on his *Chansons gaillardes*—"some old and rather naughty French poems of the sixteenth and seventeenth century," Hamnett calls them.

(1925–26) **Chansons gaillardes FP42** (anonymous), composed in Nazelles and at Clavary.

(1 July) Still estranged from his former friends, Erik Satie dies, when FP is in Vichy. He asks Raymonde Linossier (who was close to Satie) to send flowers in his name.

(18 July) Adolf Hitler publishes his autobiography, *Mein Kampf*.

(25 September) FP receives a letter from the teacher and conductor Nadia Boulanger (1887–1979) in which she expresses an interest in discussing his music. He is delighted and responds positively.

(Autumn) At the Amboise train station, FP's hand is crushed by a carriage door and two tendons of his thumb are severed by broken glass. He undergoes an operation, spends ten days in a clinic, and is able to play the piano again only after two months. This injury inevitably affects his ability to compose.

(27 November) FP's painter friend Roger de la Fresnaye, wounded in 1918, dies as a long-term result of his injuries.

(30 November) FP together with Auric, author Paul Morand, and Milhaud and his wife attend a lecture by Jean Cocteau on the subject of Orpheus.

1926 (aged 27)

FP spends the first months of the year in the south of France and visits Stravinsky there. He continues to work on his Trio for Oboe, Bassoon, and Piano.

(15 January) FP lends Charles Koechlin 2,000 francs, asking for 8 percent interest.

(2 May) First public performance of *Chansons gaillardes* FP42, a sell-out, at the Salle des Agriculteurs, Paris. The baritone Pierre Bernac, Poulenc's exact contemporary, is accompanied by the composer in a shared concert of works by Auric and Poulenc. FP's Trio also receives its first performance.

(17 May) FP participates in a Satie festival at the Théâtre des Champs-Élysées.

(11 June) FP and Bernac give a second performance of the *Chansons gaillardes* in the Salle des Agriculteurs. Thereafter, the two lose touch.

FP spends the summer months in Nazelles with "Tante Liénard," working on a violin sonata that is never completed.

Poulenc and Auric travel to Copenhagen for a joint concert of their chamber music, which does not include a new violin sonata by FP as planned.

1927 (aged 28)

(February) *Vocalise* FP44, composed in Paris.

FP begins work on a harpsichord concerto for Wanda Landowska, the *Concert champêtre* FP49.

(April) FP (along with Auric, Milhaud, Ravel, Roussel, Marcel Delannoy, Pierre-Octave Ferroud, Jacques Ibert, Alexis Roland-Manuel, and Florent Schmitt) contributes a short dance (*Pastourelle* FP45) to a project in honor of the ballet teacher, salon hostess, and Alban Berg patron Jeanne Dubost: *L'Éventail de Jeanne*. When the work is produced at the Opéra in 1929, with décor by Marie Laurencin, ten-year-old Tamara Toumanova dances the lead role.

(1927–28) *Airs chantés* FP46 (Moréas), composed in Nazelles and Paris.

FP purchases an impressive property beside the village of Noizay in the Touraine, not far from Tours (the nearest railway station)—a large country house named Le Grand Coteau. He already knows the area well: in neighboring Nazelles, he had often been a guest at the home of "Tante Liénard."

He refers to Le Grand Coteau as *"mon château,"* but it is in dire need of modernization, having been built in the sixteenth century, with additions and improvements made in the eighteenth. It would have pleased Poulenc to remember that another composer had also chosen to live in the Touraine: Chabrier, whose former beloved home, La Membrolle, was not far away.

(2 June) FP embarks for London with Henri Sauguet (whose ballet *La Chatte* is receiving its premiere there), as a rehearsal pianist for performances of Stravinsky's *Les Noces* by the Ballets Russes, the first of his countless visits to the British capital. Eugene

At the front gates of Le Grand Coteau, Poulenc's house in Noizay.

Goossens is the conductor, and the other pianists are Auric, Vittorio Rieti, and Vladimir Dukelsky (later Vernon Duke). When *Les Biches* is performed during the same season, Poulenc is extremely impressed by the orchestral playing; he also adores riding on London buses (according to Nina Hamnett). On 5 July Claire Croiza gives a recital at the Piccadilly home of the Baronne Cathérine d'Erlanger (Debussy, Poulenc, Auric, Chabrier), accompanied by Poulenc and Auric. Cocteau designed a program cover that combines the faces of his two favorite protégés.

Painter Jacques-Émile Blanche spreads rumors that FP is in love with an English girl and intends to marry her.

(August) the Poulenc family property at 4, rue de la Muette, Nogent-sur-Marne (formerly the home of the composer's maternal grandparents), is emptied and rented—the end of an era in his life. Some furniture goes to Noizay and is stored there while work progresses on FP's new home.

André Manceaux (who has recently bought Le Tremblay, a much grander château in Normandy) redesigns the gardens for FP, his younger brother-in-law, at Noizay. Costly renovations on Le Grand Coteau will continue for several years. For some of this time, the composer takes up resi-

dence in a local hotel: *"The plasterer has been working since 4 November. . . .*
I assure you that the more I go to this lovely house the more enamored I am
with it. . . . I am in a hurry to live there."[12]

1928 (aged 29)

FP begins recording with French Columbia Records (a relationship that will
last until 1934)—piano and chamber music, as well as *Le Bestiaire* and songs
by Duparc, Fauré, and Debussy with Claire Croiza (in April).

(3 March) First public performance of **Vocalise FP44**, at the Théâtre du
Vieux-Colombier, Paris. Mezzo-soprano Jane Bathori, accompanied by FP,
also gives the first performances of two songs from *Airs chantés* (i and iv).

(10 June) First public performance of the complete **Airs chantés FP46**, at
the Salle Chopin (the smaller hall of the recently opened Salle Pleyel), Paris.
In this recital of Auric and Poulenc songs, Suzanne Peignot is accompanied
by FP.

FP imagines Raymonde Linossier sharing his new home as his wife. In an
unsuccessful attempt to bring this about, he writes to her sister Alice Ardoin
(1893–1964), asking her to forward a proposal of marriage: *"Did you think*
that I have bought a large house for myself alone. . . . The longer I live, the more
I feel she is the only person with whom I would like to live."[13]

(July) FP is invited to write a new work for a costume ball to be held in
June 1929 at the mansion of Charles and Marie-Laure de Noailles, in the
place des États-Unis. This will be the "concerto choréographique" *Aubade*
FP51, for which FP will be paid an astonishing 25,000 francs.[14]

(August) FP completes work on Wanda Landowska's *Concert champêtre.*

(11 August) FP is a first-time guest at Kerbastic (affectionately known
as "Kerker"), the summer retreat of Jean and Marie-Blanche de Polignac, in
Brittany. He takes the train there, and makes his entrance to the château riding a bicycle that has been left for him under a tree. Kerbastic is described by
Germaine Tailleferre as "a group of large, typically Breton buildings, with
sets of windows in white granite" near a "splendid park in Guidel, next to
the sea."[15]

(30 August) George Gershwin's *Rhapsody in Blue* is performed by its
composer at the home of Comte Étienne de Beaumont.

FP spends much of the autumn supervising the building alterations at
Noizay and arranging his move there, which has been frustratingly plagued
by delays. He takes into his service André Rocheron and his wife Suzanne,
who remain faithfully at Noizay as wine maker and gardener, cook and
housekeeper, for the rest of the composer's life. Suzanne, fearing that Noizay
would be sold after FP's death, will commit suicide in May 1963.

At the end of 1928 and the beginning of 1929, FP writes gramophone record reviews of both instrumental and vocal music for the magazine *Arts phoniques*.[16]

1929 (aged 30)

FP subscribes, via Adrienne Monnier's bookshop, to the new French translation of James Joyce's *Ulysses*.[17]

(February) Wandering the streets of Paris, FP encounters, by chance, Richard Chanlaire (1896–1973), whom he had met some years earlier through mutual friends.[18]

(3 May) *Concert champêtre* receives its premiere (conducted by Pierre Monteux). The work is

> an early example of what would now be called polystylism, in which the whole of French music from the Middle Ages to the present, via the classical and baroque, is scintillatingly convoked to create a never-never-land that is not so much rural as suburban: a mixture of Nogent-sur-Marne and the Ermenonville of Rousseau blended with Landowska's estate at Saint-Leu-la-Forêt to the north of Paris, where parts of it were written, with for the first time just a hint of the "deserts of vast eternity" stretching beyond.[19]

Letters written in May from Poulenc to Richard Chanlaire, in an ardently romantic tone found nowhere else in the correspondence, contain the first unambiguous references to his homosexuality.[20] FP comes to accept that his feelings are unrequited, but the two men remain in contact, on and off, for the rest of their lives. The composer gradually becomes more open, particularly with close friends, about his affairs and sexual adventures. "Homosexuality and Catholicism came to exacerbate, and in a way reveal, elaborate, and dramatize the contradictory forces that were a fundamental part of his nature."[21]

Poulenc confides in Landowska, almost certainly regarding his sexuality and his unrequited passion for Chanlaire. The great harpsichordist, herself bisexual, writes to him, "Be happy and *live* your happiness with all your strength."[22]

(19 June) The commissioned ballet *Aubade* (privately complicated by the unhappiness of the Chanlaire episode) is given a successful first performance at the Noailles home. Among the guests are Paul Morand, Max Jacob, Louis Aragon, Max Ernst, Salvador Dali, and the pianist Jacques Février.

FP spends the summer first in Vichy, then with the Princesse de Poix (mother of Charles de Noailles) at Fontainebleau, once again with the Polignacs at Kerbastic, and finally with his sister and brother-in-law at Le Tremblay. Such a progress from one great house to another becomes a regular summer ritual, allowing him to save a great deal of money in the process.

(19 August) Sergei Diaghilev dies in Venice. In the light of the impending Wall Street crash two months later (29 October), the words of writer Maurice Sachs seem prescient: "Everything that we knew has now finished. There is already despair in the air because we've had enough of enjoying ourselves, of being useless, vain and frivolous. The ox, weary with acting the fool, has come down from the roof."[23]

FP spends much of the autumn working on two projects that are never to come to fruition—the long-delayed *Marches militaires* and a third attempt at a violin sonata.

After nearly two years, FP is at last able to move into a renovated Grand Coteau in Noizay. He welcomes Raymonde Linossier (for the first and last time) as his house guest on 3 November.

(6 December) At the Salle Chopin, FP accompanies Marya Freund in a program of songs by, among others, Karol Szymanowski, Henryk Wieniawski, and his own *Poèmes de Ronsard*.

(11 December) To celebrate the tenth anniversary of the founding of Les Six, an orchestral concert is given in the Théâtre des Champs-Élysées, followed on the 18th by a recital of chamber music and songs (one by each of Les Six, sung by Suzanne Peignot) in the Salle Gaveau.[24]

Songs of the Twenties

FP19 *Suite pour piano*, March 1920

FP20 *Le Gendarme incompris* (incidental music for a one-act play by Jean Cocteau and Raymond Radiguet), November 1920

FP21 *Impromptus* (piano), 1920 (rev. 1924)

FP22 *Quatre Poèmes de Max Jacob* (voice and wind quintet), September 1921

FP23 "Discours du général" and "La Baigneuse de Trouville" (from the ballet *Les Mariés de la Tour Eiffel*), 1921

FP24 *Promenades* (ten pieces for piano), summer 1921

FP25 *Esquisse d'une fanfare* (overture to Act V of *Roméo et Juliette*), summer 1921

FP26 *Trois Études* (for pianola, never performed), summer 1921

FP27 *Première Suite d'orchestre*

FP28 String Quartet (first of four abortive attempts), summer 1921

FP29 Trio for Piano, Clarinet, and Violoncello (lost or destroyed), 1921

FP30 *Marches militaires* for Piano and Orchestra (never performed), 1922

FP31 *Chanson à boire* (drinking song for unaccompanied men's voices), September 1922

FP32 Sonata for Clarinet and Bassoon, September 1922

FP33 Sonata for Horn, Trumpet, and Trombone, August–October 1922

FP34 *Caprice espagnol* (oboe and piano, lost or destroyed)

FP35 Recitatives for *La Colombe* of Charles Gounod, 1923

FP36 *Les Biches* (ballet), 1923

FP37 Quintet for Strings and Clarinet (lost or destroyed)

o   o   o

FP38 ***Poèmes de Ronsard***

    Composed in Amboise, December 1924–January 1925

    [*Suzanne Peignot, Marya Freund, Vera Janacopoulos, Mme* (Claire) *Croiza, Jeanne* (Jane) *Bathori*; Heugel]

Literary source: Pierre de Ronsard (1524–1585), *Poésies choisies de Pierre de Ronsard*, ed. Roger Sorg and Bertrand Guégan (Paris: Chez Payot, 1924). (i) p. 149, from *Les Odes de P Ronsard, gentilhomme vendomois* (1550); (ii) pp. 113–14, from *De l'Éléction de son sépulcre*; (iii) p. 86, from *Les Amours* (1555); (iv) p. 258, published posthumously in *Dernier Vers* (1586); (v) p. 108, from *Odes de Pierre de Ronsard* (1550).

(i)   *Attributs*
(ii) *Le Tombeau*
(iii) *Ballet*
(iv) *Je n'ai plus que les os*
(v)   *À son page*

Ronsard was France's greatest Renaissance poet, a scholar and reformer of verse techniques (he belonged to the constellation of poets known as La Pléiade) as well as an astonishingly original artist. His profound studies of Homer, Pindar, Horace, and Petrarch laid the foundation stones of a French literature that abandoned medieval literary precepts in favor of the Greek and Roman classics. And his fame was such that he traversed national and political boundaries, writing poems in honor of Charles IX of Spain, Catherine de Medici, Mary Queen of Scots (who sent him a gift from her captivity), and Mary's enemy Elizabeth I. When working on these songs, Poulenc may not have realized that Ronsard had spent the last twenty years of his

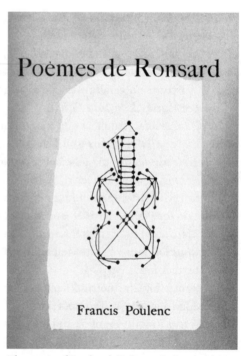

The cover of Poulenc's Poèmes de Ronsard *(1924), designed by Picasso.*

life and was buried in the Prieure of Saint-Cosme, in the Touraine. This ancient priory is not far from Noizay, where the composer was soon to make his home.

In 1924, to celebrate the four-hundredth anniversary of Ronsard's birth, *La Revue musicale* issued a handsome paperback supplement devoted to the poet's connection with music, containing eight specially commissioned settings. The most famous of the chosen composers, Maurice Ravel, with his *Ronsard à son âme*, unintentionally denied the publication a contribution from Ravel's former teacher, the dying Gabriel Fauré, who was planning to set the same poem. Fauré tore up his sketch (it would have been his last work) when he heard about Ravel's. Albert Roussel's graceful setting *Rossignol, mon mignon* (for soprano and flute) has stood the test of time and remains in the repertoire. André Caplet's *Sonnet de Pierre de Ronsard* (with harp accompaniment), a lesson in how to set a sonnet to music, should be better known. Two further sonnet settings by Paul Dukas and Roland-Manuel, as well as songs by Louis Aubert and Maurice Delage, are less interesting—the complexity and density of this kind of poetry often leads to convoluted musical solutions. But Arthur Honegger's *Plus tu connais que je brûle pour toi* is of a simplicity that rivals Ravel's and is hauntingly effective.

When it came to fellow members of Les Six, Poulenc was close friends with Auric and Milhaud (only envying Auric later on account of the money he made with film music), and he was not afraid of being outshone by Durey or Tailleferre. Honegger was another matter; there is no doubt that Poulenc resented that this composer was invited to take part in the Ronsard tribute and he was not. Even Saint-Saëns, who had died a few years earlier, is represented by an advertisement for four Ronsard settings published by Durand. It is likely that Poulenc's determination to prove himself as a Ronsard composer was initiated by pique.

The anniversary supplement is a wonderful artifact for what it tells us about musical life in 1924 Paris. Conductors announcing upcoming concerts include Walter Damrosch, Willem Mengelberg (visiting from Amsterdam with Wanda Landowska as soloist), and Serge Koussevitsky (with guest artists Serge Prokofiev and Igor Stravinsky). Soprano Ninon Vallin is accompanied by pianist Édouard Risler; Marcel Dupré is giving an organ recital; Alfred Cortot plays ten recitals in May, chronologically arranged by composer; and Arthur Rubinstein's concerts conflict with two of Cortot's dates. One of the most arresting pages is devoted to the forthcoming Paris season of the Ballets Russes, repeating at the Théâtre des Champs-Élysées their earlier triumphs in Monte Carlo: Auric's ballet *Les Fâcheux*, Milhaud's *Le Train bleu*, and above all, Poulenc's sensational *Les Biches*. Such a stellar reminder of that success must have compensated Poulenc somewhat for the announcement on the previous page of a "Festival Honegger" with the Pro Arte Quartet. Poulenc's ascendancy over his peers, taken for granted today, was far from assured, and he was acutely aware of the fact. Honegger became something of a *bête noire*, all the more so since Poulenc was a friend of singer Claire Croiza, whom Honegger would abandon in 1929, leaving her a single mother. This unofficial rift between the two composers was healed by an exchange of letters only thirty years later.

The musicological part of the *La Revue musicale* volume consists of a sequence of essays ("Ronsard et la musique") by the top French commentators and critics of the time—André Suarès, Louis Laloy, Henri Prunières, and André Schaeffner

Tombeau de Ronsard, *a booklet of eight settings of the poet published by* La Revue musicale *as a supplement in 1924.*

among them. In Schaeffner, a Belgian critic with strong ties to Parisian music, Poulenc had a true friend and supporter, and as with all such allies he nurtured the connection assiduously. No doubt aware that Poulenc was miffed at having been left out of the *Revue* project, Schaeffner sent him an anthology of Ronsard's verse (*Poésies choisies de Pierre de Ronard*) to which he had contributed a musical appendix, artfully challenging the composer to throw his hat in the ring.

The first thing to recognize in these five songs is the huge contrast in length and complexity with the fragmentary and simplistic *Cocardes* of six years earlier—solid progress in terms of creating music as an organic whole. Poulenc initially considered them *"de vraies mélodies"*—"*real songs of the length of Fauré's and Debussy's, with something rather new about them in spirit.*"[25] He felt he had arrived, in a sense, and a number of critics seemed to agree. In a letter to Auric he boasts about his well-paid contract for the songs with a new publisher (Heugel), and the fact that they were going to be performed by Claire Croiza for the Princesse de Polignac.[26] This was clearly deeply irritating for Auric, who did not admire these songs, and no doubt resented the slower progress of his own career in comparison with the unexpected comet that was Poulenc's. Poulenc described to Claude Rostand the occasion when the thrust of Auric's rapier punctured his happy complacency, and dispatched the Ronsard songs for good and all:

> I think back to the little station at Meudon one April night. We'd just spent the evening with Louis Laloy, Debussy's great friend and first biographer. The air smelt of lilacs; I was feeling in fine form. Suddenly, just as the train was coming into the station, Auric, as though someone had turned a key, suddenly said to

me: "I must tell you. Your Ronsard songs, apart from the beginning of the first one, and the end of the last, are not you. You're not made for the classical poets. Stay with Apollinaire, set Max Jacob, Éluard and Reverdy."[27]

Poulenc was confident, usually vain (sometimes insufferably so) about his music. On a good day his self-esteem would brook no obstacles. But it could quickly crumble when it met with an immovable obstacle, such as Auric's ukase. The fall from grace of the *Poèmes de Ronsard* in the composer's own eyes was spectacular: from that moment on, they were "bad" Poulenc, the result of going down the wrong path. For the following generations, they became the exiles and pariahs among the composer's vocal catalogue. Hardly ever sung in concerts, they were never taught by Bernac in master classes (at least not in my hearing), and their "failure" was always blamed on the belief that Charles Koechlin in the early twenties had somehow steered the young composer in the wrong direction.

In his article "Poulenc and Koechlin: 58 Lessons and a Friendship," Robert Orledge makes a magnificent case for the highly honorable and positive role Koechlin played in Poulenc's professional life.[28] The composer admitted his debt in 1929, calling Koechlin *"a wonderful teacher . . . whose voice I hear continually in my ear."*[29] We no doubt owe his wonderful choral music to exercises he did for Koechlin, and there is absolutely nothing to support the theory that the older composer had somehow ruined, or even diverted, a natural talent. If Poulenc was going through a phase of exaggerated experimental modernity, this was surely more to do with his awareness of the Second Viennese School and his worship of Stravinsky. Two songs (ii and v) possess a grandeur and stature that show a real affinity with the darkness of their sixteenth-century texts; *Je n'ai plus que les os* in particular achieves the kind of majesty that suggests the age of the Valois kings.

The Ronsard songs did not deserve to be entirely exiled,[30] even if they were destined to be superseded. But Poulenc, with his genius for public relations, turned their damnation to the advantage of his narrative. It suited his role as the musician of Apollinaire and Éluard (and other contemporary poets) to have "failed" with earlier poetry, so that his affinity with the modern writers was considered something almost preternatural. It was important that "ease" and "naturalness" be seen to lie at the heart of his work, as if he wanted to avoid the impression of any tortuous effort. It was also essential for the purposes of his frequent public conversations that he could openly admit to having failed at some things, and avoid seeming to be self-congratulatory on all fronts. A handful of his works appear to have been sacrificed to this purpose, and thus we have the strange phenomenon of Poulenc appearing to denounce works, like the Ronsard songs, that have their very positive merits. He did admit, however, to a certain pride in the accuracy of the songs' prosody.

(i)   *Attributs (Attributes)*
> B-flat minor; $\frac{4}{4}$; *Allegro giocoso* ♩= 132 (Bernac found Poulenc's metro-
> nome markings in these songs too fast.[31])

Les épis sont à Cérès,	The corn belongs to Ceres,
Aux Dieux bouquins les forêts,	The forests to the Satyr gods,
À Chlore l'herbe nouvelle,	The fresh grass to Chloris,
À Phœbus le vert laurier,	The green laurel to Phoebus,
À Minerve l'olivier	The olive tree to Minerva,
Et le beau pin à Cybèle;	The lovely pine to Cybele;
Aux Zéphires le doux bruit,	The sweet sound to Zephyr,
À Pomone le doux fruit,	The sweet fruit to Pomona,
L'onde aux Nymphes est sacrée,	The seas are sacred to the Nymphs,
À Flore les belles fleurs;	The lovely flowers to Flora;
Mais les soucis et les pleurs	But sadness and tears
Sont sacrés à Cythérée.	Are sacred to Cytherea.

The list of gods, and the merry abandon with which the words are set, gives this song a connection with Schubert's rollicking Schiller setting *Dithyrambe*, with its party atmosphere. Poulenc acknowledged the influence here of Stravinsky's *Mavra* (the prancing basses of the opening come from that work's overture). Critics commented on the composer's "insouciance"—his ability to create something partly serious and partly frivolous, a post-Offenbach cancan of the gods. Although he has not yet learned how to write a vocal line that seems liquid and inevitable, the concluding lines about Cythèrée are set with a typically Poulencian tenderness. Details in the accompaniment—the snaking descent of the right hand into the bass clef in bar 4, the gusting wind effect after "Aux Zéphires le doux bruit," the welling tears that rise up the bass stave eight bars from the end—show considerable pianistic ingenuity. *Attributs*, dedicated to Suzanne Peignot, was the composer's own favorite of the set.

(ii)   *Le Tombeau (The Tomb)*
> No key signature (F minor); $\frac{4}{4}$; *Modéré—sans lenteur* ♩= 88

Quand le ciel et mon heure	When the heavens and the hour
Jugeront que je meure,	Decree that I should die
Ravi du beau séjour	Stolen from the beauty
Du commun jour,	Of everyday existence,

Je défends qu'on ne rompe
Le marbre pour la pompe
De vouloir mon tombeau
    Bâtir plus beau,

Mais bien je veux qu'un arbre
M'ombrage en lieu d'un marbre,
Arbre qui soit couvert
    Toujours de vert.

De moi puisse la terre
Engendrer un lierre
M'embrassant en maint tour
    Tout à l'entour;

Et la vigne tortisse
Mon sépulcre embellisse,
Faisant de toutes parts
    Un ombre épars.

I forbid that anyone should break up
Marble for the pomp
Of wishing my tomb
    Be built more beautifully,

I'd rather that a tree
Sheltered me than a marble tomb,
A tree forever covered
    With green.

Let the earth bring forth
From me ivy
To twine around me
    Coil upon coil.

And let this twisted vine
Adorn my sepulchre,
Affording all about me
    Scattered shade.

Bernac labels the music "laboriously and artificially elaborate," and it does aspire to the complexity in simplicity (that is, not very simple at all) of the neoclassical style espoused by Stravinsky. (And why not? Ronsard is neither a Romantic nor a modern poet.) As an older composer, Poulenc would perhaps have better understood the poem's tranquility and humility; the music becomes vehement and overheated, as if Ronsard had the energy here to throw a tantrum. However, the genuine voice of Poulenc shines through the artifice. When the piano gambols in roulades on the last page to illustrate "embellisse" (pre-echoes of Louise de Vilmorin's *Violon* FP101/v), we realize the composer is unable to remain pofaced for long; four bars from the end appears the only glissando to be found in Poulenc's mélodie accompaniments. There are glints of musical inspiration here that amply prophesy the composer's future in poetry of a different kind. The dedicatee is Marya Freund, the singer associated with early performances of Schoenberg's *Pierrot lunaire* and whose eightieth birthday Poulenc would honor, forty years later, with *La Souris* FP162/i.

(iii) *Ballet*

      No key signature (F major–D minor/major); $\frac{4}{4}$ (constantly changing to $\frac{5}{4}$ or $\frac{6}{4}$); *Très animé* $\downarrow$ = 160, with changes

Le soir qu'Amour vous fit en la salle descendre	That evening when Cupid bade you come down to the ballroom
Pour danser d'artifice un beau ballet d'Amour,	To dance an artful dance of love,
Vos yeux, bien qu'il fût nuit, ramenèrent le jour,	Although it was night your eyes conjured back the daylight,
Tant ils surent d'éclairs par la place répandre.	So able were they to spread brightness all around.
Le ballet fut divin, qui se soulait reprendre,	The dancing was divine, and it managed to revive anew,
Se rompre, se refaire et, tour dessus retour,	To break off, to remake itself, and, by twist and turn,
Se mêler, s'écarter, se tourner à l'entour,	To mingle, to stand apart, to circle round and round,
Contre-imitant le cours du fleuve de Méandre.	Like the mazy motion of the river Meander.
Ores il était rond, ores long, or' étroit,	Now in a ring, now in a line, now close together,
Or' en pointe, en triangle, en la façon qu'on voit	Now tapering to a point, in a triangle, as we see
L'escadron de la grue évitant la froidure.	Flocks of cranes flying off to hotter climes.
Je faux, tu ne dansais, mais ton pied voletait	No I'm wrong, you were not dancing, your feet soared
Sur le haut de la terre; aussi ton corps s'était	Above the earth; and your body
Transformé pour ce soir en divine nature.	Was transformed for that one night into divine nature.

The ballet danced here is rather more *The Rite of Spring* than a stately occasion at the court of the Valois kings. Poulenc never wrote anything more difficult to count, a song full of stuttering rhythmic energy where "the river Meander" seems related to the Volga and menaces rather than charms. With the second verse ("Le ballet fut divin"), there is a complete change of register as Poulenc's instinct for almost-vulgar populism asserts itself, in a way that seems almost shocking (as if Richard Rodgers's "March of the Siamese Children" from *The King and I* were suddenly to appear in the middle of *Les Noces*). As though ashamed of these cheery (or perhaps cheesy) melodic sequences, the composer switches into totally unmelodic modernistic posture for the third verse; he then provides a new section (*Plus lent*) of slinky, jazz-like music for the final three lines, with splashy harmonies that add to the impression of an improvised mishmash. The last page, in calmer mood, displays some no doubt unintentional echoes of the D minor dotted rhythms of Fauré's *Danseuse* (from *Mirages*), a masterpiece of understatement written about a decade earlier. Auric's dislike of Poulenc's Ronsard style here seems somewhat justified.

(iv)   *Je n'ai plus que les os* (*I Have Only My Bones*)
No key signature (A minor/D minor); $^3_4$-$^6_8$ (frequent changes); *Adagio* ♪ = 88

Je n'ai plus que les os, un squelette je semble,
Décharné, dénervé, démusclé, dépoulpé,
Que le trait de la mort sans pardon a frappé.
Je n'ose voir mes bras que de peur je ne tremble.

Apollon et son fils, deux grands maîtres, ensemble
Ne me sauraient guérir; leur métier m'a trompé.
Adieu plaisant soleil; mon œil est étoupé,
Mon corps s'en va descendre où tout se désassemble.

Quel ami me voyant en ce point dépouillé
Ne remporte au logis un œil triste et mouillé,
Me consolant au lit et me baisant la face,

En essuyant mes yeux par la mort endormis?
Adieu, chers compagnons, adieu mes chers amis,

I have only my bones, I seem like a skeleton,
Devoid of flesh, of nerves, of muscle, of substance,
Which the unforgiving hand of death has struck.
I daren't look at my arms for fear of trembling.

Apollo and his son, two master physicians, working in tandem
Could not cure me. Their profession has led me astray.
Farewell, lovely sun; my eyes are clouded over,
My body will descend to where everything falls apart.

What friend, seeing me thus laid bare,

Would not visit me with a moist and mournful eye,
Consoling me on my sickbed and kissing my face,

And wiping my eyes, which death has put to sleep?
Farewell, dear companions, farewell my dear friends,

| Je m'en vais le premier vous préparer la place. | I am going before, to prepare you a place. |

This sonnet, written at the end of Ronsard's life, was published posthumously (in 1586) in *Dernier Vers*. Poulenc rises to the occasion magnificently, with a song that is surely the dark and unacknowledged jewel of the set. That he dedicates it to Claire Croiza, the most famous mélodie singer of the time apart from Ninon Vallin, shows that he estimated it too. The "pointless complications" of which Bernac complains seem far more troublesome in some of the other songs;[32] this one has an implacable sweep to it. Poulenc never wrote a slower song ($\jmath = 44$), and he never chose a darker text. He was not yet pastiche-master of sixteenth-century style (as he was later to become for *À sa guitare* FP79), but he caught the bleak and stoic grandeur of Ronsard's century, when a man of sixty could expect to die grateful for a long life. Ronsard, in the grip of terminal illness, describes his physical deterioration—and we hear death's stalking tread throughout the music. The pulse-racing panic toward the end is the response of the hypochondriac composer rather than that of the composed, and dying, poet. The fact that Poulenc avoids mentioning the song in his *Journal* seems less a result of musical disdain than of fear, as if the music were somehow jinxed: he had created a song that looked into a frightening abyss he did not care to revisit, particularly when he was in his sixties and experiencing strange, inexplicable—and accurate, as it turned out—intimations of his own mortality.

(v)   *À son page (To His Page)*
        C major; mainly $\frac{4}{4}$ (after opening page); *Allegro molto* $\jmath = 168$

Fais rafraîchir mon vin	Chill my wine until
Qu'il passe en froideur un glaçon;	It's colder than an icicle;
Fais venir Jeanne, qu'elle apporte	Call for Jeanne, and have her bring
Son luth pour dire une chanson;	Her lute so she can oblige us with a song;
Nous ballerons tous trois au son,	All three of us will dance to its music,
Et dis à Barbe qu'elle vienne,	And tell Barbe to join us,
Les cheveux tors à la façon	With her hair all in ringlets
D'une folâtre italienne.	Like a wild Italian girl.
Ne vois-tu que le jour se passe?	Can't you see that the day is dying?
Je ne vis point au lendemain;	I never give a thought to the morrow;
Page, reverse dans ma tasse,	Page, come recharge my cup,
Que ce grand verre soit tout plein.	Fill my big glass to the brim.

Maudit soit qui languit en vain!	A curse on those who languish in vain!
Ces vieux médecins je n'appreuve;	I don't approve of those old doctors;
Mon cerveau n'est jamais bien sain	My brain is never sound
Si beaucoup de vin n'abreuve.	Unless it's watered with lots of wine!

Although the lyric is a drinking song of great elegance, the song is extraordinarily bitty, even by Poulenc's patchwork-quilt standards. Speed and verve, rather than any attempt at organic musical cohesion, are what make it stick together. The opening stomp of Russian peasant music ($\frac{7}{8} + \frac{4}{8} + \frac{5}{8} + \frac{6}{8} + \frac{5}{4} + \frac{3}{4}$, all within seven bars) is annealed to the romp and carefree scuttle of the Folies Bergère. In this mélange the great French poet is made to drink (albeit posthumously) the uncertain health of the devil-may-care 1920s. At one point the accompaniment goes into three staves, as if to prove Poulenc's avant-garde credentials; the peroration works up a head of steam where ebullience combines with "melancholy lyricism" (Bernac), a rather effective depiction of intoxication. The postlude sounds as if the accompanist, in the grip of *delirium tremens*, is chasing a chord that continues to elude his grasp. The composer Jacques Legeurney (1906–1997), a specialist in the poetry of La Pléiade, made a wonderful setting of these words in 1944, in which a cast of four characters is more clearly delineated: an inebriated aristocrat and his page, plus the compliant Jeanne and Barbe. Poulenc ignores the erotically illustrative possibilities of such an occasion.

○　　　　　　　　○　　　　　　　　○

FP39　Sonata for Violin and Piano (a second unsuccessful attempt), 1924–25

FP40　*Napoli* (piano), 1922–25

FP41　*Dorfmusikanten-Sextett von Mozart* (a transcription of Mozart's *Ein musikalischer Spaß*, for piano), 1925

○　　　　　　　　○　　　　　　　　○

FP42　*Chansons gaillardes* (*Ribald Songs*)

　　　Composed in Navelles and at Clavary (near Cannes), 1925–26

　　　[*Mme Fernand Allard*; Heugel]

　　　Literary source: *Choix de Chansons joyeuses suplement* [sic] *à l'anthologie* (Paris, 1765). Vol. IV, *Chansons gaillardes*: (i) p. 2 with the title "Les Deux Pucelages," (iii) p. 43 with the title "La Fille sans têtons," (iv) p. 73, (vi) p. 33, (vii) p. 15 with the title "Avis à la belle jeunesse," (viii) p. 17 with the title "La Main."

　　　The two drinking songs are taken from vol. III, *Anthologie françoise, ou Chansons choisies*: (ii) p. 217, (v) p. 278. Both are printed as unaccompanied vocal duos.

(i)   *La Maîtresse volage*
(ii)   *Chanson à boire*
(iii) *Madrigal*
(iv)   *Invocation aux Parques*
(v)   *Couplets bachiques*
(vi)   *L'Offrande*
(vii) *La Belle Jeunesse*
(viii) *Sérénade*

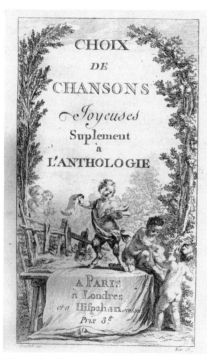

Choix de Chansons joyeuses, *the source of a number of* Chansons gaillardes FP42.

Some years before I actually visited Poulenc's library at Noizay, I had more or less given up my search for a book entitled *Chansons gaillardes* where I might reasonably have hoped to discover these anonymous texts. I had also long been hoping to acquire the literary source of Mozart's two songs in French: *Oiseaux, si tous les ans* K307 and *Dans un bois solitaire et sombre* K308. I eventually traced the Mozart poems to Monnet's *Anthologie françoise* [sic], *ou Chansons choisies depuis le 13ème siècle jusqu'à présent* (Paris, 1765), a set of four beautifully produced volumes decorated with plates and vignettes. Old French texts were here united with equally old tunes—mostly notated on single staves of melody, but sometimes arranged as duets on two staves. Both Mozart songs texts are in volume I.

Volume IV is divided into two parts, the first with music and the second subtitled *Chansons gaillardes*, and seems to have been published as an optional extra for selected, unshockable clients only. To my delight, six of the eight poems from Poulenc's cycle were here, among others equally scabrous and amusing. The two remaining Poulenc texts ("Chanson à boire" and "Couplets bachiques") are to be found in volume III, both with music (Poulenc, like Mozart, simply ignored the original "airs"). Also in volume III the composer found the "Chanson à boire" ("Vive notre Hôtesse") that he set as an *a cappella* TTBB quartet in September 1922 (FP31). It was almost comically unfortunate that this drinking song, Poulenc's first work for unaccompanied chorus, was written for the Harvard Glee Club during the Prohibition era, and received no public performances in America as a result. Poulenc had to wait until 1950 to hear it for the first time, and was astonished that he had no desire to change anything about it.

In a letter of August 1922 to the composer Jean Wiéner, the composer reports that his *Chansons gaillardes* are awaiting their first performance. Perhaps he was counting chickens before they had hatched (it was not uncommon for him to boast about projects that had not yet come to fruition), but it seems likely that at least some of the cycle, officially dated 1925–26, had already been composed;[33] Poulenc informed Milhaud that he had written some "*chansons françaises incovenantes*" (improper French songs) on eighteenth-century texts.[34] Clearly Poulenc, never a very exact historian, simply meant "taken from an eighteenth-century book," but according to the title page of the *Anthologie françoise* some of the poems go back to medieval times. The song cycle's title page has "texts from the seventeenth century," and this seems to have been a reasonable guess on account of the lyrics' language and style.

As far as the somewhat obscene texts were concerned, the singer had to bear the brunt of any possible discomfort on the part of audiences of the 1920s, in a way that was spared the pianist/composer, who did not have to face the audience. ("*You have to forgive me this innate taste for obscene songs; it is one of my French defects.*"[35]) And it was not only the young Pierre Bernac who found the texts embarrassing (in 1926)—a performance with another singer in Brussels arranged for January 1927 had to be canceled, offense having been taken at the word "pucelage." In a letter to the Belgian musicologist Paul Collaer, Poulenc commented on the "*irremediable impropriety*" of *L'Offrande* and *Sérénade*, not that he seems to have felt any regret about it.[36]

By the mid 1930s, Bernac had found a way of presenting these songs with sufficient clarity to amuse the libertines, and ambiguity enough to avoid offending the morally upright. He must have taught the *Gaillardes* a thousand times, so popular are they with baritones. In master classes he made a point of turning his back on the audience and engaging the student-singer in a mock-discreet man-to-man chat, purportedly to reveal the already obvious double entendres of the texts. In this way he simultaneously conveyed to the public that yes, the songs *were* really as rude as suggested by the printed translations, and he was spared any further public explication.

Why the Ronsard cycle should be so seldom performed and this collection should have remained ceaselessly popular is scarcely a mystery. The poetry is far less good than Ronsard's, but this is precisely what appealed to Poulenc—and the result is a much more characteristic piece of music. The tradition of outrageous *Chansons gaillardes* may be a time-honored one in French literature, but singing them on the recital platform is another matter, also perhaps to do with the age of the performer and the prevailing Zeitgeist. What seemed deliciously daring when I first performed these songs in 1975 seems far less hilarious now—to me, at least; in the same way, "épater [shocking] la bourgeoisie" was much more fun for Poulenc in 1926 than it would have been had he lived, as we do, in an age of legal pornographic surfeit. The songs are highly effective despite, rather than on account of, their obscenities. Poulenc counsels against "knowing winks" in performance,[37] but the four songs in fast tempi are impossible to distort in such a manner, and it would take an exceptionally bold and vulgar singer to act out the slow ones. What makes the cycle effective in performance are the rhythmic drive of the music, the virtuosic pianism, and the stream of vocal melody that has replaced the artful motivic constructions of the Ronsard songs. Poulenc is now writing his own folksongs, as Ravel remarked. His musical means throughout are simple and direct while remaining challenging, especially so far as the accompaniments are concerned.

(i) *La Maîtresse volage (The Flighty Mistress)*
     G minor; $\frac{2}{4}$; *Rondement* (The vocal line, as throughout this cycle, is written in the bass clef.) $\downarrow$ = 176

Ma maîtresse est volage,	My mistress is flighty,
Mon rival est heureux;	My rival is delighted;
S'il a son pucelage,	If he took her virginity,
C'est qu'elle en avait deux.	She must have had two.
Et vogue la galère,	So let the dice fall
Tant qu'elle, tant qu'elle,	As long as they, as long as they,
Et vogue la galère, tant qu'elle,	So let the dice fall, as long as
Pourra voguer.	They may fall.

The poem's heading is "Les Deux Pucelages" (The two virginities), but Poulenc preferred to reveal the joke in the telling. The music veritably crows with the glee of someone who has trounced a rival. Like the other fast songs in the cycle, this one must appear to be very youthful; Poulenc found a performance by Gérard Souzay in 1956 *"too slow, too virtuous."*[38] And it is this first song—written in the manner of a folksong "with a beat," the prototype of *Chanson d'Orkenise* FP107/i—that best suggests a seventeenth-century musical style. The composer takes his cue from Stravinksy's *Pulcinella* (1920), where the musical past is reinvented in modern terms—like a château on the Loire with ultra-modern furniture.

(ii) *Chanson à boire (Drinking Song)*
      C minor; $\frac{4}{4}$; *Adagio* $\downarrow$ = 60

SONGS OF THE TWENTIES: FP42 o 63

Les rois d'Égypte et de Syrie,	The kings of Egypt and Syria
Voulaient qu'on embaumât leur corps,	Wished to have their bodies embalmed,
Pour durer plus longtemps morts.	To last longer dead.
Quelle folie!	What folly!
Buvons donc selon notre envie,	Let us drink as much as we want,
Il faut boire et reboire encore.	We must drink and drink again.
Buvons donc toute notre vie,	Let's drink our whole lives through,
Embaumons-nous avant la mort.	Let's embalm ourselves before we die.
Embaumons-nous;	Let's embalm ourselves;
Que ce baume est doux.	How sweet the balm.

While it is not uncommon to find singers and pianists applying a wayward rubato here in the hope of appearing musically drunk, young performers need to learn that those who drink the most—reaching a state of embalmment, as the poem has it—can often appear to be the most sober. The thick, weighted chords of the accompaniment in the bass clef suggest someone so pickled that his only possible movements are carefully considered, if somewhat elephantine (some passages here predict the chordal distributions of the piano music for *L'Histoire de Babar, le petit éléphant* from 1940). There is no ducking and weaving; this kind of stately drunkenness goes beyond the talents of the common man. The pharaohs of ancient Egypt provide a time-honored justification for inebriation, and the lugubrious blocks of chords emulate the imposing dimensions of the Temple of Karnak in Luxor.

(iii) *Madrigal*
F-sharp minor; $\frac{2}{4}$; *Très décidé* ♩ = 152–160

Vous êtes belle comme un ange,	You are lovely as an angel,
Douce comme un petit mouton;	Sweet as a little sheep;
Il n'est point de cœur, Jeanneton,	There is no human heart, Jeanneton,
Qui sous votre loi ne se range.	Who is not beneath your sway.
Mais une fille sans tétons	But a girl without boobs
Est une perdrix sans orange.	Is a partridge without an orange.

The poem's original title is "La Fille sans tétons" and Poulenc substitutes the innocuous *Madrigal* to avoid giving the game away. A miniature of considerable musical skill with a remarkably agile piano part, the song is both gleefully cruel and smugly arrogant. One of the least shocking songs in the flat-chested 1920s, this loutish and misogynist insult now seems more objectionable than those with texts about self-pleasuring. (The recycling of the saucy and piquant music as Poulenc's second *Novelette* for piano, FP47/ii, has the advantage of being word- and insult-free.) Fortunately Poulenc, the least misogynistic of men, was later to expiate this *folie de jeunesse* with some of the most perfectly judged music for women, and about women, ever written.

(iv)   *Invocation aux Parques (Invocation to the Fates)*
     C-sharp minor; ¾; *Grave* ♩ = 56 (Bernac points out that Poulenc always
     played the opening eight bars at about ♩ = 50.)

Je jure, tant que je vivrai,	I promise, as long as I live,
De vous aimer, Sylvie.	To love you, Sylvie.
Parques, qui dans vos mains tenez	Ye Fates, who hold in your hands
Le fil de notre vie,	The thread of our lives,
Allongez, tant que vous pourrez,	Make mine, I beg of you,
Le mien, je vous en prie.	As long as possible.

A prayer to the Fates, and on one level very like Racine (according to Poulenc),[39] but this mock-prayer contains an in-joke first explained to me years ago by Hugues Cuenod (who also invented and sang an obscene parody-text of Poulenc's *C*, to the composer's delighted amusement). The supplication here is to make the narrator's life as long as possible, but with a nod and a wink this also applies to his penis—the size of which is said to have some link with the span of his hand. In the two closing bars Poulenc provides a postlude built on right-hand tenths—as if the pianist were demonstrating the required optimum endowment. (It might also encompass a covert boast on the composer's own part—he was, after all, the work's first accompanist.) This postlude is a taxing stretch even for pianists with large hands.

(v)   *Couplets bachiques (Bacchic Verses)*
     A-flat major; 2/4; *Très animé* ♩ = 152

Je suis tant que dure le jour	I am, all the livelong day,
Et grave et badin tour à tour.	Sad and merry each in turn.
Quand je vois un flacon sans vin,	When I see an empty wine bottle,
Je suis grave, je suis grave,	I am sad, I am sad,
Est-il tout plein, je suis badin.	If it's full to the neck, I'm merry.
Je suis tant que dure le jour	I am, all the livelong day,
Et grave et badin tour à tour.	Sad and jolly each in turn.

Quand ma femme me tient au lit,	When my wife holds me in bed,
Je suis sage, je suis sage,	I'm well-behaved, I'm well-behaved,
Quand ma femme me tient au lit,	When my wife holds me in bed,
Je suis sage toute la nuit.	I'm well-behaved the whole night through.
Si catin au lit me tient	If a trollop holds me in bed
Alors je suis badin	Then I'm merry.
Ah! belle hôtesse, versez-moi du vin	Ah! Lovely hostess, pour me more wine
Je suis badin, badin, badin.	I am merry, merry, merry.

Of all Poulenc's song accompaniments, this one, bristling with runs in double thirds and chords that dart all over the keyboard, is perhaps the hardest to play. The song is remarkably exuberant, and even genial—mainly about drinking, but including adultery in its boastful list of misdemeanors. Bernac advises the singer to show "the greatest possible effrontery."[40] Poulenc's frenetic energy makes us believe, if only for a moment, that dancers from the Folies Bergère were on hand to entertain Cardinal Richelieu. He bridges the divide between the centuries, and between serious and popular music; if we were to hear this song in a film about the three musketeers, we would not be at all surprised (apart from the sound of a modern piano). For all the musicological impossibilities, the reckless spirit of a libidinous age is riotously evoked.

(vi)   *L'Offrande* (*The Offering*)

G minor; $\frac{2}{4}$; *Modéré* ♩ = 96 (A tempo, says Bernac, that may seem on the fast side, but "Poulenc liked it that way.")

Au dieu d'Amour une pucelle	One day a virgin offered
Offrit un jour une chandelle,	A votive candle to the god of Love
Pour en obtenir un amant.	So she could find herself a lover.
Le dieu sourit de sa demande	The god smiled at her request
Et lui dit: Belle en attendant	And said, "My lovely, while you're waiting
Servez-vous toujours de l'offrande.	You can always use the offering."

Bernac tells us that the composer required a change of dynamics from those printed: the narration should remain *mezzo forte* on the first page, while reserving the *piano* dynamic for the god of Love's reply on the second. The song, in a high tessitura for baritone, could be transposed down to F minor but no lower, for fear of losing the music's heady rapture. It is extremely tempting, and rather effective, for the pianist to make a slight and subtle *accelerando* in the eight bars of the extended postlude, leading to the *mezzo forte* final chord. Then after a tiny hesitation on the bar line, there is a sudden outburst of "Ha" (not loud!) from the singer, who, if he momentarily imagines the "pucelle" transferred to a new plateau of delight, must do so with great discretion, and without getting a writhe out of the music. (One can have all sorts of accidents with a candle, especially if already lit.) Bernac also reminds us that the key to getting away with all this is to sing "without apparently understanding the obscenity of the text . . . it is a wanton little picture, but charming and poetic."[41]

(vii)   *La Belle Jeunesse (Beautiful Youth)*
        D major; $\frac{2}{4}$; *Très animé* ♩ = 176

Il faut s'aimer toujours	We should always love
Et ne s'épouser guère.	And rarely marry.
Il faut faire l'amour	We should make love
Sans curé ni notaire.	Without priests or lawyers.
Cessez, messieurs,	So gentlemen,
D'être épouseurs,	That's enough marrying,
Ne visez qu'aux tirelires,	Aim for their piggybanks,
Ne visez qu'aux tourelours,	Aim for their thingummyjigs,
Cessez, messieurs, d'être épouseurs,	Gentlemen, that's enough marrying,
Ne visez qu'aux cœurs.	Aim for their hearts.
Pourquoi se marier,	Why get married,
Quand les femmes des autres	When other people's wives
Ne se font pas prier	Are so keen
Pour devenir les nôtres?	To become ours?
Quand leurs ardeurs,	When their passions,
Quand leurs faveurs,	When their wants,
Cherchent nos tirelires,	Seek out our piggybanks,
Cherchent nos tourelours,	Seek out our thingummyjigs,
Cherchent nos cœurs.	Seek out our hearts.

Another exciting song, very fast and helter-skelter, fitting the tradition of the modern French music hall perfectly to the texts—racy poems and racing pianism. This is music for a knees-up as well as a leg-over, displaying (as in *Couplets bachiques*) a contempt for the institution of marriage. The song is list of dos and don'ts for a younger generation of seventeenth-century rakes, and one wonders how much progress we have made since. Singers and pianists have enormous fun with this side of Poulenc; before he has become a serious composer with a feeling of responsibility to Apollinaire and Éluard, here he is, youthful and unbuttoned, working up an enviable head of steam in favor of the life of the unbridled libertine. For the singer, and certainly the pianist, it can be hard work.

(viii)   *Sérénade (Serenade)*
         A minor; $^6_8$; *Modéré* ♩ = 56

Avec une si belle main,	With such a lovely hand,
Que servent tant de charmes,	Possessed of so many charms,
Que vous devez du dieu malin,	You should know how to handle
Bien manier les armes.	Cupid's darts.
Et quand cet Enfant est chagrin	And when the child comes to weep,
Bien essuyer ses larmes.	To wipe away his tears.

The poem's original title, "La Main" (The hand), was too blatant even for Poulenc. The song's title, *Sérénade,* and the transcriptions for cello and piano by Elizabeth Poston (1943) and Maurice Gendron (1950), bring its elegance as a piece of music to the fore (as a lilting *sicilienne*), rather than the meaning of its text. It makes a rather strange ending to the set, a solitary song for a solitary vice. Bernac observes that the marks of expression at the end (on the repeat of "Bien essuyer ses larmes") make the composer's intention obvious. These markings, in conjunction with the notes on the stave, do look somewhat bizarre on the page: seven upward leaps of a sixth in the vocal line, one after the other, with *crescendo* hairpins for each, forming a succession of self-indulgent (and self-pleasuring) slides. Fortunately the poem's double entendre is obscure enough for the singer to be able to present *Sérénade* more or less without embarrassment. One cannot help thinking, however, that *La Belle Jeunesse* would have made a better ender to the set, certainly more upbeat. Perhaps Poulenc intended to imply that when all was said and done, a life of orgiastic abandon was ultimately unfulfilling. The melancholy feeling left hanging in the air at the end may be an intentional reflection of his own circumstances—always a naughty boy, and seemingly too often left to his own lonely devices.

∘   ∘   ∘

FP43   Trio for Oboe, Bassoon, and Piano, February–April 1926

∘   ∘   ∘

FP44   *Vocalise*
         Composed in Paris, February 1927
         [*À la mémoire de Evelyne Brélia*; Hettich]
         B minor; $^3_4$; *Andante con moto*

An entire volume of vocalises composed by Fauré between 1906 and 1916, in his capacity as director of the Paris Conservatoire, has recently emerged. This minor music by a great composer, hitherto unknown, is an indication of the frequency with which skill in wordless instrumental singing was required of performers (specifically in French institutions) for pedagogical and examination purposes. Such exercises made ideal sight-reading material, and tested tuning and technique rather than the interpretation of poetic text, a very French victory for the head over the heart.

This "Air sans paroles" (song without words, as it was known in the Poulenc circle) was one of a series of such pieces commissioned by Amédée Hettich (1856–1937), poet and singing professor of the Conservatoire. In some editions Hettich provides a substantial (but not entirely convincing) argument in favor of writing and singing vocalises: "The Vocalise, the mother of prolific embellishment, only appears very rarely in modern compositions. Is there any reason why it should be expelled from vocal instruction? Certainly not!"[42] That it was not always meant to be excluded from the recital repertoire was demonstrated by the success of Ravel's *Pièce en forme de habanera,* which started life as a pedagogical exercise commissioned by Hettich.

In a list of the fifty-nine vocalises for high voice printed on the work's cover for the Leduc edition, Poulenc takes his place beside such composers as Fauré, Messiaen, Milhaud, Ravel, and even the young Aaron Copland. He writes a dramatic and angular piece of high seriousness that makes considerable technical demands. If it is true that in 1927 he has not yet found his "voice," the singer certainly has to find hers from the very first bar. The music, in his occasional *marche funèbre* style—albeit in triple time—reminds us of the earlier *Chanson à boire.* Its severity and bleakness are not at all characteristic of Poulenc's later vocal works, although the mood makes a rare reappearance in the Fombeure *Le Mendiant* FP117/iv, a hymn to the strength of the French working classes. The woman who sings this *Vocalise* has none of the femininity of the Vilmorin settings, but rather the unflinching endurance of Gluck's Iphigénie.

Although this was never one of Poulenc's most famous pieces, it seems to have appealed to Russian taste; during the 1970s, arrangements for trumpet or violin and piano were published in Moscow. The Russian connection can be linked with the fact that Poulenc adored Stravinsky's *Pastorale,* a beautiful vocalise for voice and instruments (or piano). Paradoxically, Poulenc's *Vocalise* displays a Stravinskian (*Oedipus Rex*) gravity, and Stravinsky's *Pastorale* an almost Poulencian charm. Poulenc wrote to the Russian composer in 1934, "*Your* Pastorale, *score in hand, enchants my evenings in the country.*"[43] The severity and mournful nature of Poulenc's music may be explained by the fact that the score was dedicated to the memory of the murdered Belgian soprano Evelyne Brélia, a friend of Paul Collaer. Brélia, the first person to purchase a painting from René Magritte, had been memorably, if disturbingly, painted by the artist 1924.

∘   ∘   ∘

FP45 *Pastourelle* (orchestral movement, part of the ballet *L'Éventail de Jeanne*), 1927

∘   ∘   ∘

FP46 ***Airs chantés pour soprano d'après des poèmes de Jean Moréas*** (*Sung Airs for Soprano after Poems of Jean Moréas*)
     Composed in Nazelles and Paris, 1927–28
     [*François Hepp, Suzanne Peignot, Jacques Lerolle, Jeanne* (Jane) *Bathori*; Rouart, Lerolle]
     Literary sources: Jean Moréas (1856–1910), *Les Stances: Les Sept Livres* (Lyon: Lardanchet, 1923) and *Jean Moréas: Les Stances* (Paris: La Connaissance, 1927). These are the two likely editions Poulenc might have used. The following list refers to the Lyon edition: (i) *Septième Livre* No. 4, p. 114; (ii) *Sixième Livre* No. 1, p. 97; (iii) *Troisième Livre* No. 8, p. 54; (iv) *Cinquième Livre* No. 1, p. 83.

     (i)   *Air romantique* (August 1927)
     (ii)   *Air champêtre* (May 1927)
     (iii) *Air grave* (May 1928)
     (iv) *Air vif* (May 1927)

"Jean Moréas" was the pseudonym of Greek-born poet Ioannis Papadiamantopoulos. Having published a collection of Greek poetry in Athens, Moréas came to Paris and made the acquaintance of Debussy, Paul Verlaine, and Stéphane Mallarmé. He was a man of formidable culture and technical gifts, but the neoclassical purity of his style (he belonged to the so-called École Romane) laid him open to charges of being a latter-day Leconte de Lisle and an emotionless pasticheur. He also took himself very seriously. Poulenc, on the other hand, and despite the fact that there were two very good mélodies to Moréas texts by Reynaldo Hahn, felt that Moréas's verse was "*suitable for mutilation*"; for the only time in his songs he indicates that his set was "after" the poems, as if to distance himself from the writer and from the responsibility of deliberately misrepresenting him. If Poulenc really intended to commit "*every possible sacrilege*" against the poetry of Jean Moréas,[44] as was his declared aim, I can think of nothing comparable in the history of song—for it goes without saying that the effort of composing a song implies the composer's affection and admiration, his respect at the very least, for the chosen text.

The truth is that Poulenc would never have set Moréas if there had not been a financial reason for doing so. The story usually told is that the publication of *Airs chantés* was conceived as a game to "tease" a friend, François Hepp, who genuinely admired Moréas. In fact, Hepp was less of a friend than a publisher-colleague and a source of revenue. A lawyer and banker by training, he had married the daughter of music publisher Alexis Rouart, and between 1921 and 1929 worked with Rouart's partner, Jacques Lerolle. Hepp was a man of conservative literary tastes, and his recommendation of Moréas as a poet worthy of Poulenc's attention took place during a meeting in the publisher's offices on 3 May 1927.

Jean Moréas, drawn by Félix Valloton (1865–1925).

An overlooked letter from Poulenc reveals the fuller story. During this meeting Poulenc evidently sensed that Lerolle, Hepp's publisher partner, was not keen on the idea of a new cycle—say, to poems of Apollinaire. The composer wasted no time in writing to Hepp, later the same day, to thank him for the "*grand service*" of revealing Moréas's work to him.[45] He asks for an advance of 1,000 francs. "*I hope I am not going against the usual way of doing things in the firm*" is what he writes; what he actually means is "Send me the money whether Lerolle likes it or not." In the few hours it took for Poulenc to return home and put pen to paper, Hepp's suggestion had miraculously turned into a "commande" (commission) for songs to Moréas texts. At the end of the letter, Poulenc pleads poverty and dire straits. As if making light of a situation that was really more serious than anyone realized—he had spectacularly extended himself by buying his château at Noizay—he claims that the money will save him from the Seine, where he will otherwise take the unborn *Airs chantés* with him to their mutual grave.

Once Poulenc had the money from Rouart-Lerolle, he could do as he liked and backtrack as he wished. He told Claude Rostand later that he only went along with Hepp's idea as a joke, and that the reason he commits real "sacrilege" only in two or three bars of *Air champêtre* was that, despite himself, he was "*a born admirer of poetry.*"[46] In 1927 the idea of a musical assassination of Moréas had seemed plausible to his modernist friends, contemporary poets who were not musical experts, but it was a scheme almost impossible to carry through in musical terms, and not without losing a great many royalties from performances.

The irony is that once the *Airs chantés* were published (the first song dedicated to Hepp), they proved not to be such a joke after all. With singing translations added in English and German, they made a great deal of money, willy-nilly, for the publisher as well as for the composer. All's well that ends well perhaps, and with such a success Hepp had few grounds to objecting to any background story that Poulenc chose to spin. Nevertheless, this is one of many examples where the facts of a situation were adjusted and tweaked to make a more colorful anecdote for the rolling series of frequently conflicting commentaries and interviews that have long served as Poulenc's ad hoc autobiography.

(i) *Air romantique* (*Romantic Air*)
E minor; $\frac{2}{4}$; *Extrêmement animé* ♩ = 152

J'allais dans la campagne avec le vent d'orage,	I wandered through the countryside with the storm wind,
Sous le pâle matin, sous les nuages bas;	Beneath the pale morning, and the hanging clouds;
Un corbeau ténébreux escortait mon voyage,	A dark crow escorted me,
Et dans les flaques d'eau retentissaient mes pas.	And my steps echoed in the puddles.
La foudre à l'horizon faisait courir sa flamme	The lightning on the horizon set its flame running
Et l'Aquilon doublait ses longs gémissements;	And the North Wind redoubled its long moans;
Mais la tempête était trop faible pour mon âme,	But the tempest was too weak for my soul,
Qui couvrait le tonnerre avec ses battements.	Which was drowning out the thunder with its throbbing.
De la dépouille d'or du frêne et de l'érable	And from the golden spoils of the ash and the maple
L'Automne composait son éclatant butin,	The Autumn gathered its brilliant booty,
Et le corbeau toujours d'un vol inexorable	And the crow, inexorably,
M'accompagnait sans rien changer à mon destin.	Accompanied me without altering my destiny in any way.

On account of the tenacious companionship of the crow, this stormy little scherzo, the third song to be composed, is a strange and unlikely companion piece to Schubert's *Die Krähe* from *Winterreise*, but a good deal more jolly. The latter fact is due to Poulenc's gleefully ignoring the poem's pessimism, although in other respects the musical scene-painting reflects the text most effectively. The song *"must be sung very fast with the wind in one's face,"* advises the composer.[47] The flight of the singer's avian companion, rendered as musically peremptory, and busy as a humming-bird, nevertheless serves as a fine little display piece for soprano and pianist alike. The twelve-bar postlude (Bernac refers to it as a "squall") is one of Poulenc's most effective.[48] Perhaps the somber postlude of the Schubert song, and that macabre crow, still lingered somewhere in his childhood memories (see Outline, 1910, p. 6).

(ii) *Air champêtre* (*Pastoral Air*)
    G major; $\frac{4}{4}$; *Vite* ♩ = 144

Belle source, je veux me rappeler sans cesse	Beautiful spring, I wish never to forget
Qu'un jour, guidé par l'amitié,	That one day, guided by friendship,
Ravi, j'ai contemplé ton visage, ô déesse,	Enraptured, I studied your face, oh goddess,
Perdu sous la mousse à moitié.	Half-hidden under the moss.
Que n'est-il demeuré, cet ami que je pleure,	If only he had lived, this friend I weep for,
Ô nymphe, à ton culte attaché,	Oh nymph, to stay faithful to your cult,
Pour se mêler encore au souffle qui t'effleure,	To be mingled still with the breeze that caresses you,
Et répondre à ton flot caché!	And to respond to your hidden waters!

Probably composed soon after Poulenc had come to an agreement with the publisher, *Air champêtre* is entirely pleasant as a song, and at first hearing its lovely melody and genial piano texture seem hardly at odds with the poem—like a modern-dress production of a classic, perhaps. A closer reading reveals Poulenc's total disregard for Moréas's tender memories of a friend who has died. The composer's cheeky delight in looking the goddess in the face is untempered by the poet's regret. And then, with the phrase "sous la mousse à moitié," he plays what he claimed was his most deadly sacrilegious card: against all rules of prosody the line becomes "sous la mou, sous la mousse à moitié," as if Toulouse-Lautrec's dancing girls were displaying frilly knickers on Olympus. At least Offenbach had kept his leggy dancers in the Underworld, but Poulenc had already effected this juxtaposition in his 1924 Ronsard song *Attributs* FP38/i. As it turned out, no one was particularly shocked, and certainly not singers who took it in their stride. On the closing phrase "j'ai contemplé ton visage, ô déesse," Poulenc momentarily, and cheekily, taps into Richard Strauss's Zerbinetta style with a high B, and very fetching it is too. The three-bar postlude is an unashamed steal from the ending of Chopin's Étude in G-flat Major (Op. 25 No. 9), clearly a favorite; over a decade later the composer was to purloin the same signing-off motif in the final bars of *Il vole* FP101/iii.

(iii)   *Air grave (Serious Air)*
        F minor; $\frac{4}{4}$; *Andante con moto* ♩ = 66

Ah! fuyez à présent, malheureuses pensées,	Ah! Begone now, wretched thoughts,
Ô! colère, ô! remords,	Oh anger, oh remorse,
Souvenirs qui m'avez les deux tempes pressées	Memories which have grasped my temples
De l'étreinte des morts;	With the grip of the dead;
Sentiers de mousse pleins, vaporeuses fontaines,	Paths thick with moss, misty fountains,
Grottes profondes, voix	Deep grottoes, voices
Des oiseaux et du vent, lumières incertaines	Of the birds and of the wind, flickering shafts of light
Des sauvages sous-bois;	In the wild undergrowth;
Insectes, animaux, beauté future,	Insects, animals, beauty to come,
Ne me repousse pas, ô divine Nature,	Do not reject me, oh divine Nature,
Je suis ton suppliant.	I am your suppliant.

This song, the last of the set to be composed, is surely the least loved of the four and also the least effective as parody. Poulenc had clearly aimed to write something clumsily over the top, with its histrionics and melodramatic appeals to "Insectes, animaux," and so on. A singer determined to make the song ridiculous might be able to do so with a lot of mummery, but in performance the neoclassical grandeur of the music is not nearly as funny, nor as impossible to take seriously, as Poulenc claimed he had intended. If he truly disliked his own song (he called it "*indefensibly conventional*"),[49] he was punished for it: for the rest of his life he had to sit through any number of performances sung by artists who admired both music and poem in equal measure.

(iv)   *Air vif* (*Lively Air*)

> C minor; $\frac{2}{4}$; *Presto—très gai* ♩ = 192 (A tempo, notes Bernac, that "may at first seem very difficult, especially for the pianist! But it is excellent and must be assumed at once and maintained without slackening."[50])

Le trésor du verger et le jardin en fête,	The bounty of the orchard and the garden in bloom,
Les fleurs des champs, des bois,	The flowers of the fields, of the woods,
Éclatent de plaisir, hélas! et sur leur tête	Burst with pleasure, and above their heads, alas,
Le vent enfle sa voix.	The wind swells up its voice.
Mais toi, noble Océan que l'assaut des tourmentes	But you, noble Ocean, which the onslaught of the tempests
Ne saurait ravager,	Cannot ravage,
Certes, plus dignement, lorsque tu te lamentes,	Certainly, with more dignity when you lament,
Tu te prends à songer.	You lose yourself in dreams.

This song ends the set with an explosion of joy, a real success despite its initial intention to shock and irritate. Moréas's poem reads portentously—"Mais toi, noble Océan" and so on—but Poulenc does what he can to mirror the rhetorical severity of the words, and the only real challenge is for the wind-borne voice, where the necessary and tricky coloratura is easier for some singers than others. The same applies to the piano writing: the deliciously deft coda, balletic for singer and pianist in turn, each one turning on a dime, is one of the best throwaway endings in the French, or any, song repertoire. Since the *Cocardes*, Poulenc's progress in song writing represented by a truly "joined-up" piece like this is enormous. But then by this time, he had an international success, *Les Biches*, already well under his belt.

o   o   o

FP47   *Deux Novelettes* (piano), 1927–28
FP48   *Trois Pièces pour piano*, 1928
FP49   *Concert champêtre* for harpsichord and orchestra, August 1928
FP50   *Pièce brève sur le nom d'Albert Roussel* (piano), 1929
FP51   *Aubade, concerto choréographique* for piano and eighteen instruments, May–June 1929
FP52   *Fanfare* (brass)
FP53   *Valse* (sketch)
FP54   Sonata for Violin and Piano (third attempt, destroyed)

· III ·

Poulenc and his beloved dog Mickey, on the terrace of Le Grand Coteau at Noizay.

Outline of a Musical Life:

1930–1939

1930 (aged 31)

FP is now leading an astonishingly energetic life, with a full and often minutely organized career. His drumming up of concert engagements alone displays a virtuoso touch, and the sheer scale of his traveling and letter-writing seems unparalleled in comparison with most of his contemporaries. In the absence of diaries, his life can be partially reconstructed by scouring letters (and other sources such as concert programs) for clues regarding his whereabouts and activities,[1] but there are gaps when he disappears from view—a conjuring trick employed by this secretive composer throughout his life.

(Third week of January) FP plays three performances of *Aubade* at the Théâtre des Champs-Élysées with the Nemtchinova Ballet.

(30 January) Raymonde Linossier dies after a brief and sudden illness (peritonitis), a devastating blow to FP. She is buried with the manuscript of *Les Biches.*

(April–20 May) FP emerges from some months of mourning to go on an extended working holiday to Spain (Madrid, Bilbao, Puerta del Sol, Seville, Málaga, Grenada). His hopes of seeing Manuel de Falla are dashed by that composer's ill health. He gives lecture-recitals and concerts and hobnobs with the highest in Spanish society while keeping in close touch with Alice Ardoin, Raymonde's sister.

(23 May) Back in Paris, FP appears with Suzanne Peignot at the Salle de l'École Normale de Musique in a hotch-potch of a concert that shows he is not yet an experienced planner of programs. An opening group of Monteverdi, Salvator Rosa, Caldara, and Pergolesi, possibly chosen with Nadia Boulanger's help, is followed by four Schubert songs, two late cycles by Debussy as well as his *Le Balcon*, a Ravel group (*Sainte* and the *Mélodies populaires greques*), an excerpt from Satie's *Socrate,* and finally Ronsard settings by Poulenc and the four *Airs chantés*—a cycle already popular with singers.

Young Poulenc and his nanny, Marie-Françoise Lauxière, c. 1911.

FP spends the summer and autumn in Noizay, making various jaunts from there to see friends and family up and down the country. He visits Charles and Marie-Laure de Noailles in Hyères, then Jean and Marie-Blanche de Polignac at Kerbastic (where he stays two weeks), his sister and brother-in-law at Le Tremblay (another two weeks), and his former nanny (in the Morvan), who is ill. Paying tribute to this guardian of his childhood, FP asks: "*Where are those far-off times, alas, when she stuffed me with jam?*"[2] He also visits beautiful towns in that region (Montjeu, Autun, Avallon, Vézelay, Auxerre).

(July) *Épitaphe* **FP55** (Malherbe), composed in Noizay. The date of the first public performance is unknown. Some years later Bernac and Poulenc would include the song in their first full recital at the Salle de l'École Normale de Musique (3 April 1935).

(9 October) FP sends manuscript copies of *Épitaphe* to Raymonde's two sisters, but the commemorative volume in her memory for which it was composed is never issued.

FP begins to work on a set of piano *Nocturnes*. The first, in C major, is dedicated to Richard Chanlaire's sister-in-law Suzette Chanlaire, with whom he maintains a close friendship.

1931 (aged 32)

Sometime in his early thirties, FP meets Raymond Destouches (c. 1904–1988), who will become his lifelong partner—a liaison conducted with an extreme discretion that is as much to do with their difference in social class as with the gay closet. Destouches lives his life between Noizay and Paris as a chauffeur; he has several rich clients who commute to the Touraine, and FP often relies on his driving skills. Raymond has a son from a first marriage, but it is his second wife, Céline, who will become a valued part of the Noizay household. He will remain devoted to FP; and the composer depends on his loyalty while concealing from this rather naïve man other long-term liaisons.

(February–March) *Trois Poèmes de Louise Lalanne* **FP57** (Laurencin and Apollinaire) and *Quatre Poèmes de Guillaume Apollinaire* **FP58** composed in Noizay.

(24 February) While working on the two new cycles concurrently at Noizay, FP makes a trip to Paris to hear Stravinsky's *Symphony of Psalms* at the Théâtre des Champs-Élysées; he dines with Stravinsky after the concert (together with the Picassos and Ernest Ansermet). Poulenc writes a laudatory review for *Le Mois*: "*Such a power of renewal confounds us and fills us with wonder . . . I salute you Jean-Sébastien Stravinsky.*" He sends Stravinsky a copy of the review on 2 April, and receives a reply four days later: "I couldn't have a better Easter present . . . you are good, and that is what I always rediscover in your music."

This spring FP lands in financial trouble. His bank, the Comptoir Lyon-Alemand, in close conjunction with the Banque Nationale de Crédit, fails and goes into liquidation—a knock-on effect of the stock market crash that had rocked the world in 1929. He keeps this financial disaster quiet, choosing to share his severely straitened circumstances with only a few friends, and then in no great detail. It is clear that with his inherited funds gone, he will have to rely exclusively on his own earnings. FP has long had a reputation for parsimony, but finding the means of earning money now becomes a veritable obsession. Likening the house in Noizay to a mistress, he writes to his publisher, Paul Rouart, that the upkeep of his country home is more ruinous than keeping Joséphine Baker would be.[3]

Avoiding film music, a genre for which he feels little sympathy, FP sees his way forward as a performer, accompanist, and lecturer. Since music publishers at the time were able to offer more money for grateful and accessible works for solo piano, he accordingly produces a large amount of piano music between 1931 and 1934.

Sometime between May and November, FP visits the Exposition Coloniale, held at the Bois de Vincennes, and is enchanted by the Balinese music he hears, which will feature in the first movement of his 1932 Concerto for Two Pianos (FP61).

(19 June) First public performances of *Trois Poèmes de Louise Lalanne* **FP57** and *Quatre Poèmes de Guillaume Apollinaire* **FP58**, at the Salle Chopin. FP accompanies Suzanne Peignot in the Lalanne and Roger Bourdin (replacing Gilbert Moryn) in the Apollinaire. This concert (originally to have taken place on 1 June) includes performances of the Trio for Oboe, Bassoon, and Piano FP43 as well as an early version of the Sextet that has not survived.

(July) FP once again holidays at Kerbastic with the Polignacs.

(August) Pulling as many strings as he wisely can, FP engineers a commission from the Princesse Edmond de Polignac (Winnaretta Singer, greatest of composers' patrons, aunt by marriage of Jean de Polignac). The resulting work will be the Concerto for Two Pianos.

This summer the former home of FP's grandparents in Nogent-sur-Marne is finally put up for sale after four years of being rented. FP stays in the empty house and composes new settings of Max Jacob.

(24 September) Marie-Françoise Lauxière, FP's devoted nanny, with whom he has always kept closely in touch, dies.

Having given up his bachelor pad at 83, rue de Monceau, FP needs a pied-à-terre in Paris. He lodges, seemingly rent-free, at 24, rue du Chevalier de la Barre in Montmartre, the home of Georges Salles (1889–1966), a specialist in Asian art at the Louvre. *"It is the only spot in Paris where I have ever been truly able to work."*[4]

(October) From Noizay, FP makes a quick visit to Paris to hear Prokofiev's First String Quartet and Gian Francesco Malipiero's Third String Quartet.

(November) FP receives another commission from Charles and Marie-Laure de Noailles, to compose a work for a "spéctacle-concert" to be given at Hyères on 20 April 1932. This will be the "cantate profane" *Le Bal masqué* FP60 (texts by Max Jacob).

(1 December) A new series created by the violinist Yvonne de Casa Fuerte (1895–1984), a musical colleague of Milhaud who later will become FP's good friend and confidante, is inaugurated. These concerts, under the title "La Sérénade," will regularly promote Poulenc's music.

(21 December) FP gives a recital in Tours with the singer Madeleine Vhita that includes a performance of his Trio for Oboe, Bassoon, and Piano.

(July–December) ***Cinq Poèmes de Max Jacob* FP59**, composed in Nogent-sur-Marne and Noizay.

1932 (aged 33)

"An exceedingly busy year," notes Carl Schmidt. "Not only did he have important commissions to complete, but attending and performing concerts drained his time and energy. . . . Poulenc was enslaved by his social involvement, which was absolutely basic to his character."[5]

(5 January) FP attends the premiere of Milhaud's opera *Maximilien* at the Paris Opéra.

(14 January) FP attends the premiere of Ravel's Piano Concerto in G Major and the first screening of Jean Cocteau's film *Le Sang du poète* two days later.

(18 January) FP performs in Mulhouse and, back in Paris, accompa-

nies Suzanne Peignot in a "Concert pour enfants" with readings by Alexis Roland-Manuel (21st).

(24 January) FP hears pianist Jacques Février (1900–1979) perform Stravinsky's *Capriccio*. Further engagements in January and early February include viewing Coco Chanel's new couture collection, attending various gatherings at the home of the Princesse de Polignac as well as Marcel Achard's new play *Domino*, and visiting Misia Sert (a patroness of the arts) to view her new apartment.

(20 February) FP performs *Aubade* with the Orchestre Lamoureux and takes part in the second "Sérénade" concert (on the 22nd, a repeat of the Salle Chopin program from 19 June 1931). The second half of the concert features Satie's one-act comedy *Le Piège de Méduse*.

(10 April) Work is completed on *Le Bal masqué* in Cannes, only ten days before its performance for the Noailles' spéctacle-concert in nearby Hyères. Baritone Gilbert Moryn is accompanied by an instrumental ensemble conducted by Roger Désormière (1898–1963). "*It is one hundred percent Poulenc. To a lady in Katchamka who would write to me inquiring what I was like, I would send her Cocteau's portrait of me at the piano,* Le Bal masqué, *and the* Motets pour un temps de pénitence. *I think that in this fashion she would get an exact picture of Poulenc-Janus.*"[6]

(15 May) FP hosts the Aurics, Prokofiev, Vittorio Rieti, and Sauguet at Noizay.

(24 May) First partial public performance of **Cinq Poèmes de Max Jacob FP59** (songs iv and v), at the Ancien Conservatoire, Paris. Suzanne Peignot is accompanied by FP. It is unknown when the first performance of the complete cycle took place.

(13 June) *Le Bal masqué* is performed in Paris at the fourth "Sérénade" concert.

During the summer, at Le Tremblay and Noizay, FP works on the Princesse de Polignac's commission, the Concerto for Two Pianos. FP informs Marguerite Long (16 July) that his eighteen-year-old niece Brigitte Manceaux, herself a skilled pianist trained at the Paris Conservatoire, has helped him rehearse the tricky passages.

(5 September) The premiere of the Concerto for Two Pianos is given by FP and Jacques Février at the Palazzo Polignac, on the Grande Canale in Venice. The playing of the La Scala Orchestra, trained by Arturo Toscanini, delights the composer. While in Venice, he spends time with Manuel de Falla, a fellow guest at the Palazzo Polignac. He hears a performance of Falla's *El Retablo*, and joins Arthur Rubinstein in the two-piano reduction of *Nights in the Gardens of Spain*.

Vladimir Horowitz records Poulenc's *Pastourelle* FP45 and *Toccata*

FP48/ii. In the absence of further commissions, FP concentrates on providing publishers with the piano music they are willing to pay for; through November and December he composes six *Improvisations*. Georges Auric is a house guest at Noizay for six weeks until the end of the year.

(20 November) FP entertains Colette, her partner Maurice Goudeket, Violet Trefusis, the Princesse de Polignac, and Auric and his wife at Noizay.[7]

1933 (aged 34)

(January) FP is summoned by Louis Jouvet to meet Jean Giraudoux to discuss providing incidental music to his play *Intermezzo*. For this new venture in the commercial theater, FP bargains hard for favorable terms.

(12 January) In Strasbourg, FP plays the piano (with Jacques Février) for a concert with works by Milhaud, Sauguet, Rieti, Nicolas Nabokov, and Igor Markevitch.

(16 January) FP plays *Le Bal masqué* in a private concert conducted by Alfred Cortot. The next day FP attends an all-Ravel concert at the Salle Pleyel, with Paul Wittgenstein performing the Concerto for the Left Hand.

(21 January) FP buys the scores of Chabrier's operas *Gwendoline* and *Le Roi malgré lui* at an auction of Vincent d'Indy's library—Chabrier is a composer he venerates. Rather than pay cash, he barters with the dealer, who accepts a cask of rosé wine.

(23 January) The first private Parisian performance by the composer and Jacques Février of the Concerto for Two Pianos is given at the home of the Princesse de Polignac.

(25 January) FP and Henri Sauguet leave for a London visit of five days.

(30 January) Adolf Hitler is appointed chancellor of Germany by President Hindenburg.

(12 February) FP and Février perform the two-piano concerto in Lyon and later in the month in London under Sir Thomas Beecham (Queen's Hall). FP plays the piano version of the *Concert champêtre* with the same conductor on the 25th.

(1 March) Jean Giraudoux's *Intermezzo*, in rehearsal throughout February, premieres. For the incidental music, FP has recycled some music from his *Villageoises* for piano.

(4 March) Franklin Delano Roosevelt is inaugurated as president of the United States.

(5 March) FP gives a concert in Marseilles, followed by the two-piano concerto (with Février) in Paris under Roger Désormière (21st).

(12 April) FP visits Monte Carlo for a Ravel festival.

(18 May) **Pierrot FP66** (Banville), composed at Noizay. If this song was

performed before its first known performance on 26 March 1996, the date is unknown.

(5 July) An early version of the Sextet FP100 is given a regional BBC broadcast with the composer, on his third British visit of the year; there will be a fourth when he and Février return for another performance of the two-piano concerto on 25 September.

FP spends three weeks with "Tante Liénard" in Nazelles, then returns to Noizay and devotes much of the autumn (apart from a performance of the two-piano concerto in Brussels) to piano music: an *Improvisation* in C Major (November) and an *Intermezzo* in C Major; the first six *Improvisations* are published collectively this year.

FP contributes music to two other stage productions in 1933: a play by Jules Romains (September), and *Pétrus* by Marcel Achard (which has its premiere on 10 December). By Christmas he has composed the second *Nocturne*, subtitled "Bal de jeunes filles."

In a review of the Sextet, the critic André George writes, "With Poulenc, it is the whole of France that comes through the windows he opens."[8]

1934 (aged 35)

(January–April) *Huit Chansons polonaises* **FP69** (early nineteenth-century Polish texts), composed in Noizay and Paris.

Riots by far-right activists are suppressed by the state in what is considered a failed coup d'état, a major political crisis for the Third Republic. As far as FP is concerned, Fascist demonstrations in Paris begin "if not to impinge directly on his life, then at least to concern him."[9]

(March) FP visits Rome.

(30 April) FP attends the premiere of Stravinsky's *Perséphone* at the Opéra.

(May) The *Improvisation* in A Minor (No. 8) and *Nocturne* No. 6 are composed in Noizay.

(23 June) At the salon of Juliette Mante-Rostand (sister of Edmond Rostand) in the rue du Bac, FP hears and admires a baritone performing Debussy; he listens from around a corner in the room, but is unable to identify the singer. To his astonishment, it is Pierre Bernac, with whom he had last worked, somewhat unsatisfactorily, in 1926. Bernac is about to travel to Salzburg to study lieder with Reinhold von Warlich, and they agree to be in touch in the autumn.

Quatre Chansons pour enfants **FP75** (Jaboune/Nohain), composed in Noizay, Besançon, Vichy, and Paris (probably begun this summer). The date of the first performance of any of these songs is unknown.

The composer with the singer Suzanne Peignot, his lifelong friend and colleague.

(9–18 July) FP holidays in Vichy and at Le Tremblay (writing a *Presto* for piano for Vladimir Horowitz during his visit). He then stays with the Polignacs in Kerbastic (composing there a second *Intermezzo* and dedicating it to Marie-Blanche) before setting off for the Salzburg festival on 13 August.

(21 August) In Salzburg, FP participates, with Suzanne Peignot, in a concert of modern French music and mingles with many of the Parisian *beau monde*. He also persuades the arts editor Paul Morand (later poet of Ravel's *Don Quichotte* songs) to let him write two articles for *Le Figaro*. Adolf Hitler had won the German elections the year before, and FP, wearing his critic's hat, describes the preponderance at Salzburg of operas by Richard Strauss (appointed president of the "Reichsmusikkammer" the preceding November) as one of several Austrian "*favors to Hitler.*"[10] He hopes the 1935 Salzburg festival will be different.

Also in Salzburg, an American eccentric, a Mrs. Moulton, has rented the superb Villa Kummer, which looks out on the Mirabel Gardens; she organizes an all-Debussy evening consisting of various concerts, one of which is conducted by the young Herbert von Karajan, and a late-night open-air song recital. She asks Bernac to sing, and he invites FP to accompany him—the beginning of a legendary song duo.

(September–October) As a means of promoting the somewhat languishing career of his friend Suzanne Peignot, FP orchestrates the *Poèmes de Ronsard*, composed nearly a decade earlier.

(October) FP settles on the idea of writing a Concerto for Organ and Strings as the result of a second commission from the Princesse de Polignac. He will take four years to produce the work.

(November) First partial public performance of **Huit Chansons polonaises FP69** at the Union Interalliée, Paris. This performance, by Maria Modrakowska accompanied by Nadia Boulanger, presents songs i–iv and viii. The first complete performance was probably with the same singer in Algeria in February 1935, accompanied by FP.

(December) FP composes *Badinage* for piano, inspired by a short verse by Raymond Radiguet. This concludes a year of numerous piano compositions, as well as recordings the composer made of his *Nocturnes* 1, 2, and 4 and *Improvisations* 2, 5, 9, and 10. Nevertheless, as he later avowed, "*my best pianistic discoveries have come to me in writing accompaniments for my songs.*"[11]

(22 December) FP entertains Louise de Vilmorin, novelist and friend of Marie-Blanche de Polignac, at Noizay for the first time; she writes a poem entitled "Musique" in his guest book.

1935 (aged 36)

With the assistance of Suzanne Peignot, FP prepares a "conférence-concert" for 16 January—a new kind of lecture-recital (and lucrative format for the future) entitled "French Song from Chabrier to the Present."

(15–30 January) FP is in Paris for rehearsals with Polish soprano Maria Modrakowska.

(9 February) FP embarks from Marseilles on his first extensive concert tour outside France, of North Africa with Modrakowska.

In Oran, Algeria, FP meets the nineteen-year-old Henri Hell, who will later become a good friend and, in 1958, his biographer.

The North African tour includes performances of the *Huit Chansons polonaises* and music by Schubert, Duparc, Fauré, Debussy, and Roussel. Further concerts take place in Mostaganem and Algiers, Algeria (14 and 19 February); and Tunis, Tunisia (22nd).

Returned from North Africa, FP and Modrakowska begin a tour in France with performances in Paris (7 March), Metz (11th), and Épinal (20th). The Paris lecture-recital is entitled "My Masters and My Friends." "Poulenc had mastered the art of eking mileage out of a finite repertoire by repackaging it for presentation in diverse venues."[12]

(March) **Cinq Poèmes de Paul Éluard FP77**, composed in Hyères and Cannes. The first public performance, by Bernac and Poulenc at Paris's Salle de l'École Normale de Musique (3 April), marked the debut of a musical partnership that would last twenty-five years. The last of these songs was written in Cannes, where FP was visiting his ailing "Tante Liénard." There seems to have been very little time left between the completion of the cycle and its first performance, requiring Bernac to learn brand-new songs with astonishing speed and precision.

The FP-Modrakowska tour continues with recitals in Lille (5 April), Paris again (8th), Lyon (9th), and Bordeaux (13th).

(21 April) FP leaves for Rome with Soulima Stravinsky to give a two-piano recital for "Concerts of Spring," a series organized by Mimi Pecci-Blunt, who will be his generous hostess whenever he visits Rome for the rest of his life.

(11 May) FP returns to Cannes to be with Virginie ("Tante") Liénard, who dies at the age of ninety.

During the summer FP composes music within ten days for *La Belle au bois dormant* FP76, an animated color publicity film for Vins Nicolas—an advertising feature, in fact.[13]

(July) FP attends Comte Étienne de Beaumont's "Le Bal d'Orgel" (The Count of Orgel's Ball, the title of Raymond Radiguet's second and last novel), for which guests dress as painters or sculptors.

(July–August) While a summer guest with the Polignacs at Kerbastic, FP, having earlier consulted Nadia Boulanger about sixteenth-century French music, begins to compose incidental music for Édouard Bourdet's play *Margot*.

(September) *À sa guitare* FP79 (Ronsard), composed in Noizay. The first public performances, by its dedicatee, Yvonne Printemps, took place during the run of Bourdet's play *Margot* (first night, 26 November). Hugues Cuenod sang the song at a lecture and Maggie Teyte in a London concert hall in 1938. FP accompanied a performance by Geneviève Touraine in Paris in 1943.

(15 September) The German Reichstag passes the Nuremberg race laws, making anti-Semitism official government policy.

(28 October) FP performs *Le Bal masqué* in Geneva.

(5 December) FP accompanies mezzo-soprano Madeleine Grey in a recital at the Salle Chopin, Paris.

(12 December) In their second recital at the Salle de l'École Normale de Musique, Poulenc and Bernac perform the *Chansons gaillardes* for the first time together since 1926. They also perform eleven songs from Schubert's *Winterreise* and music by Milhaud, Auric, and Satie.

(13 December) FP and Suzanne Peignot present the lecture-recital "French Song from Chabrier to the Present" in Le Havre.

FP and Bernac make commercial recordings on the Ultraphone label (thought to date from this year) of *Chansons gaillardes* and the first three of the *Quatre Poèmes de Guillaume Apollinaire*.

1936 (aged 37)

(22 January) FP performs *Aubade* under the baton of Alfred Cortot at the Salle Gaveau, Paris.

(Early February) FP and Suzanne Peignot perform their lecture-recital at Reims.

(Late February) FP and Bernac give a recital in Avignon at the invitation of the Société Avignonaise de Concerts. The society's secretary is an amateur pianist, Simone Girard (1898–1985), who will become a close friend and confidante of both singer and composer to the ends of their respective lives. Fifteen years later Poulenc inscribed a score to her "*Simone, the valiant, the faithful, the affectionate, the tenacious, the heroic.*"[14]

(27 February) FP and Bernac give a recital in Lyon at the home of Suzanne Latarjet (1886–1962, sister of Raymonde Linossier and childhood friend of Poulenc's sister Jeanne) and her husband André. The couple were well-known patrons of music and the duo's faithful hosts in Lyon.

(March–April) Inspired by performances of Monteverdi by Nadia Boulanger and her ensemble of singers (whom FP hears chez Princesse de Polignac in March), the composer sets poetry by Apollinaire and Éluard for unaccompanied chorus. He dedicates these *Sept Chansons* (FP81) to the Latarjets and to the amateur group of singers conducted by André Latarjet, the Chanteurs de Lyon.

Nadia Boulanger (seated) and her ensemble of madrigal singers (c. 1936). Standing at the back is bass Doda Conrad; to the right are soprano Marie-Blanche de Polignac and tenor Hugues Cuenod.

In late spring FP moves into the "maid's room" in the apartment of his Uncle Papoum at 5, rue de Médicis, overlooking the Luxembourg Gardens. He will no longer have to rely on the hospitality of Georges Salles in Montmartre. "*The style will be flea market. I have already purchased a bed, an armchair, a piano stool, a chair, all for 200 francs,*" he reports to Marie-Blanche de Polignac[15]—a communication typical of Poulenc's "inimitable fashion of pleading poverty to the rich."[16]

FP continues to work on the organ concerto commissioned by the Princesse de Polignac in 1934. He spends most of March to July at Noizay, apart from sorties to Paris for social occasions, like dining with Marie-Laure de Noailles and Misia Sert.

(3 May) The socialist Front Populaire, under its leader Léon Blum, wins the French elections with an ambitious program of social reforms. Poulenc confesses to Marie-Blanche de Polignac that he did not support the Front, preferring the cozier conservatism of a politician like Georges Clémenceau.[17]

(4 July) FP and Bernac perform a recital at the Jeu de Paumes at the American School in Fontainebleau, directed by Nadia Boulanger, the first of many such summer occasions over the years.

(11 July) FP is in London for a BBC recital with Madeleine Grey.

(17 July) After a failed coup by nationalists, civil war breaks out in Spain between the left-wing government and the Fascist forces of General Francisco Franco.

Instead of going to Kerbastic, Poulenc decides to spend August on a working holiday in Uzerche, a small town in southwestern France, where he and Bernac are to be coached by musicologist and conductor Yvonne Gouverné (she had also been Bernac's accompanist) as they prepare recital repertoire for the coming winter. FP writes to Marie-Blanche from a wet and melancholy Le Tremblay (15 August), regretting that he will not be coming to Brittany; he describes 1936 as a year he detests.

(22 August) Poulenc, Bernac, and Gouverné visit the shrine of the Black Virgin in the small chapel set into the rock face of the mountains at Rocamadour. Following this experience, FP composes *Litanies à la Vierge noire* FP82, for women's voices and organ. Although he is proud of the work, letters to friends mention nothing of the life-changing experience in the chapel that effected his reconversion to Roman Catholicism. Nearly forty years later, Gouverné remembered

Poulenc (with Yvonne Gouverné on the left) on the steps leading up to La Chapelle de la Vierge Noire at Rocamadour; a snapshot by Pierre Bernac from 22 August 1936.

that "outwardly nothing happened, yet from that moment everything in the spiritual life of Poulenc changed."[18]

(25 August) In a letter to Georges Auric from Uzerche, FP complains of feeling very low—he mentions problems with money and with publishers, bemoans the sudden death in a car accident of composer Pierre-Octave Ferroud (b. 1900) on 17 August, worries about friends caught up in the deteriorating political situation in Spain. In a letter to Henri Sauguet (28th), however, FP says that his *Litanies* convince him there are ideas that come to us from the beyond ("*de l'au-delà*").

In preparing recitals with Bernac, FP begins to learn a great deal about the wider song repertoire, including German lieder. He admits to Sauguet in the same letter of 28 August that some songs of Liszt bring tears to his eyes.

(September) FP moves into his Parisian pied-à-terre at 5, rue de Médicis, courtesy of his Uncle Papoum. This same month he begins composing a new song cycle to words from Jean Cocteau's *Plain-chant*. By November four of the six songs are composed, but Poulenc, perhaps no longer effortlessly in tune with Cocteau or his poetry, experiences difficulties with the project.

(1 October) FP completes the piano suite *Les Soirées de Nazelles*.

"*One Sunday in November,*" FP tells us, the music for *Bonne journée*, the opening song from the Éluard cycle *Tel jour telle nuit*, first comes into his head—though it was officially composed two months later. Also in November, Louise de Vilmorin sends Poulenc the poems he has encouraged her to write, which he will set in *Trois Poèmes de Louise de Vilmorin* a year later.[19]

(26 November) FP arrives in Lyon to coach Latarjet's choral singers in his *Sept Chansons*. He and Bernac appear at a concert at the Salle Molière in Lyon (30th); afterward they catch a midnight train to Paris and take a morning flight to London for a BBC broadcast, in which FP premieres *Les Soirées de Nazelles* as well as accompanying his songs (1 December).

(Early December) Five French HMV discs appear featuring the Bernac-Poulenc duo: Fauré's *Prison* and *Jardin nocturne*; Debussy's *Trois Chansons de France* (FP was particularly proud of the performance of *La Grotte*); Ravel's *Sur l'herbe* and *Sainte*; Chabrier's *L'Île heureuse* and *Ballade des gros dindons*; Auric's *Le Gloxinia*; and Satie's *Le Chapelier*, *Daphénéo*, and *La Statue de bronze*.

(12 December) The British king Edward VIII abdicates in favor of his brother, later George VI, father of Queen Elizabeth II.

(19 December) FP and Bernac give a recital chez Princesse de Polignac.

FP composes four further songs (Nos. ii, iv, vi, and vii) of *Tel jour telle nuit*. As the concert date draws near, Bernac is clearly anxious to have the music as soon as possible. "*We are preparing with Pierre our recital for 3*

February. He pulls out these songs from me, one by one, which is turning my hair gray."[20]

1937 (aged 38)

(November 1936–January 1937) *Tel jour telle nuit* **FP86** (Éluard), composed in Lyon, Noizay, Monte Carlo, and Paris. Bernac and FP give the first public performance, at the Salle Gaveau in Paris, on 3 February. No. iii of the cycle, *À toutes brides*, a tricky piece of music, was completed in Monte Carlo only on 27 January, giving Bernac less than a week to learn it. The program also included lieder by Weber and Liszt, Debussy's *Trois Ballades de François Villon,* and Ravel's *Histoires naturelles.* A letter from Paul Éluard to his former wife Gala (14 February) confirms that the event ("with 9 of my songs") was a "great success."

Some of the spring is taken up with meetings about a proposed operatic collaboration between FP and Armand Lunel, a writer and philosophy professor who lived in Monte Carlo. Lunel had collaborated with Henri Sauguet in writing the libretto for Sauguet's Stendahl opera, *La Chartreuse de Parme.*

(3 May) *Litanies à la Vierge noire* receives its French premiere in Lyon.

(28 May) Neville Chamberlain becomes prime minister of Great Britain.

Between May and November, Paris hosts an Exposition Internationale des Arts et Techniques dans la Vie Moderne, for which Poulenc has received two minor commissions: *Bourée, au Pavillon d'Auvergne* (for piano) and *Deux Marches et un intermède* (for chamber orchestra), the latter meant to accompany specific courses of a dinner given in honor of Harold Nicholson and other British intellectuals.[21] Among the other composers invited to contribute to the "Expo 1937" is Darius Milhaud, who left this account:

> In spite of the difficult period that followed the adoption of social reforms (forty-hour week, paid vacations, organized leisure), and in spite of the disturbances, lockouts, and sit-down strikes at factories, the International Exposition of 1937 went ahead. . . . There was to be an Austrian pavilion, yet the evil forces of the *Anschluss* were never very distant. Picasso's *Guernica* adorned the walls of the Spanish pavilion, but the Republic had been murdered. The pavilions of Germany and Soviet Russia, placed face to face, seemed to defy each other. One evening while we contemplated the sunset behind the huge mass of flags of all the nations that dominated the Pont d'Iéna, [his wife] Madeleine felt such deep anguish that she clutched my arm and whispered: "This is the end of Europe!"[22]

(August) FP stays in the town of Anost, in the Morvan, where his nurse was born and is buried: "*It lies at the approach to Burgundy, yet with a milder atmosphere.*"[23] He composes, in memory of his father, an *a cappella* Mass in G Major. "*I can't understand why I am so at ease in choral music, I should have lived in the 16th century.*"[24] At the same time, he rehearses with Bernac a large number of Debussy songs, for an upcoming recording for the BBC. He returns to Noizay on the 19th.

(24 August) FP destroys a diary he has kept for some years, on account of unkind references therein to the music of Albert Roussel, a composer he valued enormously as a man and friend, and who had died the day before.

Earlier in the summer, FP was approached by Edward James, a rich and eccentric English poet, friend of Salvador Dali and collector of surrealist art, to compose a cantata to four of his poems. The resulting cycle for chorus and orchestra, *Sécheresses* FP90 (September–December), is to prove perhaps Poulenc's least comfortable exercise in word-setting—almost certainly because he did not choose the texts himself.

(December) **Trois Poèmes de Louise de Vilmorin FP91**, composed in Noizay.

1938 (aged 39)

(25 January) FP and Bernac have an extraordinarily full diary of concerts for 1938, beginning at the Concertgebouw in Amsterdam.

(7 February) They give their major Paris winter concert at the Salle Gaveau: four lieder by Mozart, Schumann's *Sechs Gedichte* Op. 90, and mélodies by Gounod, Roussel, Ravel, and Debussy.

(19 February) The duo make their first British appearance this year at Haslemere. In five broadcasts between 28 February and 4 March, they perform what FP claims is the "*intégrale*" of the Debussy mélodies.[25]

(March) **Le Portrait FP92** (Colette), composed in Paris.

Less than a week after their return from England, FP and Bernac perform their second recital in Avignon, for Simone Girard. They continue on to Italy (departing 12 March) for concerts in Milan, Turin, Lugano, and Florence.

(13 March) The *Anschluss* between Germany and Austria sets off an immediate tide of Jewish emigration, including countless musicians.

(April–November) In Noizay, under pressure from the Princesse de Polignac, FP returns to work on the organ concerto.

(2 May) First performances of the Mass in G Major and *Sécheresses*.

(May) ***Allons plus vite*** (No. ii of **Deux Poèmes de Guillaume Apollinaire FP94**), composed in Noizay.

FP spends part of July in Kerbastic and at Le Tremblay before going south to Anost on the 31st. There he begins *Quatre Motets pour un temps de pénitence*, completing them in January 1939. He spends most of August (until the 28th) in the Morvan area in and around Anost, working with Bernac.

(August) *Dans le jardin d'Anna* (No. i of *Deux Poèmes de Guillaume Apollinaire* **FP94**) and *Tu vois le feu du soir* (No. i of *Miroirs brûlants* **FP98**) (Éluard) composed in Anost.

After returning to Paris, FP and Bernac leave by car for Venice for the Festival International de Musique Contemporaine de la Biennale de Venise (they are driven by Suzanne Lalé, Poulenc's neighbor in Noizay). *Tel jour telle nuit* receives a performance at the Palazzo Giustinian (7 July). They return the next day, passing through the Aveyron on their way back to Noizay.

(29 September) *Priez pour paix* **FP95**, composed in Noizay. The first performance was possibly the one given by bass Doda Conrad in Canterbury Cathedral on 27 August 1939, accompanied by Nadia Boulanger on the organ.

(30 September) Adolf Hitler and Neville Chamberlain sign the Munich Agreement, which Chamberlain claims will guarantee "peace in our time."

(October) *La Grenouillère* **FP96**, composed in Noizay. Date and locale of the first performance are unknown. The song was possibly meant to be part of the Salle Gaveau recital program on 28 November, to be given by Marie-Blanche de Polignac, its dedicatee.

(14 October) First public performances of *Deux Poèmes de Guillaume Apollinaire* **FP94**, *Tu vois le feu du soir* **FP98/i**, and *Le Portrait* **FP92**, in The Hague.

(Late October–early November) FP and Bernac give further recitals in Holland (The Hague, Amsterdam, Hilversum, Rotterdam), and recitals in France (Metz, Nancy, Besançon, Nantes).

(9–10 November) On what has become known as Kristallnacht, Jewish property is destroyed on a vast scale in Germany.

(28 November) First public performance of *Trois Poèmes de Louise de Vilmorin* **FP91**, at the Salle Gaveau, Paris (a "Sérénade" concert). Marie-Blanche de Polignac is accompanied by FP, and the critical reception is embarrassingly harsh—for the singer rather than the music.

(16 December) First private performance (conducted by Nadia Boulanger) of the Concerto for Organ FP93, in the palatial music room attached to the residence of the Princesse de Polignac, in the avenue Henri-Martin.

1939 (aged 40)

(7 January) *Je nommerai ton front* (No. ii of *Miroirs brûlants* **FP98**) (Éluard), composed in Noizay.

(26 January) In London, FP and Bernac give a recital for the Anglo-French Art and Travel Society, Seaford House, in Belgrave Square. There was also probably a recital in Dublin on the 30th.

(16 February) Bernac is accompanied by FP in *Deux Poèmes de Guil-*

laume Apollinaire, *Miroirs brûlants,* and *Le Portrait* at the Salle Gaveau in Paris. This was the premiere of *Je nommerai ton front,* the other four songs having received "try-out" performances in Holland. The recital also included lieder by Haydn and Schumann, and mélodies by Fauré and André Caplet.

(February–March) The schedule of Poulenc and Bernac's British tour gives some idea of the intensity of their nonstop travel and performances, which very few classical singers of today would find possible (some dates may represent provisional studio reservations):

—London BBC (19 February), Cardiff (21st), London BBC (22nd, 23rd, and 24th), London Queen's Hall (25th), Liverpool (26th), London BBC (1 March), Nottingham (2nd), Haslemere (4th), Cambridge (6th). At the French Embassy for the London Contemporary Music Centre (7th), they perform a program of Milhaud, Auric, Ibert, and Poulenc, and premiere Sauguet's Baudelaire setting *Le Chat.*

FP returns to Paris for the premiere of Sauguet's opera *La Chartreuse de Parme.*

(1 April) Spain becomes a dictatorship under General Franco.

(April) ***Ce doux petit visage* FP99** (Éluard), composed in Noizay. See 4 February 1941 for details of the first performance.

(April) FP contemplates writing music for a play by Édouard Bourdet based on one of Shakespeare's plays, *The Tempest* or *Pericles.* (See *Fancy* FP174.)

(21 June) Paris premiere of the organ concerto at the Salle Gaveau.

(5 July) The London magazine *Tatler* publishes photographs of the celebration in Paris of the Eiffel Tower's golden anniversary, attended by the Duke and Duchess of Windsor. FP is pictured sitting in tails at the formal dinner. The caption reads: "The Marquise de Talleyrand and Baron Poulenc," a safe enough guise for the composer to have assumed for an English publication.

(July) FP takes a cure in Vichy.

(By 15 July) Louise de Vilmorin gives FP proofs of the as-yet-unpublished collection of poems *Fiançailles pour rire,* and reads aloud sections to him, when she is on a visit to Paris from Hungary; he is not initially interested in these poems. Sometime in August he changes his mind—his concern for Vilmorin's safety in Hungarian exile during the coming hostilities plays a part in his change of heart.

(6–16 August) FP is in Kerbastic, chez Jean and Marie-Blanche de Polignac.

On his return to Noizay, FP revises his Sextet and begins composing *Les Mamelles de Tirésias.* (The main part of the work will be composed between May and October 1944.)

(26 August) As the political situation worsens, FP's home in Noizay

becomes a refuge from Paris for his Uncle Papoum and some close friends. On 1 September France declares war on Germany.

Bernac is called up for military training. As a sufferer from tuberculosis, he had been spared military duty in 1917. A soldier ("second class") for the first time at the age of forty, he has to sleep in the straw. He tells FP that "it would all be very well if the rigor of the regime was made up for by the fact that one was doing something useful, but for the moment the days are empty and drag terribly."[26]

(26 September) FP informs Nadia Boulanger that he has sketched six poems from Vilmorin's *Fiançailles pour rire* and is looking for a seventh.[27]

(September–October) *Fiancailles pour rire* **FP101** (Vilmorin) and *Bleuet* **FP102** (Apollinaire) composed in Noizay. Date and locale of the first performance of *Bleuet* are unknown.

(26 October) FP receives news from his aunt that the Rhône-Poulenc factory and all its personnel have been requisitioned by the government.

(3 November) FP begins his *Journal de mes mélodies*. On the same day, Bernac becomes a lorry driver in military service.

(19 November) Although FP has been a reservist in the Défense Contre Avions (DCA) since 1934, assigned to the Tours subdivision, he is given a special classification with the Éducation Nationale, Administration des Beaux-Arts. This effectively excuses him from military service.

Thanks to masterful string-pulling and without Bernac knowing any details, Poulenc manages to intervene with the powerful Alfred Cortot concerning the singer's military call-up. The duo are peremptorily assigned to the cohorts of the Ministère des Beaux-Arts pour la Propagande Musicale. Bernac is hugely surprised to be suddenly relieved of his truck-driving duties, and finds himself in tails and giving a recital in Lisbon with Poulenc, at the beginning of January 1940.[28]

Songs of the Thirties

FP55 *Épitaphe* (*Epitaph*)

> Composed in Noizay, July 1930
>
> [*En souvenir de Raymonde Linossier*; Rouart, Lerolle]
>
> Literary source: François de Malherbe (1555–1628). Where Poulenc found the poem is unknown, but it appears, without heading, in one of the earliest editions of Malherbe's work: *Les Œuvres de Mre. François de Malherbe | Gentilhomme ordinaire de la chambre du Roy* (Paris: Antoine de Somaville, 1638), p. 218.
>
> Tonal center of D; $\frac{3}{4}$; *Calmement*. No metronome marking, but Bernac recommends ♩ = 52.[29]

Belle âme qui fus mon flambeau,	Beautiful soul who was my torch,
Reçois l'honneur qu'en ce tombeau	Accept this homage which, in this tomb,
Le devoir m'oblige à te rendre;	Duty obliges me to pay you;
Ce que je fais te sert de peu	My deeds are of little use to you
Mais au moins tu vois en la cendre	But at least you can see in the ashes
Que j'en aime encore le feu.	That I still love their fire.

François de Malherbe, born in the Normandy town of Caen, belonged to the generation of French poets following Ronsard. He was the official court poet of both Henri IV and Louis XIII, remaining also in favor with Cardinal Richelieu. Poulenc's *Épitaphe* thus explores the deeply serious side of the epoch of the lighthearted *Chansons gaillardes* and Dumas's *Three Musketeers*. Well known for his literary severity, Malherbe set himself against the frivolity and freedom of the poets of the Pléiade. He was something of a killjoy, in fact—although the noble austerity and economy of the lines that Poulenc chose were ideal for the purpose of honoring the memory of his beloved Raymonde Linossier, who had died suddenly on 30 January 1930. Nineteenth-century editions make clear that

François de Malherbe, "Gentilhomme ordinaire de la chambre du roi."

the poem was commissioned in 1614 as an epitaph for the wife of a certain M. Puget, thus the composer's title.

Raymonde's sister Alice Ardoin had it in mind to publish a tribute to her sister consisting of a selection from her correspondence, her novel *Bibi-la-Bibiste*, and "Une violette noire," a poem written in Raymonde's memory by Léon-Paul Fargue (another of her close friends). The Poulenc song was to be part of this publication, issued by the illustrator and printer Jean-Gabriel Daragnès. But in the end nothing came of Alice's ambitious plans. In December 1930, when the song was published, Poulenc had a number of copies printed on special paper and circulated them among his good friends (Jeanne Dubost, Marya Freund, Suzanne Peignot, and others)—all of whom knew how much Raymonde had meant to him. And he sent autograph copies of the song to her two sisters, Alice Ardoin and Suzanne Latarjet.

Poulenc never wrote a more austere song than this one, and none that looked more like Stravinsky on the printed page: from the eighth bar the accompaniment is laid out in a complex arrangement in three staves, with a pile-up of bass-clef chords that adds to a feeling of doleful lugubriousness. The difficult intervals in the vocal line are also untypical; it is as if singer and pianist have been invited to take part in a ritual of grave importance, but first need to decipher the secret of the message to be relayed. This is a profound song in every sense; true to its title, an epitaph short enough to be engraved on a headstone, every word chiseled in musical marble. Poulenc compares it to a piece of the architecture of Louis XIII and directs that it should be sung *"without bombast."*[30] No doubt because of the vocal line's pivoting between major and minor thirds, Hervé Lacombe is reminded of the opening and closing songs of *Tel jour telle nuit,* which will later make much of this major-minor alternation.[31]

∘   ∘   ∘

FP56 *Nocturnes* 1–8 (piano), 1930–38

∘   ∘   ∘

FP57   *Trois Poèmes de Louise Lalanne*
 Composed in Noizay, February 1931
 [*Comtesse Jean de Polignac*; Rouart, Lerolle]
 Literary source: Marie Laurencin (1885–1956) and Guillaume Apollinaire (1880–1918), *Il y a* (Paris: Albert Messein, 1925), (i) p. 72, (ii) p. 73, (iii) p. 73

 (i)   *Le Présent* (Laurencin)
 (ii) *Chanson* (Apollinaire)
 (iii) *Hier* (Laurencin)

Poulenc found these poems—and those for almost all his Apollinaire songs—in *Il y a*, a collection of the poet's youthful and unpublished verse, some of it written for reviews and ephemeral publications. There is no information in this volume as to who "Louise Lalanne" is, or why the work of an otherwise unknown poetess should have been given a guest slot in such a distinguished volume. The three poems had first appeared in the March 1909 issue of *Les Marges*, a small but influential review whose editor, Eugène Montfort (a close friend of Apollinaire), thought that women's literary contributions should be seen to be reviewed by a member of their own sex. His attempts to recruit well-known names for the task came to nothing—until he found, or invented, Louise Lalanne. "Lalanne" (in reality Apollinaire) went on to contribute articles on such female writers as Anna de Noailles, Gérard d'Houville, and Colette.

Poulenc had only recently begun to be aware of gender issues in his songs. Although *Le Bestiaire* was always sung by mezzo-sopranos in the early years (Croiza, Bathori, Peignot, Freund), the composer had no objection to male singers performing the cycle—it was just that he had no close link to a male singer at the time. *Cocardes* is similarly suitable for either sex, as are the Ronsard settings. For reasons of their texts alone, *Chanson gaillardes* had to be sung by a male singer, and Poulenc wrote them in the bass clef accordingly.

Poulenc at Amboise in the mid-1920s, contemporary with the publication of Apollinaire's Il y a.

(Women occasionally sing them today.) The tessitura and coloratura of *Airs chantés* rule out most male singers—although Souzay recorded *Air romantique* and *Air vif* in a lower transposition, and Peter Pears sang *Air vif* in the 1963 Poulenc Memorial Concert in London.

It is difficult to know whether Poulenc ever believed in the existence of a woman called Louise Lalanne outside the pages of *Il y a,* but he had a growing desire to match the timbre of a singing voice with the poetry it was required to sing. Five years later he was to encourage a friend, novelist Louise de Vilmorin, to branch out and write poems—which he immediately turned into soprano songs. Now he needed words for a new cycle to be sung by Suzanne Peignot, and his love of modern poetry took him to *Il y a*; there in the heart of Apollinaire's collection was a guest appearance by a woman, with three poems that were impossible to resist.

The painter Marie Laurencin (Apollinaire's former mistress) was a long-standing friend of Poulenc's. She had written him in September 1921 after hearing and being enchanted by *Le Bestiaire,* to tell him that the songs had reminded her of her Guillaume's speaking voice; three years later she had provided the décor and costumes, to ravishing effect, for the Ballets Russes' production of *Les Biches* in Monte Carlo. On receiving a copy of the newly composed Lalanne songs, she was uniquely placed to solve all the mysteries relating to their texts.

> Looking at your charming score I saw that you had set to music the three poems of Louise Lalanne. Of these three poems, two are by me, "Hier" and "Le Présent." . . . At the time of going to press, Guillaume—who was idleness itself—had done nothing: and I remember we hunted through our schoolbooks, naturally full of nonsense, and ended up by finding those two early efforts . . . which are nothing out of the ordinary. . . . And there you have it! I embrace you with all my heart, my dear Francis.[32]

Poulenc had begun by looking for poems by Apollinaire, had decided on three by an unknown woman, and had ended up composing a triptych with two poems by a woman who was also a friend of long standing and the middle one by Apollinaire himself. The more famous, German parallel to this wonderful and unexpected turn of events is the unacknowledged inclusion of Marianne von Willemer's Suleika poetry in Goethe's *West-östlicher Divan* (1819), with Willemer only confessing her authorship some fifty years after they were written.

Each song introduces a type of mélodie that would later come to be considered generically typical of the composer; perhaps this is why he declared that here, with Apollinaire, he had at last found his *"true melodic style."*[33]

(i)   *Le Présent* (*The Present*)

No key signature (G minor); $\frac{3}{8}$; *Presto possibile* ♩ = 152

Si tu veux je te donnerai	If you wish I'll give to you
Mon matin, mon matin gai	My morning, my lovely morning,
Avec tous mes clairs cheveux	And with it my bright hair
Que tu aimes;	Which you love;
Mes yeux verts	And my eyes
Et dorés	Gold and green
Si tu veux.	If you wish.
Je te donnerai tout le bruit	I'll give you all the sound
Qui se fait	Which is made
Quand le matin s'éveille	By the morning as it wakens
Au soleil	To the sun
Et l'eau qui coule	And the water that flows
Dans la fontaine	In the fountain
Tout auprès;	Nearby;
Et puis encor le soir qui viendra	And then the evening that will come
vite	quickly,
Le soir de mon âme triste	Evening of my soul,
À pleurer	So sad, I'll weep.
Et mes mains toutes petites	And my tiny hands
Avec mon cœur qu'il faudra près	As well as my heart, which will have to
du tien	be kept
Garder.	Next to yours.

There are two kinds of scherzo in Poulenc, and both are announced in this little cycle: the serious, ominous scherzo with an undertone of menace, of which *Le Présent* is the first example; and the devil-may-care scherzo inspired by the café-concert, of which the next song, *Chanson*, is an augury. Poulenc is particular about explaining what inspired *Le Présent*'s unusual time signature:

> *People generally make a rhythmic mistake in* Le Présent *by not allowing the six-teenth notes at the beginning to be strictly equal. I could have written the whole song in 2/4, adjusting the rests in the first bar. However, it seemed to me more acute to write in 3/8 followed by a catch of the breath. It is for the singer to give an impression of intensity by slight breathlessness. The song must flow without a shadow of a rubato.*[34]

"Deliciously feminine," Bernac calls the poem,[35] although the sense of panic and insecurity behind the total devotion is rather too vulnerable to be delicious; Laurencin's text has none of the epicurean assurance in matters of love that we encounter in the Vilmorin poems. The song seems to describe a romantic relationship without much of a future, the breathless devotion equating to a kind of masochism.

At the end, under the final "garder" (b. 45), a moment of major-key optimism is immediately countermanded by the victory of the minor tonality and ominous triplets—this is perhaps the first song where we are allowed a glimpse of the composer's own feelings. *Le Présent* is not one of his bewitching and entertaining set pieces functioning as a smokescreen. The accompaniment, doubling the voice, hurtles through the staves like a miniature storm, the hands an octave apart throughout—inspired, as Poulenc admits, by the "wind across the graves" of the last movement (also a *Presto*) of Chopin's B-flat Minor Piano Sonata.

(ii) *Chanson (Song)*

G minor/major; $\frac{2}{2}$; *Follement vite* ♩= 132 (Although Bernac admits this is difficult to achieve, the performers should be "as near to it as possible.")

Les myrtilles sont pour la dame	Blueberries are for the lady
Qui n'est pas là	Who isn't here
La marjolaine est pour mon âme	Marjoram is for my soul
Tralala!	Tra-la-la!
Le chèvrefeuille est pour la belle	Honeysuckle is for the beauty
Irrésolue.	Who isn't sure.
Quand cueillerons-nous les airelles	When will we go cranberry-picking?
Lanturlu.	Lanturlu!
Mais laissons pousser sur la tombe	But let's leave the rosemary
Ô folle! Ô fou!	Oh folle, oh fou,
Le romarin en touffes sombres	To grow in black clumps on the grave
Laïtou!	Laïtou!

The nonsense refrains are made more of sound than sense. "Ô folle, ô fou" adds gender to madness. "Laïtou" crops up as a "tra-la-la" in children's folksongs, notably "La Jeune Grenouille." "Lanturlu" implies delight—"Whoop-de-whoop!," perhaps. J. S.

This *moto perpetuo*, more populist than *Le Présent,* is a vintage piece of so-called leg-Poulenc, with its echoes of the music hall and the hectic gaiety of the 1920s—even if the mirth is a little too breathless to betoken real happiness. The piano interlude in bars 11–14 and the zany "La-ï-tou" at the end (a word sometimes substituted by French singers for forgotten text) are typical examples of Poulencian thumb-nosing. The seven-bar postlude is also entirely characteristic. The composer insisted that the rhythm of the song *"must be imperturbable"*; he thought of it as a counting song. As for the Apollinaire text, Bernac calls it "completely meaningless. Do not seek for a meaning in this poem for none exists."[36]

(iii)   *Hier (Yesterday)*
No key signature (E minor); $\frac{4}{4}$; *Modéré mais surtout sans traîner* ♩ = 66

Hier, c'est ce chapeau fané	Yesterday, was that faded old hat
Que j'ai longtemps traîné	I dragged around for so long
Hier, c'est une pauvre robe	Yesterday, was a shabby dress
Qui n'est plus à la mode	Now long out of fashion
Hier, c'était le beau couvent	Yesterday, was the lovely convent
Si vide maintenant	So deserted now
Et la rose mélancolie	And the rosy melancholy
Des cours de jeunes filles	Of classrooms of young girls
Hier, c'est mon cœur mal donné	Yesterday, was my heart foolishly
Une autre, une autre année!	Another, another year
Hier n'est plus, ce soir, qu'une	Yesterday, tonight, is no more than a
ombre	shadow
Près de moi dans ma chambre	By my side, in my room

"Une autre année" is possibly ambiguous: either "that belonged to a different era" or "year after year." J. S.

Hier may rank in Poulenc's œuvre as the first real signpost to a genre of mélodie that was to become a benchmark of his style. The mood is languid, but also eloquent and touching; for the first of many times in his songs, long sinuous vocal lines are accompanied by flowing eighth-note chords—the shadow of a popular style that influences the mood without cheapening the music and finds its glorious apotheosis in *C* (FP122/i). Many of Poulenc's nostalgic excursions of this kind seem especially evocative of the city of his birth. One explanation of his music's popularity outside France is that listeners feel transported by it, as if walking down a Parisian boulevard with Maurice Chevalier or listening to Édith Piaf in cabaret. Even Poulenc found this song allusive; he admitted it made him think of the enchanting Yvonne Printemps (see p. 148) and of an interior painted by Édouard Vuillard. *"If you think carefully of the words you are saying,"* he advised, *"the color will come of itself."*

The sound of the piano is exceptionally important here, as it will continue to be in all the mélodies. A magical touch and a highly skilled use of the pedal are necessary to make the chords glide sensuously from one harmony to the next, the voice supported by sonic bloom rather than boom: *"The task of the pianist is to conquer the mechanism, to make the notes sing, to make his own sound* ["son

son"], *as Viñes said.*"[37] When Poulenc himself played music like this, he was told, "you give the impression of musical invention being born under your finger tips."[38] These three songs were the first of many to be dedicated to Marie-Blanche de Polignac, a future soprano in Boulanger's ensemble of madrigalists. Poulenc remembered seeing the ten-year-old Marie-Blanche (Marguerite di Pietro) when he was only eight, walking near the Champs-Élysées and dressed in beautiful clothes made by her mother's *atelier*; she wore an old-fashioned "chapeau cabriolet" secured under the chin with a pink ribbon.[39] Perhaps it was the song's opening mention of a faded hat and a shabby dress no longer in fashion—this is the only Poulenc song that mentions couture of any kind—that made the dedication seem appropriate, even if only in contradictory terms. It is curious, and perhaps no coincidence, that at the same time the song was being composed, Vuillard was working on a portrait of Marie-Blanche sitting on a bed in her sumptuous bedroom, with her dog Titillon.[40]

The poet and painter Marie Laurencin in the 1930s.

FP58   *Quatre Poèmes de Guillaume Apollinaire*

Composed in Noizay, February–March 1931

[*Marie Laurencin, Mme Cole Porter, Mme Picasso, Mme Jean-Arthur Fontaine*; Rouart, Lerolle]

Literary source: Guillaume Apollinaire (1880–1918), *Il y a* (Paris: Albert Messein, 1925), (i) p. 96, (ii) p. 50, (iii) p. 104, (iv) p. 94

(i)   *L'Anguille*
(ii) *Carte postale*
(iii) *Avant le cinéma*
(iv) *1904*

Poulenc composed these four songs at the same time as *Trois Poèmes de Louise Lalanne* (the dedication of *L'Anguille* to Marie Laurencin is a kind of cross-referencing between the two works); both sets were also published by Rouart, Lerolle at more or less the same time. If the Lalanne songs show a decidedly female slant, these seem destined for men's voices; there is nothing to say a woman should not sing them, but relatively few female singers have found them rewarding as a set, something to do perhaps with the vocal range and the rather male ebullience implicit in the first and last songs. This kind of Apollinaire—youthful, casual, transparent, above all evocative—was treasure trove for Poulenc.

(i) *L'Anguille (The Eel)*
     C major; $\frac{3}{4}$; *Mouv't de Valse à 1 temps* ♩ = 108

Jeanne Houhou la très gentille	Jeanne Houhou, that sweet girl,
Est morte entre des draps très blancs	Died between snow-white sheets
Pas seule Bébert dit l'Anguille	But not alone. Bébert, alias "The Eel,"
Narcisse et Hubert le merlan	Narcisse and Hubert the Hake
Près d'elle faisaient leur manille	Were nearby playing cards
Et la crâneuse de Clichy	And the Bigmouth of Clichy
Aux rouges yeux de dégueulade	Her eyes red from puking
Répète Mon eau de Vichy	Keeps on saying My Vichy water
Va dans le panier à salade	Off you go in the police van
Haha sans faire de chichi	Haha, and none of your nonsense
Les yeux dansants comme des anges	Her eyes dancing like angels
Elle riait elle riait	She laughed and laughed
Les yeux très bleus les dents très blanches	Her eyes so blue her teeth so white
Si vous saviez si vous saviez	If only you knew if only you knew
Tout ce que nous ferons dimanche	What we'll be doing on Sunday

> *"Manille" (line 5) was a card game all the rage early in the last century, usually (as here) for four persons. "Merlan" (line 4) is normally "whiting," but is still used (as in "passer chez le merlan") to denote having your hair cut or dressed. Perhaps Hubert is the knife-man of the gang, like Mackie in The Threepenny Opera. "Panier à salade" (verse 2) is to this day French slang for a police van with a grille at the back like a salad shaker (Black Maria in the UK; Paddy Wagon in urban America, where cops are traditionally Irish). J. S.*

This implacable *valse-musette* is a hymn to lowlife set in Clichy, a center of Parisian sleaze at the time (and not much has changed). For Poulenc, the music *"evokes the atmosphere of a shady hotel . . . with a rhythm inspired by little steps in felt shoes*" (more of his music-hall imagery; he could also have mentioned the sound, built in to the accompaniment, of a piano accordion). Yet the composer stresses that it "*should be touching. . . . Sing this song without irony, believing in it.*"[41] Apollinaire's "Parigot" (Parisian slang) includes zoological nicknames for well-known members of the underworld, as in the gangland stories of New Yorker Damon Runyon. The final vocal phrase ("If only you knew if only you knew / What we'll be doing on Sunday") is rendered subtly suggestive by the way "Sunday" is set: an augmented fourth droops just as the eyebrow is raised. Nearly a quarter of a century later, recreation on a Sunday would also feature evocatively at the end of the Max Jacob setting *Jouer du bugle* (FP157/i).

Bernac admits that Poulenc "adopts a plebeian accent" here, and avers that the composer understood better than most "the dark poetry of a certain sordid Parisian atmosphere" (a loaded observation this, considering the number of times during their decades of friendship that Poulenc had confessed his own sordid adventures to his chief interpreter). Nevertheless, Bernac continues, "it is *essential*, while giving the song its character, to avoid any hint of *vulgarity*" (his emphases).[42]

(ii)   *Carte postale* (*Postcard*)

No key signature (F minor); $\frac{4}{4}$; *Modéré sans traîner* $\downarrow$ = 96 (Bernac feels this is the maximum speed, although pianists and singers are often tempted to perform the song too slowly and too expressively. The secret is an ineluctable flow, as if the music were by Fauré.)

L'ombre de la très douce est évoquée ici,	Listen. The ghost of someone very sweet is evoked here,
Indolente, et jouant un air dolent aussi:	Indolently playing some doleful tune:
Nocturne ou lied mineur qui fait pâmer son âme	Nocturne, or lied in a minor key, which makes her soul swoon
Dans l'ombre où ses longs doigts font mourir une gamme	Deep in the gloom where her long fingers send a scale to its death
Au piano qui geint comme une pauvre femme.	At the piano which moans like a poor woman.

The poem printed in *Il y a*, with the bracketed title "Carte postale du 19 mai 1901 pour gente damoiselle Linda M da S," is one of seven poetic postcards Apollinaire addressed to Linda, sister of his friend Fernand Molina da Silva. The poet at the age of twenty was helplessly enamored of this young woman and unsuccessfully attempted to woo her by any means possible, including deluging her with twenty-one anagrams of her name and a succession of dedicatory poems. Linda had the good grace to pity him ("le pauvre garçon") and regretted she was unable to return his affection.[43] This postcard is written in the form of an acrostic (the first letter of each line spelling LINDA). The music for *Carte postale*, with its gentle but imperturbable pianism, indolent but not slow, put the composer in mind of a 1902 painting by Pierre Bonnard of Misia Sert playing the piano for her own enjoyment. The painting's mood is gently rueful, intimate and concentrated, without a touch of sentimentality, exactly as the composer wished this piece to be performed.

Poulenc dedicated the song to another, more modern Linda, the beautiful socialite Linda Lee Thomas, the unhappy Mrs. Cole Porter. Such were the circles in which the thirty-two-year-old composer already moved, at ease in the *beau monde* and completely unfazed by wealthy celebrity.

(iii) *Avant le cinéma (To the Cinema)*
No key signature (D minor); $\frac{12}{8}$; *Très animé* ♩ = 126

Et puis ce soir on s'en ira	And tonight we're all off
Au cinéma	To the cinema
Les Artistes que sont-ce donc	What are Artists?
Ce ne sont plus ceux qui cultivent les Beaux-Arts	No longer those who cultivate the Fine Arts
Ce ne sont pas ceux qui s'occupent de l'Art	Nor those who are actually working in the arts
Art poétique ou bien musique	In poetry, say, or music
Les Artistes ce sont les acteurs et les actrices	Artists are actors and actresses
Si nous étions des Artistes	And if we were those artists
Nous ne dirions pas le cinéma	We wouldn't be saying cinema
Nous dirions le ciné	We'd be saying le ciné
Mais si nous étions de vieux professeurs de province	But if we were provincial old professors
Nous ne dirions ni ciné ni cinéma	We wouldn't say ciné or cinema
Mais cinématographe	But Cinematograph
Aussi mon Dieu faut-il avoir du goût	Because, my god, one does have to have taste

Parisians can reasonably claim that the birth of the cinema occurred in their city on 28 December 1895, when the brothers Louis and Auguste Lumière presented moving pictures (workers coming out of the Lumière factory in Lyon, among other vignettes) to a paying public, on the boulevard des Capucines. Soon to follow was Georges Méliès's *A Trip to the Moon*, the first sci-fi film and the beginning of cinematic special effects. By the time Apollinaire wrote this poem in 1917, French cinema, formerly an undisputed leader in the field, had suffered setbacks as a result of the First World War, and was soon to be overtaken by Hollywood. Nevertheless, a decade later Abel Gance was to produce his vast biopic *Napoléon*, counted as a milestone in the medium. In the field of national, non-English-speaking cinema, the French have always occupied a privileged place.

Apollinaire was an enthusiast for the new "ciné," and Poulenc's teacher Charles Koechlin was an unashamed addict (his *Sept Chansons pour Gladys*, for example, is a celebration of the 1931 film *Calais-Douvres,* starring Lilian Harvey, a film star on whom he had an enduring crush). Poulenc, on the other hand, was a devotee of the theater, and more or less indifferent to the cinema—a surprising lacuna in his otherwise all-embracing passion for popular entertainment ("*At the most beautiful film I am bored*").[44] Apollinaire ruthlessly parodies the need of "provincial old professors" to use fancy terminology to define and thus make more intellectually acceptable their fascinating new interest. Or perhaps their use of the term "cinématographe" immediately identifies them as non-Parisians, behind-the-times fuddy-duddies. It is also possible that Apollinaire was poking fun at the Lumière brothers themselves, professorial figures who were far too serious to have their ennobling invention traduced as the "ciné." And these great and serious scientists came from Lyon—the provinces, as far as Parisians are concerned.

The triplets of much of the accompaniment unwind like a spool in an old cinema projector, with the piano part played in strict time until the last chord. Poulenc sometimes gives his songs excessively fast metronome markings (if his own recorded performances are anything to go by), and here is a case in point; to perform *Avant le cinéma* as a rushed patter song is to rob the music of its humor and urbanity. Setting the text fourteen years after Apollinaire wrote the poem, Poulenc allows himself a somewhat galumphing postlude in triplets that evokes the zany rhythm of the Laurel and Hardy theme ("Dance of the Cuckoos," originally for two clarinets and new in 1930), an ironic after-comment on good taste. Bernac requires that the song be sung "with almost exaggerated seriousness."[45]

(iv) *1904*

Begins in F minor, no established key; ¢; *Très animé* ♩ = 104 (according to Bernac, "almost impossible and too hurried")

À Strasbourg en 1904	Strasbourg 1904
J'arrivai pour le lundi gras	I arrived on Shrove Monday
À l'hôtel m'assis devant l'âtre	In the hotel I sat by the fire

Près d'un chanteur de l'Opéra	Next to an opera singer
Qui ne parlait que de théâtre	Who was going on about theater
La Kellnerine rousse avait	The red-headed barmaid
Mis sur sa tête un chapeau rose	Put a pink hat on her head
Comme Hébé qui les dieux servait	The like of which not even Hebe
	servant to the gods
N'en eut jamais ô belles choses	Ever wore Oh lovely things
Carnaval chapeau rose Ave!	All hail the Pink Carnival Hat!
À Rome à Nice et à Cologne	In Rome Nice and Cologne
Dans les fleurs et les confetti	In those flowers and in that confetti
Carnaval j'ai revu ta trogne	Carnival I've seen your ruddy face
Ô roi plus riche et plus gentil	Oh king far richer and kinder
Que Crésus Rothschild et Torlogne	Than Croesus Rothschild and Torlogne
Je soupai d'un peu de foie gras	For supper I had a sliver of foie gras
De chevreuil tendre à la compote	Tender venison with fruit compote
De tartes flans etc	Tarts flans etc.
Un peu de kirsch me ravigote	A shot of kirsch perked me up
Que ne t'avais-je entre mes bras	If only I'd had you in my arms

The speed of the song, one of Poulenc's whirlwinds, testifies to the poet's riotous time in the Alsatian capital in 1904 during carnival time (the poem's original title, written in 1914, was "Carnaval"). On the Monday before Mardi Gras (Shrove Tuesday), Apollinaire finds himself in a city where the eating of rich food before Lent is an honored tradition. "Rothschild" continues to be a significant name in our own time, but "Torlogne" (Torlonia), a Roman family known for their fabulous wealth, is a reference from the forgotten past.

As Apollinaire takes his fill of the delicacies of Strasbourg, his red-haired server is referred to as a "Kellnerine," a made-up word that reflects the inevitable mixes in culture as Strasbourg/Strassburg was occupied alternatively by the French and then Germans. "Kellnerin" is German for "waitress," but with the addition of the final "e," it is once more frenchified. After mention of Alsace's famous onion "tartes" and of kirsch (the cherry liqueur), the music suddenly stops. After four beats' silence, a breathless travelogue turns briefly into a lament (*Très lent, amoroso*), when the poet realizes that there was a girl missing who would have made that experience all the happier. There are other Poulenc songs of this helter-skelter kind, but the sudden poetry of "Que ne t'avais-je entre mes bras," and the way the vocal line communicates real longing, mark the singer down as not merely an epicurean dandy. The woman addressed as "you" is present only in his imagination, and the whole song is a monologue-confessional, a multilayered dream of the past.

We may also imagine a slightly different scenario: the poet, in the company of his current mistress and friends, is swept away as he recounts a riotously entertaining time he had in Strasbourg a decade earlier. After enthusing about food and wine, he is on the brink of retelling a romantic adventure (perhaps with the red-headed waitress) when he remembers where he is.[46] He pulls himself up short and, gallantly and just in time, brings his paramour of the moment into the narration ("if only *you* had been there in my arms, it would have been perfect").

The closing bars, four staccato eighth notes, capture the Gallic sigh or shrug ("Oh well, nothing to be done") to perfection. In my experience, this dry little postlude has never failed to amuse the audience.

FP59 *Cinq Poèmes de Max Jacob*

Composed in Nogent-sur-Marne and Noizay, July–December 1931

[Marie-Blanche de Polignac, Madeleine Vhita, Suzanne Peignot, *Suzanne Balguerie, Eve Curie*; Rouart, Lerolle]

Literary source: Max Jacob (1876–1944), contributions to the literary review *Commerce* (Winter 1929), No. 22. The first section of this substantial issue is given over to *Poèmes de Morven le Gaëlique* (pseudonym of Jacob): (i) p. 7, (ii) p. 9, (iii) p. 24, (iv) p. 38, (v) p. 40.

(i)   *Chanson bretonne*
(ii) *Cimetière*
(iii) *La Petite Servante*
(iv) *Berceuse*
(v)   *Souric et Mouric*

Poulenc had known Max Jacob since 1917, and their fondness and admiration were mutual. In 1921 he composed *Quatre Poèmes de Max Jacob* for voice and wind quintet; he claimed to have destroyed the work for its all too modish polytonality, but a copy survived and was published posthumously in 1993. Correspondence and contact between poet and composer were sporadic. The most important Jacob work is the 1932 "profane" cantata *Le Bal masqué* (for voice, piano, and instrumental ensemble), while the *Cinq Poèmes* were part of the glut of mélodie composition of 1931. We know very little of their genesis. It has been assumed that Jacob himself sent these Breton-folksong-like poems to the composer, but there is nothing in the letters to suggest that was the case.

Sophie Robert's magisterial essay on Raymonde Linossier in *Francis Pou-*

lenc: Music, Art and Literature suggests another possibility. By scanning
the sales ledger at Adrienne Monnier's bookshop, La Maison des Amis
des Livres, Robert was able to track
which books Raymonde had bought
or borrowed, and which poets she
had admired. As a close friend of
Poulenc (perhaps his closest), Raymonde would have communicated
these enthusiasms to the composer,
even if she was evidently unable to
convert him to an enduring admiration of Léon Paul Fargue (a poet
of Erik Satie's songs but not of Poulenc's). Possibly Poulenc was jealous
of Raymonde's connection with this
literary lion.

In Robert's essay, one fact leaps
from the page: Linossier subscribed to
Commerce, a literary review founded

*Raymonde Linossier, photographed at the
Musée Guimet, where she was in charge of
the oriental collection.*

under the aegis of Paul Valéry, Fargue, and Valery Larbaud. Not only
was Linossier a subscriber, she had
been the periodical's first administra-
tor in 1924.[47] Perhaps it was Poulenc who suggested that Max Jacob was worthy
of Raymonde's attention and his suggestion found its way to the editors of *Commerce*. But if not, the composer was certainly in a position to borrow or share
her books—including the last edition of the review published before she died,
which opens with twenty poems by Morven le Gaëlique, a pseudonym of Jacob.
The appearance in this periodical of the poems for the cycle has slipped through
the net as far as the Poulenc documents are concerned.[48]

Jacob's second-last poem, and Poulenc's fifth song, is simply entitled "Chanson," and the composer wrote Jacob to ask if he could suggest a more evocative
title. The tone of Jacob's reply on 11 December 1931 suggests that there had been
no anterior correspondence about this collaboration: "You know that I am really
very flattered to have inspired you. I say this entirely sincerely, and not just to be
polite. Call No V simply *Souric et Mouric* [the poem's opening words] . . . I authorize whatever your precious fancy dictates, O Master! That my name will have
appeared beside yours will be my only claim to fame. A hundred regards from
your fervent admirer, Max Jacob."[49]

(i) *Chanson bretonne (Breton Song)*
       No key signature (C minor); $\frac{2}{4}$; *Rondement* ♩ = 138

J'ai perdu ma poulette	I've lost my little hen
et j'ai perdu mon chat,	and i've lost my cat,
Je cours à la poudrette	I'll run all the way to the dung heap
si Dieu me les rendra.	if God gives me them back.
Je vais chez Jean le Coz	I'll go and see Jean le Coz
et chez Marie Maria.	and Marie Maria.
Va-t'en voir chez Hérode	You go and see Herod
Peut-être il le saura.	maybe he'll know.
Passant devant la salle	When I went by the hall
toute la ville était là	the whole town was there
à voir danser ma poule	watching my hen dancing
avec mon petit chat.	with my little cat.
Tous les oiseaux champêtres	All the birds of the fields
sur les murs et sur les toits	on the walls and on the rooftops
jouaient de la trompette	were playing the trumpet
pour le banquet du roi.	for the king's banquet.

"*The scene is the marketplace of Guidel in Brittany one summer morning. A peasant girl recounts, very simply, her misfortunes.*"[50] In this way Poulenc places the beginning of his cycle near Kerbastic, the country house belonging to Marie-Blanche and Jean de Polignac, where he was so often a guest; and Marie-Blanche is the song's dedicatee. A chicken dancing with a little cat adds an air of unreality to a scenario that in other ways seems convincingly, even aggressively, down-to-earth. But that is typical of Max Jacob, and here he is clearly recalling his childhood in Brittany.[51] In some ways this is a scene that might have been painted by a Breton incarnation of Marc Chagall.

The last page offers Poulenc's most extended passage of bird music in his mélodies ("*poetic and unreal*" is his description): a succession of trills and grace notes, ornamentation *à la française*, perhaps harking back to his study of harpsichord music while he was writing *Concert champêtre* (1927–28) for Wanda Landowska. Another "early music" indication is that Poulenc asks that the passage be sung with a white voice (*la voix très blanche*). Bernac (who would never have counseled a singer to remove all vibrato from the voice) requires that the sound should be "very fresh and full of wonder."

(ii) *Cimetière (Cemetery)*
A-flat major; $\overset{6}{8}$; *Sans lenteur* $\downarrow$ = 52

Si mon marin vous le chassez,	If you drive my sailor away
au cimetière vous me mettrez,	you'll send me to my grave,
rose blanche, rose blanche et rose rouge.	white rose, white rose and red.
Ma tombe, elle est comme un jardin,	My grave, it's like a garden,
comme un jardin, rouge et blanche,	like a garden, of red and white,
Le dimanche vous irez, rose blanche,	On Sunday you'll go, white rose,
vous irez vous promener,	you'll go for a walk,
rose blanche et blanc muguet,	white rose and white lily of the valley,
Tante Yvonne à la Toussaint	On All Saints' Day Aunt Yvonne
une couronne en fer peint	carries from her garden
elle apporte de son jardin	a wreath of painted iron
en fer peint avec des perles de satin,	painted iron with satin beads,
rose blanche et blanc muguet.	white rose and white lily of the valley.
Si Dieu veut me ressusciter	Should God choose to resurrect me
au Paradis je monterai, rose blanche,	I will go to Paradise, white rose,
avec un nimbe doré,	wearing a golden halo,
rose blanche et blanc muguet.	white rose and lily of the valley.
Si mon marin revenait,	If my sailor returns,
rose rouge et rose blanche,	red rose and white rose,
sur ma tombe il vient auprès,	he'll come by my grave,
rose blanche et blanc muguet.	white rose and lily of the valley.
Souviens-toi de notre enfance, rose	Do you remember when we were
blanche,	children, white rose,
quand nous jouions sur le quai,	when we'd play on the quayside,
rose blanche et blanc muguet.	white rose and white lily of the valley.

Here is vintage Poulenc in an enchanting waltz of great tenderness—a lighter-hearted version of Richard Strauss's *Allerseelen* (All Souls), where the singer envisages herself buried in a country cemetery and visited by her relatives and her sailor lover. Grocery shops near a cemetery used to sell ready-made circular wreaths for such visits, of "painted iron and decorated with satin and pearls," as Bernac describes them. At "Le dimanche vous irez," a memorable tune in A-flat major alternates with a more rhythmic section in C major, before the darker graveyard feel (E-flat minor) of "une couronne en fer." These ten bars, almost accompanied recitative, form a kind of middle section leading to an ingenious modulatory interlude (of which even a composer like Fauré would have been proud) returning us to A-flat major and the girl's vision of paradise, with an etiolated accompaniment (marked *Clair et doux*) in the treble clef in both hands. The closing passage ("Souviens-toi de notre enfance") achieves that rarefied and poetic effect of half happy, half sad that Poulenc manages to pull off whenever a poem evokes childhood nostalgia. By now we have forgotten all about the kitschy wreaths bought at the local grocer's; as is so often the case, Poulenc has transformed what might have teetered on the borders of vulgarity into something delicate and beautiful.

(iii) *La Petite Servante* (*The Little Serving-Girl*)
No key signature (D minor); $\frac{2}{4}$; *Presto–Très agité* ♪ = 132

Préservez-nous du feu et du tonnerre,	Preserve us from fire and thunder,
Le tonnerre court comme un oiseau,	Thunder runs like a bird,
Si c'est le Seigneur qui le conduit	If it's caused by the Lord
Bénis soient les dégats.	Then blessed be the damage.
Si c'est le diable qui le conduit	If it's driven by the devil
Faites-le partir au trot d'ici.	Get it out of here double-quick.
Préservez-nous des dartres et des boutons	Preserve us from sores and pimples,
de la peste et de la lèpre.	from plague and leprosy.
Si c'est pour ma pénitence que vous l'envoyez,	If you have sent them as penance,
Seigneur, laissez-la moi, merci.	Then, Lord, let me endure them, thank you.
Si c'est le diable qui le conduit	If they're driven by the devil
Faites-le partir au trot d'ici.	Get 'em out of here double-quick.
Goître, goître, sors de ton sac,	Goiter, goiter, get out of your sac,
sors de mon cou et de ma tête!	out of my neck and my head!
Feu Saint Elme, danse de Saint Guy,	St. Elmo's fire, St. Vitus's dance,
Si c'est le diable qui vous conduit	If you're driven by the devil,
mon Dieu, faites-le sortir d'ici.	my God, get him out of here.
Faites que je grandisse vite	Help me to grow up fast
Et donnez-moi un bon mari,	And find me a good husband

qui ne soit pas trop ivrogne   who isn't too much of a drunk
et qui ne me batte pas tous les soirs.   and doesn't beat me every night.

La Petite Servante represents another step forward in Poulenc's progress to mastery. The song is influenced, as he readily admitted, by Musorgsky, but also clearly by Stravinsky's Russian works before his neoclassical phase:[52] Russia here meets Brittany in the almost medieval depth of its faith and superstition. The music is divided into four different sections, to correspond with the poem's four strophes. The kind of incantation hurled out at the beginning would not be out of place during an era of witch burnings and ducking stools; as far as this excitable and fanatical little soul is concerned, the devil is a real person with a pitchfork.

Bars 1–15 feature a piano-writing style that was announced in *Le Présent*: an étude bristling with rustling octaves between the hands, sinister in effect. The second verse (bb. 16–22), another incantation, more spoken than sung, brings a list of sicknesses the servant prays will not beset her. ("*The dreaded maladies*," Poulenc instructs, "*must be pronounced precisely.*"[53]) Mild echoes of *The Rite of Spring* primitivism suggest possibilities of a different kind of religious sacrifice; this is imitation born of Poulenc's almost childlike admiration for Stravinsky, and is meant in earnest homage.

In the third verse (bb. 23–30), which ups the ante in a mood of increasing panic, the girl's terror and anguish reach new heights, or plumb greater depths, while the accompaniment prances, stabs, and thunders beneath her. Poulenc never set any lines more demented or grotesque than "Goître, goître, sors de ton sac, / Sors de mon cou et de ma tête"; on the first two words the singer is required to make two downward octave leaps in quick succession while the music whips itself up into a frenzy—more outright drama than this composer has so far attempted in song. In the terrified vehemence of this exorcism, we can discern the future creator (a quarter of a century later) of the agonies of the dying prioress in *Dialogues des Carmélites*.

And then (from b. 31) the mood suddenly changes. As tormented sixteenth notes yield to spacious half and quarter notes, lyrical melody settles on the stave like an unexpected blessing, the pedal irrigates the previously dry textures, and harmonies blossom in honor of the supplicant's flowery future. Hers is only a modest dream—a husband who is not *too* drunk or abusive—and the composer plays his violin for her, responding with what he terms "*L'archet à la corde*,"[54] a well-bowed, singing, legato melody and a recognizably Poulencian turn of phrase. The postlude is unusually eloquent, not only for the piano's luscious restatement of the melody for "Faites que je grandisse vite," but also for the bass rumblings in the accompaniment that return us to the earlier mood of sadness and disquiet. All in all, this is strange but significant music, written on the threshold of *Le Bal masqué*.

(iv)   *Berceuse (Cradle Song)*
       No key signature (G major); $\frac{3}{8}$; *Mouvement de valse* ♩ = 76

Ton père est à la messe,	Your father's at mass,
ta mère au cabaret,	your mother's at the cabaret,
tu auras sur les fesses	you're going to get such a spanking
si tu vas encore crier.	if you don't stop your bawling.
Ma mère était pauvresse	My mother was a poor girl
sur la lande à Auray	from the moors of Auray
et moi je fais des crêpes	and here I am, making pancakes
en te berçant du pied.	rocking your cradle with my foot.
Si tu mourais du croup,	If you died from croup,
coliques ou diarrhées,	from colic or diarrhea,
si tu mourais des croûtes	if you died from the scabs
que tu as sur le nez.	you've got on your nose,
Je pêcherais des crevettes	I'd be off fishing for shrimp
à l'heure de la marée	at low tide
pour faire la soupe aux têtes:	to make shrimp-head soup with:
y a pas besoin de crochets.	you can catch them without a hook.

"*In* Berceuse," Poulence explains, "*everything is topsy-turvy: the father is at mass, the mother at a tavern. A waltz rhythm takes the place of a cradle song. It is redolent of cider and the acrid smell of the thatched cottages.*"[55] The song is a precursor to *A Charm* ("Quiet, sleep!") from Benjamin Britten's *A Charm of Lullabies*— both feature babysitters from hell. Here a beggar woman's daughter, not at all enamored of children, is dangerously cooking crêpes as she rocks the cradle. In Jacob's imagination she is the same superstitious "petite servante" of the previous song, given to outbursts of verbal violence (the poem's full title in *Commerce* is "Berceuse de la petite servante").

Fantasies of terrible illnesses for the baby are accompanied by a sequence of voluptuous ninth harmonies—musical *Schadenfreude*—and then the mood melts into an unexpectedly tender closing section. Poulenc, not given to politically motivated compassion for the poor in general, is clearly touched by this girl's individual plight and her plucky response to it. She lacks the hooks that are necessary to go shrimping and will have to make do by making a thin soup from shrimp heads. The lift from E major into C-sharp major via an E-sharp at bar 51, marked *Mélancolique, subito dolce,* has the effect of opening a privileged window into her dreams. She has not become who she is without a lifetime of fending for herself. A lack of self-pity and a humorous acceptance of life's paradoxes bring an earthy charm to the music. When Poulenc slums, he can do it convincingly in both Apollinaire's Paris and Max Jacob's Brittany.

(v)   *Souric et Mouric*
      No key signature (final two pages in F major); $\frac{4}{8}$; *Extrêmement vite*
      ♩ = 116

Souric et Mouric,	Souric and Mouric,
rat blanc, souris noire,	white rat, black mouse,
venus dans l'armoire	they've come to the wardrobe
pour apprendre à l'araignée	to teach the spider
à tisser sur le métier	how to weave, using a loom,
un beau drap de toile.	a beautiful sheet of cloth.
Expédiez-le à Paris, à Quimper, à Nantes,	Send it to Paris, to Quimper, to Nantes,
c'est de bonne vente!	it'll sell really well!
Mettez les sous de côté,	Put the pennies by,
vous achèterez un pré,	and you can buy a field
des pommiers pour la saison	with apple trees for the season
et trois belles vaches,	and three fine cows,
un bœuf pour faire étalon.	and a bull for stud purposes.
Chantez, les rainettes,	Sing, tree-frogs,
car voici la nuit qui vient,	for night is falling,
la nuit on les entend bien,	you can hear them clearly at night,
crapauds et grenouilles,	the toads and the frogs,
écoutez mon merle	listen my blackbird
et ma pie qui parle,	and my talking magpie,
écoutez toute la journée,	listen all day long,
vous apprendrez à chanter.	then you'll learn to sing.

Here is another song where, despite the Breton provenance of the poetry, Stravinsky's Russia and Poulenc's France meet in the middle—at least in the first section, where the angularity of the opening vocal line suggests mechanical music, in this case the sinister spinning of a spider. Poulenc admits as much; he considers this a counting song to be delivered as fast as possible.[56] After the tumult of the opening pages, which end almost in a puff of smoke, we come to the heart of the music, introduced by three bars of somber chords marked *Très calme*—an atmospheric and seraphic F major nocturne (from "Chantez, les rainettes"). The perspective is suddenly changed: as Hervé Lacombe observes, "One no longer counts, one no longer looks, one no longer enjoys oneself, *one listens*."[57] These twenty-six bars are connected with a number of Poulenc's vivid personal memories, where reflections of childhood and adulthood find themselves in gently melancholic conjunction.

Poulenc composed the song while staying in the empty house of his grandparents, now up for sale. What Nogent-sur-Marne had meant to him is incalculable; as a holiday refuge in his youth, it had been a home away from home and a place of magical excitement and poetry. He also called up memories of his dog Mickey, who used to lie under the piano, and of a children's tea party with Eve Curie (the song's dedicatee) on the artificial Lac des Minimes in the Bois de Vincennes. In the childlike coda, with its haunting little piano motif of a quarter note followed by four descending sixteenths (a melisma initiated by "Chantez"), the soprano is requested to keep her tone *très blanc*—no doubt to emphasize her artless innocence. Nightfall comes as poetically as at the end of *L'Histoire de Babar, le petit éléphant*; the vocal line is cushioned by the piano's gently floating eighth notes with occasional decorative sixteenths; and, in this inverted universe, the blackbird and magpie must learn to sing in imitation of the tree frogs. Poulenc confessed a "*predilection for the last two pages, which give, I believe, a true impression of night*."[58] The music seems all the more seductive because it so effectively soothes the furor of the vertiginous opening; Poulenc is fast becoming a master of these kinds of contrasts. Apart from its opening (fleeting ghosts of Stravinsky's *Oedipus Rex*), *Souric et Mouric* is a song that is as original as it is genuinely touching.

∘   ∘   ∘

FP60   *Le Bal masqué* ("Cantate profane" for baritone or mezzo and chamber orchestra, on poems of Max Jacob), February–April 1932

FP61   Concerto in D Minor for Two Pianos, summer 1932

FP62   *Valse-improvisation sur le nom de Bach* (piano), 8 October 1932

FP63   *Improvisations 1–10* (piano), 1932–33

FP64   *Intermezzo* (incidental music for a play by Jean Giraudoux), 1933

FP65   *Villageoises (Petites Pièces enfantines)* (piano), February 1933

∘   ∘   ∘

FP66   Pierrot

> Composed in Noizay, 18 May 1933
>
> [*Mme Victomesse de Noailles*; Salabert]
>
> Literary source: Théodore de Banville (1823–1891), *Les Cariatides* (Édition definitive) (Paris: Charpentier, 1879), p. 181. "Pierrot" is No. vi of the section *Les Caprices en dizaines à la manière de Clément Marot*.
>
> No real tonality, feeling of A minor; $\frac{2}{4}$; *Très vite* ♩ = 144

Le bon Pierrot, que la foule contemple,	Good old Pierrot, under the gaze of the crowd,
Ayant fini les noces d'Arlequin,	Having finished with Harlequin's wedding,
Suit en songeant le boulevard du Temple.	Wanders dreaming down the boulevard du Temple.
Une fillette au souple casaquin	A girl in a flowing robe
En vain l'agace de son œil coquin;	Tries vainly to lure him with with her mischievous eyes;
Et cependant mystérieuse et lisse	And meanwhile, mysterious and smooth,
Faisant de lui sa plus chère délice,	Cherishing him above all others,
La blanche lune aux cornes de taureau	The white moon, horned like a bull,
Jette un regard de son œil en coulisse	Casts a sidelong glance
À son ami Jean Gaspard Deburau.	At her friend Jean Gaspard Deburau.

The autograph of this song was recovered from the files of the publisher Salabert in 1991, and it is highly unlikely that Poulenc ever intended to publish it. Théodore de Banville, skilled precursor of the Parnassians, was completely outside Poulenc's area of literary interest. His poetry had been set some dozen times by the young Debussy, and it was almost certainly Debussy's skittish setting of "Pierrot" (composed in 1882 but posthumously published only in 1926 as one of *Quatre Chansons de jeunesse*) that drew Poulenc's attention to the poem—which was written in

the manner of the sixteenth-century poet Clément Marot.

This is a last gasp of Poulenc's *Cocardes* style (in the circus-like trumpet voluntary of the opening) interlaced with the comic, almost atonal piquancy of the first Max Jacob settings from the twenties. The end result, however, is scarcely among the composer's most memorable works; he adopts something of that air of nervous, raffish conspiracy that is a feature of the Debussy songs about the commedia dell'arte (of which the Verlaine setting *Fantoches* is the best known).

Théodore de Banville.

Jean-Baptiste Gaspard Deburau (in the poem's last line) was a famous Czech-born mime (1796–1846) who was at his height as an entertainer in 1830s Paris, and whose eloquently mute Pierrot became his trademark. Deburau is most remembered for his appearances at the Théâtre des Funambules in the boulevard du Temple (in the poem's third line), also known as the boulevard du Crime. This epoch in Paris's theatrical history is evoked in Marcel Carné's celebrated 1945 film *Les Enfants du paradis*, in which Jean-Louis Barrault (with whom Poulenc was later to collaborate) memorably takes the role of Deburau. The name is correctly spelled in Banville's poem but misspelled "Debureau" in the Debussy publication; Poulenc follows suit, proof perhaps that the older composer's score was the source of his text. The song was almost certainly written for some party event involving the work's socialite dedicatee, Marie-Laure de Noailles.

○   ○   ○

FP67 *Pétrus* (incidental music, a single song, for a play by Marcel Achard), autumn 1933

FP68 *Feuillets d'album* (piano), 1933

○   ○   ○

FP69 **Huit Chansons polonaises** (*Osiem pieśni polskich*) (*Eight Polish Songs*)
Composed in Noizay and Paris, January–April 1934
[*Ida Godebska, Misia Sert, Elisabeth Potocka, Marya Freund, Mme Kochanska, Mme Arthur Rubinstein, Wanda Landowska, Maria Modrakowska*; Rouart, Lerolle]
Literary source: The known authors are (i) Franciszek Kowalski (1799–1862), (ii) Stefan Witwicki (1801–1847), (v) Maurycy Gosławski (1802–1834), (vi) Rajnold Suchodolski (1804–1831). Texts for the remaining songs are traditional.

(i)   *Wianek* (*La Couronne*) (Noizay, January)
(ii) *Odjazd* (*Le Départ*) (Noizay, January)
(iii) *Polska młodziez* (*Les Gars polonais*) (Paris, January)
(iv) *Ostatni mazur* (*Le Dernier Mazour*) (Paris, 30 April)
(v)   *Pożegnanie* (*L'Adieu*) (Paris, January)
(vi) *Białą chorągiewka* (*Le Drapeau blanc*) (Noizay, February)
(vii) *Wisła* (*La Vistule*) (Noizay, January)
(viii) *Jezioro* (*Le Lac*) (Paris, 29 April)

These harmonizations and arrangements of Polish melodies were undertaken by Poulenc at the request of the Polish soprano Maria Modrakowska (1896–1965), who chose the tunes and provided notes on their historical background. Poulenc thought her *"incomparably gifted"* and that she *"sang divinely."* He made a month-long tour of North Africa with the singer in February 1935, followed by concerts in the French provinces in April and May. Modrakowska had once seemed a possible permanent duo partner, but the unexpected arrival of Bernac on the scene rendered her eventually redundant. Poulenc dropped her, but later it suited him to spin the story differently: stating that to his consternation and disappointment she had disappeared inexplicably from his musical horizons, one of the reasons he stopped composing songs between 1931 and 1934. In reality, it was the soprano who felt abandoned by the man who had entered her musical life for a short period and then withdrew, but she never made a fuss.

Poulenc compared *Huit Chansons* with Ravel's arrangement of Greek folksongs (*Cinq Mélodies populaires grecques*). When writing those arrangements, Ravel had had a free hand, largely because, as Poulenc put it, he had no *"ghost of an Athenian Chopin"* to haunt him. *"In composing an accompaniment for these songs, I didn't aim for local color and originality. I simply imagined, in a French manner, a Polish atmosphere just as others have evoked Spain without knowing it. My work is similar to those delicate bronze frames in which eighteenth-century French artisans used to set porcelain from the Orient."*[59]

Poulenc's urbane confession postdated the work's publication in 1934, when he evidently sold the songs to publisher Rouart, Lerolle as if they were original mélodies, at a cost of 6,000 francs. A letter to Jacques Lerolle on 9 February, complete with demands for checks and bank transfers, provides a fascinating peek into the composer's financial dealings.[60] We get a good idea of his ability to bargain financially with determination, charm, and more than a touch of wheedling—and his lack of shame at pleading poverty: *"I'm a bit of a bore* [about money], *aren't I?"* There is also evidence of further cost-cutting: it seems that via Modrakowska, Poulenc made a rough French translation of the Polish text and passed it on to Lerolle, who then fashioned a singing translation. The expensive alternative of hiring a professional translator was thus avoided with an in-house solution.

A trio of important women musicians in Poulenc's life (1934): Maria Modrakowska, Nadia Boulanger, and Marie-Blanche de Polignac.

The result is not always felicitous, as the French texts fit the music rather than accurately reflecting the text. Occasionally rhythms are changed, and the texts do not always rhyme in the way that the poetry, or indeed the music, does. The modern performer should if possible go back to the original Polish.

Huit Chansons is, almost inevitably, a homage to Chopin, whose music Poulenc so loved. The poems come from the period when Poland was occupied by Russia, Germany, and Austria, a baleful state of affairs that gave rise to the Polish insurrection that began on 29 November 1830, known as the November Uprising, and continued into the autumn of 1831. The Uprising was a valiant revolution of patriotic combat and fervor, but with none of the big powers coming to the aid of the Poles, it was eventually crushed by Russia. Chopin had left Poland to begin his European career shortly before the Uprising, and his heart was entirely with his countrymen. Some of his own songs date from this time, when he was twenty-one. His fury at the Russian victory knew no bounds.

(i) *Wianek* (*La Couronne*) (*The Wreath*)
　　G major; $\frac{3}{4}$; *Preste et enjoué*

Targa swéj wianeczek	The maiden tears up her wreath
W rzewnych łzach dziewczyna,	Shedding bitter tears,
Że jej kochaneczek	For her beloved
Idzie do Lublina.	Is going away to Lublin.
Bo w Lublinie są Krakusy,	To Lublin, to join the Cracow boys,
Żwawe chłopcy i wiarusy.	Those spirited old campaigners.
"Nie idź, nie idź Janku,	"Janek, don't go, don't go,
śmierć tam grozi tobie,	You're doomed to die there,
Czyż ja bez ustanku,	Am I to mourn you
Płakać mam w żałobie?"	For ever and a day?"
"Uśmierz dziewczę swe katusze,	"Let your anguish be soothed, dear maiden,
Ja Ojczyźnie służyć muszę."	I must serve the Fatherland."
"Więc ty z sobą razem,	"Then take your girl
Zabierz swą dziewczynę,	Along with you,
Jak zginiesz żelazem,	If you are struck dead
I ja z tobą zginę."	Then I will die with you."

In the poem a young girl is weeping as Janek, her betrothed, goes off to join the army at Lublin. She rends in two her crown of flowers (in Lerolle's French translation she merely throws it to the ground). The original melody is entitled "The Young Girl and the Krakouss—the Soldier from Krakow," and Poulenc's arrangement is in the two contrasted speeds (*Modéré* and *Vite*) of the mazurka form. His opening ritornello, the piano writing high in the treble clef, is one of the most convincing Chopin evocations of the set.

Poulenc dedicated each song in *Huit Chansons* to an important female member of the expatriate Polish community in Paris—this first one to Ida Godebska, wife of Cipra Godebsk. The Godebskis were close enough to Ravel to count as his second family, and Ida was the sister-in-law of Misia Godebska (later Natanson and then Sert), patroness of dance, music, and painting, and dedicatee of the next song.

(ii) *Odjazd (Le Départ) (The Departure)*
     G major; $\frac{3}{8}$; *Mouvt. de Mazurka*

Rży koniczek mój bułany,	A dun horse is neighing,
Puśćcie, czas już czas!	Let me go, it's time, it's time!
Matko, ojcze mój kochany,	Mother, beloved father,
Żegnam, żegnam was.	I say goodbye, goodbye.
Cóżby życie warte było,	What would life be worth
Gdybym gnuśnie zgasł?	If I died an idle death?
Dosyć, dosyć się marzyło,	Enough of dreaming,
Teraz nie ten czas.	This is not the time.
Zdala słyszę trąb hałasy,	I hear the trumpets' distant call,
Dobosz w bęben grzmi,	The drummer is beating the drums,
Rzucam, rzucam słodkie czasy,	I am leaving, leaving the sweet times behind,
Błogosławcie mi!	Give me your blessing!

The poem, about a cavalryman bidding farewell to his family, is by a well-known poet of the period, Stefan Witwicki, friend of Chopin and dedicatee of his Op. 41 Mazurkas. Its melody is a popular song, another mazurka, this time with a slower middle section and with Poulenc's accompaniment almost entirely doubling the vocal line. Chopin's song *Wojak (The Warrior)* is an 1831 setting of the same poem with original music.

(iii) *Polska młodziez (Les Gars polonais) (Polish Youth)*
A major; $\frac{2}{4}$; *Gaiement*

Polska młodzież niech nam żyje,	Long live Polish youth,
Nikt jej nie przesadzi,	Who won't be defeated,
Bo jej ręka dobrze bije,	Because their hands know how to smite
Głowa dobrze radzi.	And their heads are full of wisdom.
Pognębieni, zapomnieni,	Oppressed, forgotten
Od całego świata,	By the whole world,
Własnych baliśmy sięcieni,	We feared our own shadows,
Brat unikał brata.	Brother avoided brother.
Niech do boju każdy biegnie,	Into battle, everyone
Piękne tam skonanie,	It's beautiful to die there
Za jednego, który legnie,	For every man who falls
Sto mścicieli wstanie.	A hundred shall rise in vengeance.
Zawsze Polak miał nadzieję	A Pole will always place his trust
W mocy Niebios Pana,	In Almighty God,
On w nas jedność, zgodę wleje,	Who will inspire us with unity and concord
A przy nas wygrana.	And victory shall be ours.

This song, cheekily harmonized by Poulenc and alternating between fast and slower tempos, was originally sung by enthusiastic crowds at Warsaw's National Theater on 8 February 1831, in honor of General Józef Chłopicki—six days before the first battle in the Russo-Polish War. Poulenc's piano writing is more inventive here, and in this "quick march" he is not afraid of the occasional clash or discord.[61]

(iv) *Ostatni mazur (Le Dernier Mazour) (The Last Mazurka)*
E minor; $\frac{3}{4}$; *Modérément lent*

Jeszcze jeden mazur dzisiaj, nim poranek świta,	Let's dance one more mazurka before dawn,
"Czy pozwoli Pana Krzysia?" młody ułan pyta.	"May I have this dance, Miss Krysia?" a young uhlan asks.
I tak długo błaga, prosi, boć to w polskiej ziemi:	He implores and begs her ceaselessly, as they do in Poland:

W pierwszą parę jąponosi, a sto par za
 niemi.

On coś pannie szepce w uszko, i
 ostrogądzwoni,
Pannie tłucze sięserduszko, i liczko się
 płoni.

Cyt, serduszko, nie płoń liczka, bo
 ułan niestały:
O pół mili wre potyczka, słychać
 pierwsze strzały.

Słychać strzały, głos pobudki, dalej na
 koń, hurra!
Lube dziewczę porzućsmutki,
 dokończym mazura.

Jeszcze jeden krąg dokoła, jeden uścisk
 bratni,
Trabka budzi, na końwoła, mazur to
 ostatni.

He leads her to the dance—a hundred
 couples follow suit.

He whispers into her tiny ear, his spurs
 are jangling,
Her heart is racing, her tiny face is
 blushing.

Heart, be still. Cheeks, stop blushing—
 the uhlan is fickle.
The battle is but half a mile from here,
 you can hear the first shots.

The shots and the reveille, "Get back
 on the horse!" "Hurrah!"
Sweet girl, don't be sad, let's finish the
 mazurka.

One more spin, one more fraternal
 embrace,
The bugle calls order us into the saddle.
 This is our last mazurka.

The original melody was created in the period of the 1830 November Uprising and sung in honor of General Chłopicki's troops (an uhlan is a light cavalryman, or lancer) as they departed for the Front. It remained famous until the First World War, when troops of General Józef Piłsudski adopted it as their theme tune. Piłsudski was the aged, and increasingly despotic, leader of Poland when Poulenc and Modrakowska first performed these songs. Little could either artist know that a mere five years later, both Britain and France would have declared war on Germany, after Hitler's brutal invasion of this plucky and deeply unfortunate country.

The mazur is a traditional dance from Masovia, the historical northeastern region of Poland, and less lively than a mazurka—the name itself a diminutive of "mazur." Whether mazur or mazurka, the song is marvelous grist to Poulenc's mill; a number of his subsequent mélodies are tinged with exactly this kind of Chopin-influenced *tristesse*—and he still manages to make it sound like genuine Poulenc. The composer summed the song up thus: "*A real set piece. During a ball the sound of the cannon is heard. A young girl dances with her lover for the last time.*"[62] The final two lines, suddenly marked *Très vite*, denote the sudden call to battle ("La trompette" in the French translation) and come as something of a clinching surprise. The song is dedicated to Poulenc's old colleague, soprano

Marya Freund, early champion of *Le Bestiaire* and of Schoenberg's *Pierrot lunaire*—as well as mother of the bass Doda Conrad, for whom Poulenc would compose *Hymne* FP144 and *Mazurka* FP145 fifteen years later.

(v)   *Pożegnanie (L'Adieu) (Farewell)*
          C minor; $\frac{3}{4}$; *Mélancolique*

Widzisz dziewczęchorągiewkę,	Maiden, do you see the pennant
Co przy mojej lancy drży?	That flutters by my lance?
Zaśpiewam ci o niej śpiewkę,	I'll sing you a song about it,
Ona piekna tak jak ty.	A song as beautiful as you.
Nie płacz luba, bywaj zdrowa,	Do not cry, beloved, fare you well,
Łzy na cięższe zostaw dnie:	Save your tears for harder times.
Co Bóg sądzi, bywaj zdrowa,	May God decide—be well,
Może wrócę, może nie.	I may return, I may not return.

This text of fateful leave-taking is by Maurycy Gosławski, known for his *Poems of a Polish Outlaw*. At the time of the November Uprising, Gosławski was a member of the Russian army, but deserted in order to join the revolutionary cause; he died in prison in Stanislawów. As in the first song, Poulenc here allows himself a postlude; this one reharmonizes the opening eight bars of vocal melody to haunting effect.

(vi)   *Białą chorągiewka (Le Drapeau blanc) (The White Pennant)*
          G major; $\frac{3}{8}$; *Modéré*

Warszawianka dla kochanka szyła	A Warsaw girl was sewing a little
białąchorągiewkę,	white pennant,
To płakała, to wzdychała, śląc modły	She cried, she sighed, she prayed to
do Boga.	God.
Warszawiaczck zrzucił fraczck	A Warsaw lad took off his frockcoat,
Przeciw cara jest czamara,	Put on a greatcoat to fight the Tzar,
Kulka w rurkę, proch w panewkę,	Load the musket, prime the powder,
I dalej na wroga.	And off to fight the enemy.

Like *Pożegnanie*, this song tells the story of a lovers' farewell in times of war. Rajnold Suchodolski, the poet, was the younger brother of January Suchodolski (1797–1875), a painter of military pictures. Rajnold was one of many talented and idealistic young Poles who lost their lives in the November Uprising. Poulenc varies the potential monotony of the triple rhythm with sixty-fourth-note decorations that sound like crushed grace notes dashed off under the hands of an improvising pianist. The white pennant sewn on the coat of the girl's lover, reflecting her hope for peace, is spurned by the patriotic young man in favor of a military uniform.

(vii)   *Wisła (La Vistule) (The Vistula)*
        B-flat major; ²⁄₄; *Animé*

Płynie Wisła płynie,	The Vistula flows and flows
Po polskiej krainie,	Through the Polish land,
A dopóki płynie,	As long as it flows,
Polska nie zaginie.	Poland shall not perish.
Zobaczyła Kraków,	It saw Cracow
Wnet go pokochała:	And fell in love with it immediately.
I w dowód miłości	And, to prove its love,
Wstęgą opasała.	Wrapped itself around it like a ribbon.
Bo ten polski naród	That's our Polish nation,
Ten ma urok w sobie,	That's the charm of it,
Kto go raz pokochał,	Whoever who falls in love with it
Nie zapomni w grobie.	Won't forget it till the grave.

The Vistula winds itself around Cracow like a ribbon, hence the metaphor. J. S.

After six songs connected with the Uprising, Modrakowska appends two folksongs. This one honors the Vistula, the longest and most important of Poland's rivers, which passes through many towns (including Krakow and Warsaw) on its way to the Baltic. The "song from Krakow" has long been popular, and even Polish singers of the younger generation today remember the melody from their schooldays. The first and third verses are simply harmonized, but Poulenc invented a descant for the second, a floating ribbon of a countermelody to complement the words and add a certain amount of color to an otherwise plain song. That the composer must have been pleased with this arrangement is shown by the fact he dedicated it to his dear friend the harpsichordist Wanda Landowska, who had first performed his *Concert champêtre*.

(viii)   *Jezioro (Le Lac) (The Lake)*
         G major; ³⁄₄; *Lent et triste*

O jezioro, jezioro:	Oh lake, oh lake:
Bystra woda w tobie jest.	Running water flows in you.
Wionku z maryjonku,	A wreath of marjoram
Na głowie mi więdniejesz.	Is withering on my head.
Jakże ja nie mam więdnieć?	How am I not to wither
Gdy już nie jestem cały.	If I am no longer whole?
Zielone listeczki,	Little green leaves,
Modre fijołecki	Little violet flowers
Ze mnie już opadają.	Are falling from me.

"While the first seven songs are urban in character, the last is rustic, sung by peasants in Upper Silesia. It depicts the despair of a young girl abandoned on the shores of a lake."[63] And it is perhaps the most original arrangement of the eight: for the first page, the vocal line is harmonized by a single stave of piano writing in the treble clef. Poulenc brings a haunting modernity to this music that is lacking from the other songs, the first five of which are, after all, character pieces from a definite historical epoch. Chopin and his style simply had to be present in music from a period when that composer was almost an active participant in political events. But here Chopin plays no role. The music brings to mind the folksong-arranger Ravel, with whom Poulenc compared himself in his *Journal*. The dedicatee was Maria Modrakowska, who had been so crucial in bringing the cycle into being.

o   o   o

FP70   *Presto in B-flat Major* (piano), July 1934

FP71   *Two Intermezzi* (piano), March–August 1934

FP72   *Humoresque* (piano), 1934

FP73   *Badinage* (piano), December 1934

FP74   *Villanelle* (from *Les Pipeaux*, anthology for pipes and piano), 1934

o   o   o

FP75   **Quatre Chansons pour enfants** (*Four Songs for Children*)

Composed in Noizay (i), Besançon (ii), Vichy (iii), and Paris (iv), 1934

[*Marie-Blanche de Polignac, Mme H. Ledoux, Mario Beaugnies* [sic] *de Saint-Marceaux, Jean de Polignac*; Enoch]

Literary source: Jaboune, also Jean Nohain (pseudonyms of Jean-Marie Legrand, 1900–1981). The poems probably all appeared in Jaboune's weekly children's newspaper, *Benjamin*.

(i)   *Nous voulons une petite sœur*

(ii)   *La Tragique Histoire du petit René*

(iii) *Le Petit Garçon trop bien portant*

(iv) *Monsieur Sans-Souci*

"Jean Nohain" and "Jaboune" were both pseudonyms for Jean-Marie Legrand, a school contemporary of the composer. Though not on intimate terms with Legrand, in December 1944 Poulenc, saluting a war hero, paid him a visit in Val-de-Grâce, a military hospital in Paris, after he had been wounded in action.

The musical language of these four songs is simple without being in any way infantile, a "style situated somewhere between Maurice Chevalier and Offenbach."[64] Although the texts are irreproachably suitable for young people to either sing or listen to, songs of this kind, with their zany melodies and verbal patter, would have been far more suggestive had they been conceived for the music hall. These innocent little sketches show the composer's genius for pastiche, his ability to write his own popular music with no apparent difficulty. Poulenc seems never to have referred to them in his writings or known correspondence; possibly he dashed them off to make some quick money from the publisher Enoch, and was not altogether proud of having done so.

The songs were published as part of an advertised series entitled "What artists are singing and recording," together with a motley array of vocal works by Chabrier, Franck, Cécile Chaminade, and André Messager among others long since forgotten—all offering what we may term the lighter side of the mélodie repertoire without crossing (officially, at least) into the realms of chanson. A footnote by Enoch indicates that it was accepted that the songs could be sung without any accompaniment, and separate voice parts were printed accordingly. Poulenc keeps the involvement of the pianist to a decent minimum, mostly doubling the voice, but touching on the harmonies in a simplified style without losing any of the piquant wit that was already his trademark. The children's illustrator Marianne Clouzot (1908–2007) provided simple but atmospheric pictures for the song covers.

(i) *Nous voulons une petite sœur* (*We Want a Little Sister*)
G major; $\frac{2}{2}$; *Gaîment*

Madame Eustache a dix-sept filles,	Madame Eustache has seventeen daughters,
Ce n'est pas trop,	It's not too many,
Mais c'est assez,	But it's enough,
La jolie petite famille	That nice little family
Vous avez dû dû dû,	You must have seen seen seen,
Vous avez dû dû dû,	You must have seen seen seen,

Vous avez dû la voir passer.	You must have seen them in the street.
Le vingt décembre on les appelle:	On the twentieth of December they are summoned:
Que voulez-vous mesdemoiselles, pour votre Noël?	Girls, what would you like for Christmas?
Voulez-vous une boîte à poudre?	Would you like a powder compact?
Voulez-vous de petits mouchoirs?	Would you like some tiny hankies?
Un petit nécessaire à coudre?	A little sewing kit?
Un perroquet sur son perchoir?	A parrot on a perch?
Voulez-vous un petit ménage?	Would you like a toy roundabout?
Un stylo qui tache les doigts?	A fountain pen that stains your fingers?
Un pompier qui plonge et qui nage?	A fireman who dives and swims?
Un vase à fleur presque chinois?	A vase that's almost Chinese?
Mais les dix-sept enfants en chœur ont répondu:	But the seventeen children answered in chorus:
Non, non, non, non, non,	No, no, no, no, no,
Ce n'est pas ça que nous voulons,	That is not we want,
nous voulons une petite sœur	We want a little sister
Ronde et joufflue comme un ballon,	Round and chubby as a balloon,
Avec un petit nez farceur,	With a funny little nose,
Avec des cheveux blonds,	With blond hair,
Avec la bouche en cœur,	With a heart-shaped mouth,
Nous voulons une petite sœur.	We want a little sister!
L'hiver suivant elles sont dix-huit,	Next winter they are eighteen,
Ce n'est pas trop, mais c'est assez,	It's not too many, but it's enough,
Noël approche et les petites sont bien em ba ba ba	Christmas is coming and the little girls are quite en-cum- cum- cum-
Sont bien em ba ba ba	Are quite en- cum- cum- cum-
Sont vraiment bien embarrassées.	Are totally en- cum- cum- cum-bered!
Madame Eustache les appelle:	Madame Eustache summons them:
Décidez-vous, mesdemoiselles, pour votre Noël:	Make up your minds, girls—what would you like for Christmas?
Voulez-vous un mouton qui frise?	Would you like a sheep that does your hair?
Voulez-vous un réveil matin?	Would you like an alarm clock?
Un coffret d'alcool dentifrice?	A box of alcoholic toothpaste?
Trois petits coussins de satin?	Three little satin cushions?

Voulez-vous une panoplie,
De danseuse de l'opéra?
Un petit fauteuil qui se plie,
Et que l'on porte sous sont bras?

Mais les dix-huit enfants en chœur
    ont répondu:
Non, non, non, non, non,
Ce n'est pas ça que nous voulons,
Nous voulons une petite sœur
Ronde et joufflue comme un ballon,
Avec un petit nez farceur,
Avec des cheveux blonds,
Avec la bouche en cœur,
Nous voulons une petite sœur.

Elle sont dix-neuf l'année suivante,
Ce n'est pas trop,
Mais c'est assez,
Quand revient l'époque émouvante,
Noël va de nou nou,
Noël va de nou nou,
Noël va de nouveau passer,
Madame Eustache les appelle:
Décidez-vous, mesdemoiselles, pour
    votre Noël:

Voulez-vous des jeux excentriques,
Avec des pil's et des moteurs?
Voulez-vous un ours électrique?
Un hippopotame à vapeur?
Pour coller des cartes postales,
Voulez-vous un superbe album?
Une automobile à pédales?
Une bague en aluminium?

Mais les dix-neuf enfants en chœur
    ont répondu:
Non, non, non, non, non,
Ce n'est pas ça que nous voulons,
Nous voulons deux petites jumelles,

Would you like the costume
Of a ballerina at the opera?
A little fold-up comfy chair
You can carry under your arm?

But the eighteen children answered in
    chorus:
No, no, no, no, no,
That is not we want,
We want a little sister
Round and chubby as a balloon,
With a funny little nose,
With blond hair,
With a heart-shaped mouth,
We want a little sister!

The next year they are nineteen,
It's not too many,
But it's enough,
When the moving time
Of Christmas comes comes comes
Christmas comes comes comes
Christmas comes comes comes around,
Madame Eustache summons them:
Make up your minds, girls, for
    Christmas:

Would you like some eccentric toys
With batteries and motors?
Would you like an electric bear?
A steam-driven hippo?
As somewhere to stick your postcards
Would you like a superb album?
A pedal-driven car?
A ring made of aluminium?

But the nineteen children answered in
    chorus:
No, no, no, no, no,
That is not we want
Two identical twin sisters,

Deux sœurs exactement pareilles,	We want two little twins,
Deux sœurs avec des cheveux blonds!	Two sisters with blond hair!
Leur mère a dit: c'est bien,	Their mother said: that's enough,
Mais il n'y a pas moyen	It just can't be done.
Cette année vous n'aurez rien rien rien.	This year you'll get nothing nothing nothing!

Nous voulons une petite sœur *was first printed in the magazine* Benjamin *(28 December 1933).*

Despite the merry marking, the composer directs that the ritornello—at "Ce n'est pas ça que nous voulons" ("That's not what we want")—should be sung with melancholy, and slower than the main tempo. The four-bar prelude sounds like nothing more than a quasi-improvised scene setter, but it manages to convey something of the importunate longing of the Eustache sisters—seventeen of them ("it's not too many, but it's enough"). The wit and charm of Madame Eustache's increasingly exasperated (and very difficult to memorize) Christmas suggestions have made this the most often performed song of the set: it makes an appealing and useful addition for song recitals with a Christmas theme. The song is also a reminder of the Third Republic's obsession with encouraging its citizens to have more children, a subject Poulenc would revisit in more extended fashion in the Apollinaire opera *Les Mamelles de Tirésias*. The dedication to Marie-Blanche de Polignac shows the composer's pride, almost despite himself, in his *jeu d'esprit*.

(ii)   *La Tragique Histoire du petit René* (*The Tragic Story of Little René*)
        G minor; $\frac{2}{4}$; *Rondement*

Avec mon face-à-main	Through my lorgnette
Je vois ce qui se passe	I can see what's going on
Chez Madame Germain	At Madame Germain's
Dans la maison d'en face.	Opposite.
Les deux filles cadettes	The two youngest girls
Préparent le repas,	Are cooking the meals,
Reprisent les chaussettes	Darning dad's socks
Et font le lit de leur papa.	And making his bed.
Emma s'occupe du balai,	Emma's sweeping the floor,
Paul va chercher le lait,	And Paul's fetching the milk,
Mais le petit René	But René,
Quoique étant l'aîné	Though the eldest,
Fait rougir la maisonnée	Is shaming the whole household.
D'un bout de l'année	From one year's end
À l'autre bout de l'année,	To the next,
Il met les doigts dans son nez.	He's picking his nose!
Les sermons, les discours	The sermons and the speeches
Dont ses parents le bourrent	Given by his parents
Semblent tomber toujours	Seem always to fall
Dans l'oreille d'un sourd.	On deaf ears.
Sa mère consternée	And for all that his distraught mother
A beau le sermonner,	Lectures him,
Le priver de dîner,	And deprives him of supper,
Et lui donner le martinet,	Hits him with a wooden spoon,
L'enfermer dans les cabinets,	And locks him in the lav,
Il se met les doigts dans le nez	He still picks his nose,
D'un bout de l'année	From one year's end
À l'autre bout de l'année,	To the next.
C'est sa triste destinée,	It's his tragic destiny!
Pauvre petit René,	So poor little René,
Pour en terminer,	To put an end to it,
On a dû lui couper le nez.	They had to cut his nose off!

The poem has something about it of Hilaire Belloc's *Cautionary Tales* for children, or Harry Graham's *Ruthless Rhymes*, particularly in the violent solution for a domestic problem—cutting off little René's nose.[65] The story is told from the point of view of a disapproving peeping Tom, and the music cleverly conveys censorious, finger-wagging disapproval, as well as the narrator's furtive pleasure in spying on the Germain family, and René in particular.

(iii)   *Le Petit Garçon trop bien portant* (*The Little Boy Who's Too Healthy*)
         F major; $\frac{2}{4}$; *À perdre haleine*

Ah! mon cher docteur, je vous écris,	Dear Mr. Doctor, I'm writing to you,
Vous serez un peu surpris.	And this might come as a surprise,
Je ne suis vraiment pas content	But I'm really not happy
D'être toujours trop bien portant.	Being in such good health.
Je suis gras, trois fois trop,	I'm fat, triple-size,
J'ai des bras beaucoup trop gros.	And my arms are miles too big.
Et l'on dit, en me voyant:	And people say, when they see me:
"Regardez-le, c'est effrayant,	"Look at him, it's downright scary,
Quelle santé, quelle santé!	Such good health, such good health!
Approchez, on peut tâter!"	Come on, have a feel!"
Ah! mon cher docteur, c'est un enfer,	Ah Mr. Doctor, it's utter hell,
Vraiment, je ne sais plus quoi faire.	And I don't know what to do.
Tous les gens disent à ma mère;	Everyone says to my mum,
"Bravo, ma chère, il est en fer!"	"He's got an iron constitution!"
J'ai René, mon aîné,	My elder brother René,
Quand il faut être enrhumé,	When it's time to catch a cold,
Ça lui tombe toujours sur le nez.	Always gets it in the nose.
Les fluxions, Attention!	And when mumps are about,
C'est pour mon frère Adrien!	My brother Adrien gets them!
Mais moi, je n'attrape jamais rien!	But I never catch a thing!
Et pourtant j'ai beau, pendant l'hiver,	And it's a fat lot of use, come winter,
M'exposer aux courants d'air,	Exposing myself to draughts
Manger à tort à travers	Or eating my way through
Tous les fruits verts, y a rien à faire.	Piles of green fruit, no use at all!
Hélas, je sais que lorsqu'on a la rougeole,	Alas, I know that when you get measles
On reste au lit, mais on ne va plus à l'école.	You stay in bed and bunk off school.
Vos parents sont près de vous, il vous cajolent.	Your parents stand by your bedside, coddling you
Et l'on vous dit	And saying
Des tas de petits mots gentils.	Loads of sweet things.
Votre maman, constamment	And your mum gives you
Vous donne des médicaments.	Loads of medicine.

Ah! mon cher docteur, si vous étiez gentil,	Ah Mr. Doctor, if you were nice,
Vous auriez pitié!	You'd have pity on my plight!
Je sais bien ce que vous feriez,	And I'm sure you'd make me up
Les pilules que vous m'enverriez!	Some pills you can send!
Être bien portant tout le temps,	Being healthy all the time
C'est trop embêtant.	Is really annoying.
Je vous en supplie, docteur,	I beg you, Doctor,
Pour une fois, ayez bon cœur,	Be nice for once,
Docteur, une seule fois.	Doctor, just this once.
Rendez-moi malade,	And make me ill,
Pendant une heure!	For just one hour!

Perhaps the masterpiece of the set, and the most perfect homage to Poulenc's admired Maurice Chevalier; we can almost hear that great singer's voice written into the music. The song has to be performed so fast that the singer loses breath, and with this slew of words few English-speaking artists are capable of bringing it off—Felicity Lott, who has performed it many times to the admiring delight of French audiences, is a joyous exception. Poulenc here allows himself a moment of biographical irony; as a self-confessed hypochondriac, he would have felt considerable identification with the boy's plight.

The song is dedicated to Mario Baugnies de Saint-Marceaux, "Mario" being a contraction of "Marie-Odile"—name of the granddaughter of the famed Marguerite de Saint-Marceaux, who presided over one of the most influential salons in Paris. In a typically acerbic entry in her *Journal* (27 March 1927), "Meg" describes a soirée where the guest of honor was Ravel: "Mme [Marguerite] Long with Ravel played *Ma Mère l'Oye* for four hands. Poulenc sang his *Chansons gaillardes* and played his *Napoli*. He plays the piano well. His compositions do not lack talent, but he isn't a genius, and I fear he believes himself to be one."[66] In that period of his life, Poulenc was wary of anyone who did not unquestioningly embrace his supremacy. He had already fallen out with Bernac, which is clearly why he had to sing these songs himself. Interestingly, Mme Saint-Marceaux was evidently unfazed by the obscenity of some of the texts; at least she makes no mention of them. The dedication of *Le Petit Garçon trop bien portant* to a younger-generation member of her family was as near as the composer allowed himself to get to this formidable woman, who (as Meg Baugnies) had played such a vital part in the life and career of Gabriel Fauré.

(iv) *Monsieur Sans-Souci (Mr. Not-a-Care)*
      B-flat major; $\frac{4}{4}$; *Modéré*

Quand les gens,	When folks have got
Ont beaucoup d'argent,	Pots of money,
Pour leur service	They have servants,
Ils ont dit-on:	Or so I'm told:
Larbins, nourrices	Underlings, nursemaids
Et marmitons.	Scullery-boys.
C'n'est pas ainsi,	That's not the way
Chez Monsieur Sans-Souci . . .	With Mr. Not-a-care . . .
Il fait tout lui-même	He does everything himself
Dans sa p'tite maison,	In his tiny house.
C'est le bon système:	It's a system that works:
Il a bien raison!	So good for him!
Il frott', il astique:	He cleans, he polishes:
Pas de domestique,	Without a maid,
Son plancher reluit . . .	His floor gleams . . .
Qu'on est bien chez lui!	What a nice house he's got!
Les petits plats qu'il aime,	The little dishes he prefers
Il se les fait lui-même	He makes himself
Et puis il s'dit merci	And then he thanks himself
Monsieur Sans-Souci.	Mr. Not-a-care.
Au printemps,	Come the spring
Il est bien content . . .	He couldn't be happier . . .
Le jardinage	Doing his garden
Prend tout son temps . . .	Takes up his time . . .
Malgré son âge	In spite of his age
C'est en chantant	It's while singing
Des airs d'antan	Songs of the old days
Qu'il se met à l'ouvrage . . .	That he potters about . . .
Il fait tout lui-même	He does everything himself
Dans son p'tit jardin,	In his tiny garden,
Et les fleurs qu'il aime	And the flowers he loves
Il les a pour rien.	He gets for free.
Il bêche, il arros',	He digs, he waters,
Il taille ses ros's	He prunes his roses,
Et dans sa villa	And in his villa
C'est plein de lilas . . .	There's lilacs everywhere . . .
Il a des chrysanthèmes	He has chrysanthemums
Qu'il cueille pour lui-même,	Which he picks for himself
Et pour les dam's aussi	And for the ladies too
Monsieur Sans-Souci.	Mr. Not-a-care.

Le bon vieux	The sweet old chap
N'est jamais envieux,	Is never jealous,
Il se contente	He's quite content
Toujours de peu . . .	With not very much . . .
Rien ne le tente;	Nothing tempts him;
Il est heureux . . .	He's happy . . .
Son seul désir,	His only desire,
C'est de nous faire plaisir . . .	Is to please us . . .
Il fait tout lui-même	He does everything himself
Pour qu'on soit content . . .	To make others happy . . .
Tout le monde l'aime,	Everyone loves him,
Il vivra longtemps.	He'll live a long time . . .
Il est centenair',	He's a hundred years old,
Et déjà Saint-Pierr',	And St. Peter is already
L'attend, m'a-t-on dit,	Waiting for him, I'm told,
Dans son paradis . . .	In paradise . . .
Il entrera sans peine,	He'll get in, no problem,
Et près du Bon Dieu lui-même	And by the side of God Himself
Nous le verrons assis,	We'll see him seated in state,
Monsieur Sans-Souci.	Mr. Not-a-Care.

The subtitle of the song is "Il fait tout lui-même" (He does everything himself), and the two bars of introduction—punctilious octaves, as if the piece were being dusted and tidied in front of our ears—are cleverly indicative of the mood of the entire poem. Here, an old man undertakes all the household tasks that would normally be entrusted to a wife at the time. The poem encapsulates Jaboune's projection of naïveté and can-do optimism that made him a famous figure in French popular culture. A member of the Free French Forces that liberated Paris in 1944, he was shot in the jaw, paralyzing one side of his face. Nothing daunted, Jaboune went on to enjoy a highly successful career in television and radio, writing and entertaining for eighteen years after the death of Poulenc, his school friend and contemporary.

Poulenc was unaccustomed to look after himself domestically, but he was extraordinarily self-reliant in other ways. He was his own creation in terms of both art and publicity: maintaining his "sans-souci" equanimity, successfully hiding disappointments and failures from all but his closest friends, and giving the impression of an imperturbable urbanity, which has persisted in the public mind as part of his persona. In Poulenc's own version of being Monsieur Sans-Souci, his professional life rolled on oiled castors. In his home he employed servants, but in professional matters he micromanaged all the details, while seeming to leave everything to chance.

∘   ∘   ∘

FP76   *La Belle au bois dormant* (film music), 1935

∘   ∘   ∘

FP77   **Cinq Poèmes de Paul Éluard**
       Composed in Hyères (i–iv) and Cannes (v), March 1935
       [*Mme la Vicomtesse de Noailles, Valentine Hugo, Suzanne Nivard, Pierre Bernac, Nora Georges Auric*; Durand]
       Literary source: Paul Éluard (1895–1952), *À toute épreuve* (Paris: Éditions surréalistes, 1930), unnumbered pages. (i) No. 13 in section *L'Univers-solitude*, (ii) No. 9 in section *Confections*, (iii) No. 7 in *L'Univers-solitude*, (iv) No. 9 in *L'Univers-solitude*, (v) in its own section, *Amoureuses*, which gave Poulenc the title for the song.

       (i)   *Peut-il se reposer*
       (ii)   *Il la prend dans ses bras*
       (iii) *Plume d'eau claire*
       (iv) *Rôdeuse au front de verre*
       (v)   *Amoureuses*

Poulenc needed a new work for his and Bernac's Paris recital on 3 April 1935, the debut of their newly established duo, and this cycle was written in rather a hurry in March. It is an early sign of Bernac's hard-working reliability that he was able to learn and memorize the music at such short notice.

Since 1931 and the three cycles of Lalanne, Apollinaire, and Jacob (twelve songs in all), Poulenc had written no real mélodies, a significant hiatus in his song-writing career. Two things now changed this stalled state of affairs: his chance reacquaintance with Bernac in a Paris salon (leading to their memorable first recital together in Salzburg) and his first encounter as a composer with the poetry of Paul Éluard. He described *Cinq Poèmes* as the key turning in the lock, the beginning of his being able to gain full access to the secrets of Éluard's poetry.[67]

> *I'd admired Éluard from the day I met him in 1917, in Adrienne Monnier's bookshop on the rue de l'Odéon. (That's where I also met André Breton and Louis Aragon.) I have to say I was immediately attracted to Éluard. First of all, because he was the only surrealist who could tolerate music. And also because all his poetry is musical vibration. But how to approach his poems as a composer? A little brochure, printed on pink paper, reached me as I was intending to write new songs for my first recital with Bernac. I took the plunge, bravely, with*

encouragement from Auric, who'd been urging me for years to "set Éluard." . . .
At last I had found a lyric poet, a poet of love, whether of human love or that of liberty.[68]

À *toute épreuve,* an exquisitely presented collection of poetry, is a small pamphlet (4½" × 2½") printed on a single sheet of paper (pink or light green) that has been folded multiple times to make sixteen small pages. The full extent of this "brochure" is only apparent when the "pages" are folded out into a single sheet—a truly surrealist production. Two sides were reserved for the front title and backpage list of the poet's works, and twenty-nine poems

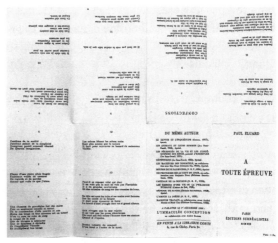

Eight pages of À toute épreuve *(including the title page), a collection printed, in surrealist fashion, on a single piece of paper folded into sixteen.*

were printed on the remaining fourteen "pages." Poulenc selected five poems for this cycle and one for his very last Éluard song, *Une chanson de porcelaine* (FP169, 1958).

(i)   *Peut-il se reposer (Can He Rest?)*

No key signature (C major with minor undertones); $\frac{5}{4}$, with changes;
Très calme ♪ = 72, with changes

Peut-il se reposer celui qui dort	Can he rest he who sleeps?
Il ne voit pas la nuit ne voit pas l'invisible	He doesn't see the night doesn't see the invisible
Il a de grandes couvertures	He has large blankets
Et des coussins de sang sur des coussins de boue	And pillows of blood on pillows of mud
Sa tête est sous les toits et ses mains sont fermées	His head is beneath the roofs his hands are clenched tight
Sur les outils de la fatigue	Around the implements of his weariness
Il dort pour éprouver sa force	He sleeps to test his strength

La honte d'être aveugle dans un si grand silence.	The shame of being blind in so profound a silence.
Aux rivages que la mer rejette	On shores rejected by the sea
Il ne voit pas les poses silencieuses	He doesn't notice the silent postures
Du vent qui fait entrer l'homme dans ses statues	Of the wind which makes a man enter his statues
Quand il s'apaise.	When it dies down.
Bonne volonté du sommeil	Willing acceptance of sleep
D'un bout à l'autre de la mort.	From one end to the other of death.

A new economy of means is evident here, with the melody in the voice and both piano staves trebled, the hands an octave apart for five mysterious bars. The piano then diverges from the vocal line for three bars of strangely dotted rhythms. Poulenc said he was "*trying to give the piano the maximum with the minimum of means. While composing these songs I often thought of an exhibition of drawings by Matisse* [at the Pierre Colle Galerie in Paris, February 1933] *for a book by Mallarmé, where the same pencil drawing could be seen full of hatching, of repetitions, finally retaining nothing but the essential, in a single stroke of the pen.*"[69] He was describing illustrations of a swan for a Mallarmé sonnet that became increasingly simple in each version—although to describe Matisse as having used a single stroke of the pen is an exaggeration. It is truer to say that more of the paper's white background is visible in each successive version.[70] Matisse's example seems to have led Poulenc away from the complexities of the Ronsard songs, or the *Chansons gaillardes*, to piano writing of much greater lucidity.

Nevertheless, after the opening nine bars, with their "perfect immobility and legato, without any rubato,"[71] we return to the clashes, jumps, and pianistic pirouettes of earlier cycles. The almost brutal change to *Subito allegro molto* on the second page conveys a jazzy heartlessness: Éluard abrupt and peremptory, the dark underside of his tenderness. Melody is replaced by a chanting that is almost *parlando*—as in the *Cinq Poèmes de Max Jacob*—with contrasting bar groupings throwing in an element of disjointed surrealist *grotesquerie*. As is often the case with Poulenc, the music hangs together simply on account of his determination that it should do so, and confidence that his reading of the poem will inspire the necessary musical adhesive. For the last four bars the music returns, once again *Très calme*, to C major—the "Bonne volonté" here being perhaps prophetic of the "Bonne journée" that opens the same poet's *Tel jour telle nuit*, in the same sunny tonality.

The dedicatee is Poulenc's hostess and sometime patron Marie-Laure de Noailles, owner of the Villa Noailles, an ultra-modern architectural marvel (or "an undistinguished cubist extravaganza," according to Picasso's biographer James Lord) designed by Robert Mallet-Stevens. Lord commented that living there was like "existing outside time in a stranded ocean liner."[72] It is tempting to imagine that a certain ultra-modern aspect to the song might have been influenced by these uncompromisingly modernist surroundings.

(ii) *Il la prend dans ses bras* (*He Takes Her in His Arms*)
No key signature (intimations of B-flat minor); $\frac{2}{2}$ at the beginning, constantly changing time signatures; *Presto* ♩ = 132

Il la prend dans ses bras	He takes her in his arms
Lueurs brillantes un instant entrevues	Flashes of light glimpsed for a moment
Aux omoplates aux épaules aux seins	On her shoulder-blades her shoulders her breasts
Puis cachées par un nuage.	And then hidden by a cloud.
Elle porte la main sur [à] son cœur	She raises her hand to her heart
Elle pâlit elle frissonne	She goes pale she trembles
Qui donc a crié?	Who was it who cried out?
Mais l'autre s'il est encore vivant	But the other man if he's living still
On le retrouvera	Will be found
Dans une ville inconnue.	In some unknown town.

Cinq Poèmes is the most metropolitan of the Éluard cycles; perhaps Poulenc intended the songs as companion pieces to the very Parisian *Quatre Poèmes de Guillaume Apollinaire*. Later Éluard cycles are seldom specific about locale, but here we guess that something sinister is happening in Paris by night, as in a fragment of mysterious and frightening film noir. After the initial *Presto,* there are three changes of tempo: in bar 7 "Puis cachées par un nuage" is marked *Céder avec liberté,* an effect difficult to arrange between voice and piano; nine bars marked *Sensiblement moins vite* give the impression of a cinema scene played in slow motion, the accompanying triplets reminiscent of unwinding spools of film, as in *Avant le cinéma*; and a sudden *Tempo presto* (b. 19) is violent and merciless, as if the composer were describing a crime scene with grim and melodramatic relish. When "he" takes "her" in his arms, it is uncertain whether love or terrible violence is in the offing; perhaps a bit of both. The melodramatic clatter of the postlude (*Très violent*) strikes a populist and deliberately vulgar note.

Bernac emphasizes the importance of the rests in this song, of observing all Poulenc's markings exactly, and of respecting the short note values at the ends of the vocal phrases. At the same time, he clearly regards the setting as less than a complete success.[73] Poulenc admitted that the song was *"terribly difficult. . . . One needs to be familiar with Éluard's work, because the tempo, which no metronome can indicate exactly, must be felt instinctively."*[74] The song is dedicated to Valentine Hugo, a close friend and admirer of Éluard and the surrealists, and sometime illustrator of their work.

(iii)   *Plume d'eau claire (Feather of Clear Water)*
        No key signature (C minor/major); $\frac{4}{4}$; *Modéré* ♩ = 72

Plume d'eau claire pluie fragile	Feather of clear water fragile rain
Fraîcheur voilée de caresses	Coolness veiled by caresses
De regards et de paroles	By glances and by words.
Amour qui voile ce que j'aime	Love which veils that which I love

This perfect nine-bar miniature is a powerfully prophetic fragment—the musical key to the poetry of Éluard grating in the lock, as the composer put it. Just as *Hier* from the Louise Lalanne songs points to that aspect of Poulenc's mature style tinged with nostalgic intimations of popular chanson, this song, with its auguries of a masterpiece like *Main dominée par le cœur* FP135 (in the same tonality), announces the true nature of the composer's love affair with Éluard's poetry. The poem is lyrical word-music, indeterminately amorous, and the vocal line is fashioned in the grateful-to-sing sinuous shape adored by singers who are drawn to this composer. The accompaniment glides in sixteenth notes and ranges over the keyboard without the slightest sense of being hectic, while the postlude makes a point of juxtaposing E-flat and E-natural within C minor/major arpeggios, something of a trademark of the Éluard settings.[75] A pedaled haze of ambiguity between major and minor keys is the perfect tonal analogue for the veiled imagery of the poem.

(iv)   *Rôdeuse au front de verre (Prowler with a Brow of Glass)*
        No key signature (B-flat minor); $\frac{4}{4}$; *Sans lenteur* ♩ = 80–84[76]

Rôdeuse au front de verre	Prowler with a brow of glass
Son cœur s'inscrit dans une étoile noire	Her heart is written on a dark star
Ses yeux montrent sa tête	Her eyes reveal her head
Ses yeux ont la fraîcheur de l'été	Her eyes have the coolness of summer
La chaleur de l'hiver	The heat of winter
Ses yeux s'ajourent rient très fort	Her eyes let in light, laugh out loud,
Ses yeux joueurs gagnent leur part de clarté.	Her eyes play and win their share of the light.

At the beginning the mood is ominous. We are never told who this prowler may be, or why she loiters; she seems to be more sybil than Parisian prostitute, a female archetype of grand power and perspicacity. Some of the language and imagery are reminiscent of the Rimbaud of the *Illuminations*. Poulenc's music is imposing and pulsates in majestic manner—with throbbing chords prophetic of *Joan Miró* in *Le Travail du peintre* (FP161/vi)—but Bernac is right to remind us that this formidable woman is "not without her share of brightness."[77] Indeed, by replacing Éluard's "sont" with "ont" in line 4, the composer makes her more real and personal, less of a metaphor: the woman's eyes have ("ont") rather than are ("sont") the freshness of summer. All credit to Poulenc for making full use of the skills of his newly inducted baritone interpreter: that is to say, strength and eloquence in the lower register balanced by an exquisite ability to sing *mezzo voce* at the top of the stave (as in b. 17, marked *Très doux*), whereby we experience the lightness and luminosity of a creature who is also potentially terrifying. For the last two lines, the composer changes key, but he adds an unusual recapitulation of the poem's first line and a prowling postlude with both hands in the bass clef. All in all, a strangely haunting song.

Poulenc described to Claude Rostand his infinite respect for verse ("*whether regular or free*") and what he regarded as a "*victory of prosody*" in connection with this poem.

> When I've chosen a poem—and sometimes I don't set it until months later—I examine it from every angle. If it is a question of Apollinaire or Éluard, I attach the greatest importance to the look of the poem on the page, to the spaces and the margins. I recite the poem to myself over and over. I listen to it, I watch out for traps, sometimes I underline difficult passages of the text in red. I note the breaths and try to discover the internal rhythm, taking it from a line <u>that is not necessarily the first one</u> [Poulenc's emphasis]. Then I embark on the musical setting, bearing in mind the differing densities of the piano accompaniment. When I'm brought up short by a detail in the prosody, I don't slave away at it. Sometimes I wait for days and try to forget the word until I can see it as new. . . . In a vibrant poem by Éluard, "Rôdeuse au front de verre," I had to set the line "ses yeux s'ajourent" ["Her eyes let in light"], *comma*, "rient très fort" ["laugh out loud"].

Rostand intervenes: "It's certainly not easy to set that plural of the verb 'ajourer,' which sounds here rather like a subordinate phrase 'à jours.'" Poulenc continues: "*Instinct, basic instinct, led me to this accent on the strong beat* [on the verb "rient"], *after a silence* [after "s'ajourent,"], *which makes any ambiguity impossible.*"[78]

The passage is fascinating for English speakers (and also composers) who sometimes fail to see where and how such ambiguities arise in the French language: a musical setting may not be wrong in terms of accentuation but may still fail to make the meaning clear, with often comical consequences. A great deal of French humor and wordplay is based on unintended (or deliberately funny) aural dislocations like these.

(v) *Amoureuses (Women in Love)*

No key signature (F major/minor); $\frac{9}{8}$; *Très vite (un peu haletant)* ♩. = 152

Elles ont les épaules hautes	They have their shoulders held high
Et l'air malin	And a cunning air about them
Ou bien des mines qui déroutent	Or else a look that leads you astray
La confiance est dans la poitrine	Their confidence is in their chests
À la hauteur où l'aube de leurs seins se lève	Just there, where the dawn of their breasts breaks
Pour dévêtir la nuit	To undress the night
Des yeux à casser des cailloux	Eyes that could smash stones
Des sourires sans y penser	And thoughtless smiles
Pour chaque rêve	For every dream
Des rafales de cris de neige	Gusts of crying snow
Et des ombres déracinées.	And uprooted shadows.
Il faut les croire sur baiser	You must believe them by their kisses
Et sur parole et sur regard	Their words their eyes
Et ne baiser que leurs baisers	And kiss only their kisses.
Je ne montre que ton visage	I'm only showing your face
Les grands orages de ta gorge	The great storms of your bosom
Tout ce que je connais et tout ce que j'ignore	Everything I know and everything I don't
Mon amour ton amour ton amour ton amour.	My love your love your love your love.

Éluard was the lover of the famous Gala (his first wife) and the equally famous Nusch (his second), and of countless other women in the free-love atmosphere that was part of his ultra-bohemian world. Poems of the uncompromising doctrinaire surrealists (such as André Breton) were never as sexy as this. The song describes Parisian women with a flavor of street music, the tinge of louche chanson and *boîte* that characterizes some of Poulenc's Apollinaire settings. Such a taste of metropolitan sleaze is scarcely to be found in any of the later Éluard songs, which are far more idealistic and high-minded. Bernac tells singers that there is "no reason to fear a slight accent of Parisian slang, but without vulgarity."[79]

"Amoureuses" is by far the longest poem in *À toute épreuve*. The waltz rhythm, with its hint of a piano-accordion texture, seems appropriately hoity-toity for the girls of Paris, just as Enrique Granados's *Tonadillas* accurately paint (through Goya's eyes) the proud *majas* of Madrid. The flow of the music is rendered vertiginous by throbbing eighth notes as the piano strums a melodic descant to the vocal line—dotted quarter notes in the tenor register, sometimes played by the right hand, sometimes taken over by the left. Singer and pianist are swept along by the pulsating music, which manages to be nonchalant and threatening at the same time. The chilling climactic *fortissimo* of "Mon amour" is backed up by a dizzying slew of chromatically ascending chords in octaves. From the beginning, the music's charm and grace have been undermined by an ominous undertone that now comes to the fore; breathless repetitions of "ton amour" bring the song, and the cycle, to an eerie close. The secret of a successful performance, as Bernac notes, is "immutable tempo throughout."

The song is dedicated to Nora Georges Auric, wife of the composer who had counseled Poulenc to set Éluard in the first place. Glamorous Nora, famed not only for her skills as a watercolorist but for her intelligence and brilliant conversation (the fact that she was rather hard-edged made her perhaps an appropriate dedicatee for *Amoureuses*) was Austrian by birth, and she was as chic as any native-born Parisienne. Poulenc wrote the song in Cannes while visiting his ailing friend Tante Liénard, who died shortly afterward at the age of ninety.

BIOGRAPHICAL INTERLUDE: PAUL ÉLUARD

THE ÉLUARD SONGS: *Cinq Poèmes de Paul Éluard* FP77 (1935); *Tel jour telle nuit* FP86 (1936–37); *Miroirs brûlants* FP98 (1938–39); *Ce doux petit visage* FP99 (1939); *Main dominée par le cœur* FP135 (1946); . . . *mais mourir* FP137 (1947); *La Fraîcheur et le feu* FP147 (1950); *Le Travail du peintre* FP161 (1956); *Une chanson de porcelaine* FP169 (1958). Seventeen further Éluard settings are for unaccompanied voices: five poems as part of *Sept Chansons* FP81; four in *Un soir de neige* FP126; and eight in the cantata *Figure humaine* FP120, the last of which is the celebrated "Liberté."

o   o   o

"If on my tomb could be inscribed: Here lies Francis Poulenc, the musician of Apollinaire and Éluard, I would consider this to be my finest title to fame."
It was the writing of this surrealist poet that most engaged the altruistic and humanistic side of Poulenc's nature, his better self. Poet and composer

Paul Éluard in the forties.

had in common an idealistic, almost religious appreciation of love and physical beauty, a shared aesthetic that made differences in their lifestyles seem irrelevant. Éluard was a poet of the Left and a voice of resistance and freedom during the Second World War. Poulenc could not claim any such credentials. But his music bridged the political gap between poet and composer in the case of the Marxist Louis Aragon's poem "C"; even more extraordinary is the amalgam of Éluard's poetry and Poulenc's music in their joint choral masterpiece *Figure humaine* FP120.

With *Cinq Poèmes* (1935), Poulenc's song-writing moved into a new sphere; we might almost say it came of age. And this intense engagement with Éluard more or less coincided with the composer's reconversion to Catholicism in 1936 after visiting the shrine of the Black Virgin at Rocamadour, and the establishment of his partnership with Pierre Bernac. *"People will never know how much I owe to Éluard, how much I owe to Bernac,"* Poulenc wrote in his *Journal.* *"It is due to them that lyricism has entered my vocal works."*[80]

"Paul Éluard" was the pseudonym of Eugène Émile Paul Grindel (Éluard was the name of his maternal grandmother), born into a comfortable middle-class household in Saint-Denis, just outside Paris, on 14 December 1895. Although Éluard was always associated with working-class causes, his father was a chartered accountant who became a successful estate agent. Three life experiences jolted the young man out of his bourgeois comfort zone: illness, war, and love. A severe pulmonary hemorrhage at age seventeen consigned him to months of enforced immobility at a sanatorium near Davos, Switzerland, where he read deeply and widely; the crystalline mountain landscapes by which he was surrounded were later to influence his poems. One fellow patient at the sanatorium was a young Russian student named Helena Dmitrovnie Diakonova, whose nickname was "Gala"; after some years of separation Éluard was to marry her in 1917, when on military leave. He had volunteered for the Front despite his ongoing infirmity, and his first published work, *Le Devoir et l'inquiétude* (1917), describes the misery, comradeship, and solidarity of soldiers in the trenches.

After his demobilization, Éluard was introduced to André Breton and Louis Aragon and soon assumed his place as a member of the Parisian avant-garde, publishing several collections of poetry. Éluard, Breton, Aragon, and Philippe Soupault together would found the movement that grew out of Dadaism called surrealism, although the term had been coined earlier by Apollinaire. In 1921 Éluard met the German painter and sculptor Max Ernst (1891–1976), the first of his many painter friends and one of the most influential on his development (he is one of thirty-two painters celebrated in the poet's 1948 anthology *Voir*). Ernst's seminal role in Éluard's career has been compared to that of Virgil guiding Dante—into the perilous regions of the dream-like inferno that was to become surrealism. The poet chose six of Ernst's collages to illustrate his collection *Répétitions*.

In 1922 Ernst left his wife and small son to settle with Éluard and Gala in a ménage à trois at Eaubonne, near Paris, where their home was decorated with Ernst's murals. At this time Éluard seemed to be as infatuated with Ernst as he was mesmerized by Gala; his bonding with a handful of men in his life, Picasso the supreme example, was strongly emotional, almost romantic. Two years later, in the wake of a personal and conjugal crisis, Éluard suddenly left Paris for Saigon. Both Ernst and Gala followed him there at his behest, and it was decided that Gala would stay with Éluard—although he was eventually to lose her to another painter, Salvador Dali, in 1929. The poet harbored a lifelong hatred of possessive jealousy, believing rather in the innocence of desire. He took the subject of love extremely seriously: the erotic freedom he espoused was never simply an excuse for libertinage, and each of his female partners was accorded the elevated role of Muse in a seamless tapestry of creativity. Like that of his good friend and alter-ego Picasso, his work was often defined by the major female figures of his life: Gala and her successors Nusch, Jacqueline, and Dominique.

Soon after Éluard and Gala returned to France from Vietnam, Breton published his *Manifeste de surréalisme* (October 1924), defining the movement as a "purely psychic automatism.... Dictated by thought in the absence of all control by reason, outside all aesthetic or moral occupations, Surrealism rests on the belief in the superior reality of certain forms of associations, formerly neglected, and in the transcendent power of dreams released from any interference by thought." It follows, then, that every reading of a surreal poem is wholly individual. When asked what Éluard's poems actually meant, Bernac always replied that he had no idea. But Poulenc's readings and the musical meanings he assigned to Éluard's poetry are both intuitive and revelatory; he seems to translate the poems into music rather than simply setting them.

Two important Éluard collections from the later 1920s and early 30s were *Capitale de la douleur* (published in 1926, the year the poet joined the Communist Party) and *La Vie immédiate* (1932). In 1930, the year of *À toute épreuve*, Éluard met Maria Benz, a destitute music-hall and circus performer from Alsace, eleven years younger, who went by the name of Nusch (Poulenc always mistakenly spelled her name "Nush"). The poet's rescue of this highly intuitive waif brings to mind an older version of Mignon, the Italian child acrobat saved by Wilhelm Meister in Goethe's novel *Wilhelm Meister's Apprenticeship*.[81] The couple married in 1934. Graceful, lighthearted, and luminously beautiful, Nusch was the poet's ideal companion and inspiration. And she was also one of Picasso's favorite models. Over the years, sixteen volumes of Éluard's poetry were illustrated by drawings or engravings by Picasso, and the collection *Les Yeux fertiles* (1936) openly celebrated their friendship. The powerful affinity of poet and painter, both personal and political, was reinforced by the rise of Fascism and the outrage of Guernica.

By 1938 Éluard had broken with Breton, whose brand of "pure" surrealism had become anathema to him. Instead, he began to develop his own kind of Promethean humanism, a joyful celebration of the fraternity of mankind where women are the spiritual mediators—a philosophy light-years away from the dour and dogmatic Stalinism of some of his former associates. *Le Livre ouvert I* (1940)—the source of Poulenc's cycle *La Fraîcheur et le feu* FP147—was one of the first collections in which the poet, now taken up by Nusch and themes of love, more or less turned his back on the didactic preoccupations of the hard-line surrealists. The occupation of France and his active participation in the Resistance reinforced his visionary optimism and determination—as in *Poésie et vérité 1942*, a title that translated Goethe's *Dichtung und Wahrheit* as a dig at the occupying forces, and *Au rendez-vous allemand* (1944). A radiant poem appearing in both collections, "Liberté" (set by Poulenc as the concluding movement of *Figure humaine*), proclaims the "power of a word" by which the poet can begin his life afresh: "I was born to know you / To name you / Liberty."

On account of his fragile health, Éluard often left Paris for sojourns in the mountains and by the sea, holidays that were facilitated by family money. Nevertheless, it was Nusch who died first—of a sudden cerebral hemorrhage in November 1946 while visiting the poet's mother. Poulenc

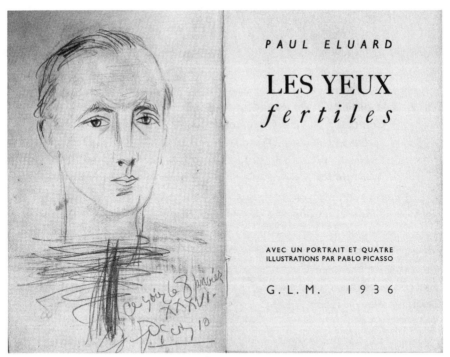

The title page of Éluard's Les Yeux fertiles *(1936), with a portrait of the poet by Picasso.*

commemorated this loss with the song . . . *mais mourir* FP137. Her totally unexpected death rendered Éluard suicidal. But he was consoled by the affections of Jacqueline Trutat, who inspired a different kind of poetry; as did Dominique Laure, who became the poet's tender and vigilant wife in 1951. He died of a heart attack on 18 November 1952.

In his perceptive pen portrait of Éluard, the writer Claude Roy (1915–1997) provided a description of his physical appearance that also throws light on the poet's inner nature:

> Éluard was large, with a large body, a large forehead, a large nose. There is a way of being large that is heavy, square massive, but Éluard was large with lightness. He had a type of slow majesty that was very remarkable, the natural majesty of the truly great of the world: nomadic chieftains, racehorses, children at play, certain fish, and grey-pink gladioli. With him, even the weightiest things had this majestic lightness.[82]

"Majestic lightness" would also be a remarkably accurate way of describing many of the Éluard settings of Francis Poulenc.

o   o   o

FP78 *Margot* (incidental music to the play by Édouard Bourdet), 1935

o   o   o

FP79 **À sa guitare** (*To the Guitar*)
      Composed in Noizay, September 1935
      [*Yvonne Printemps*; Durand]
      Literary source: Pierre de Ronsard (1524–1585). Poulenc possibly found
      the poem in the first volume of the complete works of Ronsard edited by
      Paul Laumonier: *Pierre de Ronsard: Œuvres complètes* (1924–75).
      G minor; $\frac{3}{4}$; *Calme et mélancolique* ♩ = 60

Ma guitare, je te chante,	My guitar, I sing to you,
Par qui seule je déçois,	It is only through you I that I deceive,
Je déçois, je romps, j'enchante	I deceive, I break, I enchant
Les amours que je reçois.	The loves which I receive.
Au son de ton harmonie	At the sound of your harmony
Je rafraîchis ma chaleur,	I reinvigorate my passion,
Ma chaleur, flamme infinie,	My passion, that eternal flame,
Naissante d'un beau malheur.	Born of a beautiful sorrow.

This song marks Poulenc's first collaboration with the extraordinary singer and actress Yvonne Printemps (1894–1977), by then already world famous. Printemps's first husband was the equally celebrated actor and writer Sacha Guitry, who conceived various projects to show his multitalented wife off to best advantage. In 1923 André Messager wrote the operetta *L'Amour masqué* (with its famous song "J'ai deux amants") for her, and two years later a touching little theatrical piece with music by Reynaldo Hahn, *Mozart,* took Paris by storm. During *Mozart's* wildly successful London run, even the hardened theater critic James Agate was enraptured by Printemps playing the great composer *en travesti*: "On Monday evening people were observed to cry, and by that I mean shed tears, when Music's heavenly child appeared at the top of the stairs. At that moment of her entrance this exquisite artist made conquest of the house, and subsequently held it in thrall until the final curtain."[83] Printemps's English career culminated in 1934, when Noel Coward concocted a Regency drama for her entitled *Conversation Piece.* A good deal of untranslated French was spoken onstage, and the star learned English phonetically for the rest. The Viennese Oscar Straus (1870–1954), who had composed *Mariette* for her in 1928, conceived his operetta *Les Trois Valses* (1935, filmed in 1938) for Printemps and her second husband, actor Pierre Fresnay.

Printemps's vocal skills were considerably more developed than those of the average singing actress. In 1937 she even gave a full-length classical recital (accompanied by Jean Doyen) in the Salle Gaveau, but never repeated the experience, saying it was too much like hard work. (Poulenc confessed himself *"torn apart"* by her interpretation of Debussy's *Noël des enfants qui n'ont plus de maisons.*[84]) Such was her versatility as an actress that she was often involved in large-scale theatrical projects where music was merely a subsidiary consideration. One such project was the historical play by Édouard Bourdet (1887–1945) called *Margot*—about Queen Marguerite of Navarre (1553–1615), who was also known as Marguerite de Valois or simply Margot.

Detail from the cover of the song Les Chemins de l'amour *(FP106), published by Max Eschig in 1945.*

Brilliant and temperamental, spontaneous, promiscuous, and ungovernable but nevertheless brave and resourceful, Margot was the daughter of King Henri II of France and Cathérine de Medici, and sister of three kings who reigned one after the other in relatively quick succession: François II, Charles IX, and Henri III, all of them in the shadow of their controlling mother. Margot's brother François II was briefly married to Mary Stuart, Queen of Scots; her elder sister Élisabeth, third wife of Philip II of Spain, appears in Verdi's opera *Don Carlos*; and as Marguerite de Valois, Margot is an important character in Meyerbeer's opera *Les Huguenots*, one of Joan Sutherland's great roles. Honegger's *Saluste du Bartas* (1941), song settings of the eponymous Protestant poet from these troubled times, adds yet another layer to the musical afterlife of the Valois era.

To help ease tensions between the opposing religious factions in France, Margot was made to marry King Henri of Navarre—although the whole premise of Bourdet's play is that despite their tempestuous relationship, the couple really loved each other. They married a few days before the St. Bartholomew's Day Massacre of Protestant Huguenots (1572), after which Henri narrowly escaped death with Margot's help. In Elizabethan times there was enormous British interest in French royalty in the wake of France's religious wars; Shakespeare's *Love's Labour's Lost* (1594) is set in the court of Navarre, a fantasy locale in theory, but until 1600 a reconciliation between Margot and Henry still seemed a newsworthy

Cover of Édouard Bourdet's play Margot
*(1936), with an illustration by Christian
Bérard (1902–1949).*

possibility. And we can also be certain that Queen Elizabeth I was kept informed of Margot's widely reported liaisons and emotional vicissitudes.

By the 1930s, a time when sexual freedom and female emancipation were themes of the day in France, as well as those perennial preoccupations with beauty and fashion, Marguerite de Valois, historical mistress of those categories, was an ideal subject for further exploration, provided there was someone suitably magnetic to play her onstage.[85] Taking his lead from Alexandre Dumas's 1845 novel *La Reine Margot*, Bourdet constructed something of an extravaganza (with a cast of fifty-two named characters) as a vehicle for Yvonne Printemps, with Pierre Fresnay as her leading man. It so happened that the young King Charles IX was played by Stéphane Audel, first a protégé of Poulenc's Uncle Papoum, and much later a close friend and confidant of the composer; an eleven-year-old named Charles Aznavour debuted as one of the young princes.

Both Poulenc and Georges Auric provided music for the production, which premiered at the Théâtre Marigny on 26 November 1935. Each composer also wrote a single song for Printemps, to texts by Ronsard (Auric's was entitled *Printemps,* punning on the fact that her name means "spring"). Both songs were arranged for instrumental accompaniment for the stage production, but later published with piano accompaniment.

Poulenc's song was allowed to play to its strength, the evocation of bittersweet nostalgia, by its position at the end of this long play. At the opening of the final tableau, the date is 1589 and Margot is thirty-six, saddened and chastened; she has been detained for many years by her brother King Henri III, whom she now learns has been assassinated. Her long-estranged husband, Henri of Navarre, has ascended to the throne as Henri IV. Although Margot has technically become queen—of France as well as of Navarre—her relationship with the new king, whom she still loves, is beyond repair. The closing words of the play assure us that she will never sing again ("On ne chantera plus jamais maintenant"), a sentence that places a spotlight on Poulenc's haunting music, which she has sung only minutes earlier. In 1600, after an annulment of his marriage to Margot, King Henri IV took Marie de Medici as his second wife, and together they founded the Bourbon dynasty. Margot lived on, withdrawn from the world, until 1615, some years into the reign of Louis XIII. She reportedly offered motherly affection to the children of her beloved Henri and his second queen.

À sa guitare was begun in the summer of 1935 at Kerbastic, home of Marie-Blanche and Jean de Polignac. The atelier of Marie-Blanche's mother, the couturier Jeanne Lanvin, would make the women's costumes (designed by Christian Bérard) for Bourdet's play. Ronsard's poem, part of Les Amours (1552–67), contains no fewer than twenty-two strophes, but Poulenc chose to set only the first and third, repeating (and somewhat altering) the first at the end to make an ABA structure. A five-bar introduction (echoed and shortened in the postlude) evokes the sound of a harp, evidently the accompanying instrument from the orchestral pit. When Printemps recorded the song for French HMV, her accompaniment was "enhanced by instrumental additions," Poulenc tells us. "Unfortunately, I have lost the score, a pity because it was rather pleasing."[86] It was only in 1960 that he actually wrote a piece for guitar, the Sarabande, published in an Italian anthology of guitar music.

In the ten years since composing his Ronsard cycle, Poulenc had changed as a song composer, and no longer felt the need to prove his credentials as an important modernist. He was content to write a song of mournful ennui, a quasi-modal sixteenth-century pastiche, but one with a memorable melody and full of personal feeling. Eighteen years later Benjamin Britten was to write a similarly haunting evocation of music from the same period, the second lute song of the Earl of Essex from Gloriana. À sa guitare was published by Durand late in 1935 with an unsigned color illustration by Christian Bérard (responsible for the play's beautiful sets as well as historically accurate costumes), who also provided the Auric setting with a charming cover drawing.

For the play's nonvocal music, Poulenc consulted Nadia Boulanger, who suggested that he base his music on Henri Expert's 1908 edition of the Livre de Danseries of Claude Gervaise (1525–1583). From this source the composer transcribed seven short pieces of incidental music.

o   o   o

FP80   *Suite française d'après Claude Gervaise* (piano), October 1935

FP81   *Sept Chansons* (mixed chorus, *a cappella*, to texts by Apollinaire and Éluard), March–April 1936

FP82   *Litanies à la Vierge noire* (women's or children's chorus and organ), 22–29 August 1936

FP83   *Petites Voix* (five songs for *a cappella* children's chorus, texts by Madeleine Ley), September 1936

FP84 *Les Soirées de Nazelles* (piano), 1930–36
FP85 *Plain-chant* (song settings of Jean Cocteau, destroyed), Christmas 1936

∘   ∘   ∘

FP86 ***Tel jour telle nuit*** (*As the Day, So the Night*)

 Composed in Lyon, Noizay, Monte Carlo, and Paris, November 1936–January 1937

 [*Pablo Picasso, Freddy* (Frédérique Lebedeff), *Nush* (Nusch Éluard), *Valentine Hugo, Marie-Blanche de Polignac* (v and vi), *Denise Bourdet, Pierre Bernac, Yvonne Gouverné*; Durand]

 Literary source: Paul Éluard (1895–1952), *Les Yeux fertiles* (Paris: Gallimard, 1936), with a frontispiece drawing of Éluard by Pablo Picasso. (i) p. 42, (ii) p. 33, (iii) p. 34, (iv) p. 37, (v) p. 66, (vi) p. 47, (vii) p. 69, (viii) p. 68, (ix) p. 88; this last poem had been previously published on the final (unnumbered) page of *Facile*, with photographs by Man Ray (Éditions G.L.M., 1935).

 (i) *Bonne journée* (begun in Paris, November 1936; completed in Lyon, January 1937)
 (ii) *Une ruine coquille vide* (Noizay, December 1936)
 (iii) *Le Front comme un drapeau perdu* (Monte Carlo, 27 January 1937)
 (iv) *Une roulotte couverte en tuiles* (Noizay, December 1936)
 (v) *À toutes brides* (Paris, January 1937)
 (vi) *Une herbe pauvre* (Noizay, December 1936)
 (vii) *Je n'ai envie que de t'aimer* (Noizay, December 1936)
 (viii) *Figure de force brûlante et farouche* (Paris, January 1937)
 (ix) *Nous avons fait la nuit* (Lyon, January 1937)

The musical progress from the *Cinq Poèmes de Paul Éluard* to this cycle was far from smooth or inevitable. Bernac, who kept resolutely silent about so much he knew concerning the composer's life, offered a few anecdotal set pieces, and here is one of the most memorable:

At Christmas in 1936 I was at Noizay for a short stay in order to make the most of this free time to prepare the programs for our forthcoming tours, and in particular the new songs that Poulenc had written and which we were going to perform at our annual recital in Paris. They were settings of poems by Jean Cocteau entitled *Plain-chant* [a collection from 1923]. The evening I arrived, Poulenc went to the piano and let me hear them. Frankly I did not feel enthusiastic, and he must have sensed my reaction. Suddenly, to my alarm, to my horror, Poulenc took the manuscript and threw it on the big fire that was burning in the grate. He began to laugh and said, "Don't worry, you will have something much better for February 3rd!" It was to be *Tel jour telle nuit*.[87]

Tel jour telle nuit is by far the most famous of Poulenc's song cycles, in the same way that *Dichterliebe* may be said to be the most famous of Schumann's. Just as Schumann's musical relationship with poet Heinrich Heine is perfectly expressed within the sixteen songs of *Dichterliebe*, Poulenc's affinity with Éluard is made crystal clear in these nine songs—all, strictly speaking, separate songs, but threaded together as pearls on a necklace. How it came to be that the bad boy of French music, the spoiled son of a rich family who was judged by many to be lacking in depth, found it within himself to voice the quiet radiance, the humility and grandeur, the rapture, the terror, the profound humanity and compassion of this great poet is one of the mysteries of French music. Like *Die schöne Müllerin* for Schubert, *Tel jour telle nuit* was a watershed work. And as the last songs of Beethoven's *An die ferne Geliebte* and Fauré's *La Bonne Chanson* gather together the musical strands of what has gone before in the cycle, the last song of Poulenc's cycle is a summing-up and consummation.

Much had changed in the composer's life and work since the year he had last composed mélodies. In May 1936 a new socialist government, the Front Populaire, had come to power in France. A polarization of left- and right-wing ideologies in the world marked the dawning of a new and dangerous age; and even Poulenc, uninterested in politics as he was, was aware that the time had come for the jokers of the 1920s to stand up and be counted as serious human beings. Composer Pierre-Octave Ferroud's decapitation in a car accident in August was a reminder of the arbitrary nature and fragility of existence. Poulenc seems to have found this news very distressing (although he and Ferroud were not close friends), and

he expressed a wish to visit Rocamadour, a center of religious pilgrimage since the Middle Ages. He had just begun a working holiday with Bernac and Yvonne Gouverné (the choral conductor who introduced almost all of Poulenc's choral music to the world) in

Bernac and Poulenc, c. 1938.

Uzerche, and the famous mountain shrine was an easy journey. His holiday companions, both practicing Catholics, were only too pleased to accompany him. As a result of an extraordinary experience at Rocamadour (see Outline, 1936), the composer reconverted to Roman Catholicism and wrote the *Litanies à la Vierge noire* FP82. Poulenc was also fast coming to the realization that in Bernac, a man of remarkable calm and integrity, he had found a friend of considerable import as well as an indispensable colleague.

Tel jour telle nuit, begun with the ghost of an idea during a November walk, was worked on in December 1936 in Noizay (and thus the composer had at least some of the songs up his sleeve when he so dramatically destroyed the *Plainchant* songs) and finished by January 1937; the first and last songs were completed in Lyon, related by tonality and mood and between them containing the cycle almost like matching bookends. Early in January, with the first performance only a month away, Poulenc asked the poet for a title for the work; though the songs had individual titles, the composer declined to use any of them, and *Les Yeux fertiles* would not do: "*What's good for a book isn't necessarily good for a collection of songs. I said to Éluard: Listen, the title's very visual, that's all very well when poems appear with engravings, illustrations by Picasso, but for music it's a bit awkward.*"[88] Éluard supplied four epithets; his preferred choice was *Tout dire*, but Poulenc selected his second suggestion, which encompasses both the contrast and the similarities between the opening and closing songs.

As Sidney Buckland explains, Éluard's *Les Yeux fertiles* is "structured as a progression towards facilité, towards simplicity, clarity, freedom unfettered." The titles of the three sections reflect this progression: *Le Barre d'appui* (the support, something to lean on), *Grand air* (open air), *Facile* (easy).[89] *Facile* had been published on its own in 1935 as a slim volume, with silvery-edged erotic photogravure illustrations by Man Ray; the model was no other than Éluard's wife (since 1934) Nusch. The layout of the poetry seems to cling to these bold nude images, or vice-versa; poet René Char called the book "carnal perfection."[90] It's not every poet who will present a composer with naked photographs of his wife (Éluard sent it to Poulenc as a gift in April 1936), much less parade them to the world, but this poet was no ordinary husband. He felt he had no proprietary rights over his wife's body; in turn, she did not own him or attempt to bar him from taking other lovers. Within this extraordinary freedom and trust developed one of the great love stories of French literature.

Buckland has also usefully encapsulated the mood of each poem in a single word, given below in conjunction with Éluard's original titles.[91]

   (i)   "À Pablo Picasso, I": well-being
   (ii) "Je croyais le repos possible": mystery
  (iii) "Être": despair

(i)   *Bonne journée (A Good Day)*
      C major/minor; ¾; *Calme* ♩ = 63

Bonne journée j'ai revu qui je n'oublie pas
Qui je n'oublierai jamais
Et des femmes fugaces dont les yeux
Me faisaient une haie d'honneur
Elles s'enveloppèrent dans leurs sourires

A good day. I saw again those I've not forgotten
Nor will ever forget
And flighty women whose eyes, for me,
Formed a guard of honor
They wrapped themselves up in their smiles

Bonne journée j'ai vu mes amis sans soucis
Les hommes ne pesaient pas lourd
Un qui passait
Son ombre changée en souris
Fuyait dans le ruisseau

A good day. I saw my friends free of care
And men of little weight
One who passed
His shadow magicked into a mouse
Scurried into the gutter

J'ai vu le ciel très grand
Le beau regard des gens privés de tout

Plage distante où personne n'aborde

I saw the sky, huge,
And the beautiful gaze of those deprived of everything

A distant shore where no man lands

Bonne journée qui commença mélancolique
Noire sous les arbres verts
Mais qui soudain trempée d'aurore
M'entra dans le cœur par surprise.

A good day. Which started in melancholy
Black beneath trees of green
But which suddenly drenched in dawn
Entered my heart quite by surprise.

Over thirty of Éluard's poems were written with Picasso in mind, and no fewer than sixteen collections of his poetry were to feature Picasso drawings or engravings (*Les Yeux fertiles* is dedicated to him, as is Poulenc's *Bonne journée*). The friendship of painter and poet suffered a temporary setback in March 1936, when Éluard introduced Picasso to Dora Maar, who would become his mistress.

Picasso simply disappeared from view, causing considerable disquiet, and this poem is a celebration of his sudden reappearance in Éluard's life, at an exhibition of the Austrian painter Wolfgang Paalen (Picasso was also having an affair with Paalen's wife, Alice Rahon).[92] The artist's sudden return to Paris brought Éluard great happiness, and he was also elated as a result of his ever-deepening relationship with his wife Nusch. The sense of well-being that radiates through the poem denotes a turning point for Éluard; he had at last decided to cut ties with André Breton and the doctrinaire aspects of surrealism, and this new beginning in his career gave him an enormous sense of untrammeled joy.

There is no prelude; voice and piano embark on this journey, this *journée*, together. The eighth-note accompaniment is ambulatory but calm and even, the piano's bare, oscillating Cs placed two octaves apart. The composer's insistence that the song should be sung *"with a very peaceful joy"*[93] explains the quintessential Poulencian "traveling" tempo of $\quarternote = 63$. Of utmost significance is the marking *Calme*, for there was never music more measured and genial than this. The vocal melody, ascending in optimism as if to greet the dawn of a wonderful new day, is in C major with a Lydian inflection of F-sharp. Each of the three verses begins the same way and then branches off into different harmonic directions, a semi-strophic form that lends the song a measure of gravity—as if something important and radiant were being proclaimed. In the vocal line's last six bars (from "Mais qui soudain trempée d'aurore"), which blossom at the height of the stave, the minor key seems to prevail with a harmonic ambivalence typical of Poulenc. But after the high notes of "M'entra dans le cœur" (*forte*, with a *diminuendo* to *piano*), C major wins its ascendancy via an extended dominant-to-tonic cadence on "surprise." To Bernac, this suggests "the invasion of the heart by the dawn."[94]

For the piano postlude, the eighth notes are replaced by octaves syncopated between the hands, the music still somewhat on the move. At the end of "surprise" the right hand introduces a haunting motif: a jump of a fifth (C to G) in octaves, then an octave plunge to the G below. The motif is then repeated, and it is impossible to analyze why this seems almost unbearably eloquent rather than simplistic and banal. At the last moment the left hand adds the B-flat below middle C to turn the final chord, left hanging in the air, into a seventh—a ravishing touch that prepares us for the dream-like world of the next mélodie. "There must be no hurry in beginning the next song," warns Bernac.[95]

Poulenc described how he was inspired to think of such extraordinary music:

One Sunday in November 1936, I felt very happy. I was strolling down the avenue Daumesnil, watching a locomotive in a tree. It was so pretty and so reminiscent of my childhood departures when I went back to Nogent by train from the Bastille. With trains departing from the height of a second storey [the railway track was elevated above street level], *I did not need surrealism to perch a locomotive in a plane tree. Moved by this recollection of my youth, I began to recite the poem "Bonne journée" from the collection* Yeux fertiles. *That evening the music came to me.*[96]

The image of a train in a tree brings to mind the surrealist painter René Magritte (1898–1967), whose *La Durée poignardée* (1938) depicts a train, not stuck in a tree but emerging from a marble fireplace, steam billowing from its funnel. The painting was executed for the British surrealist poet Edward James (1907–1984), and Poulenc was in touch with James at this time about writing a choral work with orchestra—the controversial *Sécheresses*.

Whether or not the composer's image of a train in a tree has anything to do with Magritte or James, it is one of the most important accounts Poulenc left us of his creative process—the way he used memory to set his compositional faculties in motion. "There, at the corner of the street," writes Hervé Lacombe, "subsequently, so to say, at the corner of a poem, he finds an image from his childhood in its entirety, and so there is the possibility of reliving a state of mind, a feeling, a special thought, of superimposing in perfect register the present moment on the moment from the past."[97] This is far from the only time a sight or a sound facilitated a kind of Proustian connection in the composer's mind. And it is uncanny that the long-accepted English translation of the work Magritte painted for Edward James was *Time Transfixed*.

Poulenc's songs are often built around such nuggets of memory, what other composers may simply term flashes of inspiration. He has by now become expert at pinning down magical and evocative moments from his past, a past of which he wrote and spoke incessantly, while simultaneously mourning the inevitable evanescence of memory. Of course, he will never again be able to take that train in the tree from the Bastille to see his grandparents in Nogent; they are no longer alive, and the house has been sold. In turning round to look at a picture from his past, this Poulenc-Proust-Orpheus both sees and then must lose his Eurydice, but not before putting down a few bars of music on manuscript paper that will germinate into a song.

Time and again in Poulenc's music, and in his mélodies in particular, some of the most powerful passages are those where the present is superimposed on the past—just as Lacombe describes. The tug between these two different places conjures a nostalgia so authentic and intense we can experience it as if it were our own. In a song like *Hôtel*, for example (the second song from *Banalités* FP107), the experience of being there in Apollinaire's hotel room in Montparnasse is almost palpable; at the same time, we mourn the fact that this is a Paris we will never know. The composer was connecting with a vivid memory of his own, a memory that brought joy and pain in equal measure: joy in the recovery of a feeling, and the pain of its renunciation, the impossibility of going back, the blurring of fantasy and reality, the yawning gap between past and present.

As we listen to *Bonne journée*, it is as though Poulenc has prepared a time capsule for us. We may find ourselves imagining what it was like to be alive on a sunny day in May 1936, when such artists as Picasso, Éluard, and Poulenc were living in the same magical city. It is the authenticity of the composer's nostalgia that enables us to experience this song, and many others, in both the present and past and on different levels of intensity. In taking Poulenc's multi-layered emotions as our point of departure, we are able to hear hidden depths in the music that will lead us, if we so wish, into all sorts of voyages of discovery, including time travel of our own.

(ii)   *Une ruine coquille vide (A Ruin, an Empty Shell)*
       No key signature (tonal base of G); $\frac{3}{4}$; *Très calme et irréel* ♩ = 60

Une ruine coquille vide	A ruin an empty shell
Pleure dans son tablier	Weeps into her apron
Les enfants qui jouent autour d'elle	The children playing all around
Font moins de bruit que des mouches	Make less noise than flies
La ruine s'en va à tâtons	The ruin stumbles along
Chercher ses vaches dans un pré	Looking for her cows in a meadow
J'ai vu le jour je vois cela	I have seen the day I see all this
Sans en avoir honte	Without any shame
Il est minuit comme une flèche	It's midnight like an arrow
Dans un cœur à la portée	In the heart within reach
Des folâtres lueurs nocturnes	Of the fleeting glimmers of night
Qui contredisent le sommeil.	Which deny sleep.

If the first song had a kind of austerity and classicism, here we are plunged into a world of impressionistic sound where a pianist's experience with the piano writing of Debussy may come in useful. It is above all the use of both pedals that assures the kind of haze of unreality that the composer requires. Bernac imagines that the apron into which the ruin weeps is "heavy masses of ivy hanging down the old walls." He is simply sharing with us the kind of personalized imagery with which performers, when confronted with this poetry, must experiment in order to make the texts (and thus the songs) come alive. In Bernac's own performances there is never any doubt that he "understands" everything he sings, or rather that the poetry has imprinted vivid images in his mind; whatever these may be, they come across to the listener as authoritative. As Buckland explains,

"Somewhere there are always 'margins of silence' around [Éluard's] poems which allow the reader to perceive them in their own way, to make those poems theirs. This is Éluard's super-reality [surrealism] in poetry."[98]

In the light of Éluard's title, "I thought that sleep was possible," Buckland interprets the text as "an insomniac vision of ruin, of emptiness and silence, of weeping, a heart wounded by the arrow midnight, 'nocturnal glimmerings,' chimeras from which there is no relief since sleep is denied."[99] The idea of being sleepy but not able to find the key into the realms of sleep is supported by the music's harmonies—gently shifting, never truly coming to rest.

Poulenc creates a dream landscape almost suspended in time, apart from the distant tintinnabulations in the pianist's left hand and beneath the gently pulsating right-hand chords. The dynamics are muted throughout; even the *mezzo forte* passages are contained within the nocturnal atmosphere. In no song have the hushed mysteries of the midnight hour ("Il est minuit comme une flèche") been more eloquently expressed; the piano's low C on the second syllable of "minuit," like a quietly resonating tam-tam, provides one of the most spellbinding colors in the composer's songs. In the extraordinarily beautiful coda, left hand crosses right, and movement and stasis are inextricably entwined.

(iii)   *Le Front comme un drapeau perdu (Forehead Like a Lost Flag)*
          No key signature (A minor); $\frac{12}{8}$; *Très animé* ♩ = 132

Le front comme un drapeau perdu	Forehead like a lost flag
Je te traîne quand je suis seul	I drag you along when I am alone
Dans des rues froides	Through cold streets
Des chambres noires	And dark rooms
En criant misère	Crying my despair
Je ne veux pas les lâcher	I can't release them
Tes mains claires et compliquées	Your bright complex hands
Nées dans le miroir clos des miennes	Born in the closed mirror of my own
Tout le reste est parfait	Everything else is perfect
Tout le reste est encore plus inutile	Everything else is more useless even
Que la vie	Than life
Creuse la terre sous ton ombre	Dig up the earth beneath your shadow
Une nappe d'eau près des seins	A sheet of water by your breasts
Où se noyer	Which one can drown in
Comme une pierre.	Like a stone.

A sudden shock, and planned as such, this is one of those songs that Poulenc placed strategically between slower, more profound ones to create a sense of contrast and excitement—a "mélodie tremplin" (a springboard, or trampoline, song) that bounces the listener into the beginning of a more substantial work. There is a brusque and frightening side to Éluard, a violence that Poulenc does not try to avoid. This is a strange and stormy outburst, a love song of sorts, with a suddenly gentle middle section ("Tout le reste est parfait") and a peroration (beginning "Une nappe d'eau") that starts ominously and winds down to a major-key resolution representing "all-engulfing oblivion" (according to Buckland).

Once again Buckland looks at the discarded title ("Être," to be) as a key to the poem's meaning: "a sense of claustrophobic enclosure and of need . . . the poet, when he is alone, drags the thought of a loved one like a lost flag (lost cause) through cold streets, dark rooms, shouting misery."[100] In the middle section he does not want to let go of her hands, he abases himself before her shadow, wishing to drown like a stone near her breasts. Buckland notes the poet's need to "blot out the autism of solitude in order 'to be' "; and thus we return to his original title. The dedication to "Nush" is an indication that Poulenc has understood that Éluard's lyric described the kind of abject love and desperate adoration she alone was able to inspire in him. If singer and pianist follow all the directions and perform the song implacably, it successfully sets up the drama of the next song.

(iv)   *Une roulotte couverte en tuiles* (*A Gypsy Wagon Roofed with Tiles*)
No key signature; $\frac{4}{4}$; *Très lent et sinistre* ♪ = 80

Une roulotte couverte en tuiles	A Gypsy wagon roofed with tiles
Le cheval mort un enfant maître	The horse dead a child in charge
Pensant le front bleu de haine	Thinking his brow blue with the hatred
À deux seins s'abattant sur lui	Of two breasts beating down on him
Comme deux poings	Like two fists
Ce mélodrame nous arrache	This melodrama rips from us
La raison du cœur.	Our heart's very reason.

The title may at first suggest van Gogh's painting *Les Roulottes, campement de bohémiens aux environs d'Arles* (1888), but the bright sunlight of the south of France fails to fall on this dark metropolitan poem. Paris was a terrible place of poverty in the years between the wars, nowhere more apparent than in "La Zone," the name of a derelict ribbon of land around Paris that provided a refuge for the criminal classes and the dispossessed.[101] Writer Blaise Cendrars and artist Fernand Léger, both members of Éluard's extended circle, visited a Gypsy camp in the "Zone" in 1924, and Cendrars left this account:

I took a path that zigzagged between the tarps, the farmyards, the little gardens, enclosed in walls topped with broken bottles, delimited with barbed-wire fences and old railroad crossing gates, filled with furious dogs ... drooling with rage, among the empty, dented, crumbling tin cans, the jagged bits of sheet metal, the bed-springs poking up from the slag, broken china and pottery ... dominated like a Golgotha by the skeleton of a tree ... a disused runt of a linden tree, the stump of its branch capped by a chamber pot, its pollarded top crowned by an old tire.[102]

Such a surreal urban moonscape is remarkably different from, say, the poetic Parisian evocations of Apollinaire, but it is a snapshot of Paris nevertheless, and one that Éluard would have recognized. And Cendrars's prose has something of the harsh and bleak quality of the poem Poulenc set to music. Éluard was a Communist who supported the idea of revolution, although his tendency was to sympathize with individual cases of injustice rather than promulgate theory. A central tenet of his poetry was brotherhood: poets could no longer inhabit ivory towers but belonged among the people, where they should speak for all men. Poulenc was completely uninterested in politics, did not support the Front Populaire government elected in 1936 (and was seemingly indifferent to the fact that the prime minster, Léon Blum, was homosexual). He claimed that his vision of the poem was of a Gypsy child on a wagon he saw one November day in Ménilmontant[103]—a comparatively salubrious working-class suburb (locale of a famous Maurice Chevalier chanson) and no match in misery to the scene depicted by Éluard, where the only color mentioned is the blue of hatred.

Buckland again throws light on the poem by returning to Éluard's title, here "Rideau" (curtain). A curtain implies a theatrical event, as does the word "melodrama." The poet remembered "losing himself" as a child (perhaps in excitement) at the rising of a play's curtain.[104] Bernac found resonances here of paintings by Picasso in the period when he depicted acrobats, *saltimbanques*, the down-and-out and disadvantaged—theatrical or circus performers of some kind.[105]

In the depression years of the 1930s, starvation and untreated illness left many a child facing the brutal responsibilities of adulthood alone on the streets. The scene here is still and ominous, as if a nightmare moment had been frozen in time. Both poet and composer also register a brooding sense of impending danger from the "child master," even if it is a long-term threat. Éluard is pointing out that the future of a society that permits such a heartless scenario can only be violent, and Poulenc seems to have been drawn into musical, if not philosophical, agreement. In the piano writing for the opening bar of this single page of music, held whole notes in octaves shelter a chromatic descent of four quarter notes doubled in both hands; this sinister undertow settles into a D minor chord on the fourth beat. The second bar is a repeat of the first, with tiny differences in the vocal line—essentially a terse monotone, inflected first with a minor third, then a major third.

These opening bars, with three separate exclamations, bring to mind the recitative style of Musorgsky, one of the few composers to write songs with working-class protagonists. Poulenc may have known Musorgsky's 1868 song *Sirotka* (*The Orphan*), a setting of the composer's own words, where the piano writing, also in phlegmatic chords, supports a vocal line that gasps and pleads in short phrases. There seems little doubt that the "enfant maître" of Éluard's poem, the child left in charge of the broken-down wagon with a dead horse, is also an orphan who has already learned to hate those who lead a happier life.

The effect of the music is atonal and fragmentary. The piano's contrary motion in bars 3–5 is a musical thumbscrew—a right-hand descent and a simultaneous left-hand ascent leading to "s'abattant sur lui"—suggesting ineluctable forces cornering the unfortunate youngster. These breasts (Éluard seldom denies himself such female imagery) bear down on the boy like fists; they may belong to a brutal or uncaring mother, or even a mother who is dead. In bar 6, when a pair of bare fifths in both hands ascend a semitone (under "Comme deux poings"), suddenly *forte*—"poings" is onomatopoetically explosive—it is as though the pianist is punching the keyboard with both hands clenched.

For the last three bars the opening music is repeated, and the entire vocal line consists of repeated Ds punctuated by silence into three separate phrases ("Ce mélodrame . . . nous arrache . . . La raison"). Buckland likens these three short phrases to the medieval custom whereby, just before curtain up, the floor of the stage is struck three times with an ornate stick (known as the "brigadier")—a custom still alive in France and a surprise for visiting British and American theatergoers.[106] A final unexpected twist to the harmony defies any sense of musical cadence or even accuracy on the part of the singer. But in this case it doesn't really matter. The words "du cœur" are to be delivered *dans un souffle*, half spoken. The *scena* (remarkably powerful considering its brevity) and its alarming social implications are left gaping open; there is no sense of closure, only a shudder.

(v) *À toutes brides* (*At Full Tilt*)
   No key signature, ends in G minor; $\frac{2}{4}$; *Prestissimo* ♩ = 112

À toutes brides toi dont le fantôme	You whose ghost, at full tilt,
Piaffe la nuit sur un violon	Prances at night on a violin
Viens régner dans les bois	Come and reign over the woods
Les verges de l'ouragan	The lashes of the hurricane
Cherchent leur chemin par chez toi	Seek their way past you

Tu n'es pas de celles	You are not one of those
Dont on invente les désirs	Whose desires can be invented

Viens boire un baiser par ici	Come and drink a kiss here
Cède au feu qui te désespère.	Give in to the fire that drives you to despair.

This flirtatious and provocative song from a man admiring and encouraging the fire of a woman's desire is another "trampoline" designed to serve as a transition between a nightmare scenario (iv) and a song of infinite and gentle sweetness (vi). Poulenc's wild *danse macabre,* producing open fifths like a violin, is his response to the imagery of unbridled female lust. He obviously cannot match Éluard's first-hand experience of the searing energies of the eternal feminine, but the two extraordinary jazzy piano interludes (bb. 7–10 and 16–17) give musical voice to the pressing nature of desire; and the driven nature of sexual attraction is something this composer understood all too well. (A bass-clef symbol is missing in the left-hand stave at the beginning of b. 7.) "Les verges de l'ouragan" (bb. 11–15) brings a suitably stormy quality, its B-flat minor tonality suggesting a strong link with the windswept last movement of Chopin's Second Piano Sonata (in the same key). After "Dont on invente les désirs," Poulenc leaves out two of Éluard's lines, whether by mistake (in the heat of the compositional moment) or intentionally has never been clear: "Tes soifs sont plus contradictoires / Que des noyées" (Your thirsts are more contradictory / Than those of the drowned). The turbulent closing moments (from b. 18, *fortissimo, éclatant*) are Éluard's invitation, a challenge even, to a woman whose sexual energy seems to be unassuageable. Rendered bold by passion, excited by the appetite for love that he discerns in his partner, he offers himself as the source of satisfaction that has hitherto eluded her. The piano here seems to pursue the vocal line; the two bars of postlude (*Très violent*) are like a Venus flytrap snapping shut.

At first it may seem as if Poulenc has totally submerged himself in the spirit of the poet's words, but he lacks Éluard's untrammeled and generous joy when it comes to matters of love. Those jazzy piano interludes appear rather driven and heartless; the sexual drive celebrated by the poet takes on an air of something diabolical, and the song ends resoundingly in the minor key. This is a composer who might match, even exceed, Éluard in the number of his lovers, but also a man who never remotely enjoyed the equality of spirit with his partners that was a central glory of Éluard's life with Nusch. But *À toutes brides* is perhaps too fast and over too quickly for such doubts to be allowed to raise their heads or take away from our enjoyment in the flawless progress of the cycle. The song serves its purpose admirably.

(vi)   *Une herbe pauvre* (*A Meager Blade of Wild Grass*)
       E minor; $\frac{3}{4}$; *Clair, doux et lent* ♩ = 60

Une herbe pauvre	A meager blade of wild grass
Sauvage	
Apparut dans la neige	Appeared in the snow
C'était la santé	It was health
Ma bouche fut émerveillée	My mouth was amazed
Du goût d'air pur qu'elle avait	By its taste of pure air
Elle était fanée.	It was withered.

This little masterpiece in E minor has a simplicity worthy of the Fauré of *Le Jardin clos*, where one harmony yields to the next in a way that is both inevitable and surprising. To Poulenc, Éluard's poem held "*a divine savor. It recalls for me that invigorating bitterness of a flower I once plucked and tasted in the surroundings of the Grande Chartreuse.*"[107] Admirers of Schumann's lieder will note a similarity to the Kerner setting *Erstes Grün*, Op. 35 No. 4, where the poet presses the first blade of grass of spring to his lips and heart. This dreamlike song, as if already a memory, has the seriousness of sacred ritual, without falling into undue reverence or mourning for something that is, after all, only a blade of grass. Nevertheless, as Sidney Buckland puts it, the poem's seriousness lies in balancing "a sense of wonderment . . . against a sense of loss."[108] The melancholy inherent in the poem's final line ("Elle était fanée") brings a tinge of resignation to the music; the blade of grass, plucky enough to stick its head out above the snow, has been withered by cold. What was perfection undisturbed in its own environment has been sullied by the plucking—a metaphor for many things, including, in some circumstances, the beloved.

Most unusually, the composer repeats the poem's first three lines to round off this haunting little elegy in the form of a stately minuet, as perfect and as simple a song as Poulenc ever wrote. I say "minuet" advisedly because even Poulenc's slow and serious music has the quality of a dance. None of his slow songs, even one as rapt as this, are slow enough to suggest stasis in their performance; the music always moves in a way to imply the trajectory of a singer's breath, or the movement of a bow across a string. No matter what the subject matter of the poem, the tempo of most French mélodies is ruled by the physicality of the dance rather than the immobility of philosophical reflection. The dedication to Marie-Blanche de Polignac is an indication of the composer's pride in a song that was one of his most eloquent to date.

(vii) *Je n'ai envie que de t'aimer* (*All That I Want Is to Love You*)
D-flat major/B-flat minor; $\frac{12}{8}$; *Très allant et très souple* ♩. = 100

Je n'ai envie que de t'aimer	All that I want is to love you
Un orage emplit la vallée	A storm fills the valley
Un poisson la rivière	A fish the river
Je t'ai faite à la taille de ma solitude	I've created you in the shape of my loneliness
Le monde entier pour se cacher	The whole world to hide in
Des jours des nuits pour se comprendre	Days and nights in which to understand one another
Pour ne plus rien voir dans tes yeux	To see no more in your eyes
Que ce que je pense de toi	But that which I think of you
Et d'un monde à ton image	And a world made in your image
Et des jours et des nuits réglés par tes paupières.	And days and nights ruled by your eyelids.

Early in my career I played this song (not the rest of the cycle) for Victoria de los Angeles. She had performed it for Poulenc at some point in the 1950s, and he had encouraged her to sing it faster, breathlessly. (There is a parallel here with the Fauré/Verlaine song *Green,* where the composer indicated a relatively sedate metronome marking but advocated that a performance should be breathless—more a matter of interpretive attitude than speed.) Poulenc's advice seems to have been a corrective to hearing many a well-meaning performance that sounded earnest and labored. The music must convey the well-being of a besotted lover, and the singer's task is to create the romantic glow of fulfillment while avoiding any sense of panic or agitation. Bernac warns that the metronome mark is, in fact, sufficiently fast, but performers must beware slowing down: he advises a slight *accelerando* on "réglés par tes paupières," the pianist getting a little slower only in the closing bars (*Céder doucement*).[109]

Here Éluard has written, by his often-unfathomable standards, an uncomplicated love poem to Nusch, and the lyrical élan of the music is a perfect match. There is just a tinge of cabaret in the music; a charming lightness of heart and the gallantry of the *cavaliere servente* are somehow reflected in the graceful *acciaccatura* ornamenting "la taille de *ma* solitude." In the opening bars the pianist experiences the sensation of dancing on the black keys in the G-flat major tonality, before sliding down to the white notes for a graceful cadence into F major in the third bar. Poulenc then takes us on a tour of sequences in flat, and then sharp, keys—no doubt carefully planned, harmony by harmony, but somehow adding up to something effortlessly elegant, as if conceived in a single, inspired arc. He wanted it *"to be sung in a single curve, one single impulse."*[110] The last phrase (beginning "Et des jours et des nuits") throbs with triplet chords that should be played like a succession of palpitations without creating the impression of a series of downbeats. Contrast between day and night is indicated by a simple but magical alternation of B-flat minor and major. And the two-bar postlude, the left hand twice crossing the right with pinpricks of melody, has the delicacy of a caress.

(viii)   *Figure de force brûlante et farouche (Face Burning with Wild Strength)*
          No key signature (D minor); $\frac{3}{4}$; *Presto—très violent* ♩ = 138; from b. 12, *Lent* ♩ = 66

Figure de force brûlante et farouche	Face burning with wild
Cheveux noirs où l'or coule vers le sud	Black hair where the gold flows south
Aux nuits corrompues	On corrupted nights
Or englouti étoile impure	Engulfed gold impure star
Dans un lit jamais partagé	In a bed never shared
Aux veines des tempes	At the veins of the temples
Comme au bout des seins	And at the nipples
La vie se refuse	Life denies itself
Les yeux nul ne peut les crever	Nothing can put out those eyes
Boire leur éclat ni leurs larmes	Nor drink their brilliance nor their tears
Le sang au-dessus d'eux triomphe	Above them blood is triumphant for
pour lui seul	itself only
Intraitable démesurée	Intractable immoderate
Inutile	And useless
Cette santé bâtit une prison.	This health builds a prison.

Poulenc explained that the reason he created such a loud and active song was to make the silence at the opening of the final song more effective.[111] That may be, but the gestural power here adds considerable weight to the cycle as a whole. It is as if the spirit of Stravinsky at his most elemental has suddenly appeared as a kind of avenging angel—although whenever Poulenc imitates another composer, the music is always refracted through a prism of his own individuality. We hear the "Russian" Stravinsky in the repetitive punched rhythms of the opening and the savagery of "Dans un lit jamais partagé"; and the composer of *Symphony of*

Psalms in the hieratic slowness of "Aux veines des tempes," with the vocal line doubled an octave higher in the piano. In truth, the song is a bit of a ragbag of different effects, but intensity of utterance binds it together. We are reminded that Éluard is no miniaturist or mere love poet; his words sometimes require a Picasso-like boldness in setting them to music.

From the poet's point of view, the words are a vehement denunciation of those moralistic forces that would deny the individual's right to give and receive love. Bearing in mind that all the surrealists were against religion, some more than others (especially those with memories of abuse in childhood), we might also see the poem as Éluard's attack on what he sees as the majesty, power, corruption, and sterility of the Catholic church, although it is unlikely that the recently converted Poulenc would have read it that way. On first reading, the poem might seem to depict the devil or some fallen angel, but more likely it describes reactionary forces marshaled to do battle with the imaginary devil, forces that are far more frightening in their lack of humanity.

In the coda (beginning with "Intraitable démesurée"), two bars of unchanging Ds in the vocal line are accompanied by oscillating D octaves in the pianist's right hand, while the left adds clashing and grinding E-flats and E-naturals. Such is the power of Éluard's denunciation of a "rigid, unyielding negation of life"[112] that those five bars are among the most taxing for the singer in all Poulenc's songs. The repeated Ds rise to an E-flat for "Inutile," to an even higher F-sharp for "santé," and then (after a brief descent) a high A for "prison," where the baritone tessitura is tested to the limits (it is easier for sopranos to sing this coda). It is perhaps paradoxical that music describing negativity (Buckland's key word for the poem is "denial") should achieve a wild kind of ecstasy in its major-key ending—a grandiose cadence into D major, emphasized both by the height of the vocal line and the emphatic and *fortissimo* participation of the piano hammering out the notes of the triad, supported by an octave deep in the bass. A final D in the treble is played with defiance as the pianist's left hand crosses the right, a *coup de grâce*. In Poulenc, as often with Schubert and other composers, we are accustomed to the "pathetic" major used to invoke sad tenderness, but this major key denotes grim triumph.

Bernac, a hard-working professional, was the composer's temperamental opposite. Could the song's dedication to him be Poulenc's subtle critique of his colleague's formidable and sometimes intractable self-control? The singer practiced an abstinence undreamed of, or never seriously contemplated, by the composer. There is no doubt that Bernac would quickly become a "figure de force" for Poulenc, without the slightest suggestion of a "lit partagé." And it is also beyond doubt that the influence of such a disciplined individual on Poulenc's musical and personal life was entirely beneficial and, at times, life-saving.

(ix)   *Nous avons fait la nuit* (*We Have Made the Night*)
           C minor/major; $\frac{4}{4}$; *Très modéré, sans traîner pourtant* ♩ = 60

Nous avons fait la nuit je tiens ta main je veille	We have made night I hold your hand I watch
Je te soutiens de toutes mes forces	I support you with all my strength
Je grave sur un roc l'étoile de tes forces	I carve into a rock the very star of your strength
Sillons profonds où la bonté de ton corps germera	Deep furrows whence the goodness of your body will grow
Je me répète ta voix cachée ta voix publique	I repeat to myself your secret voice your public voice
Je ris encore de l'orgueilleuse	I still laugh at the thought of the stuck-up woman
Que tu traites comme une mendiante	You treat like a beggar
Des fous que tu respectes des simples où tu te baignes	At the fools you respect at the simple folk in whose company you delight
Et dans ma tête qui se met doucement d'accord avec la tienne avec la nuit	And in my head so sweetly in tune with yours and with the night
Je m'émerveille de l'inconnue que tu deviens	I am amazed at the stranger you become
Une inconnue semblable à toi semblable à tout ce que j'aime	A stranger just like you just like everything I love
Qui est toujours nouveau.	Which is always new.

The poor (and also lucky) Pierre Bernac had to learn and memorize a great deal of newly composed music in time for the first performance of this cycle, on 3 February 1937. He recalled the January evening when the closing song was written: "As always when we passed through Lyon on one of our tours, we stayed with our friends Professor and Mme Latarjet [Suzanne Latarjet was a sister of Raymonde Linossier]. I remember during dinner we tried to persuade Poulenc to leave the piano—'Francis it will all be cold!' He was composing *Nous avons fait la nuit*, one of the most beautiful songs that he had ever written."[113]

Poulenc himself regarded it as one of his most moving songs, and few would argue with him. The poem, from *Facile*, first appeared in print next to one of Man Ray's many nude photographs of Nusch, although in this picture, a solarized photogravure, we do not see her face. She lies on her back, knees bent, the fourth finger of her left hand sporting a large ring and both wrists bedecked with leather straps and bracelets (how modern and timelessly chic they look). The pose gives the impression that her wrists have been secured to her ankles, but she was a former circus acrobat and needed no fancy restraints to maintain such an erotic position. Éluard is continually surprised by Nusch—her thoughts can never be guessed in advance, she can never be taken for granted. She treats the mighty with contempt and the foolish with respect, and she constantly reinvents herself. Although she resembles the person he knows and loves, she is "toujours nouveau," always new.

Such enduring fascination seems nothing less than Éluard's analysis of what makes a relationship work. It is her sheer unpredictability and generosity of spirit that have kept them together (Éluard does not attempt to analyze why Nusch remains devoted to him, but everything about this poetry suggests a state of heightened reciprocity). The physical nature of the union ("Sillons profonds où la bonté de ton corps germera") is dependent on a profound mental affinity ("ma tête . . . se met doucement d'accord avec la tienne"). Here, as Buckland points out, "Éluard's perception of the woman as mediator between himself and the outside world reaches an apogee of intensity. . . . she is situated at the creative centre of life, like the supreme force of nature, the sun:

> "Through you I go from light to light
> From warmth to warmth
> It is through you that I speak and remain at the centre
> Of everything like a sun consenting to happiness."[114]

In setting this great lyric of the melding of opposites, of yin and yang, of man and woman, Poulenc never puts a foot wrong. It is as though he has been lifted and inspired by the kind of relationship that he can admire profoundly at a distance, but can never experience himself. The extraordinary poignancy and longing, the veil of sadness that covers and gently transmutes so much of his music, even music purporting to be joyous, surely stems from his inability to achieve a state of being where love is a source of trust and security rather than guilt, anguish, and despair.

Bernac recalled Poulenc's saying that *calm in a poem of love can alone give intensity.* He also advises performers, having finished the preceding song in such a passionate manner, to wait several seconds before embarking on this one.[115] It begins in C minor with the piano doubling the voice, possibly a tonal analogue for a couple holding hands in the dark (the title implies they have just turned out the light) and feeling their way to intimacy; the tempo is as constant as a heartbeat. Gradually the harmonies fill out and become more effulgent. Once freed from doubling the treble, the left hand roves the bass clef in split octaves, often marked staccato—supplying a certain luminous clarity to the piano texture despite the constant pedal. These ambulations, sometimes etching a kind of countermelody in left-hand accents, provide the impetus for the song's unceasing movement. For despite the moderate tempo, this is music in the great lieder walking tradition of Schubert's *Winterreise* (*Gute Nacht, Rast, Der Wegweiser*), where being on the move is a sign of a journey that is as much spiritual as physical, and where trudging through snow can also seem like floating through dreams.

At bar 15 the three flats of the key signature are canceled into naturals for seven bars, essentially a shift into A minor. Then, after a descent into darker harmonic profundity, the vocal line, inflected by a bel canto intensity that any Italian composer might admire, moves into another sphere and becomes something extraordinarily eloquent. The piano writing also becomes increasingly demonstrative, with the phrase "avec la nuit" occasioning a piano chord ornamented with grace notes, a stretch of a tenth that seems a metaphor for one soul straining to become part of another. For six of the singer's last eight bars, piano and voice are anchored on a nonstop G pedal—underscoring imagery of unwavering devotion, the poet transfixed by admiration for an unknown woman ("Une inconnue") who is also the woman he already knows and loves. This pedal-point, with a few other bass notes cleverly thrown into the mix, also sets up a longing for a cadence. And on the final syllable of the phrase "Qui est toujours nouveau," we are granted this resolution in sumptuous fashion, one of the most satisfying dominant-to-tonic progressions in all song.

The thirteen-bar postlude is almost entirely on the piano's white keys, which here seem to denote purity and altruism. This music is radiantly calm, aglow with a vision of twinned souls that has moved and inspired the composer, but seems sadly out of his own reach; that sadness is quietly built in here, alongside Éluard's joy. It is unassuaged *Sehnsucht* (longing), wordlessly expressed in the piano postlude, that this cycle has most in common with *Dichterliebe*. Poulenc warns the pianist not to hurry. Years ago many an embarrassed accompanist dispatched postludes quickly in order not to delay the singer's applause a moment more than necessary, but at this moment the pianist is the star and the composer's mouthpiece. He or she must be expansive in spirit yet avoid slowing up in quixotic rubato; the music should flow, but not overflow. As so often in Poulenc's piano writing, the volume and percussiveness of the pulsating eighth notes in the thumb and first finger of the right hand must be kept to a minimum while the fifth finger sings a seraphic melody that is "conjured from nowhere" and inhabits the perfect register to suggest fulfillment and trust.

At the end we hear once again those notes from a C major triad that ended *Bonne journée,* a seeming recipe for banality that produces instead the alchemist's gold. The very end brings a delicate signing-off in the minor key, a gentle oscillation high in the treble between a flattened third (with "blue" seventh) and the dominant. This is easy to play—apart from the fact that every time I reach for those notes, having traversed this wonderful postlude, my hands are shaking, the sheer effect of this pulse-quickening music on the human heart. The cycle has come full circle, and in its twenty-three pages Poulenc has joined the ranks of the song-composing immortals. In one interview, given in America, he allowed his public mask of modesty to slip for a moment: "*Every composer eventually discovers what he considers to be his own source of greatness. I have found it in the poetry of Paul Éluard.*"[116]

∘   ∘   ∘

FP87 *Bourrée, au Pavillon d'Auvergne* (piano), 7 May 1937
FP88 *Deux Marches et un intermède* (chamber orchestra), June 1937
FP89 Mass in G Major (mixed chorus, *a cappella*), August 1937
FP90 *Sécheresses* (cantata for mixed choir and orchestra), September–December 1937

∘   ∘   ∘

FP91 **Trois Poèmes de Louise de Vilmorin**
Composed in Noizay, December 1937
[*Marie-Blanche de Polignac*; Durand]
Literary source: Louise de Vilmorin (1902–1969) gave handwritten copies of the poems to Poulenc; these were beautifully bound for his library, but were auctioned in Paris in 2017. The poems were published, somewhat altered, in *Fiançailles pour rire* (Paris: Gallimard, 1939): (i) p. 41, (ii) p. 71 with the title "Choisir n'est pas trahir," (iii) p. 33.

(i)   *Le Garçon de Liège*
(ii) *Au-delà*
(iii) *Aux officiers de la Garde Blanche*

Having recently formed a serious duo with Bernac, and having declared himself an Éluard composer, Poulenc seems to have wanted to up his game in terms of his poets. After *Tel jour telle nuit*, he realized once and for all that contemporary poetry was far better suited to his talents than anything written in the nineteenth century. The meeting between the inscrutability of modernist texts and the clarifying lyricism of the vocal line was a compact made to the advantage of both words and music; the music appears stronger and more noble when heard in conjunction with challenging texts, and the texts appear less redoubtable, more human, as if they were being unencrypted by a composer doubling as magician and sage. We can imagine how sentimental texts, only too easily understood at first glance, might have made Poulenc's delicious use of melody and harmony seem glutinously indigestible—the very situation that scuppers most of the songs of Massenet, whose chosen texts are so accessible and deferential to public taste that the addition of music in the same vein, however pretty and charming, leads to forgettably saccharine results.

Since Poulenc's death, there have been successful female performances of *Tel jour telle nuit*, Dame Felicity Lott's (coached by Bernac) among them, but it was clearly Poulenc's view that Éluard was a male poet with such a strong narrative identity that his words were better expressed by a male singer. "*I need to believe in the words that I hear sung*," Poulenc asserted. He was uncomfortable hearing a woman singer perform Fauré's *Chanson d'amour*, beginning with lines (by poet Armand Silvestre) unequivocally intended to be sung to a woman by a man.[117] Equally, the composer with some justification felt that poems from a gifted and up-to-the-minute female poet would make for authentically female songs for the soprano voice. And he even had such a singer in mind: his good friend Marie-Blanche de Polignac, the soprano in Nadia Boulanger's ensemble of singers who were the first to record Monteverdi madrigals (with piano accompaniment).

Poulenc adored women, and he adored the female voice. He worshipped female glamour and even fantasized at times about being a woman. And he was on the lookout for a candidate to be his female Éluard. Louise de Vilmorin, a talented novelist who was alluring, clever, and chic enough to move in exalted social circles, belonged to the family whose celebrated firm still supplies the well-to-do French middle classes with tree, flower, and vegetable seeds. "*Few people move me as much as Louise de Vilmorin*," wrote Poulenc, "*because she is beautiful, because she is lame, because she writes French of an innate purity, because her name evokes*

flowers and vegetables, because she loves her brothers like a lover and her lovers like a sister. Her beautiful face recalls the seventeenth century, as does the sound of her name."[118]

By the time she entered Poulenc's life, Louise had made a celebrated debut with *Sainte-Unefois* (1934), written with the encouragement of her mentor, the literary lion André Malraux, whose mistress she had become. She could already claim quite a past: by her early thirties she was the mother of three daughters with a divorced American husband, Henry Leigh-Hunt. After struggling unsuccessfully

Louise de Vilmorin, photographed by Horst P. Horst, 1937.

to accustom herself to living in Las Vegas, she had returned to her family home in Verrières-le-Buisson in the southern suburbs of Paris—a house built in 1680 by Louis XIV for his former mistress, another Louise, Mlle de la Vallière. The Vilmorin family acquired the house in 1815, and you can still visit the remarkable Arboretum Vilmorin there with its thousands of trees, plants, and shrubs, affirmation of the family's passion for horticulture and gardening.

Louise gave her friend Marie-Blanche de Polignac the third poem, "Aux officiers de la Garde Blanche," as a Christmas present in 1935. The painter Jean Hugo described how Louise wrote the poem in the library of his home in Fourques, near Arles, and uncharacteristically stopped speaking until she had finished it. He sketched her as she worked (no doubt also impatient to take her in his arms, which is what occasioned her need to write these lines), noting how from time to time, with pen poised, she lifted her head while opening wide her green eyes. When Poulenc read the poem, he immediately encouraged Louise to write more. He was charming in his insistence—as only he could be when he wanted something badly—and she eventually complied in November 1936, when she was staying with the Polignacs at Kerbastic.

All three songs were dedicated to Marie-Blanche, who gave their first performance in the Salle Gaveau on 28 November 1938 as part of the "Sérénade" concert series. The house was packed with the singer's upper-class friends and fans; but she was castigated by Paul Bertrand, critic of *Le Ménestrel,* for her unintelligible words and meager size of voice—however pretty the sound may have been within a group of madrigal singers.[119] Bertrand's review was a denunciation, in short, of an amateur singer's pretensions, while highly praising Poulenc's skill as an accompanist.

Such was the importance of Marie-Blanche in the composer's circle, and so central to his well-being was her friendship and patronage, that there is no reference to this critical bombshell in any of the documents; a veil was swiftly drawn. Neither Bernac nor Poulenc would have failed to take the singer's side. It was not, however, an experiment she was to repeat in public. For the next two decades Marie-Blanche remained ensconced in her salon, queen of her own private musical milieu, singing and playing the piano to the delight of her guests. She was the dedicatee of more Poulenc songs than anyone else. There are, unfortunately, no recordings of her singing even one of the songs dedicated to her that might have gainsaid the critic's damning verdict. Even the HMV recordings of Monteverdi madrigals, with Boulanger at the piano, give us little idea how Marie-Blanche might have performed a twentieth-century mélodie in a concert hall.

(i) *Le Garçon de Liège (The Boy from Liège)*
       C minor; $\frac{4}{4}$; *Vertigineusement vite* ♩ = 176

Un garçon de conte de fée	A fairy-tale boy
M'a fait un grand salut bourgeois	Gave me a big old-fashioned bow
En plein vent, au bord d'une allée,	On a windy day, by a country lane,
Debout sous l'arbre de la Loi.	Standing beneath the Tree of the Law.
Les oiseaux d'arrière-saison	The last birds of autumn
Faisaient des leurs malgré lapluie,	Were up to their mischief despite the rain,
Et prise par ma déraison	And I, seized by a wanton whim,
J'osai lui dire: "Je m'ennuie."	Dared to say to him: "I'm bored."
Sans dire un doux mot de menteur	Without a sweet word of a lie
Le soir dans ma chambre à tristesse	That evening in my sad room
Il vint consoler ma pâleur.	He came to comfort my paleness.
Son ombre me fit des promesses.	His shadow made me certain promises.
Mais c'était un garçon de Liège	But he was a boy from Liège
Léger, léger comme le vent	As light, as light as the wind,
Qui ne se prend à aucun piège	Who won't be caught in any trap
Et court les plaines du beau temps.	And plays the field when the sun shines.
Et dans ma chemise de nuit,	And in my nightgown,
Depuis lors quand je voudrais rire	Since then, I've wanted to laugh,
Ah! beau jeune homme je m'ennuie,	"Oh, beautiful young man, I'm bored,
Ah! dans ma chemise à mourir.	Ah, bored to death, in my nightgown."

The song's breathless tempo and ever-restless octave sixteenth notes (bb. 3–14) denote a family similarity with the Louise Lalanne setting *Le Présent*, although the musical lines here are more lyrical and infinitely more melodic. A secret of this song is that the piano writing should sound helter-skelter while the vocal line, in longer note values, preserves an unruffled elegance above the fray. Voice and piano artfully combine to illustrate simultaneous boredom and excitement.

When (from b. 15) cascades of broken chords descend the stave in elegant filigree, while the little finger of the right hand sustains a line of held half notes, a new kind of accompaniment is born in the Poulenc songs—which will reach its apotheosis in the Éluard setting *Main dominée par le cœur* FP135 (1946). This is clearly the composer's response to "audacious poetry" that in its lightness of style is "transparent," "capricious like embroidery," yet "not without seriousness."[120]

The poem's title, a pun on "Liège/liege" (the Walloon town in Belgium and the French noun for "cork"), describes a whirlwind romance with a good-looking but not particularly profound young man, a youth as light as cork and liable to float by. Vilmorin embarks on a liaison that temporarily alleviates her boredom, only to find that as the relationship comes to what she sees as its natural end, she has ended up even more bored than before. For Bernac, the phrase "l'arbre de la Loi" (which also appears in *Dans l'herbe* from the later Vilmorin cycle *Fiançailles pour rire* FP101) evoked a picture of St. Louis dispensing justice from under an oak tree; for Vilmorin, it may have had something to do with her defiance of convention and the house rules of her distinguished family, whose name had so much to do with the cultivation of gardens.

The excitement of the sexual chase and the melancholy and disillusionment that follow are admirably caught in the music's impetus and onrush, all leading ineluctably to the confessional coda. These five bars (marked *Brusque*), with a plaintive "Ah!" on a whole note F-sharp that is abetted by a trill in both hands for the pianist, sound like brakes suddenly being applied on the relationship. With the song now drained of its sixteenth notes and thus its energy and *joie de vivre*, Bernac advises that the passage must "express all the boredom possible!"[121] The phrase "à mourir," an octave leap in half notes on the first two syllables, provides a return to C major via a progression (V^7–IV–I) that perfectly conveys ennui, inconvenient rather than tragic. Here is the self-awareness of those experienced in promiscuous dalliance: such a boy can only be loved in a passing moment, and not permanently. She had been looking for a good time rather than a long time. Poulenc left one verse out; when the poem was finally published, in 1939, he was rather proud of the fact that Vilmorin had chosen to suppress that same verse.

But the poet was also capable of much longer attachments: in the war years she was happily married to a Hungarian count (see *Fiançailles pour rire*) and at the end of her life was living with André Malraux (the flame from an earlier time having been rekindled). After Paris was liberated, Louise returned to her family home at Verrières to find it uninhabitable, trashed by the German SS. She took up residency in the British Embassy and became the live-in mistress of the ambassador, Duff Cooper. Surprisingly, admiration for Vilmorin's charm and grace also came from Lady Diana Cooper, the ambassador's wife: "I wouldn't be able to say whether it was her beauty or her poetic and terribly funny conversation that was more seductive, or whether it was her songs, her Hungarian clothes or her extravagant projects."[122] Their son John Julius Norwich remembers Louise being wonderfully kind to him as a gawky teenager; she taught him any number of racy French songs with guitar accompaniment (Poulenc's not among them).[123]

Although Bernac never sang the *Trois Poèmes*, the performer is encouraged to study his thoughts on their performance. He frequently taught them, and he recommends several important changes to the printed dynamic markings, as well as the addition of an important *crescendo*.[124] We can be certain that his suggestions were made with Poulenc's full approval.

(ii) *Au-delà* (*Way Beyond*)
No key signature; $\frac{9}{8}$; *Très vite* ♩ = 138

Eau-de-vie! Au-delà!	Eau-de-vie! Way beyond!
À l'heure du plaisir,	When pleasure calls,
Choisir n'est pas trahir,	Choice is not betrayal,
Je choisis celui-là.	And I choose him.
Je choisis celui-là	I choose the one
Qui sait me faire rire,	Who makes me laugh,
D'un doigt de-ci, de-là,	With a finger here, a finger there,
Comme on fait pour écrire.	Like when you're writing.
Comme on fait pour écrire,	Like when you're writing,
Il va par-ci, par-là,	Moving here, moving there,
Sans que j'ose lui dire:	I don't dare tell him
J'aime bien ce jeu-là.	It's a game I like.
J'aime bien ce jeu-là,	It's a game I like,
Qu'un souffle fait finir,	Which ends in a breath
Jusqu'au dernier soupir	At the final sigh,
Je choisis ce jeu-là.	It's a game I like.
Eau-de-vie! Au-delà!	Eau-de-vie! Way beyond!
À l'heure du plaisir,	When pleasure calls,
Choisir n'est pas trahir,	Choice is not betrayal,
Je choisis ce jeu-là.	This is the game I choose.

Poulenc immediately connected this poem with an erotic scenario, no doubt delighted by what he must have perceived as Vilmorin's openness and lack of inhibition. He had, after all, composed *L'Offrande* in 1926, a "chanson gaillarde" to an anonymous seventeenth-century text that rather outrageously broaches the subject of self-exploration with the help of the votary's candle. In the Vilmorin poem it is far from clear whether an erotic game is being played *à deux* or *toute seule*. The song is an impressive *moto perpetuo* for a bemused singer accompanied by roving fingers (exactly whose is not clear), the pianist's exploratory left hand gently placing its fleeting eighth notes in different regions of the bass stave—all part of what the composer probably saw as a feminization of the texture.

When Vilmorin's volume *Fiançailles pour rire* was published in 1939, Poulenc was disconcerted to find that she had changed this poem (already in print as part of the song). Her title was "Choisir n'est pas trahir" (To choose is not to betray); in the second strophe "doigt" (finger) was replaced by "mot" (word), and the phrase "Jusqu'au dernier soupir" in the fourth disappeared altogether. After he questioned these changes, Poulenc received this reply:

> Mon Poupoul chéri, . . . The poem, which I had written without the slightest improper wish or thought, caused Marie-Blanche to tease me so much that I am still smarting from the onslaught. She convinced me that the poem was indecency itself and that it contained images and avowals fit to make the most broad-minded of confessors blush. And when I told her that she had taken it all the wrong way, she replied that my thoughtlessness was not, in her eyes, proof of my innocence . . . I was left with egg on my face and herb omelette at that. . . . I altered it for everybody else, and if I did not change it for you it was because I had written it for you, and because I knew that your music would have the power to bring out the innocence of its original form.[125]

There is nothing like this song in all Poulenc. Far from being over-egged, it is as light as a soufflé, with a triplet accompaniment that throbs all the way through to the very last bar, with its seven repeated Gs deep in the bass—the only time we hear anything nearly as deep-seated, the rest of the accompaniment remaining diaphanously feminine. As is so often the case in the composer's mature songs, speed does not preclude elegance, and palpitating desire does not necessarily presage panic. The overriding impression, although sybaritic, is one of wide-eyed, childlike wonder. Anything deliberately obscene (as in some of the *Gaillardes* songs) would have betrayed Poulenc's respect for Vilmorin's elegance and spirit.

   It is the interpreters' task to avoid suggesting anything frantic or peremptory. The music is never *forte* and the pace is never forced; the song unfolds in a gentle and capricious manner, the pianist's hands darting hither and thither. Poulenc directs that it should be sung *"very lightly, very simply, without emphasizing anything, but at the same time without hiding its true meaning."*[126] He announces a little melodic motif of three notes in the two opening bars of the prelude, first in the minor key, then the major, a jump of a (mostly) rising sixth followed by a drop of a third, fourth, or fifth—whatever the harmony requires. This teasing tag, appearing over thirty times, makes a perfect tonal analogue for a game that is repetitive as well as private and closed off to others. One of the great successes of the setting is a sense of something taking place within an oasis of quickening delight and private exultation. Even if the poem stems from Vilmorin's seemingly inadvertent revelations occasioned by her stream-of-consciousness writing, there is little wonder that Poulenc was adamant in retaining her original words; he had set them too well to allow their poet to backtrack in confused embarrassment.

(iii) *Aux officiers de la Garde Blanche (Officers of the White Watch)*
A minor; $\frac{3}{4}$; *Assez modéré et mélancoliquement irréel* ♩ = 69

Officiers de la Garde Blanche,	Officers of the White Watch,
Gardez-moi de certaines pensées la nuit.	Protect me from certain nighttime thoughts.
Gardez-moi des corps à corps et de l'appui	Protect me from love's combat, and the press
D'une main sur ma hanche.	Of a hand on my haunch.
Gardez-moi surtout de lui	Above all protect me from him
Qui par la manche m'entraîne	Who drags me by the sleeve
Vers le hasard des mains pleines	Toward the random chance of full hands
Et les ailleurs d'eau qui luit.	And the elsewheres of shining water.
Épargnez-moi les tourments en tourmente	Save me from the tempestuous torments
De l'aimer un jour plus qu'aujourd'hui,	Of loving him a day more than today,
Et la froide moiteur des attentes	And the cold dampness of days of waiting
Qui presseront aux vitres et aux portes	Pressing up against windows and doors
Mon profil de dame déjà morte.	My profile, that of a lady already dead.
Officiers de la Garde Blanche,	Officers of the White Watch,
Je ne veux pas pleurer pour lui	I have no desire to weep for him
Sur terre. Je veux pleurer en pluie	On earth. I want my weeping to fall like rain
Sur sa terre, sur son astre orné de buis,	On his earth, on his star, trimmed in boxwood,
Lorsque plus tard je planerai transparente	When later on I'm hovering transparently
Au-dessus des cent pas d'ennui.	Over the endless pacing of boredom.
Officiers des consciences pures,	Officers of clear consciences,
Vous qui faites les visages beaux,	You who make faces beautiful,
Confiez dans l'espace au vol des oiseaux	Entrust the birds flying through space
Un message pour les chercheurs de mesure	With a message for those who seek moderation
Et forgez pour nous des chaines sans anneaux.	And forge for us chains that have no rings.

Having returned to Paris from Las Vegas and an unhappy marriage, Vilmorin met and embarked on a relationship with André Malraux in 1930. As the result of an infidelity on her side, he left her five years later, and this poem shows her on the brink of a new affair, this time with the painter Jean Hugo. Vilmorin, pursued by many men since her youth (her lameness following a childhood illness was apparently no handicap), would seem to have been quite capable of a sexual fling without deep attachment (as in *Le Garçon de Liège*). And yet we should not doubt that she also had other liaisons in which she paid for becoming close to someone in the pain of their eventual parting. (She may have agreed with the famous lesbian writer Natalie Barney, who admitted, "In love I only like the beginnings.")

When writing this poem at Hugo's home, Vilmorin is at the stage where a deepening of friendship into love seems likely, and she regards it as a matter for the angels whether or not such a development is desirable. In French parlance, a "nuit blanche" is a sleepless night, but it can also imply a night given over to sex. Vilmorin imagines a legion of guardian angels (the "Garde Blanche," words capitalized in Poulenc's song but not in Vilmorin's poem) who are on duty during such "nuit blanches." That the liaison with Hugo was short-lived (after which she went on to have affairs with Pierre Brisson of *Le Figaro* and her publisher, Gaston Gallimard, among others) seems foretold in the poem's plea for protection, intercession, and guidance from some higher power. She longs for moderation and "a chain without rings"; she would often prefer to be simply close friends with men who wanted to take her to bed. Such an attitude would explain the strength of her friendship with Poulenc and later Bernac, both of whom loved her undemandingly, entirely for herself and her gifts.

The poem held resonances for Poulenc, whose attitudes to love and sex were complicated by guilt and a compulsive lifestyle that involved many more lovers than others might have thought wise. The "officiers" here are clearly meant to be angels, and Vilmorin the repentant sinner. Such an avowal, a renunciation garlanded in sensuality, is completely in line with the composer's reawakened Catholicism. He might have hoped that his rediscovered faith would play a part in keeping him safe from what at times seemed an uncontrollable proliferation of amorous experiences.

Apart from the Charles d'Orléans prayer *Priez pour paix* (FP95), *Aux officiers* is uniquely religious among the Poulenc mélodies, a moment of metaphysical contemplation within a corpus of songs otherwise worldly and profane—although some Éluard songs provide a spirituality of another order. His first response to the words suggests the humility of prayer. Throbbing sixteenth notes, unison repetitions on the same note in the right hand supported by left-hand notes an octave lower, create an aureole of sound that propels the music forward. Poulenc goes into some detail regarding an unusual procedure:

> *It was after much reflection that I adopted the style of the pianistic writing for* Aux officiers de la Garde Blanche. *"What poor stuff" the grouser of Geneva will exclaim on discovering the unchanging unison of the opening. All the same, it has given me a great deal of trouble. What a temptation to harmonize after the fourth bar, and yet I am convinced that this false richness had to be resisted. For my part I see more humility and misery in it.*[127]

He goes on to say that "*all is prelude* [the first thirty-two bars] *until the first invocation.*" "False richness" is indeed avoided, but something more sumptuous awaits us, even if in controlled, incremental stages. At "Gardez-moi surtout de lui," the pianist's left hand introduces an independent bass line, while the right continues doubling the voice, as it has done assiduously from the beginning. The third section beginning "Épargnez-moi les tourments" (*Plus intense*) continues the gradual employment of fuller resources in the piano writing. For "Officiers de la Garde Blanche, / Je ne veux pas pleurer pour lui," the music shifts to F minor and flowers into a more effulgent texture. This "first invocation" is the real beginning of the song. If the piano's austere shadowing of the voice part is now more or less abandoned in favor of harmonic richness, in almost every bar either the left hand or right still provides a guard-rail for the vocal line by doubling it, keeping it on the metaphorical straight and narrow.

At "Lorsque plus tard je planerai," the fifth section (the song is conceived in six verses although Vilmorin's poem is printed as a continuous lyric), there is a five-bar bridge passage with a pianistic character of its own (unwinding left-hand sixteenth notes, descending into the depths of depression, with forlorn right-hand quarters). Then all is set for the peroration, the majestic significance of which is belied by the underplayed dynamics, nothing over *mezzo forte*. In its best performances, the song now takes on an air of something both transcendental and mystical—and prophesies the music of *Dialogues des Carmélites*, composed some twenty years later.

This final invocation ("Officiers des consciences pures") returns us to A minor. As if to emphasize humility as a retreat from vocal self-indulgence, the voice part at "Confiez dans l'espace" is marked *Très blanc*, which Bernac advises singing "in a floating voice and without vibrato."[128] ("A tendency to whiteness" might have been the most accurate, if not the most flattering, way to describe the voice of the song's dedicatee and first singer, Marie-Blanche de Polignac.) The song ends with a five-bar postlude of half and quarter notes (three separate gestures are implied, as if the singer were crossing herself and then sinking to her knees in prayer). In this way the composer reminds us that the battle that has occasioned this plea for protection is far from over. In providing an Amen in a minor key, is it possible that the sadness of renunciation (all those opportunities forbidden by the Garde Blanche) trumps the ecstasy we might have been expected to feel in the presence of the angels? We can be certain that for both poet and composer, the prayer remained largely unanswered, and that the angels stood mutely by as the unabashed pair of sinners made their untrammeled way from lover to lover.

FP92 *Le Portrait* (*The Portrait*)

Composed in Paris, March 1938

[*Hélène Jourdan-Morhange*; Deiss]

Literary source: Colette (Sidonie-Gabrielle Colette, 1873–1954) gave the poem to Poulenc in handwritten or printed form "on a handkerchief." There is no known printed source.[129]

No key signature; $\frac{2}{4}$; *Très violent et emporté*. No metronome mark, but Bernac recommends ♩ = 88.

Belle, méchante, menteuse,	Beautiful, wicked, mendacious,
injuste, plus changeante que le vent	unfair, more mutable than the April
d'Avril, tu pleures de joie, tu ris de	wind, you weep for joy, you laugh
colère, tu m'aimes quand je te fais	with rage, you love me even when I
mal, tu te moques de moi quand je	hurt you, you make fun of me when
suis bon. Tu m'as à peine dit	I am good to you. You hardly even
merci lorsque je t'ai donné le	thanked me when I gave you that
beau collier, mais tu as rougi de	beautiful necklace, but you blushed
plaisir, comme une petite fille, le jour	with pleasure like a little girl, the day
où je t'ai fait cadeau de ce mouchoir	when I gave you that handkerchief as a
et tous disent de toi: "C'est à n'y	present, to which everyone said, "Now
rien comprendre!" Mais je t'ai, un	that I don't understand!" But one day
jour, volé ce mouchoir que tu	I stole that handkerchief, which you'd
venais de presser sur ta bouche fardée.	just pressed to your rouged mouth.
Et, avant que tu ne me l'aies enlevé	And before you managed to scrabble it
d'un coup de griffe, j'ai eu	back from me, I had just enough time
le temps de voir que ta bouche	to see that your mouth had painted
venait d'y peindre, rouge, naïf, dessiné	upon it, red, naïve, designed to delight,
à ravir, simple et pur, le portrait même	simple and pure—the very portrait of
de ton cœur.	your heart.

Poulenc composed a handful of songs by poets he visited only once. Charles d'Orléans (*Priez pour paix*) is from the fifteenth century, Shakespeare (*Fancy*) from the sixteenth, and Malherbe (*Épitaphe*) and Racine (*Hymne*) from the seventeenth. Théodore de Banville (*Pierrot*) is his only nineteenth-century poet. An avowed fan of contemporary poetry, Poulenc stood at some distance from all these earlier writers' work, though the songs are masterfully composed. Among

Colette, photographed by Rogi André, 1947.

contemporaries, Raymond Radiguet (*Paul et Virginie*) was a friend from his youthful years, Jean Anouilh (*Les Chemins de l'amour*) was little more to him than a theater colleague, and Laurence de Beylié was unknown to him until he chanced on her poem "Nuage." None of those songs get anywhere near the virtuosic verve and ebullience of *Le Portrait*, but then there was no one who could compare with the one and only Colette.

The famously bisexual novelist, born in Burgundy to the tax collector Jules-Joseph Colette and his wife Sidonie (later immortalized by Colette as "Sido"), left her carefree provincial environment to seek a meaningful role in Belle Époque Paris. She signed her early work "Willy" (pen name of her first husband, critic Henri Gauthier-Villars, who thus claimed credit for his wife's racy *Claudine* books of 1900–33). In her roles as journalist, critic, and sometime vaudeville performer, Colette sometimes bent society's rules: in 1907 she openly acknowledged her lesbianism (louchely encouraged by Willy) with an onstage kiss with her lover Missy, an act that outraged the public. Refusing to dissemble about something that was central to her emotional well-being, Colette found herself a *cause célèbre*, vilified by many in the establishment but also secretly admired by those with the same inclinations who were, as yet, afraid to confess them. Marcel Proust was an admirer, and the young Poulenc probably was as well. Colette's talent as a writer and her irresistible personality had turned her into a national treasure by the time Poulenc came to meet her (they were no doubt introduced by Jean Cocteau, one of her most ardent fans since his opium-smoking days).

The author was twenty-six years older than Poulenc, but she was reaching her peak at the very time Poulenc was emerging on to the musical scene. Awarded the Légion d'Honneur in 1920, she published her novel *Chéri* the same year, which was immediately adapted for the stage. Colette played the role of Lea, the older woman who has an affair with "Chéri" (Fred Peloux), a much younger man. This scenario had a real-life echo in Colette's passion for Bertrand, the sixteen-year-old son of her second husband, Henry de Jouvenel. At the age of fifty, with the publication of *Le Blé en herbes*, "Colette Willy" became simply "Colette." In

1925 she met Maurice Goudeket, another younger man, who became her third husband. And in the same year, she provided Maurice Ravel with the libretto for *L'Enfant et les sortilèges*, a text she had originally written for her daughter Bel-Gazou; it was reputedly this opera that effected Poulenc's reconversion to Ravel's music, which had left him cold ever since his unfortunate interview with the composer in 1917 (see Outline for that year).

Colette was thus a literary lion and a huge personality in French literature during most of Poulenc's working life. His relationship with her seems to have been closest in 1931, the year she published the semi-autobiographical *Ces Plaisirs . . .* , her favorite book, later to be republished as *Le Pur et l'impur*. In that summer, plans appear to have been afoot for author and composer to collaborate on a film, a project that never got anywhere—perhaps because she had suggested setting the film in the 1880s, not a favorite epoch for Poulenc in musical terms.[130] On 20 November 1932 Poulenc gave a scintillating dinner party at Noizay, where the guests included the Princesse de Polignac, Colette and Maurice Goudeket (not yet her husband), their friend Violet Trefusis (a decade or so after her stormy liaison with Vita Sackville-West), and Georges and Nora Auric. Earlier that year Poulenc had entertained the Prokofievs and Arthur Rubinstein. What other French composer in his early thirties could have dreamed of being able to host such glittering social occasions in his own recently acquired country house? Colette's pleasure at being at Noizay is expressed in an entry in the visitor's book, typical of her prose style: "A thought? ["Une pensée?"] Oh! Not here! One feels far too much at ease."[131]

Poulenc unexpectedly received the poem for *Le Portrait* in the early months of 1938. By this time, Colette had settled into her apartment on the first floor of the Palais-Royal at 9, rue de Beaujolais. While her fame as a writer was never in doubt, she had also become an esteemed theater critic, and *Claudine à l'école* had been filmed. She was beginning to show early signs of the pitiless arthritis that would cripple her, confining her to bed for ever longer periods.

> *For years Colette had been promising me some poems. One day, sitting by her bedside with [actress] Thérèse Dorny and [violinist] Hélène Jourdan-Morhange, I implored her for some. "Here take this," she said to me, laughing, as she threw me a quite large gauze handkerchief on which this pretty poem was transcribed in facsimile. I must confess that my music expresses quite inadequately my admiration for Colette.[132]*

In her Palais-Royal bedroom, Colette would reach out to a bedside shelf to read to visitors from the voluminous works of Balzac, which she knew her way around better than anyone else. Unfortunately the gauze handkerchief is not among the Poulenc artifacts that have survived.

An unpublished letter to Poulenc in the Bibliothèque Nationale indicates that Colette was interested in hearing a performance of *Le Portrait*, but we don't know whether she ever did; her lack of mobility might have prevented her from attending a Bernac recital. Poulenc clearly had it in mind to issue a small collection of Colette songs, as he had already done for Vilmorin, Éluard, and Apollinaire:[133] "In no time at all," she assured him, "we will decide about the subject matter of the two other poems." The project was never to be realized, just as the idea of a collaboration on a film never went any further than ideas exchanged by letter. Nevertheless, the two artists remained friends, if not intimates. Her pleasure in his company is expressed in a note that deliberately misquotes lines from the singing actor Louis-Jacques Boucot: "Ah! Quell'joi', quell'joi', quell'joi', / J'ai Francis Poulenc chez moi! / (chanson de Boucot) / Je vous embrasse. A vendredi. Merci. / Colette." (Oh what a joy, what a joy, what a joy, I have Francis Poulenc in my home! I embrace you. Until Friday. Thank you.)

Bernac points out that *Le Portrait* is "not one of Poulenc's most beautiful works," but he would also have to agree that it is a fine setting of a poem that is vicious and tender by turns, unsurprisingly feline in view of the writer's celebrated passion for cats. Poulenc felt free to make a musical portrait of Colette, or perhaps of one of the many tempestuous relationships that she had pursued throughout her life with both men and women; this writer was both imperiously demanding and insecure, adorable but dangerous when crossed. Bernac gave the song's first performance in 1938, but despite "quand je suis bon" (the adjectival ending signaling a male narrator), the poem seems written in Colette's voice: a woman writing of another woman in a mood of love-stricken exasperation.

The marking *Très violent et emporté* is the key to the interpretation of a song that hurtles forward in a musical tidal wave of passion and jealousy, but also contains passages where the rigid tempo yields to a kind of musing capriciousness. This is particularly noticeable in the chromaticism of bars 26 to 31, where the downward slide of the piano writing and the descent in the vocal line at "Mais je t'ai, un jour, volé" are exceptional; as is the suddenly high-in-the-stave, erotic setting of "bouche" in bar 39. The text describes the paradoxical behavior of the beloved in a similar way to the (very different) hymn to Nusch Éluard, *Nous avons fait la nuit* from *Tel jour telle nuit*. One song is a mirror image of the other: the Éluard, with enormous lyrical calm, describes the love of soulmates, in this case heterosexual; *Le Portrait* reflects the emotional turbulence and tension of a homosexual relationship teetering on the edge. In 1954, the year of Colette's death, the composer was to experience this kind of torment for himself (see "The Crisis of 1954").

∘ ∘ ∘

FP93 Concerto in G Minor for Organ, Strings, and Timpani, April–August 1938

∘ ∘ ∘

FP94 *Deux Poèmes de Guillaume Apollinaire*
Composed in Noizay, May 1938 (ii); and in Anost, August 1938 (i)
[*Reine Bénard, Georges Auric*; Rouart, Lerolle]
Literary source: Guillaume Apollinaire (1880–1918), *Il y a* (Paris: Albert Messein, 1925), (i) pp. 84–85, (ii) pp. 106–7

(i) *Dans le jardin d'Anna*
(ii) *Allons plus vite*

(i) *Dans le jardin d'Anna (In Anna's Garden)*
No key signature; $\frac{4}{4}$ with changes to $\frac{6}{4}, \frac{3}{4}, \frac{5}{4}$; *Très animé* ♩ = 100

Certes si nous avions vécu en l'an dix-sept cent soixante	One thing is for sure. If we'd lived in the year 1760
Est-ce bien la date que vous déchiffrez, Anna, sur ce banc de pierre	Isn't that the date Anna you see carved in this stone bench
Et que par malheur j'eusse été allemand,	And if I'd had the misfortune to be German,
Mais que par bonheur j'eusse été près de vous	And the good fortune to be sitting next to you
Nous aurions parlé d'amour de façon imprécise	We would have spoken of love in rather vague terms
Presque toujours en français	Almost exclusively in French
Et pendue éperdûment à mon bras	And clinging devotedly to my arm
Vous m'auriez écouté vous parler de Pythagoras	You'd have listened to me talking about Pythagoras
En pensant aussi au café qu'on prendrait	While actually thinking about the coffee we'd be drinking
Dans une demi-heure.	In half an hour's time.
Et l'automne eût été pareil à cet automne	And that autumn would have been the same as this autumn
Que l'épine-vinette et les pampres couronnent	Bursting with barberries and vine leaves
Et brusquement parfois j'eusse salué très bas	And now and then I would have bowed brusquely and low to
De nobles dames grasses et langoureuses	Various large and languorous noblewomen

J'aurais dégusté lentement et tout seul	I would have sipped slowly all alone
Pendant de longues soirées	For long evenings on end
Le tokay épais ou la malvoisie	Full-bodied tokay or malmsey
J'aurais mis mon habit espagnol	I would have put on my Spanish coat
Pour aller sur la route par laquelle	And gone out on to the road by which
Arrive dans son vieux carrosse	In her old carriage
Ma grand'mère qui se refuse	My grandmother always arrives
à comprendre l'allemand	She who refuses to understand
	German
J'aurais écrit des vers pleins de	I'd have written verse after verse
mythologie	replete with mythology
Sur vos seins la vie champêtre et sur	About your breasts pastoral life and
les dames	the ladies
Des alentours	Of round about
J'aurais souvent cassé ma canne	I'd often have smashed my stick
Sur le dos d'un paysan	On some peasant's back
J'aurais aimé entendre de la musique	I'd have loved to listen to music
en mangeant	Eating ham the while
Du jambon	
J'aurais juré en allemand je vous le jure	I swear I'd have sworn in German
Lorsque vous m'auriez surpris	When you caught me kissing full on
embrassant à pleine bouche	the mouth
Cette servante rousse	That red-headed serving girl
Vous m'auriez pardonné dans le bois	You'd have forgiven me in the
aux myrtilles	blueberry wood
J'aurais fredonné un moment	For a moment I'd have hummed a tune
Puis nous aurions écouté longtemps	And then we'd have listened long to
les bruits du crépuscule	the sounds of the twilight

The poem, a dizzying profusion of events conjured by Apollinaire's fertile and quirky imagination, was written in the autumn of 1901. During a visit to Germany in the company of the Vicomtesse de Milhau, the poet fell in love with Annie Playden, English governess to the vicomtesse's children. Guillaume and Annie had no hope of making a life together (their on-off relationship would end unhappily in London three years later). As if in defiance of this reality, the poet wrote a kind of fantasy riff inspired by a day in Alsace when the lovers had found themselves sitting on a park bench engraved with the date 1760. In that year Louis XV was on the French throne, Frederick the Great was king of Prussia, and Alsace, as always, was caught between the two ancient enemies. In this scenario the park is privately owned, and the Polish-Russian-Italian Guillaume from Paris is not afraid to set himself up as a linguistic anomaly, a German-speaking aristocrat of 1760 in a *département* ruled by France, with a grandmother who refuses to understand German. In his imagined marriage with Anna, the couple switch between the two languages, favoring French (also the preference in Potsdam of Frederick the Great, an avid admirer of Voltaire).

Apollinaire's imagined German background allows him a certain stereotypical pedantry: he lectures Anna on Pythagoras, and pens verses in the manner of the Anacreontic poets popular in eighteenth-century Germany. An added layer of irony is that the poet was visiting this region, and writing his poem, at a time (1901) when Alsace was in German hands following the disastrous rout of the French during the Franco-Prussian War of 1870–71. Germany's defeat in the First World War returned Alsace to French hands; Hitler's victory over the French made it German once more, until it reverted permanently to French possession in 1945. The poem is a mixture, if not quite a clash, of French and German cultures.

In setting this exceptionally complex lyric, Poulenc came of age as a composer of extended mélodies. He confessed to attempting to set it as early as 1931 (almost certainly as part of *Quatre Poèmes de Guillaume Apollinaire*), when he composed music for the poem's conclusion as well as the brief Spanish episode (bb. 36–39). But *"the rest would not come. As in all poems that concern an enumeration of mental images, a tempo that is continuous and strict is essential. It is this that I had not understood in 1931. I put this poem on one side vowing to return to it one day."*[134]

In May 1938 he discarded everything he had already composed seven years earlier and started fresh. About this work Bernac is more than usually eloquent:

> The poem has an extravagant degree of verve and fantasy. It displays by turns irony, tenderness, parody, it is bombastic, farcical, erotic, down to earth, poetic—all this without transitions, in phrases that follow one another in a whirl of images. It would be impossible to follow such a diversity of contrasting nuances more closely and with greater accuracy than Poulenc has done. This means that the interpreters on their part must prove to have the virtuosity of an acrobat in the rapidity and the abruptness of all these contrasts of expression, and these contrarieties of vocal color, which must never cause a change in the implacable tempo in which Poulenc never accords the singer the saving grace of a bar's rest.[135]

Poulenc somehow manages to make this highly episodic song hang together to enchanting effect. His different responses make the poet's castles in the air sound casually, and conversationally, erected on the spot. But he ensures that the musical segments, sometimes composed months apart, are sewn together to make a tight whole.

For the first four bars, the narrator adopts a brusque tone, staccato and in dry recitative style, as he outlines to Anna the rules of the make-believe game they are about to play. This is still Apollinaire speaking in 1901, before he has progressed too far into his assumed character of 1760. The staccato accompaniment seems to emphasize a certain Germanic didacticism, the poet becoming increasingly "in character." With "Nous aurions parlé d'amour," the music begins to flow in a manner that is *almost* poetic, the left hand retaining its staccato articulation: here, Poulenc inserts the marking *monotone* to discourage emotional commitment in a passage that Bernac believes calls for "feigned indifference."

At bars 10–13 ("Et pendue éperdûment"), in stark contrast, the music suddenly becomes lyrical and *forte*, as poet and composer warm to their theme. The passage displays all the confidence of a *grand seigneur* sure of his place in the world, with a touch of braggadocio. Anna is cast as an admiring "milady" who is too pretty to appreciate the significance of Pythagoras (to be fair to the poet, this patronizing attitude toward women is part of his portrait of the Zeitgeist). The next section ("En pensant aussi au café") is marked *Avec charme*, and the dynamic is suddenly *piano*. The singer, having shown off the breadth of his voice, is now challenged to the intimacy of *mezzo voce*; the idea of taking coffee in half an hour suggests the habitual daily refinements of life for the eighteenth-century bourgeoisie.

An interlude of seven bars (17–23, "Et l'automne eût été pareil") extols the beauties of autumn in sinuous music in $\frac{3}{4}$ time—an aside by the modern poet, who comments on the eternity of nature and the seasons. After this calm respite, Poulenc embarks on a gradual vocal ascent that is characteristic of the song, cleverly conveying the idea of a story being invented on the hoof, and growing taller with each bar. The courtly and ceremonial requirements of life in the eighteenth century require the narrator to bow and scrape to "large and languorous noblewomen," and the sheer indolence of the spoiled aristocracy is depicted in the extended, mocking setting of that "langoureuses"—one of several moments when the composer allows the poet's own character to peep through the disguise.

Bars 29–35 (*Très expressif*) suggest the narrator's solitary drinking of sweet and rich wines, perhaps an addiction to be concealed. This tokay is an Alsatian pinot gris, not Schubert's favored Hungarian tipple; the confusing term "malvoisie," historically the malmsey in which the Duke of Clarence drowned, could apply to many wines from different regions, including Madeira. The piano writing here sounds furtive, and the effulgent harmonies and arpeggios in G-flat major indicate intoxication. Then two bars (36–37) briefly evoke the thrumming of a Spanish guitar—perhaps the disguise of a Spanish cloak is prudent when visiting those "dames / Des alentours" mentioned a few lines later. His querulous grandmother riding in her old-fashioned carriage brings three dry and tetchy bars (38–40) that suggest dissatisfied finger-pointing and scolding on her part.

The family confrontation ends with a $\frac{5}{4}$ bar that is suddenly suspended in favor of a lyrical $\frac{4}{4}$, with another direction of *Avec charme* (bb. 41–47, beginning "J'aurais écrit des vers"), where the narrator expresses his vanity as a writer. In 1760 he would likely be writing verses in the manner of the Anacreontic poets, in praise of Anna's breasts and the pastoral life: nymphs and shepherds perhaps, or Daphnis and Chloë. Mention of other women of the region occasions a most unusual (for Poulenc) vocal trill on "alentours" and an equally unusual pianistic upward slide in rising fourths, as if the pianist's right hand were making its forbidden way up a woman's leg (and we assume it is not Anna's). The composer is attempting to convey something roguish here, true to Apollinaire's fabled promiscuity, that goes beyond the written words.

Two bars (at "J'aurais souvent cassé ma canne / Sur le dos d'un paysan") depict the casual cruelty of an *ancien régime* aristocrat, and the subservient nature of his wretched underlings. Both hands of the pianist are placed in the bass clef, as if he or she were bending to the punishing task. It is to Poulenc's credit that they pass by so easily in musical terms that we are somehow made not to take it too seriously; this is, after all, mere fantasy on Apollinaire's part, and in reality he would not have been tempted by such brutal behavior. At "J'aurais aimé entendre de la musique," Poulenc briefly evokes a vapid, rococo musical style anchored in an unchanging *faux naïf* F major, perhaps the shortest vignette of all, and akin to Stravinsky's wrong-note arrangements in *Pulcinella* of the music of Pergolesi. It is followed by a swift musical depiction of gluttony: ham quickly and inelegantly gobbled (more German than French).

Halfway through bar 51, the chromatically ascending stealth of "J'aurais juré" suggests post-prandial dirty work afoot, an approaching climax and an excited muttering. Then in two bars of forbidden and passionate (as well as *fortissimo*) canoodling, the narrator, in the manner of the count in *The Marriage of Figaro* and with the same sense of entitlement, kisses the red-haired serving wench full on the mouth. He is caught red-handed by Anna (Poulenc may have drawn here on childhood memories of having discovered the family cook entertaining her boyfriend in the basement kitchen). With a half-spoken, unaccompanied "Cette servante rousse," the girl is waved away. The song now more or less comes to a standstill—a moment of sheer black comedy—then the piano continues (strictly in the same tempo) with a discordant plunge of a ninth followed by a sequence of eight notes frozen in their tracks, as if the narrator is momentarily disoriented by guilt and embarrassment.

It is, however, part of the poet's fantasy to assume that anything he chooses to do would have Anna's obedient and loving understanding. Annie Playden would have turned out to be a more difficult partner in real life. In the poem, at least, Apollinaire is anything but repentant. There is a touch of wheedling in the music for "Vous m'auriez pardonné," and the cool insouciance of "J'aurais fredonné" suggests that he is now bored with this little incident and it's time to move on. By bars 58–61 he gets back in his stride surprisingly quickly, cajoling his way back into Anna's affections by asking for (and apparently receiving) her forgiveness. That Poulenc's music exactly conveys, within in a few bars, an entire world of male fantasy, followed by an assumption (via a musical shrug) that bad behavior brings no consequences for rich and powerful men, is astonishing.

All the poem's hectic activity has been planned to lead up to the quietus (À l'aise, très calme) of the marvelous peroration of bars 62–72, where spikiness and verve are smoothed into a nocturnal postlude ("Puis nous aurions écouté longtemps les bruits du crépuscule")—music of ravishing tenderness and assuagement, music to be shared. Bernac actually advises that there should be "a little slackening of tempo" at this point. Sumptuous harmonic vistas are now conjured that exist nowhere else in the song, the rest having been far too fractured to settle into any tonality or landscape. Poulenc creates here an atmosphere of twilight that rivals the masterly coda of Ravel's Le Grillon. As he had been practicing Ravel's Histoires naturelles for recitals with Bernac, it can surely be no coincidence that both these evocative passages are in D-flat major.

The piano's lambent sixteenth notes continue for two and a half bars after the vocal line comes to an end. By this time, the calm assurance of D-flat major has turned into a minor-key variant. The two forlorn and almost comic bars of chords and notes that end the piece, first smooth then pianissimo spiky octaves, are vintage Poulenc 1931 (rather than 1938). (There is a similarly laconic ending to the 1931 Apollinaire setting 1904. In both cases the meaning is: "Oh well, wouldn't it be nice if all this were all true—but it isn't, and tant pis.") Stylistic tics and borrowings notwithstanding, there is nothing like Dans le jardin d'Anna anywhere else in the French song repertoire.

Poulenc composed the song in the Burgundian town of Anost, his holiday retreat on a number of occasions. As we shall see, the views and sunsets of this region were to play their part in a great Éluard song written in the same month, but in the case of Anna he was thinking of neither Burgundy nor Alsace: "In spite of my eighth part of Alsatian blood (my paternal grandfather came from Colmar) I did not once think of Alsace while writing Le Jardin d'Anna. On the contrary the last lines evoke for me the end of a September day somewhere in Seine-et-Marne, toward Chartrette, with a view of the river and the forest of Fontainebleau."[136]

(ii) Allons plus vite (Get a Move On!)
No key signature (A minor/major); $\frac{4}{4}$; Très calme ♩ = 56

Et le soir vient et les lys meurent
Regarde ma douleur beau ciel qui me
l'envoies
Une nuit de mélancolie

And the evening falls and the lilies die
Look at my sadness you lovely sky
that sends it to me
A night of melancholy

Enfant souris ô sœur écoute
Pauvres marchez sur la grande-route
Ô menteuse forêt qui surgis à ma voix
Les flammes qui
brûlent les âmes

Smile my child, listen my sister,
Poor people, stick to the high road
Oh forest of lies which at my bidding
Summons up flames which
burn the soul

Sur le boulevard de Grenelle
Les ouvriers et les patrons
Arbres de mai cette dentelle
Ne fais donc pas le fanfaron
Allons plus vite nom de Dieu
Allons plus vite

On the boulevard de Grenelle
The workers and the bosses
Maytime trees like lace
Stop showing off
Get a move on for God's sake
Get a move on

Tous les poteaux télégraphiques
Viennent là-bas le long du quai
Sur son sein notre République
A mis ce bouquet de muguet
Qui poussait dru le long du quai

All the telegraph poles
Stretch down to the quayside
On its breast, our Republic
Placed this sprig of lily-of-the-valley
Which grew thick and fast along the
quayside

Allons plus vite nom de Dieu
Allons plus vite

Get a move on for God's sake
Get a move on

La bouche en cœur Pauline honteuse
Les ouvriers et les patrons

Simpering shameful Pauline,
The workers and the bosses

Oui-dà oui-dà belle endormeuse
Ton frère
Allons plus vite nom de Dieu
Allons plus vite

Oh yes oh yes you lovely temptress
It's your brother
Get a move on for God's sake
Get a move on

"Poulenc liked nothing better than crossing into forbidden territories, toppling values, turning things upside down and head over heels, inserting several vulgar elements into a concerto, or putting Apollinaire's 'Allons plus vite' into music that expresses both high and low, passing from lilies to the gutter."[137] Hervé Lacombe could also have added how delighted the composer was with the sudden topsy-turvy turnaround of the poem—a lofty Baudelairian idiom changing, at the beginning of the third verse, to the language of the street chanson. But it was Poulenc's genius to have spotted that shift and used it to his musical advantage.

Allons plus vite is the perfect foil for *Dans le jardin d'Anna*. Here Apollinaire is not a twenty-one-year-old almost idealistically in love with Annie Playden but rather a military veteran with a head wound received at the Front and a seasoned and promiscuous lover of women. With a change of gender concerning lovers, the poem chimes with Poulenc's own experiences. Poet and composer share a profound understanding of that initially exciting but ultimately melancholy search for sexual gratification with strangers: "*There are few poems that I 'hankered after' more intensely and for longer. As early as 1935 I made a sketch, subsequently burnt and, thank goodness, totally forgotten. . . . I have so often loitered at night in Paris that I think I know better than any other musician the rhythm of a felt slipper along the pavement on a May evening.*"[138] Poulenc's honesty here is remarkable, even if it is far from certain that he intended his confessional words to reach the world at large.

Apollinaire was sexually avaricious as well as a published and celebrated pornographer. His bedroom interests were more or less mainstream (with certain arcane and sometimes sadomasochistic tributaries), but sexual addiction admits no boundaries of gender or proclivity, and Poulenc knew at first hand what the poet was talking about: the sense of incompleteness, the futile hope that yet another chance encounter will lift depression and heal age-old wounds—the "flames which burn souls" framed by the most beautiful of locations, Paris in early summer. And here another aspect of this richly evocative poem needs to be examined.

The presence of lilies ("lys" and "muguet") is no accident. The first of May (in a tradition dating back to 1560 during the reign of Charles IX) was a day to celebrate spring, nature, and love, and to give a bunch of lilies as a token of affection. Hundreds of stalls were set up on Parisian streets where lilies, picked in the woods outside the city or even gathered up from the banks of the Seine, were for sale. The "Arbres de mai" (verse 3) signify a mast or Maypole, traditionally decorated with lilies—telegraph poles were adapted to this purpose. The opening line, describing the wilting of lilies that had been fresh earlier in the day, symbolizes faded hopes, the death of romantic idealism, the loneliness and melancholy of those who no longer expect to find a partner. But by 1917, the year the poem was written, the lily had also long been a symbol of workers and workers' rights. And on 1 May, not yet a public holiday, processions of workers ("Les ouvriers et les patrons") added to the mêlée of humanity out on the streets.

On his nocturnal forays, Apollinaire was a different kind of hunter from Poulenc. There was almost always a woman in his life; the long-suffering Marie Laurencin was one, but what he sought could be had for a price, and he would have respected that working girls had to make a living. Poulenc, on the other hand (as far as anyone knows), did not use prostitutes. For him, the excitement was in the chase. What he needed was usually available for free, although the search could be a lengthy and even dangerous one.

> *If the sexual melancholy of the poem is not understood, it is useless to sing the song. For Apollinaire and me the boulevard de Grenelle is as rare and poetic as the banks of the Ganges are for others. To tell the truth I was not specifically thinking of the boulevard de Grenelle while I was writing the music, but of its twin brother the boulevard de la Chapelle, which I passed through on so many evenings when I lived in Montmartre. I imagined Pauline at the door of the Hôtel Molière. Czechoslovakian prostitutes are seen there in shiny rubber boots, for a hundred sous.*[139]

In 1938, having destroyed his first attempts at setting the poem, Poulenc discovered the Parisian, Maurice Chevalier–like, A major music for "Sur le boulevard de Grenelle" (b. 14). In cases like these, he jealously preserved the original tonality of any fragment he had composed, creating new material around it. Thus the song begins in A minor, and the shifting to the magical regions of A major mirrors Schubert's partiality to the same key change. Despite the slow and calm tempo, the music's solitary quest is driven ineluctably forward by a ceaseless movement of ambulatory eighth notes. The whole of the accompaniment is powered by these eighths, often phrased away in drooping pairs, in a movement that is never fast but seems nevertheless *driven*; such quiet but determined propulsion seems to me an apt equivalent for the verb "draguer" (not used in the poem), encompassing fishing, dredging, and chatting or picking people up. The opening of the extremely expressive vocal line suggests a kind of energized lethargy, as if thinking, "Here we go on another expedition": the seesaw intervals of "Regarde ma douleur" artfully contrast with the single-note incantation of "Une nuit de mélancolie." One of my favorite moments of Poulencian word-setting has long been the bar with upbeat containing "Les flammes qui brûlent les âmes" (13), a phrase I associate with the life of this composer.

The music then, as Poulenc puts it, *"comes to earth on a Parisian pavement,"*[140] and the effect in the right singer's hands can be dazzling, with a hint of a Parisian accent on "Grenelle" (something Bernac does wonderfully well). In entering into the supposedly sleazy and popular part of the song, Poulenc's markings ensure that his interpreters do not resort to camp or send-up: the music has to be taken seriously, accompanied *Dans un doux halo de Pédales* and sung in a manner *Ému et doucement poétique* (Moved and gently poetic). The poet has moved into a milieu he clearly knows well, with the "ouvriers" and the "patrons"—their day of political marching over, all searching for relaxation of one kind or another. At

"Arbres de mai cette dentelle" (b. 16), the rush of musical adrenaline, with *crescendo* and climbing tessitura, is entirely appropriate to the chase.

The brusque instances of "Allons plus vite," first occurring in bar 18, then in 20, 26–27, and the final bar, are something of a mystery. My first impression on hearing them was that a gruff policeman is speaking as he moves the girls along, but then I remembered this was a Parisian poem, not one from a less tolerant London. With the heightening of tessitura and dynamic, it seems that the narrator wants to bring his search to an end as soon as possible. Perhaps he has been caught up in a transaction that is not going as quickly as planned. Pauline the prostitute, "La bouche en cœur" (her lips painted in the heart shape of a Cupid's bow), is introduced in a two-bar vignette where the baritone, singing at the top of his range, sounds strangely menacing. We are not to forget that many female prostitutes were really transvestites, and Poulenc's falsetto here appears to encompass that possibility (not an observation, please, to encourage singers to imitate a drag queen at this point). With the intoned words "Oui-dà oui-dà," sung with a glissando between the notes, we sense an immense weariness and cynicism about the whole tawdry charivari. For a moment a third-party commentator seems to be looking in on the commercialization of human lust with more than a touch of disgust. We might also detect in these words, as well as in their musical response, a hint of self-loathing.

At the end, perhaps Pauline has lingered a moment too long to talk with her pimp (whom she passes off as her brother, to the incredulity of her prospective client; Poulenc marks the words "Ton frère" *incrédule*). "Come on," the poet says, "*come on!*" Any erotic expectations have been nullified by the imperatives of desire and the brutality of the street. In the closing four bars the oscillations in the piano between A and B-flat, A and C-natural, punched out deep in the bass, are ominous. So much for your romantic dreams, splutters the final, low eighth note—a peremptory and brutal staccato. In a July 1939 letter to Nadia Boulanger, Poulenc revealingly insisted that it was significant that *Allons plus vite* and *Vinea electa* (the second of the *Quatre Motets pour un temps de pénitence* FP97) first saw the light of day together.[141] When Poulenc directed that parts of this song should be performed in a *halo de Pédales,* was he perhaps slyly illustrating the same duality to a group of admirers, less high-minded and more in the know, than the saintly Nadia?[142]

THE SEXUAL MILIEU OF FRANCIS POULENC

As far as the documents in the *Correspondance* are concerned, Poulenc discovered sex, as well as romance and love, at about the age of thirty. There is no mention of any sexual or emotive attachment up to that time;

and then suddenly, in July 1928, he asked Alice Ardoin to help persuade Raymonde Linossier to accept his proposal of marriage.[143] Nothing came of it, and Linossier died unexpectedly eighteen months later. It has been suggested that she was aware of Poulenc's homosexuality, and no more approved of it than did her close friend Erik Satie.[144] Then in May and June 1929, Poulenc wrote two letters to Richard Chanlaire expressing intense sexual and romantic feelings.[145] It becomes clear, however, that Chanlaire found it impossible to envisage a committed relationship with Poulenc. The conventional wisdom has it that after the failure of these two different attempts to find a long-lasting and settled *modus vivendi*, Poulenc discovered his homosexuality (as if the Chanlaire affair had been a first) and embarked on a promiscuous lifestyle. Even admitting this much about the composer's private life represents a fairly recent take on events that had long remained hidden.

Yet such a theory of a sudden and late development seems unconvincing. During the 1920s, the already extremely *mondain* Poulenc was in close contact with Jean Cocteau (who conducted well-known affairs with numerous men) and with the homosexual circle around Sergei Diaghilev (notorious for his own succession of favorites). In a letter written in late 1923 to Diaghilev, Poulenc addressed him as "*Altesse*" and mentioned that a member of the ballet company "*always seems to have a hot backside. This morning I helped him do his pirouettes.*"[146] In 1925 he spent two weeks near Cannes as part of a gay house party, and there is evidence of other high-jinks. If Poulenc, as Henri Sauguet asserts in his 1990 memoirs,[147] loved going to drag balls in the early 1920s, if he relished dancing with strangers *en travesty* (revealing his identity only at the end of the evening), how can we believe he was inexperienced about sex and unaware of his homosexuality during this decade? Do we accept that *Les Biches* (1924), with its witty, urbane, sophisticated music, was

Marcel Royer, Uncle "Papoum," brother of Poulenc's mother Jenny Royer; a silhouette in the possession of the family.

composed by a virgin? Poulenc himself later claimed that the ballet was indebted to "*the erotic atmosphere of my twenties,*"[148] its joyfulness not a matter of love, but of pleasure.[149]

Poulenc's well-loved Uncle Papoum was fascinated with lowlife locales (as they would be considered by the likes of Poulenc's upright father) and fostered his nephew's interest in music-hall performances. His lifestyle and tastes were almost certainly influential on the composer from an early age. Shortly after Papoum's death, in a letter to Stéphane Audel, Poulenc referred to his uncle as "*mon vieil ange*" (my old angel) and confided that it had caused him pain to "*reconcile my two beings: before and after the death of Papoum.*"[150] (Strong words from a nephew who never penned a word about the loss of his father.) Still, such a lively boy as Francis, living largely unsupervised in early twentieth-century Paris, scarcely needed a family member to show him the way, even if that had been the case in more than a cultural sense. He was adventurous and gregarious by nature, and lonely as very gifted children often are. He admitted to coming to a cynical understanding with the family cook, who was no doubt required to keep an eye on him (and he on her) but who craved privacy for her own sexual dalliances: two rogues of different ages conspiring to pull the wool over the eyes of the Poulenc parents.

The psychological problems and upheavals of Poulenc's later years suggest that experiences pleasurable, dislocating, and guilt-inducing all at the same time may have taken place early on:[151]

> *Incredibly young I haunted music halls and from 1912, when I was thirteen years old, I savored the cherries in eau-de-vie from the Petit Casino. . . . My parents often gave me tickets for concerts but it required incredible trickery to get me into the café-concert. A pen sold to a friend at the Lycée Condorcet assured me of entry to the Eldorado and to the Scala* [music halls in the none too salubrious boulevard de Strasbourg], *and once—the blasphemy of it!—thanks to the complicity of our cook, I was able to sell a volume of Beethoven piano sonatas to a book dealer by the banks of the Seine, which later enabled me to applaud Mistinguett at the Folies Bergère.*[152]

When Francis was not roaming the seedier *quartiers* of Paris without his parents' knowledge, he was on an equally loose leash as a frequent guest in his grandparents' house in Nogent-sur-Marne, where Parisian working-class life at leisure was transplanted every weekend to the Île de la Beauté and Île d'Amour. These magic islands of fantasy, the raunchier

A postcard of Nogent-sur-Marne at the time of Poulenc's childhood.

Disneyland of the time, and the men who frequented them in search of hook-ups (mostly but not exclusively with women), were within easy reach of a boy with an almost uncanny knowingness and *joie de vivre*. If his obsession with well-built working men started early on, the type never changed for him; his lovers had to be his social inferiors.

After the First World War, as Christopher Moore observes, "homosexuality was seen to undermine the patriotic duty of the French to repopulate the country in the wake of the massive losses in the trenches."[153] In a distinctly anti-homosexual milieu, there would have been too many people potentially shocked by Poulenc's secret preference: his sister and brother-in-law (who offered him lodging for a long period of time), friends like Raymonde Linossier, and his teacher Charles Koechlin among them. All other members of Les Six were heterosexual, as were Apollinaire, Éluard, Picasso, Satie, Viñes, and Roussel, not to mention his musical gods Debussy and Stravinsky (the latter, according to recent revelations, may have been bisexual). In the company of Cocteau and in the Diaghilev circle, it would have been possible for him to relax somewhat; it is doubtful, however, if he shared much about himself with these colleagues, being as yet unsure about what impact "coming out" would have on his career—his music being more important to him than any other aspect of his life.

Secrecy was one of Poulenc's default settings, in personal matters—one lover concealed from the other, a secret daughter (see Outline for 1946, p. 245)—and in his business dealings (publishers and promoters skillfully played off against another). Whether from 1930 or much earlier, sex with a succession of strangers became a growing need, exciting in the forbidden nature of the hunt, dispiriting and enervating after the event. His proposal to Linossier was perhaps a desperate attempt to engineer a situation that would break the habit, a way of reversing a life already running out of control. The ballet *Aubade*, the crucial work of the time, suggests an unsatisfactory amatory existence rather than simply a sexual awakening. The composer longed for a normal life, and he was one of legions of gay men who have seen marriage as the problem solver it rarely turns out to be. His emotionally unreciprocated relationship with Richard Chanlaire was surely another attempt to put an already chaotic house in order, rather than a virginal experience.

But although both efforts failed in spectacular fashion, something crucial indeed happened in 1929–30: the closet door in his highly compartmentalized life was partially opened, and Poulenc accepted something fundamental about his nature (and shared the fact with increasing frequency with his friends).[154] For the rest of his life, Linossier took on an almost talismanic position: she represented the golden dream of another kind of existence from the one to which he was seemingly condemned. And the Chanlaire friendship—on the composer's side passionate and involved, controlling and self-abasing, ultimately unsatisfying—set a pattern replicated a number of times in his life, a few islands of elusive and obsessive love floating within an ocean of sexual adventures. The unraveling consequences of the most turbulent relationship of his life reached their peak in a serious breakdown that brought Poulenc's life to a standstill (see "The Crisis of 1954," p. 383).

For Poulenc, there always remained the fantasy of a peaceful harbor, a love nest he could share with someone special. Noizay was too busily frequented a place ever to serve as a hideaway for him and Raymond Destouches (see Outline, 1931), but he found one temporarily in the final phase of his life: at a house in Bagnols-en-Forêt, in the south of France, which his lover Louis Gautier built with his own hands in 1959 (p. 364). Far less is known about the household routine Poulenc helped finance for his daughter Marie-Ange and her mother and grandmother. With this arrangement, he apparently found another kind of fleeting stability, one that gave him the illusion of continuity and normality—and one that was kept safe and concealed from the gay world he otherwise inhabited. There are many unpublished letters that bear witness to his playing out the role of an indulgent godfather, a family man by proxy.[155] His role as closet father was utterly typical of the secretive and complex nature of Poulenc's personal life.

FP95 *Priez pour paix* (*Pray for Peace*)

Composed in Noizay, 29 September 1938

[No dedication; Rouart, Lerolle]

Literary source: Charles d'Orléans (1394–1465), *Le Figaro*, 29 September 1938.[156] The song is printed with modern French text.

C minor; $\frac{6}{4}$; *Très lent, très calme.* Printed metronome mark of $\downarrow$ = 66 should be 60.[157]

Priez pour paix doulce Vierge Marie,	Pray for peace, sweet Virgin Mary
Royne des cieulx et du monde maîstresse,	Queen of the heavens and mistress of the world
Faictes prier par vostre courtoisie	By your courtesy have all the Saints
Saints et saintes et prenez vostre adresse	Pray, and address your son, beseeching his Highness
Vers vostre Fils requerrant sa haultesse	
Qu'il lui plaise son peuple regarder	To deign to look on his people
Que de son sang a voulu racheter,	Whom he chose to redeem with his blood,
En deboutant guerre qui tout desvoye;	Banishing war, which ruins everything;
De prières ne vous vueillez lasser	Do not cease your prayers
Priez pour paix, priez pour paix le vray trésor de joye.	Pray for peace, pray for peace The true treasure of joy.

Such was the international tension at the time of the Munich crisis (September 1938) that the daily Parisian newspaper *Le Figaro* ran a regular column on its second page entitled "Les Prières pour la paix." And the precarious nature of the political situation is underlined by the fact that when Poulenc discovered "Priez pour paix" there, he set it to music that same day, not at all his usual modus operandi. (That Poulenc was a daily reader of *Le Figaro* in the first place tells us that his political viewpoints, such as they were, leaned toward the conservative right rather than the socialist left.) On the following day, 30 September, Prime Minister Neville Chamberlain flew back to England from Germany with a piece of paper signed by Hitler, and proclaimed "peace in our time." Prayer worked for a while, but sadly only for less than a year.

Charles d'Orléans, one of the great *poètes courtois* of the fifteenth century, was himself a victim of war: he was taken prisoner by Henry V at the Battle

Signature of Charles d'Orléans, from an ex libris of a medieval manuscript.

of Agincourt (1415), at the age of twenty-one. In Shakespeare's *Henry V* he is the Duke of Orleans; that the Bard was well aware of his later history is shown by a line in Act III/7, when the Dauphin claims to have written a sonnet to his horse beginning "Wonder of nature," and Orleans replies, "I have heard a sonnet begin so to one's mistress"—clearly someone celebrated for his literary knowledge. In Act IV/5 he cries, "O Seigneur! Le jour est perdu, tout est perdu!" (The day is lost, all is lost), words that are singularly appropriate to Orléans's own fate.

The consequences of the Agincourt victory for the English were to make the French royal duke a prisoner of war for the next twenty-four years, as he was moved from one English castle to another. He was a political prisoner on English soil even longer than Mary, Queen of Scots. Although the conditions of his incarceration were not harsh—his royal status, in direct line of succession to the French throne as first cousin to Charles VII, was recognized—he was regarded as too valuable to be allowed back into political circulation (he returned to France only in 1440). But during his extended imprisonment the prince became an ever more accomplished and prolific poet, writing works in his chosen forms of chanson, rondeau, and ballade, the latter usually a substantial poem that concluded with a four-line envoi (concluding words).

Poulenc would have been familiar with the Debussy settings of Charles d'Orléans: *Le Temps a laissié son manteau* and *Pour ce que Plaisance est morte* (from *Chansons de France,* 1904) and *Trois Chansons de Charles d'Orléans* (1908). *Le Figaro* printed only the first ten lines of a fifty-line "Ballade" (No. XXV from the 1896 *Poèmes complets,* edited by Charles d'Héricault). There are four further ten-line verses, ending with "Priez pour paix, le vray trésor de joye," and Poulenc took the trouble to look up the poem in its entirety; but he realized that the opening verse was sufficient for his purposes:

> *All my religious music turns its back on the style that is inspired in me by Paris and its outskirts. When I pray, it is the native of Aveyron who reawakens in me. This is evidence of heredity. Faith is strong in all the Poulencs. . . . This prayer is influenced by the* Litanies à la Vierge noire, *my first religious work . . . I have tried to give here a feeling of humility (for me the most beautiful quality of prayer). It is a prayer to be spoken in a country church.*[158]

This hieratic song, fervent and grave, begins with a four-bar introduction, almost entirely in quarter notes. While the (correct) $\rfloor = 60$ metronome marking is by no means the slowest to be found in Poulenc's songs, pianists find it difficult, in the absence of any quicker note values, to keep the introduction sufficiently slow and steady. With the singer's entry in bar 5, the marking is *Très doux et confiant* and the dynamic *pianissimo.* The concluding eight bars return to this dynamic, but otherwise this prayer is not in any way hushed or deferential. From bar 11 the music progresses from *mezzo forte* to *piano* for "Vers votre Fils, requerrant sa haultesse," but it then develops into a *cri de cœur* framed in harmonies that become increasingly anguished and chromatic. Although the song has often been accompanied on the organ (its first British performance, in August 1939, took place in Canterbury Cathedral with the bass Doda Conrad and Nadia Boulanger at the console), in the second half, where the singer laments the disruptive power of war, the piano's percussive nature comes into its own, while the harmonies grow more strident and discordant before returning to the bare simplicity of the opening.

Although the musical rigors of the poet's epoch were not lost on Poulenc, the music transcends pastiche. There was a perfect reason for writing the song, and here was a perfect poem by a medieval prisoner of war that utterly reflected the concerns of the world in September 1938. Composer and poet make time stand still in every way; one cannot imagine a single note different.

FP96 *La Grenouillère* ("*La Grenouillère*")
   Composed in Noizay, October 1938
   [*Marie-Blanche de Polignac*; Deiss]
   Literary source: Guillaume Apollinaire (1880–1918), *Il y a* (Paris: Albert Messein, 1925), p. 90
   D major; $\frac{4}{4}$; *Très las et mélancolique* ♩ = 56

Au bord de l'île on voit	All along the island you see
Les canots vides qui s'entre-cognent	Empty rowboats jostling together
Et maintenant	But now
Ni le dimanche ni les jours de la semaine	Neither on Sundays nor on weekdays
Ni les peintres ni Maupassant ne se promènent	Will you see the painters nor Maupassant rowing their boats
Bras nus sur leurs canots avec des femmes à grosses poitrines	Their sleeves rolled up, with their buxom women
Et bêtes comme chou	As daft as cabbages
Petits bateaux vous me faites bien de la peine	Little boats you break my heart
Au bord de l'île.	All along the island.

 "Bêtes comme chou" (line 7) has the additional meaning of "easy as pie," possibly a comment on the painters' companions. The promenade described here could mean a walk by the river, but a "promenade en bateau" is also commonly used to mean a boat ride. Apollinaire writes "femmes à grosse poitrine" (line 6), but Poulenc prefers the plural. J. S.

As early as the 1850s, Parisians took to bathing nude along the banks of Île-de-Croissy-sur-Seine, until an edict enforced the use of *costumes de bain*. (Nudity was much less dangerous than the questionable cleanliness of the water.) An enterprising woman entrepreneur, seeing the commercial possibilities of developing a corner of this large, elliptical island (nicknamed "Madagascar of the Seine"), with its microclimate and lush vegetation, built a large ballroom, small artificial beach, and long row of bathing huts there. A park with huge trees made an ideal promenade. A visit to this establishment, called La Grenouillère (frog pond), was as near as many Parisians got to holidaying in the fashionable Normandy towns of Trouville and Deauville; it was accordingly trumpeted as "Trouville-sur-Seine." You could hire a boat for the day and eat and drink in a floating café that looked out over the water. Middle-class elegance rubbed shoulders with the demimonde; dances, held once a week, soon acquired a risqué reputation as a place to pick up a partner. La Grenouillère, only a short train ride away from Paris, was not far from Bougival, the fashionable resort where Pauline Viardot kept a villa, and where Fauré spent his family holidays—composing *La Bonne Chanson* for Emma Bardac (his neighbor in Bougival and subsequently his lover) in 1896.

The resort's heyday came in the late 1860s, the twilight of the Second Empire and well before Fauré's fin-de-siècle idyll. In 1869 both Renoir and Monet, still poor and unknown and almost certainly sitting side by side, painted the same view of a small round island known as "Camembert" or "Le Pot-à-Fleurs" (*La Grenouillère* and *Bain à la Grenouillère*, respectively). The most vivid literary description, somewhat less idyllic, is to be found in *La Femme de Paul*, a short story written in 1880 by an author who lived in the *quartier* at the time, Guy de Maupassant (1850–1893). He is mentioned in Apollinaire's poem for this very reason:

> You get to experience the full odor of society's dregs there, the genteel lewdness, the moldiness of Parisian society; a mixture of seamstresses, play actors, down-at-heel journalists, gentlemen under investigation, shady money-men, depraved revelers, raddled elderly rakes, a suspect mob of every kind of lowlife, half of them known, half of them ruined, half lost souls, half disgraced, rogues, swindlers, pimps, captains of industry with sober gait, bullies who seem to say, "The first person who tries it on, I'll break his skull."[159]

It is here, in Maupassant's story, that Paul Baron realizes that his mistress Madeleine has sexual interests that perplex and perturb him. When a boat carrying four women, two of them mannishly dressed, passes by and the women are greeted with cheers of "Lesbos! Lesbos!," Madeleine seems fascinated rather than repelled by this spectacle. Later that night, having caught Madeleine and one of the boating Amazons making love in the gardens of La Grenouillère, Paul drowns himself in the Seine.

In 1904 Apollinaire paid a visit to two friends, the fauve painters André Derain and Maurice de Vlaminck, who lived in the area. On the way home he passed by La Grenouillère; all that was left of its former glory were some abandoned buildings and empty boats bumping up against each other. Parisians now frequented bigger, livelier, and more commercial entertainment hubs like Joinville, Champigny, and above all Nogent-sur-Marne (all on the banks of the Marne), where Poulenc first developed his taste for popular culture on visits to his grandparents' house. More than thirty years after Apollinaire had written his melancholic little evocation, Poulenc, at his peak as a song composer, confessed to having had his eye on the poem for some time. "La Grenouillère *evokes a beautiful, lost past, Sundays of ease and contentment. I certainly had in mind those boatmen's lunches, as painted by Renoir, where the bodices of the women and the rowing vests of the men harmonize, and not only in terms of color.*"[160]

To Claude Rostand, Poulenc revealed another inspiration for the song, this one a painting: "*My friend the Countess Jean de Polignac, that marvelous musician to whom I've dedicated a number of my songs, often under her first name of Marie-Blanche, told me that her mother, Mme Jeanne Lanvin, had given her a wonderful Renoir for Christmas: so I decided to give her one after my own fashion. And that was the impulse behind my little song* La Grenouillère *on a poem by Apollinaire, a kind of musical evocation of a Renoir landscape.*"[161]

The composer exactly captures the poem's gently nostalgic atmosphere, with four imperturbable beats per bar that somehow convey movement within stasis. The secret here is that the quarter notes on beats 2 and 4 resonate like ripples in the wake of the stronger half notes on beats 1 and 3, higher on the stave. The pianist's hands move together, first to the right, then left, then right, then left—a sensual pianistic vamp, chords first strong then weak in hypnotic alternation, yet all in an unchanging and languid $\frac{4}{4}$ pulse. The uncannily effective result is a tonal analogue for the gentle bobbing of boats tethered closely together, with a *molto legato* vocal line gently resigned to the transitory nature of life's summers. Between bars 8 and 13 a *crescendo* of intensity peaks at a *forte* on the verb "promènent," the musical equivalent of a momentary twinge of pain felt in recalling something beautiful that is now forever consigned to the past.

For bars 14–15 (beginning "Petits bateaux"), Poulenc admitted borrowing the musical language of Musorgsky.[162] Like so many other influences, this Russian intervention is effortlessly assimilated into the song without any sense of its being a transplant; indeed, it is a powerful means of evoking the desolation of both the poet and the locale. Here are two pages of Poulencian perfection, an out-and-out masterpiece, and a supremely simple one.

o   o   o

FP97 *Quatre Motets pour un temps de pénitence* (mixed chorus, *a cappella*), December 1938–January 1939

∘ ∘ ∘

FP98 *Miroirs brûlants* (*Burning Mirrors*)
>
> Composed in Anost, August 1938 (i); and in Noizay, 7 January 1939 (ii)
> [*Pierre Bernac, Marie-Laure de Noailles*; Deiss]
> Literary source: Paul Éluard (1895–1952), contributions to *Mesures*, 15 July 1938: (i) pp. 79–80 with the title "Nous sommes," (ii) pp. 81–82 with the title "Vertueux solitaire." Later published in *Chanson complète* (1939).

(i) *Tu vois le feu du soir*
(ii) *Je nommerai ton front*

This pair of songs was *"born of chance and happy encounters."*[163] The composer found their texts in the July 1938 *Mesures*, a quarterly review and the kind of publication that Poulenc, fascinated above all by twentieth-century literature, would have read regularly. So it was a happy coincidence that the review's Parisian offices and bookshop were located in the rue de Médicis, right below his apartment.

Poulenc acquired the paperback on his doorstep before embarking on a train journey to Nevers. From there he and Bernac drove to Anost, a town nestling in the mountains of the Morvan, where he found he could work with *"lightness and oxygen."*[164] The composer set the first and last two of the Éluard poems printed in *Mesures*, originally entitled "Nous sommes" and "Vertueux solitaire." It was easy enough to adopt the first lines as alternative song titles, but he needed a title for the set as a whole; Éluard suggested *Miroirs brûlants*. Both poems appear in a Gallimard collection from 1939 entitled *Chanson complète* (on pp. 11 and 37, so clearly the poet did not think of the poems as belonging together). A copy of this collection, belonging to Bernac and signed by Éluard, has come into my possession via Rosine Seringe and Sidney Buckland. Its inscription (pictured) includes a play on words, underlined by Éluard, as a tribute to the interpreter's art: "Pour Pierre Bernac à qui ces poèmes doivent d'être <u>entendues</u>, en témoignage de mon admiration, Paul

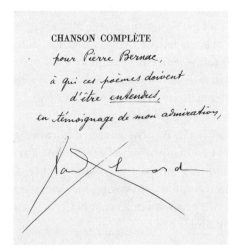

Éluard's inscription to Bernac in a copy of his Chanson complète.

Éluard" (For Pierre Bernac, to whom these poems owe being heard/understood, in witness of my admiration).

(i)   *Tu vois le feu du soir* (*You See the Fire of the Evening*)
        No key signature (tonal center of C-sharp minor); $\frac{4}{4}$; *Calme et irréel*
    ♩ = 60

Tu vois le feu du soir qui sort de sa coquille	You see the fire of evening emerging from its shell
Et tu vois la forêt enfouie dans sa fraîcheur	And you see the forest buried deep in its coolness
Tu vois la plaine nue aux flancs du ciel traînard	You see the bare plain flanked by the lagging sky
La neige haute comme la mer	Snow as high as the sea
Et la mer haute dans l'azur	And the sea high in the blue
Pierres parfaites et bois doux secours voilés	Perfect stones and sweet woods veiled relief
Tu vois les villes teintes de mélancolie	You see towns tinged with gilded melancholy
Dorée des trottoirs pleins d'excuses	Pavements full of excuses
Une place où la solitude a sa statue	A town square with a statue of solitude
Souriante et l'amour une seule maison	Smiling, and love is but one house
Tu vois les animaux	You see animals
Sosies malins sacrifiés l'un à l'autre	Evil doubles, sacrificed to each other
Frères immaculés aux ombres confondues	Unstained brothers with melted shadows
Dans un désert de sang	In a wilderness of blood
Tu vois un bel enfant quand il joue quand il rit	You see a pretty child when he laughs when he plays
Il est bien plus petit	He's even tinier
Que le petit oiseau du bout des branches	Than the little bird perched at the tip of the branches
Tu vois un paysage aux saveurs d'huile et d'eau	You see a landscape which smacks of oil and of water
D'où la roche est exclue où la terre abandonne	Where rocks are banned where the earth

Sa verdure à l'été qui la couvre de fruits	Offers up its greenness to summer which covers it in fruit
Des femmes descendant de leur miroir ancien	Women stepping down from their ancient mirrors
T'apportent leur jeunesse et leur foi en la tienne	Bring you their youth and their faith in yours
Et l'une sa clarté la voile qui t'entraîne	And one of them veiled in her own light draws you
Te fait secrètement voir le monde sans toi.	Secretly shows you how to see the world without you.

In Anost (where he spent the month of August in both 1937 and 1938), Poulenc rented a three-room apartment and had a Pleyel upright sent down from Paris, so he and Bernac could rehearse to their hearts' content and prepare concert programs for the coming season. The composer was astounded that the sunset described in this poem was exactly that to be seen from his room in Anost (he had enjoyed the same view while composing his Mass in G Major exactly a year earlier), and that the poem *"fitted so perfectly with the surrounding countryside."*[165] He was so in love with this part of France that he kept on his mantelpiece "a photo of Autun [a market town with remarkable Roman ruins, near Anost] as others have of a beloved woman."[166]

> It was not by chance that I discovered this corner of the Morvan. It is here that my nurse was born and is laid to rest. Few towns appeal to me more than Autun, few mountains reflect "the fire of evening" with greater mellowness than the hills of the Morvan. It lies at the approach to Burgundy, yet with a milder atmosphere. To reward ourselves for days of work, Bernac and I would dine at Saulieu or Arnay-le-Duc.[167]

"Tu vois le feu du soir" is another of Éluard's "litany" poems ("Tu vois" six times in all) in praise of his beloved Nusch, where an awestruck husband and votary addresses a great priestess. A kind of "Casta diva" of French song, it is a hymn to female fecundity and to the mysteries and depths of female perception—an affirmation of Goethe's *Ewig-Weibliche*, or eternal feminine. Simone de Beauvoir was among those who denounced such "gender essentialism" as patriarchal myth, but tender veneration for the opposite sex was at the heart of Éluard's work as a poet, although his went far beyond courtship or seduction. In placing Nusch on a pedestal, he never expected her to conform to the bourgeois model of a modest housewife or chaste mother (the couple never had children). It might be truer to say that he was amazed by Nusch as much as he was dazzled by her erotic charms; in some respects he considered her his teacher and mentor, a bringer of clarification and light. That Éluard regarded the two of them as journeying down the same path, hand in hand, is shown by the poem's original title, "Nous sommes"—We are.

The song shares a metronome marking ($\downarrow$ = 60) with *Nous avons fait la nuit* FP86/ix—by no means fast, by no means slow, a gentle rhythm that glides through seemingly every tonality possible while avoiding gratuitous rubato or sentimentality. In the entire song there is only one bar of piano interlude (54) where the singer is mute; and the effect of the words that follow ("Pierres parfaites") is heightened by that vocal silence. It is a miracle that the song hangs together as seamlessly as it does. Poulenc was not a composer to whom a long span of musical thought came naturally, and, unlike Fauré, he was not a master of organic development.

> *If the conception of* Tu vois le feu du soir *was spontaneous, the achievement of it none the less gave me a lot of trouble. As I have already written concerning* Dans le jardin d'Anna, *an enumerative poem calls for an unchanging flow of movement. This long song (four minutes), where not a single sixteenth note disturbs the flow, was to be saved from monotony by the subtlety of the writing for the piano and the simplicity of the vocal line.*[168]

He thus weaves together a patchwork of juxtaposing ideas, modified according to the imagery of the words—hence the special tenderness on "Tu vois un bel enfant quand il joue quand il rit"—which he carefully connects via a sequence of interconnecting harmonic doors separated by "terraced" dynamics. A good performance, poised and necessarily hypnotic, depends on the singer's having a masterful control of *mezza voce* at the top of the stave (as did Bernac, the dedicatee) and a feeling for the mystery of the text. *"No one will ever sing this song like Pierre Bernac. It is for this reason that I have dedicated it to him. I wonder if among my 'desert island discs' this might not be the song of mine I would choose to*

The manuscript of Tu vois le feu du soir *inscribed to its dedicatee, Bernac: "Pour mon vieux Pierre en souvenir de notre cher travail d'Anost, avec ma vieille amitié, Francis" (For my dear old Pierre, in memory of our precious work at Anost, in longstanding friendship).*

take with me."[169] The sumptuous piano writing is almost all in cushioned eighth and quarter notes (not a sixteenth in sight, as Poulenc points out), making his achievement in avoiding dullness all the more remarkable. It is one of Poulenc's most serious songs, and one of his greatest.

Bernac points out two important misprints in the score: in bar 45 the *ossia* for the difficult-to-achieve (for a baritone) high G-sharp is C-sharp, not E; and in the same bar the text should read "la [not "le"] couvre de fruits."

(ii) *Je nommerai ton front (I Will Name Your Brow)*
         F minor; $\frac{4}{4}$; *Molto agitato* $\downarrow$ = 144

Je nommerai ton front	I will name your brow
J'en ferai un bûcher au sommet de tes sanglots	I will make a stake of it atop your sobs
Je nommerai reflet la douleur qui te déchire	I will name as "reflection" the pain which rips you apart
Comme une épée dans un rideau de soie	Like a sword through a curtain of silk
Je t'abattrai jardin secret	I will demolish you, a secret garden
Plein de pavots et d'eau précieuse	Full of poppies and precious water
Je te ligoterai de mon fouet	I shall bind you with my whip
Tu n'avais dans ton cœur que lueurs souterraines	You had nothing in your heart but buried light
Tu n'auras plus dans tes prunelles que du sang	You will have nothing but blood in the pupils of your eyes
Je nommerai ta bouche et tes mains les dernières	I will name your mouth and your hands last of all
Ta bouche écho détruit tes mains monnaie de plomb	Your echo-mouth destroys your hands, coins of lead,
Je briserai les clés rouillées qu'elles commandent	I will shatter the rusty keys they command
Si je dois m'apaiser profondément un jour	If I am to find deep peace one day
Si je dois oublier que je n'ai pas su vaincre	If I am to forget that I can never prevail
Qu'au moins tu aies connu la grandeur de ma haine.	At least you will have known the scale of my hate.

This is without doubt the most vilified of the Poulenc songs, even more discounted than the Colette *Le Portrait*. Unlike *Le Portrait*, however, it is hard to say much in its defense when Poulenc himself is so dismissive. "*I began it at Anost. After our departure, earlier than we had anticipated (Bernac's father was dying), I did not take it up again until much later at Noizay. I had lost the thread. Tant pis.*"[170]

The dedication to Marie-Laure de Noailles is an interesting one; she was one of Poulenc's most important patrons but not nearly the kind of close friend that Marie-Blanche de Polignac was. Marie-Laure was a grand lion of the French social scene and an indefatigable supporter of avant-garde art, but she was also a needy poor-little-rich-girl capable of terrifying tantrums on the scale depicted in this song. Poulenc might have calculated that she was capable of accepting the dedication of a brilliant and virtuosic song without really caring that it was far from one of his best.

Je nommerai ton front was always meant to follow *Tu vois le feu du soir*; like a bracing lemon sorbet served between courses, it was meant to clean the palate in preparation for the next significant course. But in recitals, Bernac and Poulenc tended to replace it with *La Belle Jeunesse* (from *Chansons gaillardes* FP42) if they were in need of a "trampoline song." As Bernac comments: "Both Éluard and Poulenc were more successful in singing of love than of hate."[171] That said, the song is an effective piece of huffing and puffing, glittering with pianistic challenges and vocal energy; in fact it is difficult to conceive words like these, so untypical of the poet, receiving more effective treatment than they do here.

FP99 *Ce doux petit visage* (*This Sweet Little Face*)
        Composed in Noizay, April 1939
        [*À la mémoire de Raymonde Linossier*; Rouart, Lerolle]
        Literary source: Paul Éluard (1895–1952), *Cours naturel* (Paris: Éditions du
        Sagittaire, 1938), p. 24 (No. VII of the seven-part poem called *Passionnément*)
        A minor; $\frac{3}{4}$; *Très modéré* $\downarrow$ = 63

Rien que ce doux petit visage	Nothing but this sweet little face
Rien que ce doux petit oiseau	Nothing but this sweet little bird
Sur la jetée lointaine où les enfants faiblissent	On the far-off jetty where the children fade away
À la sortie de l'hiver	At the end of winter
Quand les nuages commencent à brûler	When clouds start to burn bright
Comme toujours	As they always do
Quand l'air frais se colore	When the cool air takes on colors.
Rien que cette jeunesse qui fuit devant la vie.	Nothing but this youth which runs away before life.

Éluard's gentle fragment is set to uncommonly moving music. "*I have tried here to transfuse musically all the tenderness of Éluard's poem. I think I have succeeded, particularly over the prosody of the long phrase 'À la sortie de l'hiver'* [bb. 10–11], *full of ticklish difficulties.*"[172] The poem, from a collection dedicated to Nusch, makes up the last part of the seven-part poem *Passionnément*. Poulenc dedicated the song to the memory of Raymonde Linossier, the remarkable woman he had wanted to marry in his youth.

In that great Apollinaire song of 1948 *Voyage* FP140/vii, the word "visage" is similarly at the heart of the poem ("It's your face which I no longer see"), and that song is also dedicated to the memory of Raymonde. Poulenc attempted to explain his fascination with facial imagery in 1954, when he was in the grip of a mental breakdown: "*Do you know my song* Ce doux petit visage? *And the line* [of Éluard] *in* Belle et ressemblante [*Sept Chansons* FP81/v]: *'A face at the end of the day, a face in the scales of silence'? May the face of Christ enlighten me one day.*"[173]

Perhaps because of its link with Raymonde, this is one of the few Éluard settings that suit a female voice better than a male (on the whole, settings of this poet are remarkably suitable for both sexes, perhaps because there is something about their power that goes beyond sex, even when erotic). Bernac warns against too slow a tempo; he admits that the meaning of the poem is inscrutable, but that the sense can be found in the simplicity of the music, as well as its expression of nostalgia and melancholy.[174]

It is the very inscrutability of Éluard's words that gives this music the dignity to refute all sentimentality. The first eight bars float like a bird in the ether of the treble clef, unanchored by the bass; from bar 10 the music exudes a warmth, and a remarkably lyrical, if not memorably melodic, vocal line. And the three bars of the postlude, which lead into a sumptuous A major cadence, sound like a blessing, one that the composer may have imagined Linossier bestowing upon him. The whole song seems made of precious memories turned into sound—perfection of a kind, and vintage Poulenc.

The composer wrote at some length about the use of pedal here, and also takes this opportunity to reflect on the pianos used by great composers, and how they influenced the work of their owners. The sound of Debussy's Bechstein was "*rich and creamy*," Ravel's "*old Erard, dry as a guitar*"; and the Pleyel that Stravinsky used in composing *Les Noces* produced a sound unlike any other piano he had heard.[175]

∘ ∘ ∘

FP100 Sextet (flute, oboe, clarinet, bassoon, horn, and piano), 1931–39

∘ ∘ ∘

FP101 *Fiançailles pour rire* (*Laughable Betrothal*)

Composed in Noizay, September–October 1939

[*Marie-Blanche de Polignac, Freddy* (Frédérique) *Lebedeff, Suzanne Peignot, Ninon Vallin, Denise Bourdet, Solange d'Ayen*; Rouart, Lerolle]

Literary source: Louise de Vilmorin (1902–1969), *Fiançailles pour rire* (Paris: Gallimard, 1939), (i) p. 37, (ii) p. 49, (iii) p. 25, (iv) p. 95, (v) p. 85, (vi) p. 67

(i) *La Dame d'André*
(ii) *Dans l'herbe*
(iii) *Il vole*
(iv) *Mon Cadavre est doux comme un gant*
(v) *Violon*
(vi) *Fleurs*

This is Poulenc's most famous cycle for the female voice, better known than the *Trois Poèmes de Louise Vilmorin,* whose music benefits from the daring and freshness of a new literary discovery. It would be easy to assume that having set three of Vilmorin's poems at the end of 1937, the composer returned to her work two years later with renewed pleasure, but the reality was not quite so simple. One of the main attractions of working on the earlier group had been that Marie-Blanche de Polignac needed a new cycle for her 1938 recital (a critical disaster for the singer, not the music, and an experiment never to be repeated). Poulenc badly wanted to write further songs for the female voice, but there was no suitable collaborator to hand. The talented soprano Denise Duval existed only in his distant future, and Suzanne Peignot, always busy performing the work of other contemporary composers, seems to have fallen temporarily out of favor.

In the meanwhile, Vilmorin, encouraged by her success as a poet at Poulenc's behest, had gone ahead and assembled a slim volume entitled *Fiançailles pour rire,* a collection of thirty-seven poems written mainly in Slovakia, where she had been living since 1937 with her second husband, Count Paul Pálffy. Poulenc's immediate response was that he should choose poems from this collection for a new cycle for Bernac. Easier said than done; Vilmorin had made alterations to a text he had already set (FP91/ii), and the collection was dedicated to her husband ("à mon cher Pali"). She apologized, only half in jest, for not having dedicated it to the composer who had brought her name to prominence in the musical world.[176]

Moreover, Georges Auric, who had known Vilmorin long before she met Poulenc, had already been allocated a number of her new poems—including "La Jeune Sanguine" (which Poulenc also wanted to set) and "Attendez le prochain bateau," which was to become perhaps the most famous of her lyrics.[177] Poulenc, while admitting that Auric had a prior claim, was clearly miffed. It is extremely rare that the composer permits us to see him in less than affable mood; and in this case we can only do so thanks to passages in his *Journal* (quoted below) that were deleted by him before publication, and were reconstituted in 1993 in a new edition by Renaud Machart.[178]

Vilmorin sent Poulenc a copy of the corrected proofs of the new book, then made a short visit back to Paris for its launch early in 1939. Although ill in bed, she read the poems aloud to the composer in a "monstrously ugly" room in the Hôtel de Crillon, on the place de la Concorde. *"Lolou read. It was pretty, but it was not at all what I wanted, not what I wished to hear, at least not at that time."* The poems "Mon Cadavre est doux comme un gant" and "Il vole" left him cold: *"The musician almost never chooses the poems that the poet wants him to. Éluard wrote for me a 'Chanson espagnole' that I have never been able to put to music . . . to write a good song one must love the poem."*[179] Vilmorin returned to Pálffy's vast estates in Hungary, and Poulenc dispatched the newly published *Fiançailles pour rire* to his bookbinder, after which the slim volume was set to be lost within his large library. That was that. She promised to send him further poems, but they never materialized.

It was almost certainly the gathering storm clouds of war that made him relent. In August 1938, holidaying in Brittany in an unsatisfactory inn at the coastal town of Le Pouldu, Poulenc was grumpy and wished he had gone to Anost instead. The nearby Polignacs took pity on him and invited him to Kerbastic, where Louise had also often been a welcome guest. Calculating that Bernac would probably be lost to him in an inevitable military call-up, the composer decided he might as well write another set of songs for soprano. He imagined "Loulou" sitting out the impending war in a kind of mournful captivity in Slovakia—only partly true (she was enjoying a time of reflection and creativity)—and was able to latch on to the note of ennui and melancholy that was to be an important part of his new work.

He wanted his first new setting to be ready as a birthday present for Marie-Blanche de Polignac, on 15 August. In 1851 Robert Schumann had set seven short poems by the child prodigy Elisabeth Kulmann (Op. 104), and Poulenc's initial aim was to compose a seven-song cycle to mirror that work. But in looking closer into the Kulmann settings, he discovered that they were far from Schumann's most interesting, and it was unlikely that sopranos attracted to his new cycle would also program the Schumann. In the end, six new Vilmorin settings proved sufficient for a cycle—although it would be more accurate to call the work a set of songs, where any one of them might appear in a recital without its confrères.

Although *Fiançailles pour rire* is sung everywhere, it has failed to win the admiration reserved for the great Apollinaire and Éluard cycles. Poulenc's change of mind was not dictated by his falling in love with the poems, and perhaps it shows. When he reassessed the songs in 1960 ("*days playing my old songs again*"), he found them contrived, comparing unfavorably with the authenticity of his *Cinq Poèmes de Max Jacob*.[180]

Bernac tactfully comments that "these charming and elegant poems are not comparable in richness and substance to the admirable poems of Éluard—a comparison reflected in the music."[181] To Poulenc's credit, the lack of richness and substance seems entirely deliberate. Instead, we have something sleek, graceful, and impertinent, lightweight in texture, with a subtle bass note of underlying melancholy (if this sounds like a description of a perfume, it is a tribute to Poulenc that the music has an elusive, Guerlain-like subtlety). On account of his identifying with what he took to be Vilmorin's unhappy wartime exile (in Hungary according to Poulenc, actually Slovakia), we can also detect a note of desperation lightly worn. A touch of eroticism is reminiscent of the graceful Poulenc of *Les Biches*, a world he said he was pleased to be able to revisit.[182]

(i) *La Dame d'André (André's Lady)*
A minor; $\frac{4}{4}$; *Modéré sans lenteur* ♩ = 126 (Bernac recommends 132.)

André ne connaît pas la dame	André doesn't know the lady
Qu'il prend aujourd'hui par la main.	Whose hand he takes today.
A-t-elle un cœur à lendemains,	Will she have a heart for the days to come,
Et pour le soir a-t-elle une âme?	Will she have a soul come the evening?
Au retour d'un bal campagnard	Returning from a country ball
S'en allait-elle en robe vague	Did she in her gauzy dress
Chercher dans les meules la bague	Go hunting in a haystack for
Des fiançailles du hasard?	Her random engagement ring?
A-t-elle eu peur, la nuit venue,	Was she scared, at dead of night,
Guettée par les ombres d'hier,	Spied on by the shades of yesterday
Dans son jardin, lorsque l'hiver	In her garden, when winter
Entrait par la grande avenue?	Swept down the great avenue?
Il l'a aimée pour sa couleur,	He loved her for her color,
Pour sa bonne humeur de Dimanche.	For her Sunday holiday humor.
Pâlira-t-elle aux feuilles blanches	Will she fade in the white pages
De son album des temps meilleurs?	Of his photo album of better days?

During the war Vilmorin had no news of her family, and worried in particular about her brothers, who were all of military age. Eventually, thanks to the son of the former German ambassador to Japan, she heard that all four were safe. Accompanying this news was a four-leaf clover in an envelope, and Louise thereafter adopted a clover-leaf monogram with an L at the bottom. Her favorite brother, André, wrote a biography of his sister in 1962, in which his knowledge of literature and deep appreciation of her poetry are very evident.[183]

The four-leaf clover monogram of Louise de Vilmorin (symbolizing her four brothers) in a signed copy of her novel Le Violon.

The poem is an elegant sisterly meditation on the suitability of André's new girlfriend; Louise wonders whether the friendship will make her brother happy. She hopes so; but if not, she must let matters take their course, as any other attitude would be vulgar. The gently discursive music superbly delineates exactly this level of engagement, with an equable mood that is free of passion while expressing sisterly concern. Poulenc had met André, but that is less important here than an ability to capture the unique inflections of Vilmorin's speech. Marie Laurencin had congratulated the composer for getting the tone of Apollinaire's speaking voice just right in the *Bestiaire* settings, and it would not surprise me if the rise and fall of this music somehow conjured the speaking voice of Louise de Vilmorin for those who knew her. The question of the new girl's suitability is left open: "*The tonal ambiguity prevents the song from coming to a conclusion* [in the final chord] *and so prepares the way for the following songs.*"[184]

(ii) *Dans l'herbe (In the Grass)*
No key signature (C-sharp minor); $\frac{3}{4}$; *Très calme et très égal* ♩ = 56

Je ne peux plus rien dire	I can say no more
Ni rien faire pour lui.	Nor do any more for him.
Il est mort de sa belle	He has died for his darling
Il est mort de sa mort belle	Died a natural death
Dehors	Outside
Sous l'arbre de la Loi	Under the Tree of the Law
En plein silence	Deep in silence
En plein paysage	Deep in the country
Dans l'herbe.	In the grass.
Il est mort inaperçu	He has died quite unnoticed
En criant son passage	Crying out in his passing

En appelant en m'appelant.	Calling calling for me.
Mais comme j'étais loin de lui	But since I was so far from him
Et que sa voix ne portait plus	And since his voice no longer carried
Il est mort seul dans les bois	He died alone in the woods
Sous son arbre d'enfance.	Beneath his childhood tree.
Et je ne peux plus rien dire	And I can say no more
Ni rien faire pour lui.	Nor do any more for him.

The pun here is on "belle," meaning a beautiful girl (lines 3–4). "Mourir de sa belle . . . mort" means to die a quiet or natural death. J. S.

While Marie-Blanche de Polignac was the dedicatee of the first song, this one is dedicated to Freddy Lebedeff (née Bucquet, 1907–1999), a woman the composer met through Richard and Suzette Chanlaire, and with whom he had something of a complicated relationship: seven years later she would become the mother of his daughter Marie-Ange (see p. 245).

This touching little threnody, an altogether deeper song than the first, possesses a kind of fierceness that is simultaneously engaged and at one remove, as in all of Vilmorin's poetry where deep emotions are contained by insouciance. When Poulenc writes, "*Mélodie sans histoire—Nothing to say about this song. Sing it with great intensity,*"[185] he is surely echoing the poet herself. We don't know whose death is referred to here, but, as in *La Dame d'André,* the feminine tone is conserved by a certain musical reserve and childlike simplicity. It may be that the poem refers to the death of one of the Vilmorins' pets, a cat or a dog—an animal is much more likely to die unnoticed in the grass than a human being— but that may be attempting to explain away more complicated imagery. Whether the loss is human or animal, there must be a sense of distance in the interpretive response to a tragedy that seems framed by arcane ritual.

The accompaniment, in stately and unrelenting quarter notes, is something of a processional. But as in all Poulenc's songs in triple time, the tempo should never be allowed to suggest the solemnity of stasis; even at this rather slow metronome marking, there needs to be the suggestion of a dance, a

Louise de Vilmorin and her brothers: (from left) Roger, André, Olivier, and Henry.

very slow waltz perhaps, in the way the accompaniment is phrased. Bars 19–20 ("Mais comme j'étais loin de lui") are so beautiful that it is hardly surprising that the composer simply repeats the music for the next line. And in the four-bar postlude, the return to C-sharp minor from D-sharp minor is a master class in ingenious modulation.

(iii)   *Il vole (Flying)*
    E-flat major; $\frac{4}{4}$; *Presto implacable* ♩ = 120 (Bernac believes this is the minimum speed, and the song could be faster.)

En allant se coucher le soleil	Just as it's setting, the sun
Se reflète au vernis de ma table	Is reflected in the varnish of my table
C'est le fromage rond de la fable	It's the big round cheese of the fable
Au bec de mes ciseaux de vermeil.	In the beak of my silver scissors.
—Mais où est le corbeau?—Il vole.	—But where is the crow?—Flying.
Je voudrais coudre mais un aimant	I'd like to sew but a magnet
Attire à lui toutes mes aiguilles.	Keeps stealing all my needles.
Sur la place les joueurs de quilles	In the square the skittle players
De belle en belle passent le temps.	Pass their time from strike to strike.
—Mais où est mon amant?—Il vole.	—But where is my lover?—Flying.
C'est un voleur que j'ai pour amant,	I have a thief as my lover,
Le corbeau vole et mon amant vole,	The crow flies, my lover steals,
Voleur de cœur manque à sa parole	The thief of hearts breaks his word
Et voleur de fromage est absent.	And the cheese thief is gone
—Mais où est le bonheur?—Il vole.	—But where is my joy?—Flying.
Je pleure sous le saule pleureur	I'm weeping beneath the weeping willow
Je mêle mes larmes à ses feuilles	I'm mingling my tears with its leaves
Je pleure car je veux qu'on me veuille	I'm weeping because I want to be wanted
Et je ne plais pas à mon voleur.	And my flighty thief doesn't fancy me.
—Mais où donc est l'amour?—Il vole.	—But where is love?—Flying.
Trouvez la rime à ma déraison	Find the rhyme in my lack of reason
Et par les routes du paysage	And by the country roads

Ramenez-moi mon amant volage	Bring me back my flighty lover
Qui prend les cœurs et perd ma raison.	Who steals hearts and robs me of my reason.
Je veux que mon voleur me vole.	I wish my thief would steal me . . .

"Il vole" means either "He flies" or "He steals." Here it means both. The skittle players in the square pass their time "de belle en belle" (line 9). A "belle" for a skittler is a successful game, but also, of course, a pretty female. J. S.

Underneath the piano stave at the opening are the words "Dans le style d'une étude pour piano." Ever since the song first appeared, it has been regarded as a special challenge for the pianist—and it is also far from easy for the singer. *"One of the most difficult of my songs. It seems to me impossible to interpret it without serious work and numerous rehearsals."*[186]

"Étude" suggests a connection with the music of Chopin, a composer (judging from the later *Métamorphoses* FP121 and *Mazurka* FP145) whose music Poulenc seems to have linked strongly with Vilmorin. And the helter-skelter virtuosity of *Il vole* is partly Chopinesque in style, with its cascades of arpeggio sequences (although partly pure Poulenc in passages like "Je pleure sous le saule pleureur"). The unison passagework an octave apart, in sixteenth notes as almost always in Poulenc, derives from the "wind whistling over graves" movement of Chopin's B-flat Minor Piano Sonata. And the pianistic pattern in the two final bars is a direct steal from Chopin's Étude in G-flat Major, Op. 25 No. 9. It is almost comical to realize how easily the ear accepts this little melodic detail as a genuine piece of Poulenc, as the master magpie strikes again.

Or perhaps on this occasion we have a deceived crow rather than a thieving magpie. "Le fromage rond de la fable" (line 3) is a reference to Aesop's "The Crow and the Fox," where the wily fox flatters the crow about its singing voice, and the crow, having been persuaded to open its beak to sing, drops a piece of cheese. Like Poulenc's very first Vilmorin setting, *Le Garçon de Liège*, *Il vole* exhibits a kind of rationalized dissatisfaction, a gracious and graceful acceptance of the realities of life, including unfaithfulness in love.

For Vilmorin, love is something that flies past her; we may almost say that it eludes her, just as it eludes Poulenc, at least in the long term. She speaks of inconstancy and betrayal, even of weeping, but as part of the charivari of life and the undependability of human emotion. Accordingly, the music offers no complaint or bitterness, only a kind of *joie de vivre* (simply the joy of being sufficiently alive to experience, and to suffer). The song's subtext and undertone, a worldly sigh of disappointment, is scarcely to be discerned amid the ebullience of the piano's rushing sixteenth notes and cascading chords; yet the modulated twists and turns of the vocal line reveal a vulnerability that exists on a somewhat different plane. The effect of voice and piano together is of a singer tempted by melancholia but dragged along on a roller-coaster ride through the breathless ascents and descents of virtuosic pianism.

At the poem's end, Vilmorin wishes that her thief would steal her. But if that does not happen, "C'est la vie" must be her response. It would be inestimably vulgar for the poet, already in her late thirties, to wail her discontent to the heavens. So instead, with Poulenc's help, she smiles ruefully and shrugs her shoulders as only the French can. How differently would this abandonment, and this longing for love, be expressed in a German lied.

(iv) *Mon Cadavre est doux comme un gant (My Body Is as Soft as a Glove)*
No key signature (E minor); $\frac{4}{4}$; *Très calme, intense et très lié* ♩ = 60

Mon cadavre est doux comme un gant	My body is as soft as a glove
Doux comme un gant de peau glacée	Soft as a glove of glacé leather
Et mes prunelles effacées	And my wiped-out pupils
Font de mes yeux des cailloux blancs.	Turn my eyes into white pebbles.
Deux cailloux blancs dans mon visage	Two white pebbles in my face,
Dans le silence deux muets	In the silence, twin mutes
Ombrés encore d'un secret	Shrouded still with a secret
Et lourds du poids mort des images.	And heavy with the dead weight of what they've seen.
Mes doigts tant de fois égarés	My fingers which have strayed so often
Sont joints en attitude sainte	Are joined in a pious pose
Appuyés au creux de mes plaintes	Against the hollow of my misery
Au nœud de mon cœur arrêté.	At the knot of my stopped heart.
Et mes deux pieds sont les montagnes	And my two feet are like mountains
Les deux derniers monts que j'ai vus	The last twin peaks I saw
À la minute où j'ai perdu	The very moment that I lost
La course que les années gagnent.	The race the years always win.
Mon souvenir est ressemblant,	My memory still resembles all this,
Enfants emportez-le bien vite,	Children, take it away quickly,
Allez, allez ma vie est dite.	Come on, come on, my life is done.
Mon cadavre est doux comme un gant.	My body is as soft as a glove.

This sumptuous song is dedicated to soprano Ninon Vallin (1886–1961), the greatest female recitalist in France of her generation. Vallin performed *Airs chantés* in a Paris recital in 1929 with Ivor Newton, and it had long been Poulenc's hope to win her back to his cause. *Mon Cadavre est doux comme un gant,* the heavyweight number of the set in terms of emotive ambitions and sovereign legato line, would have suited her superbly well, at least from a vocal point of view. Hugues Cuenod once told me that Vallin (who in any case favored Louis Beydts as a composer over Poulenc)[187] was horrified by the song's implied necrophilia (as she saw it) and absolutely refused to sing it. A pity; a Vallin-Poulenc duo might have proved a fitting sequel to her celebrated collaboration with Reynaldo Hahn, both in concert and in the recording studio.

For Hervé Lacombe, the song begins as simply as *Priez pour paix* but is quickly spoiled by complications in the harmony and in melodic inflections. He feels that the decadent side of the poem (much prized by André Vilmorin, who thought it one of his sister's more important lyrics) was not made for Poulenc's talents.[188] Vallin's reservations are not, therefore, to be totally discounted. There is something singularly uncharming about a woman viewing her corpse-to-be in the manner of a doppelgänger, at least in music as luxuriously indulgent as this. Richard D. E. Burton has pointed out that after the shocking death by decapitation of composer Pierre-Octave Ferroud in a road accident in 1936, depictions, visual or literary, of the lifeless human body appear to have made a profound effect on Poulenc.[189] But the composer seems always to have been drawn to imagery of the broken corpse (as in the dark 1925 Ronsard sonnet *Je n'ai plus que les os* FP38/iv), even if only as a means of shocking audiences out of their complacency.

From a musical point of view, the song could be a study for the future Apollinaire setting *Sanglots*, the closing song of *Banalités* FP107. The layout of the accompaniment is similar, and *Sanglots* shares a first-person narrative voice with the Vilmorin song, as well as images of death; in Vilmorin the singer's heart is "arrêté" (stopped), in Apollinaire "brisé" (broken). Usually Poulenc found music for difficult-to-understand texts that humanized the words and made them more accessible; in turn, their obscurity and literary stature saved his music from seeming sentimental and over-flowery. This is certainly the case with *Sanglots*, but somehow not with *Mon Cadavre est doux comme un gant.* As if he were trying too hard to lure Vallin's world-class voice back into his orbit, his musical contribution seems rather too allied to the effulgence, almost melodrama, of the text rather than composed as a balance to it. The words "Allez, allez ma vie est dite" require a less richly sentimental setting to avoid bathos, however harmonically gorgeous that phrase is.

(v) *Violon (Violin)*

A minor; $\frac{3}{4}$; *Modéré* ♩ = 63 (Bernac suggests 72.)

Couple amoureux aux accents méconnus	An amorous couple with unfamiliar accents
Le violon et son joueur me plaisent.	The violin and the violinist both please me.
Ah! j'aime ces gémissements tendus Sur la corde des malaises.	Oh, how I love these drawn-out wails On the string of unease.
Aux accords sur les cordes des pendus	Strung from the c(h)ords of the hangman's rope
À l'heure où les Lois se taisent	At that time when the Laws are silenced.
Le cœur, en forme de fraise,	The heart, shaped like a strawberry,
S'offre à l'amour comme un fruit inconnu.	Offers itself to love like an unknown fruit.

Lots of wordplay here on "accords" and "cordes," which imply variously chords, accords, the strings of a violin, and the hangman's rope. J. S.

Lacombe believes that *Violon* is "a rare example of irony in Poulenc's music: a little bit of hot air, several Chopinesque reminiscences, a little absurdity, a little facile lyricism and excitability. Everything is fake ["toc"], everything is somewhat second class, just like the phony Hungarian restaurant."[190]

In *Violon*, the *Fiançailles* song most often heard on its own (Poulenc encouraged such excerpting with this set), both singer and pianist are presented with the challenge of imitating the exaggerated legato of a restaurant violinist. The composer had evidently heard from Vilmorin, perhaps during that private reading at the Hôtel de Crillon in early 1939, why the poem was written: it seems that the well-meaning Count Pálffy had wanted to import a little of his own country's musical atmosphere for his new wife.

Composed with a Hungarian restaurant in the Champs-Élysées in mind, for which Louise's husband, Count Pálffy, had engaged a Hungarian Gypsy band from Budapest. I have tried to suggest only very distantly the local color because the hand that wrote the poem is French. The musician similarly transposes the rhythm of the Danube into our own atmosphere.[191]

It is also possible that Poulenc was a fellow guest on this bizarre occasion. He insists, in the same passage, that the song evokes Paris more than Hungary, and that Louise, the recipient of the serenade, was wearing a hat by Caroline Reboux, the Chanel of milliners. As for national authenticity, or willful inauthenticity, one is reminded of Poulenc's remark that the wrought-iron balconies of Chabrier's *España* came from a French department store. French music is French music, whatever origins it may claim.

The song suggests the slinky, smoky atmosphere of a nightclub, but as a result some performers, less experienced in the composer's style, tend to exaggerate the music's populist side to the point of parody—which was never his intention. As Bernac warns: "The song must not become a night club song, but should only suggest its atmosphere." For this reason he also recommends that Poulenc's metronome marking of ♩ = 63 be replaced by 72.[192] If the music is amusing, it is only gently so, and must never tip over into grotesque parody, which is what happens when singers go to town on vocal slides. Another danger is taking the music too slowly; the accompaniment should be played strictly in time, not meaningfully or exaggeratedly. Once again performers are advised that this kind of $\frac{3}{4}$ rhythm holds the ghost of a waltz, with a strong downbeat on the first beat of the bar.

The stream-of-consciousness wordplay inspired by the curvaceous shape of the violin will be heard again in another Vilmorin setting, *Paganini* (FP121/iii). In *Violon* ("Vi-yo-lon," as it must be pronounced in b. 12) the poet sees the musician and his instrument entwined like an amorous couple; voice and piano, though tasked with different things, enjoy the same kind of intimacy. The passage where the violinist/pianist skates up the fingerboard (at "et son joueur") and the *quasi parlando* at the end (where the voice murmurs "en forme de fraise" in the background while the violin/piano plays an obbligato) are charmingly effective. Most of the accompaniment, bathed in pedal, is first and foremost pianistic, but the final bars conjure violin harmonics and pizzicato; Benjamin Britten's violin evocation in a Thomas Hardy setting, *At the Railway Station, Upway* (from *Winter Words*, composed fourteen years later), employs similar imitative devices.

(vi) *Fleurs (Flowers)*
D-flat major; $\frac{3}{4}$; *Très calme* ♩ = 56

Fleurs promises, fleurs tenues dans tes bras,
    Fleurs sorties des parenthèses d'un pas,
    Qui t'apportait ces fleurs l'hiver

    Saupoudrées du sable des mers?

Sable de tes baisers, fleurs des amours fanées

Promised flowers, flowers held in your arms,
    Flowers that have sprung from the parenthesis of a footstep,
    Who brought you these flowers in winter,

    Dusted with sand from the sea?

Sand of your kisses, flowers of wilted loves,

Les beaux yeux sont de cendre et dans la cheminée	The lovely eyes are made of ash, and in the fireplace
Un cœur enrubanné de plaintes	A heart beribboned with sad sighs
Brûle avec ses images saintes.	Burns with its holy icons.

"Parenthèses d'un pas" (line 2) evokes the brackets shape briefly left around a footprint in wet sand. The "sable des mers" (line 4) reinforces the notion that these are seaside flowers. J. S.

Poulenc chose the key here, D-flat major, so that it should be tonally as far away as possible from *Violon*: *"this will safeguard the impression of a sound that comes from far away."*[193] *Fleurs* is one of the most static and most beautiful of all Poulenc's songs, and perhaps the masterpiece of the set. Once again it shows a certain passive resignation in matters of love on the part of Vilmorin and, through her, on the part of Poulenc. *"It has to be sung with humility,"* he urges.[194] The poet burns love tokens from the past—dried flowers ("the little sea pinks that grow on the shores of Brittany," suggests Bernac)[195]—and perhaps also other mementos, even old letters gathered together in a bundle and secured with a ribbon. She muses on the melancholy of life, where affection turns to ashes. Mozart's song about another Louise who burns her letters comes to mind: the Gabriele von Baumberg setting *Als Luise die Briefe ihres ungetreuen Liebhabers verbrannte* (K. 520), a lied that bristles with fury and anguish, a short sharp shock. That Austrian Luise, choking back her emotion, confesses that she still burns with love. On the other hand, the rational Vilmorin and her alter-ego Poulenc are superbly imperturbable in the lilting $\frac{3}{4}$ movement of quarter notes. Unlike her probably pregnant eighteenth-century counterpart, the French Louise is in no danger of being vilified, abandoned without money by her family. Vilmorin and Poulenc always had someone new around the corner.

It is songs like *Fleurs,* with its mood of deep, even inconsolable regret expressed without undue emphasis or exaggeration, that wins the hearts of those who feel more temperamentally drawn to the mélodie than to the lied. The older Fauré was a special master in such slow songs, where implacable quarter notes accompany a vocal line that remains relatively undemonstrative, but which nevertheless breaks the heart for all it does not permit itself to say—*"the lyricism,"* as Poulenc observes, *"coming from within."*[196] The style of this music suggests that Poulenc, Bernac's recital partner in an increasingly wide range of French song, had learned something from the later mélodies of Fauré, a composer he had earlier professed not to admire.

FP102 *Bleuet* (*Soldier Boy*)

Composed in Noizay, October 1939

[*André Bonnelie*; Durand]

Literary source: Guillaume Apollinaire (1880–1918), *Il y a* (Paris: Albert Messein, 1925), p. 110

C-sharp minor; $\frac{3}{4}$; *Modéré* ♩ = 63

Jeune homme	Young man
de vingt ans	of twenty
Qui a vu des choses si affreuses	Who has seen such dreadful things
Que penses-tu des hommes de ton	What do you think of the men of
enfance	your childhood?
Tu	You
connais	know
la bravoure et la ruse	courage and cunning
Tu as vu la mort en face plus de cent	You have looked death in the face
fois	more than a hundred times
tu ne sais pas ce que c'est que la vie	you haven't a clue what life is
Transmets ton intrépidité	Pass your courage on
À ceux qui viendront	To those who come
Après toi	After you
Jeune homme	Young man
Tu es joyeux ta mémoire est	You are full of joy and your memory is
ensanglantée	steeped in blood
Ton âme est rouge aussi	And your soul is also red
De joie	With joy
Tu as absorbé la vie de ceux qui sont	You have absorbed the lives of those
morts près de toi	who died beside you
Tu as de la décision	You are resolute
Il est 17 heures et tu saurais	It's five in the afternoon and you
mourir	will know how to die
Sinon mieux que tes aînés	If not better than your elders
Du moins plus pieusement	at least with more piety
Car tu connais mieux la mort que la	For you know death better than
vie	life
Ô douceur d'autrefois	Oh, the sweetness of vanished times
Lenteur immémoriale	Unforgettable slowness

In *Il y a*, "Bleuet," first published in the summer of 1917, is printed as a calligram—where the words are arranged on the page in order create a visual image. (Seven

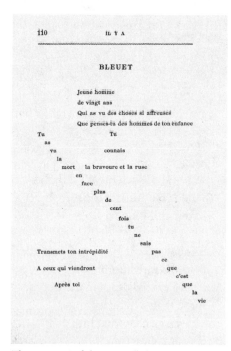

110   IL Y A
─────────────────────────────────

BLEUET

Jeune homme
de vingt ans
Qui as vu des choses si affreuses
Que penses-tu des hommes de ton enfance
Tu   Tu
  as
    vu   connais
      la
        mort   la bravoure et la ruse
          en
            face
              plus
                de
                  cent
                    fois
                      tu
                        ne
                          sais
Transmets ton intrépidité   pas
                                  ce
A ceux qui viendront   que
                                  c'est
      Après toi   que
                                  la
                                    vie

The opening of the poem "Bleuet" as it appears in Il y a, depicting two warring sides separated by a trench.

of these would be set by Poulenc in *Calligrammes* FP140, from 1948.) The verse beginning "Tu as vu la mort" is printed diagonally across the page, while the rest is ranged on either side, like opposing sides in trench warfare. The title is the diminutive of "bleu," denoting that state of inexperience English speakers refer to as "green," thus the army term for a rookie. And as a *bleuet* is also a cornflower, the name may also be connected to the blue-gray color of a soldier's uniform. Before he was wounded, Apollinaire was fighting in the war of attrition, in which soldiers were sent "over the top" at five p.m. to take a few yards of muddy terrain, and to face almost certain death.

There are surprisingly few great art songs capable of encompassing the experience of the trenches. I can think only of two Ivor Gurney songs—*In Flanders* and *By a Bierside* (the latter composed in a trench)—to match this one; the piano is usually quite the wrong domesticated instrument for the scale of such disaster, and Britten's masterly Wilfred Owen settings in *War Requiem* are bolstered by the orchestra and the text of the Mass for the Dead. If "Bleuet" had been given first-person narration, it would never have succeeded; what saves it is that we hear an observer's voice, not that of the sacrificial victim. We may think of the narrator-poet as an older and more experienced bystander, awestruck by the sacrifice required of a youth whose beauty deserves to be embraced in the arms of love, rather than by the grip of death. This young man, who never asked to be a hero, has had heroism thrust upon him by being born in the wrong time and the wrong place. The poet looks on, asking the kind of questions that must be asked silently. I am reminded of Britten's *Midnight on the Great Western: The Journeying Boy,* where the narrator, Thomas Hardy, asks a series of questions of the boy without addressing him directly; instead, within the conventions of vocal music, his colloquy is with us, the audience. He is so concerned about the child traveling alone on a train at midnight that the only way he can make sense of the situation is to ascribe to this youthful apparition the identity of an angel, perhaps one sent to avenge the venality of mankind.

Poulenc provides something of a musical halo for Apollinaire's soldier, the least mortal of the many fallen angels the composer knew in his private life. Right-hand chords in the accompaniment are marked *Très égal et estompé* (blurred), an effect that softens the contours of the music and brings to it an otherworldly quality that gradually prepares us for the transcendental conclusion. The shape of the vocal line betokens an infinite tenderness, a passion even, where the borderline between comradeship and homoeroticism is also deliberately smudged. Poulenc wrote a number of Éluard settings that pay tribute to the strength and poetry of heterosexual relationships; it would have been extraordinary if his output had not included at least one song addressed to a "jeune homme"—and this is one of two. (The other is also a setting of Apollinaire, the autobiographical *Montparnasse* FP127/i.)

Of course, many heterosexual men have written tenderly of the pity of war and the senseless loss of young lives (Apollinaire's poem is proof enough), but Poulenc's music, uniquely conceived for tenor, employs an ethereal, youthful tessitura that seems to come from another world, where the lover's caress and the comrade's salute are interchangeable. The only parallels are the A. E. Housman settings of George Butterworth and John Ireland and, once again, Britten, in the *Lacrimosa* of the *War Requiem*: a soldier's body is laid out ("Move him into the sun") in a futile attempt to revive him. Britten's music suggests the lament of a lover, also a tenor, transfixed by bitter bereavement. In *Bleuet* by Poulenc, if not "Bleuet" by Apollinaire, the young soldier is presented to us as someone brave and not at all stupid, trusting of his elders, and perhaps as naïve as the composer's beloved Raymond Destouches.

There is nothing ultimately, or conventionally, heroic about the poem and nothing heroic in the music, despite the fact that "ta mémoire est ensanglantée" is delivered *fortissimo* during a valorous (but short-lived) vocal surge into a higher tessitura. On the third page the pace quickens (*Animer un peu*) toward the deciding phrase, "Tu as de la décision," proclaimed on stentorian B-flats in the middle of the stave. Thus, moments of determination and manliness are counterpointed by sweetness, the humble readiness to die, the yielding to fate—all conveyed in music that breaks the heart. Toward the end, in a passage of ineffable beauty marked *Très calme et doux* ("Il est 17 heures"), we fancy we may be hearing the sound of the clock striking five in suspended time, in the gentle tintinnabulations of the death knell.

In the coda (*Très calme*, F-sharp minor to C-sharp major), Poulenc achieves the kind of musical lift-off for "Ô douceur d'autrefois / Lenteur immémoriale," rare even by his own exalted standards, that defeats gravity. Four bars from the end, and dovetailing with the end of the tenor's "immémoriale," the pianist crosses hands into the upper regions of the treble stave in order to play a single tiny motif in dotted rhythm, G-sharp to C-sharp—a "Taps" call. Night has fallen, five o'clock is now in the past. The left hand has one more reverential task: a final note, a D-sharp quarter tied to a half note, marked *ppp*, one step higher than where the bugle call left us. This "crossing the bar," with the lingering sound of an etiolated ninth chord, signifies release from duty and from life itself. The listener has been spirited into starlit regions where few songs by any composer are capable of taking us. Significantly, this postlude seems to have been inspired by Debussy, a composer revered by Poulenc: the last six magical bars (*Lent*) of his Verlaine setting *Chevaux de bois*, also in four sharps, conjure a nocturnal mood that is similarly ineffable and valedictory.

While eschewing the idea of conventional marble war memorials, Poulenc writes movingly of *"the mysterious moment when, leaving the mortal remains in the vestiary, the soul flies away after a long, last look at the 'douceur d'autrefois.'"*[197] It is Poulenc himself who glances back at this young hero, and the ghosts of all the young men he has loved and lost.

∘   ∘   ∘

FP103 *Française d'après Claude Gervaise* (piano), 1939

FP104 *Deux Préludes posthumes et une gnosienne* (orchestration of piano pieces by Erik Satie), 1939

· IV ·

Bernac and Poulenc boarding ship for their first American concert tour,
November 1948.

Outline of a Musical Life:
1940–1949

1940 (aged 41)

France has been on war footing for three months, still believing it can defend itself against Nazi aggression.

(2–10 January) After seeing in the new year with his sister's family at Le Tremblay, FP travels with Bernac to Portugal, under government auspices, for a series of recitals.

On the way back to Paris, having missed his train connections, FP, in the spirit of a pilgrimage, visits Saint Jean de Luz (near the French-Spanish border), where he pays homage to the memory of the region's most famous musical son, Maurice Ravel.

(13 January) FP and Bernac perform at a "Matinée poétique" organized by Édouard Bourdet at the Comédie-Française; the theme is "writers who died for France." The program includes Poulenc settings of Apollinaire, as well as Fauré's *L'Horizon chimérique* (the poet, Jean de la Ville de Mirmont, was a First World War casualty).

On an Italian tour, FP and Bernac perform recitals in Rome (14 February); Florence, at the Pitti Palace (17th); Trieste (21st); and Milan (23rd).

(14 March) FP and Bernac give a recital in Zurich that includes a Schumann group. During the next four years there would be little German repertoire in their programs.

Back in Noizay, FP informs Georges Auric that he has completed the sketch for a song, since lost or destroyed, entitled *Dimanche en mai*.[1] Poulenc reads the printed proofs of Britten's *Les Illuminations,* brought to Paris by Lennox Berkeley for a verdict from Nadia Boulanger (see p. 428).

(30 April) Bernac and Poulenc perform a recital in Avignon for the benefit of the Red Cross.

(10 May) Germany invades Belgium, France, Luxembourg, and the Netherlands. Winston Churchill becomes prime minister of England.

(25 May) Allied forces make a disastrous and dangerous retreat to

Dunkirk. The young French soldier Louis Aragon, later the poet of Poulenc's song *C*, experiences this part of the war at first hand.

(2 June) FP is mobilized into the Défense Contre Avions. The Germans bomb Paris on the 3rd. Some 2 million Parisians, fearing that their city is about to be destroyed, leave in a mass exodus (10th–14th).

The French government decamps to Tours and thence to Bordeaux. A treaty is negotiated between Marshal Philippe Pétain and the Germans on 22 June, followed by an official surrender three days later. The northern half of France is occupied by German forces, while the southern part is in the control of the collaborationist Vichy government led by Pétain.

Although Amboise and Tours were bombarded, Noizay had been spared. André and Suzanne Rocheron hold the fort at Le Grand Coteau.

FP's brief mobilization is spent in Cahors, in the south of France. He tells Marie-Blanche de Polignac of the hospitality of an elderly peasant couple with whom he is billeted, which included "*a table loaded with confits de canard, delectable vegetables, and often truffle omelettes washed down by a marvelous Cahors*" (10 July).[2] To Bernac, on the same day, he strikes an unexpectedly optimistic note: "*I have faith in the future and in our 'team,' and what is more, I feel full of music. . . . The absence of a piano has even been salutary. I like these parts. The air is buoyant. I live with peasants who give me confidence. That is all my news. You will no doubt be astounded by my calm. I assure you it runs deep.*"[3]

(18 July) FP is demobilized. Instead of going back to Paris or Noizay, he journeys 100 kilometers north to Brive-la-Gaillarde, where Uncle Papoum, his sister, nieces, and cousins have taken refuge from Paris. They will all stay there until 9 September, when a cattle truck is the only available means of transport back to the capital city. In Brive, at the piano of his friend Marthe Bosredon, FP sketches the piano piece *Mélancolie* FP105 (dedicated to Raymond Destouches, who is stuck in faraway Noizay; this work is the first of 1940) as well as *L'Histoire de Babar, le petit éléphant* FP129—a score that will take several years to complete. He also begins on a Sonata for Cello and Piano (the future FP143). In August Poulenc dines in Brive with distinguished fellow fugitives Yvonne Printemps and her actor husband Pierre Fresnay, and he agrees to write the music for Jean Anouilh's play *Léocadia*.

On returning to Noizay, FP continues work on his ballet *Les Animaux modèles* FP111.

During this summer the Battle of Britain rages in the air, with Hitler determined on an early invasion. Churchill speaks in the House of Commons in praise of British airmen: "Never in the field of human conflict has so much been owed by so many to so few" (20 August).

(1 September) Germany's Jews are forced to wear a yellow star on their clothing.

(October) *Les Chemins de l'amour* **FP106** (Anouilh), composed in Paris.

(October–November) *Banalités* **FP107** (Apollinaire), composed in Noizay and Paris.

(3 November) First public performance of *Les Chemins de l'amour* FP106 (in the play *Léocadia*), at the Théâtre de la Michodière, Paris. The singer is Yvonne Printemps. The play will run until 2 May 1941.

(9 November) FP and Bernac give a recital at the Salle Gaveau, featuring *Tel jour telle nuit* and songs by Chausson, Debussy, Fauré, and Ravel.

(December) *Colloque* **FP108** (Valéry), composed in Paris.

(9 December) First performance of the revised and definitive version of the Sextet in the Salle Chopin.

(14 December) First public performance of *Banalités* **FP107**, in the Salle Gaveau, Paris. Bernac is accompanied by FP. Other mélodies in the program are by Bordes, Debussy, Duparc, and Roussel.

During December the FP-Bernac duo record Chausson's *Le Colibri*, Duparc's *Soupir*, and Fauré's *Après un rêve* and *Lydia*. There are to be no more recordings until 1945, as Bernac refuses to have anything to do with radio broadcasts under enemy control. In common with so many singers who were at their artistic peak during the war, a travel-restricted period of no recordings, some of his best work is lost to international exposure and to posterity.

1941 (aged 42)

The year begins with a busy series of concerts for Poulenc, an indication of the immensely lively musical scene in wartime Paris—which, in contrast to other occupied European cities, avoids Allied aerial bombardment.

(18 January) FP takes up residence in Paris, having spent the New Year at Noizay. FP and Bernac give a recital of the composer's songs at the Théâtre de l'Atelier (25th).

(4 February) First public performances of *Ce doux petit visage* **FP99** and *Colloque* **FP108**, at the Théâtre des Mathurins, Paris. Bernac and the soprano Janine Micheau are accompanied by Poulenc. Other items on the program were songs by Chabrier and Debussy.

(16 February) FP performs the *Concert champêtre* at the Salle de l'Ancien Conservatoire.

(2 March) FP takes part in a performance of Stravinsky's *Les Noces* at the Ancien Conservatoire with fellow pianists Marcelle Meyer, Jacques Février, and Soulima Stravinsky.

(15 March) FP and Bernac give a recital at the Salle Gaveau. The theme

is "Baudelaire, Verlaine, Apollinaire, and five of their musicians." Poems are read by Madeleine Renaud; in addition to Poulenc, the featured composers are Duparc, Fauré, Debussy, and Honegger.[4]

(25 March) FP performs his *Aubade* with orchestra at the Ancien Conservatoire.

(May) FP completes his *Exultate Deo* and *Salve regina* at Noizay, and resumes work on his piano *Improvisations*, last worked on in September 1934.

(10 June) At a "Séance Francis Poulenc" recital at the Théâtre des Mathurins, FP accompanies Bernac and soprano Ginette Guillamat.

(July) FP is busy at Noizay making the piano score of his new ballet *Les Animaux modèles*, prior to its orchestration. On the 25th, FP and Bernac present a recital at the Casino Municipal in Biarritz, in Vichy France.

During his summer residence at Noizay, FP begins a string trio for the Trio Pasquier, which is never finished.

FP writes to Simone Girard regarding his intention to compose the music for Jean Giraudoux's film (after Balzac) *La Duchesse de Langeais*.

(Early September) Bernac visits Noizay for a week to prepare upcoming concerts. Glamorous photographs of Poulenc's house feature in the December issue of *Images de France*.

(17 September) FP offers to play the score of *Les Animaux modèles* to the Opéra director Jacques Rouché and the choreographer Serge Lifar, both of whom will be accused of collaboration after the war.

In the autumn FP declines to provide the music for the film of Louise de Vilmorin's novel *Le Lit à colonnes*, suggesting that Jean Françaix should compose it instead.

(8 October) Opening night of Charles Exbrayat's three-act play *La Fille du jardinier*, for which FP provides the incidental music, at the Théâtre des Mathurins. The play runs until January 1942.

(November) FP composes his *Impromptu* in E-flat Major, "Hommage à Schubert."

(15 November) FP and Bernac give a recital at the Salle Gaveau, featuring airs by Lully, songs by Liszt, mélodies by Ravel and Poulenc, and the premiere of Arthur Honegger's *Trois Poèmes de Claudel*.

(9 December) FP participates in a commemorative "Festival Albert Roussel" at the Salle de l'École Normale de Musique.

Just before Christmas Poulenc hears his Concerto in G Minor for Organ played by Maurice Duruflé, conducted by Charles Munch, at the Palais de Chaillot.

1942 (aged 43)

(10 January) The great fauvist painter André Derain, later accused of collaboration with the Germans, withdraws from providing the décor for *Les Animaux modèles.*[5]

(20 January) At a conference at Wannsee (in Berlin), the Nazis discuss the details that lead to a systematic program of the extermination of the Jews.

(25 January) FP plays his *Concert champêtre* in the Théâtre de Chatelet under the direction of Gaston Poulet.

(27 March) The Jean Giraudoux film *La Duchesse de Langeais,* for which FP has written the music, has its first screening.

(April) In Meknès, Morocco, where he and Bernac are performing recitals, FP sketches out a detailed scenario for *Les Animaux modèles.*

(19 May) FP and Bernac take part in a "Festival Fauré" at the Salle Gaveau, together with pianist Marguerite Long. The duo perform the cycle *La Bonne Chanson* and eight other songs of Fauré.

(21 May) First public performance of **Fiançailles pour rire FP101**, at the Salle Gaveau, Paris. Soprano Geneviève Touraine, sister of Gérard Souzay, is accompanied by the composer. Poulenc had hoped that the most celebrated French soprano of the time would premiere the cycle, "*but alas, Ninon Vallin doesn't like my music! I wipe away a large tear and press on.*"[6] Other works on the program are airs by Pergolesi, Cavalli, and Caccini and mélodies by Gounod and Roussel.

(29 May) All Jews in France are ordered to wear the yellow star.

(5 June) The Bernac-Poulenc duo present a "Récital des mélodies contemporaines" at the Salle de l'École Normale de Musique, one of their most adventurous and taxing programs, with no fewer than six first performances: *Trois Airs de Dolorès* by André Jolivet; *La Lyre et les amours* by Louis Beydts; *D'un paravent de laque* by Claude Delvincourt; *L'Adolescence clémentine* by Jean Françaix; *Le Chat* and *Deux Poèmes de Tagore* by Henri Sauguet; and *Noël* by Marcel Delannoy.

(1 July) Bernac and Poulenc take part in a "Honegger Week" at the Salle Gaveau, performing that composer's *Trois Psaumes,* the Giraudoux cycle *Petit Cours de morale,* and the early *Six Poèmes de Jean Cocteau.* Bernac also sings *Pâques à New York* with string quartet.

(3 July) FP and Bernac perform a recital at the Palais de Tokyo in Paris. Apart from Poulenc, the featured composers are Gounod, Chabrier, Auric, and Ravel.

(16–17 July) Parisian Jews are rounded up and taken to the Vélodrome d'Hiver (the "Vel' d'Hiv"), a bicycle velodrome used as a temporary holding site, before being sent on by train to Drancy and thence to Auschwitz. Max Jacob escapes this trawl, but his relatives do not.

(8 August) First performance of *Les Animaux modèles* at the Paris Opéra. It will be performed twenty-nine times before July 1944.

(19 August) In a letter to FP, Charles Koechlin confesses that he prefers *Les Biches* as a ballet to the new work; he likes the orchestration of *Les Animaux modèles*, but little else. FP thanks Koechlin for his frank remarks (c. 21th), and bemoans the quality of the string section in the Opéra orchestra: *"In the pit there were exactly 10 first violins, 7 seconds, 6 violas, 6 cellos, and 5 double basses. I know there has been a holiday period, but since the desks of political detainees ["prisonniers"] or of the Jews have not been replaced, it is clearly to the great detriment of the music."*

Under the auspices of the French National Committee, the critic Felix Aprahamian (1914–2005) arranges a series of concerts of French music at London's Wigmore Hall. At the Fauré concert (17 September), the Princesse de Polignac, now resident in Paignton (in Devon), is espied queueing for ticket returns to hear music originally dedicated to her, and is ushered into a place of honor by Aprahamian. The third concert (24th) celebrates Les Six and includes a performance of *Le Bestiaire* by the Swiss soprano Sophie Wyss. Benjamin Britten is one of the musicians taking part, on celesta.

(26 September) *"I've passed an odious and detestable summer. . . . I have often found my creations to have black holes. I resign myself to it. This will last as long as it lasts."*[7]

(October) FP composes a Sonata for Violin and Piano (FP119) inspired by the Spanish poet Federico García Lorca and dedicated to his memory. It is Poulenc's fifth attempt to write for this combination.

This same month, Poulenc reflects on the state of music in France, leading to a kind of self-evaluation: *"I know very well that I am not the sort of musician who makes harmonic innovations, like Igor, Ravel, or Debussy, but I do think there is a place for new music that is satisfied with using other people's chords. Wasn't this the case with Mozart and Schubert? And in any case, with time, the personality of my harmonic style will become evident. Wasn't Ravel for a long time regarded as nothing more than a petit maître and imitator of Debussy?"*[8]

(October–December) **Chansons villageoises FP117** (Fombeure), composed in Noizay and Paris.

(7 November) FP and Bernac give a recital at the Salle Gaveau: songs by John Dowland, Duparc, Debussy, and Reynaldo Hahn (*Études latines*), and *Chansons gaillardes*.

(Late November–early December) The duo give recitals in Cannes, Marseilles, and Lyon.

(3–8 December) FP spends five days in Brive with his friend Marthe Bosredon. Writing to Swiss conductor Ernest Ansermet, he evaluates what is happening in the French capital: "*Parisian musical life is intense. Munch is giving very beautiful concerts and each one of us tries to preserve the spiritual atmosphere of our good city. Picasso paints solitarily and superbly, Braque likewise. Éluard writes masterpieces.*"

(22 December) FP and Bernac take part in the 200th concert of the "Le Triptyque" series at the Salle de l'École Normale. They perform again Honegger's *Trois Poèmes de Claudel* and Henri Sauguet's *Quatre Mélodies*.

1943 (aged 44)

(6 February) FP and Bernac, together with pianist Nicole Henriot-Schweitzer, take part in a "Festival Maurice Ravel" at the Salle Gaveau: *Deux Épigrammes de Clément Marot, Histoires naturelles,* and *Don Quichotte à Dulcinée* (repeated on 27 March).

(March) FP goes to Bordeaux to review a performance of Fauré's opera *Pénélope*. He admires much of the music but finds the orchestration "*lamentable*."[9]

(22 March) A new series of Parisian concerts entitled "La Pléiade" (which FP has helped plan), sponsored by the publisher Gaston Gallimard and supported by the composer's great musical ally André Schaeffner, begins at the Galerie Charpentier, for the benefit of imprisoned writers and musicians.

(29 April) Ricardo Viñes dies.

(10 May) FP is present at a "Pléiade" concert at the Galerie Charpentier, where Olivier Messiaen's *Visions de l'Amen,* for two pianos, is given its first performance by Messiaen and his pupil (and future wife) Yvonne Loriod. Among the many luminaries in the audience are Cocteau, Paul Valéry, François Mauriac, Alexis Roland-Manuel, and the young Pierre Boulez.

(24 May) The soprano Suzanne Balguerie and FP present a full-length recital: mélodies by Duparc, Fauré's *La Bonne Chanson*, Debussy's *Ariettes oubliées,* and Poulenc's *Fiançailles pour rire*.

(28 May) FP joins Jacques Février for a performance (in the "Concerts du Conservatoire" series) of his Concerto for Two Pianos, conducted by Charles Munch.

(21 June) FP and violinist Ginette Neveu (1919–1949) give the first performance of his Sonata for Violin and Piano in the Salle Gaveau. (The work will be revised and published in a new edition in 1949.) The same concert includes Poulenc's *Sept Chansons* for unaccompanied chorus, Debussy's *Le Promenoir des deux amants* sung by Bernac, and choral music by Debussy and Ravel sung by the Chorale Passani.

Immediately after the Salle Gaveau concert, FP goes off to play a concert in Lyon.[10] There he finds in a bookshop a copy of the small Swiss edition of Éluard's *Poésie et vérité,* which contains the text for Poulenc's choral masterpiece *Figure humaine.*[11]

(23 June) FP and Bernac record the gently patriotic mélodie *À mon fils* by Pierre Vellones (1889–1939), for HMV France.

(28 June) First public performance of **Chansons villageoises FP117**, at the Salle Gaveau, Paris. Baritone Roger Bourdin is accompanied by the Orchestre Maurice Hewitt. Poulenc later came to realize that the best singer of this cycle (when piano-accompanied) was Bernac, sidelined in this instance because of the composer's desire to write for big voice and orchestra. The concert is the last in the "Pléiade"'s first season.

(Early July–20 August) In order to get away for the summer and compose, FP rents a two-room apartment with Raymond Destouches in Beaulieu-sur-Dordogne, Corrèze, not far from his pilgrimage site of Rocamadour. His plan is to write a string quartet and a violin concerto for Ginette Neveu, but neither aim is achieved. In the six weeks away, however, he manages to compose the unaccompanied choral cantata *Figure humaine* FP120. And despite the bad piano at his disposal, he embarks on settings of three poems by Louise de Vilmorin suitable for performance by a male singer.

(August–October) *Métamorphoses* **FP121** (Vilmorin), composed in Beaulieu-sur-Dordogne and Noizay. The first of the three songs, *Reine des mouettes*, was probably sketched earlier in the year.

Leaving Beaulieu, Poulenc goes to Brive to visit Marthe Bosredon for five days, then makes a pilgrimage to Nogent-sur-Marne, where he is saddened by the absence of the funfair atmosphere that had been such an exciting part of his youth.

On his return to Noizay, FP turns his attention to a volume of verse a friend has brought back from Switzerland: Louis Aragon's patriotic *Les Yeux d'Elsa.* The turn-around between discovering these poems, setting two of them to music, and giving their first performance—all in the space of three months—is remarkably swift by his standards.

(September–October) **Deux Poèmes de Louis Aragon FP122**, composed in Noizay.

(23 October) Jean de Polignac, husband of Marie-Blanche, ill and appalled by the Germans' taking over his home (Kerbastic), dies. FP dedicates to him the second Aragon song, *Fêtes galantes*. Since 1928 Poulenc had been the couple's frequent guest, an idyll that had now almost run its course.

(25 November) FP returns to Paris in order to rehearse with Bernac for their upcoming Paris recital. He meets the composer Jacques Leguerney, a pupil of Nadia Boulanger, at Bernac's apartment. In *The New Grove*'s assessment, Leguerney's songs "were regarded as second only to those of Poulenc."

FP himself seems not to have considered this composer (who favored poetry of the sixteenth-century Pléiade poets) much of a rival.

(8 December) First performances of **Métamorphoses FP121** and **Deux Poèmes de Louis Aragon FP122**, at the Salle Gaveau, Paris. Bernac is accompanied by the composer in a program that also includes airs by Pierre-Alexandre Monsigny, lieder by Schubert, and mélodies by Fauré and Chabrier. The inclusion of German lieder may have been designed to divert attention from the patriotic Aragon songs, which were performed without adverse reaction.

(9 December) FP travels to Belgium to play his two-piano concerto under the baton of Charles Munch.

During this year, FP records (for French Columbia) Debussy songs with soprano Lucienne Tragin, including an extract from Le Martyre de Saint Sébastien.

1944 (aged 45)

(Late January) Raymond Destouches is arrested for black marketeering. FP appears to have successfully pulled strings to effect his release, possibly with the help, via Cocteau, of the famous pianist Alfred Cortot (regarded by many as a collaborator). Also around this time, Destouches, accompanied by Poulenc's niece Rosine, crosses the border between Occupied and Vichy France in order to bury part of the Manceaux family fortune.[12] Raymond receives scant thanks from the Manceaux family and is accused of dishonesty— which seems unlikely and remains unproven. Poulenc stands firmly by him.

(21 January) FP records the music he has written to date for the Jean Anouilh film Le Voyageur sans bagage—possibly because the existing music for the play, by Milhaud, was not usable on account of German race laws. The film opens on 23 February.[13]

(20 February) FP and Bernac give a recital in Tours.

(5 March) Following his arrest by the Gestapo in Orléans, and due for deportation to Auschwitz, Max Jacob dies of bronchial pneumonia in the Drancy concentration camp, some seven miles northeast of Paris.

(19–21 March) Having been involved in the film, FP now composes the complete incidental music for the revival of Anouilh's Le Voyageur sans bagage FP123, for a production at the Théâtre de la Michodière. The music was recovered only some sixty-five years later.

(24 March) FP travels to Brussels as accompanist to violinist Ginette Neveu and for a recital with Bernac (on the 29th).

FP writes an article (published on 31 March) in homage to the recently deceased critic and champion of modern music Louis Laloy, close friend of Debussy and the cause of Satie's falling out with Poulenc twenty years earlier.

(April) *Les Animaux modèles* is once again performed at the Opéra. At a "La Pléiade" concert at the Salle du Conservatoire (4th), FP performs the *Aubade.* On the same day, Charles de Gaulle, from exile in London, takes command of all Free French Forces.

(2 May) FP's niece Rosine Manceaux marries Jean Seringe.

(May–October) FP immerses himself at Noizay in the composition of *Les Mamelles de Tirésias* FP125. He also continues work on the two Apollinaire settings *Montparnasse* and *Hyde Park,* which he will finish at the beginning of 1945. Bernac, regularly consulted about vocal matters in the new opera, writes a detailed letter of advice to Poulenc (6 June, D Day).

(8 June) A munitions train is bombarded a few kilometers from Noizay, and water and electricity are cut off in FP's house. When Amboise and Tours are bombed, FP offers refuge to his friend Marthe de Kerrieu, a famous cocotte of the Belle Époque, who fascinates him (and whose mémoire he published at his own expense). He also takes in the parents and sister of Raymond Destouches, although they eat their meals separately, in the kitchen.

Bernac, who has remained in Paris, is an important life-line of information for FP. *"Did the Messiaen performance take place and did you hear the* Litanies? *I have been through much of his music again. When he remains faithful to his* Visions *style, he is truly remarkable; in other more contrived pages* [Paul] *Dukas's influence is annoying"* (24 June).[14]

FP tries, without success, to procure a teaching appointment for Bernac at the Paris Conservatoire. The baritone's unusual voice, that he was never a Conservatoire student, and that he lacked an operatic background clearly all count against him.

Raymond Destouches travels to Paris, bringing back with him a score of the choral cantata *Figure humaine* (composed in the summer of 1943), which has already been printed by Paul Rouart. Copies are kept safe in the publisher's warehouse until after liberation.[15]

Responding badly to the everyday stress of living under war conditions in Noizay, FP complains of rheumatism in his shoulder, and later of a full-blown attack of arthritis. In a letter to Marie-Blanche de Polignac (27 July), which nostalgically evokes the pleasures and luxuries of his prewar visits to Kerbastic, he bemoans being stuck in Noizay, where conditions are becoming increasingly difficult as the Allied invasion progresses: *"A photo album of Paris charms and numbs me like a shot of morphine."*[16]

(6 August) In a letter to Bernac in Paris, FP reports that carloads of German civilians and functionaries are leaving Angers by night, events curiously reminiscent of 1940. He confides his evaluation of other composers' work, the result of hours spent at the piano in recent months reading through their scores. Some, like Rieti and Hindemith, fare badly in his reappraisal; but

"if people love Apollinaire, Éluard, Aragon, Loulou [de Vilmorin] *etc., it will always be necessary to get to them while passing me on the way."*[17]

(25 August) Paris is liberated by Allied forces, the Free French Forces and the Resistance playing a key role in a symbolic restoration of French honor. Noizay is liberated by the Americans at more or less the same time. FP describes to Bernac how female collaborators in Tours had their heads shaved and were thrown naked into the fountains of the Hôtel de Ville. There is gossip that his Noizay neighbor Suzanne Lalé (who had driven Bernac and Poulenc to Venice in 1938) would be subject to the same treatment. His letter also credits Raymond Destouches with enormous audacity and bravery in the execution of "two dangerous missions" and the saving of civilian lives in Amboise (27th).[18]

(28 August) The Germans surrender in Toulon and Marseilles in southern France, and General George S. Patton's tanks cross the Marne. The Germans surrender at Boulogne (22 September).

In late October or early November, the BBC dispatch newsreel producer Véra Lindsay to France to discuss the first British performance of *Figure humaine*. She returns to London with a score of the work.

(Late November) FP and Suzanne Peignot give a recital, their first in a considerable length of time.

(27 November) FP plays through two new works, *Les Mamelles de Tirésias* and *Figure humaine*, at the home of Marie-Laure de Noailles in Paris. Present are Picasso, Éluard, and Cocteau, who observes: "Even Francis's singing showed us how his musical intelligence heightens both the harshness and the charm of a text."[19]

(11 December) First night at the Comédie des Champs-Élysées of J. M. Barrie's play *La Nuit de Saint-Jean* (originally *Dear Brutus*), for which FP wrote incidental music for flute and percussion (the play will run until early February 1945).

(December) FP visits the poet Jean-Marie Legrand ("Jaboune"; see FP75), wounded in action, at the Val-de-Grâce military hospital in Paris.

(24 and 26 December) FP composes *Un soir de neige*, an *a cappella* cantata for six mixed voices to four texts by Éluard.

1945 (aged 46)

Duff Cooper (soon to be the new British Ambassador to France, and the lover of Louise de Vilmorin) arranges for a military aircraft to take FP and Bernac to London; they arrive on 2 January for a two-week stay full of musical activity:

—(4 January) The Committee of the London Philharmonic Orchestra gives a reception at 53 Welbeck Street, around the corner from Wigmore Hall. Among the luminaries present are Sir Kenneth Clark, Lady Colefax,

Returning to London after six years, the duo gave a recital in January 1945 at Wigmore Hall.

publisher Leslie Boosey, Benjamin Britten (his first meeting with Poulenc), Peter Pears, and three British musicologists: Scott Goddard, Edwin Evans, and Edward Dent.

—(6 January) At the Albert Hall, FP's Concerto for Two Pianos is performed by the composer with Britten, the LPO conducted by Basil Cameron.

—(7 January) In a Wigmore Hall recital ("under the auspices of the French Provisional Government"), FP and Bernac perform works by Duparc, Fauré, Debussy, and Poulenc. Bernac will remember the occasion for the rest of his life: "Imagine our joy at being able to leave France. When we stepped out on the Wigmore Hall stage, the entire audience rose and my emotion was such that instead of beginning to sing, I was overcome with tears."[20]

—(8 January) The duo record Fauré, Debussy, and Poulenc for the BBC. The taping session is followed by a dinner with leading BBC personalities: Victor Hely-Hutchinson, Julian Herbage, Edward Lockspeiser, Leslie Woodgate, Elizabeth Poston (also a composer), and Rollo Myers. Poulenc plays through *Figure humaine* for the assembled company.

—(9 January) The duo perform a recital of Fauré, Debussy, and Poulenc at the National Gallery.

(15 January) FP and Bernac depart for Paris on the first boat-train in operation from Britain to the Continent since May 1940.

(September 1941–January 1945) ***Deux Mélodies de Guillaume Apollinaire* (*Montparnasse* and *Hyde Park*) FP127**, composed in Noizay and Paris.

(17 January) Playwright Édouard Bourdet dies.

(27 January) Soviet forces liberate the death camp at Auschwitz, in Poland.

(5 February) FP takes part in a performance of Stravinsky's *Les Noces*, conducted by Manuel Rosenthal, in Paris.

(6 February) English critic Felix Aprahamian visits Poulenc and Ber-

nac at the composer's Paris apartment, becoming one of the first to hear *Montparnasse*.

(18 February) FP makes private recordings of *Mouvements perpétuels*, his Violin Sonata, and, with Suzanne Peignot, settings of Max Jacob and Ronsard.

(March) Bernac and Poulenc return to England for further concerts and recordings, with the Hyde Park Hotel in London as their base. Soon after his arrival, at a gathering of the London Philharmonic Arts Club, Poulenc listens to works by Bartók and Hindemith. During Hindemith's *Ludus tonalis*, FP passes Felix Aprahamian a note: "*My God, deliver us from fugues. Amen.*"[21]

In continuing wartime conditions, and the attendant transport difficulties, their schedule poses an almost superhuman challenge, but it is also evidence of the musical hunger of a British public eager to welcome artists from abroad after several years of musical isolation:

—(10 March) A performance of *Aubade* (with orchestra) in Brighton. BBC recording of Fauré's *La Bonne Chanson* (11th and 12th, afternoon). A violin and piano recital at Wigmore Hall with Ginette Neveu, part of which FP accompanies (12th, evening). Recital of FP and Bernac in Sheffield (13th). Recital in Birmingham (14th). Recital at the Chelsea Town Hall, the program including Lully, Chausson, Chabrier, Fauré, Poulenc, and Ravel (15th). Recital in Bletchley (16th). A performance with Ginette Neveu in Cambridge (18th). Recital in London's Fyvie Hall (Regent Street Polytechnic) honoring the memory of musicologist Edwin Evans, who died on 3 March. Harriet Cohen plays piano pieces, and the FP-Bernac duo are joined by Maggie Teyte for the final scene of Debussy's *Pelléas et Mélisande* (20th).

—(21st) Choral rehearsals for *Figure humaine*. Recital at the National Gallery of Debussy songs (Teyte) and Poulenc songs (Bernac), and the Debussy and Poulenc violin sonatas (Neveu) (22nd, lunch hour). Duo recital at Cowdray Hall, Cavendish Square (22nd, evening), organized by the London Contemporary Music Centre, followed by a reception at the Aston Grill. BBC recording of songs (23rd, completed on the 26th). The premiere of *Figure humaine* with the BBC Chorus (in Rollo Myers's English version) under Leslie Woodgate, a broadcast from the BBC Concert Hall with invited guests (25th).

—(27th) Wigmore Hall recital: first British performances of Maurice Jaubert's *L'Eau vive* and *Chants des métiers de Haute-Provence*, Jean Françaix's *L'Adolescence clémentine*, Stravinsky's *Trois Histoires pour enfants*, and the Poulenc cycles *Banalités* and *Chansons villageoises*.

—During this British visit, the duo also somehow manage to record Fauré's *La Bonne Chanson* for HMV (DB 8931–3) at the EMI studios in Abbey Road. It is perhaps little wonder that on receiving advance copies of recordings made during such a challenging and overworked time, singer and pianist decided against their release.

In Germany, the Buchenwald concentration camp is liberated by American forces (10 April) and Bergen-Belsen by the British (15th).

(21 April) Back in Paris, FP attends the Paris premiere of *Un soir de neige* at the "Pléiade" concert in the Salle du Conservatoire. He shares the program with choral works by Messiaen.

(27 April) First public performances of **Deux Mélodies de Guillaume Apollinaire FP127**, at the Salle Gaveau, Paris. Bernac and Suzanne Balguerie are accompanied by the composer in a recital given over entirely (for the first time, and not without trepidation) to his own songs. The Salle Gaveau is sold out. Other works included *Banalités*, *Tel jour telle nuit*, *Fiançailles pour rire*, and the two Aragon settings; *Priez pour paix* was the encore. In a program note, André Schaeffner avers that "Francis Poulenc contributes to our French music a little of that which, each in respect of his own country, did Schubert and Musorgsky."[22] Ecstatic reviews refer to Poulenc as "our Mozart" and praise his works' sobriety, strength, grandeur, and prosody; while Bernac, on account of "the beauty of his sound, his power," and "depth of emotion . . . remains our best singer of lieder."[23]

(30 April) Adolf Hitler commits suicide in his bunker in Berlin.

(May) At Auric's invitation, FP contributes to *Les Lettres françaises*, formerly a Resistance magazine. He spends a recuperative May and June in Noizay, with a trip to Paris in early June.

(8 June) Poet Robert Desnos dies in the Terezin (Theresienstadt) concentration camp, in Czechoslovakia.

(8 July) FP visits Rocamadour and then leaves for Larche in the Corrèze, where he takes lodgings with piano at a farm named La Chatoine. Once again his holiday companion is Raymond Destouches, who sleeps in a small room in the main farmhouse; they remain there until the end of August. FP begins work on his unaccompanied choral settings *Chansons françaises* and *L'Histoire de Babar, le petit éléphant*. Both the BBC and HMV in London persuade him to return to *Babar* (begun in 1940), as an ideal project for broadcast and gramophone record.

(From 26 August) FP returns to Paris and spends a week in discussion with Jean Anouilh and Armand Salacrou concerning Salacrou's play *Le Soldat et la sorcière*, for which he agrees to write incidental music (nearly completed by 10 September). The play runs from October 1945 to May 1946.

In Noizay, FP concentrates on the orchestration of *Les Mamelles de Tirésias*, plans a string quartet, and completes *L'Histoire de Babar*. This work, for reciter with piano interludes, is conceived for Bernac to read in French, while an English actor will read it for British audiences.

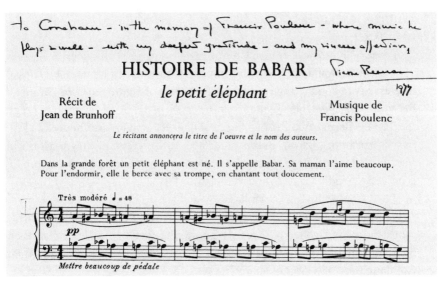

First page of L'Histoire de Babar, le petit éléphant, *inscribed to the author by Bernac in 1977.*

(10 September) In an extraordinary letter to Bernac, we glimpse some of the strategies FP employs for drumming up and organizing concert engagements. He outlines how he wishes 1946 to be divided between composing, performing, and holiday time; only three months are assigned to Noizay.[24] Poulenc also considers the possibility of composing music for Apollinaire's libretto *Casanova*. He describes to Bernac his fruitless efforts to set the poet's "Le Pont" (to be FP131 in 1946): *"I feel no more desire to write songs. Let's hope that it will appeal to me again one day."*[25]

(26 September) Béla Bartók dies.

The FP-Bernac duo perform in Reims (24 October) and Brussels (31st).

(November) Bernac and FP undertake a small tour of Ireland, including a concert in Dublin. On the 24th, the day of a recital in Belfast, his Uncle Papoum dies of cardiac arrest. *"I am having difficulty in joining together my two beings: before and after the death of Papoum."*[26]

By the end of November, Bernac and Poulenc are back in Britain for another densely packed tour—what FP later calls *"an infernal winter of concerts"*:[27] Cambridge (29 November), London (two concerts with different programs on 2 December), Harpenden (5th), Oxford (8th), Marlborough (9th).

(December) Bernac and Poulenc make eight sides of 78-rpm discs, some of their best, for HMV: Gounod's *Au rossignol* and *Sérénade*, Poulenc's *Métamorphoses*, *Deux Poèmes de Louis Aragon*, and *Le Bestiaire*, Duparc's *Élégie* and *L'Invitation au voyage*.

1946 (aged 47)

(18 January) Poulenc is named Chevalier de la Légion d'Honneur.

On Nadia Boulanger's return from American exile in January, FP tries to interest her in conducting the first performance of *Figure humaine*. Amid all his winter engagements, FP must put the estate of his Uncle Papoum in order.

The FP-Bernac duo begin a flurry of concert activity: Mulhouse (22 January), Strasbourg (25th), Besançon (26th). In Switzerland they perform in Vevey (1 February)—the hometown of tenor Hugues Cuenod (with whom FP is on very friendly terms)—and Winterthur (3rd).

(4–c. 18 March) Tour of Holland.

(27 March) Concert in Brussels, where FP and Bernac are guests of the industrialist and collector Auguste Lambiotte and his wife Rose in their home, dubbed St. Bernard's Palace. FP considers the Lambiottes and their two daughters *"my Belgian family."*[28]

(April) Back in Noizay, FP completes the final three songs of the unaccompanied *Chansons françaises* FP130.

FP had perhaps hoped to inherit from his Uncle Papoum the apartment at 5, rue de Médicis, the building where he had already lived for ten years in the "maid's room." His sister Jeanne, however, claims Papoum's former dwelling, and Poulenc tells Milhaud (4 June) he has decided to move into another flat on the sixth floor of the same building, with bedroom, sitting room, and dining room (*"at long last I will be able to have friends to dinner"*), and marvelous views of the Luxembourg Gardens.[29] FP retains the services of Papoum's domestics, Anna Zeugin (the cook, from Alsace) and her Swiss husband Charles, sharing their services from time to time with Jeanne. This will be Poulenc's home in Paris for the remainder of his life. After renovations, the move takes place in 1947.

(14 June) The first broadcast performance in Paris of *L'Histoire de Babar*, with Bernac in the reciter's role.

(17 June) FP is invested with the Légion d'Honneur. As he requires a sponsor for the event, he asks his writer friend François Mauriac to perform this service (six years later Mauriac will receive the Nobel Prize for literature).

FP and Bernac now embark on another of those "short, hectic trips basking in the English limelight":[30] Brighton (23 June). First British performance of *Babar* on the BBC's *Children's Hour*, with Robert Irwin as narrator (24th). Recital at Mayflower Barn, Jordans (Buckinghamshire), in a program that mixes Dowland and Schubert with the French repertoire (29th). BBC concerts, collaborating with the oboist Leon Goossens (30 June and 3 July). A fifteen-minute BBC-TV interview with Poulenc by Cecil Madden at London's Alexandra Palace (9 July).

Back in Noizay, FP struggles to write a string quartet, his second unsuccessful attempt. He tells Nadia Boulanger: "*I am prisoner face to face with my quartet. How difficult it is. There are days when we embrace each other, others when we slap each other in the face.*"[31]

(Late July–early August) FP and Bernac spend a three-week working holiday at Le Tremblay. The singer's presence during these days seems to have had a remarkable effect on Poulenc's productivity.

(July) *Deux Mélodies sur des poèmes de Guillaume Apollinaire* (*Le Pont* and *Un poème*) **FP131** and *Le Disparu* **FP134** (Desnos), composed in Normandy at Le Tremblay.

(August) *Paul et Virginie* **FP132** (Radiguet), completed in Noizay. Date and locale of the first performance are unknown.

(14, 18, 19 August) *Main dominée par le cœur* **FP135** (Éluard), composed in Noizay. Date and locale of the first performance are unknown.[32]

FP shows himself inspired and instructed by earlier mélodie composers. An entry in his *Journal* expresses admiration for Bizet's Hugo setting *Les Adieux de l'hôtesse arabe* (28 August); another entry mentions his affection for Musorgsky's *Nursery* cycle (8 September).

In August, FP writes for *Harper's Bazaar*, whose editor, Carmel Snow, is a friend. He contributes recipes (published in the November issue) for "Eau clairette," "Lait de poule," "Poulet à l'Aveyronnaise" (his father came from the Aveyron district), and "Crème bachique"—titles chosen to reflect his "Poulet" or "Poupoule" nicknames or, in the case of the last recipe, a song (*Couplets bachiques* FP42/v). "*I grew up in a family where gastronomy was a rite . . . it is my culinary ancestry.*"[33]

(13 September) Birth of FP's daughter Marie-Ange (who will remain unacknowledged as such during his lifetime). Her mother was Frédérique ("Freddy") Lebedeff, whom the composer had known since 1929 through Richard Chanlaire. Freddy's husband, Vladimir Lebedeff, abandons her on the birth of the little girl. Marie-Ange grows up believing FP is her godfather (*parrain*) and uses her mother's surname.

(October–November) FP and Bernac rehearse at Noizay for concerts in the upcoming season. A particularly difficult challenge is a new cycle by Luigi Dallapiccola, *Rencesvals: Trois Fragments de la Chanson de Roland*.

(6 November) First public performances of *Deux Mélodies sur des poèmes de Guillaume Apollinaire* **FP131** and *Le Disparu* **FP134**, at the Salle Gaveau, Paris. Bernac is accompanied by the composer in a program that includes airs by Grétry, lieder by Schumann, English settings by Hindemith, and mélodies by Debussy and Poulenc. *Main dominée par le cœur* may have been the encore.

(14 November) Manuel de Falla dies.

In the late part of the year, FP finishes his string quartet at last, but a play-through with the Calvet Quartet proves an embarrassment: "*I threw my manuscript into a drain on the Place Péreire! I went straight to a café and phoned Auric. . . . There were just three nice tunes but only if played by wind instruments.*" Auric advises him not to forget the three tunes. "*These themes now appear in my* Sinfonietta *and, remembering our phone conversation, I dedicated this piece to Auric.*"[34]

(28 November) Nusch Éluard dies suddenly of a cerebral hemorrhage.

(2 December) *Figure humaine* is performed for the first time in Belgium, with 140 singers under the direction of Paul Collaer. In Brussels FP also performs *Babar* in a Flemish translation, and hears Milhaud's early song cycle *Alissa* performed at the Lambiottes' house.

(16 December) FP performs his Sextet with the Quintette à Vent at the Paris Conservatoire. He spends the remaining part of the month in Monte Carlo.

Toward the end of the year FP meets the soprano Denise Duval (1921–2016) for the first time. He is immediately struck by her talent and beauty, and conceives an instantaneous enthusiasm to cast her in the lead role of *Les Mamelles de Tirésias*.[35] "*Just think of what the good fairies have put into her cradle—a voice of sunlight, real gifts as an actress, beauty and chic.*"[36]

1947 (aged 48)

Much of the work at the beginning of the year is taken up with preparing for the premiere of *Les Mamelles de Tirésias* in early June. Now that FP had found his ideal Thérèse in Denise Duval, it was full steam ahead for the production. But even this big project could not get in the way of his profitable English tours:

—(9 February) FP and Bernac perform at London's Wigmore Hall in a program of Grétry fragments from *Le Jugement de Midas*, Schumann's *Dichterliebe*, Lennox Berkeley's *Five Songs of Walter de la Mare*, and Poulenc's *Chansons villageoises*. BBC recordings penciled in on 10, 13, 26, 27 February and 4, 5, 6 March. Recital at Welwyn (21 February). Concert at Chelsea Town Hall with the Leighton Lucas Orchestra, featuring Poulenc's Sextet and *Aubade* (28th). Chamber music recital for the London Contemporary Music Centre at Wigmore Hall. FP plays his Sextet with the Dennis Brain Wind Quintet, and Natasha Litvin (Mrs. Stephen Spender) performs Lennox Berkeley's Piano Sonata (4 March).

(20 March) Lecture with Bernac, "My Melodies and Their Poets," at the Université des Annales in Paris: "*Above all I ask my interpreters to sing, always sing, really sing, as if it were a Lied by Schumann or a song by Gounod. I love singing for singing's sake. . . . Understanding every word carries no weight*

with me if the singer, of whichever gender, has no legato and if technical short-comings produce breaks in the musical line. If an interpreter is intelligent, as a bonus, so much the better!"[37]

(15 April) The first read-through with the cast of *Les Mamelles de Tirésias*.

(7 May) A "Concert Public Radio" recital includes Bernac and Poulenc performing Dallapiccola's *Rencesvals*, Hindemith's English songs, and Éluard settings by Poulenc.

(12 May) FP plays his Violin Sonata with Françoise Soulé at the Conservatoire.

(22 May) The French premiere of *Figure humaine* is conducted by Paul Collaer at the Théâtre des Champs-Élysées.

(3 June) *Les Mamelles de Tirésias*, dedicated to Darius Milhaud in celebration of his return to France, premieres at the Opéra-Comique. There is a public scandal when some regular patrons object to the vulgarities of Apollinaire's text, but most reviews are highly favorable for a work that is the worthy successor of Chabrier's *Le Roi malgré lui* and Ravel's *L'Heure espagnole*. In a review (4th), the critic Claude Rostand for the first time refers to Poulenc as a combination of "moine et voyou," monk and ragamuffin. FP's designation as "Poulenc-Janus" followed shortly after.

Another short, event-packed trip to England: duo recital at the Mayflower Barn, Jordans, Buckinghamshire (7 June), BBC recordings (8th and 13th) as well as a private party at 3 Belgrave Place. FP meets Paul Hindemith on this trip; he likes that composer's *Variations for Piano and Strings*, but finds his *Hérodiade* "*always against Mallarmé*" (as Poulenc writes, unusually for him, in English).[38]

(Beginning of July) FP is invited to provide incidental music for Anouilh's play *L'Invitation au château*.

FP goes for a short break to the Corrèze and visits Rocamadour. He returns to Paris by the end of July, and then to Noizay on 1 August.

The BBC commissions an orchestral *Sinfonietta* from Poulenc, to celebrate the first anniversary of the Third Programme. Despite assiduous summer work at Noizay, and the fact that he is using material discarded from the abandoned string quartet, FP is not able to finish the work on time (it would be delivered only in September 1948). Fearing that this failure will endanger his relationship with the BBC, he promises very good financial terms for the work when it is at last finished.[39]

Between 24 July and 1 August, FP meets the actor and director Jean-Louis Barrault in Paris to discuss composing incidental music (to be conducted by Pierre Boulez) for Molière's *Amphitryon*. By 23 September he is able to assure Bernac that the score would be "*very special*," although "*it was horribly difficult to do*."[40]

(Summer–September) *Trois Chansons de F. García Lorca* **FP136**, composed in Noizay.

FP is commissioned by the Choir of St. Graal in Amsterdam to orchestrate the *Litanies à la Vierge noire* from 1936. The finished manuscript is dated 1 September.

FP begins a series of radio broadcasts entitled *À bâtons rompus* (Chitchat, or This and That)—thirty-minute radio talks, interspersed with gramophone recordings, made between September 1947 and late April or early May 1948. The first subjects are "Maurice Chevalier," "Spain I and II," "Paris and Symphonic Music," "Three Great Singers: Claire Croiza, Maggie Teyte, Ninon Vallin," "Maurice Ravel," "André Messager," and "Walton and Britten."

(3 October) FP and Bernac make another brief visit to England, followed by further radio broadcasts when they return to Paris.

(21 October) *. . . mais mourir* **FP137** (Éluard), composed in Noizay. Date and locale of the first performance are unknown.

(5 November) First night of Anouilh's *L'Invitation au château* at the Théâtre de l'Atelier. The play runs until July 1948.

(12 November) First performance of *Trois Chansons de F. García Lorca* **FP136**, at the Salle Gaveau, Paris. Bernac is accompanied by the composer in a program of Rameau, Schubert, Stravinsky, and Ravel (*Histoires naturelles*).

During yet another UK visit, FP and Bernac appear on television (3 December), give a recital (4th), and present a BBC recital of Debussy and Ravel (7th). They also record four Fauré songs for HMV: *Soir, Le Secret, Automne,* and *Les Berceaux.* These are the last song recordings made by the duo for EMI at Abbey Road. Their next recordings were made in February–March 1950, during their second American tour.

(5 December) Molière's *Amphitryon* (décor and costumes by Christian Bérard) opens at the Théâtre Marigny in Paris. FP is in the UK at the time.

1948 (aged 49)

After a recital in Lisbon (9 January), FP and Bernac undertake a fifteen-concert tour in Holland: to Amsterdam (19th) and The Hague (2 February). Concerts in Rome, Palermo, Tunis, and Algiers follow in March.

(February–April) FP continues his radio talks in the *À bâtons rompus* series: "Sergei Prokofiev," "Sacred Music," "Music Bad and Exquisite," "Folklore in Twentieth-Century Music, II & III,"[41] "Darius Milhaud," "The Influence of the Fair," "Igor Stravinsky and Asceticism," "Charles Gounod," "Carl Maria von Weber," and "Francis Poulenc and His Mélodies."

(April–May) In Noizay FP makes preliminary sketches later to be incorporated in *Calligrammes*. He attempts to arrange a performance of the *Sinfo-*

nietta (not yet complete or delivered to the BBC) before 22 October, when he will depart for the USA.

This spring FP meets the American two-piano team of Arthur Gold and Robert Fizdale at a lunch with Germaine Tailleferre and Georges Auric. FP will write three works for this duo.

(1 June) FP and Bernac take part in a BBC program devoted to the music of Mozart and Poulenc. FP goes directly from London to Strasbourg, where he performs his *Le Bal masqué* (15th).

(Mid-July) FP makes his customary summer visit to Le Tremblay, where he works on the *Calligrammes* songs, the Cello Sonata, and the last movement of the *Sinfonietta*. He is able to assure Bernac (on the 18th) that there will be "*a beautiful new cycle that I already love as much as* Tel jour telle nuit" for their second New York recital.[42]

(19 May–18 August) **Calligrammes FP140** (Apollinaire), composed in Noizay and in Normandy at Le Tremblay. Bernac takes delivery of the songs at Noizay on 28 August and returns on 13–15 September, knowing them well enough to rehearse for the upcoming American tour.

(August) FP's nephew Frère Jerôme Poulenc asks him for a choral work for the Convent of Carrières-sous-Poissy. Back in Noizay, FP composes *Quatre Petites Prières de Saint François d'Assise* FP142.

Music listened to on gramophone or radio at Noizay by the end of the summer includes Schoenberg's Violin Concerto, Hindemith's opera *Cardillac*, and works by Dallapiccola and Bartók. FP also coaches the bass Doda Conrad in Henri Sauguet's new Max Jacob song cycle, *Visions infernales*. Much time is devoted to rehearsing with Bernac for their upcoming six-week tour of the United States.

(15 September) Ahead of his first American visit, FP sends a supplicatory letter to composer and critic Virgil Thomson (in private, he has recently mocked Thomson's music to the pianists Gold and Fizdale).[43] He wonders what the "*famous Virgil Thomson*" will make of his new cycle *Calligrammes*. The two seem to know each other already (perhaps since the 1920s), as FP employs the "tu" form in a letter that serves as a carefully aimed charm offensive.[44]

(16 October) As a prelude to their American tour, Bernac and Poulenc give a private performance of *Calligrammes* at the home of Marie-Blanche de Polignac in Paris, an evening that also includes the premiere of Sauguet's *Visions infernales*, sung by Doda Conrad. Among the guests are Arthur Rubinstein, Marguerite Long, Jacques Leguerney, Marya Freund, Suzanne Peignot, René Chalupt, and Robert Veyron-Lacroix.

(22 October) Traveling in the company of Doda Conrad, Bernac and Poulenc leave Le Havre for New York, probably arriving on the 28th. Decades later Conrad will write that the composer left France suffering from a terri-

bly sore throat, terrified he had cancer; Conrad claims to have guessed it was gonorrhea of the throat and arranged treatment in New York.[45]

(24 October) Roger Désormière conducts the first performance of the *Sinfonietta* at the BBC in London, in the composer's absence.

FP, once installed in a two-room apartment (with a Baldwin piano) in the St. Moritz Hotel in New York, calls on Virgil Thomson (29 October). From the beginning, the tour with Bernac is a huge success, both musically and socially. FP dines with Christian Dior, who has just opened a new boutique in New York. He re-establishes links with old friends Wanda Landowska, Vittorio Rieti, Yvonne de Casa Fuerte, Natalie Paley, and Nicky de Gunzbourg (editor of *Vogue*). New friends are made: Leonard Bernstein will conduct the last of FP's works fifteen years later; the soprano Rose Dercourt and her husband Fred Plaut will become close friends and ever-helpful factotums. Bernac and Poulenc also take part in madcap outings with "the Boys" (pianists Gold and Fizdale) to Chinatown and Harlem.

(30 October) FP hears a performance of his Organ Concerto in Boston.

In a rare visit to the cinema, FP sees an Alfred Hitchcock thriller—*Rope*, starring James Stewart—in which his *Mouvements perpétuels* has been used without permission. He immediately instructs his publishers to chase the appropriate royalties.

(4 November) FP and Bernac make their American recital debut at Dumbarton Oaks, Washington, D.C.: three excerpts from Lully operas, three Debussy mélodies, and Poulenc's *Tel jour telle nuit* and *Chansons villageoises*.

(6 November) Back in New York, FP attends an orchestral concert conducted by Arturo Toscanini.

(7 November) Repeating the program performed in Washington, the duo make their New York debut at Town Hall. They are greeted by three minutes of applause, and *Tel jour telle nuit* receives seven curtain calls. "*Pierre has been fantastic. He deserves his triumph.*"[46]

(2–8 November) **Hymne FP144** (Racine), composed in New York. The date on the music is January 1949.

(8 November) Metropolitan Opera soprano Lily Pons (who had long ago performed Poulenc's *Airs chantés*) gives a reception in the composer's honor; Vladimir Horowitz is another special guest.

(9 November) Duo recital at Jordan Hall in Boston.

(11, 12, 14 November) FP performs his *Concert champêtre* (piano version) under the baton of Dmitri Mitropoulos at Carnegie Hall.

(15 November) Duo recital at Sage Hall in Northampton, Massachusetts, sponsored by Smith College.

(20 November) First public performance of **Calligrammes FP140**, at Town Hall, New York. In this second (sold-out) Town Hall concert, the new

cycle receives seven curtain calls. There were five encores, and FP notes that he and Bernac took twenty-three bows in all. The program also included songs by Gounod, Schumann, Fauré, and Ravel.

(21 November) The duo leave for a tour of the "provinces": Quebec, Chicago (Chicago Arts Club, 28 November), Los Angeles (arriving on the 29th, with a concert at the Wilshire Ebell Theater on 1 December). FP tells reporters meeting his train in Los Angeles, *"J'adore Hollywood. . . . I want to marry Greta Garbo and live here for the rest of my life."*[47] He meets Edward G. Robinson and Ingrid Bergman, and he and Bernac lunch with Igor and Vera Stravinsky (2 December).

During his Californian sojourn, FP also visits Darius and Madeleine Milhaud in Oakland (Milhaud divides his time between living in Paris and teaching at Mills College). Their tour takes Poulenc and Bernac to San Francisco, Denver, and Salt Lake City (by 5 December).

(11 December) Their last New York recital is under the auspices of the League of Composers, honoring Poulenc with a concert devoted entirely to his music at the Museum of Modern Art.

(12 December) Recital in Pittsburgh. Recital in the Barclay Hotel ballroom, Philadelphia (13th).

(14 December) FP and Bernac depart New York for Le Havre, arriving in France on the 23rd. Misia Sert is hugely amused by FP's slew of stories on his return, and laughs helplessly at his newfound enthusiasm. "He's just discovered America," she exclaims.[48] *"It fascinates me, although I only feel at home in Paris."*[49]

(28 December) First public performance of *Hymne* **FP144**, at Town Hall, New York (postponed from the 12th). Doda Conrad is accompanied by Erich Itor Kahn.

1949 (aged 50)

(7 January–17 March) FP returns to his *À bâtons rompus* series, having brought back with him from America gramophone recordings (not available in Europe) that he will use to illustrate the lectures. His subjects, much influenced by his recent transatlantic tour, are "Return from America,"[50] "Igor Stravinksy: American Portrait," "Samuel Barber and Gian Carlo Menotti," "Wanda Landowska," "Francis Poulenc and His Instrumental Music," "Claude Debussy," "Béla Bartók and Alban Berg," "Henri Sauguet," "Ravel the Orchestrator," "Italian Song," "Erik Satie," and "Louis Ganne."

Bernac and Poulenc embark on a twelve-day British tour: In a performance of *L'Histoire de Babar*, FP accompanies British newsreader and broadcaster Bruce Belfrage (8 February). BBC broadcast with FP and Bernac (10th). Recital in Edinburgh (11th). Recital in Amersham (13th). BBC recital with the first British performance of *Calligrammes* (14th). Recital in Doncaster (16th). Recital in Cambridge (17th). BBC broadcast, including a performance of *Le Bal masqué* (20th).

(11 February) One of FP's closest friends, Christian Bérard (b. 1902), dies in Paris of a cerebral embolism. FP will dedicate the *Stabat Mater* FP148 to his memory.

FP spends most of March in Paris, but he and Bernac give a recital in Perpignan (29th), followed by a two-week working holiday in Madrid and Barcelona. Poulenc is disappointed with the artistic climate of Madrid, but enjoys meeting the composer Federico Mompou in Barcelona.

(May) Simone de Beauvoir publishes the first volume of her study *Le Second Sexe*. In discussing the treatment of women throughout history, she launches a second wave of feminism.

FP spends May at Noizay, working on a piano concerto (to be FP146). He envisages that it will be the central work for his second American tour.

(18 May) Poulenc and Pierre Fournier give the first performance in Paris of the Cello Sonata FP143 (along with the Debussy Sonata) at the Salle Gaveau. Poulenc likens Fournier's musical precision to Bernac's.[51] He asks Marie-Blanche de Polignac's one-off permission for the working-class Raymond Destouches to attend the private premiere at her home. FP, when alone and on home ground, was no snob. There were card parties at Noizay with innkeepers, drivers, and carpenters, with whom he felt supremely comfortable. Stéphane Audel: "'I only like the aristocracy and the common people,' [Poulenc] said to me one day. He might have added 'and my friends.'"[52]

(June) Another English visit, this time accompanying Pierre Fournier: BBC broadcast of the Cello Sonata (15th); cello recital at the Mayflower Barn, Jordans, Buckinghamshire (18th); another BBC recital (19th).

Back in Paris, FP attends a Gold and Fizdale two-piano recital and tells them he intends to write a work for them. The resulting sonata will eventually be delivered in 1953.

(25 June) FP participates, with Bernac and soprano Janine Micheau, in a Chausson Festival at the Salle Gaveau to celebrate the fiftieth anniversary of Ernest Chausson's death.

(26 June) Bernac and Poulenc perform at the Abbé de Royaumont: Jolivet's *Poèmes intimes*, Poulenc's *Calligrammes*, and the premiere of Jean Françaix's *Huit Anecdotes de Chamfort*.

(6 July) The young American composer Ned Rorem (b. 1923), in the company of Henri Hell, calls on Poulenc, as prearranged. They are told to return on the 8th, which becomes the first of many occasions that Rorem spends in FP's company, often confiding his frank and sometimes unfavorable impressions to his diary.

FP spends three weeks in July at Le Tremblay.

(By 16 July) *Mazurka* **FP145** (Vilmorin), composed in Normandy at Le Tremblay.

(September) FP completes work on his Piano Concerto.

(27 October) FP attends a reception in honor of Aaron Copland, given by Rosamond ("Peggy") Bernier. Among the guests are Auric, Messiaen, Nadia Boulanger (Copland's former teacher), and Marie-Laure de Noailles. Copland laconically commented that "Messiaen seemed very self-concentrated and looked somewhat seedy, but poetic. Auric was friendly, Poulenc amusing."[53]

(28 October) Thirty-year-old violinist Ginette Neveu, one of FP's most prized chamber music partners, is killed with her twin brother in an airplane crash in the Azores.

(6 November) First public performance of *Mazurka* **FP145** (as part of *Mouvements de cœur*), in Town Hall, New York. Doda Conrad is accompanied by David Garvey.

(28 November) FP and Bernac give a recital in Rome.

(December) FP practices his newly composed Piano Concerto at the Gaveau studios in Paris, his niece Brigitte playing the orchestral reduction on a second piano. She has become his indispensable helper in many ways, a kind of secretary and personal assistant within the family in whom he can confide anything—including his clandestine love affairs (she makes the arrangements to keep them secret). Of the child Marie-Ange, however, Brigitte knows nothing.

(8 December) Before departing on their second American tour, Bernac and Poulenc perform a recital at the Salle Gaveau. No new songs were composed for Bernac this year, thus there is no premiere. The program is lute songs by John Dowland and Robert Jones (with piano accompaniment), songs by Fauré, Schumann, and Chabrier, Poulenc's *Calligrammes*, and Ravel's *Trois Chansons hébraïques*.

Bernac and Poulenc fly to the United States on 28 December.

Poulenc with his niece, also his closest friend, Brigitte Manceaux.

Songs of the Forties

FP105 *Mélancolie* (piano), August 1940
FP106 *Léocadia* (incidental music), October 1940

o   o   o

FP106 *Les Chemins de l'amour* (*The Paths of Love*)
     Composed in Paris, October 1940
     [No dedication; Eschig]
     Literary source: Jean Anouilh (1910–1987), written for the play *Léocadia* but not included in the printed version
     D-flat major; $\frac{3}{4}$; *Modéré mais sans lenteur*

Les chemins qui vont à la mer	The paths that lead to the sea
Ont gardé de notre passage,	Still have, from when we passed,
Des fleurs effeuillées	Some scattered flowers
Et l'écho sous leurs arbres	And the echo, beneath the trees,
De nos deux rires clairs.	Of our bright laughter.
Hélas! des jours de bonheur,	Alas! Days of happiness,
Radieuses joies envolées,	Radiant joys, now vanished,
Je vais sans retrouver traces	As I wander I can't find a trace of them
Dans mon cœur.	In my heart.
Chemins de mon amour,	Paths of my love,
Je vous cherche toujours,	I'll always look for you,
Chemins perdus, vous n'êtes plus	Paths that are lost, you're no longer there
Et vos échos sont sourds.	And your echoes are hollow.
Chemins du désespoir,	Paths of despair,
Chemins du souvenir,	Paths of memory,
Chemins du premier jour,	Paths of that first day,
Divins chemins d'amour.	Divine paths of love.

Si je dois l'oublier un jour,	If one day I'm forced to forget him,
La vie effaçant toute chose,	Since life erases everything,
Je veux, dans mon cœur, qu'un souvenir repose,	I'd wish one memory to stay my heart,
Plus fort que l'autre amour.	Stronger than any other love.
Le souvenir du chemin,	The memory of the path
Où tremblante et toute éperdue,	Where, trembling and quite bewildered,
Un jour j'ai senti sur moi	One day I felt upon me
Brûler tes mains.	Your burning hands.
Chemins de mon amour,	Paths of my love,
Je vous cherche toujours, etc.	I'll always look for you, etc.

In 1940 Jean Anouilh, already celebrated as a creator of dark and dramatic theater, decided to try his hand at plays of greater charm. He was apolitical by nature (thus rather a good fit for Poulenc), even if his most famous play, the later *Antigone* (1944), was taken to be a criticism, sufficiently veiled to have survived Nazi censorship, of Marshal Pétain and Vichy France. Anouilh referred to *Léocadia* (its English title was first *Time Remembered* and then, when revived in Chichester in 2002, *Wild Orchids*) as a *pièce rose*—as opposed to his more ambitious *pièces noires, brillantes,* or *costumées*—but it still contained a serious message about the necessity of being oneself when trying to connect with others. The plot concerns a prince, Albert, who has enjoyed only three blissful days with his lover, an actress named Léocadia Gardi, before she suffers a fatal accident. Like the dancer Isadora Duncan in 1927, Léocadia is strangled by a scarf; and like the title character in Daphne du Maurier's *Rebecca* (1938), she lends her name and haunting presence to a story in which she never appears in person. Prince Albert's aunt, the Duchess, resolves to recreate the surroundings of her nephew's love for the actress, and furnishes a park with auberge, taxi, nightclub, and Gypsy orchestra. She also arranges for a milliner named Amanda, who resembles Léocadia, to impersonate the dead paramour; the levelheaded Amanda finds the whole setup preposterous. But as the Duchess's schemes to perpetuate a fantasy life for her nephew slowly unravel, true love (and reality) wins through.

In August 1940, freshly demobilized from the army, Poulenc was staying in Brive-la-Gaillarde, near Cahors, with members of his family and others who had fled Paris. There he dined one evening with Pierre Fresnay and Yvonne Printemps (the French Laurence Olivier and Vivien Leigh of the time) at the home of their mutual friends Paul and Georgette Chadourne. The actors, already thinking ahead of how best to survive the Occupation, asked Poulenc to compose the music for a production of *Léocadia* in the Théâtre de la Michodière later in the year. He had already written *À sa guitare*, a Ronsard setting, for Printemps in 1935. Bernac once told me that Fresnay's speaking voice was the most beautiful he had ever heard, and Poulenc was similarly in awe of the great actor. Another reason to work with such stars was in order to keep afloat financially, and the composer managed to negotiate 6 percent of the play's profits. Finishing the score, as he revealed to Nora Auric (on 1 January 1941), in addition to relieving some of his money worries, lifted his spirits from the *"menace of the occupation that weighs on my house—what a sad epoch is ours, and when and how will it all finish up?"*

Printemps adored playing ingénue roles where her character was smarter than toffs and intellectuals; here, as Amanda, she trounces the bossy Duchess as well as the posthumous sway of the somewhat pretentious Léocadia. She breaks into song at the end of the fifth tableau (Printemps's public had come to expect music from her, even in straight plays), and Anouilh clearly took some trouble to craft a lyric that was gently associated with the plot, even if it is not to be found in printed editions of the play. The first verse refers to the past, with "paths of my love" that are no more. In the second verse Amanda wishes for a real lover to touch her with burning desire, as she touches him. Such are the different paths of love: one way, echoes and fallen petals; the other, reality and new happiness. Albert should realize that life is for the living.

Poulenc provided about twenty minutes of music, most of it orchestral "Ouvertures" to five acts. In the only solo song, *Les Chemins de l'amour*, he pens the kind of lilting *valse-chantée* mastered by such operetta composers as André Messager, Reynaldo Hahn, Henri Christiné, and Maurice Yvain. This is certainly the Poulenc song heard most often in concert halls today, frequently chosen by singers who have studied no other vocal music by Poulenc—and when this is the case, it shows. Unashamedly "Poulenc-lite," it is not a mélodie, nor is it discussed in any detail in Bernac's indispensable *Francis Poulenc: The Man and His Songs*. A pity, because *Les Chemins de l'amour* is regularly butchered by sopranos (and their pianists) who weigh it down with an inappropriately opulent sentimentality. If taken too seriously, and slowly, it loses that sense of containment and proportion that is at the heart of French music, even music in the popular vein. The two verses in C-sharp minor (as opposed to the refrains in D-flat major) are such an impeccable pastiche of quasi-conversational French popular style that we can almost hear Édith Piaf singing them.

The main tune claims an operatic antecedent: the most famous waltz from Richard Strauss's *Der Rosenkavalier*, a melody that jumps a sixth (from the fifth of the scale to the third above the tonic) and then descends, rocking to and from the repeated fifth step. Poulenc similarly begins "Chemins de mon a-" with an upward sweep and subsequent pivoting. But at the sixth note of his melody, he departs from his too-famous model and utterly individualizes his tune by writing an E-flat instead of a D-flat on the syllable "-mour," creating a ninth harmony not to be found in Strauss. So like, and yet suddenly so unlike: this is musical legerdemain of an extraordinarily audacious order.

The French EMI recording of Printemps accompanied by a pit orchestra of violin, clarinet, bassoon, double bass, and piano was almost certainly made with Poulenc's participation, and thus shows us the correct tempo—although few singers today would dare to emulate Printemps's vocal *portamenti*, exaggerated even by the standards of the time. A notable feature of that recording was the *Molto più mosso* of the postlude; it was also no doubt the fashion then to hurry postludes, although it makes the singer's long-held high note at the end far more achievable, and the effect is charmingly evanescent. *"She transforms everything she touches . . . the allure of her voice gives to the few songs I have composed for her an impression of success that I search for in vain when I look at them on the printed page."*[54]

Léocadia ran for 173 performances at the Michodière theater, from 3 November 1940 to May 1941. Two years later Poulenc wrote the film music (not a medium he enjoyed, either as an audience member or as a composer) for Anouilh's *Le Voyageur sans bagage* (FP123). Their final collaboration came after the war, in 1947, for the play *L'Invitation au château* (FP138).

FP107 *Banalités* (*Banalities*)

Composed in Noizay, October 1940 (ii, iv); and Paris, November 1940 (i, iii, v)

[*Claude Rostand, Marthe Bosredon, Mme Henri Fredericq, Paul Éluard, Suzette* (Chanlaire); Eschig]

Literary sources: Guillaume Apollinaire (1880–1918), (i) from "Oniro-critique," final chapter of *L'Enchanteur pourrisant* (1908), reprinted in *Il y a* (Paris: Albert Messein, 1925), pp. 237–38; (ii) and (iv) from five poems with the title *Banalités,* published in *Littérature* (8 October 1919); (iii) and (v) from *Il y a*, pp. 114 and 108

(i)   *Chanson d'Orkenise*
(ii) *Hôtel*
(iii) *Fagnes de Wallonie*
(iv) *Voyage à Paris*
(v)   *Sanglots*

In selecting these poems from a variety of sources, including a 1919 issue of the review *Littérature* (*"where so many beautiful poems had appeared in such a modest guise"*),[55] Poulenc affirms his enduring loyalty to Apollinaire. As the Nazis invaded France, it was good to remember that the great poet had been a welcome immigrant, and that his enthusiasm as an art critic for new waves of modernity and surrealism forever changed the landscape of art. So much for the Germans' condemnation of "degenerate art"; Apollinaire and his band of "degenerate" brothers would survive the invaders and triumph in the end.

Poulenc clearly thought of *Banalités* as a set of songs rather than a cycle; perhaps he had too much respect for the poet to attempt to construct a cycle from three different literary sources. The title suggests a medley of everyday banal things, a selection of "this and that," and Poulenc's anthology became a portmanteau of his Apollinaire styles: folksong, atmospheric vignette, scherzo, café-chanson, and extended and ennobling mélodie. The composer had no hesitation in performing single songs from this collection, and neither should the performer of today. However, there have been countless concert performances of *Banalités* as a whole, and Poulenc made sure that this was also rewarding. As a unifying theme to the work, Hervé Lacombe sees a journey of "the sensitive heart," which, in traversing the banal activities of everyday life, "lives and feels, crosses town, a wood, musing, toys with indifference, laughter, becomes intoxicated by simple pleasures, grows sad and shuts itself away in an inner life, that of memories."[56]

Title page of Apollinaire's Il y a (1925), the posthumous collection of poetry and prose that was a source of sixteen Poulenc songs.

(i) *Chanson d'Orkenise* (*Song of Orkenise*)
F major; $\frac{3}{4}$; *Rondement, dans le style d'une chanson populaire* ♩ = 126

Par les portes d'Orkenise	Through the gates of Orkenise
Veut entrer un charretier.	A wagon driver wants to enter.
Par les portes d'Orkenise	By the gates of Orkenise
Veut sortir un va-nu-pieds.	A tramp wants to leave.
Et les gardes de la ville	And the guards of Orkenise
Courant sus au va-nu-pieds:	Running up to the tramp, ask,
"—Qu'emportes-tu de la ville?"	"—What are you taking out of town?"
"—J'y laisse mon cœur entier."	"—I'm leaving my whole heart here."

Et les gardes de la ville	And the town guards
Courant sus au charretier:	Running up to the wagon driver, ask,
"—Qu'apportes-tu dans la ville?"	"—What are you bringing into town?"
"—Mon cœur pour me marier."	"—My heart, so I can be married."
Que de cœurs, dans Orkenise!	No shortage of hearts in Orkenise!
Les gardes riaient, riaient.	The guards laughed and laughed.
Va-nu-pieds la route est grise,	Tramp, the road is hazy,
L'amour grise, ô charretier.	Wagon driver, love makes you woozy.
Les beaux gardes de la ville	The handsome guards of Orkenise
Tricotaient superbement;	Countermarched superbly;
Puis les portes de la ville	Then the gates of Orkenise
Se fermèrent lentement.	Slowly closed.

> *"Tricoter" (last verse, line 2) means "to knit." So maybe the soldiers were doing just that; the Apollinaire story from which this poem is extracted is full of surreal fancy. Soldiers do, though, to this day, perform marching displays at the closing and opening of border posts. "Gris" (last line in fourth verse) means "gray," but also "drunk."* J. S.

Having decided to end his set with the imposing "Sanglots" from *Il y a*, and wanting to begin with something upbeat and rhythmical, Poulenc suddenly remembered a poem, *"a little Maeterlinck in style, that Apollinaire had inserted in a strange and mysterious prose piece"* from *L'Enchanteur pourrissant* (*The Rotting Magician*), a phantasmagorical tale about the wizard Merlin, full of biblical allusions as well as references to classical and Celtic mythology. The poem is introduced by a paragraph that seems influenced by Arthur Rimbaud's *Illuminations*:

> The embers from the sky were so close that I was afraid of their heat. They were on the point of burning me. But I was aware of the differing eternities of men and women. . . . Among the myrtles an ermine was turning white. We asked it for the reason for the false winter. . . . Orkenise appeared on the horizon. We made our way toward that town, missing the valleys where the apple trees sang, whistled and reddened. But the song of the tilled fields was marvelous. "Par les portes d'Orkenise."

Real-life events in June 1940 were scarcely less far-fetched. Two weeks before the armistice, Poulenc was briefly called up to serve in an anti-aircraft battalion before taking refuge in Brive-la-Gaillarde: *"Marching as a soldier on the road to*

Cahors I began to whistle, I don't know why, 'Par les portes d'Orkenise.'"[57] He slept in a barn, found an old couple he dubbed Philemon and Baucis to look after him, and was deliriously happy: "I live with peasants, which gives me confidence."[58] Even by this time, months before its composition, he knew he wanted to set the poem about the gates of Orkenise.

To Apollinaire, Orkenise was the fortress of King Arthur; Poulenc, on the other hand, tells us that his idea of Orkenise was a road in Autun (in Burgundy) leading to the Roman gate,[59] probably the imposing Porte d'Arroux. This suggests he imagined a medieval context to the song, and perhaps explains the vigorous opening—which could easily be scored for squealing shawm and tabor, with a touch of organum in open fifths—and the shades of the Dorian mode governing the key of F minor. The music is wonderfully lively and down-to-earth, a vein Poulenc was soon to explore again in Chansons villageoises, and we sense that his wartime interlude in the open air, far away from the big city and its temptations, had done him the world of good.

Like many of the best folksongs, Chanson d'Orkenise is at the same time heartless and heartfelt, both earthy and otherworldly. The two strands of dialogue, with the wagon driver and the tramp, are integrated into a kaleidoscope of changing harmonies deployed with nonchalant ease. For the cynical laughter of the guards, "Les gardes riaient, riaient," Poulenc manages an echo of popular song that is uncannily effective. Longer note values on "Se fermèrent lentement" describe the slow closing of the city gates: underneath a vocal high F on tied dotted half notes, a grinding bar of piano music is mechanically repeated three times, then two further bars lead back to the tonic—as if a key inserted in a gigantic lock were slowly turning and then clicking shut with a change of tonality. These splendid musical machinations are followed by a spirited coda drawn from the introduction.

In Apollinaire's lyric, the tramp and wagon driver are at least permitted their hearts' desires—one leaves the fortress town, the other enters—before the gates close behind them. Poulenc's Jewish friend Darius Milhaud had only just managed to escape from France to America, via Portugal, and the composer was astonished to hear how difficult the journey had been; he was so wrapped up in his own concerns that it is unclear how well informed he was about conditions for displaced and persecuted minorities on his own doorstep. As he composed this music, the banalities of evil were not far away: border guards asking mocking questions, preventing ingress, denying egress, terrifying the helpless supplicants at their mercy. No laughing matter.

(ii) *Hôtel (Hotel)*
    D major; $\frac{3}{4}$; *Très calme et paresseux* ♩ = 50

Ma chambre a la forme d'une cage	My room's shaped like a cage
Le soleil passe son bras par la fenêtre	The sun's reaching in through the window
Mais moi qui veut fumer pour faire des mirages	But I want to smoke to make mirages
J'allume au feu du jour ma cigarette	So I light up my cigarette by the fire of the sun
Je ne veux pas travailler je veux fumer	I don't want to work I just want to smoke

If someone were looking for a representative Poulenc song, to get a good idea of his style in the shortest possible time, *Hôtel* would be a strong contender. The song certainly played an important role in my own life: hearing a performance on LP with Régine Crespin and John Wustman in 1971 instigated a lifelong enthusiasm for Poulenc's mélodies.

When Apollinaire wrote the poem, he was living on the top floor of 202, boulevard Saint-Germain. But he was quite the traveler, and there is nothing here that tells us he was on home territory at the time. It is Poulenc who is unequivocal about its locale, at least as far as his own imagination was concerned: "*Hôtel is again Paris, a room in Montparnasse*,"[60] a somewhat seedy part of the city and all the more poetic, for the composer, for that very reason. In Montparnasse there were cheap establishments (known as "hôtels de passe") where it was possible to rent rooms for an hour or two. We might imagine the poet, perhaps not wanting to be seen leaving the hotel at the same time as his latest conquest, enjoying his cigarette in the golden glow of the afternoon sun, lost in a reverie that is both post-prandial and post-coital.

The music, describing an oasis of indolence in Apollinaire's hectic life, is the absolute antithesis to the stomping folksong with which *Banalités* begins. The tempo is one of infinitely leisurely inhalation and exhalation—music for castles in the air, or spiraling smoke pictures. These "mirages" waft in the rhythm of a very slow waltz. We can almost hear the self-satisfied stretching of lazy limbs (Blake's "lineaments of gratified desire" come to mind) in the piano's wide-spaced tonic and submediant chords with their added seconds, ninths, and sixths—activity within inactivity, the texture gently aglow in a harmonic haze. In the sinuous vocal line, a gleam of fire in the head voice on the *subito piano* of "J'allume" spirits us back to a time when no one gave a second thought to smoking indoors. The brazenly emphatic verb "fumer," quite unashamed, comes at the end of the last sentence; and the postlude in plush *mezzo forte* chords seems to snuggle back deep into the pillows of an already warm bed as if to say, "I've really worked hard today, and I deserve a further moment of relaxation."

A more obvious interpretation—waking up to an early-morning cigarette and feeling too lazy to go to work—may seem to be supported by the music's similarity (in both key and tempo) to *Le Petit Jour*, break of day on the farm, in the opening of the ballet Poulenc was composing at the time, *Les Animaux modèles*. However, D major for Poulenc means sunlight at any time of day (see *La Grenouillère* FP96), and to close the ballet he recapitulates his D major dawn music for the plush languor of *Le Repas de midi* (The midday meal). Was the composer thinking "my room" or "our room"? The more decadent alternative has too many real-life Poulencian resonances to be entirely ruled out.

(iii)   *Fagnes de Wallonie* (*High Fens of Wallonia*)
          F-sharp minor; $\frac{2}{2}$; *Très vite, d'un seul élan* ♩ = 92 (Bernac advocates 88.)

Tant de tristesses plénières	So much utter sadness
Prirent mon cœur aux fagnes désolées	Seized my heart on the deserted uplands
Quand las j'ai reposé dans les sapinières	When, in the forest of firs, I wearily set down
Le poids des kilomètres pendant que râlait	The weight of the miles I'd trodden, amid the rattle
Le vent d'ouest	Of the west wind
J'avais quitté le joli bois	I'd left the pretty woods
Les écureuils y sont restés	The squirrels stayed there
Ma pipe essayait de faire des nuages Au ciel	My pipe tried to make clouds In the sky
Qui restait pur obstinément	Which resolutely stayed cloud-free
Je n'ai confié aucun secret sinon une chanson énigmatique	I shared no secrets save an enigmatic song
Aux tourbières humides	With the dank peat-bogs
Les bruyères fleurant le miel	The honey-smelling heathlands
Attiraient les abeilles	Attracted the bees
Et mes pieds endoloris	And my aching feet
Foulaient les myrtilles et les airelles	Trampled blueberries and cranberries
Tendrement mariée	Tenderly intertwined
Nord	North
Nord	North
La vie s'y tord	There life is warped
En arbres forts	Into twisted sturdy trees
Et tors	

La vie y mord	Where life
La mort	Bites deep
A belles dents	Into death
Quand bruit le vent	With the murmur of the wind

We know this poem had long appealed to Poulenc; its vitality makes us realize why he found the "moss-grown paths" and "vaporous fountains" of Moréas's *Airs chantés* so ridiculously pompous and unreal by comparison. But it is very different from his usual Apollinaire, a rare description of nature by a poet far from Paris. The Fagnes de Wallonie make up a high plateau in the Ardennes, the moors and forests of Wallonia—French-speaking Belgium—which Apollinaire visited in 1899, the farthest north he had ever ventured. This song must contain the only poetically viable setting of the word "kilomètres" in the French song repertoire.

Poulenc fails to mention *Fagnes de Wallonie* in his *Journal*, but he had reason to be proud: these five pages of music are a truly cogent musical achievement, unfolding inevitably, all of a piece, with a clever deployment of recurring motifs. Although contrasts of dynamic between louder and softer passages should be scrupulously observed, the song is basically a single journey from sorrow to acceptance. As the singer traverses the somewhat forbidding landscape, and after confiding his enigmatic thoughts to the peat bog, his spirits lift and he feels himself swept along by something bigger than his own emotions.

Unlike the vertical harmonic sensuality of *Hôtel*, the music here moves horizontally, like wind sweeping across bare plains, with an accompaniment denuded, like the vegetation, of effulgent foliage. Bernac calls the song a single "great gust of wind," an impression enhanced by the way the vocal line seems to ride on the back of the music as though it were surfing on top of a wave of implacable eighth notes. The piano's doubling of the voice in the opening bars (as in FP77/i and FP91/iii) gives an impression of leanness and terseness, but the music gradually broadens into more complex harmonic interactions with the pianist's agile fingers.

Poulenc's music seldom achieves such organic momentum. And it's a rollercoaster ride for the pianist, particularly in the postlude, where the accompaniment branches out with great élan into three staves with no suggestion of a *ritenuto*. Although this part of the Ardennes was an important theater of war in conflicts between France and Germany, the mood is neither tragic nor ominous; having begun in sorrow, the young Apollinaire ends up excited and invigorated by his contact with the great outdoors, so different from the south of France where he had grown up. Four years after this song was written, despite fading Nazi resistance elsewhere, the Battle of the Bulge took place in the forests of the Ardennes, with huge American casualties.

(iv)   *Voyage à Paris* (*Trip to Paris*)
        E-flat major; $\frac{3}{4}$; *Très allant, valse à 1 temps* ♩. = 96

Ah! la charmante chose	Ah, what a lovely thing
Quitter un pays morose	To leave some dreary place
Pour Paris	For Paris
Paris joli	Gorgeous Paris
Qu'un jour	Which once upon a time
Dut créer l'Amour	Love must have created
Ah! la charmante chose	Ah, what a lovely thing
Quitter un pays morose	To leave some dreary place
Pour Paris	For Paris

The capitalization of "l'Amour" (line 6) implies that it was the god of Love who once founded Paris. J. S.

"*To anyone who knows me at all it will seem quite natural that I should open my mouth like a carp to snap up the deliciously stupid lines of* Voyage à Paris. *Anything that concerns Paris I approach with tears in my eyes and a head full of music.*"[61] Poulenc opts here for a madcap *valse-musette,* with the exuberance of a music-hall chanson. He evokes the style of Maurice Chevalier, with touches of devil-may-care falsetto and the cheeky humor of Parisians who pity anyone not lucky enough to live in their city. When Bernac and Poulenc—both inveterate Parisians—were on tour, a train or car ride away from the capital, they made a point of performing this song, deliciously malign, as their final encore.

And performing *Voyage à Paris* is a lot harder than it looks. In the ten-bar introduction, the pianist's right hand is required to bounce, trampoline-like, from one end of the upper keyboard to the other in search of the correct chords—the kind of thing that seems easier in rehearsal when one is not thinking too hard about it than in a concert, when it suddenly appears very challenging. Then that same right hand needs to play rather large, sumptuously colored chords quickly and deftly. Still, speed cannot be allowed to rule out poise and elegance; Bernac makes the case for a "Parisian badinage which never descends into vulgarity."[62] He was unforgettable in teaching this song, his facial expressions priceless without being ridiculously exaggerated. He always insisted that instead of "ParEE," the emphasis should be on the other syllable, "PARee," in order to give the impression of a Parisian accent (another of many similar instances occurs in *Allons plus vite*: "boulevard de GREnelle" rather than "GreNELLE").

The singer should be a master of charm for the second appearance of "Ah! la charmante chose," and for the falsetto high note on the second "joli." Intonation here is also a challenge: above all in the final phrase "charmante chose," where the singer's A-flat must contend with an A-natural in the piano. After a thicket of difficulties for all concerned, the pianist may be somewhat relieved to arrive at the four-bar postlude, straight out of a tub-thumping music-hall finale.

(v) *Sanglots* (*Sobs*)
    F-sharp minor; ¾; *Très calme* ♩ = 66

Notre amour est réglé par les calmes étoiles	Our love is ruled by the calm stars
Or nous savons qu'en nous beaucoup d'hommes respirent	Now we know that in us many men are breathing
Qui vinrent de très loin et sont un sous nos fronts	Who came from far away and are one beneath our brows
C'est la chanson des rêveurs	This is the song of the dreamers
Qui s'étaient arraché le cœur	Who tore out their hearts
Et le portaient dans la main droite	And held it in their right hand
Souviens-t'en cher orgeuil de tous ces souvenirs	Be sure to remember dear pride all these memories
Des marins qui chantaient comme des conquérants	Of the sailors who sang like conquerors
Des gouffres de Thulé des tendres cieux d'Ophir	Of the chasms of Thule, of the sweet skies of Ophir
Des malades maudits de ceux qui fuient leur ombre	Of the cursed invalids of those running from their own shadows
Et du retour joyeux des heureux émigrants	And of the joyous return of happy exiles
De ce cœur il coulait du sang	From this heart flowed blood
Et le rêveur allait pensant	And the dreamer went his way thinking
À sa blessure délicate	About his wound, so delicate,
Tu ne briseras pas la chaîne de ces causes	You will never break the chain of these causes
Et douloureuse et nous disait	And so painful, and said to us
Qui sont les effets d'autres causes	Which are the effects of other causes
Mon pauvre cœur mon cœur brisé	My poor heart my broken heart
Pareil au cœur de tous les hommes	Like every man's heart
Voici voici nos mains que la vie fit esclaves	Here here are our hands which life has enslaved

Est mort d'amour ou c'est tout comme	Has died of love or might as well have
Est mort d'amour et le voici	Has died of love and here it is
Ainsi vont toutes choses	That's the way of all things
Arrachez donc le vôtre aussi	Therefore tear out your hearts too
Et rien ne sera libre jusqu'à la fin	And nothing will ever be free not
des temps	till the end of time
Laissons tout aux morts	Let us leave everything to the dead
Et cachons nos sanglots	And hide our sobs

In its visionary amplitude, *Sanglots* is the most Éluard-like of Poulenc's Apollinaire settings (although it was the populist *Voyage à Paris* that was actually dedicated to Éluard). It shares with the great Éluard song *Tu vois le feu du soir* (FP98/i) the key of F-sharp minor, and the first two bars of the vocal lines in both songs share the same pitches, but the references to exotic faraway places (remember Don Pedro d'Alfaroubeira at the opening of *Le Bestiaire*?) are very particular to the breadth of Apollinaire's reading. Singers know Thule (line 9) from "Der König in Thule," Goethe's poem from *Faust*, set by Schubert, about a dying king in a remote kingdom; and "Ultima Thule "came to mean the end of the map, as in the Thomas Weelkes madrigal *Thule the Period of Cosmography.* "Distant Ophir" is the wealthy port of biblical times from where the "quinquireme of Nineveh" (in John Masefield's poem "Cargoes") sets out on its journey. Both places, as here, are the stuff of maritime legend.

In 1953, the Apollinaire scholar J. W. Cameron put forward the theory that "Sanglots" was actually two poems woven together, or superimposed one on the other—the first written in expansive alexandrines, the second, more personal and less metaphorical, in octosyllables.[63] Thirteen years earlier, Poulenc had independently come to the conclusion, based on the poem's changes of meter, that "Sanglots" was two poems in one. His musical solution was to bring forward, sometimes by change of dynamic, sometimes by change of texture and speed, first one part of the multi-layered poem and then the other. That he was able to project alternative poetic viewpoints without any loss of continuity, and while preserving the song's long, gradually unfolding lyrical thread, is a miraculous achievement—even when he allows his musical instincts to overrule some of the mood switches suggested by the versification of Apollinaire's printed text.

Bernac used to encourage singers to carefully differentiate two kinds of declamation by obeying the subtle tempo markings and scrupulously observing the "terraced" dynamics (sudden differences, almost always on the bar line, between shades of loud and soft). As a student, I marked up my score with asterisks to show the beginning of passages where the focus shifts from the first inner poem (in alexandrines) to the second (in octosyllables) and back again. In the beginning, the long-arched alexandrines are interpreted in a calmer and more philosophical way, whereas the shorter octosyllabic lines (and resulting shorter musical phrases) tend to express a controlled drama and vehemence.

Unusually for Poulenc, the song begins with an extended seven-bar prelude: this is in a ravishing nocturnal mood, perfectly depicting the image of "calmes étoiles,"[64] with a hypnotic pedal F-sharp throbbing on the beat for sixteen bars. Bars 17–23 (from "C'est la chanson des rêveurs" to "dans la main droite") bring the first appearance of the interpolated second poem, underlined by a change from F-sharp minor to E-flat minor, and a gradual thickening of the piano texture as rippling chords and a marking (*Animer un peu mais très progressivement*) whip up the tension in progressive stages. The more ponderous alexandrines return at "Souviens-t'en cher orgueil de tous ces souvenirs." The words "Et du retour joyeux des heureux émigrants" seem uncomfortably apposite in light of the persecuted millions forced to leave their homes at this time, only some of them (including, happily, Darius Mihaud) eventually able to return after the war. The formerly reflective alexandrines now switch roles with the shorter lines, becoming more agitated and buoyed along by an *accelerando* that helps paint feverish and visionary pictures.

At bar 39, *Tempo I* returns us to the calm of the opening, and now octosyllabic lines (from "De ce cœur il coulait du sang") provide the song's contemplative interiority. This mood pertains until bars 47–48: a brutal *forte* alexandrine interjection ("Tu ne briseras pas la chaîne de ces causes") is followed by an octosyllabic line ("Et douloureuse et nous disait") that Poulenc treats as a contrast, in a *piano* dynamic (not *mf* as printed, Bernac warns), before a reversion to a more querulous *forte* for "Qui sont les effets d'autres causes." As the two strands of the already difficult-to-decipher poem switch back and forth, it may appear that the song was composed for a ventriloquist; but a wonderful singer is capable of embracing this duality without appearing ridiculous. Possessed he or she may seem to be, but of a visionary charisma, as though speaking in tongues.

With the confessional, octosyllabic "Mon pauvre cœur mon cœur brisé," we have reached the lyrical, and deeply personal, heart of the music. Then the vehement interjection of "Voici voici nos mains que la vie fit esclaves," followed by a bar of piano interlude, sets up the song's most magical passage: a heady and heartfelt eloquence, influenced by popular song, that we must wait until the Aragon setting *C* to find again in Poulenc's melodies. "Est mort d'amour ou c'est tout comme" is followed by exactly the same (softer) notes for the slightly different "Est mort d'amour et le voici"; seldom has such a simple repetition seemed so inevitable and eloquent, and once again we think forward to the repeated sequences of *C*.

By bar 64, when the key signature changes from E-flat minor back to the home key of F-sharp minor, we no longer care how many syllables are in any line.

Poulenc has achieved a kind of musical momentum and grandeur that brings the ship sailing home to port with an imposing inevitability. There is one more interjection, however, for "Et rien ne sera libre jusqu'à la fin des temps" (for which Bernac counsels *mf* rather than the printed *forte*). With a return to *piano* for the poem's two final lines, a beautiful major ninth leaves the word "sanglots" dangling in the air on an A-sharp.

If the poem is something of a jigsaw puzzle, there is little doubt that Poulenc's negotiation of it is testament to his imaginative devotion to a poet he revered. Éluard's lofty poems (like "Tu vois le feu du soir") are usually better suited to the composer's pronouncements as a Prospero, sage or seer, but *Sanglots* is an Apollinaire exception. Even if he later felt unsure about the song,[65] Poulenc, in daring to sing of the emotional fragility of the entire human race, provides an unexpectedly grand and important conclusion to a set of songs that had promised only banality in its title.

FP108 *Colloque* (*Colloquy*)

>Composed in Paris, December 1940
>[*Solange Lemaître*; Salabert]
>Literary source: Paul Valéry (1871–1945), *La Nouvelle Revue française*, 1 June 1939. The poem was reprinted in *Poésies* (1942) as "Colloque (pour deux flûtes)" and dedicated "À Francis Poulenc, qui a fait chanter ce colloque" (To Francis Poulenc, who made this colloquy sing).
>F minor; $\frac{3}{4}$; *Modéré sans traîner*

A

D'une rose mourante
L'ennui penche vers nous;
Tu n'es pas différente
Dans ton silence doux
De cette fleur mourante:
Elle se meurt pour nous . . .
Tu me sembles pareille
À celle dont l'oreille
Était sur mes genoux,
À celle dont l'oreille
Ne m'écoutait jamais:
Tu me semble pareille
À l'autre que j'aimais:
mais de celle ancienne
Sa bouche était la mienne.

A

From a dying rose
Ennui inclines toward us;
You're no different
In your sweet silence
From this dying flower:
It is dying for us . . .
To me you're no different
From the woman who rested
Her ear on my lap,
The woman whose ear
Never listened to a word I said!
To me you're no different
From the other woman I loved:
Except that that former love's
Mouth was all mine.

B

Que me compares-tu
Quelque rose fanée?
L'amour n'a de vertu
Que fraîche et spontanée . . .
Mon regard dans le tien
Ne trouve que son bien:
Je m'y vois toute nue!
Mes yeux effaceront
Tes larmes qui seront
D'un souvenir venues! . . .
Si ton désir naquit
Qu'il meure sur ma couche
Et sur mes lèvres
Qui t'emporteront la bouche . . .

B

How can you compare me
To some wilted rose?
Love has no force
Unless it's fresh and spontaneous . . .
My gaze in yours
Only finds what it needs;
I see myself quite naked!
My eyes will wipe away
Your tears which have sprung
From some old memory! . . .
If your desire was born
Then let it die on my bed
And on my lips, which
Will bear your mouth away . . .

Valéry was unquestionably one of France's greatest poets and men of letters. Older than Apollinaire (although as a young man he was published in the same literary reviews) and unaffected by surrealism, he created his own modernism, which owed a debt to the symbolist poets. It was a style little suited to Poulenc's music; the composer wrote a single Valéry setting, as he did for Charles d'Orléans, Malherbe, Racine, Anouilh, Colette, Radiguet, and Beylié. Each collaboration resulted in a fine song, a memorable dalliance, but for one reason or another hardly an enduring liaison.

Colloque has the further distinction of being Poulenc's only duet (the poet's subtitle is "for two flutes")— although he prefers, in the manner of many of Schubert's so-called duets, that one voice should follow the other (in this case baritone followed by soprano) rather than coalesce. The piano's eighth notes in the introduction, an octave apart, are strangely

Paul Valéry, photographed by Laure Albin-Guillot in 1937.

reminiscent of the opening of the *Cinq Poèmes de Paul Éluard*, where the composer was also feeling his way with a new poet. The poem, less obscure than much of Valéry's verse, is more of a conventional love lyric than anything by Éluard, and Poulenc clearly finds this a disadvantage. Instinctively shying away from anything as hackneyed as stagey romantic lyricism, he keeps the male part of the colloquy lean and serious, permitting a flowering of romantic emotion only with the entrance of the soprano at "Que me compares-tu / Quelque rose fanée?" Here we can perceive what Poulenc's love songs may have been without the strength of Éluard's poetry—nearer the immediate sentiment of *Les Chemins de l'amour* than the sublimity of *Tel jour telle nuit*.

There are, nevertheless, some lovely and characteristic harmonic progressions. At "Si ton désir naquit / Qu'il meure sur ma couche," the drooping intervals, spiraling gently downward in sequence (a Poulencian motif), echo the composer's *Nocturne* in G Major (1938). Here we glimpse Poulenc denuded of that armory of literary mystery that renders many of his songs revelatory rather than sentimental. In a revealing 1947 letter, he tried to explain what drew him to some poets and not to others. Something that lay between the lines gave him the music's atmosphere; and *"this imponderable thing I do not sense in Verlaine and Mallarmé, and even less in Valéry."*[66]

The vocal line is eloquent enough, and truly approachable music is lavished *à deux* on love's faded roses. Two singers exchanging such avowals teeters precariously on the borders of operetta: if the music were just a little more conventionally melodious, their colloquy would not be out of place in Noel Coward's *Conversation Piece*, composed for Yvonne Printemps. Poulenc decided almost straightaway to drop *Colloque*, and he never permitted it to be published. My first copy (long before it was published) was a photostat from Bernac, who had preserved a hand-written copy in his archive and occasionally allowed students to perform it. He held a particular affection for Valéry as artist and man.

o   o   o

FP109 *Exultate Deo* (motet, unaccompanied SATB), May 1941

FP110 *Salve Regina* (mixed chorus, unaccompanied SATB), May 1941

FP111 *Les Animaux modèles* (ballet after La Fontaine), 1940–42

FP112 *La Fille du jardinier* (incidental music for a play by Charles Exbrayat), 1941

FP113 *Improvisations* 11–12 (piano), June and November 1941

FP114 Untitled piece for solo flute, 1941

FP115 String Trio (two violins and cello, lost)

FP116 *La Duchesse de Langeais* (film music), 1941–42

o   o   o

FP117 ***Chansons villageoises*** (*Village Songs*)

Composed in Noizay, October 1942 (i, v, vi); Paris, December 1942 (iii, iv); and Paris and Noizay, October–December 1942 (ii)

[*Louis Beydts, Jean de Polignac, Roger Bourdin, André Schæffner, André Lecœur, André Dubois*; Eschig]

Literary source: Maurice Fombeure (1906–1981), *Chansons de la grande hune* (Paris: Les Amis de Rochefort, 1942). Poulenc's settings are from the second part, "Chansons de la petite terre": (i) pp. 34–35, (ii) pp. 29–31, (iii) pp. 36–37, (iv) pp. 47–48, (v) pp. 49–51, (vi) pp. 45–46.

(i)   *Chansons du clair-tamis*
(ii) *Les Gars qui vont à la fête*
(iii) *C'est le joli printemps*
(iv) *Le Mendiant*
(v)   *Chanson de la fille frivole*
(vi) *Le Retour du sergent*

While composing his wartime ballet *Les Animaux modèles*, Poulenc discovered that he rather enjoyed working with sumptuous orchestral forces, and decided that his next song cycle would be for large voice and orchestra. He found a book of newly published poetry by Maurice Fombeure with texts of an unbridled, rustic nature to suit what he hoped would be a country-style "hoedown" *à la française*. Whether or not intentional, the cycle would turn out to be a defiant celebration of the French way of life in face of the German Occupation. Fombeure's aim was to "refresh" poetry, to "wash it, brush it up, take it for a walk in the grass, in the wind and the woods. Let's listen to our hearts—the head has played its part and failed—we now need a little freshness on earth, poetry made of drops of water."[67] Accordingly, he invested his work with the wit and energy of popular music and old folksongs. In his nautically titled *Chansons de la grande hune* (Songs of the maintop), Fombeure's lyrics are divided into two sections: "Chansons de la grande mer," concerned with sailors and life on the ocean wave; and "Chansons de la petite terre," in the style of country folksongs on dry land. His poems were

Maurice Fombeure.

MAURICE FOMBEURE

Chansons de la Grande Hune

LES AMIS DE ROCHEFORT

Chansons de la grande hune, *a collection of poems by Fombeure (1942).*

also set by such composers as Florent Schmitt and Claude Arrieu.

It was Ravel who once remarked to Manuel Rosenthal that Poulenc was capable of inventing his own folksongs,[68] but this was folk music of another kind. Fombeure's descriptions of country life appear to have awakened memories of Nogent-sur-Marne, and hanging around the amusement arcades and dance halls where working-class men and women came by train for a day's relaxation by the riverside, and where whirlwind liaisons were negotiated with many a pheremone left hanging in the air. Another inspiration was the countryside around Autun, where he had spent idyllic summers in the thirties, and where girls and boys of the district danced in marquees erected for festive occasions. Poulenc found these poems sexy—the men he imagined inhabiting them, as well as the brawny men he first imagined singing them—and Bernac simply did not fit this bill.

The orchestration included horns, trumpet, and large woodwind and percussion sections, and to match them he wanted the songs sung by someone heavier of vocal timbre, the kind of voice that could manage Iago in Verdi's *Otello*. He had no experience in writing for a heavier voice; the estimable singer Roger Bourdin (1900–1973) gave the first performance in June 1943 (three years earlier he had played the role of the singer Johann Michael Vogl in the French film *Sérénade*, about the life of Schubert). A composer who engages a big operatic voice to sing his music and then expects to hear the kind of interpretive detail he customarily receives from an experienced recitalist is hoist by his own petard. As soon as Poulenc could make a piano-accompanied version of the cycle (published within months of the orchestral version in 1943), Bernac took it into his repertoire. Gabriel Bacquier was a marvelous interpreter of the work in later years.

(i)   *Chansons du clair-tamis (Songs of the Clear Sieve)*
        E-flat major; ¢; *Très gai et très vite* ♩ = 84

Où le bedeau a passé	Where the beadle passed by,
Dans les papavéracées	Down among the poppies,
Où le bedeau a passé,	Where the beadle passed by,
Passera le marguillier.	The churchwarden will pass as well.

Notre vidame est mort,	Our lord and master is no more,
Les jolis yeux l'ont tué.	Pretty eyes were the death of him.
Pleurons son heureux sort.	Let us bewail his happy fate.
En terre et enterré	In the earth, and buried
Et la croix de Lorraine sur son	With the Croix de Lorraine pinned to
pourpoint doré,	his gilded doublet,
Ils l'ont couché dans l'herbe,	They laid him to rest in the grass
Son grand sabre dessous.	With his great sword beneath him.
Un oiseau dans les branches	A bird in the branches
A crié: "Coucou."	Cried "Cuckoo!"
C'est demain dimanche	Tomorrow it's Sunday
C'est fête chez nous,	It's our local fair,
Au son de la clarinette	With sound of the clarinet,
Le piston par en-dessous,	The cornet playing underneath,
La piquette, la musette,	Cheap wine, accordions,
Les plus vieux sont les plus saoûls.	The oldest are drunker than the rest.
Grand'mère à cloche-lunettes	Grandma with her specs askew
Sur ses jambes de vingt ans,	With the legs of a twenty-year-old,
Vienne le printemps, mignonne,	Bring on the spring, my pretty,
Vienne le printemps.	Bring on the spring.
Où la grenouille a passé	Where the frog passed by
Sous les renonculacées,	Down below the buttercups,
Où la grenouille a passé,	Where the frog passed by,
Passera le scarabée.	The beetle will pass as well.

Odd that in such a rustic ditty, the poet chose to use the botanically correct Latin terms for poppy and buttercup, "papaveraceae" (first verse) and "ranunculu." (last verse). J. S.

As much in a feudal society as during the German Occupation, downtrodden peasants paid minimum lip-service to those who wielded power, and disregarded and covertly undermined their masters with malicious glee. In this poem the lord of the manor has died (the words hint at sexual excess); Saturday is the ceremonial funeral, and joyous dancing at the village fête follows on the Sunday. Life goes on. The imagery is almost surreal, and certainly Fombeure as a poet flirted with the surrealists, but the incongruous juxtapositions here reflect the "little people" determined to live their lives to the full.

Poulenc's music is an irrepressible onslaught of quixotic individualism. Jaunty staccato passages, accompanied by slapdash chords that care not a hoot about *lèse-majesté*, are juxtaposed with bars in unctuous legato, suggesting utterly insincere sympathy for the demise of the "vidame." At "Ils l'ont couché dans l'herbe" the accompaniment, suddenly *piano*, changes to churchy quarter notes, as if all the peasants were expected to go through a ritual of crossing themselves in reverential memory of the deceased. But then a bird shouts "Cuckoo," providing a riotous denial of any mock piety. Fombeure's mention of a duet for clarinet and cornet, a gift for Poulenc, prompts a zany passage marked *turbulent*; though great fun in the original orchestration, it is piquant enough under a good pianist's fingers. The unexpected vivacity of Grandma's dancing adds a flavor of resurrected energy; she must have spent an entire lifetime hating the village squire, and now she no longer needs to hide the fact. Frogs among the buttercups make wonderful croaking noises with the piano's *accacciature* slipping on to staccato eighth notes, something Poulenc no doubt learned from the "grenouilles vertes" who populate the first of Debussy's *Chansons de Bilitis*. While Debussy's frogs croak gently and allusively in the left hand, Poulenc's are in the right hand and, unsurprisingly, full-voiced and vulgar.

A mere guess at the meaning of the poem's title would be that with the death of a hated village dignitary the swamp has finally been drained, the sieve is at last clear of the dregs, and man and nature can sing their various songs of gratitude.

(ii) *Les Gars qui vont à la fête (The Lads Who Are Off to the Fair)*
    F major; $\frac{4}{4}$; *Follement animé et gai* ♩ = 144

Les gars qui vont à la fête	The lads who are off to the fair
Ont mis la fleur au chapeau,	Have stuck a flower in their hats,
Pour y boire chopinette,	To down a slug of wine,
Y goûter le vin nouveau,	And to sample the new vintage,
Y tirer la carabine,	To have a shot on the rifle range,
Y sucer le berlingot.	And to suck on sugar-candy.
Les gars qui vont à la fête	The lads who are off to the fair
Ont mis la fleur au chapeau	Have stuck a flower in their hats
Sont rasés à la cuiller,	They are meticulously shaved,
Sont raclés dessous la peau,	Scraped to beneath the skin,

Ont passé la blouse neuve,	Wearing their best bib and tucker
Le faux-col en cellulo.	With a plastic collar.
Les gars qui vont à la fête	The lads who are off to the fair
Ont mis la fleur au chapeau,	Have stuck a flower in their hats,
Y faire danser les filles,	Getting the girls to dance
Chez Julien le violoneur,	At Julien the Fiddler's,
Des polkas et des quadrilles	Polkas and quadrilles
Et le pas des patineurs.	Not forgetting the skaters' dance.
Le piston, la clarinette	The music of the cornet and clarinet
Attendrissent les costauds.	Softens up those tough nuts.
Les gars qui vont à la fête	The lads who are off to the fair
Ont mis la fleur au chapeau	Have stuck a flower in their hats
Quand ils ont bu, se disputent	Once they're drunk, they argue
Et se cognent sur la peau,	And get into punch-ups,
Puis vont culbuter les filles	Then it's a tumble with the girls
Au fossé sous les ormeaux.	In the ditch beneath the elms.
Les gars qui vont à la fête	The lads who are off to the fair
Ont mis la fleur au chapeau	Have stuck a flower in their hats
Reboivent puis se rebattent	They drink some more, then fight some more
Jusqu'au chant du premier jô,	Till the dawn chorus strikes up,
Le lendemain on en trouve:	The next morning you can find them
Sont couchés dans le ruisseau . . .	Sleeping it off in the gutter . . .
Les gars qui vont à la fête	The lads who are off to the fair
Ont mis la fleur au chapeau.	Have stuck a flower in their hats.

Young working-class men, "strapping fellows" with flowers stuck in their hats, have come to dance at the village fair. Poulenc (who finds the lads both attractive and touching) imagines them "rasés à la cuiller"—shaved to the underskin—and doused with "*the common odor of Sunday aftershave*" as they dance at Julien the fiddler's. "*In the Morvan,*" Poulenc notes, "*it is possible to buy portable ballrooms with polished floors, crochet curtains, plush seats, copper candelabras,*"[69] and this dance takes place in one of them. He furnishes music that Bernac describes as having a certain "truculence" and "a certain peasant coarseness (quite different from Parisian slang), the wholesome gaiety of country folk out for a spree at the village fair."[70]

Distinctions between Parisian and country slang notwithstanding, of all the many Poulenc songs in Parisian music-hall manner, this is one of the few that could have been transplanted to that milieu without a note or word altered. We can imagine it performed by Maurice Chevalier in a tone or accent designed to gently, even affectionately, mock hayseed country cousins.[71] Poulenc admitted that Chevalier's repertoire had taught him a lot when it came to setting songs like this one: "*I repeat the words, I cut them. I imply them even, as at the end of* Gars qui vont à la fête."[72] Here Poulenc adds a line of his own in the spirit of Chevalier: "Les Gars qui vont à la fête / Chapeau"—as if both Maurices, Fombeure and Chevalier, were doffing their hats in homage to the brave lads, some of them likely to be risking their lives in Resistance activities.

The poem's scenario is rather too raw and raucous to go down well in Paris—brawling over women is hardly chic—but that is precisely what Poulenc finds delicious about it. The clumsiness of clod-hopping dancing feet (the emphasis is on the "gars," not the girls) is paralleled by right-hand chords that splash up and down the keyboard, almost always off the beat, in the manner of a drunken stag night. How different this is, musically, from the George Butterworth / A. E. Housman gathering *The Lads in Their Hundreds* (from *A Shropshire Lad*, 1911), where a similar occasion is described in a manner far more genteel. The French party sounds more fun, although an undeniable sexual undertone runs through both poems. The lines "Le piston, la clarinette / Attendrissent les costauds," where music softens the hearts of the strapping lads, might have been made for Poulenc, who was attracted to the working-class type.

Most of the English farming lads in their Housman hundreds would no doubt have preferred the kind of occasion Poulenc describes in this mini-opera, with side scenes conjured in a few bars (the alcoholic kind as well): swigging wine; a shooting range (right-hand chords firing off shots); a popular violinist's scraping and sawing; polkas and quadrilles (where the music cleverly suggests stiffly rehearsed steps); a discordant middle section of fighting, followed by tumbling with the girls, in rather perfunctory fashion; further fighting and jollification; and then sleeping senseless in a ditch. As the lads' inhibitions are progressively unbuttoned by drink, all these activities are limned by tiny illustrative details in the accompaniment, without the infectiously tuneful song missing a beat. The music manages to sound both deft and clumsy—meticulous and at the same time casual, a masterpiece of its kind.

(iii)   *C'est le joli printemps* (*It's Pretty Springtime*)
D-flat major; $\frac{3}{4}$; *Très calme* ♩ = 63

C'est le joli printemps	It's pretty springtime
Qui fait sortir les filles	That brings out the girls
C'est le joli printemps	It's pretty springtime
Qui fait briller le temps	That makes the weather shine
J'y vais à la fontaine	I'm off to the fountain
C'est le joli printemps	It's pretty springtime
Trouver celle qui m'aime	To find the one who loves me
Celle que j'aime tant	The one I love so much
C'est dans le mois d'avril	It's in the month of April
Qu'on promet pour longtemps	That you make long-lasting promises
C'est le joli printemps	It's pretty springtime
Qui fait sortir les filles	That brings out the girls
La fille et le galant	The girl and her lover
Pour danser le quadrille	To dance the quadrille
C'est le joli printemps	It's pretty springtime
Qui fait briller le temps	That makes the weather shine
Aussi profitez-en	So enjoy it while you may
Jeunes gens, jeunes filles	Young folk, young girls
C'est le joli printemps	It's pretty springtime
Qui fait briller le temps	That makes the weather shine
Car le joli printemps	For the pretty springtime
C'est le temps d'une aiguille	Is but a needle-prick in time
Car le joli printemps	For the pretty springtime
Ne dure pas longtemps.	Doesn't last that long.

Here, at the heart of the cycle, is a real jewel, one of Poulenc's most beautiful and yet most simple creations. The accompaniment is remarkably spare, particularly at the beginning: in the first eight bars, left-hand eighth notes oscillate between D-flat (above middle C) and its neighboring E-flat, while the right hand, an octave higher, doubles the outline of the vocal melody. For a singer with a large baritone voice (like the dedicatee, Roger Bourdin), or for practically any male singer other than a tenor, the height of this tessitura is punishing, particularly in conjunction with the *piano* and *pianissimo* dynamics and markings like *Extrêmement doux*. The average operatic baritone would request a downward transposition.

In an ideal performance, such difficulties would never be evident. "*The singing of this song*," advises Poulenc, "*must be as clean and sad as an April day.*"[73] His vocal line wafts and weaves with the greatest sweetness, and spring sunshine is streaked with the tender melancholy of Poulenc's trademark harmonies. The sentiments are not quite those of Shakespeare's "O mistress mine," a lyric that woos and cajoles: "Then come kiss me, sweet-and-twenty / Youth's a stuff will not endure." Fombeure's country verses might be better compared with the lyrics of Robert Herrick, who addressed his seventeenth-century plaint to fair daffodils that will "haste away so soon" in the early morning sun.

> We have short time to stay, as you,
> We have as short a spring;
> As quick a growth to meet decay,
> As you, or anything.

An echo of such intimations of mortality is to be heard in the song's postlude, with a closing cadence in G-flat, the subdominant of the home key of D-flat. We are left hanging in the air, uncertain of where we are going. The final chord adds a sixth (E-flat), a luxury typical of Poulenc, but any complacency is undermined by clashes between "impure" octaves: D-flat in the bass, D-natural in the treble, and then E-flat in the bass and F-flat (E-natural) in the treble. Such is the sincerity and depth of the setting that we cannot refrain from making personal connections. We sense that even at the age of forty-three, Poulenc already feels himself past his prime—left behind in love, or simply aware that "youth's a stuff will not endure."

(iv) *Le Mendiant (The Beggar)*
No key signature; 4/4; *Lent mais allant malgré tou* ♩ = 66

Jean Martin prit sa besace	Jean Martin took up his bundle
Vive le passant qui passe	Long live the traveling man
Jean Martin prit sa besace	Jean Martin took up his bundle
Son bâton de cornouiller	And his dogwood stick
S'en fut au moutier mendier	Went off to the friary to beg
Vive le passant qui passe	Long live the traveling man
Va't-en, dit le père moine	Run along, said the father superior
N'aimons pas les va-nu-pieds	We don't want vagrants here

S'en fut en ville mendier	Went off to the town to beg
Vive le passant qui passe	Long live the traveling man
Epiciers et taverniers	Grocers and innkeepers
Qui mangez la soupe grasse	Slurping your rich soup
Et qui vous chauffez les pieds	And warming your feet
Puis couchez près de vos femmes	And snuggling down with your wives
Au clair feu de la veillée	By the light of the evening fire
Jean Martin l'avez chassé	You chased away Jean Martin
Vive le passant qui passe	Long live the traveling man
On l'a trouvé sur la glace	He was found on the ice
Jean Martin a trépassé	Jean Martin has passed away
Tremblez, les gros et les moines	Tremble, you fat slobs and you monks
Vive le passant qui passe	Long live the traveling man
Tremblez, ah! maudite race	Tremble, you vile breed
Qui n'avez point de pitié	You haven't a scrap of pity
Un jour prenez garde ô race	One day all of you beware
Les Jean Martin seront en masse	The Jean Martins will rise as a rabid mob
Aux bâtons de cornouiller	With their dogwood sticks
Ils vous crèv'ront la paillasse	They'll beat you to death
Puis ils violeront vos garces	They'll ravish your bitches
Et chausseront vos souliers	And they'll be wearing your shoes
Jean Martin prends ta besace	Jean Martin, pick up your bundle
Ton bâton de cornouiller.	And your dogwood stick.

The poem, whose title is "Complainte de Jean Martin," is the nearest we get in all Poulenc's songs to the subject matter of his opera *Dialogues des Carmélites*, set during the French Revolution. Fombeure was not a political activist, but there is nothing as angry as this in all the settings of Éluard (who was a Communist), and it is all the more brutally effective for its sudden appearance in the middle of a rural idyll. Poulenc's own politics were scarcely left wing. "*I am not 'Popular Front,*'" he wrote to Marie-Blanche de Polignac in August 1936, a few months after the Front Populaire had been elected and begun a program of overdue socialist reform. "*Am I wrong? I am an old French Republican who once believed in liberty. . . . For me, you see, the Republic was men like Clemenceau, whose maxim I think of so often: on your feet."*[74]

Poulenc's *haute bourgeoisie* background gave him the status and wealth to mingle easily (and delightedly) with aristocrats, although in cultural and social matters he was more liberal than most of the people he saw as his social equals. He was certainly no dyed-in-the-wool right-winger, but unlike some of his well-heeled friends and colleagues (Marie-Laure de Noailles, for example), he was no friend of the left either; indeed, he considered that Ravel had leaned *"notoriously to the left."*[75] He once put forward a theory that artists needed to be independent of politics, because it often happened that the most innovative and revolutionary artists were conservative (he cited Debussy's unexpected position as an anti-Dreyfusard), and the most conservative politicians were the most radical in cultural terms. As Poulenc thought himself far from a conservative musician, it seems clear that his observation was something of an indirect justification for his less-than-left-leaning political stance.[76]

If he is not very personally engaged with Jean Martin's grievances, especially those against the church, Poulenc understood that this poem would immeasurably strengthen a work that might otherwise appear lightweight. This is the one song in the set that calls for an appreciably higher level of vocal stamina. Fombeure's fury is directed at the fat cats of monastery and manor who were more than happy to benefit from Jean Martin's bravery at the time of the 1914 war, but declined to help an aged veteran down on his luck. At the end, the poet envisages a rerun of the French Revolution—the future background, as it happens, for *Dialogues des Carmélites,* where the composer's sympathies were nothing to do with Jean Martin's.

The seven-bar introduction carries echoes of the *Chanson à boire* from *Chansons gaillardes,* FP42/ii (where we learn of the embalming of Egyptian and Syrian kings); but it is a more exact quote from a work Poulenc had begun two years earlier (1940), *L'Histoire de Babar, le petit éléphant* (following the spoken words "Babar se promène très heureux, sur le dos de sa maman" (Babar takes a ride, very happily, on his mama's back). We thus hear the recycling of music that has been imposing enough for dead and embalmed kings as well as for lumbering elephants, able to crush everything underfoot once they are angry. Poulenc imagines an abused and dangerous species, personified by Jean Martin, gradually waking up to the injustice of its plight. The song begins in a laconic march of vocal quarter notes accompanied by lugubrious chords. This is hardly a vocal melody in any usual sense; rather is it a kind of dramatized speech to go with an unpunctuated poem. A debt to Musorgksy is acknowledged by the composer—especially *Songs and Dances of Death,* says Bernac,[77] and he is right in terms of the piano writing, although other Musorgksy songs (like *The Orphan/Sirotka,* to a text by Musorgsky) more directly contrast a beggar's plight with the comforts of the rich bourgeoisie.

At Figure 23 in the score ("Va't-en, dit le père moine"), the accompaniment's dry staccato eighths reflect the persnickety fastidiousness of church authorities. Then Jean Martin's rage begins to kick in, and from Figure 24 the texture is one of seething sixteenths, with piano writing thick enough to challenge all but the most persistently defended vocal hegemony. Singers have to work hard here not to get swamped, and pianists must be careful not to get carried away. Bernac shares a useful tip that is absent from the score, the result of working with the composer: there should be a gradually controlled *accelerando* to increase the tension between Figures 24 and 29, a sweep of twenty-six bars. Such a gathering of momentum is splendid if well managed by the performers, and by the end it is as if the tumbrils are rolling to the scaffold. *Le Mendiant* is Poulenc's *Mélodie fantastique*, unlike any other he wrote, with music ominous and angry that covertly imagines the underdog turning its fury against its foes, whether domestic tyrants or alien aggressors.

(v)   *Chanson de la fille frivole* (*Song of the Flighty Girl*)
       B-flat major; 4/4; *Prestissimo possible* ♩ = 168

Ah! dit la fille frivole	Ah, says the flighty girl
Que le vent y vire, y vole	Let the wind blow where it may
Mes canards vont sur l'étang	My ducks are swimming on the pond
Belle lune de printemps	Lovely springtime moon
Ah! dit la fille frivole	Ah, says the flighty girl
Que le vent y vire, y vole	Let the wind blow where it may
Sous les vergers éclatants	Under the bursting orchards
Belle lune de printemps	Lovely springtime moon
Ah! dit la fille frivole	Ah, says the flighty girl
Que le vent y vire, y vole	Let the wind blow where it may
Et dans les buissons chantants	And in the singing bushes
Belle lune de printemps	Lovely springtime moon
Ah! dit la fille frivole	Ah, says the flighty girl
Que le vent y vire, y vole	Let the wind blow where it may
Je vais trouver mes amants	I'm off to find my lovers
Sous lune de printemps	Under the lovely springtime moon
Ah! dit la fille frivole	Ah, says the flighty girl
Que le vent y vire, y vole	Let the wind blow where it may
L'âge vient trop vitement	Old age comes too quickly
Sous lune de printemps	Under the lovely springtime moon

Ah! dit la fille frivole	Ah, says the flighty girl
Que le vent y vire, y vole	Let the wind blow where it may
Plus tard soucis et tourments	Cares and worries come too soon
Sous lune de printemps	Under the lovely springtime moon
Ah! dit la fille frivole	Ah, says the flighty girl
Que le vent y vire, y vole	Let the wind blow where it may
Aujourd'hui guérissez-m'en	Spare me them for today
Belle lune de printemps	Under the lovely springtime moon
Ah! dit la fille frivole	Ah, says the flighty girl
Que le vent y vire, y vole	Let the wind blow where it may
Baisez-moi bien tendrement	Kiss me sweetly as you can
Sous la lune de printemps.	Under the lovely springtime moon.

"Baiser" (last verse) also means a great deal more than "kiss." I have erred on the side of decency here! J. S.

As though embarrassed by the intensity of *Le Mendiant*, Poulenc now veers to a dizzy extreme of frivolity, with a trampoline song to bounce us from one serious mélodie into another. Although breathless vocal scherzi had been a Poulenc specialty ever since the *Trois Poèmes de Louise Lalanne*, here he excels himself, with sixteenth notes, often an octave apart between the hands, roving the keyboard windswept and devil-may-care. Bernac speaks of the girl's "insouciant volubility,"[78] and if she chin-wags as much as this and at this speed, what a trial she must be, her other charms notwithstanding. Staccato eighths in the left hand prance saucily, like plucked double-bass notes adding their piquant twang to the texture of a jazz ensemble. The music is so fast that there is scarcely time to sing anything. It is almost like a recitation on closely adjacent pitches, and a vocal line descending in short phrases adds to the impression of breathless activity—of whatever kind one may care to imagine.

At the beginning, the pianist's right hand, shadowing the voice, fingers a riotous succession of broken chords in diminished fifths and augmented fourths, followed by sweeping arpeggios and other cascading figurations. If Poulenc often composes songs in four- or two-bar phrases and somehow stitches them effectively together, here he has made a convincing unity out of a dizzyingly clever succession of one-bar phrases. This is fast and naughty music for a girl who is also fast and naughty; she may be too rustic to lay claim to any metropolitan sophistication, but in observing her and depicting her mercilessly, the composer shows himself the epitome of that very thing.

(vi) *Le Retour du sergent (The Sergeant's Return)*
A minor; $\frac{4}{4}$; *Mouvement de marche enlevée* ♩ = *strictement* 138

Le sergent s'en revient de guerre	The sergeant comes home from the war
Les pieds gonflés, sifflant du nez	With swollen feet and a snuffly nose
Le sergent s'en revient de guerre	The sergeant comes home from the war
Entre les buissons étonnés	Between the astonished bushes
A gagné la croix de Saint-Georges	He was given the Croix St. Georges
Les pieds gonflés, sifflant du nez	With swollen feet and a snuffly nose
A gagné la croix de Saint-Georges	He was given the Croix St. Georges
Son pécule a sous son bonnet	His stash of cash beneath his cap
Bourre sa pipe en terre rouge	He fills up his red clay pipe
Les pieds gonflés, sifflant du nez	With swollen feet and a snuffly nose
Bourre sa pipe en terre rouge	He fills up his red clay pipe
Puis soudain se met à pleurer	Then suddenly he starts to weep
Il revoit tous ses copains morts	He sees again his fallen chums
Les pieds gonflés, sifflant du nez	With swollen feet and a snuffly nose
Il revoit tous ses copains morts	He sees again his fallen chums
Qui sont pourris dans les guérets	Who've rotted in the fallow fields
Ils ne verront plus leur village	Never again will they see their village
Les pieds gonflés, sifflant du nez	With swollen feet and a snuffly nos,
Ils ne verront plus leur village	Never again will they see their village
Ni le calme bleu des fumées	Nor its calm blue plumes of smoke
Les fiancées, va marche ou crève	Their fiancées—well it's dog eat dog
Les pieds gonflés, sifflant du nez	With swollen feet and a snuffly nose
Envolées comme dans un rêve	They've disappeared as in a dream
Les copains s'les sont envoyées	The chums have helped themselves
Et le sergent verse une larme	And the sergeant sheds a tear
Les pieds gonflés, sifflant du nez	With swollen feet and a snuffly nose
Et le sergent verse une larme	And the sergeant sheds a tear
Le long des buissons étonnés.	All along the astonished bushes.

Poulenc's *Marches militaires* (FP30), a work for piano and orchestra from the early twenties, was lost or destroyed. This song, with its returning, down-at-heel refrain ("Les pieds gonflés, sifflant du nez"), is as near as Poulenc ever came to publishing a military march—even if it is a minor-key processional for a solitary demobilized sergeant who is only continuing to march from ingrained habit. Eighth-note chords strictly on the beat ensure an implacable rhythm, and the subtleties of the song's various inflections (including the sudden incursion of dotted rhythms on the last page) are not allowed to get in the way of the seeming simplicity of its mournfully cheery progress. The marching chords are sometimes replaced by legato quarter notes, in a return of the mock-pious church motif employed in the cycle's first song to describe the death of the lord of the manor. In slightly different form we hear the motif at "A gagné la croix de Saint-Georges" and at further mention of death and loss. No one in *Chansons du clair-tamis* really mourned the lord of the manor, and the Cross of St. George likewise is of absolutely no use to this poor demoralized soldier, whose innate piety and patriotism have been betrayed by his superiors, just as he has been betrayed at home by his fickle womenfolk.

Fombeure's poetry had long been associated with the military, as shown by his collection *Soldat* (1935), and particularly its humorous side. This poem, however, is not at all funny. It appeared in a book of poems hot off the press in 1942, and might just as well refer to the Second World War as the First. In June 1940, Poulenc had been among the French soldiers who were demobbed after a short and futile struggle against the Germans, and the humiliation of defeat was felt as keenly by simple working folk as by intellectuals—such as Louis Aragon, poet of *C* (FP122/i).

Tramping back to his village, the sergeant remembers his dead chums and, while retaining his disciplined bearing (indicated by the implacability of the march), sheds a tear for them. We can tell as the song continues that he is not well. He has been spared death but suffers, probably without realizing it, from trauma and shellshock—a state of mind admirably reflected in the poem's lack of punctuation. Poulenc, who knew personally about depression, has managed to write a song that is both jaunty and very dark: there is a terrible aridity in the life now facing the soldier. No matter what kindness or love he may receive at home, he will always carry within him the horrors of what he has seen and done. We feel this in the jarring discords of music that undermine the simplicity of what should have been a cheery folksong. A cycle that has begun in such a merry way, in a French countryside impermeable to change, has gradually found its way back to 1942 and harsh twentieth-century realities. It is this pertinent mixture of moods and styles, lighthearted fantasy and harsh reality, that makes *Chansons villageoises* one of Poulenc's most interesting and red-blooded collections of songs.

∘   ∘   ∘

FP118 *Intermezzo* in A-flat Major (piano), March 1943
FP119 Sonata for Violin and Piano, summer 1942–Easter 1943
FP120 *Figure humaine* (cantata for double mixed choir, *a cappella*), summer 1943

∘   ∘   ∘

FP121 **Métamorphoses** (*Metamorphoses*)

Composed in 1943 (i); in Beaulieu-sur-Dordogne, August 1943 (ii); and in Noizay, October 1943 (iii)

[*Marie-Blanche de Polignac, Marthe Bosredon, Jeanne Richter*; Rouart, Lerolle]

Literary sources: Louise de Vilmorin (1902–1969), (i) *La Nouvelle Revue française* 343 (September 1942); (ii) and (iii) *Le Sable du sablier* (Paris: Gallimard, 1945), pp. 75–76 and 21–22

(i) *Reine des mouettes*
(ii) *C'est ainsi que tu es*
(iii) *Paganini*

After the huge success of *Tel jour telle nuit* in early 1937, in which Pierre Bernac had played a significant part, Poulenc initially intended to write another male cycle, but he set six poems from Vilmorin's *Fiançailles pour rire*, for soprano, instead. According to Poulenc, Bernac was rather "jealous" of these soprano songs and, as a friend of Vilmorin in his own right, asked her for some new poems suitable for a male singer.[79] The resulting lyrics found their way to Poulenc, who was fortunately moved to set some of the consignment. Two of them later appeared in 1945 in Vilmorin's next collection, *Le Sable du sablier* (*The Sand of the Hourglass*), and she inscribed a copy "À Pierre Bernac / Notre amitié est plus forte / que les mouettes et les / sables. Louise de Vilmorin, Noël 1945, Paris" (Our friendship is stronger than the seagulls and the sands). The HMV red-label recording the duo later made of *Métamorphoses* on a single side of a 78-rpm record (DB6267) was one of their most successful. How could it not be, with the even more famous *Deux Poèmes de Louis Aragon* on the other side?

(i) *Reine des mouettes* (*Queen of the Seagulls*)
A-flat major; $\frac{4}{4}$; *Très vite et haletant* ♩ = 108

Reine des mouettes, mon orpheline,	Queen of the seagulls, my orphan girl,
Je t'ai vue rose, je m'en souviens,	I've seen you go pink, I remember it,
Sous les brumes mousselines	Beneath the muslin haze
De ton deuil ancien.	Of your old mourning clothes.
Rose d'aimer le baiser qui chagrine	Pink from loving the kiss which troubles you
Tu te laissais accorder à mes mains	You let yourself be attuned to my hands
Sous les brumes mousselines	Beneath the muslin haze
Voiles de nos liens.	The veils that bind us.

Rougis, rougis, mon baiser te devine	Go on, blush, blush. My kiss has found you out,
Mouette prise aux nœuds des grands chemins.	Seagull caught at the knot of the great highways.
Reine des mouettes, mon orpheline,	Queen of the seagulls, my orphan girl,
Tu étais rose accordée à mes mains	I've seen you go pink, attuned to my hands,
Rose sous les mousselines	Pink beneath your muslin.
Et je m'en souviens.	And I remember.

Vilmorin wrote the first two poems in this set specifically for a man to sing to a woman. Yet the male genesis of *Métamorphoses* has been all but forgotten on account of Poulenc's delight in the suitability of Vilmorin's poetry for the female voice. After he first set her poems in 1936, the entire corpus of his Vilmorin settings (apart from *Mazurka,* for bass) is usually taken these days to be soprano territory.

And *Métamorphoses* works so well for the female voice. Although (or perhaps because) *Reine des mouettes* is addressed to a woman (presumably by a man, unless Vilmorin was playing Colette-like games), it can seem the most musically feminine of the three songs, diaphanous and capricious, delicate and curvaceous. Here the narrative voice, that of the wooing male lover, is submerged by the song's *becoming* the love object; this "reine des mouettes" has been so convincingly conjured by the music that the ardent lover's presence is almost squeezed out of the picture, and a soprano voice singing these words seems perfectly plausible.

The skillfully written piano part displays certain characteristics not found elsewhere in this composer's œuvre: rising and falling waves of sound evoke a memory of the sea rather than the sea itself, with the sound of breakers muffled in mists and veiled in muslin ("brumes mousselines"). Left-hand chords in a gently pulsating rhythm (like the flapping of seagulls' wings wrapped in silk) produce, in conjunction with adroit use of the pedal, a special shimmer of sound ("no feeling of agitation," Bernac instructs).[80] With no disrespect to the great singer, none of this imagery seems especially masculine. The delicate tracery of the right hand, sometimes shadowing the vocal line and sometimes limning the melody in playful and graceful descant, propels the music into a kind of rapturous flight. Indeed, it can sometimes seem, in mid-performance, as if the piano's filigree has dematerialized into droplets of sea spray.

The song is high. It requires a softly sung high F—not possible for all baritones—which is why Bernac's recording remains a *version de référence*; his unique timbre caters to the ambiguity of the male narrative voice being all but supplanted by feminine caprice. All in all, the song is an enchanting confection that only Poulenc could have composed, and it is over in a graceful, evanescent flurry. The accompaniment seems the very definition of musical legerdemain, but it is the collusion of voice and piano that most astonishes. A moment of delicious rapport flies by in the final section: at "Rose sous les mousselines," while the voice is high in the stave (that challenging F) and *pianissimo*, the left hand touches the depths of the keyboard, and then rolls upward in a soft scale of lambent sixteenths that floods the bass stave with a tide of harmonic warmth. With a singer and pianist in top form, this passage makes the Poulenc enthusiast swoon. The five-bar postlude is another delight: a right-hand melody sings in the piano's middle register, and then arpeggios evaporate into the heights as though dissolving into thin air.

Perhaps Vilmorin tried to make Poulenc smile by opening her first phantasmagorical poem for Bernac with a pun? *Reine de musette* was the title of a 1927 hit by the famed accordionist Emile Vacher. The prevalence of the word "rose" explains the song's dedication (also possibly the poem's) to Marie-Blanche de Polignac: "rose Polignac" was an exclusive shade of pink created in honor of Marie-Blanche by the fabric specialists working for her mother, the couturier Jeanne Lanvin.

(ii) *C'est ainsi que tu es* (*That's How You Are*)
B minor; $^6_4$; *Très calme, très à l'aise* ♩= 60

Ta chair, d'âme mêlée,	Your flesh, mixed with soul,
Chevelure emmêlée,	Your tousled hair,
Ton pied courant le temps,	Your foot pursuing time,
Ton ombre qui s'étend	Your shadow, stretching out
Et murmure à ma tempe,	And whispering at my temples.
Voilà, c'est ton portrait,	That's it, that's your portrait.
C'est ainsi que tu es	That's the way you are
Et je veux te l'écrire	And I wanted to write it down for you
Pour que la nuit venue,	So that come nightfall,
Tu puisses croire et dire	You can believe, and say
Que je t'ai bien connue.	That I knew you really well.

Vilmorin entitled her poem "Portrait," but since *Le Portrait* was already the published title of a song (FP92) to a poem by Colette, Poulenc took the seventh line of the poem as his title. It has often been used as a program heading for musical portraits of the composer, and the song is so often performed as to be considered one of Poulenc's "signature" works.

The four-bar introduction is a test for all pianists who would wish to claim competence in the Poulenc style. Rubato is involved (with all those grace notes—*les appoggiature sans hâte*—and spread chords), but not the excessive rubato of sentimental expressiveness, nor rubato that halts the ineluctable progress of the melody and its attendant harmonic progressions. Many problems in performance begin with the unwise adoption of a tempo slower than marked, in a doomed attempt to increase expressivity. If we take Chopin as a stylistic model here, his most aristocratic, not his most heart-on-sleeve, interpreters should be emulated. Another source of both inspiration and possible derailment is Poulenc's affinity with popular music. We need to comprehend the considerable distance that separates Poulenc the evoker of the cabaret, the conjuror of memories behind the veils of youth, from the cabaret itself.

These caveats notwithstanding, it seems to have been Bernac's experience as a teacher that *C'est ainsi que tu es* was often performed woodenly and too "straight"; thus his caution that "this very beautiful song is *almost* romantic [my italics], and the two interpreters should not fear to surrender to it."[81] If being somewhat laid back at the opening is advisable, this approach should not come at the expense of traces of passion; and while it is also laudable to play exactly the notes on the page, the *laissez-faire* of a pianist improvising nostalgically in the half-light is also an important ingredient.

All in all, quite a conundrum. When we come to nostalgia, perhaps the most significant Poulencian emotion, student performers have as yet fewer memories to fall back on. They must take into account that events from long ago, now transmuted into song, have been softened by the years, and that ecstasy or catastrophe from the past can engender a gentle, less than explicit response. William Wordsworth's lines about the hour "of splendour in the grass, of glory in the flower" replaced by "strength in what remains behind" fit the mood of quite a number of Poulenc songs.[82] Perhaps this distancing, a dignified refusal to wallow in sentimentality, is what the composer means when he urges that the song be sung "*without affectation*."[83]

The vocal line, conceived to accommodate both the depths and *mezza voce* heights of Bernac's voice, is persuasive, even seductive. If this lover is saying "farewell and thank you" for ardor that once burned bright, the marking *Very much at ease* indicates that spent passion has not been wasted: to have been so close to someone is cause for gratitude rather than bitterness. Such infinitely civilized transience is a Vilmorin specialty. The frequently doubled vocal line in the piano suggests a final unanimity of purpose, and the last phrase, "Que je t'ai bien connue," seems to encapsulate the wisdom born of a "métamorphose"—passion deepening into friendship. Although "connue" in the printed text indicates the female gender, the difference between "connu" and "connue" on the platform is inaudible, an ambiguity entirely appropriate in an all-embracing song of this kind.

In the beautiful postlude (where Bernac begs pianists to observe the composer's fingering),[84] the first two bars are identical, the second arguably an echo of the first, while the last two bars unwind toward an ingratiating cadence in the major key. Here we sense the rise and fall of an inner sigh, a former happiness experienced in softer focus and an acceptance of mortality. The song is self-effacing, but from first to last it possesses that aura of perfection (not a note could be added or taken away) that is perceptible only in the composer's greatest mélodies. In 1943 Vilmorin gifted Poulenc with a handwritten copy of the poem with the following dedication: "Francis, don't forget that it was you who asked me to write poems. Without you I would only have been Louise de Vilmorin, and through you I am Louise de Vilmorin, your grateful friend."

(iii)   *Paganini*
E-flat minor; $\frac{3}{4}$; *Prestissimo* $\downarrow$ = 100

Violon hippocampe et sirène	Violin seahorse and mermaid
Berceau des cœurs cœur et berceau	Cradler of hearts cradle and heart
Larmes de Marie Madeleine	Tears of Mary Magdalene
Soupir d'une Reine	Sigh of a Queen
Echo	Echo
Violon orgueil des mains légères	Violin pride of fleet hands
Départ à cheval sur les eaux	Off on a horse-ride over the sea
Amour chevauchant le mystère	Love bestriding mystery
Voleur en prière	Thief at prayer
Oiseau	Bird
Violon femme morganatique	Violin morganatic wife
Chat botté courant la forêt	Puss in Boots roaming the forest
Puits des vérités lunatiques	Well of lunatic truths
Confession publique	Public confession
Corset	Corset
Violon alcool de l'âme en peine	Violin alcohol for souls in pain
Préférence. Muscle du soir	Preference—muscles at evening
Épaules des saisons soudaines	Shoulder of sudden seasons
Feuille de chêne	Oak-leaf
Miroir	Mirror
Violon chevalier du silence	Violin silent knight
Jouet évadé du bonheur	Toy that's escaped delight
Poitrine des milles présences	Bosom of a thousand presences
Bateau de plaisance	Pleasure yacht
Chasseur.	Huntsman.

In Le Sable du sablier, *"Echo" (line 5) is replaced by "Sanglots," and the order of verses 3 and 4 is reversed. In the printed score, "Puit" for "Puits" (verse 3, line 3) is a publisher's misprint. J. S.*

Vilmorin's title is "Métamorphoses," and if Poulenc had not adopted it for the set as a whole, it would have made rather a helpful title for this captivating, stream-of-consciousness lyric, where the shape of the violin "morphs" from one thing to another in a dizzying sequence of images, as if aided by advanced computer technology.

Perhaps the title *Paganini*, provided by Vilmorin, suggested to Poulenc the legendary violinist's great contemporary Franz Liszt; in any case, the merciless, and rather driven, élan of this whirlwind song is more reminiscent of a Liszt *Valse oubliée* than anything by Chopin. Pianists will appreciate the ingenuity of how the two opening bars are laid between the hands for virtuosic effect, para-doxically worthy of "the devil's violinist," with perilous double-stoppings in the piano writing.[85] Prancing basses underpin a dizzy succession of broken chords (all in waltz rhythm), the pianist's right hand almost always silent on the first beat of the bar.

And yet with all this difficulty, nonchalance reigns. The whole elegant scherzo is a sheer piece of *trompe l'oreille* wizardry. Poulenc composed other fast songs of this kind, where the words come almost automatically out of a sing-er's mouth before he or she has time to think of what they might be. With most texts, such an approach usually makes nonsense of a singer's responsibility to tell a story, but not having any time to consider the words is exactly how stream-of-consciousness works. *Paganini* is one of the finest examples of the genre—distantly derived from the music hall and the automatic speech of surrealism.

Poulenc judged the song *"une mélodie très médiocre,"*[86] but nevertheless use-ful as a bridging song before the Aragon setting C (see below), where the change between E-flat minor to A-flat minor is precisely calculated. In recital he often replicated the order of the first performance of this set, on 8 December 1943: *Tu vois le feu du soir, Métamorphoses, Deux Poèmes de Louis Aragon.*

FP122 *Deux Poèmes de Louis Aragon*

Composed in Noizay, September (i) and October (ii) 1943
[*Papoum* (Marcel Royer), *Jean de Polignac*; Rouart, Lerolle]
Literary source: Louis Aragon (1897–1982), *Les Yeux d'Elsa*, Collection des Cahiers du Rhône (Neuchâtel: Éditions de la Baconnière, 1943), (i) p. 55, (ii) p. 49

(i) *C*
(ii) *Fêtes galantes*

Like Poulenc, Louis Aragon was a Parisian. He was a wartime friend of Apollinaire, and together with Paul Éluard and Philippe Soupault developed that poet's ideas of surrealism after his death in 1918; Aragon's *Manifeste du surréalisme* and series of essays called *Le Libertinage* were published in 1924. When an affair with the shipping heiress Nancy Cunard ended unhappily, Aragon joined the French Communist Party, in 1927. A lifelong relationship with Elsa Triolet (the Muscovite Ella Yurievna Kagan, 1896–1970) dates from this time, and echoes Éluard's relationship with Nusch, his muse (although the Aragon-Triolet partnership lasted far

Louis Aragon, photographed by Jean Roubier in 1936.

longer). Triolet, a woman of strong personality and willpower, served as Aragon's enthusiastic guide and sponsor in the Communist world. His poem *Le Front rouge* (1931), advocating revolution in France, earned him a five-year suspended sentence, yet he continued to denounce bourgeois culture and was a critical opponent of André Gide, being diametrically opposed to him on every level.

Poulenc first met Aragon in his late teens, in Adrienne Monnier's bookshop in the rue de l'Odéon, but the poet's left-wing views ruled out any enduring friendship. In a letter to André Breton (3 June 1918), Aragon wrote: "Saw Poulenc, whom I can't stand (lazy, a snob, sure of himself, talking through his nose) but who was very friendly and enquired after Soupault, with whom he evidently believes me to be very close."[87] Poulenc was clearly an expert networker, even at the age of nineteen. Two days later, Aragon wrote to Breton once more: "I spoke too soon, I didn't know him, I judged him on his rather disagreeable exterior, a slow and nasal way of speaking that seemed to give him an impertinent assurance he is far from having. . . . I judged him on his *Rapsodie nègre*, which is a very unfaithful mirror of his talent."[88] Making a "group" was an obsession of the time, and Poulenc was being considered as the possible musical member of a Breton-Aragon alliance, but the idea came to nothing.

After the invasion of France in 1940, and having lived through the nightmare of Dunkirk as a soldier, Aragon believed it his duty to publish anti-Fascist poetry; he became regarded as the great poet of the Resistance on account of the popular accessibility of his verse. During a period of exile in the south of France, he formed a close friendship with Henri Matisse (whose biography he would later fashion in the shape of a novel) and wrote poetry that was printed illegally, to be circulated to sympathizers in France or published in Switzerland. A tone of anger (*colère*) was present in much of his work; his collection *Le Musée Grevin* was published under the nom-de-plume of François La Colère.

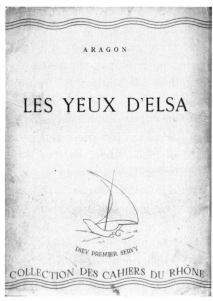

Poulenc received a smuggled copy from Switzerland of *Les Yeux d'Elsa*, a collection of twenty-four poems, hot off the press in 1943. The poem in praise of Elsa's eyes that lends the book its title (Aragon was also to write *Les Mains* [hands] *d'Elsa*) is understandable when you see Triolet's piercing gaze in photographs. Poulenc would probably have skipped the pontifications of the twenty-three-page preface and alighted upon a sequence of night poems, including "La Nuit de Dunkerque";[89]

The cover of Aragon's Les Yeux d'Elsa, *a collection of poems printed in Switzerland in 1942.*

in the wake of the Dunkirk disaster, this guardian of Communist Party purity had turned *chansonnier*. The composer's attraction to two poems later in the book was immediate, and the songs were composed within a week.[90] As he had for *Miroirs brûlants*, he conceived a diptych, a deeply serious song followed by a helter-skelter scherzo.

(i)   *C*

A-flat minor; $\frac{3}{4}$; *Très calme* ♩ = 54

J'ai traversé les ponts de Cé	I crossed the bridges of Cé
C'est là que tout a commencé	It was there it all began
Une chanson des temps passés	A song of days gone by
Parle d'un chevalier blessé	Tells of a wounded knight
D'une rose sur la chaussée	Of a rose on the pavement
Et d'un corsage délacé	Of an unlaced bodice
Du château d'un duc insensé	Of the castle of a mad duke
Et des cygnes dans les fossés	And of the swans in its moats

De la prairie où vient danser	Of the meadows where
Une éternelle fiancée	An eternal fiancée comes to dance

Et j'ai bu comme un lait glacé	And I drank in like cold milk
Le long lai des gloires faussées	The long ballad of false glories

La Loire emporte mes pensées	The Loire swept away my thoughts
Avec les voitures versées	Along with the overturned cars

Et les armes désamorcées	And the decommisioned weapons
Et les larmes mal effacées	And the ill-concealed tears

Ô ma France! ô ma délaissée	Oh, my France! oh my abandoned one
J'ai traversé les ponts de Cé.	I crossed the bridges of Cé.

In June 1940, at Les Ponts-de-Cé (a commune near Angers, Maine-et-Loire, site of a battle in the Hundred Years War), Aragon witnessed the Germans crossing the river Loire, France's last line of resistance. The poem "C" is a Marxist summation of his country's benighted (as he saw it) past, leading to an inglorious present: taking some historical license regarding the town and its bridges, Aragon traces a link between the abusive sixteenth-century aristocracy in their Loire châteaux (a castle, a mad duke, and an unlaced corset are references to the decadent libertinage of the ruling classes, with their "droit du seigneur") and France's defeat by the Nazis. It was the "long lai des gloires faussées," something to be faced and drunk medicinally, "like cold milk," that had inevitably led to the total demise of a country long weakened by corrupt rule.

The poem, written in nine two-line strophes ("distiques") in octosyllables, is technically modeled on the medieval *lai*—appropriate for the Loire, cradle of the Valois kings and their minstrels. It is also a virtuoso exercise in end rhymes, with lines that end in the same spoken (if not written) vowel. (The poet's love of wordplay extends into the dedication he wrote into Bernac's copy of the song.[91]) His lyrics were admired by a number of left-wing popular singers (such as Léo Ferré in a later generation), but Poulenc is not interested in agitprop, only in the pathos of France's demise. His music changes the angry, even bitter tone of the poem to one of tenderness. Not wishing to castigate the aristocracy (among whom he numbered his best friends), the composer embraces France as if the country were a wounded lover (*Infiniment doux* is the marking at b. 21); underneath the sadness there is pride, and we can somehow also discern a belief in the beloved's eventual recovery. To make this musical embrace all-enfolding, he borrows from popular culture, adding a hint of nightclub and boulevard (the song is dedicated to his Uncle Papoum) without in the least trivializing the mood.

The piece begins gravely with an organic four-bar piano prelude for the left hand that traces the arch of a bridge before our very ears. In a vocal phrase of infinite melancholy, now accompanied by right-hand thirds, fifths, and sixths that evoke the mournful sound of the hunting horn of medieval times, the poet tells us he has crossed the "ponts de Cé." A sudden change of dynamics from *pp* to *mf* brings a touch of rancor. *Everything* has begun there, he says, but the tragedy of this "tout" prompts a phrase sung from the heart in fuller voice. If there is perhaps a touch of medievalism (as in *Priez pour paix*) in the phrase "Une chanson des temps passés," it forms a natural part of a vocal line that unexpectedly reaches for a high A-flat, sung *pianissimo*, on "Parle"—very hard for the singer technically while at the same time a cabaret mannerism. An effect that could have been cheapening is, in this context, a moment of perilous beauty, precisely because it is achieved at great cost: here is a wounded knight singing his swan song in praise of times gone by. Seldom had the sensuality of a vocal "float" been invested with such painful multiplicities of meaning.

After singing of a thrown-away rose and an unlaced corset, a less gifted *chansonnier* would have meandered chromatically through further imagery. Instead, Poulenc assigns a ravishing and tuneful curve to an intoxicated duke and swans in the moat, the second phrase a melting sequence of the first. We can already discern the outlines of music with a popular tinge, and wonder how he means to continue. Instead of retreating, he moves boldly forward with a bow to the people, an acknowledgment of a popular style that has rendered this song immortal. (Aragon also meant his poem to be "for the people," and poet and composer, in an unlikely unity, somehow achieve a populist approach from different sides of the political spectrum.)

Building on the previous sequence and subtly changing the melody, harmony, and bar-line accentuation, Poulenc gifts us with a gloriously harmonized phrase for "De la prairie où vient danser," followed by its haunting melodic sequence ("Une éternelle fiancée"). These memorable lines move through a progression of ever flatter keys—A-flat and D-flat, then the even richer realms of G-flat and C-flat (the relative major of the song's A-flat minor tonality)—with the vocal line alternately rising and falling in intervals of fourths and fifths.

In case we forget the poem's serious intent, the turbulence of its subject matter is now given its head. After all that *pianissimo*, we return to *mf* for the salutary drinking of cold milk, and then a *forte* phrase ("false glories") that is as near to anger as the song ever comes. Nothing gets out of hand, however; in Poulenc's elegy, even anger is tempered by love. Music for the Loire begins in a gently neutral manner, but an unusual (for Poulenc) *crescendo* culminates on the astonishing word "versées": alongside the poet's "pensées," overturned motor cars are floating down the river, a grotesquely modern image of war that intrudes into the picture unexpectedly, and dramatically.

Poulenc makes the crucial decision not to allow drama and anger to disturb, much less ruin, the poetry of his own special compassion. We now hear that extraordinary musical sequence again, this time ("Et les armes désamorcées") rendered even more magical by a change in the register of the accompaniment, making the same music seem more ethereal. The apparent conflict between words describing unprimed weapons and their musical expression could have seemed amusing, but instead turns out to be heartbreaking; a *rallentando* for "Et les larmes mal effacées" invests those badly hidden tears with a massive dignity.

The noble setting of "Ô ma France" is to be expected, but "délaissée," set to another *pianissimo* high A-flat, is very daring. By now we are completely under the spell of the music, and touching echoes of the popular chanson seem an inevitable and authentic way of mourning the loss of France's freedom. Through Poulenc's eyes, we have seen a dream of what has been, and an affirmation of what will be again, because French music (where chanson and mélodie briefly come together as one) is an indestructible national tradition.

Inexperienced singers and pianists may be determined to swoon their way through this music, but it is too important and too noble to be treated as a luxurious vocal commodity. If it is true that Poulenc once remarked, "*I need a certain musical vulgarity as a plant lives on compost,*"[92] he neglected to add that the compost needs to be dug into the soil and not strewn over the plant's leaves. Bernac reveals the secret of achieving *gravitas* here: "Do not vary the equality of the eighth notes."[93] A casual or quasi-improvised treatment of rhythm, acceptable in a lot of other cabaret-inspired music, trivializes the song's seriousness; a steady rhythm preserves its dignity. This success of this masterpiece was immediate and profound. The Dutch almost always stand to applaud, but on the occasion of this song's first performance, in Amsterdam, and to the surprise of German officers seated in the audience, they stood up in silence.

(ii) *Fêtes galantes*
     F major; $\frac{4}{4}$; *Incroyablement vite, dans le style des chansons-scies de café-concert* ♩ = 152 *au moins*

On voit des marquis sur des bicyclettes	You see marquis on bicycles
On voit des marlous en cheval-jupon	You see pimps on hobby-horses
On voit des morveux avec des voilettes	You see snot-nosed brats with veils
On voit des pompiers brûler les pompons	You see firemen burning their pompoms
On voit des mots jetés à la voirie	You see words chucked on the trash heap
On voit des mots élevés au pavois	You see words praised to the skies
On voit les pieds des enfants de Marie	You see the feet of the orphan girls
On voit le dos des diseuses à voix	You see the backs of cabaret singers

On voit des voitures à gazogène	You see cars which run on Gasogene
On voit aussi des voitures à bras	You see handcarts too
On voit des lascars que les longs nez gênent	You see rogues whose long noses get in the way
On voit des coïons de dix-huit carats	You see eighteen-carat assholes
On voit ici ce que l'on voit ailleurs	You see what you see elsewhere
On voit des demoiselles dévoyées	You see depraved young ladies
On voit des voyous, On voit des voyeurs	You see yobs, you see voyeurs
On voit sous les ponts passer des noyés	You see drowned people floating under the bridge
On voit chômer les marchands de chaussures	You see out-of-work shoe sellers
On voit mourir d'ennui les mireurs d'œufs	You see egg-candlers dying of boredom
On voit péricliter les valeurs sûres	You see established values falling apart
Et fuir la vie à la six-quatre-deux.	And life rushing by in a big fat mess.

The title of Aragon's poem turns on its head the idea behind the courtly *Fêtes galantes* poems of Paul Verlaine (inspired by Antoine Watteau's paintings) of outdoor parties in the gardens of Louis XV's Versailles, where wooing and flirtations were governed by elaborate etiquette. Here everything is up for grabs: Aragon jeers at the loss of elegance in a nation that has vainly prided itself on that very quality, even if nonchalance remains indestructible. Bernac writes of being "ready to laugh at everything for fear of being obliged to weep,"[94] while Richard Burton finds the depiction of the ups-and-downs of occupied Paris "disarmingly offhand."[95] Another way of interpreting the poem is to imagine everyone heaped together on one long, crammed road. And when did that happen? In June 1940, the entire Parisian population was apparently convinced (inaccurately, as it turned out) that the arrival of the "Bosch" would lead to bombardment and large-scale destruction, and left the city *en masse*—which seems to me exactly what Aragon here describes, with the relish of *Schadenfreude*. There is a grim calling to account: descendants of "aristos" whose japes on the lawn of Versailles typified a feckless existence are now forced into a game where their power and privilege count for nothing, and where they must compete for survival, huggermugger, with the working classes.

Poulenc, still enlisted at the time, was not involved in this bizarre exodus, which resulted in almost surrealist reversals of normality amid an unprecedented mixture of humanity (thrillingly described in *Tempête en juin*, from Irène

Némirovsky's novellas *Suite française*).[96] Poulenc's decision to cast his song in the implacable rhythm of a *chanson-scie* (a music-hall genre featuring obsessive repetition—in this case the "On voit" beginning each line) softens Aragon's contempt, and finds an excuse for hoopla of the we-are-all-in-this-together variety. Once again the composer trades a left-wing sneer at the suddenly downgraded aristocracy and bourgeoisie for something far more genial. For Aragon, the phrase "true values in jeopardy" reveals his hopes for the coming Bolshevik revolution, whereas for Poulenc, the whole scene is a blip in the *comédie humaine*.

Nevertheless, an intelligent performance makes of the song something a little more ominous than a good-natured romp, and the pressure put on singer and pianist to master all the words and notes at breakneck speed generates an appropriate tension. On Poulenc and Bernac's recording, the first page is slightly under tempo and becomes gradually faster, hitting the definitive tempo only in bar 6. This may be explained by the necessity of allowing a little more time for the low notes of the baritone to "speak" at the beginning. Students are advised to study all the recordings of this duo, a performance legacy that is just as important as the printed scores.

Fêtes galantes is dedicated to Jean de Polignac, husband of Marie-Blanche and good friend of the composer: "*I finished this song, on the day before his death, without being in any doubt about how near his end was.*"[97] Aragon survived Poulenc by almost twenty years, and worldwide sales of the *Deux Poèmes* would have mounted up, over the years, to a decent sum of royalties for him from Salabert. But the poet probably never realized what wonderful songs they are: according to Poulenc, "*Aragon listened willingly enough* [to music], *but in the end without great pleasure.*"[98] He continued on the Communist path until Elsa Triolet died in 1970. After her death he completed his two-volume biography *Henri Matisse, a Novel*, and came out as bisexual. As an old man, Aragon was frequently to be seen taking part in gay pride marches, stirring up a different kind of controversy with not such a different kind of enemy.

o   o   o

FP123 *Le Voyageur sans bagage* (incidental music to a play by Jean Anouilh), 1943
FP124 *La Nuit de la Saint-Jean* (incidental music to a play by James Barrie), 1944
FP125 *Les Mamelles de Tirésias* (*opéra-bouffe* in two acts and a prologue), 1939–44 (rev. 1962)
FP126 *Un soir de neige* (chamber cantata for six mixed voices or choir, *a cappella*, to poems by Paul Éluard), December 1944

o   o   o

FP127 *Deux Mélodies de Guillaume Apollinaire*

Composed in Noizay and Paris, September 1941–January 1945 (i) and January 1945 (ii)

[*Pierre Souvtchinsky, À la mémoire d'Audrey Norman Colville*; Eschig]

Literary source: Guillaume Apollinaire (1880–1918), *Il y a* (Paris: Albert Messein, 1925), (i) p. 91, (ii) p. 93

(i)   *Montparnasse*
(ii) *Hyde Park*

(i)   *Montparnasse*

E-flat minor/major; $\frac{2}{4}$; *Très calme* ♩ = 58

Ô porte de l'hôtel avec deux plantes vertes	Oh door to the hotel with two green plants
Vertes qui jamais	Greenery which will never
Ne porteront de fleurs	Bear any flowers
Où sont mes fruits?	Where are my fruits?
Où me planté-je?	Where shall I plant myself?
Ô porte de l'hôtel un ange est devant toi	Oh door to the hotel there's an angel in front of you
Distribuant des prospectus	Handing out leaflets
On n'a jamais si bien défendu la vertu	Never has virtue been so well defended
Donnez-moi pour toujours une chambre à la semaine	Give me forever a room by the week
Ange barbu vous êtes en réalité	Bearded angel in actual fact you're
Un poète lyrique d'Allemagne	A lyric poet from Germany
Qui voulez connaître Paris	Who wants to get to know Paris

The first page of Montparnasse *(1945), inscribed to the soprano Winifred Radford, Bernac's closest British friend.*

Vous connaissez de son pavé	Already you know the cracks between
Ces raies sur lesquelles	her pavements
il ne faut pas que l'on marche	The ones you're not supposed to walk on
Et vous rêvez	And you dream
D'aller passer votre Dimanche à Garches	Of spending your Sundays in Garches
Il fait un peu lourd et vos cheveux	It's a heavy sort of day and your hair's
sont longs	getting long
Ô bon petit poète un peu bête et trop	Oh good little poet a bit dim and too
blond	blond
Vos yeux ressemblent tant à ces deux	Your eyes are so like those two big
grands ballons	balloons
Qui s'en vont dans l'air pur	Floating up into the pure air
À l'aventure	Haphazardly

The more I reread Apollinaire, the more I am struck by the poetic role that Paris plays in his work. That is why, for example, in the tumult of Les Mamelles *I have always respected the oasis of tenderness created by the words "Seine" or "Paris."... "Montparnasse" is a marvelous poem written in 1912. Let us imagine this Montparnasse all at once discovered by Picasso, Braque, Modigliani, and Apollinaire.*[99]

The artistic migration south to Montparnasse from Montmartre, the move from Right Bank to Left Bank, coincided with Poulenc's late teens and the composition of his first songs: *"Already in 1915, Montparnasse had become the artistic capital of the world, where life was full of joy. Thanks to that period of open liberty and open good humor, an art like that of Les Six could logically flourish."*[100]

Poulenc clearly had it mind to write a kind of "tale of two cities," Paris and London, to correspond with Apollinaire's own story. In this poem Apollinaire looks back on his youthful days as a penniless, jobbing journalist and wannabe poet in bemused reminiscence, evoking his former self with an almost romantic tenderness. In music lyrical and wistful, Poulenc similarly enfolds in posthumous embrace the blond and bearded young man whose poetry has long bewitched him—and turned him into a great song composer.

Apollinaire was fascinated by Paris (even the rather ordinary suburb of Garches, later flattened by First World War bombardment, seemed glamorous to the recently acclimatized Parisian), but it was clearly Montparnasse, with its growing colony of writers and artists, that exerted a powerful fascination; if anyone were to show any interest in his writing, it would be there. And it was in Montparnasse, he tells us, that he longed to live forever, in a cheap hotel room (the hotel's entrance framed by two artificial green plants). In the meantime, he stands at the hotel door feeling down on his luck and deracinated, distributing to passersby leaflets offering his odd-job literary services.

Montparnasse offers a superb example of Poulenc's patchwork-quilt method of composing:

> *The music for the line "Un poète lyrique d'Allemagne" came to me in Noizay, in 1941. . . . All the end part (after "Vous connaissez de son pavé") at Noizay in 1943. . . . The first two lines in 1944, in Paris. . . . Several lines still remained, including the terribly difficult "Donnez-moi pour toujours une chambre à la semaine." . . . This came to me during the flight to Noizay in 1943. . . . After that I let these fragments macerate and perfected the whole in three days, in Paris in February 1945. . . . I once had the opportunity to see the manuscripts of the Countess of Noailles [the poet Anna de Noailles, 1876–1933], who often worked in this way, fixing, after some suspended lines, a certain word in the middle of a line that was to come. . . . As I never transpose music I have just conceived for a certain line, or even for several words, into another key, it follows that the linking up is often difficult and I need to stand back in order to find the exact place where I am at times obliged to modulate.*[101]

The music that resulted is a kind of arioso, giving the impression of being half spoken and half sung. And the text's meditative nature exactly suits this treatment until the double lines at bar 14, when all six flats in the melancholy key signature dissolve into naturals, forming a gateway into a roving, chromatic free-for-all of nostalgia and recaptured longing. "Ô porte de l'hôtel un ange est devant toi" is made of two short phrases, the second a sequence of the first, with a lyricism that recalls the composer of *C*. The passage's *forte* dynamic lends it a slightly melodramatic air, suitable for Apollinaire's ardent self-mythologizing; he was rather good at rewriting his own history, as was Poulenc himself.

The four-bar build-up from "Ange barbu" to the impassioned release of "Un poète lyrique d'Allemagne" is one of the most passionately lyrical passages in all the Poulenc songs: a culminating cadence in E minor (with a high F-sharp for both voice and piano on the second syllable of "po-ète") is supported by a piano arpeggio encompassing a ninth—necessitating left hand crossing over right, itself an emotionally extravagant gesture. This is followed by a sensual descending passage for the voice, almost just a scale but very memorable (alighting on a plagal cadence on "d'Allemagne"); and then the wonderful afterthought of "Qui voulez connaître Paris," modulating to B major on the second syllable of the beloved city's name. Bernac recommends a slight hesitation before "Paris" to indicate the awed affection felt by poet and composer. There is a glow about this whole twelve-bar passage, the birth-moment of a song that seems to have been conceived as the result of an almost deliriously loving engagement with the text and its young protagonist. As with the same poet's *Bleuet* FP102, one cannot imagine the words set to music in the same way by a heterosexual composer.

Having reached B major on "Paris," the D-sharp in that chord changes enharmonically to E-flat, and the rest of the song is more or less centered on E-flat major, linking with the E-flat minor of the opening. Another well-known phrase, "Et vous rêvez / D'aller passer votre Dimanche à Garches," once again manages to convey a manner both self-mocking and affectionate. The harmony now wilts: added D-flats, a marvelous realization of heavier skies and the lassitude of humidity, underline the eroticism of the lines "Il fait un peu lourd et vos cheveux sont longs / Ô bon petit poète un peu bête et trop blond." The piano writing here brings out a beautiful descant over a gracefully descending vocal line suggesting a gentle benison. In this passage Bernac, for me, is incomparable (HMV DB6299)—particularly on his "blond" (both consonants and vowel), supported by the caress of a sumptuous C major chord, blondest of tonalities, and Poulenc's magical touch at the keyboard.

The song's closing section is lit by a touch of humor as the young man's eyes are likened to floating balloons, but the three-stage glissando on "l'aven-*ture*," too easy to exaggerate, make for a moment of the most tender enchantment rather than comedy or parody. The six-bar postlude is something of a miracle in itself, a sequence of chords in the bass clef that suddenly find a magical way back to the home key. My old friend Felix Aprahamian told me how exciting it was to be among the first to hear *Montparnasse* (with Bernac singing), on 6 February 1945, in Poulenc's Paris apartment shortly after the song had been completed at last.[102]

(ii)   *Hyde Park*
       No key signature; $\frac{2}{4}$; *Follement vite et furtif* ♩ = 126

Les Faiseurs de religion	The bible bashers
Prêchaient dans le brouillard	Were preaching in the fog
Les ombres près de qui nous passions	The shadowy figures we passed
Jouaient à collin-maillard	Were playing blindman's buff
A soixante-dix ans	At seventy
Joues fraîches de petits enfants	Fresh cheeks of little children
Venez venez Éléonore	Come along Eléonore
Et que sais-je encore	And who knows what else
Regardez venir les cyclopes	Look at the Cyclops coming
Les pipes s'envolaient	The pipes were flying into the air
Mais envolez-vous-en	But fly away too
Regards impénitents	Unrepentant looks
Et l'Europe l'Europe	And Europe Europe

Regards sacrés	Pious looks
Mains énamourées	Loving hands
Et les amants s'aimèrent	And the lovers kept on loving
Tant que prêcheurs prêchèrent	While the preachers kept on preaching

To Poulenc, the very name "Hyde Park" evoked something special: memories of visits to London, where he was the guest of a stage designer named Audrey Parr (née Margotine Audrey Manuella Enriquetta Pabst), a friend of Darius Milhaud. Mrs. Parr was beautiful, glamorous, and a little mad (which Poulenc loved), and she lived in Hyde Park Gardens on the north side of Bayswater Road.[103] When she later became Mrs. Audrey Norman Colville, she remained a generous hostess at a wonderfully central address. *Hyde Park* is dedicated to her memory.

The date (January 1945) suggests that Poulenc dashed this fast scherzo off as a pendant to *Montparnasse*, once that masterpiece was near completion. "*It is a bridging song, nothing more,*" he wrote. Apollinaire had visited London in 1903 in futile pursuit of his paramour Annie Playden, and his poem evokes Speakers' Corner—the park's northeast corner, near Marble Arch—where freedom of speech encouraged eccentricity and bigotry in an era of hypocrisy. Little girls are hurried along by their governesses; young couples canoodle on the grass as the preachers promise eternal condemnation; and in the pea-souper, men's pipes appear to be the glowing eye of Cyclops (that, at least, is one interpretation of lines that could mean quite a lot of things). Apollinaire seems to have diagnosed the Empire's capital as beset by a fog of insular, and rather wacky, national blindness. (Some would say "plus ça change.")

In the song's precipitous speed, Poulenc transports Apollinaire's Edwardian lines into the frenetic 1920s or 30s, the years when he attended Mrs. Parr's lively parties. In the very un-French introduction, left hand crosses over right to punch out the second beats, giving the dotted rhythms in bars 5–6 a sleazy energy. London's popular music, influenced above all by American jazz, was quite different from that of Paris. And then again, Audrey Parr, on account of her closeness to Milhaud, must have been associated in Poulenc's mind with such jazz-inspired works as Milhaud's 1923 ballet *La Création du monde*.

The tempo marking *furtif* is extraordinary, and revealing. How and why is the piece to be performed furtively? Poulenc was possibly referring to the men and women in the grass, but he more likely had in mind the boys in the bushes. In his time and for decades afterward, Hyde Park was a male cruising ground of considerable notoriety. Under cover of darkness, and perhaps of fog, a great deal went on that would have made the preachers even more furious (and who cares? says the song's laconic two-bar postlude). During his many visits to London, the incorrigible composer could easily have taken nocturnal strolls not far from Audrey Norman Colville's doorstep. In 1808, the British home secretary had ordered that the gates of Hyde Park be locked at night to "prevent those scandalous practices in such a way that the public is kept ignorant of the disgrace of them."[104] When Poulenc wrote *Hyde Park*, London was still in blackout, full of American servicemen, most of them soon bound for war in France and beyond. According to testimony of the time, the park was as busy and *furtif* as ever.

∘   ∘   ∘

FP128 *Le Soldat et la Sorcière* (incidental music for a play by Armand Salacrou), September 1945

FP129 *L'Histoire de Babar, le petit éléphant* (for reciter and piano), 1940–45

FP130 *Chansons françaises* (for *a cappella* choir), 1945–46

∘   ∘   ∘

FP131 ***Deux Mélodies sur des poèmes de Guillaume Apollinaire***
Composed at Le Tremblay (Normandy), July 1946
[*À la mémoire de Raymond Radiguet, Luigi Dallapiccola*; Eschig]
Literary source: Guillaume Apollinaire (1880–1918), *Il y a* (Paris: Albert Messein, 1925), (i) p. 102, (ii) p. 101

    (i) *Le Pont*
    (ii) *Un poème*

(i) *Le Pont (The Bridge)*
    F minor/major (bb. 1–16: key signature in three flats, then all naturals); $\frac{3}{4}$; *Très vite, d'un seul élan* ♩. = 60

Deux dames le long du fleuve	Two ladies along the river
Elles se parlent par-dessus l'eau	Talking to each other over the water
Et sur le pont de leurs paroles	And over the bridge of their words
La foule passe et repasse en dansant un dieu	The crowd come and goes, dancing a god
c'est pour toi seule que le sang coule	it is for you alone that the blood flows
tu reviendras	you will come back
Hi! oh! Là-bas	Hey-ho, below
Là-bas	Below
Tous les enfants savent pourquoi	All children know why
Passe mais passe donc	On you go, yes on you go
Ne te retourne pas	Never come back
Hi! oh! là-bas là-bas	Hey-ho, below, below!

Les jeunes filles qui passent sur le pont léger	The young girls crossing the delicate bridge
Portent dans leurs mains	Carry in their hands
Le bouquet de demain	The bouquets of tomorrow
Et leurs regards s'écoulent	And their glances flow
Dans ce fleuve à tous étranger	Into this river so strange to all
Qui vient de loin qui va si loin	Which comes from afar and flows so far
Et passe sous le pont léger de vos paroles	And passes beneath the delicate bridge of your words
Ô Bavardes le long du fleuve	Oh silly girls chattering along the river
Ô Bavardes ô folles le long du fleuve	Oh silly girls oh chatterers along the river

" 'Le Pont' is certainly one of the trickiest of Apollinaire's poems to set to music. It is these that generally attract me the most, that is why I have always preferred for my personal use the collection Il y a to Alcools."[105] Like the poem "Bleuet," this one was originally printed as a calligram in Il y a, and the typography of the title "Le Pont," curved in the shape of an old-fashioned stone bridge, survived into the title of the song (as published by Eschig). Like Montparnasse, it took some time to compose:

> I found in 1944 at Noizay the music for the line "Qui vient de loin qui va si loin"; in 1945, at Larche (Corrèze), "Et passe sous le pont léger de vos paroles." . . . I worked again at the whole song in May 1946 and finished it at one go in Normandy in July, during a spell of rehearsing with Bernac. . . . I hope that despite the long polishing, Le Pont gives the impression of an easy flow. I needed above all to give the palpitating impression of the water and of the conversation above the water, conversation that becomes "the bridge of their words." . . . The day, and that day only, when I solved the problem of expressing intelligibly the formidably difficult "c'est pour toi seule que le sang coule" (bars 18 21), I ventured to write this song.[106]

(In Il y a the words "c'est pour toi seule que le sang coule" are printed on the right side of the page, arranged in a pillar of eight lines with one word per line. Poulenc chose to run them on from the preceding words, "un dieu," although there is no way of being certain how the poet's design was to be deciphered.)

Le Pont, a delightful piece of gentle water music, is one of Poulenc's most skillful (and lesser-known) songs. The piano writing is limpidly economic, the right hand softly purling for six and a half bars before the left hand joins it. With the tempo an even and commodious one-to-a-bar (both Poulenc and Bernac stress evenness as a central characteristic here), the conversations on opposite sides of the riverbank are without stress or undue haste. Bernac makes the point that the song should not be fast or gabbled—a breakneck tempo would negate everything the composer was attempting to achieve in terms of civility and urbanity. Such qualities only serve to underline the depth of that single pillar of intense emotion printed on the right side of the page, ingeniously slipped into the body of the song amid pleasant images of children and the politesse of everyday life.

What this restraint is costing the singer is briefly glimpsed with "ô folles" at the end of the song. The "Bavardes" have no idea what is running beneath the surface of the river, and beneath the surface of the poem. Poulenc directs that the piano solo is not to slow down. Even though *Céder un peu* appears five bars from the end, Poulenc's performance with Bernac (Vega C35 A33) confirms he wanted hardly any *rallentando* at all. This recording also demonstrates Bernac's mastery of the *passagio*: most baritones would find it almost impossible to sing the high-lying "Les jeunes filles qui passent sous le pont léger" in a *piano* dynamic.

The composer dedicated the song to the memory of the writer Raymond Radiguet (see FP132 below), whom he had known quite well; Radiguet is a name he associates with the Cocteau set, and golden days spent at his grandparents' home on the banks of the Marne, not far from where Raymond was brought up. *Valses-musette* in genial mood (something like this song), which could be heard in the working-class dance halls and fairs along the riverbank, instantly became part of his musical vocabulary (compare *L'Embarquement pour Cythère*, for two pianos, FP150).

(ii)   *Un poème (A Poem)*
        No key signature; $\frac{3}{4}$; *Excessivement lent* ♩ = 44

Il est entré	He came in
Il s'est assis	He sat down
Il ne regarde pas le pyrogène à	He doesn't see the red-headed
cheveux rouges	match-holder
L'allumette flambe	The match flares
Il est parti	He is gone

> *The red tips of matches protrude from the top of a "pyrogène," a china pot for storing matches once found on café tables. Matches were struck on the side of this match-holder. J. S.*

"Un poème" appears in *Il y a* opposite "Le Pont." Its brevity as well as its mystery encouraged the composer to write a single-page exercise in quasi-atonal style—dedicated to Luigi Dallapiccola, with whom he enjoyed warm relations. Dallapiccola's three *Rencesvals* songs (texts from the medieval *Song of Roland*) were written for the Bernac-Poulenc duo, and the Italian composer's expressed admiration for the recently composed *Figure humaine* might have played a part in this dedication.[107]

Although Apollinaire died before *Ulysses* was published in Paris, the writer who comes to mind here is James Joyce, who was absolutely aware of Apollinaire's role as the impresario of Parisian modernism. One passage in Joyce's great novel (Poulenc was a subscriber to the first French edition) is a similarly tersely expressed scenario that serves as the text for Samuel Barber's *Solitary Hotel*: "In a dark corner young man seated. Young woman. Restless, solitary. She sits. She goes to window. She stands. She sits. Twilight. She thinks."[108] If Poulenc was discreetly making fun of Dallapiccola's atonality (the final, C major chord, voluptuously subversive, seems provocative in that regard), he said nothing that might imply that this song, the size of a postage stamp as he put it, should be sung with anything other than great seriousness. Indeed, he wanted it sung *quasi-parlando and terribly slowly*, as the poem *"expresses in so few words a great silence and a great emptiness."*[109] Apart, that is, from the *pianissimo* high notes on "flambe," accompanied by a soft whoosh of grace notes in the piano, when the match sparks into flame.

FP132 *Paul et Virginie* (*Paul and Virginie*)

> Composed in Noizay, August 1946 (begun in 1920)
>
> [*Lucien Daudet*; Eschig]
>
> Literary source: Raymond Radiguet (1903–1923), *Les Joues en feu, Poèmes anciens et poèmes inédits, 1917–1921* (Paris: Éditions Grasset, 1925), pp. 32–33. In 1920 Poulenc was given access to the extremely rare first printing of the poem, or worked from a handwritten copy.
>
> A major; $\frac{3}{4}$; *Très calme* ♩ = 50, with changes of tempo

Ciel! les colonies.	Heavens, the colonies!
Dénicheur de nids,	Bird-nester,
Un oiseau sans ailes,	A bird with no wings,
Que fait Paul sans elle?	What is Paul doing without her?
Où est Virginie?	Where is Virginie ?
Elle rajeunit.	She is getting younger.
Ciel des colonies,	The sky of the colonies,
Paul et Virginie:	Paul and Virginie:
Pour lui et pour elle	For him and for her
C'était une ombrelle.	It's a parasol.

Raymond Radiguet, photographed by Man Ray, c. 1922.

The young novelist Raymond Radiguet was a postwar literary phenomenon, a 1920s equivalent of Paul Verlaine's lover-nemesis Arthur Rimbaud. Radiguet took avant-garde Paris by storm, with Jean Cocteau, fourteen years older, as both his teacher and his besotted disciple (the comparison with Verlaine and Rimbaud is thus not far-fetched; both bisexual younger men insisted on freedoms that made their older mentors jealous). Radiguet's two novels, *Le Diable au corps* (1923, the probably autobiographical story of a married woman's affair with a sixteen-year-old boy) and the posthumously published *Le Bal du comte d'Orgel*, are stylistic marvels for a writer only just out of his teens. The homophobic, and probably jealous, Ernest Hemingway remarked that the bisexual Radiguet knew how to use not only his pen, but his pencil as well. Even without the proselytizing of Cocteau's publicity machine, Radiguet's career and his literary position would soon have achieved cult status; his sudden death in 1923 at the age of twenty was the most profound sorrow the older poet was ever to endure.

Poulenc counted himself a friend of Radiguet's in his own right; Raymond was raised on the Marne, born only four kilometers from Nogent, which Poulenc regarded more or less as home territory. It is also perhaps for this reason that he was friendly with the writer's parents. After Raymond's death, Maurice Radiguet wrote Poulenc to ask for his picture, as one of his son's close friends.[110]

The poem is from Radiguet's only collection of poetry, *Les Joues en feu*, written on holiday on the beaches of the Mediterranean coast. In his preface the poet takes some trouble to make it clear to the reader that he has heterosexual preferences: "On these ancient banks, for me, a naive inhabitant of the Île de France, mythology shows itself as something living and nude. After the nymphs of the Marne, a bathing Venus is certainly enough to turn your head!"[111] "Paul et Virginie," one of several idyllic boy-girl stories in the collection, was inspired by a Jean-Jacques Rousseau–influenced novel (1788) of the same name by Bernardin de Saint-Pierre (1737–1814). In this famous story with a tragic ending, the eponymous couple, both fatherless and in love from an early age, are brought up in Mauritius (thus the poem's references to "les colonies"). Radiguet's lines are a

Depiction of Paul and Virginia in an eighteenth-century edition of Paul et Virginie, *the novel by Bernardin de Saint-Pierre.*

slender evocation of the tropical scenario, far from the corruption of Western society, that had enchanted him when reading the novel as a child. He went so far as to write, together with Cocteau, an opera libretto on the same subject for Erik Satie (no trace of this music survives).

In Poulenc's copy of Max Jacob's *Cinématoma*, the poet's inscription (dated 7 September 1920) reads, in part: "Book signed while Francis Poulenc sings me *Paul et Virginie* of Radiguet, romance."[112] The song Jacob heard was never finished, but decades later the composer still felt a sense of responsibility toward this lyric:

> *These few lines of Radiguet have always had a magical savor for me. In 1920 I set them to music. . . . At that period, lacking technical control, I ran into difficulties, whereas today I believe I have found the means to progress without any real modulation for that sudden pause, that silence which makes the ultimate unprepared modulation into C-sharp* [in the last four bars] *unexpected and as though perched right on the top of a tree. . . . One rainy day a feeling of great melancholy helped me to find the tone that I believed to be right. I think it useful to bear in mind how modern poems are placed on the page. It was this that gave me the idea of respecting the blank space in the printing of the poem before "Elle rajeunit"* [bb. 11–12]. *. . . If the tempo is not maintained strictly throughout, this small song, made of a little music, of much tenderness and of one silence, is ruined.*[113]

The dedicatee, Lucien Daudet, was an accomplished painter who succeeded Reynaldo Hahn as Marcel Proust's lover; he had died in January 1946. It is possible that he was the original dedicatee in 1920, an aspect of the song Poulenc decided to leave intact for old time's sake. *Paul et Virginie*, something of an evanescent trifle, is one of three very early Radiguet settings mentioned by Poulenc in a letter to Milhaud (3 April 1920); the others, not heard of since, were entitled *Côte d'Azur* and *Victoire*.

∘   ∘   ∘

FP133 String Quartet (second attempt, destroyed), 1945

∘   ∘   ∘

FP134 *Le Disparu* (*He Who Has Disappeared*)
>   Composed at Le Tremblay (Normandy), July 1946
>   [*Henri Sauguet*; Rouart, Lerolle]
>   Literary source: Robert Desnos (1900–1944), *État de veille*, illustrations
>   by Gaston-Louis Roux (Paris: Godet, 1942); reprinted in the posthumous
>   Desnos anthology *Domaine public* (Paris: Gallimard, 1953), p. 384
>   A major; $\frac{3}{4}$; *Tempo de Valse à 1 temps* ♩. = *76, très allant*

Je n'aime plus la rue Saint-Martin	I don't like the rue Saint-Martin any more,
Depuis qu'André Platard l'a quittée.	Not since André Platard left it.
Je n'aime plus la rue Saint-Martin,	I don't like the rue Saint-Martin any more,
Je n'aime rien, pas même le vin.	I don't like anything much, not even wine.
Je n'aime plus la rue Saint-Martin	I don't like the rue Saint-Martin any more,
Depuis qu'André Platard l'a quittée.	Not since André Platard left it.
C'est mon ami, c'est mon copain,	He's my friend, he's my mate.
Nous partagions la chambre et le pain.	We shared a room, we shared our bread.
Je n'aime plus la rue Saint-Martin.	I don't like the rue Saint-Martin any more.
C'est mon ami, c'est mon copain,	He's my friend, he's my mate,
Il a disparu un matin,	One morning he disappeared.
Ils l'ont emmené, on ne sait plus rien,	They took him away, that's all we know,
On ne l'a plus revu dans la rue Saint-Martin.	No one's seen him in the rue Saint-Martin.
Pas la peine d'implorer les saints,	No point in praying to the saints.
Saints Merri, Jacques, Gervais et Martin,	St. Merri, St. Jacques, St. Gervais, St. Martin,
Pas même Valérien qui se cache sur la colline.	Not even St. Valerian, who's hiding up on the hill.

Le temps passe, on ne sait rien,	Time passes, no one knows anything.
André Platard a quitté la rue	André Platard has left the rue
Saint-Martin.	Saint-Martin.

Like Poulenc, Desnos was a born Parisian. His father was a local politician and union representative for merchants of poultry and game, and from 1902 to 1913 his family lived at 11, rue Saint-Martin, in the Halles district. Poulenc first encountered Desnos in the 1920s: *"If I was never really a part of the group of surrealists, I had a number of friends apart from Breton, Aragon, and Éluard. Thus I very much liked René Crevel and Desnos. Sometimes I used to go and meet them in a bar named Cintra in the Passage de l'Opéra."*[114]

Robert Desnos as a young man.

Desnos played an important role in the early days of surrealism, when he was able to dictate a stream of words in any condition—he had only to close his eyes, or even be more or less asleep, and poetry erupted from him. His large and soulful eyes were actually his most notable feature; the poet Tristan Tzara believed that "never were human eyes as wide open as those of Desnos." Always left-wing, but too individualistic to become identified with dogmatic Communism, Desnos was eventually spurned by his more hard-line surrealist colleagues, and moved into a period of radiophonic experimentation. His broadcasts with such artists as Kurt Weill were valued at the time for their imaginative and avant-garde use of the medium. He became something of a radio celebrity, and a talent with words and allusive writing made him a sought-after creator of advertising slogans for firms like Cinzano and Peugeot. Desnos also worked with Milhaud on a cantata, and on films with Honegger. The later part of his life and his tragic end are described in the commentary for *Dernier Poème* FP163.

Desnos's title for this 1942 poem is "Couplets de la rue Saint-Martin," and Poulenc rated it *"allusive, rather than of true quality. We are far from Aragon, already himself far from Éluard or Apollinaire."*[115] He would have been surprised to learn that Desnos has fared rather better with later composers than Éluard, and not only with his popular *Bestiaire*-like children's poems in *Chantefables* and *Les Chantefleurs*. Witold Lutosławski set poems from both collections (1989–

91), and he also took a two-page Desnos poem from 1926 for his orchestral song cycle *Les Espaces de sommeil* (1975), composed for Dietrich Fischer-Dieskau;[116] Henri Dutilleux included "Dernier Poème" as part of his orchestral song cycle *Les Temps de l'horloge* (2007), written for Renée Fleming.

In July 1946, France was attempting to come to terms with the war and its aftermath of bitterness, meting out brutal justice to collaborators and honoring those who had fought on the side of the angels. As a martyr, Desnos belonged, of course, to the latter category; it was an apposite, and a perfectly safe, time to compose this song. On first hearing it, I imagined there had been something clandestine about its composition, that it was somehow contemporary with the Gestapo arrests of Resistance fighters, when feelings of outrage had to be expressed in code. It was a little disappointing to discover that *Le Disparu* was not actually a wartime song, but one that memorialized past dangers.

Desnos's poem, anticipating, in eerie prophecy, his own arrest two years later, bemoans the disappearance of the fictional André Platard as the Gestapo close in on a cell of the Resistance. People all over France had lost loved ones in this way. Poulenc's decision to invoke the popular muse ("*in the style of Môme Piaf*")[117] is scarcely surprising: "*An immutable rhythm, that of the Boston waltz, passes through three colors: the dance with accordion band, the peal of bells, the funeral march.*"[118] (The funeral march allows the composer to suggest a layer of information lacking in the poem: Platard has been executed, and his body returned for burial to discourage others.) He casts the whole song as a *valse-musette*, while crediting American dance for its influence on French music. Changes of key for the three sections—a progression of thirds (A major, D-flat major, F major, and thence back to A major/minor)—ratchet up the narrative tension, while the texture changes from effulgent to denuded and bare-as-bones by the end of the song's four pages. After the somewhat faster music for the poem's third verse (*Presser, mais très peu*), with the tessitura rising as though in panic, the final page seems lost and hopeless, bereaved, while never really relaxing the pulse.

The popular nature of this music is such that "one could easily imagine it played on the accordion."[119] The one-in-a-bar texture poses a challenge for pianists required to bring out (and connect) the dotted half notes in the little finger of the right hand while sounding the dotted halfs in the bass with the left-hand little finger. At the same time, the pulsating quarter notes played by both hands in the middle of the texture, to suppress any tiresome sense of repetition, should glide gently along, providing a glow of harmony while avoiding undue emphasis: "*If the pianist does not observe the preliminary indication 'bathed in pedals,' the chords scarcely separated, the half notes brought out a little, the game is lost. I am waiting for you, dear Mademoiselle A, dear Monsieur T (it's not only the women to blame, of course), I am waiting for you with my gun under my arm. And if you don't listen, watch out, I'll shoot the pianist.*"[120]

FP135 *Main dominée par le cœur* (*Hand Ruled by the Heart*)
Composed in Noizay, August 1946
[*Marie-Blanche de Polignac*; Rouart, Lerolle]
Literary source: Paul Éluard (1895–1952), *Poésie et vérité* (Neuchatel: Éditions de la Baconnière, 1942), pp. 102–3, with the title "La Main Le Cœur Le Lion L'Oiseau"
C minor; $\frac{4}{4}$; *Très allant* ♩ = 100, *très exactement*

Main dominée par le cœur	Hand ruled by the heart
Cœur dominé par le lion	Heart ruled by the lion
Lion dominé par l'oiseau	Lion ruled by the bird
L'oiseau qu'efface un nuage	The bird erased by a cloud
Le lion que le désert grise	The lion intoxicated by the desert
Le cœur que la mort habite	The heart where death lives
La main refermée en vain	The hand closed in vain
Aucun secours tout m'échappe	No help, everything deserts me
Je vois ce qui disparaît	I see what is vanishing
Je comprends que je n'ai rien	I can see that I have nothing
Et je m'imagine à peine	And I can barely imagine myself
Entre les murs une absence	Between the walls an absence
Puis l'exil dans les ténèbres	And then exile into the darkness
Les yeux purs la tête inerte	The eyes pure the head inert

> *Once the music for a line of a poem has come to me, I never transpose the key in order to make my task easier at the expense of the poem. It follows that my modulations pass at times through a mouse hole. . . . Here having begun the song at the first line, and knowing what the music of the last line was to be, I have manipulated the modulations to benefit the words directly. Two arabesques of seven lines passing from C to C, with the key of D as the highest point (reached each time by different degrees) form, in my estimation, a logical whole. . . . During the first seven lines the words return so delightfully to their source that Éluard proposed a title for me (too enigmatic for the public): La Gamme [The Gamut]. I prefer* Main dominée par le cœur.[121]

In a marking of *Très allant,* the nonstop sixteenth-note accompaniment may look hectic on paper, but the song shares with other masterpieces inspired by the same poet a kind of genial calm, with music that is ardent and above the fray at

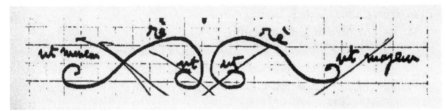

Poulenc's two arabesques outlining the palindromic harmonic structure of Main dominée par le cœur *(C minor–D–C ‖ C–D–C major). First published in the unexpurgated edition of* Journal de mes mélodies.

the same time—a gnomic pronouncement. We might think it owes a great deal to *Plume d'eau claire* from the *Cinq Poèmes de Paul Éluard* (1935), even before learning that Poulenc himself admitted to the fact, adding that one is permitted to steal from oneself. He also reveals that the tempo was modeled on Fauré's *Le Don silencieux*, one of that composer's most inscrutably beautiful songs, which Poulenc had learned to love (almost despite himself, as no admirer of Fauré).

This is one of the most graceful and sinuous of the Éluard songs, with nine of its twenty-nine bars in three flats, in the minor key, and the remainder basking in the sunlight of naturals. The play between C minor and C major cannot help but remind us of the opening and closing songs of *Tel jour telle nuit*, in those same tonalities. The song's closing section ("Les yeux purs la tête inerte") is swathed in graceful arpeggio arabesques, the piano imitating the melody of the vocal line; and this passage leads to one of the most seraphic perorations (eight bars) of any Poulenc song, ending with an immensely satisfying, and deliciously extended, C major cadence. Bernac notes: "While remaining exactly *a tempo*, the last line, owing to the long note values of the voice part, will suddenly give an impression of immobility."[122] Hervé Lacombe comments that the song's strange and calmed conclusion "corresponds to the 'yeux purs' of the poet, like a thought washed of all thought," as if accepting "the vanity of all things"; or as if underlining an earlier line in the poem, "Je comprends que je n'ai rien."[123]

The song was dedicated to Marie-Blanche de Polignac for her forty-ninth birthday, on 31 August 1946. Sending it to her in advance as his *"little vase of flowers,"* Poulenc tells her he is rather proud of it, and that as long as she likes it, it doesn't really matter that Nadia Boulanger would have sent it back with a severe expression behind her pince-nez. Apollinaire was his mainstay in the 1940s, with two great cycles at either end of the decade. It took a birthday to remind Poulenc that Éluard, who had dominated the second half of the 30s, could also inspire slender and intimate miniatures. The manuscript is dated 14–18–19 August, followed by this observation: *"Three days is perhaps a lot for so little, but it is already very fast for me, who, alas, am no Schubert!!"*[124]

FP136 *Trois Chansons de F. García Lorca*

Composed in Noizay, summer (i) and September (ii, iii) 1947

[*Geneviève Touraine, Mme Auguste Lambiotte, Gérard Souzay*; Heugel]

Literary source: Fédérico García Lorca (1898–1936), *Canciones 1921–1924* (1927); French translations by Félix Gattegno in *Anthologie poétique de Fédérico García Lorca* (Paris: Charlot, 1946. (i) In section *Au delà du monde*, p. 54; (ii) in *Andalouse*, p. 41; (iii) in *Chansons pour finir*, p. 62.

(i)   *L'Enfant muet*
(ii) *Adelina à la promenade*
(iii) *Chanson de l'oranger sec*

García Lorca, one of the greatest of Spanish poets and playwrights, was renowned for his lyrical vision and intensity. He was born near Granada, and we can trace his Andalusian roots (including his later friendship with Manuel de Falla and his discovery of Spanish folklore and the *cante jondo*) in much of his work. He was a gifted pianist and painter, and, having studied composition at the University of Grenada, was devoted to music (especially Beethoven, Chopin, and Debussy). In his student days in Madrid, where he was officially studying law and philosophy, García Lorca became friendly with a wide range of avant-garde artists, including Luis Buñuel and Salvador Dali. His first book of poems was published in 1921; the following year, after meeting the famous singer of flamenco Manuel Torres, he joined forces with Falla to promote a festival, the Concurso de Cante Jondo, dedicated to this great Andalusian musical tradition.

Canciones was the book where the poems Poulenc set are to be found, but it was *Romancero Gitano* (1928), a Gypsy anthology and a hymn to Andalusian culture, that made García Lorca truly famous; from then on, he fought against being typecast as a Gypsy poet. Between 1925 and 1928, his friendship with Dali was particularly intense, although any hopes of physical reciprocation cherished by the gay poet were dashed after the artist's marriage to Gala (see p. 144); to make matters worse, he believed a film made by Dali and Buñuel, *Le Chien andalou*, was designed as a personal attack against him. Depressed and troubled by his homosexuality, and Spanish society's hostile attitude, he spent some time in the United States, personally witnessing the fallout from the Wall Street crash of 1929.

García Lorca's return to Spain in 1930 coincided with the establishment of the Second Spanish Republic. The new left-wing government was sympathetic to bringing the arts to disadvantaged people, and the poet became director of a student theater company, La Barraca (The Shack), which toured rural Spain and also performed for African American communities in the United States. He found his life's cause in the theater: from this period come his great plays *Blood*

Wedding, Yerma, and the *House of Bernarda Alba* (known as the *Rural Trilogy*), all of which question bourgeois assumptions prevalent in Spanish life; he eagerly addressed such issues as class divides and the rights of women and minorities. To some, García Lorca must have seemed a thoroughly dangerous young man, as much on account of his lively and passionate personality as his socialist views.

At the outset of the Spanish Civil War, the poet's brother-in-law, who had agreed to take on the impossible position of mayor of Grenada, was assassinated. On that same day, 18 August 1936, García Lorca was arrested; the next day he was murdered by nationalist militia somewhere between the villages of Víznar and Alcafar—whether on account of his political leanings or his homosexuality, or both, is not certain. His body has never been found, and mysteries abound.

Without ever having met him personally, Poulenc felt a profound affinity, and dedicated his 1942 Violin Sonata (FP119) "*à la mémoire de Fédérico García Lorca*": "*What difficulty I have in proving musically my passion for Lorca. My sonata for piano and violin, dedicated to his memory, is, alas, very mediocre Poulenc, and these three songs are of little importance in my vocal work.*"[125]

(i)   *L'Enfant muet (The Mute Child)*
     F-sharp minor; $\frac{4}{4}$; *Modéré mais sans traîner* ♩ = 66, *Rigoureusement au même mouvement jusqu'à la dernière note*

L'enfant cherche sa voix.	The child is looking for his voice.
(C'est le roi des grillons qui l'a.)	(The king of the crickets has it.)
Dans une goutte d'eau,	In a drop of water,
L'enfant cherchait sa voix.	The child was looking for his voice.
Je ne la veux pas pour parler;	I don't want it in order to speak;
J'en ferais une bague	I'm going to turn it into a ring
Que mon silence portera	Which my silence can carry
À son plus petit doigt.	On its littlest finger.
Dans une goutte d'eau,	In a drop of water,
L'enfant cherchait sa voix.	The child was looking for his voice.
(La voix captive, loin de là,	(The captured voice, far away,
Met un costume de grillon.)	Takes the shape of a cricket.)

Poulenc was unnecessarily harsh on these songs, as he was on his Violin Sonata, which, in the right performance, can be an impressive work. And while the García Lorca settings are no match for his Apollinaire or Éluard songs, as mélodies with a Spanish flavor and evocations of the poet's personality, profound and gently playful by turns, they belong to an honorable tradition of quasi-Spanish music by French composers, and they possess considerable charm. *L'Enfant muet*, in one of Poulenc's favorite tonalities, F-sharp minor, is limpid and spare in texture, an early example of his "songs for children" style that would eventually lead to the transparent settings of *La Courte paille*. The gentle *acciaccaturas* that depict, at the same time, the sound of crickets and drops of water containing traces of the child's lost voice are a unique touch. Perhaps because of these graceful pianistic ornaments, Poulenc confessed to a similarity between this song and Debussy's Verlaine setting *Les Ingénus* (*Fêtes galantes*, second book).[126] Modulations leading back to F-sharp minor at the end are unusually convoluted and whimsical.

(ii) *Adelina à la promenade* (*Adelina Out for a Walk*)
      G-flat major; $\frac{6}{8}$; *Follement vite—dans un tourbillon* ♩. = 138

La mer n'a pas d'oranges	The sea has no oranges
et Séville n'a pas d'amour.	and Seville has no love.
Brune, quelle lumière	Brown-haired girl, all that burning
brûlante!	light!
Prête-moi ton parasol.	Lend me your parasol.
Il rendra vert mon visage	It'll make my face look green
—jus de citron et de limon—	—lemon juice and lime juice—
et tes mots—petits poissons—	and your words—like little fish—
nageront tout à l'entour.	will swim all around.
La mer n'a pas d'oranges	The sea has no oranges
Ay amour,	Ay love,
et Séville n'a pas d'amour!	and Seville has no love!

Like the wrought-iron balconies of Chabrier's *España* that come from a French department store, *Adelina à la promenade*, with its cheeky sixteenth triplets, is an evocation of a Spanish dance (so fast that the pianist's fingers almost clack like castanets as they dash around the keyboard) that is more Parisian than genuinely Iberian. The composer described it as "*a jota, a little 'Plaza Clichy' as Satie used to say.*"[127] Although it is over in a flash, the song is more skillful and effective than he was prepared to admit.

(iii) *Chanson de l'oranger sec* (*Song of the Barren Orange Tree*)
       C minor; $\frac{3}{4}$; *Tempo de Sarabande* ♩ = 69

Bûcheron.	Woodcutter.
Abat mon ombre.	Chop down my shadow.
Délivre-moi du supplice	Deliver me from the torment
De me voir sans oranges.	Of seeing myself without oranges.
Pourquoi suis-je né entre des miroirs?	Why was I born between mirrors?
Le jour me fait tourner	The day makes me spin
Et la nuit me copie	And the night imitates me
Dans toutes ses étoiles.	With its multitude of stars.
Je veux vivre sans me voir.	I want to live without seeing myself,
Les fourmis et les liserons	The ants and the tumbleweed,
Je rêverai que ce sont	I'll dream that they're
Mes feuilles et mes oiseaux.	My leaves and my birds.
Bûcheron.	Woodcutter.
Abat mon ombre.	Chop down my shadow.
Délivre-moi du supplice	Deliver me from the torment
De me voir sans oranges.	Of seeing myself without oranges.

This song is a sarabande, a time-honored musical means (used by Hugo Wolf in No. 7 of his *Spanisches Liederbuch,* among others) of evoking Spanish serious-ness and the depth of the country's religious belief. Here, even a barren orange tree is depicted begging for death in a stately rhythm. Although it is an impos-ing and stylish song, Poulenc confessed that it was "*nobly French*" rather than "*gravely Spanish.*"[128] The E-flat minor phrase "Je veux vivre sans me voir" is eerily similar to the "Télégraphe oiseau" phrase in *Voyage,* the closing song of the con-temporary cycle *Calligrammes* (see below).

Chanson de l'oranger sec was dedicated to the young baritone Gérard Souzay (1918–2004), the most talented of Bernac's pupils from the younger generation—although it was clearly Poulenc's intention (and Bernac's) that Souzay should per-form all three songs in the set, accompanied by his talented pianist, Jacqueline Bonneau. (*L'Enfant muet* was dedicated to Souzay's sister, soprano Geneviève Tour-aine.) Indeed, Poulenc took the trouble to ensure that the range of these songs did not fall outside what was comfortable for Souzay, who (despite his more obviously beautiful voice) did not have the same flexibility at the top of the stave as his teacher.

When Poulenc sent the García Lorca songs to Bernac, he wrote: "*Here, I hope, is something that will leave you 'muet' with admiration!!!! . . . I believe that with your voices (you and Gérard) and in our fingers (mine and Bonneau), that should result in something mysterious and translucent.*"[129] Evidently he planned simulta-neous first performances in different venues. If it seems extraordinary that Poulenc would be writing songs for another baritone with Bernac's blessing, in 1947 Bernac's devotion to his pupil Souzay, and his belief in a glorious future for the handsome baritone, was at its height. After some weeks Souzay had not acknowledged receiving the newly minted songs, and such *lèse-majesté* did not go unnoticed. *"Perhaps he thinks they're rotten,"* Poulenc mused to Bernac. *"Pity, as I'm quite pleased with them."* If Souzay did indeed think they were not Poulenc's best (a verdict later echoed by the composer), it was clearly not considered his place to say so with the snub of ungrateful silence. This was to be the only time that Poulenc wrote a piece with this or any other younger baritone in mind. But his admiration for Spanish art—music, painting, and literature—continued long after these songs were composed. At the end of 1949, in rereading Cervantes' *Don Quichotte* during his second American tour, he pronounced it an *"incomparable marvel."*[130]

FP137 ... *mais mourir* (... *but to die*)

Composed in Noizay, 21 October 1947
Literary source: Paul Éluard (1895–1952), *La Vie immédiate* (Paris: Éditions des Cahiers libres, 1932), p. 94
["*À la mémoire de Nush*" (sic); Heugel]
E minor; $\frac{9}{8}$; *Modéré, sans lenteur* ♩. = 66

Mains agitées aux grimaces nouées	Restless hands with twisted grimaces
Une grimace en fait une autre	One grimace turns into another
L'autre est nocturne le temps passe	The other one is nocturnal—time passes
Ouvrir des boîtes casser des verres creuser des trous	To open boxes to smash glasses to dig holes
Et vérifier les formes inutiles du vide	And to verify the pointless shapes of empty space
Mains lasses retournant leurs gants	Weary hands turning down their gloves
Paupières des couleurs parfaites	Perfectly colored eyelids
Coucher n'importe où	To sleep anywhere
Et garder en lieu sûr	And to safeguard
Le poison qui se compose alors	The poison which then forms
Dans le calme mais mourir.	In the calm ... but to die.

Nusch Éluard died suddenly of a cerebral hemorrhage on 28 November 1946, and Poulenc was acutely aware that his revered poet had lost his beloved muse, the *raison d'être* of his life and his art. In searching for a poem he could set in her memory, Poulenc remembered that Nusch had beautiful hands, and alighted on this poem, originally called "Peu de vertu" (Little virtue). As the 1932 publication of *La Vie immédiate* falls within the Nusch period of Éluard's life, it is safe to assume the poem refers to her.

Nusch Éluard (Maria Benz), photographed by Man Ray, c. 1935.

"*I like this song composed in memory of Nush Éluard*," Poulenc tells us,[131] and one must admit that it is extraordinarily well made without, perhaps, managing to hit the jackpot. Although it cannot boast the memorability of other Éluard "singles"—the liquid unfolding of *Main dominée par le cœur* FP135 or the rapt *Ce doux petit visage* FP99—it is more interesting than *Une chanson pour porcelaine* FP169 and, if truth be known, better than some of the songs sheltered within the larger Éluard cycles.

. . . *mais mourir* begins in E minor and ends in E major, and the vocal line ranges unusually far and wide for an Éluard setting at this speed. There is a real independence between voice and piano; melodic shapes traced in the accompaniment have a life and eloquence of their own, as if Poulenc were thinking of hand movements at the piano as he wrote the music. In the last five bars (for "mais mourir"), the pianist plays the melody against a held vocal note, an effect that is suffused with tender melancholy; the final cadence, moving from C major to E major, is gently persuasive. If I think involuntarily of *La Grâce exilée* (from *Calligrammes*), in almost the same tonality though faster, when I play this song, it may be because Poulenc is already turning his thoughts yet again to Apollinaire. Once he had surmounted a period of creative inactivity, it was his oldest poetical collaborator who would next claim his attention.

o   o   o

FP138 *L'Invitation au château* (incidental music for a play by Jean Anouilh), 1947
FP139 *Amphitryon* (incidental music for a play by Molière), September–December
    1947

o   o   o

FP140 *Calligrammes* (*Calligrams*)

> Composed in Noizay, May 1948 (i, vii); Le Tremblay (Normandy), July 1948 (ii, iii, v); and Noizay, August 1948 (iv, vi)
>
> [*Simone Tilliard, Pierre Lelong, Jacqueline Apollinaire, À la mémoire de Emmanuel Faÿ, À ma sœur Jeanne* (Manceaux), *Jacques Soulé, À la mémoire de Raymonde Linossier*; Heugel]
>
> Literary source: Guillaume Apollinaire (1880–1918), *Calligrammes, Poèmes de la paix et de la guerre (1913–1916)* (Paris: Mercure de France, 1918). (i) From section *Obus couleur de lune*, p. 162; (ii) and (iii) from *Case d'Armons*, pp. 94, 100; (iv) from *Ondes*, p. 62; (v) from *Lueurs des tirs*, p. 117; (vi) from *Obus couleur de lune*, p. 164; (vii) from *Ondes*, pp. 58–59.

- (i)   *L'Espionne*
- (ii)   *Mutation*
- (iii)   *Vers le sud*
- (iv)   *Il pleut*
- (v)   *La Grâce exilée*
- (vi)   *Aussi bien que les cigales*
- (vii) *Voyage*

Poulenc had known these poems since they first appeared in the spring of 1918; he bought his copy of the large-format first edition (published by Mercure de France, with a drawing by Picasso of the poet, a war hero with a bandaged head) in Adrienne Monnier's bookshop in the rue de l'Odéon. Mallarmé, one of Poulenc's favorite childhood poets, had already experimented with typography in *Un coup de dés* (1914), playing with space on the page and turning words into pictures; but Apollinaire took things a step further. How extraordinary and exciting, how boldly modern these "calligrams" (drawn poems, poems-in-pictures, ideograms, bold typographical experiments, call them what you will) must have seemed in 1918!

Apollinaire's collection, written and designed by him between 1913 and 1916, recounts the reactions of a poet in his mid-thirties and in love (when was Apollinaire not in love?) as he survived emotional vicissitudes and a cruel and senseless war. The collection's subtitle (*Poèmes de la paix et de la guerre*) emphasizes that before and even during his time at the Front, he experienced periods of repose and delight. The same could be said of Poulenc's own far more limited wartime experiences—in 1918 (he could claim to have participated, even if only at the margins, in the same war as his beloved poet) and in 1940, both extremely productive years for him: "*At that time I was in an anti-aircraft section, stationed at Tremblay. Once again chance led me to the banks of the Marne of my childhood. When we were not leaping on to the nearest Vincennes tramways taking French leave, I would end each day in the little bistros of Nogent. It was actually in one of*

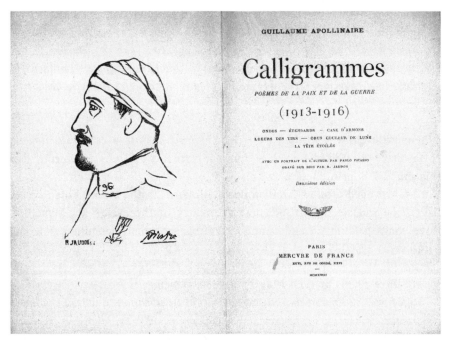

The title page of Apollinaire's Calligrammes *(1918), with a woodcut of a drawing of the poet by Picasso.*

these bistros that I first read the volume of Apollinaire, thus blending what I was going to live through with the poetic inventions of Calligrammes*."*[132]

The poems germinated in Poulenc's brain for thirty years, during which time he burnished his skills with regard to Apollinairian music. An evening in homage to the poet at the Comédie-Française (23 January 1943), when extracts from *Calligrammes* were read and projected onto a screen, was probably the event that brought the work back into Poulenc's mind. But his earlier settings *Bleuet* FP102 and *Le Pont* FP131/i, both printed as easier-to-solve calligrams, had possibly whet his appetite for further challenges. The resulting songs were *"the culmination of a whole range of experiments in setting Apollinaire."*[133]

Looking forward with some trepidation to his first North American tour with Poulenc in the autumn of 1948, Bernac received the following letter in July from the composer, holidaying in the Morvan:

I have been here a week and I have already done an incredible amount of work. Here, in spite of the gloomy weather, I have found the calm of those beautiful Anost summers. Music keeps flowing out of me and is a constant joy. Very often my winter irritability is due to my lack of creativity. Let me tell you a piece of GOOD NEWS: for our second New York concert you will have a beautiful, brand-new cycle, which I already love as much as Tel jour telle nuit. *In* Calligrammes *I have really found what I was looking for. What do I not owe to Apollinaire! I have already written four songs (two were vaguely sketched at Noizay in May); there will be seven altogether and I know exactly what they will all be like. Even more carefully constructed than* Tel jour, *this cycle has a true internal structure.*

When the cycle was printed by Heugel, Poulenc chose a calligram for the cover that reflected the work's "*internal structure*": "Dans ce miroir" (In this mirror) is printed as a symmetrical oval of single words (and parts of words), arranged around "Guillaume Apollinaire" in the center. This mirror-like shape reflects the palindromic symmetry of the cycle's key structure: three songs leading to, and from, a pivoting song in B-flat minor. Poulenc continued:

All these poems of 1913–15 bring a flood of memories from my Nogent past and from the time of the 1914 war. Hence the dedication to all my childhood friends. . . . During my last few days I took myself off to the village—Vincennes, and so on—and very gradually during the course of my solitary walks, my song cycle took shape. Two mélodies like soldiers' songs will contrast happily with the rest. I can guarantee that you will have the whole cycle for New York. You can well imagine that if I undertake this responsibility, it is because I am sure of myself. Whenever you like I will copy out the first four for you, and you will have the rest by the beginning of September by the latest. They are made to measure for you, more in the lower than the upper register.[134]

(i) *L'Espionne (The Spy)*
     F-sharp minor; $\frac{3}{4}$; *Très modéré* ♩ = 60

Pâle espionne de l'Amour	That pale spy of love
Ma mémoire à peine fidèle	My memory never the most reliable,
N'eut pour observer cette belle	Had only to survey this beautiful fortress
Forteresse qu'une heure un jour	One hour one day
Tu te déguises	You disguise yourself
A ta guise	As you please
Mémoire espionne du cœur	Memory the heart's spy
Tu ne retrouves plus l'exquise	You never rediscover that exquisite
Ruse et le cœur seul est vainqueur	Cunning, and the heart alone prevails

Mais la vois-tu cette mémoire	But do you see this memory
Les yeux bandés prête à mourir	Blindfolded, ready to die,
Elle affirme qu'on peut l'en croire	Affirming that we can believe her
Mon cœur vaincra sans coup férir	My heart will prevail with not a shot fired

The poem is printed simply, three strophes without a design; in fact, only three songs in this cycle are real calligrams. Apollinaire sent it in a love letter to his fiancée Madeleine Pagès, whose unassailable virtue is described as a "forteresse" here (he has been unable to be alone with her for an hour, much less a day). For her imaginary Mata Hari–type execution as a spy, eyes blindfolded, the poet avoids bandages in favor of badinage. The tempo is one favored in the Éluard settings (♩ = 60), and from the first two bars we might imagine ourselves to be in the sound world of *Tu vois le feu du soir* (from *Miroirs brûlants*, FP98/i).

Not for long, however: there is a sensuality and suave eroticism in this poet, and in this music, that would be out of place in Éluard's more rigorous humanistic vision. In performance, the weaving and teasing vocal line ("poetic, but very virile," says Bernac),[135] always persuasive, always charming, is a portrait of Apollinaire at the Front—the soldier beset by sexual longing and caught up in every detail of the photographs he carries in his pocket of his beloved.

Poulenc was proud of a certain technical aspect of the song: "*I feel that 'Mais la vois-tu—cette mémoire—Les yeux bandés—prête à mourir,' with its rhythm regular but broken, is one of my most exact prosodies.*"[136]

(ii) *Mutation*
No key signature (E-flat minor); $\frac{3}{4}$; *Presto, très rythmé* ♩ = 192

Une femme qui pleurait	A woman was weeping
Eh! Oh! Ah!	Eh! Oh! Ha!
Des soldats qui passaient	Soldiers were passing
Eh! Oh! Ah!	Eh! Oh! Ha!
Un éclusier qui pêchait	A lock-keeper was fishing
Eh! Oh! Ha!	Eh! Oh! Ha!
Les tranchées qui blanchissaient	Trenches were turning white
Eh! Oh! Ha!	Eh! Oh! Ah!
Des obus qui pétaient	Shells were exploding
Eh! Oh! Ha!	Eh! Oh! Ha!
Des allumettes qui ne prenaient pas	Matches refusing to light
Et tout	And everything
A tant changé	Totally changed

En moi	In me
Tout	Everything
Sauf mon Amour	Except my love
Eh! Oh! Ha!	Eh! Oh! Ha!

The mutation described in the poem, another one without a printed design, is the metamorphosis of Apollinaire from civilian to soldier; and there is a certain brutality to the process, as the rough-edged "Eh! Oh! Ha!" refrain makes clear. Poulenc had already visited this world of gruff soldierly camaraderie in *Chanson d'Orkenise* (from *Banalités*, FP107/i).

The poet, perched on a wagon and in charge of a machine gun, passes through three tableaux, scenes of grief, war, and peace; indentations in the printed poem suggest something of a rocky ride. The trenches have been dug in the white chalk of the Champagne region, and shells explode ("péter" is to crackle, to pop, also to fart) all around. Though experiences of war have changed him, he is still as much in love as ever. The pulse is that of a foot-stomping folksong—lusty and bawled to the rooftops by a group of soldiers. Their bravado has a hollow ring to it, but the devil-may-care nature of the music emphasizes that there is nothing for it but to go forward. This is surely one of Poulenc's most implacable songs. Paradoxically, although it was Éluard who was the Communist and "man of the people," it is Apollinaire, connoisseur of rough living and impoverishment, who mucks in with the proletariat in a way that Poulenc finds irresistible.

(iii)   *Vers le sud* (*To the South*)
        No key signature (E major); $\frac{3}{4} = \frac{9}{8}$; *Calme mais allant* ♩. = 54

Zénith	Zenith
Tous ces regrets	All those regrets
Ces jardins sans limite	Those boundless gardens
Où le crapaud module un tendre cri d'azur	Where the toad sings forth his soft blue cry
La biche du silence éperdu passe vite	The fawn of bewildered silence scurries by
Un rossignol meurtri par l'amour chante sur	A nightingale bruised by love sings over
Le rosier de ton corps dont j'ai cueilli les roses	The rosebush of your body, from which I have plucked the roses
Nos cœurs pendent ensemble au même grenadier	Our hearts hang side by side from the same pomegranate tree
Et les fleurs de grenade en nos regards écloses	And the pomegranate blossoms blooming under our gaze

En tombant tour à tour ont jonché le sentier	Falling one by one have strewn the path

This poem (once again without a drawing) looks back with affectionate nostalgia on a week spent in the south of France with "Lou" (Louise de Coligny-Chatillon) in December 1914 (see p. 28). In *Frühlingstraum*, the eleventh song of *Winterreise*, Schubert uses the musical language of Mozart to describe a dream of a romantic idyll from happier times, and the five-bar introduction to *Vers le sud* similarly invokes old music (baroque neoclassicism, suggesting to Jeremy Sams the "ancienne musique" of Ravel's *Tombeau de Couperin*) to suggest a liaison from the past. The gently melancholic E minor of this expressive preamble warms into brighter E major with the entry of the voice on "Zénith," as if struck by a sunbeam. Pivoting between the minor and major keys, by means of G-natural and G-sharp, becomes a feature of this setting.

"Ces jardins sans limite" (marked *Sensiblement plus vite*, ♩ = 66) describes a memory of the fecund flora in the south of France as well as the present reality of gardens dug by the soldiers in Champagne; the song of the southern toad ("crapaud") is also the sound of a whizzing German shell ("crapaud" or "crapoussin"). Toward the end, the vocal climax on "Et les fleurs de grenade" denotes a profusion of pomegranate flowers as well as the exploding hand grenade that takes its death-bringing name from the shape of the fruit.

The nightingale illustrated at "Un rossignol meurtri par l'amour" with delicate piano ornamentation is a distant relative of Debussy's songster, courtesy of his Verlaine cycle *Fêtes galantes*.[137] Unlike in the Éluard settings, rubato (meticulously organized) is the order of the day here; Poulenc marks eight changes of tempo to denote the subtle pull-and-push of a style—passionate, gallant, quixotic, ever inventive—that is in fact a portrait of Apollinaire himself. Little wonder that Poulenc dedicated the song to his widow, Jacqueline Apollinaire.

(iv)   *Il pleut (It's Raining)*
No key signature; *Aussi vite que possible, très rythmé dans une buée de pédale* ♩ = 104 *au moins*

Il pleut des voix de femmes comme si elles	It's raining women's voices as if they
étaient mortes même dans le souvenir	were dead even in memory
c'est vous aussi qu'il pleut merveilleuses	it's also you who it is raining marvelous encounters of my life oh
rencontres de ma vie ô gouttelettes	droplets
et ces nuages cabrés se prennent à hennir	and those rearing clouds begin to whinny

tout un univers de villes auriculaires	a whole universe of auricular cities
écoute s'il pleut tandis que le regret	listen for whether it's raining while
et le dédain pleurent une ancienne	sorrow
musique	and disdain weep an ancient music
écoute tomber les liens qui te	listen to the fall of the bonds that
retiennent	restrain you
en haut et en bas	from on high and below

The layout of this poem, with downward-slanting lines, is reflected in the downward lines in the printed piano part. The sound of the rain, as it were. J. S.

"Il pleut," one of the most famous of Apollinaire's calligram drawings, dates from 29 July 1914, a few days before a declaration of war that took him by surprise. The design depicts rain falling at something of an angle, with the poem printed in five lines that are neither exactly vertical nor parallel. Poulenc's response in the printed piano music is sixteenths attached to vertical lines that resemble a Hokusai rain painting—the first of his several attempts in the cycle to mirror Apollinaire's designs not only with the sound of the music but also with its appearance on paper. Here the composer seems to have imagined rain windswept in gusts, unlike the even drizzle of Debussy's *Il pleure dans mon cœur*,[138] or the crystalline droplets of Roussel's *Le Jardin mouillé*.

For this summer storm, Poulenc invents an ingenious (and fiendish) piano étude with sextuplet sixteenth notes alternating between the hands

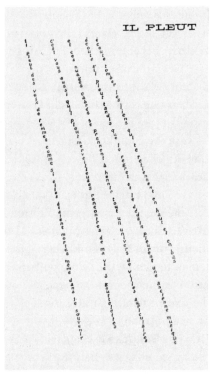

Apollinaire's ideogram for "Il pleut," from Calligrammes (1918).

with finger-punishing exactitude (although pedaled) and moving at considerable speed up and down the keyboard. The result is squalls of sound, and those finding themselves in the path of these gusts of pianistic downpour would be soaked to the skin, as well as elbowed at the keyboard. The vocal line, propelled forward by the energy of the accompaniment, soars over the stave in arcs of sound while ducking and weaving with virtuosic nonchalance. In bar 9 ("merveilleuses rencontres de ma vie") Jeremy Sams detects a quote from Ravel's *L'Enfant et les sortilèges*. In his heady flight of memories, Apollinaire recalls "marvelous encounters of my life"—the rain like women's voices, women whose long-forgotten names are now flooding his mind with erotic memories. In the music's giddy rapture, we can see how easily Poulenc transferred the sentiments expressed by Apollinaire to his own recaptured memories of Vincennes and Nogent.

(v)   *La Grâce exilée (Grace in Exile)*
    No key signature (E major); $\frac{6}{8}$; *Très allant* ♩. = 88

Va-t'en va-t'en mon arc-en-ciel	Go away my rainbow go away
Allez-vous-en couleurs charmantes	Go away charming colors
Cet exil t'est essentiel	To be banished is essential for you
Infante aux écharpes changeantes	Infanta of the ever-changing scarves
Et l'arc-en-ciel est exilé	And the rainbow is banished
Puisqu'on exile qui l'irise	Since what makes it shine is banished too
Mais un drapeau s'est envolé	But a flag has blown away
Prendre ta place au vent de bise	To take your place in the north wind

Poulenc has understood that this poem of love is not exactly a full-blown love poem. Addressed to the painter Marie Laurencin (Apollinaire sent it to her from the Front), it glows at a different temperature and with a different intensity from the rampantly erotic communications with Madeleine Pagès. Apollinaire had had a tempestuous affair with Laurencin between 1908 and 1912 (see p. 28); by the time he wrote "La Grâce exilée," the pain of their parting had been assuaged by new relationships on both sides. Laurencin had married a German artist, Otto von Wätgen, in 1914, and the couple were forced into exile in Spain at the beginning of hostilities—thus the reference to "Infanta." The "charming colors" and "ever-changing scarves" evoke her delicate style as a painter, and the latter phrase carries a strange personal resonance in Poulenc's private life: the first lover he considered setting up a home with, Richard Chanlaire, was also a painter of scarves.[139]

Apollinaire makes the point that the French flag has taken the place of painting as a matter of priority in times of war; or perhaps he means he is now enrolled under the new colors of Madeleine, to whom he had recently proposed marriage. The music is simple, valedictory, and affectionate, the final cadences charming; all in all, a perfect foil for the musical explosion that follows.

(vi)   *Aussi bien que les cigales (Just as Well as the Cicadas)*
        No key signature (E-flat major/minor); $\frac{2}{4}$; *Aussi vite que possible; dans un tourbillon de joie* ♩ = 120

Gens du midi gens du midi vous n'avez donc pas	Men of the south men of the south you haven't
regardé les cigales que vous ne savez pas creuser que vous	observed the cicadas for you don't know how to dig
ne savez pas vous éclairer ni voir Que vous manque-t'il donc pour voir aussi bien que les cigales	nor to make light nor see What are you lacking that you cannot see as well as the cicadas
Mais vous savez encore boire comme les cigales ô gens	But you still know how to drink like the cicadas men
du midi gens du soleil gens qui devriez savoir creuser et	of the south men of the sun who should know how to dig and
voir aussi bien pour le moins aussi bien que les cigales	see as well at least as well as the cicadas
Eh quoi! vous savez boire et ne savez plus pisser	So what? You know how to drink but no longer how to piss
utilement comme les cigales le jour de gloire sera celui où vous saurez	usefully like the cicadas the day of glory will be when you know
creuser pour bien sortir au soleil	how to dig your way out into the sun
creusez voyez buvez pissez comme les cigales gens du	dig see drink piss like the cicadas men of
Midi il faut creuser voir boire pisser aussi bien que les	the south you have to dig see drink piss as well as the
cigales pour chanter commes elles	cicadas in order to sing like them
LA JOIE ADORABLE DE LA PAIX SOLAIRE	THE ADORABLE JOY OF SUNLIT PEACE

The composer and publishers agreed that one could sing "siffler" (whistle) if "pisser" (verse 3) was deemed too unbuttoned. J. S.

Of all the songs in *Calligrammes,* this is the one most directly connected with war—and in fact it could not be more imbued with the mud and sweat of male activity. Apollinaire sent a handwritten copy of the poem to Madeleine Pagès, the final seven words in large capital letters to emphasize his joy in contemplating

Apollinaire's ideogram for "Aussi bien que les cigales," from Calligrammes (1918).

```
        AUSSI BIEN QUE LES CIGALES

   gens du midi          ne savez pas                    M
   gens du mi            creuser que                   ais
   di vous n'         vous ne sa                     vous
   avez donc        vez pas vous                  savez
   pas regar    éclairer ni              encore
   dé les ciga   voir Que vous        boire com  le jour
   les que vous manque-t-il      me les ci  de gloire
        donc pour           gales ô          se
       voir aus          gens du mi      c        ra
      si bien         di gens du      reusez      ce
     que les        soleil gens qui   voyez bu  lui
    ciga          devriez savoir      vez pissez  où
  les           creuser et voir        comme  vous
        aussi bien pour le           les ciga  sau
        moins aussi bien              les      rez
      que les cigales                          creu
   Eh quoi! vous savez  gens du Midi il faut   ser
   boire et ne savez    creuser voir boire     pour
 plus pisser utile      pisser aussi bien que  bien
ment comme les              les cigales        sor
 cigales    LA JOIE         pour chan          tir
            ADORABLE        ter com            au
            DE LA PAIX      me elles           so
            SOLAIRE                            leil
```

their marriage in a time of peace. The words are lined up on the page as two opposing sides with a diagonal ribbon of white space between them, each side containing about half the verbal participants—some in the direct line of fire, others ranged in clumps of back-up forces. So highly developed was Poulenc's sheerly visual response to these calligrams that for the poet's right-slanting design he provides quirky, and otherwise inexplicable, slants in the black lines connecting the stalks of the piano's eighth notes (bb. 4 and 7, 18 and 19).

Apollinaire's regiment (the 96th, from the south of France where he had grown up and gone to school) was dug in at Champagne. The "Gens du midi" are likened to courageous cicadas (the Apollinaire of *Le Bestiaire* was knowledgeable about insects) that burrow in the earth and, when coming to the surface, squirt urine at their enemies. "Cigales" was also slang for shrapnel, and the burrowing of cicadas a metaphor for the laborious construction of trenches.

After a fanfare of frantic sixteenth-note activity, Poulenc assigns to the piano music to be found nowhere else in his songs, staccato eighths that suggest digging. Heavy chords in thirds and seconds, spaced an octave apart, alternate with the confident masculine swagger of *marcato* sixteenths. On the third page the music really takes off, as the singer, instructed to be *éclatant*, almost gibbers commands to his comrades. The music is borne along by wave after wave of bravado and babbled gung-ho optimism, growing faster and wilder (*Surtout ne ralentizssez pas, au contraire*) as the poet exhorts the soldier-insects to imitate the industry of the cicadas and to dig, to see, to drink, to piss, in order to be able to sing *like them*.

And where will all this hard work lead? A *Subito largo maestoso* ($\downarrow$ = 58), with mighty chords (each preceded by lunging left-hand leaps), underpins a vocal paean (high Gs) for the singer at the top of his tessitura. The composer's *fff* dynamic matches the poet's capital letters: THE ADORABLE JOY OF SUNLIT PEACE. And when this peace comes, the poet will at last be free to marry

Madeleine Pagès. Proust dipping his madeleine in a cup of tea is too refined an exercise for Apollinaire, who longs to make free with a Madeleine of his own, dipping himself into her. The burrowing soldiers' earned moment of triumph, and their emergence at last into the open air, take on the elemental majesty of a sunburst—"*in a rhythm that recalls the sunshine of* Les Animaux modèles,"[140] a work that defied the pessimism of a more recent war. But here the unified emotion of many men fighting for the same cause in 1916 is shouldered by the voice of a single heroic singer and a hard-working pianist.

(vii)   *Voyage (Journey)*
F-sharp minor; $\frac{3}{4}$; *Bien calme, sans aucun rubato et strictement en mesure* ♩ = 58

Adieu amour nuage qui fuis	Farewell love cloud that flees
et n'a pas chu pluie féconde	and has not shed fertile rain
refais le voyage de Dante	retrace Dante's journey
Télégraphe oiseau qui laisse tomber	Telegraph bird which drops
ses ailes partout	her wings everywhere
Où va donc ce train qui meurt au loin	Where is it bound for, that train dying in the distance
Dans les vals et les beaux bois frais du tendre été si pâle?	In the valleys and the lovely cool woods of tender pale summer?
La douce nuit lunaire et pleine d'étoiles	This sweet moonlit night full of stars
C'est ton visage que je ne vois plus	It's your face which I no longer see

Voyage is one of the greatest of Poulenc's songs, and the composer thought so too ("*certainly one of the two or three songs I value most*").[141] He produces exceptionally lucid music with an unmistakable rhythm of travel: the slow rhythm of a ghost train departing on an otherworldly journey, like the journey undertaken by Dante in the company of Virgil. This mood of infinitely dignified melancholy undoubtedly betokens a final farewell; it is dedicated to the memory of the composer's beloved friend Raymonde Linossier. The poem is also by far the most complicated calligram he had to decipher, spread extravagantly over two pages and featuring a wide variety of typefaces in seemingly quixotic, sometimes perplexing, patterns of words. For a drawing of electric wires, clearly meant to illustrate "Télégraphe," Poulenc produces a musical equivalent in an effulgent E-flat minor seventh chord (b. 12), two beats before that very word. It is a magical

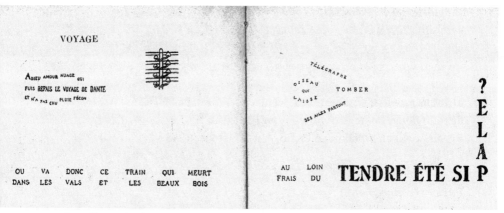

Part of Apollinaire's ideogram for "Voyage," from Calligrammes (1918).

beginning of the song's second section, both aurally and visually. Apollinaire's telegraph pole, its insulators piled on top of each other as though in the spaces of a musical stave, is eerily rebuilt on the musical page by Poulenc's similarly spaced seventh chord spread across both staves, with satellite eighth notes representing the pole's attached wires.

The final page brings a further feast of Poulencian sevenths, with the nocturnal beauty of "La douce nuit lunaire et pleine d'étoiles" (C-sharp7 to E7) succeeded by the heartbreaking "C'est ton [G7] visage [D-flat7] que je ne vois plus," as though *"the clouds had all at once unveiled a ray of moonlight. . . . Now added to that is the irrevocable departure of a face that I have never replaced and a beautiful, alert intelligence that I shall miss forever."*[142] His strange postlude (anchored in F-sharp minor, as is the beginning of the song as well as the beginning of the entire cycle) evoked for Poulenc the distant chugging of trains (parallel octaves representing parallel train tracks) that he could hear from the terrace of his grandparents' Nogent home on July evenings. As a child he thought they were only *"leaving on holiday,"* but the adult composer well knew that *"the journey of Dante"* knows of no return.[143]

Calligrammes received its official first performance in New York on 20 November 1948, the second of two recitals Bernac and Poulenc gave in Town Hall. The composer wrote to Marie-Blanche de Polignac the next morning:

I awoke this morning in a great fit of melancholy. In spite of the view of Central Park in the sun, below my window, I am suddenly very homesick for my place de la Concorde. I am delighted with my stay here, but what joy it will be to return. . . . And yet, what a success!! I am stunned by it. The second recital last night was pure delirium. House full, seven recalls after the first performance of Calligrammes, *five encores at the end of the concert—so, all in all, we took twenty-three bows.*

One needs a hall to seat 15,000 for the stentorian voice of Pierre, so rejuvenated by this success. You can imagine how pleased I am for him.[144]

∘   ∘   ∘

FP141 *Sinfonietta* (orchestra), 1947–48
FP142 *Quatre Petites Prières de Saint François d'Assise*, summer 1948
FP143 Sonata for Cello and Piano, April–October 1948

∘   ∘   ∘

FP144 Hymne (*Hymn*)
    Composed in New York, 2–8 November 1948
    [*Doda Conrad*; Salabert, New York]
    Literary source: Jean Racine (1639–1699), translated from the Roman Breviary
    No key signature (B-flat minor); $\frac{4}{4}$ (with changes to $\frac{3}{4}$ and $\frac{2}{4}$); *Largo* $\downarrow$ = 60

Sombre nuit, aveugles ténèbres,	Dark night, blind shadows,
Fuyez: le jour s'approche et l'Olympe blanchit;	Fly away: the day is approaching and Olympus is growing pale;
Et vous, démons, rentrez dans vos prisons funèbres;	And you, demons, slink back to your funereal prisons;
De votre empire affreux, un Dieu nous affranchit.	A God is freeing us from your dreadful rule.
Le soleil perce l'ombre obscure;	The sun is transpiercing the darkness;
Et les traits éclatants qu'il lance dans les airs,	And the blinding shafts it hurls into the air
Rompant le voile épais qui couvrait la nature,	Bursting the thick veil, which was covering all nature,
Redonnent la couleur et l'âme à l'univers.	Give color and soul back to the universe.
Ô Christ, notre unique lumière,	Oh Christ, our only light,
Nous ne reconnaissons que tes saintes clartés.	We acknowledge only Thy holy flame.
Notre esprit t'est soumis; entends notre prière,	Our soul is subject to Thee; hear our prayer,
Et sous ton divin joug, range nos volontés.	And beneath thy divine yoke arrange our will.

Souvent notre âme criminelle	Often our culpable soul
Sur sa fausse vertu téméraire s'endort;	Rashly goes to sleep upon its false virtue;
Hâte-toi d'éclairer, ô lumière éternelle,	Make haste, oh eternal light, to shine on
Des malheureux assis dans l'ombre de la mort.	Wretches who crouch in the shadow of death.
Gloire à Toi, Trinité profonde,	Glory unto Thee, profound Trinity,
Père, Fils, Esprit Saint: qu'on t'adore toujours,	Father, Son, Holy Ghost: may you ever be worshipped
Tant que l'astre des temps éclairera le monde	As long as the star of time illumines the world,
Et quand les siècles même auront fini leur cours.	And when the centuries have run their course.

Racine, the greatest of seventeenth-century dramatists, published a number of *Cantiques spirituels* and *Hymnes traduits du Breviaire romain* in 1688 (Fauré's 1865 *Cantique de Jean Racine* was a setting of one of these *Hymnes*). They were written some ten years after the famously pagan *Phèdre* and before the far more biblical *Esther* and *Athalie*, both latter works commissioned by Madame de Maintenon (morganatic wife of Louis XIV) and signifying stricter religious observances in the later part of the king's reign. It is not known how Poulenc came upon his text; possibly he brought it with him to America from France.

It was largely thanks to the bass Doda Conrad (1905–1997) that Poulenc and Bernac found themselves with a full list of engagements and in the midst of high society when they first visited the United States as recitalists. Conrad was the son of Marya Freund (1876–1966), a Polish soprano resident in France who had been a pupil of Julius Stockhausen, a renowned interpreter of Brahms's lieder. Freund's enthusiasm for modern music knew no bounds: she was an important colleague of Schoenberg (she sang in the first performance of *Gurrelieder* in 1917) and Satie (the first performance of *Socrate* in 1925), and an early enthusiast for Poulenc's music. Everyone loved Marya Freund. Her rather less talented son thus had an extraordinary access to the musical world. Conrad's musical accomplishments were never sufficiently profound for people to forgive his acerbic tongue, but he was a devoted admirer of Poulenc. Whether the composer counted him a friend is uncertain, but he was certainly a useful ally. He also had the advantages of inherited wealth and of being in the swim with all the socialites in New York City (he kept an apartment on Madison Avenue).

Before the war, Conrad was a member of Nadia Boulanger's ensemble, performing and recording the bass line in works by Monteverdi, Rameau, and Brahms (he "had the low notes"). He was also an aspiring recitalist with strong ideas about self-promotion and program planning. As Freund was Jewish, mother and son had to leave France for America, where Doda became a naturalized citizen and served in the American army. A knowledge of art allowed him to play a significant role in rescuing and preserving important artworks that would otherwise have been destroyed. He returned to Paris after the war but preserved his American connections.

New York managements were initially unwilling to take on the risk of touring a French composer; yet Doda persevered, found amenable agents, and prepared the ground for one of the most successful tours ever undertaken by the baritone and his composer pianist. (The duo's later American tours, for which Conrad played no part in the planning, seem to have been less well managed and rather less glamorous.) Their Town Hall recitals took place in November 1948. Doda had a concert of his own scheduled for 28 December, when he intended to give the first performance of Henri Sauguet's impressive cycle for bass on texts of Max Jacob, *Visions infernales*. Doda wanted a second new piece, and Poulenc, clearly in his debt, composed a musical "thank you" in the St. Moritz Hotel (now the Ritz-Carlton) in a few days.

This curious but eloquent song (marked *Largo*) is an incantation, as might be sung by a French Sarastro. The vocal line is notated in the bass clef, and for the first ten bars the pianist's hands also remain there, effecting an initially dark and murky texture. The high priest begins by invoking Olympus in classical manner but redeems himself with an address to Christ, "notre unique lumière." Poulenc's harmonies underline the majesty we associate with *le grand siècle* and its ceremonial musical flourishes; throughout, a dotted-rhythm motif evokes the sound of a muffled drum (both hands darting down to the bass clef). *"There are parts of this hymn that satisfy me well enough, others where I would have liked more suppleness. It is impossible to set alexandrines to music when the rhythm is not felt in a living mode. This is how I see it."*[145] He manages the alexandrines only by alternating freely between $\frac{3}{4}$ and $\frac{4}{4}$.

Hervé Lacombe's verdict on the piece is not favorable: "Embarrassed by the classical verse, Poulenc fails to animate the poem; his music borders on the grandiloquent and the harmony, like the melodic line, is often tortuous."[146] But the fact is that a beautiful bass voice, not simply a baritone but a singer with real bass quality, can make something rather marvelous of this unusual song.

FP145 *Mazurka*, from *Mouvements de cœur* (*Movements of the Heart*)
    Composed at Le Tremblay (Normandy), July 1949
    [Doda Conrad; Heugel][147]
    Literary source: Louise de Vilmorin (1902–1969), *Mouvements de cœur*
    (suite by six composers in homage to Chopin)

Les bijoux aux poitrines,
Les soleils aux plafonds
Les robes opalines,
Miroirs et violons

Bejewelled bosoms
Suns on the ceiling
Shimmering gowns
Mirrors and violins

Font ainsi, font, font, font

So they make, make, make

Des mains tomber l'aiguille
L'aiguille de raison
Des mains de jeunes filles
Qui s'envolent et font

Needles fall from hands
Needles of reason
From the hands of young girls
Who fly away and make . . .

Font ainsi, font, font, font

So they make, make, make

D'un regard qui s'appuie,
D'une ride à leur front
Le beau temps ou la pluie
Et d'un soupir larron

With an unrelenting look
With a crease on their brow
Sunshine or rain
And a thievish sigh.

Font ainsi, font, font, font

So they make, make, make

Du bal une tourmente
Où sage et vagabond
D'entendre l'inconstante
Dire oui, dire non

The ball a torment
Where the wise or the wild
Hear the fickle girl say
"Say yes, say no"

Font ainsi, font, font, font

So they make, make, make

Danser l'incertitude
Dont les pas compteront,
Oh! le doux pas des prudes,
Leurs silences profonds

The dance of uncertainty
Whose steps will be important.
Oh, the soft steps of the prudes
Their deep silences.

Font ainsi, font, font, font

And so they make, make, make

Du bal une contrée
Où les feux s'uniront.
Des amours rencontrées

Of the ball, a landscape
Where fires will combine
From the loves encountered

Ainsi la neige fond, fond, fond

And so the snow, melts, melts, melts

The refrain "font, font, font" quotes a well-known children's song, "Ainsi font font font les petites marionettes." Perhaps Vilmorin was thinking of young girls at a ball as dancing puppets. "Font" means "do" or "make," and is punningly reinvented in the last line as "fond," "melts." J. S.

The year 1949 was the centenary of Chopin's death, and Doda Conrad, ever on the lookout for additions to his bass repertoire, commissioned Louise de Vilmorin to write seven poems evoking episodes in Chopin's life, set in Warsaw, Vienna, Paris, Majorca, and Nohant, and evoking his ardent patriotism and nostalgia for the country of his birth. Once she had delivered the poems, Conrad embarked on the considerable task of persuading six composers to set them to music as quickly as possible. He needed the songs printed within four months, a seemingly impossible deadline.

While Conrad no doubt had the financial means to encourage composers and publishers to work faster than they otherwise might, there is no record of money changing hands, apart from the royalties due to poet

A U R I C FRANÇAIX MILHAUD POULENC P R E G E R SAUGUET

MOUVEMENTS DU CŒUR

UN HOMMAGE A LA MÉMOIRE DE

F R É D É R I C C H O P I N

1849 - 1949

SUITE POUR CHANT ET PIANO
SUR DES POÈMES DE

L O U I S E D E V I L M O R I N

HEUGEL & Cⁱᵉ

The cover of the collection Mouvements de cœur *(1949), a cycle for bass with songs by six composers to texts by Louise de Vilmorin.*

and composers from the publisher, Heugel. Arrangements could have been made "under the counter," but Conrad was a forceful character and a clever impresario. Once he had Poulenc's song in hand, his first task was to convince Heugel to collaborate. Then the race was on, like a round robin. Such was Poulenc's renown in the wake of his American success that other composers, no matter what they thought about Conrad, the poetry, or the project as a whole, would waste no time in contributing to the *recueil*:

> I sent the poem for *Mazurka*, No. 2 of the suite, to Poulenc. . . . it was thus up to him to choose the general tonality of the whole.[148] This *Mazurka* was sent to Auric, from whom I had commissioned the *Valse*. I left it to him whether or not to attune the character of his composition to the music of Francis. Then came the turn of Jean Françaix, who found himself entrusted with the *Scherzo impromptu*. He had under his gaze the work of his two predecessors.

Léo Préger, for whom I had reserved the *Étude*, was a strange person—a Corsican, with all the characteristics of this little, insular race: miserable, proud, obstinate, irritable, arrogant and . . . enormously talented. He was . . . one of the most original musicians I had ever seen go through the hands of Nadia Boulanger . . . who was perfectly aware of the rarity of his talent. . . . He died young and the *Étude* of Louise de Vilmorin was the only Préger work to be published. . . . The *Ballade nocturne* was destined for [Milhaud], and I sent to him in California photocopies of the four works that had already been set to music. Milhaud never received these, and I had to describe to him the keys and characteristics of the existent pieces. Almost by return of post I received his contribution: Milhaud composes with a disconcerting facility. Finally Henri Sauguet was charged to open proceedings with the *Prélude* and to conclude the suite with the *Postlude-Polonaise*. The title, found by him, *Mouvements du cœur*, was just right. Heugel worked amazingly fast to print the suite, which was on sale in the lobby of Town Hall on the day of my recital.[149]

Yet it was Poulenc who gave Conrad more trouble than he was expecting. This concerned the order of the published work. He was happy (*"me gusta mucho"*) that his *Mazurka* should come after Sauguet's *Prélude*, but he was adamant that he did not want Françaix's *Scherzo* to follow. In the end, Doda agreed that Auric's song would follow Poulenc's; it was as if the composer felt safe only in the company of close friends.[150]

(i) Sauguet, *Prélude* (*"Une forêt surgit des flots"*: E-flat minor, $\frac{6}{8}$, *Andantino quasi allegretto*)

(ii) Poulenc, *Mazurka*

(iii) Auric, *Valse* (*"Les Flots du silence ne porte"*: B-flat minor, $\frac{3}{4}$, *Mouvt. de valse lente*)

(iv) Françaix, *Scherzo impromptu* (*"Promesse au cœur de vos sourires"*: F major, $\frac{3}{8}$, *Allegrissimo leggiero* 80)

(v) Préger, *Étude* (*"Seigneur, venez à mon secours"*: C major, $\frac{4}{4}$, *Moderato*)

(vi) Milhaud, *Ballade nocturne* (*"Dames du soir"*: no key signature, $\frac{6}{8}$, ending B-flat minor, *Modérément animé*)

(vii) Sauguet, *Postlude: Polonaise* (*"Dans les campagnes de Pologne"*: E-flat minor, $\frac{3}{4}$, *Alla Polaka*)

Poulenc's song has a somber majesty about it, reminiscent of another Chopin-inspired work he composed in 1933: the *Nocturne* in A Major for piano, which moves at the same dreamlike pace in $\frac{3}{4}$. In connection with both pieces, Poulenc mentioned the dreamlike ball scene from Alain-Fournier's novel *Le Grand Meaulnes*. He described the music as *"quite piano, melancholy and sensuous,"* and made a point of telling Vilmorin how difficult it was to set the word "font" (and then "fond") again and again. About the song's quality, he blew hot and cold. He wrote enthusiastically about it to Vilmorin, indeed offered to come to Verrières to play it for her, as well as to Marie-Blanche; but the Comtesse de Polignac, Poulenc's adorable friend, was not the person she once was, owing to a gradual deterioration in her health that lasted nearly a decade (described in painful detail in Conrad's *Dodascalies*).

By the time he came to record the song in his *Journal*, Poulenc felt no need to soft-pedal his opinions to avoid offending Doda: "Mazurka—*In the style of Poulenc by a Poulenc who was bored by an affair like this*."[151] Composer and singer had likely fallen out by this time; in any case, whatever debt the composer felt he had owed to Doda Conrad, or even to his friendship with Marya Freund, had now been well and truly paid.

∘   ∘   ∘

FP146 Concerto for Piano and Orchestra, May–October 1949

· V ·

Portrait of a long-term partnership, scarcely acknowledged: Poulenc with Raymond Destouches at the Luxembourg Gardens, Paris.

Outline of a Musical Life:

1950–1959

1950 (aged 51)

After landing in New York and spending two days there (29–30 December 1949), FP goes to Boston for rehearsals for his Piano Concerto with the Boston Symphony Orchestra under Charles Munch, followed by performances on 6 and 7 January.

Early in this tour Bernac and Poulenc visit Samuel Barber to hear two songs on Rainer Maria Rilke texts he has composed for them, part of the future *Mélodies passagères*.

(12 January) FP performs his Piano Concerto in Washington, D.C., and in New York's Carnegie Hall (14th) under Munch. He senses disappointment with the last movement, where he feels the audience's interest waning.

(15 January) FP visits Wanda Landowska in New York: "*How wonderful it is, as is also the case with Colette, when old age is a perpetual enrichment.*"[1]

"*As soon as Bernac reached the New World, he regained his youthfulness.*"[2] The duo give recitals in Philadelphia (16 January), Jordan Hall in Boston (18th), Town Hall in New York (22nd). A concert in Toronto (24th) marks the beginning of a ten-day visit to Canada.

(18 January) Jean Giraudoux's play *Intermezzo* opens at the Lyceum Theater, with music by Poulenc.

(1 February) Writing to his niece Brigitte after performing his Piano Concerto in Montreal, FP boasts of a one-night stand with a forty-year-old Canadian industrialist knowledgeable about French art, not at all the composer's usual type.[3]

(4 February) FP performs the Piano Concerto at the Pittsfield High School in Massachusetts. On the 5th, he spends a memorable evening in New York in the company of Vladimir Horowitz, who plays him, among other works, Samuel Barber's recently completed Piano Sonata.

(7 February) FP is enchanted with New York's architecture: "*In this country where everyone is in such a hurry, I offer myself the luxury of slowly walking*

and contemplating, nose in the air, the strange decorations of the Hotel Pierre's Louis XIV–style copper roof, the Gothic manor that is the next building, the Venetian terrace of a store on Third Avenue."[4]

FP visits the Metropolitan Museum in New York (7 February) and a Van Gogh exhibit at the Art Institute of Chicago (18th). He is in Chicago, and then Toledo, Cleveland, and Portland (17th–24th), presumably for local recitals (he never turned down dates with small audiences) that are now all but untraceable. His departure for the Midwest causes him to miss the first American performance of *Figure humaine* in New York (17th).

Writing from America, Poulenc exhorts his recently appointed biographer, Henri Hell, to finish work quickly, to help explain Poulenc to the Americans: "*One has to kill the legend of being a miniaturist in this country of Sibelius* [referring to the popularity of Sibelius's symphonies there]—*my music is not only vocal.*" He threatens that Claude Rostand will write the biography if Hell is not quick enough.[5]

(26 February) FP and Bernac give a successful recital at the St. Francis Hotel in San Francisco; an important critic praises the music and bemoans the composer's local enemies—a reference to conductor Pierre Monteux, who had chosen not to invite Poulenc to perform his concerto with the San Francisco Symphony. FP gleefully writes to Brigitte, having made a friendly call to the Monteaux feigning ignorance of the snub. He and Bernac then relax in Carmel (28 February–3 March). From Carmel, FP informs Paul Collaer of plans to compose new songs to texts from Éluard's *Le Livre ouvert I* (the future *La Fraîcheur et le feu* cycle).[6] The duo proceed to Tucson, Colorado Springs, and Santa Barbara (where Lotte Lehmann, "*the greatest of German singers since Lilli Lehmann,*"[7] attends their recital on 11 March).

(17 March) The duo give a recital at the Phillips High School in Birmingham, Alabama, and then fly back to New York, where they spend an evening with Stravinsky (18th).

(21 March) FP dines with Christian Dior. The couturier's 1950 New York exhibition introduces evening gowns named after such great composers as Mozart, Schubert, and Poulenc.

(22 March) FP attends, for the second time, a performance of Gian-Carlo Menotti's *The Consul* and finds it underwhelming ("*A kind of masterpiece without music*").[8]

(Afternoons of 25–27 March) FP and Bernac have a second recording session with Columbia Records for what will be a two-LP set of mélodies by Poulenc, Ravel, Chabrier, Debussy, and Satie.

(28 March) FP shares a box with the Stravinskys at Carnegie Hall for a performance of Virgil Thomson's new Cello Concerto. The next day FP and Bernac fly back to Paris. Poulenc describes the tour as "*un succès avec tremolo.*"[9]

In the spring, probably in the south of France, FP meets a forty-two-year-old traveling salesman named Lucien Roubert, with whom he will form an intimate relationship that lasts until Roubert's death in October 1955. Roubert lives in Toulon with his wife, whom he will divorce some time after meeting Poulenc.

(April–July) *La Fraîcheur et le feu* **FP147** (Éluard), composed in Noizay and Brive.

(24 July) FP gives the first European performance of his Piano Concerto in Aix-en-Provence, to a mixed critical reception.

(July–August) FP spends three weeks at Le Tremblay, where he begins work on the

Lucien Roubert, a commemorative picture sent to friends after his death in 1955 and kept by Poulenc in the pages of his prayer missal.

Stabat Mater, written in memory of the artist and designer Christian (Bébé) Bérard. The work, in twelve sections, is finished in Noizay by 3 October.

(28 October) FP accompanies Rose Dercourt-Plaut in *Fiançailles pour rire* at the Salle Gaveau, Paris.

(1 November) First public performance of *La Fraîcheur et le feu* **FP147**, in Town Hall, Birmingham, UK. Bernac is accompanied by the composer at the beginning of a three-week English tour.

(6–17 November) Bernac and Poulenc work at the BBC during the London leg of their tour. FP plays the *Stabat Mater* to Edward Lockspeiser at the BBC, who writes a disparaging internal memo about the work to his colleagues, an unusual mark of disapproval from an organization that for so long had been completely under Poulenc's spell.

(8 and 9 November) FP plays his Piano Concerto under Basil Cameron at the Royal Albert Hall. He and Bernac give a recital at Wigmore Hall (15th): songs by Verdi, Brahms, Mompou, Debussy, Poulenc (*La Fraîcheur et le feu*), and Stravinsky.

(18 November) FP and Bernac return to Paris. They give a recital at the Salle Gaveau (22th), more or less repeating the Wigmore Hall program from the week before.

(26 November) FP gives the Paris premiere of the Piano Concerto at the Théâtre des Champs-Élysées under André Cluytens.

(13–14 December) The duo are in Brussels on 6 December, probably as a prelude to a recital in Holland. In Amsterdam, FP performs his Piano Concerto with Otto Klemperer. Legend has it that the maestro turned to the orchestra leader at the end of the piece and sarcastically asked, "What was that?"[10]

1951 (aged 52)

(Mid-January) FP attends a party in Paris given by Marie-Blanche de Polignac in honor of Samuel Barber. He plays a recording of Barber singing his *Dover Beach* and encourages the American composer, an unusually gifted and sweet-voiced baritone, to perform more songs.

FP embarks on an Italian tour, playing his Piano Concerto: Rome (with Clemens Krauss), Florence, Turin (2 February), Milan (the *Concert champêtre* in the piano version), and Bologna.

(11 February–2 March) After traveling to Lyon, Aix-en-Provence, and Cannes, FP secretly spends time with Lucien Roubert in Marseilles.

(2 March) FP and Bernac embark on a tour of Morocco and Algeria, where Poulenc also plays his Piano Concerto.

(Early June) FP sits on the jury, one of twenty-three celebrity musicians, of the Marguerite Long–Jacques Thibaud Competition in Paris.

(22 April) The orchestration of the *Stabat Mater* FP148 is completed, and receives its premiere in Strasbourg on 13 June.

FP visits Marthe Bosredon in Brive between 14 and 23 June, then Marie-Laure de Noailles in Hyères. Marie-Laure's semi-permanent house guest, Ned Rorem, notes in his diary: "Lunched with Poulenc who, with Auric, becomes less and less sure of himself and manifests this by speaking of the inadequacies of others."[11]

FP spends most of August in Noizay. The film *Le Voyage en Amérique*, with Poulenc's music, is premiered in Cannes (14th). The only music to have survived, after reworking, is the *valse-musette* for two pianos entitled *L'Embarquement pour Cythère*.

(2 September) Bernac and Poulenc give a recital of Debussy mélodies at the Edinburgh Festival. At noon the next day, they make a BBC prerecording. FP plays the Piano Concerto in Bournemouth (6th).

(September) FP completes *Thème varié* FP151 (a theme with eleven variations) for piano, begun in February; the final variation, the theme more or less backward, amounts to a half-hearted dalliance with serial technique. In a letter to Doda Conrad, FP expresses his admiration for Stravinsky's new opera, *The Rake's Progress*.

(31 October) Bernac, FP, Jean Françaix, and cellist Maurice Gendron appear at a concert in Paris's Salle Marceau-Chaillot, in the "Friends of Chamber Music" series.

(2 November) FP visits Brussels for a performance of the *Stabat Mater*.

(November) From Aix-en-Provence (where he accompanies a recital with Bernac arranged by Simone Girard), FP delivers to Pierre Souvtchinsky a commissioned article on the piano music of Prokofiev, the most detailed response to another composer's work he would ever write. The article appeared only in 1953, by which time Prokofiev had died.

(10 December) While staying in Marseilles, FP writes to Simone Girard, one of his confidantes (along with Bernac and Rose Dercourt-Plaut in New York) regarding his relationship with Lucien Roubert—the first reference to the affair in the correspondence. Poulenc confesses to the fears, jealousy, and "*black thoughts*" that will come to characterize and undermine this tempestuous attachment.[12]

At the end of the year, FP begins work on *Quatre Motets pour le temps de Noël* as a kind of counterpart to *Quatre Motets pour un temps de pénitence* of 1938–39.

1952 (aged 53)

In early January, before leaving for his third tour of the United States, FP has to have his beloved terrier Mickey ("Toutou") put down ("*He couldn't go on any longer. . . . I cried my eyes out when I kissed him for the last time, just before the end*").[13]

(4 January) FP flies to New York and stays at the Wyndham Hotel. Bernac follows him on the 13th. After Poulenc has performed his Piano Concerto in Cincinnati (11th), singer and pianist meet in Ottowa for a recital on the 14th, and another in Montreal (16th). FP observes that Bernac is "*rejuvenated by 20 years, as he always is when he gets away from his humdrum Parisian routine.*"[14] The concert schedule is less rigorous than on the two previous tours, centering around New York, with a foray to South America.

(21 January) Bernac and Poulenc give a recital at Dumbarton Oaks, Washington, D.C., that includes the first performance of Samuel Barber's *Mélodies passagères*.

(By 26 January) FP hears Richard Strauss's *Salome* at the Metropolitan Opera with Ljuba Welitsch in the title role. He attends a performance of Bach's *Mass in B Minor* conducted by Robert Shaw (27th).

(1 February) In Caracas, Venezuela, FP plays his *Concert champêtre* with the visiting Berlin Philharmonic under its handsome Romanian conductor, forty-year-old Sergiu Celibidache, by whom the composer is entranced, per-

sonally and musically. FP and Bernac give recitals there on the 2nd, 4th, and 6th, returning to New York on the 7th.

(10 February) At a Town Hall recital, Bernac and Poulenc perform once again the Barber cycle; this performance pleases Barber even more than the one at Dumbarton Oaks. *New York Times* critic Carter Hayman found Poulenc's pianism "little more than adequate," while "M. Bernac's voice may not be what it once was, but his interpretations had such conviction that they swept aside such limitations and brought his listeners deep into the music."[15] Socialite Elsa Maxwell gives a party after the recital. A collective greeting card signed by Maxwell, Franz Osborne, Bernac, Menotti, and American composer Marcelle de Manziarly is sent to Louise de Vilmorin with the words "C'est ainsi que tu es" (FP121/ii).

After two concerts in Connecticut, FP visits Wanda Landowska in Lakeville. Contrasting her tact with Nadia Boulanger's "*musical bulimia*," he reports to Doda Conrad (12 February) that Wanda plays only four preludes and fugues from her new Bach recording before stopping the phonograph. He bemoans the fact that Rose Dercourt-Plaut is in love with him whereas he fancies her husband, and reveals that he is also attracted to the manager of the Wyndham Hotel, who charges him only $8 a night for bedroom, sitting-room, and kitchen. "*Perhaps I don't displease him either?*"[16]

(15–16 February) Bernac and Poulenc record Barber's *Mélodies passagères* for Columbia, unpublished, now released on YouTube. FP replies to an American musicologist, Edith Borroff (b. 1925), declining her request for composition lessons, and claiming to understand little English and speak even less.[17]

(18 February) FP and Bernac give a recital in Buffalo, New York, and the following night appear on TV in New York City.

(21–22 February) Bernac, with Poulenc's blessing, makes a recording for Columbia of Schumann's *Dichterliebe* with the distinguished solo pianist Robert Casadesus. FP is content to network and relax: lunching with Dimitri Mitropoulos, dining with Vladimir Horowitz, attending Shaw's *Caesar and Cleopatra* at the invitation of Laurence Olivier, tracking down "real" penicillin with which to treat his former lover Richard Chanlaire. Gérard Souzay gives a New York recital on the 25th, well received but not with the critical reverence reserved for FP and Bernac: "*Pierre is not jealous of Gérard whom he adores, but he is pleased not have been dethroned by him.*"[18]

(9 March) FP and Bernac return home on the steamship *De Grasse*. FP travels to the south of France to see Lucien Roubert, with whom he has been corresponding, via his niece Brigitte, from America.

(19 March) Bernac and Poulenc travel to Munich for a recital and radio recordings. After a week there, they move on to London for a recital at Gold-

smith's Hall (27th), a BBC recording (28th), and a Wigmore Hall recital (29th), where the program is Milhaud's *Quatre Poèmes de Léo Latil*, Jacques Leguerney's *La Solitude*, and works by Ravel, Roussel, and Poulenc.

There are further recital engagements in the spring, but in April FP turns his attention to a portmanteau composition for large orchestra entitled *Guirlande de Campra*, a tribute to the French composer André Campra, who was active between Lully and Rameau. Poulenc's contribution is *Matelote provençale*; the other composers included Auric, Honegger, Sauguet, and Tailleferre.

(21 April) In a letter to a close confidante, Yvonne de Casa Fuerte, FP mentions the domestic happiness of his long-term partner Raymond Destouches, who has married for the second time; his bride Céline is *"adorable,"* and the couple have a new home in Noizay.[19] FP's affair with Lucien Roubert remains hidden from Raymond.

(28 April) At the opening of a "Works of the Twentieth Century" Festival in Paris, organized by the composer Nicolas Nabokov, FP's *Stabat Mater*, conducted by Fritz Munch (brother of Charles), is performed at the church of Saint-Roch.

(May) At Nabokov's festival, the Vienna State Opera (Staatsoper) offers Berg's *Wozzeck*, which FP adores, and the Royal Opera House presents Britten's *Billy Budd*. The hall is half full for the Britten, and FP leaves after Act II, stating that he much prefers Virgil Thomson's *Four Saints in Three Acts*.[20] Toward the end of the multi-city festival, Bernac and Poulenc give a recital at the Château de Brède in Bordeaux (23rd).

FP entertains his biographer, Henri Hell, together with Virgil Thomson at Noizay for the last weekend in May.

(Early June) Home at Noizay with a new record player: *"I devour my discs with mad passion: the quartets of Bartók are sublime."*[21]

Bernac and Poulenc set off on another English tour, which includes a BBC recording (20 June) and a recital in Hampstead, London, of Rameau, Fauré, Wolf, Debussy, Poulenc, and Ravel (22nd). An appearance at Britten's Aldeburgh Festival, penciled in for the 27th, does not take place.

(Early July) At Le Tremblay, FP ponders ideas for a ballet that was commissioned by Ricordi Editions for La Scala; this project will eventually be replaced by *Dialogues des Carmélites*.

(August) FP suffers from an eye infection at Noizay. He composes *Ave verum corpus* for women's voices (an American commission), which receives its first performance in Pittsburgh on 25 November.

(10 September) Nadia Boulanger visits Noizay for the first time, praising "your house, your motets, and Mon Dieu, I almost forget, your grapes."[22]

In Noizay, FP composes *Capriccio d'après "Le Bal masqué"* for two pianos, and dedicates it to Samuel Barber.

(18 November) Paul Éluard dies suddenly of a heart attack in Charenton. FP is devastated. He attends the funeral four days later.

(23 November) FP and Bernac give a recital in Freemasons' Hall, in Edinburgh.

(Late November–20 December) FP spends time in Lyon and Avignon and makes several trips to Marseilles, where he stays at the Hôtel Beauvau (furnished with piano). He spends three days with the American pianists Gold and Fizdale, and shows them his work in progress on the Sonata for Two Pianos. The purpose of the visit, however, is to be with Lucien.

(15 December) In the Salle Gaveau, Jacques Février gives the first performance of the forcedly "modern" *Thème varié*, which Poulenc, still in Marseilles, does not attend.

Bernac is FP's Christmas guest at Noizay.

1953 (aged 54)

New Year's day dinner takes place at Noizay with the Belgian actor Stéphane Audel (1901–1984), Bernac, Raymond and Céline Destouches, and Suzanne Peignot. Despite his legendary parsimony, Poulenc is usually a lavish host for such occasions, and this one was no exception: potage aux champignons, quenelles sauce Natua, Poularde truffée, fromages, gâteaux, fruits, café, vin moelleux, liqueurs.

(4–28 January) FP takes up residence in the Hôtel Beau-Rivage, overlooking Lake Leman in Ouchy-Lausanne, where he will record six autobiographical conversations for Swiss radio with Stéphane Audel. At the same time, he scrupulously prepares a series of seemingly spontaneous conversations with the critic Claude Rostand for French radio to be recorded and broadcast later in the year.

(2 March) FP and Bernac give a recital in Avignon. Afraid that correspondence arriving at Noizay may give him away, Poulenc tasks Simone Girard in Avignon with making all the hotel arrangements for his assignations in the south of France with Lucien (Brigitte is also complicit).

(5 March) Sergei Prokofiev dies.

(March) FP rehearses with cellist Pierre Fournier for a forthcoming Italian tour.

After making several radio recordings in Naples (and meeting there Renata Tebaldi and Ingrid Bergman), FP and Fournier make their debut in Turin (18th) with a program that includes the Debussy and Poulenc cello sonatas, Schubert's *Arpeggione* Sonata, Schumann's *Fantasiestücke,* and Stravinsky's *Suite italienne.* Concerts follow in Bergamo and Assisi. FP is delighted to work with Fournier and announces to Simone Girard that the duo has "*lost its virginity.*" He also adds: "*Fournier is a love, a real love, but he is not my Pierre.*"[23]

In passing through Milan, FP confesses to the director of Ricordi Editions, Guido Valcarenghi, that a commission for a ballet on the life of St. Margaret of Cortona, the so-called second Magdalene, is a nonstarter. When he says he would prefer to write an opera, Valcarenghi proposes a libretto based on the *Dialogues des Carmélites,* by Georges Bernanos (1888–1948). FP, having both read and seen the play, is stupefied by this suggestion . . . and says yes. So he writes to Bernac on 26 March. But Poulenc tells the story differently in 1957: after a highly successful recital with Fournier in Rome (early April), by chance he finds in a bookshop a copy of the *Dialogues.* He sits for over two hours on the terrace of the café Tre Scalini in the Piazza Navone and rereads the play. To test his musical response to the text, he opens it at random to a passage for the First Prioress, and immediately finds the melodic curve; by 2 p.m. he has telegraphed Valcarenghi to accept the commission.[24]

(3–11 April) FP is the guest of Marie-Blanche de Polignac in her home in Bastide du Roy, in Antibes. He thanks her for a time that has recaptured his youth, an Easter of paradise.[25] During this visit he plays *Aubade* in Monte Carlo, in a concert that also features his *Sinfonietta* and *Les Biches* (10th). He also visits Lucien in Marseilles, returning to Paris on the 14th.

FP works on dividing the Bernanos play into viable operatic scenes (which he does by June) and sets about informing friends of the new project, vaunting the prospects of performances in Milan, Buenos Aires, Naples, Covent Garden, London, Berlin, and perhaps even Paris.

(1 June) In a letter to the composer and musicologist Henry Barraud, FP congratulates him on his article on Musorgsky in the newly appeared *Musique russe,* but deplores the clinical analysis by Pierre Boulez of Stravinsky's *Rite of Spring* in the same publication.[26]

(23 July) At Le Tremblay, FP completes the Sonata for Two Pianos begun in Marseilles the previous December. He confesses to Simone Girard that the *Andante lyrico* movement owes its existence to Lucien Roubert ("*l'inspiration toulonnaise*").[27] He entrusts the autograph to Samuel Barber to deliver to the sonata's dedicatees, the duo Gold and Fizdale ("Les Boys"), in America.

(2 August) FP performs *Aubade* in Deauville and gives a recital with Fournier in Menton in the south of France (11th). He flies from Nice to Paris (14th) and is joined by his sister Jeanne Manceaux at Noizay. Other events in August include a fine performance of Stravinsky's *The Rake's Progress* in nearby Tours, and a reception given by Poulenc for fifty students from Nadia Boulanger's American Conservatory at Fontainebleau.

(15 August) In Noizay, work on the opera begins in earnest. The already written dedication on the score reads: "*To the memory of my mother who revealed music to me, of Claude Debussy who gave me the taste to compose it, of Claudio Monteverdi, of Giuseppe Verdi, and of Modest Musorgsky who have served me here as models.*" FP tells Bernac (22th) that "*my phonograph is not lying idle. Operas, operas, operas.*"[28]

Continuing correspondence between Bernac and Poulenc concerns the range of singers' voices, the different vocal colors that may be appropriate for each role and for the kind of voices for which he has never composed songs, the balancing of different female tessiture. Bernac's command of vocal pedagogy and of Italian opera is superior to Poulenc's, although the composer soon becomes a knowledgeable fan of Verdi in particular.[29] It is partly thanks to Bernac's assiduous advice over many months that *Dialogues des Carmélites* has remained a valued and viable ensemble work in the world's opera houses. As Hervé Lacombe points out, the opera's "five great roles for women require the vocal means represented by Thaïs (Blanche), Amneris (the First Prioress), Desdemona (the Second Prioress), Kundry (Mother Marie) and Zerlina (Constance)."[30]

The first three scenes of *Dialogues* are drafted by early September. Rather than stem the flow of his operatic creativity in Noizay, FP decides against attending recording sessions for *Les Mamelles de Tirésias* in Paris with conductor André Cluytens. Instead, he provides Cluytens with tips and tempo suggestions in a long memorandum (mid-September).

(31 October) FP is invested with the rank of Officier de la Légion d'Honneur at a ceremony chez Colette. Also present at the brief ceremony are the Aurics, Marie-Blanche de Polignac, André Dubois, and Brigitte Manceaux. The investiture is followed by a buffet (at FP's expense) at Le Grand Vefour, the restaurant downstairs from Colette's apartment in the Palais-Royal.

FP returns to Lausanne and the Hôtel Beau-Rivage to work on the difficult fourth scene of Act I. He writes almost daily to inform Bernac of his progress. (These letters, sold in Bernac's old age to the Morgan Library in New York, enabled the singer to remain in the suddenly rent-hiked apartment in Paris where he had lived all his life.)

(4 December) FP hears a performance of Stravinsky's *Cantata* sung by Cuenod, a work he finds "*overwhelmingly sterile*": "*It is one of the most Russian and oriental of Igor's works, which has nothing at all to do with the Elizabethan texts. . . . It's dreadful to think that Stravinsky will compose from now on in English and that his whiskey will always smell of vodka. Oh! The danger of America. In Paris he would have remained a cosmopolitan.*"[31]

Despite the opera's becoming more and more of an obsession, FP keeps up his work as a pianist in the south of France: he performs the *Concert champêtre* in Lausanne (7 December) and *Aubade* at Nyons (11th). He also makes a recording of (mostly) his songs with the Swiss tenor Hugues Cuenod.

(9 December) Cuenod records a recital, including six Poulenc songs with the composer, for Radio Suisse Romande.[32]

(23 December) FP returns to Paris (via Lyon to see Lucien), having completed the first act of his opera.

1954 (aged 55)

After many years, FP is once again in contact with Arthur Honegger, whose *Une cantate de Noël* is performed in Paris while its composer lies in a hospital in Basel. This turn of events finds Poulenc at his kindest and most compassionate; in a letter of 9 January he recalls former times of Les Six, while observing, not without a trace of envy, that Auric's success with the film music for *Moulin Rouge* has made him a millionaire.[33]

(13 January) FP attends the inaugural concert of "Domaine musicale," a series directed by Pierre Boulez and supported by Jean-Louis Barrault and Madeleine Renaud. He finds conductor Hermann Scherchen's performance of Stravinsky's *Renard* incomprehensible, but later remarks that the link between Boulez and the poet René Char in *Soleil des eaux* is similar to the bond he and Auric had felt with Éluard.[34]

(15 January–15 February) In the midst of an exceptionally cold winter, FP moves to warmer Cannes, where he takes a suite in the Hôtel Majestic, hoping to work on his opera. But his first week there is ruined by a bad case of food poisoning as well as bad weather. He completes Act II, scene 1, on 27 January.

(3 February) Bernac arrives in Cannes to work on the music for a forthcoming tour of Egypt. FP returns briefly to Paris to play excerpts of *Dialogues* to friends (15th). He also accompanies Marya Freund, now seventy-eight, in a memorable performance of Satie's *Socrate* at the salon of Comte Étienne de Beaumont.

Bernac and Poulenc leave for their Egyptian tour, which begins with Poulenc sitting on the jury of the Cairo Conservatoire. The first recital is an all-Poulenc program in Alexandria (9 March). Ten days in Alexandria are spent profitably: thanks to the French consul, FP has a room with piano in the Consulate, where he finishes Act II, scene 4, of the opera. A recital in Cairo (19th) is followed by further concerts in smaller cities. At the end of the tour, singer and pianist visit Luxor, then Greece (28th–29th). They rent a large car and tour Salonika, Corinth, and Mycenae: "*Marvelous, I lost my head—what eyes! What mouths! What charm!*"[35]

(30 March) FP and Bernac arrive in Rome, where they stay for a week as guests of Mimi Pecci-Blunt. Poulenc learns that after its first performance in New York, the Sonata for Two Pianos was described by a critic as "a mas-

terwork from a master hand." On the way back to Paris, the duo visit Marie-Blanche de Polignac in Antibes (7–9 April).

There is now an unforeseen gap in the composition of the opera. For the first time in four years, FP turns his attention to song composition.

(April) *Parisiana* **FP157** (Jacob), composed in Noizay.

(Late April) *Entretiens avec* [Interviews with] *Claude Rostand* is published. It was Rostand who, in a review of the recent Piano Concerto, had coined the antithesis that FP was both "monk and ragamuffin" ("moine et voyou").[36]

(4–5 May) FP plays concerts in Brussels, where he stays with the Lambi-ottes. Honegger, having just read the Rostand *Entretiens* with great pleasure and emotion, writes to Poulenc (10th): "Do not find me presumptuous if I put myself beside you to say 'We are two honorable men.'"[37]

(May) *Rosemonde* **FP158** (Apollinaire), composed in Noizay.

(End of May) FP attends a recital given at the Salle Pleyel with Pierre Fournier and Wilhelm Kempff; his own performing partnership with Fournier has proved to be of limited duration, probably on account of the opera.

(2 June) FP makes his will, apportioning precious possessions to relatives and close friends (including Raymond and Lucien) and granting Brigitte the sole right to "*deal with the posthumous destiny of my works . . . the best part of me, my spiritual legacy.*" The contents of this "Testament" and of the accompanying letter to Brigitte, in which he confesses the existence of his daughter Marie-Ange, will become known to her only after his death. In the letter, Poulenc's devotion to Marie-Ange is shiningly obvious; she reminds him, in her every gesture, of his mother. "*She is 100% me. . . . I ask you always to look after her as I adore her . . . and never abandon Raymond* [Destouches]. . . . *Think of me without bitterness, as I have loved you so much (you have been a second Raymonde* [Linossier] *to me).*" Brigitte had inherited a large diamond from her mother, and FP asks her to give it to Marie-Ange on her eighteenth birthday; "*it's fairer that way*" (Brigitte will no longer be alive to do so).[38]

(13 June) FP cancels his participation in Britten's Aldeburgh Festival. He is experiencing problems with his gall bladder. He visits Arrens, a town high in the Pyrenees and in the vicinity of Lourdes, where he hopes for a miracle cure—spiritual and mental as much as physical.

Poulenc is tormented by permissions difficulties with *Dialogues des Car-mélites*. The copyright of the story that initially inspired playwright Georges Bernanos is owned by an American writer, Emmet Lavery, who is on bad terms with Bernanos's heirs. There is a distinct possibility that Poulenc may not be able to adapt the play, a situation that won't be resolved until the following year. FP also becomes convinced that he is suffering from undiagnosed stomach cancer, and is worried about Lucien's deteriorating health.

(8 August) FP visits Rocamadour, and the faithful Raymond Destouches comes to Poitiers to drive him back to Noizay. With Poulenc's sister Jeanne there to look after him, Noizay has a temporarily healing effect; most unexpectedly, and out of sequence, he finds the music for the end of the opera, and is able to begin orchestrating the work on the 16th. By the first week of September, Act I is orchestrated.

(2–15 September) Stéphane Audel arrives at Noizay to replace Jeanne as Poulenc's "nurse." He finds the composer in an alarmingly changeable emotional state, and listens to endless recitations of illness and emotional anguish. Bernac arrives to rehearse on the 11th.

(13 September) FP writes to Marie-Ange on the occasion of her eighth birthday, signing the letter "Payen," which derives from her childish pronunciation of "parrain," godfather.[39]

(14 September) FP, Audel, and Bernac visit the grave of Ronsard at the nearby Saint-Cosme Priory, and the museum at Tours.

(15 September) On returning to Paris, FP, afraid to be alone, asks Audel to stay with him in the rue de Médicis until the 27th. On 10 October he departs with Bernac for a ten-day concert tour of Holland.

(12 October) First public performances of *Parisiana* FP157 and *Rosemonde* FP158, in the small hall of the Concertgebouw, Amsterdam. These concerts are not the happiest of events; Poulenc is not well, and he can talk of little besides his emotional turmoil.

(October) After leaving Holland, FP travels to the south of France to see Lucien. He writes to Simone Girard, *"Alas! I am no longer the master of my will, of my poor nerves. I am completely adrift. It is shaming."*[40]

(4 November) After learning of an emotional crisis that has temporarily ended the relationship between Poulenc and Lucien, Bernac sends the composer a firm and frank letter that casts doubt on the viability of their forthcoming German tour. Bernac also doubts his own ability to survive vocally when he has to deal with nonstop talk about Lucien on top of FP's other obsessive and erratic behavior. Poulenc's "Crisis of 1954" (p. 383) takes the narrative of his life to the end of this year.

At the end of the year, in a letter to Marthe Bosredon written from the home of Marie-Blanche de Polignac in Antibes, Poulenc is still referring to the unhappy state of his *"poor nerves."* He will recuperate in the south of France until 6 January 1955.

During this year, an LP on the Boîte à musique label is released with Poulenc accompanying Geneviève Touraine in songs by Debussy, Roussel, and Poulenc.

1955 (aged 56)

Bernac and Poulenc (now partially recovered) travel to London, arriving on 13 January. They record a BBC recital on the 15th (broadcast the next day). On that evening (the 16th) FP is at the Festival Hall performing his Concerto for Two Pianos with Benjamin Britten and the Liverpool Philharmonic conducted by John Pritchard. FP had requested that the two pianists be allowed to use the scores, "*better for my convalescent memory.*"[41]

FP and Bernac give recitals in Carlisle (18 January) and Newcastle upon Tyne (20th), then return to France on the 23rd.

(26 January) FP visits Brussels, and returns to Paris to hear Denise Duval's debut as Massenet's *Manon* (27th).

(2 February) FP and Bernac perform their twentieth-anniversary concert at the Salle Gaveau (the actual anniversary date would have been 3 April). The concert of songs by Fauré, Debussy, Roussel, Ravel, and Poulenc draws a full house (seats onstage) and is a great critical success. Nevertheless, this date proves something of a turning point for the duo. On account of the opera, there will now be far fewer recitals. This is scarcely healthy for Poulenc's finances—although in due course he will benefit from opera royalties—but it is Bernac who, without a word of complaint, is left high and dry at a time when there are few performing years left to him.

(20 February) Lucien Roubert is diagnosed with lung cancer, a revelation that heals the breach between the composer and his lover. Lucien is so unwell that Poulenc has no further grounds for jealousy or suspicion; Lucien belongs to him entirely. He had considered selling the house in Noizay and moving to the south of France, but now "*Raymond and Noizay have won.*" It would be a short-lived victory.[42]

(1 March) FP departs for Cannes to be close to Lucien, living at the Hôtel Majestic and resuming work on his opera. He completes scenes 3 and 4 of Act II and at last receives permission to adapt the Bernanos play (5th). Feeling a great deal better, he attends the Cannes Film Festival, where he pays particular attention to the film music and writes a detailed article about it (published in *Cahiers de cinéma*, July 1955).

(31 March) Peter Pears and Benjamin Britten give a poorly attended recital in Cannes. A photograph taken by FP's distinguished acupuncturist, Felix Mann, shows the two composers and singer walking together on the promenade the next morning, an overcoated Poulenc looking old for his age and every inch a convalescent. (He has just checked in to the Hôtel Majestic, where he will stay for twelve days.) The two Englishmen flanking him clearly find the weather in the south of France pleasantly clement in comparison with what they are accustomed to in Aldeburgh.

(5 April) Lucien, who has been in Cannes with FP, is taken back to Toulon. Poulenc returns to Paris on the 12th, and on the 18th gives a recital with Bernac for a medical charity.

(19 April) FP and Bernac give a recital in Toulouse, "French Song from Gounod to Poulenc." The composer cancels plans to go on to Noizay and returns to Cannes to spend more time with the terminally ill Lucien. While there, he completes Act III, scene 1, of *Dialogues* and begins scene 2. (It had only recently been decided during a visit from the La Scala team that the opera should be in three acts rather than two.)

(12 May) FP and Bernac give a recital in Paris.

With only a few scenes of the *Dialogues* left to compose, FP turns his attention to the Éluard song cycle *Le Travail du peintre*. Alice Esty, a soprano and one of Bernac's wealthy American pupils, is prepared to commission such a work provided she sings the first performance (accompanied by the composer) and receives the autograph.

(6 June) FP meets with Alice Esty at Noizay, discusses the commission, and suggests that she also purchase the manuscript of the Sonata for Two Pianos. Gold and Fizdale are thus spared from paying for a work they had unwittingly accepted as a gift.

(17 June–3 July) After returning to the Hôtel Beau-Rivage in Lausanne, FP goes to Evian-les-Bains for a cure. He then travels to Le Tremblay (beginning Act III, scene 3, of the opera) and visits Aix-en-Provence in the middle of July.

(19 June) Bookseller Adrienne Monnier dies in Paris. FP learns some months later that it was a suicide.

Declining an invitation to stay in Hyères with Marie-Laure de Noailles, in early August FP rents a room with piano at the Hôtel Grive Dorée in Tourrettes-sur-Loup, a mountain village thirty kilometers north of Nice; his old friend Richard Chanlaire owns a boutique there where he sells painted scarves. In Tourrettes, while attending to the desperately ill Lucien in the room above his own, FP completes the third scene of Act III.

(12 August) FP chooses a poem, Laurence de Beylié's *Nuage*, to set as a song for Rose Dercourt-Plaut in thanks for all she does for him in America. He warns her to get her handkerchiefs ready for his opera, noting that he "*no longer feels ill*" and that "*ma ménopause est finie!*"[43]

(16 August) A setback in Lucien's health sends Poulenc back to Cannes. FP writes to Bernac that if Raymond Destouches is the secret of the *Mamelles de Tirésias* and *Figure humaine*, Lucien is the secret of the *Stabat Mater* and *Dialogue des Carmélites* (19th).[44]

After growing a mustache (partly to amuse Lucien, who has one), FP conducts a bizarre survey among his friends to learn who is for or against it.

Five (including Bernac) are against, and nine (all women, apart from Richard Chanlaire) are in favor. He lays out plans to Bernac for a recording of two 10-inch LPs of his own mélodies for the French firm Véga (9 September). The discs, released in 1958, feature some of the most definitive of the duo's performances.[45]

(27 September) Poulenc completes *Dialogues des Carmélites*, in Noizay.

(21 October) Lucien Roubert dies in Toulon, probably in his mother's arms. Poulenc writes to Simone Girard on the 31st: *"Lucien delivered from his martyrdom ten days ago, the final copy of* Les Carmélites *completed (take note) at the very moment the poor boy breathed his last. I got up from the table and said to my faithful Anna* [his cook]: *I have finished, Monsieur Lucien will die now."*[46] Anna had never met "Monsieur Lucien," who as far as we know had visited Poulenc neither in Noizay nor Paris. Poulenc will continue to interpret Lucien's death in the spirit of Blanche's death in his opera: Lucien had died of the illness from which Poulenc had convinced himself he was suffering (a transference of death). "It seemed to him after some months that Lucien Roubert was a necessary drama, and, in the broader scheme of things, his own personal experience of the transfer of grace."[47]

(16 November) FP and Bernac give an all-Schumann recital at Chaumont, somewhat prematurely honoring the centenaries of the deaths of Schumann (d. 1856) and the poets Heinrich Heine (d. 1856) and Joseph von Eichendorff (d. 1857).

(21 November) FP records a group of Satie piano pieces with the pianist Marcelle Meyer.

(27 November) Arthur Honegger dies, the first of Les Six to do so. FP attends the funeral on 2 December and is distressed by the service.

(28 November) FP and Bernac give a recital in Tours and repeat the Schumann recital for the Concertgebouw in Amsterdam (16 December).

An LP on the Boîtes à musique label is released this year with Poulenc playing the piano music of Satie. On a Discophiles français LP, Poulenc and Marcelle Meyer perform duets by Chabrier.

1956 (aged 57)

(6 January) FP is invited as guest of honor to the annual reunion of former pupils at the Lycée Condorcet.

(14 February) FP, with false beard, dresses up as Chabrier (and Denise Duval goes as Manon) in a "Bal des artistes."

(8–13 March) FP and Bernac give concerts in Athens and Thessaloniki, Greece. After five days in Rome, where FP is installed as an honorary member of the Accademia Santa Cecilia (together with Copland, Shostakovich, and Messiaen), he writes to his friend Luigi Dallapiccola from Rome about the *Carmélites*: "*It is terribly tonal. Love me nevertheless, as I love you*" (16th).[48] In Milan (19th), FP plays his new opera to an enthusiastic Victor de Sabata, music director of La Scala. He hobnobs with celebrities like Herbert von Karajan and Elisabeth Schwarzkopf at the Biffi restaurant. "*I was treated like Wagner!!*" he delightedly writes to Brigitte. Commenting in the same letter on Stravinsky's adoption of serial style, he says that his favorite composer now "*puts on hats that are too young for his age.*"[49]

(22 March) After returning to Paris, FP attends a "Domaine musicale" concert at the Petit Marigny and hears the first Parisian performance of Boulez's *Le Marteau sans maître*, which he finds "*remarkable,*" although "*the prosody was like the tooth-edge of a saw, which made the text unintelligible.*"[50]

(27 March) FP and Jean Françaix perform the Concerto for Two Pianos in Liverpool. They repeat the concerto in Cannes on 5 April. FP returns to his favorite room in the Hôtel Majestic, where he finishes orchestrating Act II of *Dialogues*. He revisits Rocamadour with Marthe Bosredon, and completes the orchestration of the entire opera in Brive on 11 June.

After giving a lecture in London (22 June), FP finally makes his debut at Britten's Aldeburgh Festival two days later. In the morning he lectures (in French) on his music, and in the evening he performs *Aubade* under Paul Sacher's baton (both events at the Jubilee Hall); he finds the Swiss conductor ill-suited to his music. Between these two events he attends a concert in nearby Thorpeness by the Aldeburgh Music Club, entitled "Music on the Meare." Invited to sit in a barge on the water, he apparently expresses his fear and discomfort at having to do so in surprisingly fluent English. In his letter of thanks to FP for taking part in the festival, Britten excuses himself for writing in English, but "we all know you speak English perfectly, even if it's necessary for you to be in a boat, or on the water, to speak it . . . !!!"[51]

(Beginning 26 June) FP spends a holiday at the Hôtel Splendide in Evian. Joining him is Claude (surname unknown), a new boyfriend from Nantes who works for Citroën.

(3 July) FP writes to Jacques Leguerney about recently published letters between Reynaldo Hahn and Marcel Proust: "*Without* [the influence of] *Reynaldo, Proust would have adored* Pelléas, Strauss, Debussy, Ravel, Stravinsky. . . . *Full of spirit and intelligence, Reynaldo, Louis* [Beydts], [Bernard] *Gavoty represent delicious Parisian mediocrity.*"[52] The critic Gavoty ("Clarendon" of *Le Figaro*) was no Poulenc enthusiast, and a rival on the lecture circuit.

(8 July) FP departs departs by car from Evian to Venice in the company of Claude. They then travel to Milan, where Poulenc enters discussions about the production of his opera. He later refers to Claude (in a letter to Bernac on 17 August) as "*a poor tortured boy.*"

(4–28 July) FP and Bernac give master classes on Poulenc's music at Nadia Boulanger's American Conservatory at Fontainebleau, with an opening recital on the 24th.

(31 July) In a letter to Wanda Landowska, FP recalls his love for Lucien and his almost mystical role in the composer's life: "*I took care of him, and that cured my anxiety and nervousness.*"[53]

(Late August) FP stays at Le Tremblay to finish **Le Travail du peintre FP161**, the new cycle about painters to poems of Éluard, which shares some of the melodic themes of his new opera. He copies the score and posts it to Alice Esty in New York.

FP spends time at Noizay—with trips to Paris for meetings with opera personnel—preparing for the two premieres of *Dialogues*. For the first, in Milan in January 1957 (*Dialoghi delle Carmelitane*), he has no control over the cast, production, or decor. He has considerably more say in the French premiere in June 1957 at the Opéra, and discussions about the producer, conductor, and designer are detailed and ongoing (late August–September).

(7 September) After listening to a radio broadcast from Venice of the premiere of Stravinsky's *Canticum sacrum*, FP writes to him: "*I found it sublime. . . . you always give us a lesson in youth, faith and lucidity.*"[54] But to Milhaud some months later, he confesses that he truly dislikes "*St-Marc d'Igor*" and disparages Robert Craft's influence on Stravinsky ("*Misérable Craft*").[55]

(September) **Deux Mélodies** (**La Souris** and **Nuage**) **FP162** (Apollinaire and Beylié), composed at Noizay.

In the UK, Bernac and Poulenc perform recitals in Birmingham (6 November) and Oxford (8th), and for a BBC broadcast (10th).

(19–20 November) FP is in Milan to hear the first read-through of the orchestra rehearsals for *Dialogues*. There is a recital with Bernac in Berlin on the 25th.

(December) Using all his powers of persuasion, FP attempts to arrange for his daughter Marie-Ange (aged ten) to be accepted into the Opéra's ballet school, but is unsuccessful.

(1–25 December) FP stays at the Hôtel Majestic in Cannes, where he works on the Flute Sonata and a new mélodie.

(December) **Dernier Poème FP163** (Desnos), composed in Cannes. Date and locale of the first performance are unknown.

A 10-inch Véga LP is released this year of Poulenc and an instrumental ensemble accompanying Bernac in *Le Bal masqué*.

1957 (aged 58)

(7 January) FP arrives in Milan to work on *Dialogues* and attend rehearsals. He writes to Marie-Ange that he must work from 10 a.m. to midnight. He

is happy with the cast and director (Margarita Wallmann), but less so with the visual aspects.

(19 January) Work begins in Paris on the French production of the opera. *Dialogues des Carmélites* has its glittering and hugely successful premiere at La Scala, Milan, on the 26th. FP invites Simone Girard and Bernac to the general rehearsal. Ninety-four critics from around the world are present, and the Carmelite nuns of Compiègne keep a day of silence in honor of the work.[56] The premiere appears to mark the beginning of the end of FP's relationship with Claude from Nantes—unusually for the composer's attachments, an opera fan.[57]

(7 February) FP returns to Paris exhausted after a month of constant activity, including work on the publication of the opera's piano vocal score.

(February–March) At the Hôtel Majestic in Cannes (for this period of his life as much his composing base as Noizay), Poulenc makes adjustments and revisions to the opera's score in the light of the first performances. He meets twenty-nine-year-old Louis Gautier, an infantry sergeant in the former French colonial forces, who will be Poulenc's "secret" lover (hidden from Raymond Destouches) for the next five years.

(By 8 March) In Cannes, Poulenc completes two of three movements of the Flute Sonata, his work apparently hastened by the excitement of his new liaison. "*The Sonata for Flute is proof of the beneficial effects of the French army on the morale of an old maestro.*"[58] Picasso, who lives in Cannes, makes a graphite drawing of a dapper Poulenc sitting in a chair (13th). FP is almost certainly not present for the sitting.

(17 March) FP returns to Paris, via Avignon and Marseilles. He views a Picasso exhibit at the Galerie Louise Leiris and prepares for the first performance of his Éluard cycle about the painters, sung by soprano Alice Esty.

(25 March) The Treaty of Rome establishes France as one of six founder members of the European Economic Community and the European Atomic Energy Community.

(1 April) First public performance of *Le Travail du peintre* FP161, at the École Normale de la Musique, Paris. American soprano Alice Esty (who commissioned the work) is accompanied by the composer. Other songs in the program are accompanied by the American pianist David Stimer.

(3 April) FP flies to Basel for the first German-language performance of *Les Mamelles de Tirésias* (*Die Wandlung des Tiresias*), returning to Paris on the 6th.

(12–15 April) FP visits Milan at the invitation of the Ricordi director Guido Valcarenghi, to see Maria Callas in *Anna Bolena* at La Scala.

(Late April) FP records *L'Histoire de Babar* with Noël Coward in a visit to the UK. The "Master" seems to have made little impression on him.

(10 May) FP and Bernac take part in a concert for the fiftieth anniversary of the Salle Gaveau in the company of the Trio Pasquier, Marguerite Long, and Jean-Pierre Rampal, among others.

(7 June) FP mails the Flute Sonata FP164 (commissioned by the Coolidge Foundation and dedicated to the memory of Elizabeth Sprague Coolidge) to Washington, D.C.

(18 June) First performance, by Jean-Pierre Rampal and Poulenc, of the Flute Sonata for the Strasbourg Festival. Arthur Rubinstein happens to be in Strasbourg and is treated to a preview on the morning of the concert.

(21 June) First performance in France of *Dialogues des Carmélites* at the Paris Opéra. FP is delighted with his protégée Denise Duval in the role of Blanche (she had worked for six weeks with Bernac on the music) and by Régine Crespin as the Second Prioress, and the press is mostly favorable. The first-night audience includes Maurice Chevalier, Jean Cocteau, Georges Auric, Maurice Yvain, Christian Dior, and the widow of Georges Bernanos. FP also takes note of who is not there, namely baritone Gérard Souzay.[59]

FP makes his yearly pilgrimage to Rocamadour. From there he travels to Cologne for the first German performance of his opera (14 July), accompanied by Claude (without Louis Gautier's knowledge). There are seventeen curtain calls, though critical reception is not good. He spends two days with Hervé Dugardin, director of Ricordi in Paris and increasingly a good friend, listening to the latest music by young composers ("*wallowing in Darmstadt dodécaca*"),[60] and then on to Aix and Avignon.

(1 August) FP replies positively to Britten's invitation to take part in performances of *Les Mamelles de Tirésias* at the 1958 Aldeburgh Festival, the orchestral reduction to be played by the two composers on two pianos. FP volunteers to make an arrangement, but this never materializes.

(August) Brigitte Manceaux has acquired, with her father's help, some land near St. Tropez where she will build her own small house, La Brigida. Poulenc, who now spends much time in the south of France, is delighted.[61]

(23 August) FP begins a Sonata for Bassoon and Piano, mentioning it to Robert Douglas Gibson of Chester Music, but no trace of the music has survived.

(1 September) Horn player Dennis Brain is killed in a car accident, an echo of the death of Pierre-Octave Ferroud, which had so shaken the composer in 1936. It may not have escaped FP's superstitious attention that Brain was traveling back from the Edinburgh Festival at almost the same time that the composer was making his way there with Bernac—another transfer of deaths, perhaps. Later in the month FP begins to compose an *Élégie* for horn and piano, in Brain's memory.

(Early September) After visiting London to drop off an autograph score of the Flute Sonata at Chester's, FP and Bernac make three appearances (and a recording of Gounod mélodies) at the Edinburgh Festival, where their performance of *Le Travail du peintre* is misadvertised as the premiere.

(5 September) First public performances of **Deux Mélodies** (**La Souris** and **Nuage**) **FP162**, at the Edinburgh Festival. These songs were performed in the same recital as *Le Travail du peintre*.

(16 September) For Nadia Boulanger's seventieth birthday, a surprise party is organized in Switzerland by Doda Conrad, with 125 guests arriving from around the world. Unable to attend, FP contributes a five-bar vocal fanfare ("Vive Nadia la chère Nadia Boulanger, la très chère Nadia"). Copies are distributed to the guests, who perform the music. Before his departure for Edinburgh, FP promised Boulanger an *Ave Maria* in her honor, which was sketched but never completed.

(25 September) In a letter to Guido Valcarenghi of La Scala, FP declares his intention to compose Cocteau's *La Voix humaine* for Denise Duval, a suggestion that had come from Hervé Dugardin. FP regards it as providential that Hans Werner Henze is no longer interested in setting the text.[62]

(24 October) FP's friend Christian Dior dies.

(2–4 November) FP is a member of the jury (he relishes such work) at the competition of Queen Elizabeth of Belgium. He attends another performance of *Dialogues des Carmélites* in Paris and then travels to Cannes (11th), where he plans to spend a month at the Hôtel Majestic.

After only three days in Cannes, FP flies back to Paris and into the arms of his doctors, having succumbed to an attack of nervous anxiety and fearing a recapitulation of the problems of three years earlier. He works at Noizay on the *Élégie* for horn. Louis Gautier comes to spend four days with him over Christmas; it's not clear how the visit was explained away to Raymond Destouches.

A Discophiles français LP is released this year of *L'Histoire de Babar*, with the great actor Pierre Fresnay and FP. The American label Turnabout also releases an LP of Poulenc songs sung by Rose Dercout-Plaut accompanied by the composer; the inadequate vocal performance alone makes this Poulenc's least distinguished recording.

1958 (aged 59)

(5 January) FP and Jacques Février perform the Concerto for Two Pianos with the London Symphony Orchestra, conducted by Alexander Gibson.

(16 January) *Dialogues des Carmélites* (sung in English) receives its British premiere at the Royal Opera House, Covent Garden. The Blanche is Elsie

Morrison, whose husband, Rafael Kubelik, conducts; and Joan Sutherland, a year before achieving world stardom in *Lucia di Lammermoor* at the same house, sings the role of the Second Prioress. In a letter of congratulation to Poulenc, Edward Sackville-West describes Sutherland as "usually a gawky schoolgirl with too much chin," but he praises her "authority and touching dignity" in the role.[63]

(16–18 January) FP makes BBC recordings of his Flute Sonata (with Gareth Morris), *Élégie* for horn and piano (with Neill Sanders), and Sextet (with the Brain Wind Ensemble). He then flies to Rome for a recital with Bernac.

(February) FP is in Milan, and then in Cannes at the Hôtel Majestic. He begins to work seriously on Cocteau's *La Voix humaine*, hoping that Maria Callas will sing this one-woman opera in Milan and Denise Duval in Paris.

(14 February) Marie-Blanche de Polignac, in poor health for years, dies at sixty-one of a brain tumor. FP feels an *"atrocious dizziness"* at this loss.[64]

FP visits Rome as the guest of Mimi Pecci-Blunt. He attends the first night of a new production of *Dialogues* (17 March), then returns to Cannes on the 21st.

(March) **Une chanson de porcelaine FP169** (Éluard), composed in Cannes. Date and locale of the first performance are unknown.

FP is so enthused by his progress on *La Voix humaine* that he dispenses with all his medication apart from the sedatives Equanil and Soneryl (Butobarbital), to which he is addicted. In a letter to Hervé Dugardin and his wife Daisy, later to be the joint dedicatees, FP is unusually frank about its origins: *"Blanche was me, and Elle* [the anonymous protagonist of *La Voix humaine*] *is me again and . . . Louis, looking into the future, as life will take him away from me in one way or another. . . . He is charming to me and (except at certain moments!) a tender, polite and deferential son."*[65]

FP spends three days in Lisbon, where his opera is performed at the San Carlo theater (18 April). *"Not only do I no longer believe that I have cancer, but I know that everything is in order with my 'machine.' Only my unfortunate state of mind takes pleasure in torturing me. Doubts about my music, doubts about my love to whom I am too attached and who adores me."*[66] He returns to Noizay on the 21st and finishes the *La Voix humaine* by June. He boasts that the work was written in record time and will spend July making a fair copy from his working sketches.

(Early May) FP and Louis Gautier on holiday discover Bagnols-en-Forêt, a perched hilltop village in the Pays de Fayence, which will become their future home. At the local hostelry, Auberge des Chasseurs, FP asks the proprietor, Mimi Martin, for an aspirin—and thus begins one of the warmest and least complicated friendships of his later years.[67]

As his work with Bernac becomes increasingly infrequent, FP embarks on a new recital partnership with Denise Duval, the star (Blanche and Thérèse) of his two operas. Their first appearance is at the beautiful Château de la Brède, near Bordeaux, on 16 May (as part of the Mai Musical de Bordeaux).

(13 June) Having earlier canceled his participation as a duo pianist at the Aldeburgh Festival in a production of *Les Mamelles de Tirésias*, FP writes to Britten on the day of its first performance there, bemoaning his inability to travel, as *"my doctor has once more forbidden me the sea."* In the absence of the promised two-piano arrangement by Poulenc, the vocal score is speedily "cooked" by Britten with the help of Viola Tunnard, who performs in Poulenc's place. Peter Pears and Jennifer Vyvan sing the principal roles.

(23 June) A week after *Les Mamelles* has been performed without him in Aldeburgh, FP travels to London, staying at 28 Hamilton Terrace with his friends Vere and Honor Pilkington, whom he had met through composer Lennox Berkeley. In Oxford he receives a Doctorate of Music, *honoris causa*, along with Shostakovich (25th). (In the Latin citation, Les Six are "sexviri Franco-Gallici" and the Bernanos opera is "Carmelitidum Dialogos."[68]) In London for another two days, he attends the dress rehearsal of Stravinsky's *The Rake's Progress* in Glyndebourne and lunches with Robert Douglas Gibson, his publisher at Chester Music, returning to Paris on the 27th.

(July–August) FP takes a cure at Evian, visits the festival Aix-en-Provence to see *Don Giovanni*, and then spends three weeks in Tourrettes-sur-Loup. He finishes the vocal score of *La Voix humaine* and visits Menton to attend concerts. He rejoices in time spent with Louis Gautier, who is building his own house in Bagnols-en-Forêt—a little village of the Var, near Saint-Raphaël, that will become Poulenc's retreat in these closing years of his life.[69]

Bernac is spending much more time teaching, particularly in America and England. His (and Poulenc's) good friend Simone Girard begins to accompany the singer on these journeys abroad (as she continues to do after Poulenc's death). FP tells Girard that he is no longer worried about Bernac's future, realizing that he will be in great demand as a teacher.

(25 August–19 September) Back in Noizay, FP completes the orchestration of *La Voix humaine*. Denise Duval visits and declares herself delighted with her new role: "Merci mon Poupoule chéri."[70]

FP journeys to Milan and Venice, then arrives at the Villa D'Este in Cernobbio, on Lake Como, on 27 September. As a member of a jury (together with Malipiero, Ildebrando Pizzetti, Frank Martin, and Goffredo Petrassi), he judges 123 operas—none of which is awarded a prize. By 6 October FP and Louis Gautier are in Venice again, then travel slowly back to Paris via

Poulenc with his lover Louis Gautier, standing at the house built by Louis in Bagnols-en-Forêt.

Florence, arriving on the 21st. *"I want to be 20 again, and live my life like a bad boy. . . . If I were truly wise, although my boy from the South is handsome and kind, I'd send him packing, but here I am, my 60 years reveling in the 30 years difference."*[71]

(8 November) FP travels to Barcelona to hear his *Stabat Mater*. Back in Paris he plays through the score of *La Voix humaine* for friends at Bernac's apartment (10th).

(December) Denise Duval's husband is operated on for brain cancer and dies; her four-year-old son Richard is ill and also in the hospital.

In the final days of the year, FP confides in Stéphane Audel (a constant companion through this December) that he believes Louis is deceiving him; he is racked with jealousy, suffers from insomnia, and fears creative impotence and becoming a fuddy-duddy (*"un vieux birbe"*). When Louis returns to Cannes to meet a younger lover, terrible scenes ensue in front of Henri Hell, Chanlaire, and Audel in the rue de Médicis apartment, including threats of suicide (28–29 December). The drama of *La Voix humaine* is being played out in real life, and the composer's behavior is so "outrée" that Audel wonders if he is play-acting. Audel is charged with letting Louis know how the composer is suffering.

(30 December) FP phones Audel at 1 a.m. to tell him that Louis is disappointed with the younger man and is missing the composer's tenderness: "*Alleluia.*" The mollified Poulenc sends Louis a handsome check to help with the building of his house in Bagnols. The one helpful suggestion in this month—that FP should compose a *Gloria*—comes from Bernac.[72]

1959 (aged 60)

(2–7 January) Because Jean Cocteau is not well enough to come to Paris, FP and Denise Duval travel to Nice to work on the staging of *La Voix humaine*. Duval is impressed by Cocteau's helpfulness, different from that of any other stage director with whom she has worked. Cocteau describes her voice as "an angel's trumpet" and is astounded at the composer's ability to make an old rehearsal piano sound so beautiful.[73] On Poulenc's sixtieth birthday (7th), there is a general rehearsal with an audience of close friends, including Hervé Dugardin and Picasso's friend Francine Weisweiller. These days in Nice afford FP a chance to be with Louis, although the relationship continues to torment him.

(7 January) FP is elected an honorary member (together with François Mauriac, Marc Chagall, and Harold Nicholson) of the American Academy of Arts and Letters.

(8 January) Charles de Gaulle becomes the first president of the newly established Fifth Republic; unlike presidents of the previous republics, he holds considerable executive powers.

(11 January) Back in Paris, FP and Audel listen together to a recording of Ravel's *Daphnis et Chloé* as the composer moans and weeps like a sick child. His friends are both deeply concerned and exasperated.

(14 January) Rehearsals begin at the Palais Garnier for *La Voix humaine*. FP flies to Barcelona to attend an unsatisfactory performance of *Dialogues des Carmélites* (21st) and then back to Paris. He returns to Nice for two days, ostensibly to discuss production details one last time with Cocteau, in reality to be once again with Louis. Duval, despite singing three performances of *Dialogues* at the end of the month, is universally admired by those who see her in rehearsal for *La Voix humaine*; she reduces even the stage technicians to tears.[74]

(6 February) Premiere of *La Voix humaine* at Paris's Opéra-Comique, sharing the bill with *Isoline*, a one-act opera by André Messager derided by the critics. Cocteau, in his sickbed in Nice, is informed by telephone of a sensational success shared by composer, poet-playwright, and singer.

(9 February) FP and Duval arrive in Milan to prepare for the premiere of the new opera at La Scala. Poulenc flies to Vienna for the premiere of *Dialogues des Carmélites* at the Staatsoper, with Irmgard Seefried as Blanche and

Anneliese Rothenberger as Constance (12th), and returns to Milan in time for the first performance of *La Voix humaine* on the 14th. Cocteau, alerted by mutual friends to the composer's ups and downs, writes in his diary of Poulenc's "singular obsession with a rather sordid love story."[75]

(23 February) FP travels to Naples to see a production of *Dialogues* (much admiring the Blanche of the beautiful Rosanna Cartieri, a singer he would later engage to record his *Gloria*). He writes to Brigitte (on the 25th) that he now hates Paris because of how everyone attempts to look after him there.[76]

After visiting Nice (7–9 March), Poulenc joins Bernac for a recital in Avignon. There follows a recital in Marseilles of songs and chamber music. In Cannes, FP completes his *Laudes de Saint Antoine de Padue*. He spends a week in Rome with Mimi Pecci-Blunt, returns to Cannes on the 28th, then travels to Catania to hear *Dialogues* and receive the Bellini Centenary Medal (8 April).

(23 April) Bernac sends Poulenc the Latin text (with translation) of the *Gloria*.[77] The composer works on it with the idea of renewing an old commission, formerly declined, from the Koussevitsky Foundation in Washington. Bernac sends a letter to Poulenc informing him of his heart trouble—an arterial malfunction with which he will struggle, while continuing to teach, for the next twenty years. If it were not for having to earn a living, he would like to retire to Villeneuve-lès-Avignon to share a quiet life with Simone Girard. In a letter to Brigitte, FP finds this ambition incomprehensible.[78]

(24 April) Denise Duval sings *La Voix humaine* (conducted by Georges Prêtre) in Toulouse, after which FP spends time in Bagnols-en-Forêt with Louis.

(27 May) In honor of their joint sixtieth birthday year, Bernac and Poulenc take part in an all-Poulenc concert at the Salle Gaveau—by mutual consent, their last recital together. On the ambitious program are *Le Travail du peintre* as well as chamber music and unaccompanied choral music (including *Figure humaine*). "*Yesterday I appeared on the stage with Bernac for the last time. He sang better than ever. . . . The public accorded a triumph to this exemplary artist. My fingers trembled a little in beginning* Le Travail du peintre. *Then I regained control of myself. The end of such a fraternal association is very sad.*"[79]

(30 May) FP returns to Vienna to see another performance of *Dialogues*, which is presented twenty-five times at the Staatsoper in 1959–60. He also hears splendid performances of *Siegfried* and *Wozzeck*, and is enchanted with the city ("*there I don't feel chez l'ennemi*").[80] He finds the performance of his own opera impeccable, if clinical: what pleases him most is that it is given "*before a full and enthusiastic house, with not a friend among them!!!!*"[81] This success and that of the Paris recital bolster his confidence.

(4–15 June) From Vienna, FP journeys to Bagnols-en-Forêt, where Louis Gautier has finished building his house, naming it La Gardiette. Returning to Paris in mid-June, FP goes on to Brive, where he always works happily (composing a *Novelette on a Theme of Manuel de Falla*), then makes his yearly visit to Rocamadour and spends ten days at Le Tremblay.

(7 July) FP receives news from Washington that the board of the Koussevitsky Foundation has approved a $2,000 commission for the *Gloria*.

(27 July) Writing to Brigitte, FP compares *Le Travail du peintre* with the late work of Fauré, adding, *"with what art Pierre sings them."*

(Mid-July to end of August) FP, to Louis's delight, spends six weeks in Bagnols working on the *Gloria* and the beginning of the Sonata for Clarinet and Piano. He also sketches an *Élégie* for two pianos in memory of Marie-Blanche de Polignac.

(28 July) Marion, Countess of Harewood, invites FP to write for a children's book of songs to which Britten and Kodály will also contribute. Knowing of her closeness to Britten, FP considers this a commission from the composer himself and, no doubt feeling guilty about his 1958 Aldeburgh cancellation, composes the song in record time, after asking Bernac questions about English prosody.

(August) *Fancy* **FP174** (Shakespeare), composed in Bagnols-en-Forêt and Noizay. Date and locale of the first performance are unknown.

(16 August) The death of Wanda Landowska leaves the composer *"horribly sad."*

(September) FP receives various friends at Noizay, including Hervé and Daisy Dugardin, Rose Dercourt-Plaut, Richard Chanlaire, and his sister Jeanne. He works on a short book about Emmanuel Chabrier, and visits Bagnols, Brussels, and Ghent in October.

(November) *La Puce* (Apollinaire, no FP number), composed in Noizay. Date and locale of the first performance are unknown.

(25 November–27 December) Shortly after FP takes up residence in Bagnols-en-Forêt, one of France's greatest catastrophes strikes (2 December): the Malpasset dam on the river Reyran bursts near Fréjus, a neighboring town, and kills over 420 people. Louis Gautier is caught up in rescue missions, Poulenc is appalled by the devastation. He takes a side trip to Milan (8–10 December) to hear *Otello* (with Mario del Monaco) and *Tosca* (with Renata Tebaldi, Giuseppe di Stefano, and Tito Gobbi) at La Scala.

(21 December) Poulenc finishes his *Gloria*, as well as his book on Chabrier. He and Louis spend Christmas day with Brigitte at La Brigida. As far as Raymond in Noizay is concerned, the composer has spent the entire holiday period staying with his niece.

Songs of the Fifties

FP147 ***La Fraîcheur et le feu*** (*The Coolness and the Fire*)
Composed in Noizay and Brive, April–July 1950
[*Igor Stravinsky*; Eschig]
Literary source: Paul Éluard (1895–1952), *Le Livre ouvert I (1938–1944)*
(Paris: Gallimard, 1947), (i) pp. 76–77, (ii) p. 77, (iii) p. 77, (iv) p. 78, (v) p.
78, (vi) pp. 78–79, (vii) p. 79. The original title of this seven-part poem was
"Vue donne vie" (Sight gives life).

(i)   *Rayons des yeux*
(ii) *Le Matin les branches attisent*
(iii) *Tout disparut*
(iv) *Dans les ténèbres du jardin*
(v)   *Unis la fraîcheur et le feu*
(vi) *Homme au sourire tendre*
(vii) *La Grande Rivière qui va*

Between late December 1949 and March 1950, as Poulenc and Bernac undertook
their second, successful North American tour, the composer was pondering a
new Éluard cycle. On his return to France, he went straight back to Noizay and
started work on a composite poem exactly as printed by the poet, making a cycle
unique in his output. Dissatisfied with "Vue donne vie" as the work's title, he
asked Éluard for an alternative, which ended up being taken from the fifth of the
poem's seven numbered sections.

Thirteen years had elapsed since *Tel jour telle nuit*, and Poulenc thought of
this new work as the "*most integrated*" of his song cycles:

> *I have written so many songs up to now that I have lost my inclination for them,
> and doubtless I shall write less and less of them. If these are successful, and I
> believe they are, it is because a technical problem stimulated my appetite. In*

reality it is not so much a cycle as one single poem set to music in separate sections exactly as the poem is printed. A rhythmic unity (two tempi, one rapid, one slow) lies at the base of the construction. The admirable progression of the poem made it easy for me to take as the culminating point the last song but one (Homme au sourire tendre). There is something of the litany in Éluard (Liberté is the most admirable example of this),[82] which blends with my own religious feeling. There is, besides, a mystical purity in Éluard. These songs are terribly difficult to perform well. I fear that after Bernac I shall never hear them attain the golden mean ["mesure exacte"]. The piano here is economical to a degree. I thought again of Matisse. That is why the timings of the pauses between the songs are not left to chance. The metronomic speeds are implacable. The technical performance must be rehearsed again and again with cold precision; then, sure of oneself, forget it all and give the impression of improvising and being led purely by intuition.[83]

The cycle is dedicated to Stravinsky, whose music Poulenc had admired since his teens (he once said that he regarded himself as the spiritual son of Stravinsky). The older composer was now resident in America, and Poulenc was becoming discreetly less enthusiastic about his more recent works.[84] He wrote to Milhaud that he was pleased to be able to dedicate something to *"grand Igor"* in a form (song) for which Stravinsky did not possess the secret.[85]

(i) *Rayons des yeux (Beams of Eyes)*
    No key signature (F minor); $\frac{4}{4}$; *Allegro molto, emporté* ♩ = 132

Rayons des yeux et des soleils	Beams of eyes and of suns
Des ramures et des fontaines	Of branches and fountains
Lumière du sol et du ciel	Light of the earth and of the sky
De l'homme et de l'oubli de l'homme	Of man and of man's oblivion
Un nuage couvre le sol	A cloud covers the earth
Un nuage couvre le ciel	A cloud covers the sky
Soudain la lumière m'oublie	Suddenly the light forgets me
La mort seule demeure entière	Death alone remains whole
Je suis une ombre je ne vois plus	I am a shadow, I no longer see
Le soleil jaune le soleil rouge	The yellow sun the red sun
Le soleil blanc le ciel changeant	The white sun the changing sky
Je ne sais plus	I no longer know
La place du bonheur vivant	Where living happiness lies
Au bord de l'ombre sans ciel ni terre.	On the edge of darkness with neither sky nor earth.

Whatever the composer may have written about wanting to achieve the simplicity of a Matisse, the pianistic introduction to the cycle is three bars of defiant Romantic bravura that momentarily suggest Rachmaninov—very far from the style of the dedicatee, Stravinsky. Poulenc clearly wished to thrust forward something grandly rhetorical to fit the broad-brushed humanistic notions of the first text. When writing this extended poem, Éluard was already under the influence of Nusch and disengaged with surrealism and Communism. He was horrified by political developments in Europe ("a cloud covers the earth") and was soon to begin working for the French Resistance.

Rayons des yeux is a state-of-the-nations address, a lament for a dislocated universe. The vocal line is rather more turbulent than is normally associated with an Éluard lyric, the piano chasing the voice up and down the stave with an implacable pattern of two sixteenth notes in the right hand, two in the left. On "le ciel changeant" (b. 20) the motif of the introduction returns in transposed form, but only for a bar. The song begins in F minor and ends in the same key with another atypical flourish crashing between the hands (*très brusque*).

(ii)   *Le Matin les branches attisent (At Morning the Branches Stir Up)*
       No key signature; $\frac{4}{4}$; *Presto, très gai* ♩ = 132

Le matin les branches attisent	At morning the branches stir up
Le bouillonnement des oiseaux	The flurry of the birds
Le soir les arbres sont tranquilles	At evening the trees are still
Le jour frémissant se repose.	The quivering day comes to rest.

This piquant and devilishly difficult little scherzo has as its inspiration the twittering of birdsong. The attenuation of the piano writing, completely different stylistically from that of *Rayons des yeux*, looks forward to some songs in *Le Travail du peintre*. There is a marked contrast between the bird-like flight of the first page and the second, suddenly smoother and more suave. Once again the music ends in F minor, although this time the equivocation of an A-natural undermines the minor-key coloring and turns it into a battle of tonalities, a familiar thumbprint from other Éluard songs.

(iii)   *Tout disparut (Everything Vanished)*
        No key signature (A major); $\frac{3}{4}$; *Très calme* ♩ = 69

Tout disparut même les toits même le ciel	Everything vanished. Even the roofs, even the sky
Même l'ombre tombée des branches	Even the shade that dropped from the branches

Sur les cimes des mousses tendres	On top of the soft moss
Mêmes les mots et les regards bien accordés	Even harmonious words and looks
Sœurs mirotières de mes larmes	Like sisters mirroring my tears
Les étoiles brillaient autour de ma fenêtre	The stars twinkled round my window
Et mes yeux refermant leurs ailes pour la nuit	And my eyes folding their wings for the night
Vivaient d'un univers sans bornes.	Were living in a universe without limits.

In honor of the cycle's dedicatee, Poulenc pulls a trick that we find nowhere else in his songs: an actual quote from another composer (three bars, acknowledged as such in a footnote in the score)—Stravinsky's *Serenade in A* (1925), appearing in its original A major tonality. The *Hymne* from Poulenc's earlier *Trois Pièces pour piano* (1928) was similarly inspired by the *Hymne* movement from this same *Serenade*, as would be the opening of the *Gloria* (1960). In all three instances, the music sounds entirely Poulencian.

The poet falls asleep, and the vocal line, almost a recitative, remains dream-like as it pivots around the A major tonality of the opening bars. At "Sur les cimes des mousses tendres" the music falls into a flat-key tonality, as if entering deeper into the realm of the unconscious. The otherworldly quality of "Sœurs mirotières," with the twinkling of the stars outside the poet's window, is vintage Poulenc, as is the *subito pianissimo* phrase, infinitely lyrical, of "Vivaient d'un univers sans bornes." (No other composer knew as well as this one how to use harmonic up-lighters to cast a glow on an entire phrase—in this case an octave on C-sharp, reverberating gently in the bass.) The song ends with a restatement of its first bar (Stravinsky), with three further bars and a cadence of suspended animation tacked on (very much Poulenc).

(iv)   *Dans les ténèbres du jardin (In the Darkness of the Garden)*
        No key signature; $\frac{3}{4}$; *Molto vivace* ♩ = 132

Dans les ténèbres du jardin	In the darkness of the garden
Viennent des filles invisibles	Invisible girls come
Plus fine qu'à midi l'ondée	Finer than a midday shower
Mon sommeil les a pour amies	They are best friends to my slumber
Elles m'enivrent en secret	Secretly they intoxicate me
De leurs complaisances aveugles.	With their blind acquiescence.

As the poet here recounts an erotic dream, the composer provides as phantasma-gorical a page as he ever wrote, a single page that shows, surely, his knowledge of the miniature lieder of Berg and Webern; while declining to enter their harmonic world, he values their aesthetic brevity. There are few dream songs in the repertoire as fast and breathless as this one. The fugitive nature of "Plus fine qu'à midi l'ondée" evokes a musical dew that evaporates on a blade of grass. And the imagery of the invisible girls, and their blind deference, inspires a marvelously evanescent cadence engineered over three bars of piano writing, from *forte* to *pianissimo*, a playful and erotic yielding.

(v) *Unis la fraîcheur et le feu (Unite the Coolness and the Fire)*
     No key signature; ¾; *Très calme* ♩ = 66

Unis la fraîcheur et le feu	Unite the coolness and the fire
Unis tes lèvres et tes yeux	Unite your lips and your eyes
De ta folie attends sagesse	Wait for wisdom from your folly
Fais image de femme et d'homme	Make a likeness of woman and of man.

At the center of the cycle stands another single-page song of the kind that seems engraved in stone, a gnomic utterance. Its introductory music, marked *fortissimo*, possesses grandeur and depth while remaining utterly calm. The thirty-second-note baroque roulade in the third bar is a bow to the mannerisms of neoclassical Stravinsky, but when the vocal line begins, Poulenc uses minimalist atonality to underline the gravity and austerity of the implied ritual: the ceremony of an "unthinkable union of opposites."[86] For "De ta folie attends sagesse" he writes a phrase (b. 13) that is exaggeratedly tonal on the white keys, the voice singing more or less a C major arpeggio, with an added sixth on "sag*esse*."

The final cadence at the end (at "femme et d'homme") veers, typically, between C minor and C major by alternating E-flat with E-natural. This pot-pourri of effects, a conjurer's bag of tricks in slow motion, serves its purpose: to herald the grand and universal theme, man and woman, of the following song. "'Unite the coolness and fire,' says the poet. The composer has followed this difficult advice, and has been rewarded accordingly."[87]

(vi) *Homme au sourire tendre (Man with a Tender Smile)*
      No key signature; ¾; *Très lent* ♩ = 50

Homme au sourire tendre	Man with a tender smile
Femme aux tendres paupières	Woman with tender eyelids
Homme aux joues rafraîchies	Man with fresh cheeks
Femme aux bras doux et frais	Woman with sweet cool arms

Homme aux prunelles calmes	Man with calm eyes
Femme aux lèvres ardentes	Woman with burning lips
Homme aux paroles pleines	Man with full words
Femme aux yeux partagés	Woman with shared eyes
Homme aux deux mains utiles	Man with useful hands
Femme aux mains de raison	Woman with sensible hands
Homme aux astres constants	Man with steadfast stars
Femme aux seins de durée	Woman with enduring breasts
Il n'est rien qui vous retient	Nothing can stop you my masters
Mes maîtres de m'éprouver.	From putting me to the test.

Éluard returns here to one of his favorite themes: male and female as eternal opposites. The cycle's title indicates as much—"La" and "le," coolness and fire. As a man, he is completed, instructed, inspired, transformed, by the power of the eternal feminine (what Goethe calls in *Faust* "Das ewig-weibliche"). In hieratic two-bar phrases, Poulenc expresses Éluard's radiant, almost religious confidence that the future of mankind is assured, despite all the horrors of 1940 and beyond, by the impermeable power of humanity as exemplified by male and female archetypes.

It is not often that Poulenc as a composer of religious music is evident in his secular melodies, but he is here. He achieves something sublime with a litany that would be leaden in other hands—except perhaps in those of a younger contemporary, Olivier Messiaen. Since 1936, Messiaen had represented for Poulenc the threatening face of youthful modernity, yet his music (or some of it) held a strong fascination. In July 1950 Poulenc wrote Messiaen expressing his admiration for *Les Corps glorieux, Les Visions de l'Amen,* and *Cinq Rechants.* The quieter and more rapt passages in the last work, sung by an exactly balanced ensemble of female and male unaccompanied singers, must have made a great impression on him.

In this haunting song, the poetry conjoining and contrasting man and woman is sung softly at first, growing in power and majesty as the accompanying chords gradually become richer and culminate in the *fortissimo* of "Homme aux astres constants." The final phrase, addressed to "Mes maîtres," possesses the serenity of someone about to be submitted to a grueling test while remaining aware that he has eternity on his side, the winning hand. It is perhaps here that we realize that the cycle as a whole was composed only five years after the downfall of Nazism, and in the afterglow of the founding of the United Nations. It seems as though Poulenc, from the vantage point of 1950, intended to declaim with wonder and gratitude the words of a poet whose confidence in the endurance of humanity had been vindicated, for the time being at least.

(vii)   *La Grande Rivière qui va (The Big River That Flows)*
        No key signature; $\frac{4}{4}$; *Allegro moderato* ♩ = 120

La grande rivière qui va	The big river that flows
Grande au soleil et petite à la lune	Big in the sunlight small in the moonlight
Par tous chemins à l'aventure	Hither and thither at random
Ne m'aura pas pour la montrer du doigt	Will not have me to point it out
Je sais le sort de la lumière	I know the fate of the light
J'en ai assez pour jouer son éclat	I have enough of it to play with its radiance
Pour me parfaire au dos de mes paupières	To perfect myself behind my eyelids
Pour que rien ne vive sans moi.	So nothing will live without me.

Its intensity makes this song a bookend match for *Rayons des yeux*. Earth and sky imagery in the first poem is here replaced by the idea of a river that flows in all directions at once—reflected perhaps by the way the pianist must dart all around the keyboard in search of the right notes, borne this way and that by the music's current. There is the same accompanying pattern of two sixteenth notes in the right hand, two in the left, with left-hand notes sometimes flowing with the same current as the descending sixteenths of the right, sometimes in the opposite direction. This gives the piano writing an unusual feeling of swimming upstream—something more effortful than swathes of graceful arpeggios. The ending (*Très violent*) is a recapitulation of two bars of the cycle's introduction, plus a rather hackneyed descending scale in a rush of sixteenth quintuplets, and minor and major chords in quick juxtaposition as a thundered conclusion.

It was Marie-Blanche de Polignac's idea to return to the work's dramatic, pianistic beginning in the interests of cyclic unity (for which advice Bernac credits her for infallible musical judgment).[88] I, for one, believe that the ending sounds somewhat randomly attached, and fails to avoid a certain bombastic banality. If Poulenc had wanted a sense of having come full circle (as he so gloriously achieves in *Tel jour telle nuit*), he needed to do more than pin the tail on the donkey, at no matter whose behest. It would be instructive to see his first ideas, but sadly the autograph of *La Fraîcheur et le feu* has inexplicably vanished. Lacombe's somewhat harsh verdict is that these songs are "soignées, but lack the breath of fresh air that animates *Tel jour telle nuit*, or the melodic charm of some of his other productions."[89] In their defense, the songs have the effect of a succession of vivid haikus, with beautiful moments that show the composer almost at his best; when well performed, they pack a powerful punch in a mere eight minutes.

○   ○   ○

FP148 *Stabat Mater* (soprano solo, chorus, and orchestra), 1950–51

FP149 *Le Voyage en Amérique* (film music for two pianos), 1951

FP150 *L'Embarquement pour Cythère* (two pianos), July 1951

FP151 *Thème varié* (piano), February–September 1951

FP152 *Quatre Motets pour le temps de Noël* (mixed chorus, *a cappella*), 1951–52

FP153 *Matelote provençale* (from *La Guirlande de Campra*) (collaborative instrumental ensemble), June 1952

FP154 *Ave verum corpus* (female choir, *a cappella*), August 1952

FP155 *Capriccio d'après "Le Bal masqué"* (two pianos), September 1952

FP156 Sonata for Two Pianos, 1952–53

○   ○   ○

BIOGRAPHICAL INTERLUDE: MAX JACOB

THE JACOB SONGS: *Cinq Poèmes de Max Jacob* FP59 (1931); *Parisiana* FP157 (1954). Outside the scope of this book are the instrumentally accompanied *Quatre Poèmes de Max Jacob* FP22 (1921) and the "cantate profane" *Le Bal masqué* FP60 (1932).

○   ○   ○

The son of a tailor, Jacob was born on 12 July 1876, in Quimper (Brittany), an area of France that was very Catholic and at the time mystically superstitious—a good description of the poet himself, despite his Jewish birth and upbringing. Arriving in Paris at age eighteen, he attached himself to the world of avant-garde painters and poets. He was said to have taught Picasso, whom he met in 1901, how to speak French. Both Picasso and Apollinaire were fascinated by Jacob's endless verbal dex-

Max Jacob.

terity and sense of fantasy; as an able painter ("something between Corot and Monet," he told Poulenc),[90] Jacob also became part of the Bateau-Lavoir community—a decrepit old wooden house in Montmartre that swayed and creaked in the wind like the washing boats on the Seine, inhabited by a number of poets and painters (Picasso painted his *Les Demoiselles d'Avignon* there).

One of Poulenc's most precious memories was of being taken by Raymond Radiguet in 1917 (poet and composer were hardly more than schoolboys) to meet Jacob, who lived in the rue Gabrielle, Montmartre, near the Sacré-Cœur basilica: "a little man with a bald head with beautiful bright eyes," in Auric's words, "almost always jovial in his welcome," whose "ironical and tender words" could easily become "bitter and pitiless."[91] Jacob had a way of greeting guests with a barrage of compliments thrown out while he was clearly thinking of other things.[92] Radiguet (who had not yet met Jean Cocteau) was saluted as "a novelist of genius," and Poulenc as an "immense" musician.

Poulenc's evocations of the time (if we are to believe everything he says) show how remarkably well read he was for an eighteen-year-old: he already knew the prose poems of Jacob's *Le Cornet à dés* (an "*astonishing volume*") and was perspicacious enough to class it, together with works by Baudelaire and Rimbaud, as one of the key literary precursors to surrealism. As an admirer of Apollinaire, Poulenc knew that Jacob enjoyed the same sort of fruitful relationship with his hero (who was still alive in 1917) as Picasso had enjoyed with Braque. When Apollinaire presented *Les Mamelles de Tirésias* as a stage play that same year, Jacob sang in the chorus with an "*incredible*" (not in a good way) voice.[93]

By now most of the bohemian world of painters, apart from Braque, had abandoned Montmartre for Montparnasse (see FP127/i), but the religious Jacob remained there because of the proximity of Sacré-Cœur. He had been converted to Catholicism in 1909, at the age of twenty-three, when Christ had appeared to him on the wall of his bedroom; a reappearance occurred in 1915 on a cinema screen (the "Cinématographe"; performers of *Avant le cinéma* FP58/iii, take note). One of the poet's recurring nightmares was of a divine emissary descending from a flying chariot to announce that "Max Jacob has lost the right to happiness on earth."[94] It was undoubtedly the fear of divine retribution for his sexual sins that governed his demeanor, subservient on one level and wickedly iconoclastic on another.

Poulenc believed that Jacob's life was governed by fear: "*fear of displeasing Picasso, fear of tangling with Breton, fear of Éluard, fear of Cocteau.*"[95] For this reason he was an accessible friend to the young composer, no stranger to fear himself, whose overtures to the great writers (at least at this early stage) were more often rebuffed than he cared to admit. Their friendship (Jacob was not too grand to write poems specially for Poulenc) resulted in *Quatre Poèmes de Max Jacob* (1921) for flute, oboe, clarinet, bassoon, and trumpet, a defiantly polytonal (and ultimately uncharacteristic) work in the Dada spirit of the times, which the composer subsequently destroyed.[96] After his Diaghilev ballet *Les Biches* had premiered in Monte Carlo, in 1924, Jacob sent him a long laudatory poem where "Monte-Carle" is made to rhyme with "parle": "entire newspapers are filled with your name.... They speak of you from the banks of the Ganges to the Phlegethon ... all geniuses are not, like you, easy."[97] Jacob, with a lack of self-esteem that bordered on self-hatred, habitually placed himself at the service of those he regarded as geniuses in order to feel himself protected under the umbrella of their reflected glory. The high point of his collaboration with Poulenc came in 1932 with the instrumentally accompanied "cantate profane" *Le Bal masqué* FP60.

Jacob was torn between the sexual addiction that tormented him and a life of religious contemplation. He retreated for some years to the Benedictine community of Saint-Benoît-sur-Loire near Orléans, where he found solace living within the shadow of the monastery. Then in 1928, bored with the life of a monk, he returned to live in Montmartre (rue Nollet), giving himself up to a life of dissipation until, once again utterly disgusted with himself, he returned more or less permanently to Saint-Benoît in 1937. *Rivage* (1931) was the last book of poetry published in his lifetime. As Henri Hell observes, "Today one forgets, or no longer knows, how much is owed to Jacob by such different poets as Jean Cocteau, Maurice Fombeure and Jacques Prévert."[98]

Long convinced he would die a martyr, forbidden by the Germans to publish anything on racial grounds, Jacob was arrested by the Gestapo at the end of February 1944. Some of his friends had been aware that he was in danger. Know-

MAX JACOB

RIVAGE

AUX ÉDITIONS DES
CAHIERS LIBRES
57, Avenue Malakoff - PARIS

Title page of Jacob's Rivage *(1931).*

ing that Jean Cocteau had links to actor Sacha Guitry (former husband of Yvonne Printemps), who was well connected with the German authorities, Jacob had appealed to Guitry, via Cocteau, to save his sister and handicapped nephew from deportation. Guitry responded that he was unable to help them, but he could do something for Max himself if he were ever in danger. Jacob's last letter was written to Cocteau on 29 February 1944: "I am writing this in a cattle truck owing to the kindness of the gendarmes who have shut us in here. We will soon be in Drancy. That's all I have to tell you. Sacha, when people spoke to him about my sister, said 'If it were him, I would be able to do something.' Well, it's me" ["Eh bien, c'est moi," the poet's last written words].[99] Five days later, 5 March, Jacob was dead of bronchial pneumonia at the notorious holding camp of Drancy, where Guitry was himself to be imprisoned for a while, as a collaborator, after the liberation of France. The two Jacob songs that Poulenc published in 1954 as *Parisiana* were almost certainly intended as a posthumous tribute to the poet on the tenth anniversary of his death.

Max Jacob, although later described as "buffoon and dervish ... Faust and Pinocchio,"[100] was loved by many, and his martyrdom conferred on him a kind of heroic sanctity. In gleefully acknowledging his own monk-and-naughty-boy duality,[101] Poulenc permitted the persona of a well-loved saint and sinner to add a touch of spice to his own image. He was, however, playing a game that turned deadly serious. The 1950s were to reveal less winsome parallels between composer and poet in the realms of guilt and shame, and there were several occasions when Poulenc *in extremis* came near to experiencing Jacob's tortured self-abasement and terror of divine retribution.

FP157 *Parisiana*

Composed in Noizay, April 1954

[*À la mémoire de Pierre Colle, Paul Chadourne*; Rouart, Lerolle]

Literary source: Max Jacob (1876–1944), (i) *Le Laboratoire central* (Paris: Au Sans Pareil, 1921), p. 133; (ii) *Rivages* (Paris: Éditions Cahiers Libres, 1931), p. 9

(i)   *Jouer du bugle*
(ii) *Vous n'écrivez plus?*

July 1944: "*An album of photographs of Paris charms me and numbs me like a shot of morphine.*"[102] 1954: "*Paris takes me out of myself and in a sense that is one of its blessings, there are so many days when I don't like myself! It is also the only place in the world where I can endure great sorrow, anguish, or melancholy.*"[103]

(i) *Jouer du bugle* (*Playing the Bugle*)
> No key signature (G minor); $\frac{4}{4}$; *Au pas = 72 (sans broncher jusqu'à la fin), sans ironie, très poétique*

Les trois dames qui jouaient du bugle	The three ladies who played the bugle
Tard dans leur salle de bains	Late at night in their bathroom
Ont pour maître un certain mufle	Have as their master a certain ruffian
Qui n'est là que le matin.	Who's only there in the mornings.
L'enfant blond qui prend des crabes	The blond child who is catching crabs
Des crabes avec la main	With his bare hands
Ne dit pas une syllabe	Doesn't utter a syllable
C'est un fils adultérin.	He's a bastard child.
Trois mères pour cet enfant chauve	Three mothers for this bald child
Une seule suffisait bien.	One would have been enough
Le père est nabab, mais pauvre.	The dad's a toff, but poor
Il le traite comme un chien.	He treats him like a dog.
(SIGNATURE)	(SIGNATURE)
Cœur des Muses, tu m'aveugles	Heart of the muses, you blind me
C'est moi qu'on voit jouer du bugle	I'm the one you see playing the bugle
Au pont d'Iéna le dimanche	On the Pont d'Iéna every Sunday
Un écriteau sur la manche.	With a placard on my sleeve.

This song, with its bizarre scenario—Poulenc had orginally intended to use the poem in *Le Bal masqué* (1932)—needs to be sung as though such bohemian madness and dysfunction were everyday aspects of life. The child suffering from crabs is a Parisian relative of the disadvantaged Breton baby described in the earlier Jacob setting *Berceuse* FP59/iv. One unusual effect here is created by the left-hand staccati, an articulation Poulenc almost never asks for in music that is not fast and cut-and-dried. He directs that the notes should be a kind of cushioned *mezzo staccato* (*doucement ponctué, mais avec beaucoup de pédale*), as though he had imagined them played by a tuba rather than a bugle. The final verse—an envoi preceded by the rubric (SIGNATURE)—casts Jacob himself as the busker playing cornet at the foot of the Eiffel Tower for Sunday tourists.

Poulenc takes the poet's command for a SIGNATURE seriously. At the time, he was working on *Dialogues des Carmélites* at the expense of almost everything else, and his obsessive engagement with the new opera is indicated by the appearance of an ornamental phrase in bars 15–19: the so-called *motif de la réligion* that opens Act III/3 and leads into the aria of the Second Prioress. Poulenc's introducing this music, even subconsciously, as part of what is effectively Jacob's "signature" indicates, surely, that he considered the poet, for all his faults, to have been essentially a holy man. To have been connected with the Carmelite order in this way would likely have given the devout Jacob pleasure. Needless to say, mention of a great Parisian landmark like the Pont d'Iéna prompts music that tenderly evokes shadows of popular song.

(ii)   *Vous n'écrivez plus?* (*You've Stopped Writing?*)
        No key signature; $\frac{4}{4}$; *À fond de train* ♩ = 176

—M'as-tu connu marchand d'journaux	—Did you know me when I was selling papers
à Barbès et sous le Métro	at Barbès and on the Metro
Pour insister vers l'Institut	To persist in trying for the Institute
il me faudrait de la vertu	I'd have needed some nerve
mes romans n'ont ni rang ni ronds	my novels are neither classy nor lucrative
et je n'ai pas de caractère.	and I lack character.
—M'as-tu connu marchand d'marrons	—Did you know me when I was selling chestnuts
au coin de la rue Coquillère?	on the corner of the rue Coquillère?
tablier rendu, l'autre est vert.	I gave back my apron, the other one's green.
—M'as-tu connu marchand d'tickets	—Did you know me when I was selling tickets
balayeur de W.-C.	a toilet cleaner
je le dis sans fiel ni malice	I say it with neither spite nor malice
aide à la foire au Pain d'Épice	helper-out at the Gingerbread Fair
défenseur au juge de Paix	defendant at the Magistrate's Court
officier, comme on dit office	officer, i.e., washer-upper
au Richelieu et à la Paix.	at Le Richelieu and La Paix.

"W.C." (verse 3, line 2): Poulenc helps the singer by writing "double V. C." in the score. Neither poet nor composer noticed, when proofreading their publications, that "rue Coquillère" (verse 2, line 2) does not exist; the famous street in Les Halles is "rue Coquillière." "Tablier rendu" (verse 2, line 3): When you leave a job in a kitchen, you give back your apron. "L'autre est vert" is more obscure; did he have another apron that was green? Did his colleague or successor have a green apron? J. S.

If this little pair of songs give the impression of marking time, that's because they are doing exactly that; 1954 was hardly a good year for Poulenc, despite ongoing work on *Dialogues des Carmélites*. The composer, after a tour of North Africa that failed to bring him any real pleasure, found himself on the edge of a depression that was soon to engulf him in a period of mental anguish more serious than he had ever experienced. Nevertheless, on the surface the music seems supremely cheerful, a Parisian equivalent of the rural party atmosphere of *Les Gars qui vont à la fête* (FP117/ii).

Both poems in *Parisiana* revel in the predicament of the artist who is past his best, almost down-and-out; the fellow-feeling between a poet who had met such a tragic end and the perpetually insecure Poulenc is palpable. The failed writer in this song responds to the question "Don't you write any longer?" with a list of his various part-time jobs—selling newspapers and chestnuts on the streets (the rue de Coquillière is in the Halles district, associated with food), cleaning lavatories, and finally washing dishes in the scullery (the "office") attached to two restaurants famous to this day, Le Richelieu (at the Louvre) and the even more historic Café de la Paix (near the Opéra). He even confesses to having been hauled up in court, probably for vagrancy. But the good humor of it all is not to be taken all that seriously; it conceals the poet's bitter disappointments with his professional life. And as it happens, in December 1958 the Café de la Paix was the scene of a harrowing supper lasting until two in the morning, when Poulenc subjected Stéphane Audel to a tearful jeremiad concerning his health and his lack of fresh ideas—he felt "washed up."[104]

Those who held his hand at times of crisis sometimes thought of Poulenc's depressions as the self-indulgent woes of a spoiled child from a posh background. But the bravado with which Jacob's confession of literary failure is recounted is in the great tradition of working-class defiance, taking bad luck on the chin, and central to the tradition of French chanson. In France it was possible to be a working-class singer striving to be a great writer or, at the very least, a successful *chansonnier*. Maurice Chevalier ("all the pedestrians of Paris in one person," in the opinion of Adrienne Monnier) would have been at home with this music. Poulenc, as we have seen, was an ardent admirer of Chevalier as the working-class charmer who can spin a line, vocal or otherwise: *What touches us most, us other Parisians* ["Parigots"], *is how this voice from Ménilmontant* [a poor, working-class district] *has been turned into something sublime, and with such an art that even thousands of kilometers from Paris it goes straight to the heart of a public that wouldn't even recognize the Faubourg Saint-Martin from a postcard.*"[105]

Chevalier's singing, like much music by Poulenc, makes people who have never visited Paris long to do so, and induces a nostalgia in those who know and love the city well. It is perhaps largely thanks to music that we are able to experience, side by side with the city's natives, a feeling for the allure of Paris and an understanding, easier to feel than to analyze, of what makes it unique in the world.

FP158 *Rosemonde*

Composed in Noizay, May 1954

[*Comtesse Pastré*; Eschig]

Literary source: Guillaume Apollinaire (1880–1918), *Alcools* (Paris: Gallimard, 1913), p. 104 (the only Poulenc song to be taken from this collection)

C major; $\frac{2}{4}$; *Calmement* ♩ = 63

Longtemps au pied du perron de	For a long time at the foot of the stairs
La maison où entra la dame	To the lady's house
Que j'avais suivie pendant deux	Whom I followed for two good hours
Bonnes heures à Amsterdam	In Amsterdam
Mes doigts jetèrent des baisers	My fingers sprinkled kisses
Mais le canal était désert	But the canal was deserted
Le quai aussi et nul ne vit	As was the quayside so no one saw
Comment mes baisers retrouvèrent	How my kisses reached
Celle à qui j'ai donné ma vie	The woman to whom I devoted my life
Un jour pendant plus de deux heures	For one day for over two hours
Je la surnommai Rosemonde	I dubbed her Rosemonde
Voulant pouvoir me rappeler	Never wanting to forget
Sa bouche fleurie en Hollande	Her mouth which bloomed in Holland
Puis lentement je m'en allai	Then slowly I went on my way
Pour quêter la Rose du Monde	On the quest for the Rose of the World

The third verse is multilingual. "Her mouth which bloomed in Holland" leads us to Rose (the bloom) and "Mond" ("mouth" in Dutch), i.e., Rose-monde. That name becomes in the last line "Rose du Monde"—rose of the world or, in Latin, Rosa Mundi, a still-popular rose type (hybrid of the Rosa Gallica, or French Rose). J. S.

Apollinaire took holidays in Holland in 1905, 1906, and 1908, and the incident recounted here (whether his pursuit ended fruitlessly or successfully is less than clear) could have happened during any one of them; or it need never have happened at all. There was never a real Rosemonde in the poet's life (the longer-term lovers are well documented). The name may have been inspired by a lied: Auric claimed that Apollinaire had loved certain Schubert lieder, and the *Romance* from *Rosamunde* was well known in France. There is, however, another clue: lines in one of Apollinaire's earlier Orpheus poems, inserted between some of the animal quatrains of *Le Bestiaire*, that mention in passing "the seven wonders of the world / And the palace of Rosemonde."

The palace of Rosemonde may be the same building as *Le Manoir de Rosemonde*, the title of a song by Henri Duparc (with a poem by Robert de Bonnières that has long mystified singers). In Duparc's song, suggesting a context of medieval balladry, the narrator is bitten by an obsessive love, and is unable to find Rosemonde's "blue manor." As far as Apollinaire is concerned, Rosemonde is the secret and beautiful lover, shut away from the eyes of the world in Amsterdam.

Apart from a tiny fragment from *Le Bestiaire* (see FP162/i below), this song serves as Poulenc's farewell to a poet who had played a crucial part in his life as a song composer. The contours of the piano writing, entwining with the voice, have something in common with the opening section of *Allons plus vite* without approaching that masterpiece in depth or subtlety. Stylistically, we are already standing on the brink of the three sonatas for wind instruments.

Rosemonde was given its first performance in Amsterdam on 12 October 1954, during an exceptionally unhappy tour (see below). Since the city is mentioned in the poem, Poulenc may well have chosen it with that upcoming visit in mind, but there were also other resonances in the poem: Apollinaire's Rosemonde, pursued and then shut away in her palace, is only one of his many women (real and imagined); Poulenc's secret lover Lucien Roubert is accused of infidelities while the composer continues his quest for other excitements. There are those, poet and composer among them, who go on searching for their Rosamondes, in vain, in every town in the world.

THE CRISIS OF 1954

During the composition of *Dialogues des Carmélites*, an extended battle for the rights to use Georges Bernanos's text made Poulenc fear that progress on his opera would be thwarted by legal technicalities. At times, he thought that his Carmelite ladies, who had lost their heads ("*these terrible women*"), were expecting him to sacrifice his own in return.[106] Troubles with the opera have traditionally served as an explanation for why the composer suffered a major nervous breakdown in late 1954— although relatively few people knew at the time that he was seriously ill. Even fewer were aware that the real reason for Poulenc's torment was a traveling salesman named Lucien Roubert, nine years his junior, with whom he had been conducting a secret and tempestuous relationship in the south of France since late 1950. The composer's possessiveness and mistrust of Lucien had become unmanageable, and resulted in a temporary breakup.

One of the most telling documents in the *Correspondance* is a letter Bernac wrote to Poulenc on 4 November 1954. The long-suffering singer, though deeply fond of the composer, was not afraid to speak his mind; he sometimes appointed himself the voice of Poulenc's conscience because he believed his friend and colleague deserved better of himself. The duo had just returned from a concert in Amsterdam (including the first performance of *Rosemonde*), and before they set off on their next tour, this time to Germany, Bernac felt compelled to make clear just how difficult it was to focus on his own work as a singer when Poulenc was obsessed by Lucien and could speak of little else:

> Unfortunately, through your lack of moral virility, you have worn down the affection of this loyal but not very interesting boy. I am sorry for you if you really love him as much as you think you do, something of which I am not entirely convinced. You loved the character you wanted him to play at your side. If you had really loved him you would have loved him for himself and not for you. But that was not the case. As proof, I merely observe that before this breakup you would not have hesitated to form other attachments, yet you were jealous of any that he might have made. In fact, what I would wish most for you now is to see you find someone else, if indeed you have honestly not yet succeeded in finding another formula for your time of life.[107]

The breakup between Lucien and Poulenc proved to be only temporary, and the composer's reply to Bernac, if any, has not survived. But the crisis grew worse. The composer collapsed in mid-tour in Germany and returned to Paris. Conductor Manuel Rosenthal delivered him to a clinic at L'Haÿ-les-Roses in the southern suburbs of Paris, where he was placed in the care of Dr. Maillard Verger.[108] Heavily sedated, Poulenc slept eighteen hours daily for a week, then flew to Cannes and recuperated in Antibes as a guest of Marie-Blanche de Polignac, where he remained until early January 1955.

The tensions of November-December had been building up since at least June of that year, when Poulenc was convinced he had stomach cancer despite medical assurances to the contrary—an imaginary ailment to mirror Lucien's all-too-genuine lung cancer. Less imaginary were ongoing concerns over copyright issues for his opera. His deteriorating mental and physical state was an enormous source of concern for his friends (Auric and Milhaud rallied round with letters of support), and they closed ranks as far as the outside world was concerned, refusing to talk about it. As it happens, two "outsider" Americans are the most revealing witnesses of this period.

John Howard Griffin (1920–1980), a Texan writer, journalist, humanitarian, and social critic, was educated in France; by chance he had been a piano-playing schoolboy in Tours in the late 1930s, near Poulenc's home in Noizay, and had often seen the composer out and about. Having served in the war as an American soldier, he returned some years later to the Touraine, this time as a guest in a local chateau: "Poulenc was to come to lunch that day. None of us looked forward to it. He was too cloying, too precious," and "left one with an oversweet taste and always an undercurrent of panic, of suspected tragedy—of some man helplessly trapped behind a mask."[109]

Griffin was something of an expert on masks. He was later to write *Black Like Me* (1961), an exposé of racial prejudice, after traveling through the South disguised as an African American. But he was fated to encounter Poulenc again in another context, quite different from lunch. Having reached a catastrophic standstill in the summer of 1954, Poulenc wrote the Discalced Carmelite Fathers at the Mount Carmel Seminary in Dallas, begging for their spiritual help so that his opera honoring the history of their order might be completed. Griffin, now back in Texas, was a lay member of the Carmelite order and was appointed its French-speaking (and -writing) spokesman. It was a wonder that Poulenc felt able to unburden himself in letters, almost in the manner of a confession, to a stranger—who was, nevertheless, not the complete stranger he imagined. His initial request for help ("*Will you ask the Carmelite Fathers of Dallas to make a novena that I recover my health and that I may be able to glorify God and the blessed martyrs of Compiègne with my music?*")[110] led, in later letters, to a complete unburdening of his soul. Here is an extract from one of them:

> I find myself so unworthy of your letters, and your concern, that I
> hardly dare write to you. I am a poor sinner and in a state of the
> blackest neurosis. I can no longer play the piano, I can no longer
> work, I have such contempt for myself . . . I have truly the impression
> that I am the devil's puppet. . . . I have sinned so terribly, but how

much I suffer for it. Pray that my soul be saved from eternal fire, because my body and my heart burn on this earth.[111]

When Griffin offered to put Poulenc in touch with a distinguished Dominican "master of souls," his reply was: "*Please, no. I feel bludgeoned by the intelligence of Dominicans. A Dominican would make me lose the remnants of my poor faith in five minutes. No, please send me a poor, ignorant parish priest, someone who is good and will not beat me to death with theology.*"[112]

The second American was the distinguished music and dance critic Allen Hughes (1921–2009), who found himself an observer, at close quarters, of Poulenc's dramatic period of turmoil. In a letter to Virgil Thomson (who may have introduced him to Poulenc), Hughes made an observation that seems never to have occurred to the Parisian insiders: "Just how much Poulenc's Catholicism keeps him from getting the full benefit of psychiatric assistance I don't know. I do feel, however, that this possibility has not been thoroughly enough investigated."[113] The famously hypochondriac Poulenc saw an array of doctors of every kind, but (although he had quoted from the writings of Freud in a 1947 lecture)[114] there was a tendency in Europe of the fifties to scorn the American obsession with psychotherapy. In hindsight, and as we discover more about Poulenc's life (particularly since the publication of the *Correspondance* and the groundbreaking biography of Hervé Lacombe), Hughes's opinion seems perfectly valid.

Poulenc received official permission to use the Bernanos text for *Dialogues* only in March 1955. His recovery was sporadic and gradual, but although he completed *Dialogues des Carmélites*, he seems never to have regained the energy and confidence that characterize his work before 1955. If we divide the composer's life into the conventional early, middle, and late periods, the mid-fifties mark the beginning of the final part of his life and work.

∘ ∘ ∘

FP159 *Dialogues des Carmélites* (opera), 1953–55
FP160 *Bucolique* (from *Variations on the Name Marguerite Long*) (piano), May 1956

∘ ∘ ∘

FRANCIS POULENC AND PAINTING

"Since my earliest childhood I have been passionately fond of painting. I owe to it just as many profound joys as to music."[115]

"If for my piano works I am abstract, for my songs I am, on the contrary, irremediably visual. A poem has to have a picture to tempt me."[116]

Perhaps it was Poulenc's artistic uncle "Papoum," Marcel Royer, who first introduced Francis to painting. At the age of ten he was able to tell the difference between a Cézanne and a Renoir.[117] At thirteen he was looking through art catalogues, in particular that of Henri Rouart (father of music publisher Alexis), who owned a famous collection of impressionists. His route back home from the Lycée Condorcet, via rue Caumartin in the direction of the Faubourg Saint-Honoré, took him to the place de la Madeleine, where he visited the Durand showroom in search of the latest works by Debussy. Nearby on the boulevard de la Madeleine, the Galérie Bernheim-Jeune offered paintings for sale by Bonnard, Vuillard, Cézanne, Seurat, Van Dongen, Le Douanier (Henri) Rousseau, Modigliani, Dufy, Matisse, Utrillo, and Vlaminck.[118] If Debussy was the symbol of the Durand showroom (where Francis was welcomed on account of his precocious interest in music), Renoir was a habitué at the Bernheim. In the eyes of the self-confessedly lonely schoolboy, the showroom and gallery were twin pillars of modern French culture.

During the First World War, when Poulenc was still a teenager, a remarkable series of concerts was given in the Montparnasse studio of the painter Émile Lejeune (1885–1964), named "Lyre et palette," with Erik Satie serving as the musical center of the enterprise. One could see works of Modigliani, Matisse, Picasso, Kisling, Vlaminck, and Gris, and hear readings from the poetry of Max Jacob, Apollinaire, Cocteau, and Blaise Cendrars. In the company of Georges Auric, Poulenc attended concerts devoted to the works of Debussy and Ravel. Hervé Lacombe observed that Poulenc "liked to group together musicians, painters and poets very much in his own way in order to sum up an aesthetic, or sharpen one of his own impressions (for example in comparing Falla and Goya, Duparc and Bazille, Messiaen and Rouault), but also sometimes in his own works, as, for example, was the case when *Le Bestiaire* united Dufy and Apollinaire."[119] *Cocardes* (FP16) goes back to Roger de la Fresnaye, *L'Anguille* (FP58/i) to Toulouse-Lautrec, *Hier* (FP57/iii) to Vuillard.

From these years (1920s to early 30s) also date Poulenc's close friendships with the portrait painter Jacques-Émile Blanche and the painter-poet-designer Marie Laurencin.

To Claude Rostand, Poulenc confirmed that he was attracted to the painting

> *of every period, every country, every school. I have only one kind of memory, visual memory that for my enjoyment prolongs the vision of a work of art or a country scene. I sit down in an armchair, I doze, and suddenly there I am in a particular street in Toledo; I call to mind a simple bunch of white iris in Assisi, or else the long hand on the hip of Donatello's David in the Bargello. . . . Painting has any number of saints whom I revere, whom I venerate: Titian, Tintoretto, Bellini, Raphael, Zurbarán, Goya, Chardin, Watteau, David, Corot, Degas, Cézanne, and so on.*[120]

When asked by Rostand who were his six favorite twentieth-century painters, Poulenc named Matisse, Picasso, Braque, Bonnard, Dufy, and Klee (three of whom would appear in his cycle *Le Travail du peintre*). It is extremely rare to come across a composer able to speak so fluently about painters (in this respect Poulenc resembles Chabrier, an early admirer and purchaser of Manet, Degas, and Cézanne; or Frederick Delius, who owned several Gauguins). Bernac said that "he was not at all interested in discussing philosophy, or politics, but on subjects that appealed to him—music, of course, or literature, and above all, painting. . . . He used to say that he liked painting as much as music, and his memory, not at all good musically, was infallible visually, especially for painting."[121] During his second tour of the United States, in January 1950, Poulenc recorded in a diary his impressions of visits to museums in Boston, New York, and Chicago.[122]

> [Boston] *In a deserted room I found myself suddenly face to face with one of the many paintings of Saint Francis by Zurbarán. . . . My shock was so great at discovering it that I could easily have fallen to my knees. . . . .Depicted in cold grays, muted beiges, terrifying blacks, the painting I say today attains the limits of the sublime.*
>
> [New York] *In a room superbly dominated by three paintings by Ingres, a large oil by David takes my breath away. It is the portrait of Mlle. de Valdogne. I shake off my companion so that I can remain in front of this mysterious masterpiece. . . . Mlle. de Valdogne's expression is at once ironic, mischievous and pensive.*

[Chicago] *Van Gogh exhibition. The more I admire this artist the less I like him. He, Gauguin and El Greco are the three Gs that I could do very well without. Long halt, on the other hand, in front of the famous still-life with white cloth by Chardin. . . . This picture, painted with a sensual perfection, plunges me . . . into an abyss of gourmandise.*[123]

In the unedited version of his *Journal,* Poulenc describes how he and Bernac would plan their recital programs as if they were hanging an exhibition, with oblong diagrams (representing canvases) that contained the names of the songs juxtaposed in the right way to get the correct balance. In one case, the less important songs form a border to the "gallery's" centrepiece: the song *Bleuet.*[124]

FP161 *Le Travail du peintre* (*The Work of the Painter*)
Composed at Le Tremblay (Normandy), August 1956
[*Mme Alice Esty*; Eschig]
Literary source: Paul Éluard (1895–1952), *Voir* (Geneva and Paris: Éditions des Trois Collines, 1948). The book is richly illustrated in color paintings and black and white drawings taken partially from Éluard's own collection. Picasso's drawing of Nusch Éluard, who died on 28 November 1946, precedes the first pages devoted to the painters; the book is thus clearly dedicated to her memory.

(i)   *Pablo Picasso*: p. 12, opposite Picasso's *La Bouteille de rhum* (1911)
(ii) *Marc Chagall*: p. 20, opposite Chagall's *Entre chien et loup* (1938–43)
(iii) *Georges Braque*: p. 38, opposite Braque's *Guitariste (L'Homme à la guitare)* (1914)
(iv) *Juan Gris*: p. 24, opposite Gris's *Poèmes en proses* (1915)
(v)   *Paul Klee*: p. 46, opposite Klee's *Blaubetonter Kopf* (1933)
(vi) *Juan Miró*: p. 56, opposite Miró's *Figure* (1935)
(vii) *Jacques Villon*: p. 29, opposite Villon's *À quatre mains* (1942)

Among the twenty-five other painters illustrated in *Voir,* each with a dedicatory poem by Éluard, are Fernand Léger, Max Ernst, Man Ray, René Magritte, Salvador Dali, Valentine Hugo, Balthus, and Jean Dubuffet.

Poulenc had had his eyes on these poems for quite a long time. He had already selected as his cycle's title Éluard's heading for a group of seven poems about Picasso.[125] He spoke to Éluard about the possibility of setting these poems before the poet's sudden death in 1952: "*I thought it would stimulate my work to paint musically. . . . I asked him for a poem on Matisse, whom I adore. Paul half-promised me. I say half-promised because he did not share my passion for this painter. To my mind, Matisse would have closed the cycle in joy and sunshine. As it is, Villon closes it lyrically and gravely."*[126]

Poulenc had learned a great deal about economy of musical style from studying the drawings of Matisse, which inspired him to pare down to essentials his piano writing,[127] and Apollinaire writes movingly about the painter in *Il y a*. Éluard, however, was so close to his beloved Pablo that he could display only a lukewarm appreciation of Picasso's most serious rival. Still, the composer was undeterred. He wrote to Bernac in 1953: *"More than ever I am determined to write Le Travail du peintre. I shall dedicate the whole cycle to you in letters of gold and*

PAUL ÉLUARD

The cover of Voir, *Éluard's anthology of poems on his favorite artists, illustrated with paintings and drawings largely taken from his own collection.*

I would like to give the first performance in a concert celebrating the twentieth anniversary of our association. I myself will underwrite the financial risk."[128] This was something of a rash promise, as Poulenc already had *Dialogues des Carmélites* on his plate; the offer of a cycle seems to have been something of a promissory note, or consolatory thank you for all Bernac's help and technical advice during the opera's composition. The cycle materialized in August 1956, eighteen months after the anniversary concert, and only after Bernac had found a way of financing it that effectively scuppered his chances of receiving the dedication.

One of the American singers who, thanks to the duo's enormous reputation in the United States, regularly visited Paris to study French song was the soprano Alice Esty (1904–2000). (Another Alice from New York, the celebrated patroness Miss Tully, had also studied French song in Paris, with Jean Périer, the first Pelléas.) A Broadway actress and singer, Alice Swanson had married William Esty, owner of a powerful New York advertising agency, and developed an interest in classical music and French song in particular. She was a straightforward and amicable woman, and, apart from the Princesse de Polignac (Winnaretta Singer) from an older generation, she became the most important of American patrons when it came to the art of the mélodie—a role initiated by contact with her teacher, Bernac. He explained to her that Poulenc had started to compose a cycle based on poems from *Voir*, and that he needed some kind of impetus to get him back to work on the songs. The impetus turned out to be, unsurprisingly, the $1,000 fee that Poulenc soon afterward negotiated in return for the dedication of the cycle, possession of the original manuscript, a first performance with the composer at the piano, and a recording (this last condition was never fulfilled).

Esty also agreed to pay another $1,000 for the manuscript of the Sonata for Two Pianos, which Poulenc had written for the American duo Gold and Fizdale. (To her credit, she nevertheless allowed the pianists to keep the manuscript, which they later donated to the Library of Congress.) On 3 September 1955 Bernac wrote Esty (in English) to inform her that as the opera was nearly complete, Poulenc would be turning to the task of her songs.[129] She visited Noizay soon afterward to sing to Poulenc, occasioning a snide comment from Auric: "This Sunday I imagine you are going to form an opinion on the vocal talents of Mrs. William Esty. I fear that they will not equal those she has shown as a patroness."[130] It was nearly a year later, in August 1956, that the composer sent a postcard from Le Tremblay, informing his American patron that the cycle was at last ready.

Alice Esty gave the first performance of *Le Travail du peintre* at the École Normale de la Musique on 1 April 1957 in a mixed recital, with Poulenc accompanying only his songs (her American pianist played the remainder). Bernac and Poulenc then performed the work at the Edinburgh Festival on 5 September, where it was advertised as a world premiere (and Poulenc afterward always referred to this event as the work's first performance). Esty sang the first American performance the following February in Carnegie Recital Hall, in New York. The dedicatee may not have been a great singer, but her career was honorable, and her ongoing support for song composers had the undoubted effect of encouraging interesting repertoire.[131]

Éluard and Picasso: Castor and Pollux
Éluard wrote his first poem about Picasso in *Capitale de la douleur* (1926), but it was the Spanish Civil War and his towering response to *Guernica* ("La Victoire de Guernica") that cemented one of the greatest artistic friendships of the century. Éluard was not shy about expressing his awe: "From the moment Picasso came onto the scene, the walls caved in." For his entire life the poet was in thrall to the artist-creator "who strove to see all, to project onto man's vision everything that he could understand, accept or transform, represent or transfigure."[132] As Claude Roy put it: "There was between them the only kind of affection that is completely above suspicion—that of equals."[133]

Painter and poet shared their holidays at Mougins in the company of Roland

Penrose and Lee Miller, plus Man Ray and his girlfriend Ady (Adrienne Fidelin), in the three summers of 1936–38. During the war they spent much time together in Paris, at the Café de Flore or the painter's studio in the quai des Grands-Augustins. Nusch Éluard posed again and again for Picasso; there are some seventy portraits of her in all. The great photographer Brassaï, a friend of the painter, described the portrait made in 1941 (*Portrait de Madame Paul Éluard*) as a masterpiece: "Picasso has painted this ethereal creature with all the sweetness and delicacy of which his brush is capable."[134]

During the war years, their collaboration reached its height. In April 1941, Éluard made fifteen handwritten copies of his *Divers poèmes* (later incorporated into *Le Livre ouvert II*), for which Picasso made fifteen different sets of original drawings. It is no wonder that the poet referred to the painter as "mon ami sublime." After Nusch's death, Picasso and his companion Françoise Gilot were witnesses at the marriage of Éluard to his second wife, Dominique. Another of

Picasso and Éluard at Vallauris (in southeastern France), 6 August 1950.

Picasso's companions, Geneviève Laporte, wrote of holidays in St. Tropez with Paul and Dominique, and how enchanting it was to hear the two men "recounting their memories, and discussing painting and poetry."[135]

Poulenc and Picasso: A Friendship Pursued

"Picasso understands music only through astonishing intuition and then more by looking at the composer than listening to his music."[136]

From early on, the young composer saw (and no doubt spoke to) Picasso at various events, including the first performances of *Les Mamelles de Tirésias* and Satie's *Parade* in 1917. He was often a guest at gatherings where Picasso and his wife Olga were also present. On one occasion when Poulenc and Auric performed Couperin, Scarlatti, and Satie, "Picasso confessed that he had a terrible problem staying awake while their compositions were being performed."[137]

Poulenc's *Correspondance* includes ten communications sent to Picasso over the years, with never a sign of a written reply. The first note was from June 1919, when the artist was staying at the Savoy Hotel in London (and thus beginning in English, *"My dear Picasso"*). This was shortly after writing his first letter to Serge Diaghilev, starting with a name-dropping flourish to make even a Russian smile: *"Thanks to Picasso I have at last your address."*[138] A postcard to Picasso from Vienna in 1922 described Poulenc's meeting with Schoenberg and made fun of the Austrian art and music scene; another communication from the same year announced *Les Biches*, two years before it was performed. The young composer was trying his best.

In 1925 Poulenc had to remind the master about a *"promised guitar"* that was to be printed on the cover of his *Poèmes de Ronsard*. It speaks volumes for Poulenc's persistence that he got his drawing, leaving the Picasso *Guitare* to Georges Salles (see Outline, p. 80) in his will.[139] It appears that the painter turned up chez Noailles in 1944 to hear a run-through of Poulenc's *opéra-bouffe Les Mamelles de Tirésias*. According to Cocteau, when he remarked on the "grace, pungency and exquisite freshness" of Apollinaire's text, Picasso replied, "It is perhaps to do with Poulenc that we notice it." Nevertheless, this rare compliment scarcely represented the *amitié intime* with Picasso to which the composer clearly aspired.

Poulenc's request for the painter to make a cover for *Le Travail du peintre* occasioned a small flurry of activity in the spring of 1957. Picasso, in a genial moment, picked up a brush and executed the cover in a trice—almost scrawling the title and the names of poet and composer. Perhaps Poulenc had hoped for more—a design, perhaps even another drawing. On 3 March 1957 Picasso made a graphite drawing of Poulenc sitting in a chair (now preserved in the Musée Picasso in Paris). The drawing, a three-quarter view, somewhat cubist, appears to have been done without a sitting. That December Poulenc wrote his last letter to the painter, regretting not yet having seen his portrait and asking if it could be brought to him by Francine Weisweiller; he hoped it would be possible to reproduce the image on the cover of his forthcoming biography by Henri Hell.[140] This is the last we hear of Picasso's drawing: the book was published with a different cover, and Poulenc did not have the drawing in his possession. Whether he ever paid a visit to Picasso in Cannes (as he had promised in his last letter) is unknown. One did not "drop in" on Picasso unless invited to do so.

(i) *Pablo Picasso*
  C major; $\frac{3}{4}$; *Modéré* ♩ = 63

Entoure ce citron de blanc d'œuf informe	Encircle this lemon with shapeless egg white
Enrobe ce blanc d'œuf d'un azur souple et fin	Coat this egg white in supple delicate blue
La ligne droite et noire a beau venir de toi	That straight black line may well come from you
L'aube est derrière ton tableau	But dawn is behind your painting
Et des murs innombrables croulent	And countless walls crumble away
Derrière ton tableau et toi l'œil fixe	Behind your painting while you, staring fixedly
Comme un aveugle comme un fou	Like a blind man like a madman,
Tu dresses une haute épée dans le vide	Wield a sword high in the void
Une main pourquoi pas une seconde main	A hand—why not one more hand
Et pourquoi pas la bouche nue comme une plume	And why not the mouth naked as a feather
Pourquoi pas un sourire et pourquoi pas des larmes	Why not a smile why not tears
Tout au bord de la toile où jouent les petits clous	At the edge of the canvas where the little nails are playing
Voici le jour d'autrui laisse aux ombres leur chance	This is another man's daylight let darkness take its chances
Et d'un seul mouvement des paupières renonce.	And with a twitch of the eyelids—renounce.

> Picasso *opens the collection: Honor to whom honor is due. Its initial theme, like-wise found a long time ago, served as rootstock for the theme of Mother Marie in* Dialogues des Carmélites. *Here as in the opera* [at the beginning of Act III, marked *Tempo di Sarabande*], *it takes on a tone of pride well suited to the sub-ject. The song, in C major, very distantly recalls the beginning of* Tel jour telle nuit, *but many years have passed since then, and for the musician, C major no longer means peaceful happiness. . . . It is the progress of the prosody with its long run-on lines that gives a lofty tone to this song. Note, before the end, the vocal half-note rest preceding the word "renounce," which to my mind underlines the imperious side of Picasso's painting.*[141]

As Poulenc freely admits, this majestic song sounds like an amplification and metamorphosis of *Bonne journée* from *Tel jour telle nuit*. Hervé Lacombe refers to the dotted-rhythm opening, with its air of Spanish grandeur, as a Baroque French overture—a combination of national attributes that seems an ideal mix for a Spaniard who spent most of his life in France.[142] The song is sung *forte* almost throughout; two *piano* passages (bb. 17–20 and 29–34) adopt the more hushed dynamic seemingly on account of being awestruck by the painter and his creative fecundity (easy to imagine if the observer is Éluard). The art critic J.-C. Gateau proposes that in this poem, "the depths of the painter's unconscious" is speaking; or, as Peter Low puts it, "the silent commands given to Picasso's con-scious mind by his inner genius."[143] Chords, half notes or dotted-half notes in each hand, dominate the song; they suspend their harmonic aura over the follow-ing two beats, as if each colorful cluster of notes represents a brush stroke, or an act of creative willpower on Picasso's part.

Bar 29, one of those rapt *piano* passages, begins a section devoted to the idea of "pourquoi pas"—why not. Why should the artist not paint exactly as he wishes? Who will dare stop or gainsay him? He is someone of enormous, even frighten-ing, energy and utterly uninhibited in creating the picture exactly as he wishes it to be. As the song progresses, it is as though we are seeing a painting take shape before our eyes by an artist who, in defying all convention and happily breaking all the rules, knows no fear and admits no boundaries. His brushstrokes con-tinue until the moment *he* decides his work is finished. Here is the moment of renunciation—the song's final line and the sudden triumphalism of the closing flourish of chords. (With this final, unresolved seventh chord left hanging in the air, we may be reminded of Paul Valéry's line about a poem never being finished, only abandoned.) This is the nearest that Poulenc ever came to creating a portrait in song of a living person. The other painters in the cycle were less known to him personally (with the exception of Juan Gris), and their mélodies seem to evoke an appreciation for their painting; awe and veneration for the person together with the work is Picasso's due alone.

Éluard and Chagall: A Late-Blossoming Friendship

Marc Chagall (1887–1985) was born in Vitebsk, Russia (now Belarus), in a financially impoverished but culturally rich Hasidic community, and eventually studied with Léon Bakst in St. Petersburg. In Paris in 1910, he met, among others, Max Jacob and Apollinaire—becoming part of the artistic life of Montparnasse that Poulenc was too young to experience for himself. Chagall spent the years of the First World War back in Russia as a member of the (temporarily admired) avant-garde before returning to France in 1923. During the Second World War, following a dangerously late decision to flee France in 1941, Chagall became an honored refugee in the United States; he moved back to France in 1948.

Chagall's whimsical and dreamlike art, often resembling a film montage, was influenced by his Jewish and Russian roots: images such as clowns, flying lovers, fantastic animals, and biblical figures abound in a processional melee of ideas that is entirely his own, and that prompted Apollinaire first to think in terms of surrealism. In the course of an exceptionally fecund and energetic career, Chagall also became a printmaker and designer of stage sets. We know from a 1938 sales catalogue that Éluard owned several Chagalls then, and photographs taken of the Éluard apartment in the rue de la Chapelle two years later show two of them, including a cubist still life from 1912.

The painter opened up his collection of drawings and paintings to Éluard, who penned words in response to his selected images—the opposite procedure of the one usually followed in illustrating a literary work, but an approach that produced most satisfactory results. Éluard's *Le Dur désir de durer*, nineteen poems with Chagall illustrations, was published at the end of 1946. His poem "Marc Chagall" first appeared the following year, in the preface to an illustrated volume of thirteen Chagall paintings entitled *Peintures 1942–1945*.

Poulenc and Chagall: An Arranged Marriage

Both Chagall and Poulenc nourished magical connections with their past in order to enrich their work. Chagall's open letter to his hometown of Vitebsk, written years after he had left Russia, confides, "I didn't have a single painting that didn't breathe with your spirit and reflection."[144] The same may almost be said of Poulenc's musical connection with Nogent-sur-Marne. In their own ways, painter and composer drew on memories of an idealized and magical childhood (though hugely different) for the rest of their creative lives.

Poulenc seems to have had no personal contact with Chagall before composing a song in his honor. When he finished the cycle, he sent copies of the score to the five painters who were still alive; three did not respond, but Chagall did, with great charm and humility: "I am flattered and delighted at the same time to have received your songs on the painters—including me—on poems by our great friend and poet Paul Éluard. It is true that I am only a lover of music heard by ear. . . . I was present at the first performance of *Les Biches* given by the Ballet russe [*sic*]. Thank you again, I shake your hand cordially."[145]

Chagall was commissioned to paint the ceiling of the Paris Opéra in 1964, and he created large murals for the newly built Metropolitan Opera in New York two years later. His greatest engagements with music and musicians thus post-date the composition of this cycle.

(ii)   *Marc Chagall*
          No key signature; $\frac{3}{4}$; *Molto prestissimo* ♩. = 96, one in a bar

Ane ou vache coq ou cheval	Donkey or cow cockerel or horse
Jusqu'à la peau d'un violon	Down to the skin of a violin
Homme chanteur un seul oiseau	A singing man a single bird
Danseur agile avec sa femme	An agile dancer with his wife
Couple trempé dans son printemps	A couple steeped in their own springtime
L'or de l'herbe le plomb du ciel	The gold of the grass the lead of the sky
Séparés par les flammes bleues	Separated by the blue flames
De la santé de la rosée	Of the health-giving dew
Le sang s'irise le cœur tinte	The blood glistens the heart rings
Un couple le premier reflet	A couple the first reflection
Et dans un souterrain de neige	And in a cavern of snow
La vigne opulente dessine	The opulent vine draws
Un visage aux lèvres de lune	A face with lips like the moon
Qui n'a jamais dormi la nuit.	Which has never slept at night.

"Chagall *is a kind of rambling scherzo*," Poulenc tells us. "*Strange objects pass in the sky. A poetic somersault brings us back to the human being.*"[146] Lacombe finds it "a *valse-musette* that encompasses a dream world."[147] When compared with the imposing solidity of *Picasso, Chagall* is entirely different in texture. If the first song is analytical, this one is fantasist. These are wisps of sound and melody, fanciful and fleet, that are amusing and finally touching. The entire song is derived from the opening bars, a triumph of motivic variation in which various aspects of Chagall's phantasmagorical imagination are tied together into a creative unity. The last page (beginning "Un visage aux lèvres de lune"), *pianissimo*, becomes a magical nocturne—the madcap pace calmed from three fast quarter notes in a bar to vocal duplets supported by strands of piano arpeggios gently sidling up and down the keyboard.

Having begun in the somewhat grotesque key of E-flat minor, the second half of the song is in a consolatory F-sharp major. The piano writing throughout must sound fanciful and fragile. An impish five-bar postlude, suddenly returning to the minor tonality, is like a signature mischievously affixed to a canvas and brings the listener down to earth with a knowing wink. *Chagall* is a song that teases, above all the busy fingers of the pianist.

Éluard and Braque: Disdain, Admiration, Distance

Many a study has been made of the important friendship between Picasso and Georges Braque (1882–1963). In the years before the First World War, they were almost the Freud and Jung of cubism: they worked so closely at one point that it was inevitable that there should be alienation, and that each should subsequently follow his own path.

In a 1921 issue of *Littérature,* in which Dadaists were asked to "mark" great artists and musicians with scores between plus and minus 25, Éluard accorded Braque the embarrassingly low grading of minus 10. Nevertheless, Éluard bought a number of Braques in the early 1920s, the most important of which is illustrated in *Voir.* The painter developed a close relationship with the important poet René Char (1907–1988), whom Éluard no doubt considered a rival (and by whose work Pierre Boulez was endlessly fascinated).[148] Char's *Lettera amorosa* was illustrated by Braque.

Braque's paintings are robust, serene, and meditative. He was first influenced by Cézanne and Les Fauves in 1905; later, through the dealer David Henry Kahnweiler, he met Apollinaire, who in turn took him to Picasso's Montmartre studio, where he encountered the shock of *Les Demoiselles d'Avignon* (1907). When Braque added Cézanne-inspired geometrical forms to what he learned from Picasso, cubism was born, and it was as if the two painters were roped together like Alpine climbers in the exploration of modernity (1911–14). Braque initiated the concept of "papier collé" (collage made of pasted papers) and, with stenciled letters and wallpaper, the concept of a picture as an autonomous object rather than a representation.

Braque's career was long, distinguished, and extremely prosperous. After the war he concentrated on groups of paintings on a single subject: billiard tables, studio interiors, and large birds that seem to be symbols of something ancient and profound. His life's work was crowned by many public honors.

Poulenc and Braque: The Work, Not the Man

Braque came from the same kind of upper-middle-class background as Poulenc. Unlike the composer, he was a sportsman and as fit as an athlete, a strikingly handsome figure on the Parisian scene, and his friends included Poulenc's piano teacher, Ricardo Viñes. An amateur flautist, Braque was present at the first performance of Satie's *Socrate* in June 1919 and collaborated with Auric on the Molière-based ballet *Les Fâcheux,* in Monte Carlo for the Ballets Russes, five years later. He acquired Satie's piano from Arcueil after that composer's death.[149]

Poulenc remembered sitting on the terrace of Monte Carlo's Le Café de Paris, after ballet rehearsals in 1924, with a group that included Braque and Picasso;[150] and he numbered Braque third (after Picasso and Matisse) on his list of favorite painters. And yet on the composer's side there seems to have been little desire to form a friendship with this patrician and rather formidable man, one of whose aphorisms separates him definitively from Poulenc's aesthetic: "I love the rule that corrects emotion."[151] But the composer's admiration of Braque's painting, and his pleasure in it, are evident in his song.

(iii)   *Georges Braque*
No key signature; $^6_8$–$^2_4$; *Surtout pas lent (sans traîner)* ♩ = 63

Un oiseau s'envole,	A bird takes flight,
Il rejette les nues comme un voile inutile,	He shrugs off the clouds like a redundant veil,
Il n'a jamais craint la lumière,	He has never feared the light,
Enfermé dans son vol,	Trapped in his flight,
Il n'a jamais eu d'ombre.	He has never had a shadow.
Coquilles des moissons brisées par le soleil.	Harvest husks split by the sun.
Toutes les feuilles dans les bois disent oui,	All the leaves in the woods say yes,
Elles ne savent dire que oui,	All they know is to say yes,
Toute question, toute réponse	Every question, every answer,
Et la rosée coule au fond de ce oui.	And the dew flows at the heart of that yes.
Un homme aux yeux légers décrit le ciel d'amour.	A light-eyed man describes the sky of love.
Il en rassemble les merveilles	He gathers its miracles
Comme des feuilles dans un bois,	Like leaves in a forest,
Comme des oiseaux dans leurs ailes	Like a bird in its wings
Et des hommes dans le sommeil.	Like men in their sleep.

"Braque is the most subtle of the songs, the most detailed in the collection. It is perhaps too mannered, but that is how I feel about Braque. It must be accompanied with precision, and above all, from the beginning a tempo must be taken that is not too slow, suitable for the concluding 'Un homme aux yeux légers.'"[152]

Although there are no birds in the Braque paintings illustrated in *Voir*, birds certainly seemed to be associated with Braque in the mind of Éluard as he wrote this poem. More important, Poulenc must also have thought of the painter in avian terms: the cycle was composed around the time of a series of bird paintings Braque created in 1955–62, and it is possible that Poulenc had visited a recent exhibition; in any case, the painter had designed a postage stamp of a bird in flight that was almost certainly attached to some of the composer's letters.

The song is divided into two distinct sections. In the first, birdsong is heard in the pianistic decorations of the second bar, and the flight of large birds—wafting and floating rather than darting—is meticulously depicted. The music is written in two-bar and one-bar phrases, and the harmonic language is chromatic in a way that is unusual for this composer; we might almost call these twistings and turnings too mannered, too fastidious. Even the precision Poulenc calls for requires the pianist to think harder than usual merely to play right notes. In comparison with the broad sweep of many a Poulenc mélodie, a word to sum this music up may be "intricate"—or, less flattering, "fiddly."

Such intricacy may be Poulenc's reaction to Braque the mathematically precise craftsman. But the composer admired his canvases, and that the song is nevertheless a beautiful one goes without saying. With the human tenderness of "Un homme aux yeux légers" the music changes course and deepens—we now glimpse the great painter as opposed to the formidable artisan. The quietly rocking left-hand eighth notes that drift up the stave like dreams, inspiration rising from the depths, are unlike anything else in Poulenc; indeed, the same may be said about the entire song. The imagery of birds' wings and of men asleep dovetails most beautifully at the end.

Éluard and Gris: Early and Enduring Admiration

Juan Gris (pseudonym of José Victoriano González-Pérez, 1887–1927) was born in Madrid and studied there as an engineer. He began making drawings in Art Nouveau style, and moved to Paris in 1906, where he lived in the Bateau-Lavoir (see p. 28) at the time Picasso and Braque were developing their mutually challenging explorations of cubism. Éluard owned at least four still lifes by Gris.

Before the war, the painter came up with a style known as synthetic cubism. In Robert Hughes's words, "Dickering with his bottles, violins, fruit dishes, newspapers, pipes, siphons, and fruit, Gris—so the conventional account runs—wanted to construct an ideal world, a nirvana of the inanimate, whose planes and contours fitted together in their complex reversals and transparencies like a perfectly thought-out puzzle: metaspace, as it were, a place beyond touch, in which only the eye can travel."[153]

After the First World War, Gris developed an increasingly personal style, liberated from rules and more lyrical. His friendship with Matisse, from 1914, considerably influenced that painter; Picasso remarked of Gris, "Disciples see more clearly than their masters."[154] Gris's lucidly composed still lifes represent rigorous Castillian theory and control, as opposed to the Catalan flair and improvisation of Picasso, but are not without their own warmth and fantasy. Éluard clearly admired Gris, but the poem that honors him was written specially for *Voir* in 1948, the first time the poet had penned any response to his work.

Poulenc and Gris: The Dove of Memory

Gris is the only artist in *Le Travail du peintre* that Poulenc knew better (on first-name terms) than Éluard did. He was also the only one of the cycle's painters with whom Poulenc could claim to have collaborated. As diverting sideshows for the splendid 1924 season of the Ballets Russes at Monte Carlo, Diaghilev directed four composers to write new recitatives for three *opéras comique*: Satie was to provide the music for *Le Médecin malgré lui*, Auric for *Philémon et Baucis*, and Poulenc for *La Colombe* (all by Gounod); Milhaud was entrusted with Chabrier's *Une éducation manquée*. Diaghilev also assigned designers to the various works; for *La Colombe*, the artist was Juan Gris. Poulenc confessed to Milhaud in July 1923 that he had hidden *La Colombe* in the depths of a cupboard; "*for the mise-en-scène of* Colombe *I have Gris. I would have preferred something else.*"[155]

The production was counted a great success for Poulenc, whose skill in writing pastiche went hand in hand with his ability to copy the music of earlier composers for his own purposes. But Gris had a harder time of it: "I have had a lot of trouble with *Colombe*, as on the day we put it up in the theater—last Tuesday—I saw that the colors were nothing like those of the design. The painters have got to repaint all the scenery. . . . [Spanish soprano Maria] Barrientos' dress . . . is nothing like my design and does not look right. . . . I cannot wait to get away from this infuriating milieu."[156] Thirteen weeks working in such an atmosphere contributed to a slow downturn in Gris's health. Long subject to uremia and cardiac problems, he died in Bolougne on 11 May 1927 of renal failure, just when he was gradually overcoming the obstacle of being overshadowed by Picasso and Braque. The tone of Poulenc's entry in his *Journal* indicates that his association with Gris was far more than brusquely professional: "Gris *is the song that I had first sketched out several years ago. I have always greatly admired this painter, and very much liked him as a man, this poor worthy and unfortunate Juan who is only beginning to take the place he deserves.*"[157]

That this was the first of the Éluard songs about poets that Poulenc attempted suggests that he was probably drawn to its subject matter on account of nostalgic memories of those days in Monte Carlo—an "infuriating milieu" perhaps, but one that in retrospect, at least, was part of a golden age of music and art.

(iv)   *Juan Gris*
A minor; $\frac{3}{4}$; *Très calme* ♩ = 56

De jour merci de nuit prends garde	By day give thanks by night beware
De douceur la moitié du monde	Of sweetness which is half the world
L'autre montrait rigueur aveugle	The other half showed blind rigor
Aux veines se lisait un présent sans merci	In its veins you could read a merciless present
Aux beautés des contours l'espace limité	In the beauties of its contours bounded space
Cimentait tous les joints des objets familiers	Cemented all the joints of familiar objects
Table guitare et verre vide	Table guitar and empty glass
Sur un arpent de terre pleine	On an acre of earth full of
De toile blanche d'air nocturne	White canvas of night air
Table devait se soutenir	Table to keep itself upright
Lampe rester pépin de l'ombre	Lamp to stay at the core of the darkness
Journal délaissait sa moitié	Newspaper relinquished half of itself
Deux fois le jour deux fois la nuit	Twice the day twice the night
De deux objets un double objet	From two objects a double object
Un seul ensemble à tout jamais.	One single whole for ever more.

"*The whole song is poignantly melancholy*," Poulenc writes, and the tone of the poem itself is elegiac; Éluard as well as Poulenc had been affected by the story of a hugely gifted man who had not reached his full potential. J.-C. Gateau sees the poem as "first a criticism of realistic painting, which showed only the beauty of contours and surfaces, and then praise for Gris's synthetic cubism, capable of showing objects as a single whole."[158]

Poulenc illustrates these two facets with the contrast between minor and major tonality. It is the most sparse of the cycle's songs in pianistic terms—the composer might say the most Matisse-like, appropriate to an artist who claimed the kind of close links to Matisse that most followers of Picasso did not. The marking is *mezzo forte* and the mood one of strength and determination, despite the slow tempo. The left hand begins alone, then is joined by the right hand, drifting down the keyboard in a spare countermelody that only adds to the music's calm and majestic equilibrium. The opening vocal line ("De jour merci de nuit prends garde") announces the duality of minor and major tonality that we might call an Éluard motif (see the opening and closing songs in C major/minor in *Tel jour telle nuit*). Here the difference is between A minor and A major, a shift with positively Schubertian resonances; and Poulenc's favorite Schubert songs were the last two in *Winterreise, Die Nebensonnen* (in A major) and *Der Leiermann* (in A minor).[159]

At "Aux beautés des contours" harmony and dynamic burst into a glorious effulgence, together with Poulencian hallmarks: cushioned chords in both hands, *forte* yet without bombast; and a quieter movement of subsidiary eighth notes, in the wake of dotted half notes and incorporated into their radiance. Six bars in this rhetorical dynamic are followed by "Table guitare et verre vide," words that incorporate a minor third (F, G, A-flat); then "Sur un arpent de terre pleine" and a major third, F, G, A-natural. In a mere semitone, a change from minor to major tonality, we sense the clearing of an obstacle, an epiphany in the creative process—Gris discovering something profound about his art or the spectator being taught to *see* (the real meaning of *Voir*), in a different way.

The lines "Table devait se soutenir / Lampe rester pépin de l'ombre" return us to the A minor/major of the opening. Then "Deux fois le jour deux fois la nuit" is lifted into a higher region of the stave, wavering between C-sharp minor and major. The song thus creates an impression of organic development, the artist growing and spreading his wings, even if in a dream or in another life. And the C-sharp minor ending leaves us suspended in time, with unfinished business and a destiny unfulfilled. Apart from the fact that *Juan Gris* is primarily a setting of Éluard's words, we sense that it was written with tender affection. One could be fond of this vulnerable painter, in a way that it was impossible to be "fond" of a Picasso or, by analogy, a Beethoven.

Éluard and Klee: A Foreign Master

Paul Klee (1879–1940) was born near Bern, Switzerland, although throughout his life he retained German citizenship through his father. During a Swiss exile from Germany that began in late 1933, he was excoriated by the Nazis, and his works were held up as terrible examples of degenerate art. He died before the Swiss, despite his "offensive modernism," had agreed to make him a citizen. Of all the cycle's painters, Klee was the probably the most musical, certainly the most musically educated: his mother was a singer and his father a music teacher. Young Paul was an accomplished violinist, poet, and writer. His youthful dislike of twentieth-century music played a role in his decision to pursue modernity in visual forms instead.

Klee studied with the genre painter Franz von Stuck in Munich, and visited Italy (realizing that his greatest task would lie in the assimilation of color) before returning to Bern and the black-and-white caricatures that expressed his sardonic nature. In 1911 he met Wassily Kandinsky and Franz Marc, becoming part of the editorial team of the *Der blaue Reiter* almanac. By 1920 he was able to mount a retrospective exhibition of 300 paintings. Lectures on art for the Bauhaus in Weimar (1925–31) initiated the geometric phase of his output and the pointillist paintings, with their mosaic-like surfaces of colored dots.

In 1928 Éluard sent a collection of his poems to Klee in Weimar; the painter, then teaching at the Bauhaus, replied that he would like to illustrate some of them, but sadly, nothing came of it. Picasso, another enthusiast, visited Klee in Switzerland before the war. Despite the menace of Nazism, the 1930s were an incredible period of productivity for Klee. *Blue-Toned Head*, printed in *Voir*, dates from 1933, the year he was chased out of Germany for his "offensive" art. It was one of three Klee paintings in Éluard's possession (he also owned several watercolors)—the head painted in various shades of blue and brown, above it green, the nose white, a slab of yellow at the chest, and the eyes black.

Poulenc and Klee: Germanic Modernism

It seems likely that Poulenc visited a 1925 Klee exhibition in the Galerie Vavin-Raspail in Paris, for which Éluard wrote the *Voir* poem; it is the kind of event that the young composer would have attended with relish. On Poulenc's list of favorite painters, as shared with Claude Rostand in 1954, Klee was the only one who had never resided in France. We hear nothing from the composer about specific pictures he might have admired, but he must have known those belonging to Marie-Laure de Noailles.

Apart from the great masters and a few contemporary exceptions, Poulenc pooh-poohed Teutonic attempts at modernity; most were lacking in elegance and élan, in his eyes. A postcard he sent to Picasso from a trip to Vienna in February 1922 pokes schoolboy fun at what he took to be Austrians' misguided attempts to master such styles as cubism, and their clunky and lugubrious attempts at modern poetry, poetry he was not able to understand anyway. "*Vive Paris*," he writes chummily to the painter.

The strangest juxtaposition in all the Poulenc photographs is one taken of him in 1922 with Arnold Schoenberg (in Mödling, Austria), a composer whose music he claimed to revere before and during that fleeting visit to Vienna, but later openly disliked. One had to admire *Pierrot lunaire*, but the later Schoenberg? In one of his extremely rare polemical outbursts, in an article written in

1945, he declares, *"I cannot imagine more than one reader in a hundred being able to take an interest in Schoenberg's music, 'predodecaphonic' or not."*[160] He also refers in the same article to *"la lucidité poétique de Paul Klee"* (in comparison with Kokoschka's Expressionism, clearly rotten in his eyes).[161] But we have a right to ask ourselves whether, after those early years of admiration, the art of Paul Klee still spoke to Poulenc in 1956 as "lucidly poetic." Did he truly like the *Blue-Toned Head*? The deliberate aridity of his song raises certain doubts.

(v) *Paul Klee*
No key signature (B-flat minor); $\frac{2}{4}$; *Implacablement vite* ♩ = 166

Sur la pente fatale le voyageur profite	On the fatal slope the traveler benefits from
De la faveur du jour, verglas et sans cailloux,	The favor of the day, iced over and without pebbles,
Et les yeux bleus d'amour, découvre sa saison	And his eyes blue with love, he can find his season
Qui porte à tous les doigts de grands astres en bague.	Which wears on each finger huge stars as rings.
Sur la plage la mer a laissé ses oreilles	On the beach the sea has left its shell-like ears
Et le sable creusé la place d'un beau crime.	And churned up sand the scene of some lovely crime.
Le supplice est plus dur aux bourreaux qu'aux victimes	The execution is tougher on the hangman than the victim
Les couteaux sont des signes et les balles des larmes.	Knives are clues and bullets are tears.

Paul Klee confirms that the composer was understandably more concerned to plan an effective song cycle (*"I needed a presto here. It is a dry song that must go with a bang"*)[162] than to create accurate portraits of the selected poets and/or their work. And when the painter was Klee, someone whom he had almost certainly never met, a German speaker who had been dead sixteen years, "poetic lucidity" had to be sacrificed for something more brutal and lively, a bridging song to "trampoline" the listener into the next significant musical statement (*Joan Miró*). We could argue that lively brutality is included in Klee's list of attributes, alongside his delicacy. It seems to me, however, that here we are getting Poulenc's sketch of the crotchety aridity of the German temperament, all the better to highlight the resplendent Latin muse of Miró—good program-planning in a way, but unfair in terms of art history, considering how much Miró owed to Klee's example. One cannot help thinking that the stature of Klee as one of the greatest of all modern artists deserved something better than this music.

Of all the explosive and rather empty trampoline songs Poulenc wrote (*Je nommerai ton front* FP98/ii is another), *Paul Klee* is surely the most brusque; "the poem and the music not among the best," says Bernac ruefully, "it does not need subtlety of interpretation."[163] Perhaps Poulenc was aiming for music of a Swiss precision to reflect the geometric patterns of the painter's work, everything sounding vertical without a sign of a horizontal line. In any case, *Klee* is the least "French" song by Poulenc, and probably the least lyrical of them all.

This may have been an emotional reaction to the forces that were rocking Poulenc's world. As he came to the end of his song-writing career, all the modernisms he had gleefully flirted with or embraced as a young man now threatened to engulf him and his music. He had been in the vanguard of fashion; but he was now threatened by a new German invasion, a more sinister manifestation of the modernity that he had once espoused. Pierre Boulez and other Parisian disciples of René Leibovitz (1913–1972, a pupil of Webern and Schoenberg) were being furnished with their weapons for the coming twelve-tone war by the same Germanic armory Poulenc had found so diverting and easy to flirt with and patronize in 1922 Vienna.

As for paintings, it tells us something that when Poulenc visited galleries in the United States in 1959, he chose to dwell on the art of Zurbarán, David, and Chardin rather than the innumerable twentieth-century masterpieces on display.

Éluard and Miró: Posthumous Collaboration

Joan Miró (1893–1983), born in Barcelona, son of a watchmaker and goldsmith, made his first drawings when he was eight years old. In his teens he read magazines featuring the work of Apollinaire, Max Jacob, and Pierre Reverdy. In 1917 he met and absorbed the Dadaist ideas of Francis Picabia, recently returned from New York, and was further influenced by Klee and by a study of the Dutch realists. During the war Miró got to know Marie Laurencin, living in Spanish exile with her German husband.

In the winter of 1920, inevitably, Miró came to Paris and set up a studio. There he met Andre Breton, Louis Aragon, and Éluard, and contributed paintings to the "Exposition surréaliste" at the Galerie Pierre in 1925. The art historian John Richardson found Miró to be a "very small, very courteous, very reticent man with just a touch of the troglodyte. . . . Although the Surrealists acclaimed Miró's attainments, they were slightly ashamed of his lack of Surrealist nerve and verve and intellectual clout."[164]

But Miró found the companionship of this group of artists essential to his well-being, and attached great importance to Éluard's opinion of his work.[165] The

Éluard poem here first appeared in *Capitale de la douleur* (1926), at a time when the painter's work most leaned toward surrealism. In Monte Carlo, Miró collaborated with Max Ernst on the décor for the 1926 ballet *Roméo et Juliette* (music by Constant Lambert) for the Ballets Russes, and provided the sets for Bizet's *Jeux d'enfants* (choreographed by Léonide Massine) in 1932. For the Republic of Spain's pavilion at the Paris World Exhibition of 1937, Miró painted the brutal *Le Faucheur* (*The Reaper*, or *The Catalan Peasant in Revolt*, since disappeared), a rare political statement; Picasso's contribution to the same pavilion was *Guernica*.

Miró returned to Spain during the Second World War, and afterward divided his time between Spain and Paris as he continued to work in multifarious fields—accepting gigantic public commissions and creating monumental murals. In May 1948 he agreed to illustrate Éluard poems in woodcut for a new edition of *À toute épreuve* (originally published in 1930). The link was the painter's native Catalonia, where Éluard and his wife Gala had visited Salvador Dali at the time the poems were written. Such was Miró's perfectionism that by the time of Éluard's death in 1952, only a third of the woodcuts were ready. The new illustrated edition of *À toute épreuve*, published by Gerald Cramer in Geneva, finally appeared in 1958.

Poulenc and Miró: A Distant Sun

Miró is the youngest of the painters depicted in Poulenc's cycle, less than six years older than the composer, but perhaps the least accessible on account of his shyness. John Richardson again: "Picasso, who had been one of Miró's first collectors and had known him well for half a century, said that you could live with him for years on end without learning the first thing about him."[166]

What hope, then, had Poulenc of friendship with this man? Miró's outlook on life and art, his determination to remain the Catalan *petit bourgeois*, were singularly unsuited to Poulenc's conversational urbanities. The painter disliked people he took to be glamorous and superficial, despite the considerable money he made—particularly in later life from a succession of rich patrons with exactly these attributes. His pictures were displayed at Marie-Laure de Noailles' avant-garde home in Hyères—which once led Jeremy Sams to wonder if she intoned, "Oh Miró, Miró, on the wall," as she gloated over her legendary collection.

(vi)   *Joan Miró*
No key signature; $\frac{4}{4}$; *Allegro giocoso* ♩ = 144

Soleil de proie prisonnier de ma tête,	Sun of prey imprisoned in my head,
Enlève la colline, enlève la forêt.	Get rid of the hill, get rid of the forest.
Le ciel est plus beau que jamais.	The sky's more beautiful than ever.
Les libellules des raisins	Dragonflies grapes

| Lui donnent des formes précises | Can lend it precise shapes |
| Que je dissipe d'un geste. | Which I erase with a wave of the hand. |

Nuages du premier jour,	Clouds of the first day,
Nuages insensibles et que rien	Unfeeling clouds which nothing
n'autorise,	sanctions,
Leurs graines brûlent	Their seeds burn
Dans les feux de paille de mes regards.	In the straw fires of my glances.

À la fin, pour se couvrir d'une aube	Finally, to cover itself with dawn
Il faudra que le ciel soit aussi pur que	The sky has to be as pure as night.
la nuit.	

A saying attributed to Miró more or less describes what it feels like to play this song: "I work in a state of passion, transported. When I begin a canvas, I'm obeying a physical impulse, the need to throw myself; it's like a physical outlet . . . for me a painting should give off sparks."[167] The song *Joan Miró* conveys exactly this éclat—a sunlit joy in color and a celebration of the visual sensuality of painting. John Richardson writes that Miró would "barricade himself in his studio and, as he confessed, go completely wild," dipping all ten fingers into the paint and playing with it "like a pianist."[168] One remembers Poulenc's throbbing celebration of the "Midi" (even more riotous in pianistic terms) in *Aussi bien que les cigales* (*Calligrammes*, FP140/vi).

Elsewhere, Miró calls his pictures "tiny forms in huge empty spaces. Empty spaces, empty horizons, empty plains—everything which is bare has always greatly impressed me."[169] The wonderful five-bar introduction here is an extraordinary evocation of just this kind of sunlit space. It has a Stravinskian energy and is in fact a distant, more energetic variant of the A major motif from that composer's *Serenade in A* (which opens *Tout disparut* FP147/iii), where the music seems stuck in an A major groove that doubles back on itself, as if savoring its own euphony. In this music, euphony is replaced by jubilance: A major chords, anchored in a similarly repetitive groove, are jarringly, magnificently decorated by the addition of G-sharps. These flagrant clashes are what generate the heat, enabling a quasi-orchestral burst of color from the piano that lasts twelve bars.

The remainder of the song is somewhat different from this bracing introductory paean. Following an extraordinary single bar (b. 12), a *fortissimo* flourish at the piano of spontaneous painterly temperament, the singer has some breathing space to begin the line "Les libellules des raisins," suddenly *piano*. Music of childlike wonder, poised high in the voice, now addresses the introspective aspect of Miró's art. Interestingly enough, Poulenc devotes the few lines he writes about the song to the interpretation of this very passage: "Miró: *The most difficult to interpret with its sudden passing from strident outburst to softness and lyricism on the words 'Les libellules des raisins.' The* céder beaucoup *on 'Que je dissipe d'un geste' and the* [gradual] *return to the tempo cannot be explained—it must be felt.*"[170]

There are other unusual tempo changes. Within a *rallentando,* the "wave of the hand" mentioned in the text is made to sound thoughtful and careful rather than reckless and imperious. Thus we have the two sides of Miró's art perfectly illustrated, the utterly spontaneous and the almost laboriously considered. The final phrase, "aussi pur que la nuit," takes flight into an aerial sphere, ornamented by pianistic birdsong. Back in the tempo of the opening, the postlude retraces the melodic contours of the introductory paean, now reduced to its essentials—as though an idea tamed and given more economical shape by Miró's legendary, and self-questioning, discipline.

Éluard and Villon: The Light Seen from Within

Jacques Villon (1875–1963) was born into a prosperous family in Normandy, and suffered from the fact that he was the eldest of a veritable dynasty of gifted artists: Raymond Duchamp-Villon (1876–1918) was a sculptor, Marcel Duchamp (1887–1968) was a modernist painter who quickly acquired the kind of legendary (and deserved) fame that would dampen the ambitions of any sibling, and Suzanne Duchamp-Crotti (1889–1963) was also a painter. In order to differentiate himself from his more famous brother Marcel, Jacques took the surname of his favorite medieval author, François Villon. He moved to Paris in 1894, when he was old enough to fall under the influence of Degas and Toulouse-Lautrec. Although he was drawn into the circles of the fauvists and cubists, he had an impressionist's command of color. He did not disdain the more commercial world of drawings and enjoyed illustrating books.

Villon's decision to leave Montmartre and return to Puteaux in the quiet outskirts of Paris, in order to develop at his own pace, contributed greatly to an isolation that did not help his cause in terms of marketability. (He was to die in the same Puteaux studio at the age of eighty-eight.) His important work in drypoint and printmaking were part of this voluntary withdrawal. In the end, Villon was one of those artists who had been around for so long that he was regularly taken for granted and overlooked. The first publication about his work was an illustrated monograph of twenty-five pages that appeared in 1944, when he was sixty-nine.

Éluard owned a number of Villon canvases, and a drawing of a nude from 1942 that was dedicated to him. The poet seems to have decided that something needed to be done to publicize the work of an essentially forgotten master, and in 1948 he published a book entitled *Jacques Villon, ou L'Art glorieux*—the very title of which conveys the poet's high opinion. This push on Villon's behalf (for which he seems to have been modestly grateful) led to a reassessment of his work. When the painter was seventy-eight (1953), two retrospective exhibitions were held in New York. And in 1956, the year Poulenc composed the cycle, Villon was awarded the Grand Prix at the Venice Biennale—an international success Éluard did not live to see.

Poulenc and Villon: Illuminating the Obscure

When Poulenc decided to end his cycle with a big and important song about Villon, the painter was no longer the nonentity or poor relation of some years earlier. His stock was at last on the rise, and about time too, at age eighty-one. When Poulenc sent out scores to the five artists who were still alive, Villon's was the second of the two replies he received: "Cher Monsieur, Mon cher Maître, I have just received *Le Travail du peintre*. Believe me that in associating me with your work you do me great honor, and I am very aware of that. I thank you for this. . . . I would take great pleasure in meeting you when I return to Paris in October."[171] Whether the meeting took place, whether Poulenc bothered to make it happen (he normally left some record of his interactions with celebrated people), we shall probably never know. Perhaps, as was his wont, Villon slipped just as invisibly and enigmatically out of Poulenc's ken as the poem of Éluard had brought him into it.

(vii) *Jacques Villon*
No key signature (B-flat minor/major); $\frac{3}{4}$; *Modéré* ♩ = 66

Irrémédiable vie	Incurable life
Vie à toujours chérir	Life to be cherished forever
En dépit des fléaux	In spite of scourges
Et des morales basses	And of low morals
En dépit des étoiles fausses	In spite of false stars
Et des cendres envahissantes	And intrusive ashes
En dépit des fièvres grinçantes	In spite of grating fevers
Des crimes à hauteur du ventre	Of belly-high crimes
Des seins taris des fronts idiots	Of dried up breasts of stupid brows
En dépit des soleils mortels	In spite of mortal suns
En dépit des dieux morts	In spite of dead gods
En dépit des mensonges	In spite of lies
L'aube l'horizon l'eau	Dawn horizon water
L'oiseau l'homme l'amour	Bird man love

L'homme léger et bon	Man light-hearted and good
Adoucissant la terre	Soothing the earth
Éclaircissant les bois	Brightening the woods
Illuminant la pierre	Illumining the stone
Et la rose nocturne	And the nocturnal rose
Et le sang de la foule.	And the blood of the crowd.

Éluard's poem transcends its subject and signifies the beauty and power of mankind "brightening the woods" and "illumining the stone," forever driven to create the art that mirrors the joys and struggle of life. "Villon *is*, with Gris, *the song I like best*," writes Poulenc. "*It is known how much I like the litanist side of Éluard's poetry. The prosody of 'L'aube, l'horizon, l'eau, l'oiseau, l'homme, l'amour' brings human relief to this severe and violent poem.*"[172]

It is hard not to imagine, in the opening bars, Poulenc being influenced by Éluard's title *Jacques Villon, ou L'Art glorieux*—for the music is grand and immense, yes, glorious in its way; and it joins hands, full circle, with the quasi-Baroque pomp of the cycle's opening, *Pablo Picasso*. The piano writing is marked *éclatant*, and the left hand traverses two octaves in three B-flats, *staccatissimo*, crossing over the right for the last, as if hammering nails into the corners of the picture frame to stretch and secure the canvas. Yet despite the occasional clashes of harmony, there is nothing angry about the music. *Villon* is a great lyrical song for a baritone at the height of his powers (it was conceived for Bernac, no matter who stumped up the money for the actual dedication).

The one-bar phrases "Des seins taris" and "des fronts idiots" play with the switching between major and minor that was such a memorable feature of *Juan Gris*. And the declaiming of "En dépit" (six times) gives the music the force of oratory, with a kind of moral and humanistic authority that Poulenc is only ever able to achieve in conjunction with Éluard. As in *Gris* (at "Table guitare et verre vide"), the lyrical heart of the song is cast in a plush F minor, a passage that Bernac claims was "the only subject of argument I ever had with Poulenc concerning the interpretation of his songs."[173] Their disagreement was over an appropriate dynamic for "L'aube l'horizon l'eau / L'oiseau l'homme l'amour": Poulenc thought the passage should be sung *forte*, while Bernac believed that softer dynamics (a *subito piano* on "L'aube l'horizon") would produce a more magical effect. Whatever the dynamic, the way these words are set is a marvel: each is separated and each is given its weight and meaning, with the final "l'amour" crowning the litany in a surprisingly profound yet unsentimental manner.

We have no idea what the concluding words—"la rose nocturne" and "le sang de la foule"—actually mean. Peter Low avers that the latter is "not spilt blood, but the living blood of the common people of many nations," and he goes on to quote J.-C. Gateau: "Without renouncing the 'nocturnal rose' of the imaginary, or the existence of mysterious beauty, the poem culminates in the civic and revolutionary responsibility of the creative artist who illuminates 'the blood of the masses.'"[174]

That may indeed be what Éluard had in mind, although it is difficult to imagine Poulenc being stirred by a socialist vision of this kind. Whatever he thought it meant, it is moving, and a fitting end to a work that looks back to Poulenc's friendships with the painters, a reconnection with his life in the twenties rather than the opening of a new chapter, and a salute to creative geniuses whose fame equaled or exceeded his own.

At this late stage of his life, Poulenc was pessimistic about his future as a composer of mélodies: every song, once completed, was now always threatening to be his last. "*My swansong in this domain?*" he asks about the cycle,[175] also referring to the songs as the last embers ("*nos derniers feux*") of his collaboration with Bernac.[176] As for the future of music itself, his thoughts on the subject were summed up in a passage that linked the twelve-tone system with modern painting: "*There were three great painters, Picasso, Braque and Juan Gris, for whom cubism was the natural form of expression. In the same way there were three great composers, Schoenberg, Alban Berg and Webern, who found twelve-tone music their natural form of expression. For these painters and these composers, cubism and dodecaphony were their natural means of expression. For others it's like breathing within an iron lung.*"[177]

At the end of *Jacques Villon*, by way of signing off, the boldness of the *fortissimo* ninth chord (B-flat major with a clashing C-natural) in the treble clef shelters a much more timid echo in the bass. The spatial effect, if well pedaled and played with control of touch, is a veritable halo of suspended sound. Such juxtaposition of foreground and background could also signify the vivid present sheltering a shadowy past, but with Poulenc we are approaching a time when the past rings out far more radiantly than either his present or his unknown future. For the moment at least, thank heaven there was still his great opera in the pipeline to keep his spirits up, as well as to torment him.

FP162 *Deux Mélodies 1956*

>Composed in Noizay, September 1956
>
>[*Marya Freund, Rose Dercourt-Plaut*; Eschig]
>
>Literary sources: (i) Guillaume Apollinaire (1880–1918), *Le Bestiaire, ou Cortège d'Orphée*, woodcuts by Raoul Dufy (Paris: Deplanche, Éditeur d'Art, 1911); "La Souris" is the eleventh poem in unnumbered pages. (ii) Laurence de Beylié (1893–1968), *Lueurs* (1968); Poulenc's source was a typescript copy of the poem sent to him by Lily Pastré.

(i)   *La Souris*
(ii) *Nuage*

(i)   *La Souris (The Mouse)*
      E-flat major; **3/4**; *Assez lent et doucement mélancolique* ♩= 56

Belles journées, souris du temps,	Lovely days, the mice of time,
Vous rongez peu à peu ma vie.	You're slowly nibbling away at my life.
Dieu! Je vais avoir	God, I'm going to be twenty-eight
vingt-huit ans,	years old,
Et mal vécus, à mon envie.	Years worse spent than I'd have wished.

The genesis of this song owes everything to Doda Conrad (see FP144 and FP145), who in his memoirs describes a special eightieth-birthday celebration for his mother, Marya Freund, on 12 December 1956.[178] Conrad habitually spared no effort in planning every detail of projects to amplify his reputation or that of his family—in this case, finding the right music paper to send to eighty potential contributors (mostly musicians) and pressing them to compose or write something in his mother's honor. He asked his friends Chagall, Villon, and Cocteau to contribute drawings, and he chose a box (designed by himself and made by Hermès in red morocco leather) to contain these treasures. Poulenc answered the call immediately. Although Marya Freund was not a particularly close friend, she was part of his musical past, and there was a deep psychic need on his part that his past should be continually revisited and burnished.

> *Without hesitation I took from my shelves the collection of* Le Bestiaire *of Apollinaire, for it is Marya Freund who had imposed the* grave *style on* Le Bestiaire, *the only valid style for it. Since, alas, time nibbles away our years like a mouse, I am setting this poem of Apollinaire to music. Immediately the melancholy I felt when I was twenty comes back to me and I imagine myself back again at Pont-sur-Seine, where I was a soldier in 1919.*[179]

His manuscript bears the inscription "*Dear Marya Freund. Your heart will always be twenty! Alas the composer of* Le Bestiaire *is now a lot older than twenty-eight!*"[180]

At eleven bars, *La Souris* ranks as a real miniature, but it is an enchanting one. The composer chose a deliciously apposite verse for someone who could scarcely believe how the years 1919–56 had slipped away. He was the first of the song's many performers to feel that pang of surprise. I first performed it, well before the age of twenty-eight, with my beloved colleague Richard Jackson; and I know all about the melancholy of returning to the text from a decidedly different vantage point ("what happened to all those years?") more than three decades later.

Two identical, gently drifting bars in the introduction imply the measured passing of time, while eighth notes descending down the two treble staves in intervals of fifths and a sixth suggest the falling sands of an hourglass. The exclamation "Dieu!" in bar 7 occasions the "holy" motive often to be found in *Dialogues*, a cadence with flattened mediant (G-flat major) leading to the dominant, with a hint of ceremonial piety, a blessing as swift as crossing oneself. This mouse of time is rather staid apart from a single bar of scampering recitative—the delectable throwaway sixteenth notes of "Je vais avoir vingt-huit ans," bringing to mind the marvelous aside "On n'a jamais si bien défendu la vertu" of the Apollinaire *Montparnasse*. Here Poulenc adopts the same tenderness for his younger self as he had lavished on that much longer masterpiece. And although the piece goes back, in a way, to the *Bestiaire* style, it could never have been written by the twenty-year-old composer in 1919; he would have needed to be at least twenty-seven and a half. Poulenc had every right to conclude: "*I think my* Souris *is rather pleasing.*"[181]

(ii) *Nuage (Cloud)*
  No key signature; $\frac{4}{4}$; *Allegretto* ♩ = 76 (Bernac recommends 72.)

J'ai vu reluire en un coin de mes âges	I saw something shining in a corner of my days
Un souvenir qui n'était plus à moi.	A memory that was no longer mine.
Son père était le temps	Its father was time
Sa mère une guitare	Its mother a guitar
Qui jouait sur des rêves errants.	Which played on wandering dreams.
Leur enfant tomba dans mes mains	Their child fell into my hands
Et je le posai sur un chêne.	And I placed him on an oak tree.
Un oiseau en prit soin,	A bird looked after him,
Maintenant il chante.	And now he sings.
Comment retrouver son père,	How can we find his father,
Voilé de vent,	Veiled in the wind,
Et comment recueillir les larmes de sa mère	And how can we gather up his mother's tears
Pour lui donner un nom.	So we can give him a name.
Dans le passage d'un nuage	In the passing of a cloud
Nous verrons poindre l'éternité	We will see eternity being born
Chassant le temps.	Chasing time.
En ce point tout est écrit.	In this moment all is written.

Poulenc received "Nuage" in typescript from Countess Lily Pastré, a friend and wealthy patroness of the arts with a château on the coast near Marseilles, and one of the first supporters of the festival in Aix-en-Provence. She was the dedicatee of *Rosemonde.*

It was rare for this composer to be interested in poems chosen by others—many had tried and failed to send him settable lyrics, but that was in the days when he was still inspired by Apollinaire and Éluard. With *La Souris* he had set his last Apollinaire, and he was now all but finished with Éluard. And he appears to have had no interest in the new post-surrealist poets that were emerging in the 1950s, or at least there is no sign of any such interest in his library. In the wake of the gargantuan efforts to complete his opera, Poulenc seems not to have been interested in scaling new mountain ranges as far as literature was concerned. Rather was he drawn to simplicity and clarity, as is shown by the childlike texts of the remainder of his mélodies—with the exception of *La Dame de Monte-Carlo,* in itself a return to his youth of the 1920s.

The poet, Laurence de Beylié, was pleased with the song, writing to Poulenc: "I couldn't have dreamt of anything better."[182] It was dedicated to the composer's New York friend Rose Dercourt-Plaut, an all but amateur singer who was Polish by birth and a friend of Marya Freund.[183] Poulenc's affinity for warm-hearted Polish women of some temperament goes back to Wanda Landowska and the various dedicatees of the *Huit Chansons polonaises,* including the redoubtable Misia Sert. The American LP he made with Rose (Turnabout TV4489) includes "her" song, *Nuage,* but he was certainly aware that making this record did neither him nor his music much credit. According to Hugues Cuenod, he shrugged it off as something he had to do for an old friend. *"It has delicate and manifold overtones. The cascade of modulations that underlines 'Comment retrouver son père, / Voilé de vent, / Et comment recueillir les larmes de sa mère / Pour lui donner un nom' is not without an echo of the* Valse oubliée *of Liszt, no doubt because during these last few days I have been listening to the old recording, divine, of Horowitz."*[184]

Apart from its pleasing gentleness, the mellifluous drift of the opening (eminently cloud-like), and the feast of Lisztian harmonic meanderings (in bb. 19–25), the song is prophetic of the three late, lucid sonatas for wind instruments (flute, clarinet, oboe) and piano.

Almost all the music that Poulenc composed in his last period is linked by a relationship to the opera on one side and the sonatas on the other. At bars 17–19, Mother Marie, the assistant Prioress from *Dialogues,* emerges in the piano writing. We have heard the double-dotted rhythm of the opening of her Sarabande, at the beginning of Act III, in the grandeur of *Pablo Picasso,* but in *Nuage,* at "Un oiseau en prit soin," we notice another motif from the same orchestral introduction: a scale decorated with a downward rush of thirty-second notes, something that could pass here for birdsong. Bernac points out that Poulenc liked this kind of descending figuration at the end of such songs as *Souric et Mouric* and *Jouer du bugle.*[185]

The composer ends his *Journal* entry for *Nuage* with a sudden, unexpected outburst of feeling: *"The taste for this musical form is coming to an end, so I am told. So much the worse. Long live Schubert, Schumann, Musorgksy, Chabrier, Debussy, etc. . . . etc. . . . "*[186]

FP163 *Dernier Poème* (*Last Poem*)

> Composed in Cannes, December 1956
> [*Youki Desnos*; Eschig]
> Literary source: Robert Desnos (1900–1945), *Domaine public* (Paris: NRF Gallimard, 1953), p. 408. This comprehensive anthology of Desnos's writings includes the complete *Corps et biens* (1930) and *Fortunes* (1942); "Le Dernier Poème" is the last item in the book.
>
> No key signature (E minor); $\frac{4}{4}$; *Assez lent et doucement mélancolique* $\quad \natural = 52$

J'ai rêvé tellement fort de toi,	I have so dreamt of you,
J'ai tellement marché, tellement parlé,	So talked, so walked,
Tellement aimé ton ombre,	So loved your shadow,
Qu'il ne me reste plus rien de toi.	That there's nothing of you left to me.
Il me reste d'être l'ombre parmi les ombres,	All that's left for me is to be a shadow among shadows,
D'être cent fois plus ombre que l'ombre	To be a hundred times more shadow than shadow
D'être l'ombre qui viendra et reviendra	To be the shadow that comes and goes
dans ta vie ensoleillée.	in your sun-soaked life.

The earlier part of Desnos's biography was outlined in the commentary for *Le Disparu* FP134 (p. 310). Suspected of Resistance activities (evidence surfaced, years after the event, that he had been targeted by a French collaborator and journalist who held an old grudge against him), Desnos was arrested by the Gestapo on 22 February 1944. After undergoing interrogation and spending four weeks in French camps, he was sent to Buchenwald as part of a consignment of 1,700 men. From there he was transported with 84 others to Flöha in Saxony, to manufacture parts for Messerschmitt airplanes. Letters written to his wife Youki somehow reached her, as did packets smuggled to him by the Resistance. His communications show a fierce will to survive; in a letter to Youki dated 15 July and published in *Domaine public*, Desnos promises on his return to deliver to the publisher Gallimard the manuscript of a love novel in a completely new genre.

On 12 April 1945 Flöha was evacuated in the face of Allied advances, and Desnos was among the prisoners sent to Theresienstadt (Terezin) in Czechoslovakia. On 3 May the SS abandoned the camp; by the 8th, when Theresienstadt was liberated by the Red Army and Czech partisans, Desnos was lying on a straw mattress, delirious with fever.

A few weeks later, Joseph Stuna, a Czech literature student who was working as a health volunteer, happened to see Desnos's name on the camp's list of patients. Stuna, a devotee of Éluard and Breton, instantly recognized the name. Together with another volunteer whose spoken French was better than his, Alena Tesarova, he searched among the living skeletons until at last they found the poet, who was barely able to identify himself: "Oui, oui Robert Desnos, le poète, c'est moi." Despite the loving care that Stuna and Tesarova administered, Desnos died on 8 June—one of many for whom food and care and medicine came too late. One dramatic but incorrect version of events was that this poem was written at Theresienstadt on cigarette paper, a secret message smuggled from a Nazi torture chamber. In reality, Desnos was in no state to write anything; obtaining paper was less of a problem than summoning the strength to write on it.

To honor the dead poet, on 1 July the Czech newspaper *Svobodne Boviny* published "À la mystérieuse" (in Czech translation), an ardent love poem Desnos had written in 1926 to the celebrated music hall singer Yvonne George (later published in his 1930 collection *Corps et biens*). Its last verse begins "J'ai tant

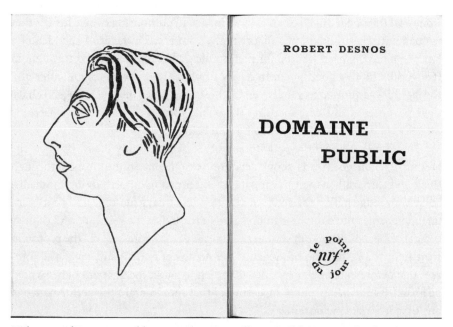

Title page of Domaine public, *a posthumous collection of the poetry of Robert Desnos (1953), drawing by Georges Malkine (1898–1970).*

rêvé de toi," thus seemingly similar to the poem set by Poulenc. Joseph Stuna had evidently gone to some trouble to select for the newspaper something from Desnos's œuvre that was representative of his work and suited the gravity of the obituary.

Meanwhile the writers' association Centre National des Écrivains (CNE) had sent Louis Aragon to bring the body back to France. Aragon, who misunderstood the Czech article, believed that the work printed there was the last poem Desnos had written in Theresienstadt. In the absence of the French original, and clearly with local linguistic help, he translated the Czech poem—rather beautifully— back into French. It is for this reason that "Dernier Poème" so resembles the Desnos poem written for Yvonne George: it is indeed the same poem, altered by two layers of translation.

Poulenc dedicated the song to Desnos's widow, Youki, a famous beauty and model of the 1920s. Her real name was Lucie Badoul, and Oyuki ("snow rose") was the name bestowed on her by her first husband, the famous Japanese art- ist (renowned for his drawings of cats) Tsuguharu (Léonard) Foujita. On that fateful evening in February 1944, Desnos had actually had time to escape the Gestapo (he had been warned of their coming), but he refused to leave Youki, who would have been tortured if he had abandoned her. Some say she was on a drugged "high" with ether at the time, and unable to leave their apartment. She denied this, but the poet's selflessness was a source of guilt, not only for her but also for many others who were spared, thanks to his resourceful bravery. It is an irony that the poem linked to Youki was in fact an outpouring of love for another woman entirely—though, not surprisingly, Youki was in favor of the idea of a last poem having been written for her. It quickly became celebrated throughout the world, and as a good poem in its own right (Aragon was Aragon, after all), the legend was allowed to stand even by those who knew the truth. Legends have their purpose: in this case focusing the public's attention on Desnos's patriotic sacrifices and his rare qualities as a human being.

That Poulenc knew the real story by 1956 seems highly likely. By then the Desnos-Aragon poem was about devotion to someone in dark times, through thick and thin, rather than passionate lines penned in a poet's dying moments. Such knowledge makes the song's dedication less than gruesome and sentimen- tal, and enables the composer to preserve in his music the restraint and dignity typical of Desnos. Bernac describes the song as being expressive of "the profound weariness of a being who has reached the depths of human suffering, and fore- sees that before long only his shade will be left to haunt the memory of her whom he loves."[187] It is this "profound weariness" that should drain the performance of any inappropriate melodrama.

The music is closely related to that of the Flute Sonata. Prevarications in the opening bars between minor and major tonality are typical Poulenc, as are the "singing thumbs"—a melody brought out by the right thumb for which the other fingers provide less important harmonic interjections. Although Bernac writes of the "lashing character of the coda," there should be no attempt to superimpose a firing squad, or some such melodramatic mise-en-scène, on the music. Poulenc pronounced the song *successful enough.* But when an always-unimpressed Swiss critic (Robert-Aloys Mooser, 1876–1969) claimed that it was the best thing the composer had ever done, his response was *"poor him, poor me."*[188]

o   o   o

FP164 Sonata for Flute and Piano, 1956–57

FP165 *Ave Maria* (voices and organ), promised to Nadia Boulanger in 1957 but never composed

FP166 Sonata for Bassoon and Piano (abandoned)

FP167 *Viva Nadia* (song for Nadia Boulanger), 1957

FP168 *Élégie* (horn and piano), September–December 1957

o   o   o

FP169 *Une chanson de porcelaine* (*A Song of Porcelain*)

> Composed in Cannes, March 1958
>
> [*Jeanne* (Jane) *Bathori*; Eschig]
>
> Literary source: Paul Éluard (1895–1952), *À toute épreuve* (Paris: Éditions Surréalistes, 1930), No. 8 in unnumbered pages (for a description of this unusual publication, see *Cinq Poèmes de Paul Éluard* FP77). Also *La Vie immédiate* (Paris: Éditions des Cahiers Libres, 1932), containing an altered reprinting of *À toute épreuve*; since Poulenc used the second collection for the more recent . . . *mais mourir* FP137, it is likely that this publication is the source.
>
> No key signature; $\frac{3}{4}$; *Andante semplice*

Une chanson de porcelaine bat des mains	A song of porcelain claps its hands
Puis en morceaux mendie et meurt	Then in pieces begs and dies
Tu te souviendras d'elle pauvre et nue	You will remember it poor and naked
Matin des loups et leur morsure est un tunnel	The morning of the wolves their bite is a tunnel
D'où tu sors en robe de sang	Whence you emerge robed in blood
À rougir de la nuit	To blush at the night
Que de vivants à retrouver	So many of the living to find again
Que de lumières à éteindre	So many lights to extinguish
Je t'appellerai Visuelle	I will call you Visual
Et multiplierai ton visage	And will replicate your face.

Poulenc's last setting of the poetry of Paul Éluard was composed as a tribute to a great champion of contemporary French music, singer Jane Bathori (1877–1970), in honor of her eightieth birthday. For the enthusiast of French song, Bathori (her real name was Jeanne-Marie Berthier) is a major figure, well worthy of celebration. She had a beautiful and distinctive voice, but she was even more remarkable for her musical skills, which included stellar sight-reading (she stepped in to sing the first performance of Ravel's orchestral song cycle *Shéhérazade* in 1904, learning it in a matter of days) and singing to her own accompaniment; her performances of Ravel's *Histoires naturelles,* which she premiered in 1906, survive on gramophone record. Debussy, Satie, Roussel, and Milhaud all wrote for her. In addition, as director of the Théâtre du Vieux-Colombier from 1917, she was responsible for a series of concerts during the 1920s that promoted new music (including that of Les Six).

Poulenc had already dedicated two songs from the twenties to Bathori, *À son page* FP38/v and *Air vif* FP46/iv. On completing *Une chanson de porcelaine*, he sent Bathori the following message on a postcard, revealing that his mind was on bigger and better things: "*Here, finally, is your mélodie. I hope you will like it, because I created it with tenderness for you, while thinking about our wonderful past. Presently I am composing* La Voix humaine. *I hope that it will be as horrific as one can wish. Who would have thought back then that I would become a somber musician.*"[189]

The poem, extremely obscure even by Éluard's inscrutable standards, was chosen from the same collection, *À toute épreuve,* with which Poulenc had begun his musical association with Éluard in 1935—making a full circle and perhaps the result of deliberate choice. After having tasted worldwide fame as composer of *Dialogues des Carmélites,* and with his partnership with Bernac winding down slowly on account of the singer's age, there seemed to be no incentive for Poulenc to devote himself to song writing in the same way as before.

With its A minor tonality and spareness of style, the opening recalls *Juan Gris* from *Le Travail du peintre,* without attempting to match that song's visionary mood. Although *Une chanson de porcelaine* displays an ease in setting Éluard's words that could only have been achieved after nearly a quarter of a century's practice, there is little here that seems new. Since the

The singer Jane Bathori.

smaller songs of 1956, the composer has developed a late style that spins out pleasing, and even touching, music without aiming for the *niveau* of the mélodies from the great composing years of the thirties and forties. No one other than Poulenc could have composed them, and in that respect they remain inimitable. But he is treading water and marking time, sometimes believing himself capable of *grands projects* that were going to replace song as his most impressive calling card. The *Six Mélodies*, a disparate collection issued by Eschig in 1960 (*Une chanson de porcelaine, Paul et Virginie, Rosemonde, La Souris, Nuage*, and *Dernier Poème*), contain moments of genuine inspiration, and one would not be without them. But taken together, they feel something like an afterthought.

○   ○   ○

FP170 *Improvisations* 13–14 (piano), March 1958

FP171 *La Voix humaine* (Jean Cocteau, lyric tragedy in one act), February–June 1958

FP172 *Laudes de Saint Antoine de Padoue* (male chorus, *a cappella*), 1957–59

FP173 *Novelette on a Theme of Manuel de Falla* (piano), June 1959

○   ○   ○

FP174 Fancy

> Composed in Bagnols-en-Forêt, August 1959
> [*To Miles and Flora*; Anthony Bland]
> Literary source: William Shakespeare (1564–1616), *The Merchant of Venice*, Act III, scene ii
> G major; $\frac{4}{4}$; *Calme et mélancolique*

Tell me where is Fancy bred,
Or in the heart, or in the head?
How begot, how nourished?
Reply, reply.
It is engender'd in the eyes,
With gazing fed; and Fancy dies
In the cradle where it lies.
Let us all ring Fancy's knell:
I'll begin it,—Ding, dong, bell.

Poulenc had first toyed with the idea of setting English poems to music in 1919. He was in constant touch at the time with the London firm of Chester, publisher of his early instrumental works, and with the French poet and critic Georges Jean-Aubry, who worked as editor of their house journal, *The Chesterian*. Jean-Aubry's French poems had been set by such Chester-published composers as

Falla, Lord Berners, Eugene Goosens, Malipiero, and Roussel. When Jean-Aubry wrote to ask Poulenc if he was interested in setting his poems, the composer replied, "*I could think of nothing better than to put some of your poems to music. I would very much like the patter of English clowns, the words being in English.*"[190]

Nothing came of the clowns' songs, but Poulenc had already learned how to be diplomatic with those who might possibly further his career. Perhaps he was counting on the fact that Jean-Aubry, though he worked in London, was not interested in writing poems in English. Poulenc's first response to Shakespeare was *Sketch for a Fanfare* FP25 (1921), an overture to Act V of *Romeo and Juliet*—the result of a request from either Cocteau or the short-lived British periodical *Fanfare*, which numbered Philip Heseltine (Peter Warlock) among its editors and had already published fanfares by Milhaud, Malipiero, Arnold Bax, and Egon Wellesz.[191] In 1939 Poulenc spoke to both playwright Édouard Bourdet and actor Jean-Louis Barrault about writing incidental music for *Périclès*; three years later he was still thinking about this play and its convoluted plot, but in the end did not write a note of music for it.[192]

Fancy was the result of a request from the Countess of Harewood (b. Marion Stein in Vienna, 1926–2014) for a contribution to a new anthology of children's songs. Her father, Erwin Stein, a pupil of Schoenberg, was Benjamin Britten's publisher. When Britten and Pears returned from America in 1942, they shared the Steins' London flat. Britten regarded Marion as a younger sister, and was delighted when she married George, Earl of Harewood, the queen's eldest cousin and an ardent admirer of his music. Britten, Poulenc, and Zoltán Kodály were each to compose a song to Shakespeare's poem. As it turned out, the songs were delightfully contrasted: Britten's was marked *Quick and fantastic*, Poulenc's calmly sad and languorous, Kodály's *Moderato* and conceived for three-part children's chorus and piano. It took some time for the book to be prepared—Britten and Kodály were much slower than Poulenc in providing their responses—and in the end Poulenc did not live to see his song in print.

Fancy first appeared (supposedly as a choral item) in *Classical Songs for Children* (1964), edited by Marion Harewood and Ronald Duncan (the librettist of Britten's *Rape of Lucretia*) and accompanied by eight line drawings of Milein Cosman. Nearly a decade later it reappeared as *The Penguin Book of Accompanied Songs* (1973), minus the drawings except for one of lutenist Julian Bream, as a frontispiece. It was this publication that brought the settings of *Fancy* by Poulenc and Britten to the attention of singers.

For advice in setting an English text, Poulenc turned once again to Bernac: "*Marion Harewood has asked me so nicely to contribute to a little collection of choruses for children with Ben, Kodály etc. that I can't refuse, but . . . help me with the accents and the exact meaning of the text, which I am only guessing at. Does one sing 'where is' on two notes—yes, not so? Of course I'll show you the whole thing before I send it off.*"[193] For the first time in their correspondence, Poulenc sketches two staves of a song and writes out the voice part of the first eight bars, only two of which contain the notes of the final version. It is extremely instructive to see how the composer later finessed the shape of the vocal line, making it sound more natural and inevitable; what had been a mere G major arpeggio in the first two bars was simply, but marvelously, transfigured into a real melody. The accompaniment and the gently striding left-hand eighth notes were added later, the right hand shadowing the vocal line throughout (Poulenc did not envisage this as a solo song, although it works superbly well as such, and he probably felt that a children's chorus would be better supported by a doubled vocal line). The feeling of a "knell"—the passing bell for those dying in Catholic countries (and Shakespeare was almost certainly Catholic)—is caught in the halo of sound occasioned by the pedal and the subtlety of the pianist's touch, particularly with the evocative depiction of bells sounding ever higher and farther away in evanescent tintinnabulation at the end.

Though notes may be different in the final version, the note values stayed the same, the result of Bernac's reply: "Here is the translation of the Shakespeare: but your English appears to me to be excellent. There is no problem with the accentuation of all these little short words. What you have done works out marvelously."[194] An English musician might have advised against placing "Or" in the line "Or in the heart, or in the head" on the first beat of two successive bars; but the double "or" (before "either/or" came into use) on the first beats of the bar is impeccable Elizabethan usage. Perhaps "*the* head" should not have occurred on the relatively strong third beat. And the accentuation of "begin it" is also suspect—BEgin rather than beGIN—as if Poulenc were working on a translation by Bernac that contained the word "*commencer.*"

There is no record of what Britten thought of the song; it is after all only a trifle, however often it touches audiences with its haunting simplicity. He may, however, have felt it necessary to give Poulenc seventeen out of twenty for his English prosody (see the following essay).

POULENC AND BRITTEN: CROSS-CHANNEL CURRENTS

Poulenc was an avid reader of musical reviews; like many artists, he subscribed to a press-cutting service and kept well informed about the activities of most composers throughout the world. It was probably clear to him from the 1930s that Britten was considered the great white hope of English music. And he heard more about Britten from his English composer friend Lennox Berkeley, who studied in Paris with Nadia Boulanger. Such knowledge was useful for the series of half-hour radio programs known as *À bâtons rompus* (*Chitchat,* or *This and That,* 1947–49), where Poulenc presented a series of biographical outlines in a mixture of scripted speech and music.

In a 1947 talk on contemporary English music, in which he concentrated on Britten and William Walton,[195] the Britten passages were presented in the context of personal acquaintance. In January 1945 the two composers had performed Poulenc's Concerto for Two Pianos at London's Albert Hall, in a performance conducted by Basil Cameron. Poulenc had expected to find there an adequately prepared colleague; instead, "*Oh stupeur! Britten était un pianiste de grande classe,*" as he put it during the broadcast. Philip Reed points out that the concerto, drawing in part on gamelan techniques, may have been influential in turn on Britten's later study of Balinese music.[196] Signed scores were exchanged in Albert Hall: the English composer presented Poulenc with a wartime edition of *A Ceremony of Carols,* inscribed "To Francis Poulenc, from his English admirer, Benjamin Britten . . . London 1945."

Poulenc's survey of Britten's music in the broadcast was cursory: three opera titles reeled off in a sentence, with the strange observation that the "*irresistible funniness*" ("*cocasserie*") of *Albert Herring* (a work not yet recorded, and it is doubtful Poulenc had plowed through the score) was reminiscent of the tone of Britten's conversation. (Maybe he thought Britten's attempts at spoken French were funny, but the English composer's conversation was hardly a laugh a minute.) Poulenc observed that the Pears-Britten duo had been formed along the lines of his own with Bernac, and he played discs of one of the *Sonnets of Michelangelo* and an extract from the *Serenade for Tenor, Horn and Strings* with Pears and Dennis Brain. The short talk would have been an unexceptional class in music appreciation in any British secondary school of the time, but that it was broadcast in France and at a French composer's behest makes it notable.

In January 1955 Britten and a convalescent Poulenc performed the two-piano concerto again at the Festival Hall in London, this time with John Pritchard as conductor. A few months later Britten and Pears gave a poorly attended song recital in Cannes, where Poulenc happened to be staying at the Hôtel Majestic. He was always good at turning up to support friends, and a well-known photograph of him flanked by the much younger Britten and Pears was taken the following day. Poulenc, wrapped in a winter coat, was still suffering from the long-term effects of his 1954 breakdown.

According to the ledgers of Ibbs and Tillett, the foremost London concert agency of the period, Poulenc had been penciled in for a date in Britten's Aldeburgh Festival in 1952. He did not perform there that year, and he canceled a participation two years later, but he did appear in 1956 for a lecture (in French) in the Jubilee Hall on the morning of 24 June, and that evening played the piano solo in *Aubade*. Although Poulenc no doubt was treated as an honored guest at the festival, he was clearly uncomfortable—quite apart from the legendary episode when he was made to sit in a boat on Thorpeness Meare for a concert of the Aldeburgh Music Club, which brought on a sudden attack of the jitters. It was highly unusual for him to be in a place where a younger colleague was the center of attention—there is some evidence that he disliked sharing the limelight, even with much less gifted composers[197]—and where much of the music that had engendered the public's admiration was unknown to him. (He refused, when in America in 1949, to visit the Tanglewood Music Festival, confessing that he intensely disliked *"musical fairs."*[198]) Poulenc would not have been the first or last composer visiting Aldeburgh to feel out of his element in this milieu.

More important, his attempts to arrange for Bernac to sing a recital, or *Le Bal masqué*, in Aldeburgh had been politely stonewalled. A letter from Britten on 8 November 1954 had dangled the future possibility of a Bernac appearance while showing the composer/festival director at his smoothest and most evasive.[199] Poulenc could not have failed to notice that the instrumental resources supposedly too expensive for *Le Bal masqué* were later happily provided to accompany the solo piano in his *Aubade*.

The 1956 festival was the last occasion when the two composers saw each other. Poulenc pulled out of a June 1958 Aldeburgh production of *Les Mamelles de Tirésias*, where he was due to play a two-piano reduction of the orchestral score with Britten—an arrangement that he had offered to make himself (*"I shall try to make a*

Poulenc flanked by Peter Pears and Benjamin Britten in Cannes, 1 April 1955.

brilliant transcription!!!!" he assured Britten) but which was never delivered.[200] His excuse for the cancellation was that his doctor had "*once more
forbidden me the sea.*" In the end, Britten and the pianist Viola Tunnard
cobbled together their own arrangement of the score. Poulenc wrote a
well-timed letter of enormous charm ("*I think of you constantly with wild
regret . . . my defection was melancholy as it was involuntary*") on the day
Les Mamelles was first performed at Aldeburgh.[201] No one could match
Poulenc in his ability to smooth feathers, to keep irons in the fire that
could prove useful later, to allow (carefully selected) others to bask in the
warmth of his attention.

And yet his ill health had not prevented him from accompanying
Denise Duval in a prestigious recital at the Bordeaux festival on 16 May,
and his aversion to the sea did not deter him from crossing the waters ten
days after writing to Britten, to receive a Doctor of Music degree at Oxford
(alongside Dmitri Shostakovich); he spent several jovial days with friends
in London on either side of the ceremony, plus a visit to Gyndebourne to
hear Stravinsky's *The Rake's Progress* (a Britten bête noire), before returning to France. Plans to visit the 1960 festival to hear Britten's *A Midsummer Night's Dream* were similarly canceled at the last minute.

Britten was someone with whom it was notoriously easy to fall out,
but despite his distinctly non-Francophile tendencies, he seems to have
been as determined to maintain a cordial friendship with Poulenc as
Poulenc was with him. This was a friendship too important to fail. It was
known that Poulenc's health, both physical and emotional, was a little
shaky, but as far as Britten was concerned, the music was sanely tonal and
on the side of the angels in the battle against the adherents of twelve-tone
music. (He had performed the profound *Tel jour telle nuit,* after all, and
was a genuine admirer of *Les Mamelles de Tirésias*.[202]) Poulenc's charm,
both face-to-face and as a correspondent, offset unpredictable behavior
that would have led to a permanent rupture between Britten and any
British colleague who behaved in a similar manner. He remained for
Britten and Pears a "typical" Frenchman, a kind of musical equivalent of
the great comedian Jacques Tati, someone rather "dotty" (the word Pears
used to describe Poulenc to me in 1984), "a delightful friend and lovable
musician . . . too innocent to be insincere."[203]

"Innocent" is not a word to be used lightly in conjunction with Poulenc. He was capable of maintaining relations of the utmost cordiality
with Britten while privately harboring reservations. He would have been
aware, for example (and this was widely talked about in the gay community at the time), that Britten was very prim when it came to suggestive
remarks; there was none of the relaxed, camp badinage in Aldeburgh of

the kind Poulenc was accustomed to making with his other gay friends.[204] What was important to him, and for this he was truly grateful to Britten and Pears, was that *Les Mamelles de Tirésias* should be produced in Aldeburgh, the work receiving first-class performances from which he would receive the publicity and royalties.

That Poulenc genuinely admired Britten and Pears as performers and festival directors is beyond doubt.[205] His fulsome thank-you letter characterizes the festival made in Britten's image as "*all intelligence, finesse and heart.*"[206] Poulenc's opinion of Britten's music is harder to fathom. How much of it did he actually know? The English language in the vocal works was undoubtedly a stumbling-block, although he singled out Britten's skill in finding good librettists "*appropriate to his talent.*"[207] In 1961 he named Britten, Dutilleux, and Sauguet (a trio of spectacularly disparate significance) as exceptional "*independents,*" praising Britten's "*richness of invention and his finesse*" without attaching those words to any named works, in that interview or anywhere else.[208] Poulenc always responded best to music he had heard in the flesh; but Britten's was performed rather seldom in France then. And he was in an awkward position regarding his lifelong friend Stravinsky, a sworn Britten antagonist.

Poulenc seems not to have known *Peter Grimes* (all that sea!). He walked out halfway through a performance of *Billy Budd*—yet more sea—in Paris in 1952 (Britten certainly never knew *that*), commenting that he preferred *Four Saints in Three Acts* by Britten's arch enemy, Virgil Thomson.[209] His knowledge of *Turn of the Screw* (he told Britten he had bought the records) was sufficient for him to dedicate his only English setting, *Fancy* FP174, to Miles and Flora, the opera's two child characters. But if Poulenc had truly admired a work as important as that opera, we would surely hear about it in his correspondence, and there is no such mention. In a warm congratulatory letter for Britten's fiftieth birthday in 1962, he saluted the composer as being "*as glorious as a young Verdi,*" claiming that the recently composed *War Requiem* had "*slightly shaken the little fortress*" of his own religious works. But there is no evidence that he had ever heard the *Requiem*, not yet recorded; perhaps he was aware of the reviews.

While Britten and his partner went out of their way to show their affection for Poulenc at every turn, they reserved their dislike for Bernac, who traveled to London specially to attend a concert in Poulenc's memory at the French Embassy in 1963, for which the British duo performed *Tel jour telle nuit*. Pears felt that Bernac, whom he thought a pedant, did not deem his French pronunciation good enough (it was certainly not flawless). In fact, he felt Bernac's presence at the event, sitting in the audi-

Program for the Poulenc memorial concert organized at the French Embassy in London, May 1963, in which Peter Pears was accompanied by Benjamin Britten.

Francis Poulenc
(1899 – 1963)
CONCERT 'IN MEMORIAM'
The Arts Council of Great Britain
4 St. James's Square, Londres, S.W.1
Mardi 7 mai 1963 à 21 heures

ence, was intentionally malicious— unjustly, I think.[210]

The Britten-Pears hostility to Bernac was something that probably went back to 1940. The previous year Britten had composed *Les Illuminations,* an orchestral song cycle with Rimbaud texts, originally for the Swiss soprano Sophie Wyss, although Pears later made it his own. Somehow Poulenc saw the score before it was first performed or published, and some twenty years later in America revealed that he had given it a score of seventeen out of twenty for prosody, believing that Britten did not breathe like a French composer.[211] As the two composers only first met in 1945 (and there is no record of any prior correspondence), there was only one way Poulenc could have seen the music of *Les Illuminations* before it was published: via Lennox Berkeley, who visited Paris in March 1940 and took a proof copy of Britten's cycle to show his former teacher, Nadia Boulanger.[212] She was critical, claiming to hear no individual voice in the music. Berkeley strongly disagreed, and the two had a spirited argument. After this rebuff, Berkeley likely sought an alternative opinion, and Poulenc happened to be in Paris at the time with Bernac, between concerts in Zurich and Avignon.

The forthright Bernac thought Britten's work was seriously flawed in its prosody. He said this to me in London, in 1977,[213] and it is my theory that in 1940 he made his feelings known to Berkeley and probably others. It seems likely that Bernac's criticism also reached, as such things do, the ears of Britten and Pears. As a result, he remained forever in bad odor at the Red House in Aldeburgh. Boulanger was an old enemy anyway (Britten gleefully told me a story about accidentally spilling a ladleful of ice cream on Boulanger's black velvet dress at a pre-concert dinner at the Connaught Rooms in the 1930s), and Bernac, one of a handful of great recitalists of the day, was pointedly never invited to appear at the Aldeburgh Festival in recital.

While Poulenc shared Bernac's reservations about Britten's French prosody, he was far too diplomatic to say so to Berkeley; he was also too clever to let on how deeply disappointed he was never to have been invited to give a recital of his own songs with his chosen singer at this important festival. Underneath the surface, on Poulenc's side at least, the *entente* was not entirely as *cordiale* as it may have seemed. He might have felt justified in withdrawing from a challenging engagement in Aldeburgh with an unnervingly superior pianist, especially as he had left it late enough to ensure that performances of his opera would go ahead in any case.

The relationship between Poulenc and Britten is now generally taken to have been an idyll of mutual understanding; in reality it was not, and in some ways they stood worlds apart. While Britten did not hesitate to state his views, making enemies along the way, Poulenc avoided confrontation at all costs. Britten's work gained a foothold in France very late, only after his death and then only as a result of international demand for his operas. Poulenc became the darling of London's recital audiences in the thirties, and nothing has ever really disturbed his reputation's roseate glow for the British public. Apart from the threat of the twelve-tone school, Britten, at least in his younger years, knew that his talent was too big to fail; from the beginning Poulenc believed his own too fragile to survive without charm offensives. Yet in terms of one composer promoting the music of another, it was undoubtedly Poulenc who got the better deal. Britten performed *Les Mamelles de Tirésias*, the two-piano concerto (at least twice), and *Tel jour telle nuit* (many times) on English soil, and Poulenc's music appeared in festival after festival in Aldeburgh.

It is surely to the credit of both of these extraordinary and insecure geniuses that they took the trouble to demonstrate a measure of patience and solidarity in dealing with each other that made allowances for their considerable differences of taste and temperament. When Pears and Britten presented a recital in memory of Poulenc as part of the 1964 Aldeburgh Festival (15 June, at the Workmen's Club, Thorpeness), it was a sincerely meant tribute; and Poulenc would certainly have much preferred the sexy (at least to him) resonances of this venue to the terrifying waters of Thorpeness Meare.

∘   ∘   ∘

FP175 *Elégie (en accords alternés)* for two pianos, summer 1959
FP176 *Improvisation* 15 (piano), summer 1959
FP177 *Gloria* (soprano solo, chorus, orchestra), 1959–60

·VI·

Poulenc and Denise Duval after a performance of La Voix humaine.

Outline of a Musical Life:
1960 to 30 January 1963

1960 (aged 61)

For Poulenc, January is marred by liver complaints and bouts of nervous anxiety.

(6 February) FP writes to Virgil Thomson that he is counting on the protection of the still powerful composer-critic during his upcoming American tour. He makes a rare reference to current events—in this case the Algerian war of independence from France (1954–62).[1]

(13 February) France explodes its first atomic bomb in the Algerian Sahara as part of General de Gaulle's determination to re-establish France on the world stage, and to redress the country's loss of "grandeur" during the war.

(18 February) FP embarks on a fourth American tour in the company of Denise Duval and Georges Prêtre, who had recently conducted *La Voix humaine*. Once again the composer stays at the Wyndham Hotel in New York. The schedule is much less strenuous than on previous visits, perhaps because Duval was unwilling to sing the number of recitals formerly undertaken by Bernac.

(23 February) Semi-staged Carnegie Hall performances of *Les Mamelles de Tirésias* and *La Voix humaine*, conducted by Prêtre and starring Duval, with repeat performances at the Academy of Music in Philadelphia (25th), are a huge success with the public and critics.

By now accustomed to the operatic standards of La Scala and Vienna, FP compares the state of New York's Metropolitan Opera unfavorably even with that of his local theater near Noizay, the opera house in Tours.[2]

(27 February) Duval and Poulenc fly to Ithaca, New York, for a recital, then two days later to Chicago (staying at the Ambassador Hotel) for a recital on 1 March. In addition to *La Voix humaine* (with piano accompaniment), their program consists of an aria from Debussy's *L'Enfant prodigue*, two numbers from Ravel's *Shéhérazade*, an aria from Ravel's *L'Heure espagnole*,

and Poulenc's *À sa guitare* and *Air champêtre*. Apart from the Poulenc songs, all the music was originally conceived for orchestra—this is far from the hallowed tradition of the mélodie recital as cultivated by Bernac in the previous twenty-five years. Although there are some rumblings in the press, FP seems too happy with his American success to care.

(3 March) FP is awarded the New York University Medal, honoring distinguished visitors to the university, after which he and Duval perform extracts from *La Voix humaine*.

(6 March) Recital at the Detroit Institute of Arts auditorium.

(10 March) Town Hall recital in New York with Duval: Debussy, Ravel, Gounod, and Poulenc, ending with an aria from *Les Mamelles de Tirésias*. FP is horrified by the piano (a Baldwin, *"worse than the worst Gaveaus"*), comparing it with the piano he had played in a Bernac recital in Tangiers.[3]

In the following ten days, FP pays a visit to Washington, composes a *Sarabande* for solo guitar, and records his Sextet for Columbia (17 March), returning to Paris on the 20th. *"Decidedly I love America, and America loves me."*[4]

(April) After a brief stay in Noizay, and performing the *Concert champêtre* in Marseilles, FP goes to Bagnols-en-Forêt, where he orchestrates the *Gloria*; five of six movements are complete by 25 April.

(30 April–5 May) FP visits Rome for a concert.

(22–26 May) FP goes to Brussels for a week to serve on the jury of the Queen Elizabeth Competition, followed by a four-day visit to London. He returns to France the first week in June for his last project with Bernac: a Véga recording of *Banalités*, *Tel jour telle nuit*, *Calligrammes*, and *Le Travail du peintre*, an LP with which Bernac, on vocal grounds, was later to express profound dissatisfaction.

Although FP intended to return to England to give a talk and for the 11 June premiere of Britten's *A Midsummer Night's Dream* in Aldeburgh, he cancels those arrangements to hear the first performance of *La Voix humaine* (with orchestra) in Belgium.

FP spends late June and early July in Brive, making excursions with Marthe Bosredon to Rocadamour and Espalion. He boasts to Stéphane Audel that he has found there a thirty-eight-year-old lover who likes old men;[5] he confesses to being "an old tart" (*"une vieille grue"*). He begins his last vocal work with orchestra, *Sept Répons des ténèbres*, and also a new song cycle conceived for Denise Duval, *La Courte paille*.

(July–24 August) FP spends the rest of the summer in Bagnols, with visits to the festival Aix-en-Provence to give a lecture, hear Duval in *La Voix humaine*, and attend a performance (28 July) of Purcell's *Dido and Aeneas* in Britten's realization, sung by Teresa Berganza and Gérard Souzay. He also visits Richard Chanlaire in Tourrettes-sur-Loup.

(July–11 August) *La Courte paille* **FP178** (Carême), composed in Bagnols-en-Forêt. FP plans for the cycle to be premiered during a forthcoming Italian tour with Duval in November, which he has meticulously planned (as though he were still working with Bernac). Having overextended herself with performances and travel, the soprano cancels the tour. FP then suggests Charleroi (near Carême's home) for the first performance, on 31 January 1961. This seems not to have taken place either. Duval did not take to the cycle and never gave a complete performance of it.

(October–December) Bagnols-en-Forêt is now FP's base, however unofficially. The metamorphosis from song composer of Noizay to opera and religious composer of the south of France is all but complete. He never sleeps at Louis's house, La Gardiette, but rents a single room (at 532, rue Grande) belonging to his friend Mimi Martin; he sometimes serves behind the bar of her hostelry when she's busy. He spends time in Milan and serves on the juries of two competitions in Rome (24–28 October and 17–22 November). He expends much time organizing his fifth American tour for January 1961—it was to be his last—demonstrating, even by his standards, an obsessive concern with detail.

1961 (aged 62)

At the beginning of the year, Russian cellist Mstislav Rostropovich asks FP for a cello piece, but there is no record of a reply. A similar request from Rostropovich to Britten results in an important collaboration.

(13 January) Sharing a flight with the organist Marie-Claire Alain, who is seduced by his charm, FP arrives in the United States for his fifth visit; he is without a singer, and New York and Boston are the only two cities visited, with no concerts in New York. He writes to Bernac: "*I am looking for you—as is sung in* La Voix: *'I am no longer accustomed to traveling alone.'*"[6]

(16–23 January) He stays once more at the Wyndham Hotel in New York, and at the Sheraton Plaza Hotel in Boston. In Boston he takes Rose Dercourt-Plaut to hear a concert with Marlene Dietrich (19th). "*This country pleases me but it also terrifies me. One must sail really high to be unassailable as far as the press and the public, even stranger than ours, are concerned.*"[7]

(21 January) In Boston, Charles Munch conducts Poulenc's *Gloria* and Concerto for Two Pianos (repeated the next day). FP has problems with Munch, who seems not to understand the tempi of the *Gloria*; the composer takes over the rehearsal and adjusts the tempi. His fellow pianist in the concerto is the "*excellent*" Evelyne Crochet; he also enthuses heartily over the singing of Adele Addison in the *Gloria*. "*Marlene Dietrich was there, baisers* [kisses], *rebaisers, photos, rephotos,*" he writes Simone Girard. "*Who will you find for me in Avignon? Lollobrigida?*"[8]

(24 January) Returning to New York, FP spends six days socializing. He meets Leontyne Price (after her Metropolitan Opera debut in Verdi's *Il Trovatore,* with Franco Corelli); he visits Horowitz and Rubinstein and sees Laurence Olivier in a production of Jean Anouilh's *Becket.* He returns to Paris on the 30th.

FP complains of food poisoning and tinnitus brought on by the transatlantic flight. He arrives in Milan (7 February) to hear Duval's performance in *Don Quichotte* by Jean-Pierre Rivière, which has won the Ricordi prize (given to an opera by a newcomer). From there he travels on to Bagnols-en-Forêt.

(14 February) Temporarily back in Paris, FP attends the European premiere of his *Gloria* (at the Théâtre des Champs-Élysées), sung by Rosanna Cartieri and conducted by Georges Prêtre. When the reviews fail to match the enthusiasm of the American press, Poulenc suffers a crisis of confidence. He reads that Messiaen and André Jolivet are regarded as the two most "important" composers in France, and fears he has been forgotten. *"I will always give my premieres abroad—that will enable me calmly to face the Parisian public with its 'ifs,' its 'buts,' . . . its shit."*[9]

Louis Gautier has embarked on a new career as a plumber, and FP continues to *"play house"* in Bagnols-en-Forêt: *"How right I am never to have chosen my gigolos from a musical milieu. . . . I play rummy in the evening with the owner of the bistro* [Mimi Martin]. *Bravo!"*[10]

(February) FP's monograph *Emmanuel Chabrier* is published. His friend Geneviève Sienkiewicz, to whom the book is dedicated, writes to thank him and to comfort him at a time of his depression: "Three notes of Poulenc, three notes of Schubert, three notes of Mozart, three notes of Stravinsky, can never be mistaken for anything else. . . . *Originality,* that is what counts."[11]

(Mid-March) FP comes across a copy of Jean Cocteau's *Théâtre de poche* (1949) in a Cannes bookshop. (In another version of the story, he finds the book in Monte Carlo while visiting his Chinese acupuncturist.[12]) This collection reprints various libretti, ballet scenarios, and monologues—including "La Dame de Monte-Carlo," written for the actress Marianne Oswald in 1946.

(April) In Bagnols, FP returns to working on *Sept Répons des ténèbres* (he abandons large portions composed in 1960 and starts again) as well as setting "La Dame de Monte-Carlo" for Denise Duval.

La Dame de Monte-Carlo FP180 (Cocteau) composed. Although Monte Carlo is given as the place of composition at the foot of the score, there is no record of Poulenc living or working there when he wrote it. He may have regarded Nice (and Bagnols) as near enough to claim a connection going back to childhood holidays. *"I love Monte Carlo like others love Venice. To leave Paris on a snowy evening and pick, the next day, a lemon in the sun, always seems to me a pleasure from* The Thousand and One Nights.*"*[13]

(1 May) An internal memo at the BBC concludes that FP's *Gloria* is not worthy of its dignified text, and that resources should not be allocated for a work that will not enhance its composer's reputation. After decades in which Poulenc could do little wrong at the BBC, this is less a sign of his waning powers than of a wind of change blowing through a corporation now controlled by younger personnel.[14]

(May) FP spends the month in Noizay with his friend and former lover Richard Chanlaire, apart from a trip early in the month to Bordeaux to hear the premiere of Henri Sauguet's cantata *Plus loin que la nuit et le jour.*

(4 June) At Noizay, FP plays *La Dame de Monte-Carlo* to Stéphane Audel and Geneviève Sienkiewicz. This same month he attends two performances in a week of Leonard Bernstein's *West Side Story* at the Théâtre de l'Alhambra–Maurice Chevalier and declares himself fascinated with it.[15]

FP travels to Strasbourg to hear the *Gloria*, continues on to Bagnols, and returns to Paris on 25 June. He visits Rocamadour and Brive in early July and then goes via Avignon to the south of France, where Louis Gautier has been operated on for appendicitis. He gives a talk on the music of Milhaud in Aix-en-Provence (24 July).

(17 August) Enclosing a photograph of the upright piano put at his disposal in Bagnols by Mimi Martin, FP writes Brigitte that he has finished *Sept Répons des ténèbres.*

(26 August) The future Poulenc scholar Carl B. Schmidt meets FP in Noizay. FP makes progress on *Sept Répons* (September) and accompanies Duval in a recital in Amboise to benefit the restoration of the church in Noizay. After a visit to Brussels, he leaves for the south of France on 26 September.

(End of October) After serving as jury member for the Ricordi prize in Milan, FP plays his Concerto for Two Pianos with Jacques Février in Lausanne, where he resides at his favorite hotel, the Beau-Rivage.

(November) First public performance of **La Dame de Monte-Carlo FP180**, in Monte Carlo. Denise Duval is accompanied by FP. The orchestral version, conducted by Georges Prêtre, is given in the Théâtre des Champs-Élysées on 5 December.

(13 November) FP, staying at the Hotel Piccadilly, gives a small recital in London, then performs *Aubade* in Braunschweig, Germany, on the 17th.

(December) FP dines with novelist, critic, and poet François Mauriac, who writes a portrait of the composer in vol. 3 of his *Bloc-notes* (five volumes of memoirs). Poulenc manages to give Mauriac the impression that he is as young and energetic as he was forty years earlier.

(7 December) FP hears *La Voix humaine* in Marseilles.

Sometime this year, FP and Suzanne Peignot are involved in a serious

road accident, from which they escape unscathed. Poulenc confided to Peignot, "*I would rather have died in that fashion, from a brutal death without
warning.*"[16]

1962 (aged 63)

(6 and 7 January) FP plays his Concerto for Two Pianos with Jacques Février
at the Théâtre des Champs-Élysées, under the baton of Georges Prêtre.

(9 February) FP and Duval embark on an Italian tour, a modified replace-
ment for the one that was canceled in December 1960: Florence (10th), Trieste (12th), Rome (16th), Perugia (18th). In Trieste and Perugia their program
included Debussy (the *Proses lyriques* and *Chansons de Bilitis*), and in Rome
it was all Poulenc: *À sa guitare, Air champêtre, Voyage à Paris, La Dame de
Monte-Carlo*, the aria from *Les Mamelles de Tirésias*, and in the second half
La Voix humaine. Poulenc suffers from a trapped nerve in his right arm.

(19 March) After eight years of strife and warfare, Algeria, a colony of
France, obtains its independence.

From Italy, FP goes straight to Bagnols, then back to Paris and again to
Bagnols. This "bagnolaise" period of his life is drawing to a close. He informs
Bernac (26 March) that he has finished *Sept Répons des ténèbres* (FP181):
"*With the Gloria and the Stabat, I have, I believe, three good religious works.
May they spare me a few days in purgatory, if I do narrowly avoid going to
hell. . . . After providing the rare, few rich of Bagnols with showers, sinks and
WCs,* [Louis Gautier] *has no more* work . . . *so he has decided to look for work
in Cannes.*" Poulenc announces himself free from the obsessive relationship
with Louis, whom he now regards as a beloved child rather than a lover; the
same transformation had happened earlier with Raymond Destouches. His
letter ends with sad words for all those who value Poulenc's unique contribution to the mélodie: "*What a lot of talent I had for this genre, a thing of the
past for me now.*"[17]

(9–13 April) FP travels with Duval to Venice, where she sings the role of
Mélisande in Debussy's *Pelléas et Mélisande*. Bernac, who helped prepare her,
tells Poulenc that he finds her too knowing and dramatic in the role.

(May) Back in Paris, FP suddenly feels extremely unwell in a bar following a concert at the Théâtre des Champs-Élysées, and is helped into a taxi and
taken home. In retrospect, Richard Chanlaire, with him at the time, believed
that the episode was a warning of the more serious attack that would take his
life seven months later.

(June) Jean Françaix orchestrates *L'Histoire de Babar*, a task Poulenc had
declined to take on and now finds masterfully done.

(13–15 June) FP and Bernac collaborate in a pair of joint master classes
on the songs of Debussy at the École Normale de Musique, to celebrate that

composer's centenary. It is the only occasion when they share a teaching project of this kind in Paris.

(18 June) In Milan, FP hears a performance of Falla's opera *Atlantide*. In Paris, he attends a performance of Strauss's *Salome* (25th) and then one of Hans Werner Henze's *Le Prince de Hombourg*, which he regards as a mixture of old and new that does not convince.

(1 July) First public performance of **La Courte paille FP178**, at the Abbey of Royaumont, near Asnières-sur-Oise. Soprano Colette Herzog is accompanied by Claude Helffer. The composer did not attend.

The summer is especially frantic with travel in the south of France. FP spends time in Brive with Marthe Bosredon (where he sketches the Oboe Sonata), and passes some blessedly peaceful hours at Rocamadour on 3 July.

(22–25 July) FP travels to the Festival in Aix-en-Provence, where he hears Mozart's *Die Entführung aus dem Serail*, a recital with Teresa Berganza (wonderfully accompanied by her husband, Felix Lavilla), Milhaud's *Les Malheurs d'Orphée* (for which he finds the Eurydice, Denise Duval, unsuited), and Stravinsky's *Les Noces*.

The ebony statuette of the Black Virgin at Rocamadour.

(25 July) Bernac writes to Poulenc from the University of Illinois in Urbana, where he is giving master classes. He complains that French students do not come to study with him. "Life is rather severe and the countryside is ugly and impoverished . . . I don't see you being here."[18]

(29–31 July) In Menton, FP accompanies a former pupil of Bernac's, the talented baritone Bernard Kruysen, as well as flautist Christian Lardé. The program includes eight Debussy songs and Poulenc's Flute Sonata.

(August) FP composes incidental music (now lost) in Noizay for the Cocteau play *Renaud et Armide*, to be given in Baalbek, Lebanon. He is in Milan on the 20th, but is unable to travel to Baalbek on account of an angina attack. He flies back to Paris and, after seeing his doctor, goes at once to Le Tremblay.

(September) Rose Dercourt-Plaut is Poulenc's guest at Noizay as he works on sonatas for clarinet and oboe. The first is dedicated to the memory of Arthur Honegger, the second to the memory of Sergei Prokofiev.

In the autumn Suzanne Latarjet, sister of Raymonde Linossier, dies. After attending her funeral, Poulenc returns to the south of France, where Louis Gautier has sold the house in Bagnols-en-Forêt and taken over the management of a gay bar in Cannes. Two years after Poulenc's death, Louis will be jailed for receiving stolen goods and drug trafficking.[19]

(October) FP writes his contribution, to be published in November 1963, to a Festschrift celebrating the fiftieth birthday of Benjamin Britten.[20] He leaves for several weeks' holiday in Cannes (22nd)—in the middle of the Cuban missile crisis, a stand-off between Russia and the United States when the world stands on the threshold of nuclear war.

FP plans another visit to the United States for April 1963, to include premieres of *Sept Répons des ténèbres* (with the New York Philharmonic) and the sonatas for clarinet and oboe, as well as a program of his mélodies with Donald Gramm, a gifted young American bass approved of by Bernac.[21]

(3–6 December) FP serves on a jury for the Trieste prize (awarded to an opera), chaired by Gian Francesco Malipiero, in Asolo, Italy. A few days at the Gritti Palace in Venice are followed by a visit to Milan to discuss a Piccolo Scala production of *Les Mamelles de Tirésias* for April 1963. He then makes his last visit to Bagnols (13th) and returns to his recently refurbished apartment in Paris to share New Year celebrations with Raymond Destouches and his wife Céline.

1963 (aged 64)

(Early January) FP spends time in Noizay with Richard Chanlaire and Stéphane Audel (who is planning another series of radio conversations) and continues work on the two wind sonatas and correcting proofs of *Sept Répons*.

FP's plans for an American visit in April include the participation of Suzanne Peignot, Bernac, and "Dolly" de Tinan (née Bardac), Debussy's step-daughter (and some say Fauré's daughter), whom he often consulted when performing Debussy. He is angry that his American agent has permitted the publication of choral excerpts from *Dialogues des Carmélites* (the "Ave verum" and "Salve Regina"), which he expressly forbade.

At Noizay, Audel and Poulenc listen together to recordings of Schubert, Webern, Bartok, Verdi, Puccini, Wagner, and Wolf. Audel provides this description of his last evening with Poulenc, before they returned to Paris on 14 January:

> Francis lit a great wood-fire on the hearth, settled himself comfortably on a chair, and gave himself up to the pleasure of conversation. He was daz-

zling. Once again I admired the range of his culture. His knowledge of music, painting and literature was bewildering. Evoking the memories of youth, he brought to life again with spirit, buffoonery and a fantastic sense of observation the surrealists, the Princesse de Polignac, Diaghilev, Wanda Landowska, Anna de Noailles, not forgetting Satie, Georges Auric, Cocteau, Éluard, and Marcel Proust, from whose *Sodome et Gomorrhe* he read a passage about Monsieur Charlus.[22]

(18 January) FP posts the Clarinet Sonata to Robert Douglas Gibson at Chester's Music in London and promises to mail the Oboe Sonata the following week.

In Paris, Audel attends two plays with Poulenc. Their parting words on the métro confirm plans to meet on 30 January in order to continue their recorded conversations: "He made his way to the exit in the lazy way peculiar to him, his feet lightly turned outward, the felt hat set back on his head like a halo, the roomy Raglan overcoat swaying to the rhythm of his step."[23]

FP spends four days with Denise Duval on a tour of Holland. Their last concert is at Maastricht on 26 January. Poulenc plays his *Concert champêtre* with orchestra, and Duval sings *La Dame de Monte-Carlo* and arias from *Les Mamelles de Tirésias*. After the concert Poulenc sends a bouquet of flowers to her hotel room with the message *"My Denise, it is to you that I owe my last joy. Your poor Fr."*[24]

(28 January) FP returns to Paris, and asks Duval to lunch with him on the 30th (the thirty-third anniversary of the death of Raymonde Linossier). On that day he gets up early and washes and shaves before having to return to bed with a searing pain in his chest. At 9 a.m. Audel receives a call from Poulenc's sister Jeanne (who lives in the same building); she has tried to contact his doctor without success. Audel, and then Bernac, also fail to reach him. A maid is sent to fetch a doctor who lives in the same building, but by the time they arrive, it is too late: the composer has vomited blood and died of a rupture of the aorta.[25]

A friend of Brigitte, alerted to the composer's death, fetches her by car from the other side of Paris, but on the way only dares to tell her that her uncle is gravely ill. At the foot of the staircase leading to the sixth-floor apartment, Brigitte senses the truth and collapses. A few days later she opens Poulenc's will from 1954 (addressed to her), in which she is tasked with the distribution of his paintings, furniture, silverware, books, and music to friends and family. A supplementary letter, eloquent and rueful, reveals to her the existence of his daughter (and thus her cousin) Marie-Ange Lebedeff, who is now sixteen and the will's principal beneficiary. This is a shock from which, it is said, Brigitte never recovers; she dies three months later.

Songs of the Sixties

FP178 *La Courte paille* (*The Short Straw*)

     Composed in Bagnols-en-Forêt, July–August 1960

     [*Denise Duval et Richard Schilling*; Eschig]

     Literary sources: Maurice Carême (1899–1978): *La Cage aux grillons* (Paris: Éditions Bourrelier, 1959), (i) p. 32, (ii) p. 56 with the title "La Puce et l'éléphant," (iv) p. 43, (vi) p. 49 with the title "La Carafe et le carafon"; *Le Voleur d'étincelles* (Brussels: Henri Kumps, 1956), (iii) p. 28 with the title "Vitres de lune," (v) p. 44, (vii) p. 22

     (i)   *Le Sommeil*

     (ii) *Quelle Aventure!*

     (iii) *La Reine de cœur*

     (iv) *Ba, be, bi, bo, bu*

     (v) *Les Anges musiciens*

     (vi) *Le Carafon*

     (vii) *Lune d'avril*

By 1960, having decided that there was nothing else in Apollinaire and Éluard he wanted to set to music, Poulenc appears to have relied on chance and circumstance to direct his song-composing agenda: celebratory poems for two singers, Marya Freund and Jane Bathori (occasioning excuses for quick returns to his two favorite poets), a poem sent through the post for *Nuage,* and a Shakespeare lyric

Maurice Carême at his desk.

(*Fancy*) requested by Marion Harewood. With the advent of Denise Duval into his life as protégée and recital partner, he must have initially expected the kind of collaboration that would continue where his concert life with Bernac had left off. But in an interview given in America in April 1960, some months before the composition of *La Courte paille*, he sounds as though he had already given up hope: "*Today, poets do not write in a manner that inspires me to song. I once told the young French composer Boulez that I was too old for René Char and that he was too young for Éluard. But aside from all that, I have written well over 100 songs, and to write more would be to force myself in a direction in which I really have nothing further to say.*"[26]

And Duval was first and foremost an opera singer; she was simply not destined to become a true recitalist in the manner of Bernac. The disciplined conventions of the recital platform, which require that emotion should be contained by form (above all in the singing of mélodie), have inhibited many singers' ability to function in this discipline—including some of the most celebrated, the great Maria Callas among them. Duval's concert appearances with Poulenc featured some Debussy and the easier Poulenc songs (like *Voyage à Paris*), but the focal point was dramatic extracts from *Les Mamelles de Tirésias* or *Dialogues*, as well as performances with piano of *La Voix humaine*.

In 1947, when Duval sang the role of Thérèse in *Les Mamelles de Tirésias*, Poulenc became her adviser in all things musical, but also in matters of dress (the couture of his friend Christian Dior suited her) and making her way in high society. Talented as she was, Poulenc prided himself on the fact that Duval was, in a way, his invention, and she regarded him as her beloved mentor. Poulenc may not have known Shaw's *Pygmalion*, but there was a side of him that delighted in the grooming of such a beautiful young woman, perhaps the kind of woman he himself would have loved to be in another life.

In the summer of 1960, in an attempt to kick-start an enthusiasm for song on her part, Poulenc selected seven poems of Maurice Carême for a cycle called *La Courte paille* (a title, derived from a children's game, suggested by the poet), to be sung by Duval at the end of January 1961 in Charleroi, near the poet's home. (He initially hoped the songs would be premiered in Italy during a tour that the singer canceled.) As Duval was the mother of a young son, it is perhaps unsurprising that he should think of texts for children. "*On some charming poems by Maurice Carême, halfway between Francis Jammes and Max Jacob, I have composed seven short songs for Denise Duval or, more exactly, for Denise Duval to sing to a little boy of six. These sketches ["croquis"], by turns sad or mischievous, are unpretentious. They should be sung tenderly. That is the surest way to touch the heart of a child.*"[27]

Carême was a minor poet but a highly talented one. He had consecrated his entire career to the writing of poetry that was accessible, neither symbolist nor surrealist but full of fantasy, wit, and elegance, inhabiting that special category of writing from which child and adult can derive equal pleasure. Poulenc was careful not to write anything too demandingly esoteric, but still he made a rare mistake regarding Duval's musical and literary tastes: they offer little opportunity for her kind of singer to tell a story or dominate the stage. The performance in Charleroi was never to take place; the first performance was given by the soprano Colette Herzog in Royaumont on 1 July 1962.

In Carl Schmidt's *Entrancing Muse,* we learn that "Duval disliked the music . . . and never did sing the cycle," an unfootnoted observation that must have stemmed from a personal conversation between Schmidt and the singer.[28] It was a refusal (unprecedented, except for Ninon Vallin's declining to sing the Vilmorin *Fiançailles pour rire* nearly a quarter of a century earlier) that must have disappointed Poulenc, perhaps even devastated him. He had surely hoped that Duval's reaction would be more like Carême's:

> It is truly a royal reward for a poet to be set to music by Francis Poulenc. How have you managed to extend, as far as the stars, the suggestions simply put to you by the verse? I am literally astounded by this transfiguration, by this changing of lead into fine gold. As narrated by you, *Quelle Aventure!* indeed! *Les Anges musiciens* or the *Carafon* becomes just as unforgettable. You have built a castle of the moon, more mysterious than the castles of fairytales. *Ba, be, bi, bo, bu* is of a mischievous, boisterous gaiety. I love the lullaby of *Sommeil* and you have made of *Lune d'avril* a kind of masterpiece both real and surreal at the same time—its final chords prolong themselves endlessly in the mind of the listener.[29]

Duval's lack of interest (she blamed her management and full diary, as singers often do when not really eager to take up musical challenges),[30] the lack of the kind of symbiosis he had enjoyed with Bernac, confirmed his feeling that his song-writing days were over. The failure of his chosen singer to perform his latest cycle sounded the death-knell of Poulenc's song-composing career.

Today, however, *La Courte paille* has become so popular that apart from the ubiquitous *Les Chemins de l'amour,* these are often the first Poulenc songs taken on by singers and pianists. They work well as a final group in a recital, light-hearted but with more than a compensatory streak of melancholy, and typical of what many believe French song should be. Singers or pianists coming to these songs after having experienced the great mélodies of the thirties and forties could well be struck by how Poulenc has purposefully limited his expressive ambitions; some would also notice a diminution in the scope and energy of his invention. Yet he has deployed those slimmer compositional resources with consummate skill. There is an admirable economy in this music, not a note wasted, the fruit of a lifetime's experience.

(i) *Le Sommeil (Sleep)*

No key signature (C major); $\frac{4}{4}$; *Très calme* ♩= 48

Le sommeil est en voyage,	Sleep's gone off on a journey,
Mon Dieu! où est-il parti?	Heavens, where's he gone to?
J'ai beau bercer mon petit,	It's no good rocking my little one,
Il pleure dans son lit-cage,	He's crying in his cot,
Il pleure depuis midi.	He's been crying since noon.
Où le sommeil a-t-il mis	Where has Sleep put
Son sable et ses rêves sages?	His sand and his lovely dreams?
J'ai beau bercer mon petit,	My baby's tossing and turning,
Il se tourne tout en nage,	Drenched in sweat,
Il sanglote dans son lit.	He's sobbing in his bed.
Ah! reviens, reviens, sommeil,	Ah, come back, Sleep, come back
Sur ton beau cheval de course!	On your beautiful racehorse!
Dans le ciel noir, la Grande Ourse	In the dark sky the Great Bear
A enterré le soleil	Has buried the sun
Et rallumé ses abeilles.	And lit up his bees again.
Si l'enfant ne dort pas bien,	If the child doesn't have a good sleep,
Il ne dira pas bonjour,	He won't say good morning,
Il ne dira rien demain	He won't say a word tomorrow
À ses doigts, au lait, au pain	To his fingers, to his milk, to the bread
Qui l'accueillent dans le jour.	Which will welcome him come morning.

Le Sommeil is the one song in the cycle that Duval might have enjoyed in terms of characterization. A mother is at her wits' end, although the poem's despair seems to be contradicted by the music: gentle syncopations signify the rocking of a cradle, and a tempo marking calls for calm. The most exasperated performance I ever accompanied was by that stylish French soprano Mady Mesplé, who had a way of incorporating impatience into the song without disturbing its pulse. (French singers are often able to achieve this effect, using a kind of rubato in their diction while remaining faithful to the written rhythm of the music.) Here is well-to-do maternal angst, a long way from Poulenc's earlier Max Jacob setting *Berceuse* FP59/iv, where a working-class Breton nursemaid threatens to spank a child's bottom if it goes on crying. In most performances the mood of *Le Sommeil* is gentle and serious, taking its cue from the music rather than the words—"a little anxious" is how Bernac describes the mother's attitude.[31] But it might be argued that Mesplé was right, and the composer was aiming for something rather more droll. How Duval would have presented this song remains a fascinating might-have-been.

The sense of daylight illuminating the picture at the final cadence (on "dans le jour") is almost palpable—one of the special final chords in a cycle remarkable for the sensuality (as here) or dryness of the codas.

(ii) *Quelle Aventure! (What Goings-On!)*
No key signature (F major); $\frac{2}{4}$; *Très vite et rythmé* ♩ = 138

Une puce, dans sa voiture,	A flea, in a car,
Tirait un petit éléphant	Was towing an elephant
En regardant les devantures	While looking at the shop windows
Où scintillaient des diamants.	Which were twinkling with diamonds.
—Mon Dieu! mon Dieu! quelle aventure!	—My God! My God! What goings-on!
Qui va me croire, s'il m'entend?	Who'd believe me if I told them?
L'éléphanteau, d'un air absent,	The baby elephant, with a vacant stare,
Suçait un pot de confiture.	Was hoovering up a pot of jam.
Mais la puce n'en avait cure,	But the flea didn't seem to care,
Elle tirait en souriant.	And carried on pulling, smiling the while.
—Mon Dieu! mon Dieu! que cela dure	—My God! My God! It doesn't stop
Et je vais me croire dément.	I'm going to think I'm going mad!
Soudain, le long d'une clôture,	Suddenly, along a fence,
La puce fondit dans le vent	The flea vanished into air
Et je vis le jeune éléphant	And I saw the baby elephant
Se sauver en fendant les murs.	Running away, smashing the walls.
—Mon Dieu! mon Dieu! la chose est sûre.	—My God! My God! It definitely happened,
Mais comment la dire à maman?	But how am I going to tell my mum?

Poulenc asked Carême's permission to change the poem's title, originally "La Puce et l'éléphant"—pointing out that one should not give the game away in the title and thus spoil the joke. Poulenc seems to have felt a certain affinity with elephants, so large and shambolic in appearance, so clever and sensitive within. This helter-skelter miniature for the ridiculous notion of a flea pulling an elephant is reminiscent of *L'Histoire de Babar*'s motor-car music (in the ninth section), and the day-dreaming elephant sucking a pot of jam recalls the more reflective harmonies in *Babar* (thirteenth section), when the kind old lady pictures her beloved elephant and wonders if she will see him again.

Poulenc does not shrink from depicting the flea, an uppity insect famous in Goethe settings by Beethoven and Musorgksy for making ladies and gentlemen of the court itch furiously:[32] staccato eighth notes poking out cheekily between the pianist's hands at the opening suggest the minute size and feisty character of the little bloodsucker. The excitable words "Mon Dieu" have surely never been better set to music, capturing exactly the inflection of the spoken phrase; but their octave leaps are also inspired by the idea of a flea jumping, while the piano leaps down the same octave, F to F, in a kind of counterpoint of astonishment—music-hall hoopla of the most innocent kind. As in *Babar*, the elephant is essentially a good-hearted if somewhat clumsy creature, and the way Poulenc changes the atmosphere of the song in a trice (at "L'éléphanteau, d'un air absent"), without changing the tempo, shows the touch of a master. The song contrasts and joins together the different personalities of the two creatures, one biting and bracing, the other emollient and gentle. Here an old, breathless style is reworked to charming effect.[33]

(iii) *La Reine de cœur (The Queen of Hearts)*
No key signature (E minor); $\frac{6}{8}$; *Très calme et languide* ♩. = 42

Mollement accoudée	Leaning gently, her elbow
À ses vitres de lune,	Against her windows of moonlight,
La reine vous salue	The queen is waving to you
D'une fleur d'amandier.	With a sprig of almond blossom.
C'est la reine de cœur.	She is the queen of hearts,
Elle peut, s'il lui plaît,	And should she wish, she can
Vous mener en secret	Secretly lead you
Vers d'étranges demeures	To strange dwellings
Où il n'est plus de portes,	Where there are no more doors
De salles ni de tours	Nor rooms nor towers
Et où les jeunes mortes	And where dead girls
Viennent parler d'amour.	Come to speak of love.
La reine vous salue:	The Queen is waving to you,
Hâtez-vous de la suivre	Quickly, follow her

Dans son château de givre	Into her castle of frost
Aux doux vitraux de lune.	With its lovely windows of moonlight.

This song, so often sung by students, so simple to play and not difficult to sing adequately—and yet hugely difficult to sing and play really well—is full of gentle heartache. It is a perfect distillation of a type of Poulenc song that has won him countless admirers and adherents, and it certainly played a part in my conversion to his cause.

At this slow metronome marking, the piece (beginning in $\frac{6}{8}$, but mainly in $\frac{9}{8}$) has the lilt of a sad and dreamlike waltz, a reminder that so much of what is touchingly nostalgic in Poulenc's music is dependent on dance. Whenever the composer talked about such music (as, for example, his *Nocturne* in C Minor, *Bal fantôme*), he invoked Alain-Fournier's *Le Grand Meaulnes*, a magical novel that also features a château—not made of frost as in *La Reine de cœur*, but a construction of fragile adolescent dreams. Here it is the young who are dead, and as in Ravel's *Là-bas, vers l'église* (from *Cinq Mélodies populaires grecques*), we are tempted to think of youthful soldiers slain in war. The poet writes of dead young girls, however, so this is no war song. (For me, since first hearing *La Reine de cœur* sung forty years ago by Régine Crespin, the music evokes the strange melancholy, with a hint of otherworldly menace, of Hans Christian Andersen's *The Snow Queen*.)

In his first mélodie in this vein, *Hier* (FP57/iii), Poulenc demonstrated his ability to invoke the ghost of heartfelt popular song. A hint of cabaret style is distilled to a harmonic shadow of the original, and yet it is still potent enough to deepen an atmosphere of nostalgia; on this account, some would call *Hier* the first song to reveal the composer's unique musical voice. As if coming full circle toward the end of his career, *La Reine de cœur* shares that earlier song's key of E minor. In other hands the music would turn out sentimental and mawkish, but here there is a kind of perfection in simplicity, and everything Poulenc does has a classiness that avoids the cheap or sensational. Even the hackneyed change of minor to major for the concluding bar

The cover of Carême's collection Le Voleur d'étincelles *(1956).*

somehow avoids banality; it is one of his most beautifully engineered endings. If the song is merely an echo of the composer's past splendors, the dreamlike world of the poem inhabits a world of echoes in itself, and Poulenc conveys its essence in the fewest possible notes—in short, masterfully.

(iv)   *Ba, be, bi, bo, bu*
　　　No key signature (E-flat minor); $\frac{4}{4}$; *Très gai, follement vite* ♩ = 152

Ba, be, bi, bo, bu, bé!	Ba, be, bi, bo, bu, bé!
Le chat a mis ses bottes,	The cat's put on his boots,
Il va de porte en porte	And is going from door to door
Jouer, danser, chanter.	Playing, dancing, singing.
Pou, chou, genou, hibou.	Pou, chou, genou, hibou.
"Tu dois apprendre à lire,	"You've got to learn to read,
À compter, à écrire,"	To count, to write,"
Lui crie-t-on de partout.	That's what everyone's shouting at him.
Mais rikketakketau,	But ricky-ticky-toe,
Le chat de s'esclaffer	The cat bursts out laughing
En rentrant au château:	As he goes back to his castle.
Il est le Chat botté! . . .	He's Puss in Boots! . . .

There are a few other ditties like this one in the Poulenc repertoire (*Chanson* FP57/ii, *Fêtes galantes* FP122/ii, *Chansons du clair-tamis* FP117/i)—the nonsense lyric, learned by rote and performed full tilt as a patter song, or like a playground counting game. The words "pou, chou, genou, hibou" are a mnemonic to remember which nouns take an x to form their plurals, and the singer, on automatic pilot, has no time to put them across as something she has experienced or felt.

In devising programs of animal songs, singers almost never consider *Ba, be,* forgetting that it is about a cat—though it displays none of the feline and slinky charm to be found in Henri Sauguet's songs about his favorite pet (Poulenc was more of a dog person).[34] The final two bars could easily illustrate a moment of wizardry in a pantomime: a $\frac{5}{4}$ bar with five *forte* quarter notes in the vocal line is accompanied by a bluster of descending eighth-note octaves in the bass . . . and then, as if in a sudden puff of smoke, Puss in Boots materializes with a bang, followed by a snatched staccato chord, a circus flourish. Bernac's judgment is hard to refute: "This little scherzo of 23 seconds obviously does not demand any subtlety. . . . rhythmic precision . . . percussive diction, that does the trick."[35]

(v) *Les Anges musiciens* (*The Angel Musicians*)
No key signature (B-flat major/E minor); $\frac{4}{4}$; *Très lent et tendre* ♩ = 50

Sur les fils de la pluie,	On the strings of the rain,
Les anges du jeudi	The angels of Thursday
Jouent longtemps de la harpe.	Play the harp unceasingly.
Et sous leurs doigts, Mozart	And beneath their fingers, Mozart
Tinte, délicieux,	Tinkles deliciously
En gouttes de joie bleue,	In drops of blue joy,
Car c'est toujours Mozart	For it's always Mozart
Que reprennent sans fin	Which is endlessly played
Les anges musiciens	By the Angel Musicians
Qui, au long du jeudi,	Who, all Thursday long
Font chanter sur leur harpe	On their harps, pluck out the song
La douceur de la pluie.	Of the sweetness of the rain.

A kind of neoclassical Poulenc occurs here and there in his piano works and chamber music but not in his songs, where he is more likely to show his dab hand at medieval pastiche (*À sa guitare* FP79, *Priez pour paix* FP95). But here the poem's references to Mozart occasion a not-quite quotation from the B-flat major slow movement (*Romanze*) of the D Minor Piano Concerto, K466—a slow-motion evocation of its opening. The pianist's hands are poised in the same part of the keyboard as for the Mozart, and there is a similar euphony (tenths between the hands) as the tune pivots from F at the top of the tonic chord to E-natural (with a C-sharp in the bass), and back to the F and up to the neighboring G—just about enough to summon the ghost of the concerto for those who know it. The poem's mention of Thursdays (a half-day holiday for French children) evokes images of pupils practicing the piano after school on rainy Thursday afternoons. We can be certain that memories of such Thursdays held some significance for the composer; the whole song has an air of seraphic melancholy.

Mozart, a composer whose music is unsullied with trappings of the Romanticism yet to come, is a byword for purity and calm. And Poulenc attempts to conjure an atmosphere of angelic innocence at the beginning, the same kind of nostalgia Schubert achieves in the opening ritornello of *Frühlingstraum* from *Winterreise*. After the first two bars, the Mozartian point has been made, and we move on into the more familiar realms of Poulenc's chromatic harmony. It is a pity that in *Les Anges musiciens* he allows the music to teeter on the edge of sentimentality, on the second page in particular. But the blame can be laid equally at Carême's door; the chocolate-box Mozartian angels playing on instruments that were not best favored by the composer verge on the twee, and we sense that Poulenc chose the poem chiefly on account of its musical references.[36] There is something predictable and uninspired about bars 7–10 (beginning "Car c'est tou- jours Mozart"). Was Poulenc remembering how much he longed as a child to play modern music rather than the classics? Is he trying to let it be known that even as an adult, he found the idea of endless Mozart an exasperating and boring prospect? If so, he has succeeded to my ears, but it is an in-joke; any singer would find it all but impossible to put across these words at anything other than their beatific face value.

This passage leads to one of his downward-modulating harmonic spirals, inspired by Liszt's *Valse oubliée*, which are more or less a cliché in the late songs. Although we have begun in B-flat major (Poulenc would never notate a musical memory in any key other than the one that first occurred to him), the song ends in E minor with a return to the opening melody, and at the close a lush E major seventh chord.

(vi) *Le Carafon (The Baby Carafe)*
No key signature; 4/4; *Très vite* ♩ = 132

"Pourquoi, se plaignait la carafe,
N'aurais-je pas un carafon?
Au zoo, madame la Girafe
N'a-t-elle pas un girafon?"
Un sorcier qui passait par là,
À cheval sur un phonographe,
Enregistra la belle voix
De soprano de la carafe
Et la fit entendre à Merlin.
"Fort bien, dit celui-ci, fort bien!"
Il frappa trois fois dans les mains
Et la dame de la maison
Se demande encore pourquoi
Elle trouva, ce matin-là,
Un joli petit carafon
Blotti tout contre la carafe
Ainsi qu'au zoo, le girafon
Pose son cou fragile et long
Sur le flanc clair de la girafe.

"Why?" moaned the carafe,
"Why can't I have a baby carafe?
Mrs. Giraffe down in the zoo
Hasn't she got a baby giraffe?"
A sorcerer who was passing by,
Sitting astride a phonograph,
Recorded the lovely soprano voice
Of the carafe
And played it to Merlin.
"Superb," said Merlin, "superb!"
He clapped his hands three times
And the lady of the house
Is to this day still wondering why
She found, that morning,
A pretty little baby carafe
Snuggled up to the carafe
Just as the baby giraffe in the zoo
Puts his long and fragile neck
Against the pale flank of the mummy
    giraffe.

In a footnote Carême acknowledges that "girafeau" is the normal term for a baby giraffe, but claims the mistake is the carafe's, not his. J. S.

This word game dressed up as a fairy tale rescues us from the cloying sweetness of the preceding number—in a kind of song Poulenc hardly ever composed, the recounting of a story in song. It is a very silly story, but still a narrative in six distinct episodes, all of which he skillfully differentiates while making us scarcely aware that we are listening to anything other than a graceful, organic whole.

We begin with the squeaky and plaintive voice of the carafe; a masculine voice will follow later, so there needs to be a different tessitura and articulation for the glassy voice of this pint-sized soprano. Staccato eighth notes between the hands add a certain petulant impatience, the plaint of someone who is being denied her nonhuman rights to a happy family life. The accompaniment makes clear the power of the anonymous sorcerer (big, masculine chords splashing an octave apart in the treble clef), his bumpy ride astride a gramophone illustrated by galumphing piano writing.

The third section involves the recording of the carafe's voice (the rather unworldly Carême fails to make clear how a "phonograph" is capable of making a recording, but we have found ourselves in the world of Harry Potter *avant la lettre*). Poulenc had some experience with records and recordings, but in 1960 the LP was brand-new, and most people still had libraries of 78s. At "Enregistra la belle voix" he conjures the sound of a gramophone needle on shellac (and making the kind of low-level background sound you hear before the music begins) in repetitive left-hand eighth notes, stuck in a groove of minor seconds for five bars. As for the singer, Bernac directs that "the legato should be exaggerated to the point of parodying a bad opera singer"; the carafe's "belle voix" was taken by Poulenc (according to Bernac) to be an ironic description.[37]

The next section introduces the character of Merlin, the Welsh wizard of Camelot and mentor of King Arthur. The great magician, evoked in two bars (12–13), is marvelously decisive and affable; in his reaction ("Fort bien") he shows himself amused with the whole scenario, a nuance clearly conveyed in the music. He claps his hands three times, the repeated bar in the accompaniment signifying a ritual, the casting of a spell. The fifth section is devoted to the anonymous "dame de la maison": descending the stairs of the stave in ladylike manner and finding, in either the kitchen or dining room, something profoundly astonishing and delightful. With no slowing up, the music has been led inexorably from the F-sharp major of bar 16 to an expectant cadence in the dominant (C-sharp major) in bar 21, on the words "ce matin-là."

This moment of surprise and hiatus is resolved by a return to F-sharp major. The final section describes the arrival of the baby carafe. For "Un joli petit carafon" the vocal line is made up of A-sharp followed by A-natural, and then back to A-sharp. The propinquity of these notes and the cozy and affectionate aura of the harmony in rippling right-hand eighth notes by which they are supported, a gentle oscillation between tonic and dominant in F-sharp major (bb. 17–20), provide an exact musical analogue for the nestling together of mother and child. In the concluding seven bars, with its description of a giraffe with her "girafon" (a real word this, unlike "carafon"), the music for "Pose son cou fragile" lies suitably high in the stave, suggesting the extent of the giraffe's long neck.

What follows is the absolute apotheosis of Poulenc's penchant, circa 1956–60, for a chain of modulations spiraling down the stave. After beginning in G-flat major (enharmonic to F-sharp) and after a good many flats and double flats in spindly eighth-note figurations (I imagine a long-legged but still unsteady girafon leaning on its mother and tottering to keep its balance), we reach a chord (essentially D minor) from which a sudden return to a staccato chord in F-sharp minor is possible. There is so much emotion here, all of it based on a ridiculous premise, that the only thing to do is to stop almost midstream, with a quick curtain (to tighten the pace, Poulenc cut a bar from the original version).[38] All in all, this is a most distinguished song, with more thought and detail behind it than we might first suspect, the art that conceals art.

(vii)   *Lune d'avril* (*April Moon*)
No key signature (C major); $\frac{2}{4}$; *Très lent et irréel* ♩ = 48

Lune, belle lune, lune d'avril,	Moon, lovely moon, April moon,
Faites-moi voir en mon dormant	Let me see in my slumbers
Le pêcher au cœur de safran,	The peach tree with the saffron heart,
Le poisson qui rit du grésil,	The fish who laughs at the sleet,
L'oiseau qui, lointain comme un cor,	The bird whose call, as distant as a horn,
Doucement réveille les morts	Sweetly awakens the dead
Et surtout, surtout le pays	And most, most of all, the land
Où il fait joie, où il fait clair,	Where all is joy, where all is light,
Où, soleilleux de primevères,	And sunshine and primroses,
On a brisé tous les fusils.	Where they have smashed all the guns.

For Bernac (who never sang *La Courte paille* but taught it everywhere), this song is the "most beautiful and the most intense of the collection. The poem is more substantial than the others."[39] After being put in mind of an elephant in *Quelle Aventure!*, Poulenc's thoughts may have returned again to the music of *Babar*. *Lune d'avril* is reminiscent of the early *Lent et mélancolique* piano solo (p. 16 of the score), where Babar's benefactress misses her adopted elephant and worries about him—just as here a mother dreams ("mon dormant") of a sunny future for her son in a world where dangerous weapons have been destroyed. The poem was written at a time of ban-the-bomb demonstrations, when nuclear disarmament was on everyone's mind. The composer was the father of a fourteen-year-old girl, although few knew about her at the time, but the idea of Poulenc as a campaigner for any cause is laughable.

Both pieces feature a quietly pulsing left hand in syncopation, off the beat (an F in the piano piece, a C in the song)—providing a rapt atmosphere that is somnolent in its lulling effect but also tense in the persistence of its rhythmic displacement. After seven bars the song's C major has changed into C minor, and those single repeated Cs are replaced by menacing octaves (*pianissimo* nevertheless); the song gradually unfolds into something much more intense and grand than the hushed opening has led us to suppose.

Now we encounter Carême at his most serious and symbolist. After images of laughing fish and birds awakening the dead, the nub of the poem ("le pays / Où il fait joie, où il fait clair") abandons the imagery of the nursery to imagine a better world, and an echo of Poulenc's altruistic Éluard style inspires a climax of some power. Since composing his last Éluard cycle, Poulenc had achieved world renown with *Dialogues des Carmélites*, and there is something about this *fortissimo* vocal line, accompanied by a succession of imposing seventh chords, that suggests operatic scale and grandeur. One factor is the sudden, unexpected sunburst of sound on "Où, soleilleux de primevères." Even the seemingly jarring prosody of making the highest note, and the most powerful moment in the phrase, occur on "Où" is vindicated by the phrase that runs on afterward, the crucial "On a brisé tous les fusils": music that returns to *pianissimo* in a setting that sounds more like a whispered prayer than a statement of fact. That expansive "Où" expressed the poet's hopes for a dream state, a Nirvana without weapons.

Carême's poem ends with "les fusils," but like so many composers, Schumann above all, Poulenc could not resist a recapitulation of convincing opening material. The first four bars of the song are now exactly repeated, but the final word, another "lune" (marked *pppp dans un souffle*), trails off and is left hanging on an inconclusive A-flat. Poulenc's farewell to song trails into the distance with one of his longest yet least eventful postludes, the right hand wavering between A-flat and G, the left hand insistently pulsating (but ever so softly) with that syncopated C in the bass. After eight bars this hypnotic succession of notes, only minutely altered with each half note, melts into a most voluptuous dominant seventh. The addition of that crucial and luxuriously decadent B-flat in the final C major chord creates a haunting, questioning resonance; while the left hand's *pppp* tintinnabulations sound the passing bell, the death knell, of Poulenc's life as a great composer of piano-accompanied mélodies.

o   o   o

FP179 *Sarabande* (guitar), March 1960

o   o   o

La Puce (without FP number) (*The Flea*)

> Composed in Noizay, 9 November 1960
> Literary source: Guillaume Apollinaire (1880–1918), *Le Bestiaire, ou Cortège d'Orphée*, woodcut illustrations by Raoul Dufy (Paris: Deplanche, Éditeur d'Art, 1911), eleventh poem in unnumbered pages
> No key signature (G minor); $\frac{3}{4}$; *Lent et mélancolique*

Puces, amis, amantes même,	Fleas, friends, lovers even,
Qu'ils sont cruels ceux qui nous aiment!	How cruel those who love us can be!
Tout notre sang coule pour eux.	All of our blood flows for them.
Les bien-aimés sont malheureux.	Being a beloved can hurt.

La Puce, perhaps the least known and least substantial of Poulenc's songs, was so well hidden in an expensive art book published in a limited edition that it failed to appear in Carl Schmidt's otherwise exhaustive 1995 catalogue. It is Poulenc's last setting from *Le Bestiaire*, and his last Apollinaire setting of all, forty-two years after the first. Written in memory of Raoul Dufy (who had made the woodcuts illustrating the poems), the song was published posthumously in Marcelle Oury's beautifully produced anthology in tribute to Dufy, *Lettres à mon peintre* (1965), to which Stravinsky and Milhaud, among others, also contributed.

Poulenc's memories of Dufy reached back to 1917, as one of the celebrities he remembered having seen at the premiere of Apollinaire's play *Les Mamelles de Tirésias*. With a composer as sensitive to images as Poulenc, it seems more than likely that the Dufy woodcuts, severe and serious yet droll, compact yet full of detail, influenced the tone of the *Bestiaire* songs in 1919. Dufy also designed the 1920 "Spectacle-Concert" organized by Cocteau, when Poulenc's *Cocardes* was performed. The composer's fondness for the painter as a man (he calls him *"cher Dufy"* in a letter of 1960) almost certainly dates back to this time.[40] In November 1956, while walking the streets of Berlin with a German music critic, *"I was wondering how to explain to him the evocation of my music of Parisian suburbia, when suddenly I caught sight in a bookshop window of a big reproduction of a celebrated picture by Dufy,* Boatmen on the Banks of the Marne. *'Look,' I said, 'that is my Nogent music.' I have always thought, moreover, that Dufy and I had more than a little in common."*[41]

It is no surprise that Poulenc identified with a painter, extremely versatile in several media, whose desire to delight his audience was important to him but not so important as to deflect him from his vocation. Dufy was dismissed as a superficial painter as often as Poulenc was thought to be a superficial composer; those who undervalued both artists because of their accessibility were often forced to concede, after evaluating the range and depth of work, that they were geniuses of their own kind, each *sui generis*. Even though they stood outside the establishment, their claim to fame was based not on their international significance (like some of their more famous heavyweight colleagues), but rather on the fact that they were irremediably French. And then "significance" is no longer an issue with the rest of the world, but rather music and painting that is overwhelmingly attractive and touching for having stayed at home, effortlessly representative of *l'esprit de France*.

Although Poulenc set "La Puce" in 1919 as one of the original twelve settings in *Le Bestiaire*, the song seems to have been destroyed. This setting from 1960 was evidently a new one. Its twelve bars are much nearer in style to *La Courte paille* than to anything in the 1919 cycle—particularly at the piano writing beneath "Tout notre sang coule pour eux" (where Poulenc surprises us by setting "coule" across the bar, with the final syllable on a higher note and a strong beat). Another unusual feature is the droll setting of "malheureux" as a plunging major seventh, D to E-flat; perhaps Poulenc had the leaping of a flea in mind. In the second and third bars of the postlude, the pianist's right hand jumps down a sixth, the second time tapping into a vein; in the middle of the chord, the B-flat of the first attempt at bloodsucking resolves to C-natural. Once anchored, it hangs there tenaciously for three and a half beats.

FP180 *La Dame de Monte-Carlo* (*The Lady of Monte Carlo*)

> Composed in Monte Carlo, April 1961
>
> [*Denise Duval*; Ricordi]
>
> Literary source: Jean Cocteau (1889–1963), *Théâtre de poche* (Paris: Éditions Paul Morihien, 1949), pp. 103–8. Among other items in this Cocteau anthology are the scenario for Satie's *Parade*; the plot for Milhaud's *Le Bœuf sur le toit*; the libretto for Milhaud's opera *Le Pauvre Matelot*; monologues written for Édith Piaf, *Le Bel Indifférent* and *Le Fantôme de Marseille*; and radio monologues for the actor Jean Marais.
>
> No key signature, $\frac{3}{4}$ *Lent et triste* ♩ = 50

Quand on est morte entre les mortes,	When you are dead among the dead,
Qu'on se traîne chez les vivants—	When you drag yourself around among the living,
Lorsque tout vous flanque à la porte	When life chucks you out of the door
Et la ferme d'un coup de vent,	And the wind slams it shut,
Ne plus être jeune et aimée . . .	No longer to be young and loved . . .
Derrière une porte fermée,	Behind a door that's closed,
Il reste de se fiche à l'eau	All that's left is to drown yourself
Ou d'acheter un rigolo.	Or to buy a revolver.
Oui, messieurs, voilà ce qui reste	Yes, gents, that's all that's left
Pour les lâches et les salauds.	For cowards and bastards.

Mais si la frousse de ce geste	But if your terror at such a step
S'attache à vous comme un grelot,	Clings and jingles like a cat's bell,
Si l'on craint de s'ouvrir les veines,	If you're too scared to open your veins
On peut toujours risquer la veine	You can always try your luck
D'un voyage à Monte-Carlo.	On a trip to Monte Carlo.

Monte-Carlo! Monte-Carlo!	*Monte Carlo! Monte Carlo!*
J'ai fini ma journée.	*My day is done.*
Je veux dormir au fond de l'eau.	*I want to sleep on the seabed*
De la Mediterranée.	*Of the Mediterranean.*
Monte-Carlo! Monte-Carlo!	*Monte Carlo! Monte Carlo!*

Après avoir vendu votre âme	After having sold your soul
Et mis en gage des bijoux	And pawned your jewels
Que jamais plus on ne réclame,	Which you'll never redeem,
La roulette est un beau joujou.	The roulette wheel is a tempting toy,
C'est joli de dire: je joue.	And it's lovely to say "I'm gambling."
Cela vous met le feu aux joues	It brings fire to your cheeks
Et cela vous allume l'œil.	And a twinkle to your eye.
Sous les jolis [de joyeux] voiles de deuil	Under your lovely mourning veils
On porte un joli [noble] nom de veuve.	You can bear the fine name of "widow."
Un titre donne de l'orgueil!	It's a title to be proud of!
Et folle, et prête, et toute neuve,	And mad, and ready, and fresh as a daisy,

On prend sa carte au casino.	You sign in at the casino.
Voyez mes plumes et mes voiles,	Look at my feathers and my veils,
Contemplez le strass de l'étoile	Look at the sequins of the twinkling star

Qui me mène à Monte-Carlo.	That leads me to Monte Carlo.

La chance est femme. Elle est jalouse	Luck is a woman. She is jealous
De ces veuvages solennels.	Of my widow's weeds.
Sans doute elle m'a cru l'épouse	She probably thought I was the wife
D'un véritable colonel.	Of a real colonel.
J'ai gagné, gagné sur le douze.	I won! I won on the twelve.
Et puis les robes se décousent,	And then your dresses come unstitched,
La fourrure perd ses cheveux.	Your furs begin to moult.
On a beau répéter: "je veux,"	No use repeating "I want"
Dès que la chance vous déteste,	When luck starts loathing you,
Dès que votre cœur est nerveux,	When your heart is a bundle of nerves,
Vous ne pouvez plus faire un geste,	You can't move a muscle,

Pousser un sou sur le tableau

Sans que la chance qui s'écarte
Change les chiffres et les cartes
Des tables de Monte-Carlo.

Les voyous! les buses! les gales!
Ils m'ont mise dehors . . . dehors . . .
Et ils m'accusent d'être sale,
De porter malheur dans leurs salles,
Dans leurs sales salles en stuc.
Moi qui aurais donné mon truc

À l'œil, au prince, à la princesse,
Au duc de Westminster, au duc,
Parfaitement.—Faut que ça cesse,
Qu'ils me criaient, votre boulot!

Votre boulot? . . . Ma découverte.
J'en priverai les tables vertes.

C'est bien fait pour Monte-Carlo.

Monte-Carlo!

Et maintenant, moi qui vous parle,
Je n'avouerai pas les kilos
Que j'ai perdus à Monte-Carle,
(Monte-Carle ou Monte-Carlo)
Je suis une ombre de moi-même . . .
Les martingales, les systèmes
Et les croupiers qui ont le droit
De taper de loin sur vos doigts
Quand on veut faucher une mise.

Et la pension où l'on doit

Et toujours la même chemise
Que l'angoisse trempe dans l'eau.

Or push so much as a penny onto the table

Without Luck as she exits,
Changing the numbers and the cards
On the tables of Monte Carlo.

The hoodlums! The vultures! The scabs!
They threw me out . . . out . . .
They accused me of being filthy,
Of bringing bad luck into their hallowed halls,
Into their filthy stuccoed halls.
Me, who would happily have divulged my system

To the prince, the princess,
To the Duke of Westminster,
The Duke, no less!—This has to stop,
Them shouting at me, "This job of yours!"

This job!? No, my discovery.
I'm going to withhold it from the green baize tables.

And serve you right, Monte Carlo.

Monte Carlo!

And right now, I who am speaking to you
Won't own up to the kilos
I've lost at Monte Carlo
(Monte Carle or Monte Carlo)
I am a shadow of my former self . . .
The formulas, the systems
And the croupiers who have the right
To rap you on the knuckles from afar
When you're trying to snaffle someone's stake.

And the digs where you owe them money

And always wearing the same blouse
Soaked in the muck sweat of fear.

Ils peuvent courir. Pas si bête.	Well, forget about that. I'm not that stupid.
Cette nuit je pique une tête	Tonight I'm going to dive headfirst
Dans la mer de Monte-Carlo.	Into the sea at Monte Carlo.
Monte-Carlo!	*Monte Carlo!*

> *The language is full of old-fashioned slang, from the Lady's prime, one presumes. Notably, "rigolo" (line 8)—gangster slang for a revolver. A "shooter" maybe, a "piece," or a "gat"?* J. S.

Cocteau conceived "La Dame de Monte-Carlo" for the singer-actress Marianne Oswald (1901–1985)—a recitation in the grand manner where only the "Monte-Carlo, Monte-Carlo" refrain (appearing three times) is sung, accompanied by piano (music not by Poulenc but allegedly by the poet himself). Cocteau described the decaying atmosphere of this gambling paradise in 1924, at about the same time as Poulenc's *Les Biches* received its premiere there: "The pilgrims mark down their losses in registers. They wet their pencils while, game over, the roulette wheel turns on with the motley slowness of racehorses returning to the paddock. A few bringers of good fortune and ill are circulating between the tables; charming, crazy, old English ladies who sleep standing up and make their way, not having changed their dress since the reign of Victoria."[42]

Cocteau's "Dame" is an aging courtesan who makes one last pilgrimage to the casinos of Monte Carlo in pursuit of Lady Luck, in the company of highflyers and extravagant gamblers. One such playboy is actually mentioned obliquely in the text: Hugh Grosvenor, second Duke of Westminster, a notorious womanizer and Coco Chanel's lover for ten years. Poulenc almost certainly had a "Dame" of his own in mind, a courtesan from Belle Époque times: Marthe de Kerrieu (1870–1958), who had been a good friend and near neighbor in Noizay. Marthe's scabrous tales of the sexual excesses of her past tickled the composer no end; he wrote a glowing preface to her *Mélie, Histoire d'une cocotte de 1900*, a novel in the form of thinly disguised memoirs that appeared in 1936 with the publication costs paid, amazingly, by himself.[43]

For Poulenc, the poem invited him to experiment with writing vocal music less theatrical than *La Voix humaine*—with more melodic continuity than that fragmentary work—but still utterly unlike song. Can this work nevertheless be regarded as a mélodie? Poulenc seemed to think so; as he concludes his *Journal*, he is unusually informative about its background:

> *Suddenly a phantom invaded my music. Monte Carlo. Monte Carlo, the Venice of my twenties!! . . . Bought by chance at Cannes the* Théâtre de poche *of*

La Dame de Monte-Carlo
*with a drawing by Cocteau,
from* Théâtre de poche
(1955).

Quand on est morte entre les mortes,
Qu'on se traîne chez les vivants —
Lorsque tout vous flanque à la porte
Et la ferme d'un coup de vent,
Ne plus être jeune et aimée...

105

*Jean Cocteau about a fortnight ago. . . . The monologue delighted me because
it brought back to me the years 1923–1925 when I lived, together with Auric, in
Monte Carlo, in the imperial shadow of Diaghilev. . . . I have often enough seen
at close quarters those old wrecks of women, light-fingered ladies of the gaming
tables. In all honesty I must admit that Auric and I even came across them at
the pawnshop where our imprudent youth led us once or twice. . . . How strange
it is that my collaboration with Jean Cocteau should come so late. Likewise with
La Voix humaine. I would not have dreamed, in his time, of putting this text
to music. I think that coupled with the solo from* Les Mamelles de Tirésias, La

Dame de Monte-Carlo *would make an excellent number for Denise Duval, to whom I have dedicated it.*[44]

Whether delight was the only emotion Poulenc felt on reading the text is debatable. Nine months after composing the work, he described it as

the heartbreaking story of an old, wretched, abandoned tart who, instead of committing suicide, goes to try her luck at Monte Carlo and finally throws herself in the Mediterranean. I'd never have thought of setting it to music if Denise Duval hadn't existed. I knew it would please her because she dreams of my writing an opera on The Madwoman of Chaillot *[Giraudoux's 1945 play* La Folle de Chaillot*]. It's strange how this ravishing lady wants to play old women.*[45]

Having recently learned his lesson regarding Duval's lack of interest in mélodie, Poulenc felt that here was a character for the singer to sink her teeth into: an aged cocotte, down at heel and also fatally down on her luck. As Carl Schmidt points out, she can't even steal successfully.[46] And like the heroine of Gounod's opera *Sapho*, she throws herself into the sea at the end. Poulenc creates a *scène* in several sections with a main tempo of *Lent et triste*—basically sad and pathetic amid her displays of helpless outrage that she is no longer treated with respect in the establishments to which, and in which, she has sacrificed her virtue. "*This monologue presented a major difficulty: how to escape monotony while conserving an immutable rhythm. That is why I have tried to give a different color to each verse of the poem. Sadness, pride, lyricism, violence and sarcasm. In the end miserable tenderness, anguish and a splash into the sea.*"[47]

Originally conceived for orchestral accompaniment, the piece is seldom heard in that version; the required ensemble is large for such a short work (about six and a half minutes) and thus needs to be part of a program where the soprano soloist sings something else as well. Poulenc's royalties were more substantial when it was performed with orchestra—a major reason for his having put a strict embargo on piano-accompanied performances of *La Voix humaine*[48]—but such orchestral evenings are few and far between, and the composer clearly foresaw the piece as a useful item for his own recitals with piano.

The style of *La Dame de Monte-Carlo* will feel familiar under the fingers of pianists who have played the scores of *Dialogues des Carmélites* and *La Voix humaine*. Nothing in the succession of chords and changing harmonies has been conceived specifically for the pianist, no figuration or turn of phrase that recalls Poulenc the virtuoso of yore. Given the numerous held notes and slower passages, the designation "operatic reduction" seems appropriate. In the orchestral version, the emotive power of strings (where notes continue and don't die away as on a piano) makes quite a difference, not to mention the added colors of wind and brass, castanets, vibraphone, cymbals, and *coup de tamtam* at the moment of death, all providing atmosphere outside the piano's possibilities.

Most of the music is a kind of accompanied arioso, never as dry as recitative (never as crazy or disjointed as the *parlando* passages in *La Voix humaine*), hardly ever blossoming into full-scale melody. It is difficult to guess what kind of emotional effect Poulenc is aiming for. We have little idea whether he feels any empathy for the old lady who opts for suicide when there seems to be no other option. With her "fixed and rather haggard vocal line" (as Henri Sauguet described it), she is revealed as a grotesque and somewhat unsympathetic character. Our first reaction may be that the composer is not as involved with her in the same way as he was with his "Dames" (as he called the Carmelite nuns of his opera) or with the lovesick protagonist of *La Voix humaine*. But it was the perceptive and tactful Sauguet, emerging from the first Parisian performance, who first realized that all these female characters were drawn from Poulenc's own experiences of fear, jealousy, anger, and desperation: "Your Dame de Monte-Carlo is sister of Blanche de la Force and of Thérèse-Tirésias . . . you depict yourself in depicting them."[49]

Monte Carlo itself is the star of this piece, the magical place Poulenc had first known as a child on holiday with his parents. For the choruses of "Monte-Carlo" dotted throughout the music (which Marianne Oswald sang, rather than spoke, in the original production), Poulenc creates a motif where the name is set to three rising pitches supported by voluptuous chords. In the oases of tenderness created by this motif, Poulenc gives full rein to lyricism and nostalgia and rekindles the sensuality of *Les Biches,* the Diaghilev ballet that foretold a career to outstrip that of any French composer of his generation. At the score's Figure 3, the same rising chords are suffused in the *grand luxe* of G-flat major. The old woman is almost in love with the idea of an easeful death in the Mediterranean, until the motif is violently disrupted by her sudden determination to make a last-ditch effort to save herself, while indulging her penchant for gambling.

The central section of the song, set at the gaming tables, reveals the hard-hearted brilliance at the center of this piece. She plays to win with an almost savage glee ("It's lovely to say 'I'm gambling.'/ It brings fire to your cheeks / And a twinkle to your eye"), and we sense the dopamine rush in the music, while she stalks a win in a kind of hunting frenzy—a corollary perhaps to the pursuit of happiness through chance encounters that ruled a part of Poulenc's life. When the woman loses, she attempts to steal; when this fails, she is expelled from the casino while making threats and screeching recriminations. She is an addict in the grip of a need that is slowly killing her, and the only way out is death.

The last words she sings are a repeated "Monte-Carlo"—the first soulfully and *pianissimo* (after which the pianist plays an abbreviated version of the cushioned-chord motif), and then a *forte* repetition as she jumps into the sea—the final staccato in the piano signifying a small, inconsequential splash. Too inconsequential, one suspects, for sopranos who might have wished for a peroration a little more dramatic. But the point is that no one knows or cares about her lonely exit. W. H. Auden, describing the mythological character Icarus falling into the sea (where "the splash, the forsaken cry" go unnoticed), remarks how individual suffering takes place "while someone else is eating or opening a window or just walking dully along."[50] We might suspect that Poulenc saw rather too much of himself in this Dame de Monte-Carlo, and at this stage of his life was repelled by the similarity. We can certainly see in the scenario signs of his own fear that he had written himself out. The avant-garde composers of the "Domaine musicale" and Darmstadt are the nightmare bully boys at the casino, threatening to expel him, not interested in tricks he had used to great effect in earlier years. Hervé Lacombe, though less tactful than Sauguet, reaches a similar conclusion: "This ageing cocotte who drags herself among the living, who attempts to entertain in spite of everything, to play the game, to create illusions, who feels only a shade of her former self, who feels herself to be washed up and sweats with anguish, this is in fact Poulenc."[51] And this work is his last, desperate throw of the dice.

The piece is so personalized to Poulenc's depressive state of mind, so inward looking and short on compassion and forgiveness, including self-forgiveness, that it's not hard to understand why relatively few sopranos sing it. There is less scope for acting or characterization than we might imagine. As for drama and pathos, the music generates tension without offering a climactic transformation; there is scarcely time for any moment of release, without which the piece is stony ground for artists who might wish to move their audience to tears.

"La Dame de Monte-Carlo *should be sung like the prayer of Tosca,*" Poulenc writes in the closing sentence of his *Journal*. "*Mais oui!*"[52] Yes, certainly! Yet Poulenc does not exactly provide us with music for a Tosca. Puccini was in love with his leading character and respected her; Poulenc could not say the same, and we are not sure if he is laughing at his old lady or weeping by her side. Strange that of all the generously

"La Tosca after the murder," a drawing by the twelve-year-old Poulenc following an open-air performance of Puccini's opera in Luchon (in southwestern France), August 1911.

voiced arias the composer could have chosen as a model, he should have selected "Vissi d'arte"—"I have lived for art." Poulenc first saw *Tosca,* aged twelve, in an open-air production in Bagnères-de-Luchon; he made a drawing of the heroine after she murdered Scarpia. Tosca (one of Denise Duval's roles) exudes a nobility of purpose, willing to sacrifice her life for her lover, that is far from the addicted and self-centered gambler. Nevertheless, the aria may hold a clue to Poulenc's troubled state of mind when creating his last work for solo voice and piano. Only a great composer of religious music, including the *Stabat Mater* and the *Litanies à la Vierge noire,* could claim that the words of an operatic heroine sung shortly before her suicide could have been equally sung by him: "I have lived for art, I lived for love, I never harmed a living soul! . . . I donated jewels to the Madonna's mantle, and offered songs to the stars and to heaven, which then shone with greater beauty. In this hour of grief, why oh Lord, do you reward me thus?"

BIOGRAPHICAL INTERLUDE: JEAN COCTEAU

THE COCTEAU SONGS: *Toréador* FP11 (1918); *Cocardes* FP16 (1919); *La Dame de Monte-Carlo* FP180 (1961). Outside the scope of this book is the *tragédie lyrique* for soprano and orchestra *La Voix humaine* FP171 (1958).

o   o   o

When Poulenc died suddenly on 30 January 1963, Cocteau came to the rue de Médicis to view the body and pay his respects. Visibly shaken, he told Poulenc's niece that it was he, ten years older, who should have been lying there instead (he died just over ten months later, on 11 October). There was indeed a link between these two figures that made their fates seem entwined. Other poets were more important to Poulenc the song composer, yet Cocteau was the first (*Toréador* FP11) as well as the last (*La Dame de Monte-Carlo* FP180) he set to music. Bookending Poulenc's œuvre in this way seems emblematic of Cocteau's role in his life: the poet's energy, daring, invention, and capacity to make artistic capital out of almost any given situation provided Poulenc with an invaluable signpost as to how to manage his own career; the master of Greek mythology showed Poulenc how to create his own Parisian fables.

Cocteau was born on 5 July 1889 into the well-to-do bourgeoisie of Paris, the same milieu from which Poulenc would later emerge. No one at home seems to have effectively prevented him from falling in, while still a teenager, with the likes of the decadent actor Édouard de Max, as well as Marcel Proust, Reynaldo Hahn, and the Comte Robert de

Montesquiou. "Cocteau would always tend to regard homosexuality as purer, nobler than heterosexuality," writes Claude Arnaud, "and in this he must have reflected the unconscious view of his moralistic mother."[53] Poulenc almost entirely bypassed any contact with this generation of wearers of the green carnation, and his attitudes and those of his parents were more conventionally schooled; he would find his way to his sexuality by a more devious route. (The profoundly different views of homosexuality in the two artists' backgrounds made an enormous difference to the way they led their subsequent lives.) The cultured Parisian attitude to the arts, however, was the same in both families. Without their parents' money, and without Paris as their youthful playground, these privileged sons of the Belle Époque (Poulenc just manages to scrape into the same time frame) could never have experienced all those ballets, operas, plays, concerts, art exhibitions, music halls, and circuses, the memories of which fueled and shaped their work for the rest of their lives. A nostalgia for their "youth" was already being apostrophized as such when they were barely out of their teens.

The strands of friendship are difficult to disentangle after a cen-

Jean Cocteau, photographed by Man Ray, c. 1922.

tury, and amid the maelstrom of activity in Paris leading up to the First World War and beyond. Poulenc was no draughtsman, Cocteau never played a musical instrument (though he fancied himself a percussion player),[54] but both artists instinctively understood the need to connect with celebrity as a way of discovering outlets for their creative talents. Even someone as unabashed as Poulenc needed introductions, and a strategy, if he was going to succeed. His piano teacher, Ricardo Viñes, opened many doors; and the composer's connection to Cocteau was facilitated by the formidably intelligent Georges Auric, whose opinion (while still a teenager) was sought by Apollinaire. Erik Satie and Max Jacob also knew Cocteau well, and those *éminences grises* Serge Diaghilev and Comte Étienne de Beaumont pounced on anything they might appropriate from younger artists, canaries in the coal mine of the avant-garde. When Cocteau, wanting to please Diaghilev at any price, asked what he should do, the impresario famously replied, "Étonne-moi"— astonish me! In the following decades Cocteau, almost unnervingly multifaceted, did just that, by employing his prolific talents as poet, novelist, playwright, painter, designer, decorator, and film producer.

Cocteau's letters to his collaborators habitually demand, wheedle, cajole, encourage, warn, even inspire. He was a program planner par excellence, and he had learned that readings were never as powerful as poetry recitals with music. As if stepping into the entrepreneurial shoes of the recently dead Apollinaire, he wrote Poulenc on 2 September 1918 to ask about including the composer's as yet incomplete *Le Jongleur* (destroyed) in a "Séance–Music Hall" of his devising that never came off (see p. 17).[55] Never mind; the second such event was a triumph. Cocteau, thoroughly despised and denounced by the surrealists Aragon and Breton (whom Poulenc also longed to impress), entered the cultural wars with a famous polemical tract devoted to music: *Le Coq et l'arlequin— notes autour de la musique*, a booklet with a frontispiece portrait of Cocteau by Picasso, and a large collection of (mostly) music-related aphorisms. For example: "TACT IN AUDACITY CONSISTS IN KNOWING HOW FAR WE MAY GO TOO FAR"; "A POET ALWAYS HAS TOO MANY WORDS IN HIS VOCABULARY, A PAINTER TOO MANY COLORS ON HIS PALETTE, AND A MUSICIAN TOO MANY NOTES ON HIS KEYBOARD."[56]

Another letter from Cocteau to Poulenc followed on 13 September, this time enclosing all twelve verses of "Toréador," effectively launching Poulenc's career as a composer of songs with piano.[57] At the time of these letters, still employing the formal "vous," Poulenc was in uniform and stationed outside Paris; he asked Cocteau the following February to fabricate a letter to the authorities to help him obtain leave, enabling him to come up to Paris.[58]

Cocteau published his first book of poems, *Le Cap de Bonne-Espérance*, in 1919. The following year, after the critic Henri Collet dubbed a group of young composers Les Six, Cocteau invested time and energy in making those composers the musical arm of his entourage. He drew them with enchanting flair, and shamelessly mythologized them. It was clear from the start (and from the iconography of the time) that Auric and Poulenc were Cocteau's favorites, although he did write the plot of Milhaud's ballet *Le Bœuf sur le toit* (1920). No young artists could have asked for a more skilled publicist. The three slight but charming songs of Poulenc's *Cocardes* (to Cocteau's texts; see p. 30) became almost the signature tunes of Les Six at their informal gatherings, and they worked their magic in strengthening Cocteau's bond with the composer.

Other shared musical projects with Cocteau included *L'Album des Six* (for which Poulenc contributed a *Valse*); *Le Gendarme incompris,* a one-act *opéra-bouffe* with a text by Cocteau and Raymond Radiguet; and *Les Mariés de la Tour Eiffel* (to which five of Les Six contributed instrumental pieces, Poulenc's entitled *Discours du général* and *La Baigneuse de Trouville*). The first performance of *Les Mariés* was interrupted by a demonstration of Dadaists, who "had good reason to loathe Cocteau. He had taken their iconoclastic shtick and diffused it into sophisticated, meretricious entertainment."[59]

By the time the second volume of Cocteau's poems appeared (*Vocabulaire,* in 1921), the poet was able to dedicate it to his composer friends. He may have thought of them as disciples, but they were never exactly that. In their correspondence, Poulenc and Cocteau were now close enough to "tutoyer." They were both gay, but how they lived their lives was utterly different. Cocteau was much more open about his sexual preferences, and openly neurotic about his love affairs, more prone to becoming desperately attached to people (often unsuitable; his literary protégé, the teenager Raymond Radiguet, was basically heterosexual) and to wearing his heart on his sleeve. His lovers, culminating with a fruitful relationship with the actor Jean Marais, defined periods of his life and creativity in almost the same way as Picasso's did. Poulenc's liaisons, on the other hand, were a succession of unknown, more or less invisible, shadows.

Cocteau's *Plain-chant* (poems modeled on sixteenth-century authors) was published in 1923 (see FP86), as was the novel *Thomas, l'imposteur.* At the beginning of 1924, Poulenc's long-term connection with Cocteau was rewarded with a commission from Diaghilev for the ballet *Les Biches*, produced with enormous success in Monte Carlo. But the shockingly early death of Radiguet in 1923 had left the poet completely distraught and increasingly dependent on opium, and one feels that this kind of addiction was a step too far from the traditions of bourgeois life for Poulenc's comfort. Never as radical as Cocteau, he grew out of disrupting the status quo simply for the hell of it; from the middle 1920s poet and composer drifted apart.

After writing one of his most important poems, "L'Ange Heurtebise" (1925), and providing the text for Stravinsky's *Œdipus Rex* (1927), Cocteau diversified—"reinvented himself" in today's cliché—and became a playwright (*Orphée*, 1926; *Antigone*, 1922; *La Machine infernale*, another treatment of the Oedipus theme, 1932) as well as novelist (*Les Enfants terribles*, 1929, later filmed). A brief reconversion to Roman Catholicism (via the famous Maritains, husband and wife) was not a success, a very different story from Poulenc's 1936 self-managed reconversion at Rocamadour. The poet weaned himself with difficulty (and never entirely) from opium—his 1930 recovery journal is entitled *Opium*; that same year his one-woman play *La Voix humaine* was first performed and published. Cocteau made his first film in the early 1930s, the avant-garde *Le Sang du poète*, to be followed by such films as *La Belle et la bête* and *Orphée*, while his literary output continued unabated. "To enclose the collected works of Cocteau," W. H. Auden commented in 1950, "one would need not a bookshelf, but a warehouse."

Cocteau was a bewitching verbal presence. Ezra Pound said he could "talk without interruption for two hours and over, with never a word that wouldn't have been good reading." Gertrude Stein even thought that he "spoke too well to write anything lasting."[60] The brilliance of his gifts brought charges (fueled also by homophobia) of superficiality and lightweight achievement. Had Cocteau been someone different, much of what he did may have been saluted as the work of a genius. By the time Poulenc returned to the arms of his "*faithful and exquisite friend*,"[61] for *La Voix humaine* and then *La Dame de Monte-Carlo*, it was like coming home to the welcome of a prodigal son. By now the poet had painted the City Hall murals in Menton and decorated the Chapel of Saint-Pierre at Villefranche.

These late collaborations between two old friends were, on the whole, happy ones, although Cocteau privately expressed disappointment at aspects of the composer's self-centered eccentricities. Poulenc was impressed once again with Cocteau's prodigious musical understanding, and Cocteau believed that the composer had "fixed once and for all the way in which my text should be spoken."[62] A year before his death, Poulenc thought that *La Machine infernale* would make a wonderful subject for a new opera.

What Poulenc learned from Cocteau was crucial: a person could make of himself anything he liked; presentation was all, and history could be written and rewritten at will. In reviewing Claude Arnaud's magisterial biography of Cocteau, Anne Stillman noted the poet's "perpetual imagining of reality as semi-fictive. . . . 'I wonder how a man can write the lives of the poets,' [Cocteau] wrote, 'since the poets themselves could not write their own. There are too many mysteries, too many true lies, too many tangled branches.'" For instance, Cocteau claimed to have spent a year in Marseilles as a boy:

> He had run away at 16, after a second failed attempt to pass the *baccalauréate*. He resolved to become a cabin boy, but found himself wandering the piers of the Vieux Port. An elderly Vietnamese woman picked him up off the rue de la Rose; he found work in a Chinese restaurant; he took refuge in a boys' bordello, where he tried opium for the first time and lived for a year—or two, or four—using the papers of a young drowned man. Finally, two gendarmes took him back to Paris.

But "Arnaud thinks the lack of any evidence, and his mother's vigilance, make this escapade improbable."[63]

The present-day biographer of Poulenc is confronted with some of the same difficulties as those faced by Cocteau's, precisely because of the way Poulenc imitated the poet as raconteur, shaping and reshaping the contours of his life. The composer similarly learned how to use the spoken and written word as his myth-making weapons and as an adjunct to the power of music. Dinner parties were fixed for the entire purpose of hearing Francis tell one of his famous shaggy dog tales. He would not have had the effrontery to claim that he had worked in a boy brothel in Marseilles, but thanks to Cocteau,

Poulenc and Cocteau working together on La Voix humaine *(1958).*

he realized that if something was true as fantasy, it was as good as being true in fact; the ground just had to be prepared and the foundations well laid. It is paradoxical that in an age of "fake news" we should come to realize that "true lies" are the prerogative of artists who seek to make their lives a carefully shaped work of art, as much as any book, play, film, or painting. That this is an age-old ploy is evidenced by Goethe's self-confessional phrase for the same thing—*Dichtung und Wahrheit* (poetry and truth), the title of an autobiography half real, half imagined.

Cocteau's reputation for unreliability and superficiality stems from his stories catching up with him; certain castles in the air, like the brothel in Marseilles, evaporated. Over a lifetime such revelations gnaw away at readers' confidence. Poulenc fared better: his "true lies" are never as fanciful, his bending of the truth never in the same fantastic league. But what he did, with great skill, was to construct a view of himself that has remained faithfully reflected in almost everything written about him since; there has scarcely been a dissenting voice—diary entries from composers Ned Rorem and Michael Ciry could be (I think unfairly) dismissed as merely the product of jealousy. Perhaps the surprisingly fresh way of looking at the life in Hervé Lacombe's biography (2013) heralds a new start. Most people are unaware of a wind of change, and prefer the old Poulenc, the stereotypically dotty, adorable Frenchman. In that sense, Poulenc's castles in the air have proven far more durable than Cocteau's. With the poet there were mainly words to question; in Poulenc's case it is the music that has carried the day, taking his assiduously crafted apologia along for the ride.

∘   ∘   ∘

FP181 *Sept Répons de ténèbres* (soprano solo, mixed choir, and orchestra), 1961–62

FP182 *Nos Souvenirs qui chantant, d'après un thème de Francis Poulenc* (voice and piano), 1961 (An adaption with new words of Thérèse's waltz song from *Les Mamelles de Tirésias,* for which Heugel held the copyright; it is not clear whether Poulenc gave his permission for this venture.)

FP183 *Renaud et Armide* (incidental music for the Cocteau play), April–June 1962

FP184 Sonata for Clarinet and Piano, summer 1962

FP185 Sonata for Oboe and Piano, summer 1962

∘   ∘   ∘

At his death, Poulenc left no work that was incomplete; considering his lifelong habit of composing works in ongoing stages, this is astonishing.

Poulenc's funeral mass, organized according to his wishes as relayed to his niece Brigitte Manceaux, was celebrated on Saturday morning, 2 February 1963, at St. Sulpice (Paris), where Marcel Dupré was organist. The organ music was by François Couperin and Nicolas de Grigny, and other music was by Bach. That there was no Poulenc played was at the composer's instruction, although (also at his behest) lots of bells sounded to shake up the soul (*"bringuebaler l'âme"*). He was interred at Père Lachaise Cemetery, where the graves of Apollinaire, Éluard, and Marie Laurencin are to be found. When Brigitte Manceaux died a few months later (21 April), she was placed in the same family vault as her beloved uncle; her sister, Rosine Seringe, joined them when she died in 2017.

The last photograph taken of the composer: after a concert in Maastricht, Holland, with Denise Duval, 26 January 1963.

Poulenc's People: Patrons, Friends, Colleagues, Dedicatees, Publishers

HIS PATRONS

By 1920, Poulenc's "know-how in building influential and useful circles of friendships as far as his career was concerned was already completely operational in France and abroad."[1] The composer from a bourgeois background worked hard to be accepted as an equal by the highest echelons of Parisian society. Music was his *carte d'entrée*. The gifted singer and pianist Marie-Blanche, Comtesse de Polignac, played the part of a modern Duchesse de Guermantes to Poulenc's Proust, and Francis, like Marcel, seemed overwhelmed and flattered to belong to the circle of a woman of such cultural refinement and beauty. She called him "Ma poule jolie" or "Poulette jolie," and could laugh at his dirty stories;[2] a photograph of him in drag at the Polignac country retreat at Kerbastic is a measure of how comfortable he felt with her. Her Parisian salon in the rue Barbet-de-Jouy was almost his second home. He was less fond of the more temperamental and less beatific Marie-Laure de Noailles (Ned Rorem's patron) and the older Winnaretta Singer, Princesse de Polignac (Marie-Blanche's aunt by marriage)—although both of these fabulously wealthy women were important patrons in his earlier career.

HIS FRIENDS AND FAMILY

Alongside these *monstres sacrés* (and *aimés*), there were other women who were essential to him—indeed, he would have insisted that the love of his life was his childhood friend Raymonde Linossier, to whom he unsuccessfully proposed marriage in 1928. She acquired, after her untimely death in 1930, an iconic status in his life, and her photograph accompanied him wherever he traveled. Virginie Liénard ("Tante Liénard") from Nazelles, near Noizay, became a mother-figure after the early death of Jenny Poulenc. Geneviève Sienkiewicz, a family friend, who had recommended that the young Francis study with Ricardo Viñes, was an indispensable early mentor, unwavering in her support and outliving him. The counsel of the bisexual harpsichordist Wanda Landowska helped the composer

Poulenc's niece Mme Rosine Seringe, with the author at Noizay in 1978.

to accept himself as a gay man. With Simone Girard, Denise Bourdet, and Yvonne de Casa Fuerte, women nearer his own age, he was able to confide the details of his emotional and sexual ups-and-downs. In his final decade, Poulenc's friendship with the much younger soprano Denise Duval bordered on the romantic; he sometimes imagined what she might have been to him if he had been another sort of "Poupoule."[3] His elder sister Jeanne had been something of a mother figure, and his brother-in-law André Manceaux was a trusted legal and financial adviser. Poulenc's niece Brigitte Manceaux was undoubtedly closer to him in his adult life than anyone else in the family, and almost anyone out of it. But the influence of his uncle Marcel ("Papoum") Royer, his mother's brother, was enormous in his adolescent years. Poulenc would have been amazed to learn that Brigitte's younger sister Rosine (later married to Jean Seringe) would play a matchless role after his death as guardian of the Poulenc flame.

Suzette Chanlaire, sister-in-law of Poulenc's first known lover, Richard Chanlaire, was also a close friend. It was through her that the composer met, and some years later had a fleeting affair with, Frédérique (Freddy) Lebedeff, mother of his daughter Marie-Ange (b. 1946). Unpublished letters indicate that the composer frequently visited mother and child, taking pleasure in playing the role of godfather in a secret family household.[4] But the nineteenth-century *pudeur* that drove him to conceal his fatherhood from the outside world, and from Marie-Ange herself, seems particularly sad, an obfuscation more worthy of Goethe's *Wilhelm Meister* than mid-twentieth-century France. Only members of Poulenc's most inner circle were aware of this situation: they included actor Stéphane Audel; the indispensable Simone Girard in Avignon; and of course Pierre Bernac, who ranks as the most significant musician in Poulenc's life on account of the extraordinary services he rendered the composer both on and off the concert platform for nearly twenty-nine years (see p. 490).

Musical colleagues to whom Poulenc was close included Georges Auric, valued artistic counselor from his teenage years, but of whom he was capable of feeling jealous; the sage, patient, and great-hearted "Da," Darius Milhaud; the pianist and choral conductor Yvonne Gouverné; the amateur pianist Marthe Bosredon, initially his hostess in wartime Brive; and the soprano Suzanne Peignot, earliest of his close singing colleagues. Of all his poets, Louise de Vilmorin was perhaps the chummiest, although Max Jacob was intimate with Poulenc in the 1920s and early 30s, as was Jean Cocteau at both the beginning and end of Poulenc's career. Marie Laurencin is the one artist and friend from his youth from whom he seems to have become permanently estranged. Paul Éluard, whom he admired more than any other living writer, was a cordial and involved colleague-correspondent.

Most of Poulenc's letters are models of urbanity and good manners. He did everything he could to smooth over rifts, having learned early on that avoiding confrontations was the best way forward for his career. He was someone who tirelessly turned up: at concerts, operas, plays, exhibitions, receptions, conferences, salons, private parties (in France, Europe, England, or America), where his presence lifted the mood of any gathering, and where he was able to forge personal connections that would be useful in the ongoing *grand projet* of promoting his music. Poulenc never knew the term "networking," but it is a concept that he developed to a fine art even if unaided by modern technology.

Friends who lived outside Paris and frequently offered cost-free hospitality included Audrey Parr (London), Mimi Pecci-Blunt (Rome), and Poulenc's well-to-do hostess in Brussels, Rose Lambiotte. Rose Dercourt-Plaut in New York was a tireless factotum during his visits to the United States, and Doda Conrad laid the groundwork in organizing his first American tour in 1948. Face-to-face contact with useful fans was supplemented by a brilliantly managed regime of letter writing. No twentieth-century composer had as many "friends" in the Facebook sense, *avant la lettre*. Colleagues and critics were marshaled into being adherents in a way that other contemporary composers had neither the inclination nor energy to organize. (The music may have generated such devotion on its own and without further ado, but Poulenc tended to dot i's and cross t's.) In Milan on the day of the premiere of *Dialogues des Carmélites* (26 January 1957), Poulenc himself met the 7 a.m. train arriving from Paris with all the French critics, and handed each of them a personal invitation to a glittering reception that would follow the performance, given by one of his wealthy supporters. Later in the day he was negotiating terms with the head of the claque that clapped or booed from the La Scala balconies. For Poulenc, already world famous, such efforts were all in a day's work.[5]

HIS COMPOSER COLLEAGUES

Poulenc was vain about his music, yet on another level he appears to have had little confidence that it could make its way in the world on merit alone. To give it a head start, he tried to ensure that rival composers held no animus against him, and that he was seen to be transparently friendly and generous (though such courtesy did not extend to such minor composers as Maxime Jacob, Marcel Delannoy, or Jacques Ibert, whom he seems to have been unafraid of snubbing).[6]

In the case of the much younger Pierre Boulez in the 1950s, his charm offensive proved to be a useful strategy. Boulez, the leading light of the French avant-garde, was no fan of Poulenc's music and could easily have condemned it out of hand. That he refrained from doing so was no accident. Poulenc was not an interesting composer, said Boulez years later, but he was a nice man. He had turned up religiously to Boulez's "Domaine musical" concerts and written letters afterward that struck just the right note of interest and positive comment, mingled with a permissible touch of perplexity. While Poulenc in fact preferred Boulez to Messiaen,[7] it is also true that he had seen the danger of his music's being relegated to the dustbin by a powerful new presence in French music, and successfully averted it. Meanwhile, a 1950 letter to Messiaen had poured expertly aimed oil on troubled waters by tempering some disapproving remarks Poulenc made about the *Turangalîla* Symphony, which had unfortunately come to Messiaen's ears.[8] Later, when Poulenc changed his opinion of that work, he wrote to say so. Messiaen's response praised the older composer's "noblesse" and "probité artistique."[9]

With that mighty Russian import Igor Stravinsky, there was a cordial relationship based on Poulenc's hero-worship. Stravinsky was someone he occasionally criticized in whispered tones, but only during the Russian master's later dodecaphonic period. With Serge Prokofiev (whom Poulenc also imitated) he was surprisingly close in the thirties; Poulenc told Audel that he had no doubt that Prokofiev thought badly of his music, but that he didn't mind.[10] Manuel de Falla, highly strung and somewhat remote, was an inspiration, especially on account of the depth of his religious commitment.[11] And Poulenc enjoyed amicable relationships with Vittorio Rieti, Gian Francesco Malipiero (serving on juries with him in the later years of his life), and Luigi Dallapiccola, whose challenging songs he performed with Bernac.

Of the members of Les Six, besides Auric and Milhaud, Poulenc was friendly enough with Germaine Tailleferre and less so, at least in the early days, with the inscrutable Louis Durey and the temperamentally very different Arthur Honegger. In 1919, when he heard that Durey had set Apollinaire's *Le Bestiaire,* he immediately dedicated his own *Bestiaire* songs to him—a typical Poulencian ploy to sidestep any awkwardness. But in later life Poulenc exchanged warm letters with both men, especially with Honegger shortly before that composer's death; as older composers, they came to see eye-to-eye on what they felt were the less attractive developments of the modern musical world.

Poulenc often supported music by people who represented no threat to his own reputation; he was a master of gentle praise bordering on the patronizing, but it was seldom taken as such, thanks to his tact. He was extremely fond of Henri Sauguet, whose permanent partnership with the painter Jacques Dupont was in marked contrast to Poulenc's ongoing clandestine arrangements. (I was fortunate to meet Sauguet in 1981, finding myself bowled over by his charm and culture.) Poulenc took a great deal of trouble to repay decades of loyalty and friendship from Sauguet, whose various successes scarcely rivaled his own. When American music eventually came into Poulenc's orbit in the late 1940s, he was impressed by Samuel Barber's music, less so by Gian Carlo Menotti's, and he assiduously wooed Virgil Thomson,[12] one of the most influential, and potentially nasty, critics in America—as Benjamin Britten had discovered to his cost some years earlier. Poulenc's relationship with Britten, his equal in terms of international fame, merits a separate essay; see page 423.

HIS DEDICATEES (THE SONGS)

Poulenc selected his song dedicatees with quite some care and discernment; he regarded the bestowal of such dedications as an instrument of friendship. They betokened his affection, admiration, gratitude, and respect, although sometimes they also simply showed good manners in the repayment of favors. Some of the friends and colleagues mentioned above were dedicatees of Poulenc compositions more substantial than mélodies.

Fourteen songs were assigned to **Marie-Blanche de Polignac**, including two cycles: FP57, FP59/i, FP75/i, FP86/v–vi, FP91, FP96, FP101/i, FP121/i, and FP135. The *Élégie* for two pianos (FP175) was dedicated to her memory. Her husband, **Jean de Polignac**, won the dedications of songs in music-hall manner—FP75/iv, FP117/ii, and FP122/ii—and Marie-Blanche's aunt by marriage, the Princesse de Polignac, dedications of instrumental works. **Marie-Laure de Noailles** received FP66, FP77/i, and FP98/ii, as well as *Le Bal masqué* (FP60, together with her husband Charles de Noailles).

The composer's beloved **Raymonde Linossier** (his "unattainable anima figure or goddess")[13] has three songs dedicated to her memory—FP55, FP99, and FP140/vii—as well as the ballet *Les Animaux modèles* FP111. **Denise Bourdet** received FP86/vii and FP101/v, and **Wanda Landowska** FP69/viii. Poulenc's uncle **Marcel Royer ("Papoum")** was gifted with the famous FP122/1, and his sister **Jeanne Manceaux** with FP140/v. (*Dialogues des Carmélites* was dedicated to the memory of Poulenc's mother.) **Suzette Chanlaire**, sister-in-law of Poulenc's first lover, Richard Chanlaire, is dedicatee of FP107/v, and **Frédérique (Freddy) Lebedeff** (mother of his daughter) received FP86/i and FP101/ii, well before the birth of Marie-Ange.

Among his composer colleagues who were also close friends, **Georges Auric** is dedicatee of FP16 and FP94/ii, and **Darius Milhaud** of *Les Mamelles de Tirésias* but also FP22, unpublished at the time and for decades thought to be lost. The choral conductor **Yvonne Gouverné** has one of the composer's greatest songs, FP86/ix, and his hostess in Brive, **Marthe Bosredon**, two of his most loved, FP107/ii and FP121/ii. Dedications in thanks for hospitality came to **Rose**

Lambiotte, Poulenc's refuge in Brussels (FP136/ii); **Audrey Norman Colville** in London (FP127/ii); and **Paul Chadourne** in Corrèze (FP157/ii).

The most important composer to receive a song dedication from Poulenc (an entire cycle, FP147) was **Igor Stravinsky**, although some would argue that **Erik Satie**'s (FP3) was just as significant in being associated with one of the composer's very first works. **Louis Durey** received the dedication of a cycle (FP15a) after Poulenc discovered he had set the same texts in 1919. **Henri Sauguet** is dedicatee of FP134, and **Louis Beydts**, a prolific composer of songs though not a friend, unexpectedly received FP117/i. **Luigi Dallapiccola** is dedicatee of FP131/ii.

It was perhaps inevitable that many of the dedicatees should have been singers, listed here alphabetically: the soprano **Suzanne Balguerie** (FP59/iv); the mezzo-soprano **Jane** (Jeanne as Poulenc has it) **Bathori** (FP38/v, FP46/iv, and FP169); the indispensable **Pierre Bernac** (FP77/iv, FP86/viii, and FP98/1); the singer-entertainer **Pierre Bertin** (1895–1984) (FP11); the operatic baritone **Roger Bourdin** (FP117/iii); in memory of the tragically murdered soprano **Evelyne Brélia** (FP44); the bass **Doda Conrad** (FP144); **Claire Croiza**, the most distinguished female mélodie singer of her generation (FP38/iv); the amateur American soprano **Rose Dercourt-Plaut** (FP162/ii); **Denise Duval**, Poulenc's recital partner after Bernac's retirement (FP178 and FP180); the mezzo-soprano **Marya Freund** (FP38/ii, FP69/iv, and FP162/i); the Brazilian soprano (one of Pierre Bernac's teachers) **Véra Janacopoulos** (1896–1956) (FP38/iii); the Polish soprano and Poulenc's recital partner **Maria Modrakowska** (FP69/viii); one of the composer's closest friends and musical partners, soprano **Suzanne Peignot** (FP38/i, FP46/ii, FP59/iii, and FP101/iii); the famous singing-actress **Yvonne Printemps** (FP79); the celebrated baritone **Gérard Souzay** (1918–2004) (FP136/iii); Souzay's sister, the soprano **Geneviève Touraine** (1903–1981) (FP136/i); the most famous French soprano of the time, **Ninon Vallin** (FP101/iv); the operatic contralto **Madeleine Vhita** (FP59/ii).

There are three visual artists among the song dedicatees: **Valentine Hugo** (née Gros, 1887–1968) (FP77/ii and FP86/iv), **Marie Laurencin** (FP58/i), and **Pablo Picasso** (FP86/i). Only a handful of poets and writers make the list: a simple but delicious waltz song was given to **Paul Éluard** (FP107/iv), a dedication was made to **Lucien Daudet** in the year of his death (FP132), and one in memory of **Raymond Radiguet** (FP131/i). A unique dedication was inscribed to the memory of the literary executor of Max Jacob, **Pierre Colle** (1909–1948) (FP157/i); the dedication to **Soulange Lemaître** (1899–1979), mutual friend of Paul Valéry and Poulenc, also pays tribute to a poet at one remove (FP108).

Following a nineteenth-century custom often honored by Gabriel Fauré, the composer sometimes dedicated songs to the wives (or widows) of distinguished artists and creators: **Nora Auric** (FP77/v); **Jacqueline Apollinaire** (FP140/iii); **Youki Desnos** (Louci Badoul, 1903–1964) (FP163); **Nusch Éluard** (Maria Benz)

(FP86/iii and FP137, the latter in her memory); **Olga Picasso** (FP58/ii); **Mme Cole Porter** (Linda Porter, FP58/ii); **Mme Arthur Rubinstein** (Nela Młynarska, FP69/vi).

Poulenc occasionally dedicated songs to patronesses on the Parisian musical scene, women neither ennobled nor fabulously wealthy but situated at the heart of the salon world, particularly at the beginning of his career: **Mme Fernand (Germaine) Allard** (FP42); **Soulange d'Ayen** (Duchesse d'Ayen, FP101/vi); the famous **Misia Sert** (1872–1950), dedicatee of *Les Biches* and of FP69/ii, and Misia's sister **Ida Godebska** (FP69/i). **Lily Pastré**, Comtesse Pastré, was a society hostess in Marseilles (FP158); **Jeanne Richter** (FP121/iii) was a glamorous concert promoter, a friend of Jacques Février and Ned Rorem; the dedication of a children's song to **Mario (Marie-Odile) Beaugnies** [recte **Baugnies**] **de Saint-Marceaux** (FP75/iii) was meant as a bow in the direction of the little girl's formidable grandmother, Marguerite (Meg) de Saint-Marceaux, whose salon, crucial in Fauré's story, had passed its peak by the time Poulenc briefly attended it.

Performers were rewarded with dedications in other areas of the composer's output. Among the song dedicatees there is only violinist **Hélène Jourdan-Morhange** (1892–1961), friend of Ravel and Colette (FP92). We also encounter the choral conductor **Suzanne Nivard** (FP77/iii); the writer and critic **Claude Rostand** (1912–1970) (FP107/i), who shared a remarkable sympathy with the composer; the Belgian musicologist **Andre Schaeffner** (FP117/iv); and the Russian musicologist **Pierre Souvchintsky** (FP127/i).

Friends from Poulenc's childhood and early years sometimes received dedications. One of the longest-lived of all his contemporaries was the journalist and pianist **Ève Curie** (1904–2007), daughter of Marie Curie, born five years after the composer but outliving him by forty-four years (FP59/v). It was **Emmanuel Faÿ** (1897–1923), boyhood friend of Poulenc in his Nogent days and whose memory is celebrated in FP140/iv, who introduced the young composer to soprano Suzanne Peignot, his cousin; Faÿ committed suicide for love of Jean Cocteau. Other dedicatees from the same cycle (*Calligrammes*), honoring the composer's early friendships, were **Pierre Lelong** (FP140/ii), **Simone Tilliard** (FP140/i), and **Jacques Soulé** (FP140/vi); the latter wrote a privately printed essay, "Francis Poulenc dans ses jeunes années," that provides fascinating insights into the teenaged Poulenc's precocious attitudes to life and music.

Finally, there are quixotic dedications that are either impulsive or mysterious, or show glimpses of the composer's private life that have remained obscure. One of his most beautiful songs (FP102) is dedicated to an unknown local man from near Noizay, whom Poulenc believed had been killed in action; when it became clear that **André Bonnelie** was still alive, the dedication remained in place. The politician and prefect of police **André Dubois** (1903–1998) (FP117/vi), something of a shadowy figure, was a man with many useful wartime connections. A mysterious "**Lambert**" (FP15b) was one of the composer's chums from Les Halles, and Poulenc's connection with **André Lecœur** (FP117/v) appears also to have been of a personal or romantic nature. The most fanciful dedication (for FP174) was inscribed to "**Miles and Flora,**" the two child characters in Britten's opera *The Turn of the Screw.* The only song dedication for money (but not the only such dedication in the composer's output) was to the American soprano **Alice Esty** (FP161).

HIS PUBLISHERS

Poulenc struck up long-standing friendships at the publishers Chester; Rouart, Lerolle; and later Ricordi; but he liked to juggle his allocations, hedge his bets, and ensure that no one took his music for granted. Disagreements and infidelities were frequent, as were reconciliations. Exacting when it came to the appearance of his music, a tireless (sometimes wheedling) negotiator, constantly concerned with sales figures and nagging about efficient distribution, he was a demanding and sometimes tiresome client.

J & W Chester (London), founded in 1874 and established in London under new management in 1915, was Poulenc's first and last publisher (he had been recommended to them by Stravinsky, who handed over the novice's manuscripts himself, and Diaghilev).[14] Apart from the Intermède from FP3, no mélodies by Poulenc appeared with Chester, but the firm published almost all the early piano and chamber music works, as well as *L'Histoire de Babar* and the sonatas for flute, clarinet, and oboe in the last years of his life.

Éditions de la Sirène (Paris), publisher of FP15 and FP20, was the most chic and avant-garde of Poulenc's publishers. The firm was founded in 1917, and its music-publishing arm folded in 1922, even shorter lived than the literary, but Poulenc must have been delighted that his *Le Bestiaire* appeared under the same imprint that had brought out the Apollinaire poems with Dufy woodcuts, as well as Cocteau's *Le Coq et l'arlequin.* He would have been less delighted with its inefficiency.

Of the three song dedications to publishers, two are to men who worked at **Rouart, Lerolle & Cie** (Paris): François Hepp (1887–1983) (FP46/i) and the fatherly Jacques Lerolle (1880–1944), nephew of Ernest Chausson (FP46/iii). Poulenc had been aware of Henri Rouart's art collection as a boy, and Henri's son Alexis (1869–1921) was a friend of his Uncle Papoum. His closest relationship was with Alexis's son Paul (1906–1972). If Poulenc could be said to have had a "house" publisher, it was this one (Britten's youthful relationship with Boosey & Hawkes comes to mind as having been somewhat similar); he was mostly able to persuade its league of gentlemen to accede to his terms.[15] Ten song sets and five individual songs appeared between 1928 (FP46) and 1954 (FP157). The Rouart, Lerolle catalogue was bought by Salabert in 1941, although the firm, still nominally under the control of Paul Rouart, was permitted for a while to retain its name on the song covers alongside Salabert's.

Poulenc had two periods of dealings with the family firm of **Au Ménestrel, Heugel**, or **Heugel & Cie** (Paris, established in 1839, known for publishing Massenet and Charpentier). In the 1920s he published two song cycles (FP38 and FP42) with Jacques Heugel (1890–1979), whom he came to regard as hopelessly inefficient.[16] When the young Philippe Heugel (1924–1992) took over, Poulenc gave the firm another try, starting with *Les Mamelles de Tirésias*. Although he was initially enthusiastic, publishing with them two cycles and a single song, as well as participating in the Vilmorin cycle *Mouvements de cœur*, disenchantment seems to have set in on both sides.

Alphonse Leduc & Cie and **Enoch & Cie** (both Paris) published five songs between them—the solitary *Vocalise* (FP44) at Leduc, and four children's songs (FP75) composed for a popular market at Enoch.

Durand & Cie (Paris), the preeminent French publisher of Saint-Saëns, Debussy, and Ravel, had a showroom near the Madeleine, which Poulenc had frequented with awe on his way home from school. This was during the heyday of Jacques Durand, whose correspondence with Debussy was later avidly studied by the older Poulenc. The composer closed a deal with the firm's director, René Dommange, in 1935, but it did not last. The handsome appearance of the Durand scores happens to coincide with Poulenc's greatest songwriting period (three important cycles, FP77, FP86, and FP91) and the beginning of his choral mastery. His infidelities (flirting with Deiss or returning to his old publishing haunts) may have been a real spoiler here—Durand's composers tended to be exclusive. Poulenc may have been irritated by Dommange's enthusiasm for Messiaen, whose important works were keeping the Durand presses constantly busy.

The personable Raymond Deiss (1893–1945) of **R Deiss** (Paris) maintained a friendly connection with Poulenc through Milhaud and Charles Koechlin. Apart from five songs between 1933 and 1939, Poulenc consigned to him his Concerto for Organ. Deiss, to whom Milhaud entrusted his manuscripts before fleeing France in 1940, was the brave publisher of the first Resistance newspaper, *Pantagruel* (after which Poulenc seems to have prudently distanced himself); Deiss was arrested in 1941 and decapitated by the Gestapo in 1943.[17] His firm was swallowed up by Salabert in 1946.

Francis Salabert (1884–1946) was something of a business genius. He was first and foremost a publisher and arranger of popular music, who made enough money gradually to buy up between 1930 and 1946 the catalogues of six publishers, including Rouart, Lerolle and Deiss—finding himself at the head of an empire of serious French music, **Éditions Salabert** (Paris), without having had to deal personally with most of its composers. Poulenc was thus in the position of having about forty of his songs owned by a publisher he did not know. As the shared arrangement with Rouart, Lerolle gradually faded, Salabert's name appeared alone on the printed covers. Poulenc met his business match in Mica, the publisher's widow (the formidable Mme Salabert) but managed to remain on coolly cordial terms with her. F144, printed by the firm's American branch, and a duet (FP108) printed posthumously are the only original Salabert songs.

Éditions Max Eschig (Paris) was established in 1907 by the Czech Maximilian Eschig (1872–1927), and was later managed by the brothers Jean and Philippe Marietti. Poulenc was familiar with this establishment from his teens; he remembered buying Schoenberg's *Six Petites Pièces* (*Sechs kleine Klaveristücke)* there in 1913.[18] Eschig eventually became Poulenc's second "house" publisher at a time when he clearly wanted to avoid working (for different reasons) with Deiss, Salabert, or Durand. Between 1941 and 1957 (FP107 to FP178), Eschig published four important cycles and ten further songs. There may have been little personal chemistry between the composer and the Mariettis, but the firm turned out to be an efficient and enduring mainstay (and a safe pair of hands during the war).

In the last decade of his life, Poulenc was increasingly abandoning Noizay for sojourns in the south of France. As he embarked on *Dialogues des Carmélites,* a La Scala commission, it was propitious that he found himself in contact with **G. Ricordi & C.** (Milan). This firm, founded in 1808, had published Bellini, Rossini, and Verdi (new enthusiasms for Poulenc). Hervé Dugardin (1910–1969) was director of Éditions Amphion (where he published Dutilleux and Boulez) and also of Ricordi's Paris branch. An Italian publisher with an office in Paris was an ideal solution for Poulenc's last years (although he returned to Salabert for his *Sept Répons de ténèbres*); charmed by both Dugardin and his wife Daisy (née Singer, niece of the Princesse de Polignac), he dedicated *La Voix humaine* to them both (FP171).

The Masks and Myths of Francis Poulenc, and His Eventual Triumph

THE SELF-PRESENTED MAN

Poulenc's appearance was unusual enough to inspire occasional flights of verbal fancy, as it did from Jean Cocteau in the 1920s: "a young dog who plays with gloves and joyfully digs up the flower beds. . . . He enjoys himself enormously even if his eyes and his mouth are always solemn."[1] A journalist in the early 1950s, noting Poulenc's "distracted attitude and arms hanging down by his sides," also observed that "his loosely held chin pulls his face downward as if waiting for some surprise. His eyes betray innumerable nuances of amazement and sleepiness. . . . In a voice that drops from the nose down into the throat, and then back again, together with a couple of elevations of the eyebrows, he describes the pleasures of his youth. . . . He gives a gaping laugh that stretches down to his tie."[2] His nasal speaking voice was given to exaggeration and wonderful changes of pitch. Another writer was struck by "the way Poulenc says, almost as if singing,'J'adore, J'aime, J'ai une passion,' this loving warmth, I can never forget it."[3]

Poulenc was a winsome child, but he shot up in ungainly fashion in adolescence. His large nose made his face look to Ned Rorem (in the 1950s) like a "combination of weasel and trumpet."[4] Nobody ever claimed that he was handsome, but it would not have occurred to him to bemoan his appearance. What was attractive, magnetic even, was his almost sublime self-confidence: he could effortlessly dominate most social gatherings and was an unabashed gate-crasher, all part of his game-plan. As Sidney Buckland and Myriam Chimènes write: "The nonchalant, self-assured image which he wanted to project of himself—in interviews, in his dealings with publishers, promoters and concert-organisers—was a carefully studied one."[5]

Right from the beginning, the composer displayed a mixture of carefully calibrated behavior and occasional mad indiscretion. Whether performing a striptease for a roomful of people, dressed (or undressed) as "La belle Poulenka" (see Outline, 27 March 1920), or allowing himself to be photographed in drag,[6] Poulenc could camp it up in outrageous fashion: one side of him wanted to hide his true nature, but it was the breath of life to him to be the center of attention. He seldom doubted himself, either personally or professionally, yet when his confidence was seriously undermined, and when he felt he was no longer in charge of a given situation (particularly in intimate relationships), he went to pieces. His self-esteem was considerable, but it was also unexpectedly fragile, and the composer went to great lengths to avoid placing himself in situations where his charm (consisting of "a malicious gaiety," as the critic Bernard Gavoty put it) no longer worked.[7]

THE SELF-PROMOTED MUSIC

It has often been the fate of Poulenc's music to be undervalued as deliciously lightweight, albeit not by those who have taken the trouble to listen to it carefully. The last thing many listeners might ever imagine was that Poulenc was a man who was frequently overcome by distress and depression, or that he was remotely in need of psychiatric help. When *Dialogues des Carmélites* appeared in the late fifties, the opera was seen by many as a perplexing new departure rather than as the logical crowning achievement of his composing life, a successor to such other works of fear and panic as the Concerto for Organ, *Sécheresses, Sept Chansons*, and the Sonata for Two Pianos. As far as the wider general public is concerned, the Poulenc who matters is the ever-relaxed composer of *Mouvements perpétuels*, the embodiment of an era after the First World War when France led the world in zaniness and freedom.

Yet the persistent impression that Poulenc's life was one of tirelessly cheery bonhomie (he once said that the person he would most like to have been in life was Maurice Chevalier) is not entirely the fault of careless listeners; it was the composer's intention to create a self-portrait to match Chevalier's seductive breeziness. By speaking about himself and his music in countless interviews, on the radio and at "conference" recitals that combined performances with verbal explications, Poulenc created a personal mythology of self-referential anecdotes that were often improved and burnished, a nightmare for those who must now choose between one version of a story and another, where neither really stands up to scrutiny.

This technique of musical press-conferencing without much regard for accuracy was learned in the 1920s from Jean Cocteau, but Poulenc tailored his image to his own bourgeois listening public; his anecdotes were far less shocking than the poet's avant-garde, out-of-the-closet somersaults. The composer was happy enough, later in his career, to admit to the well-known dichotomy of being both monk and ragamuffin, but he never let on what "ragamuffin" really meant, and what this dichotomy had cost him, and lost him. Poulenc's painstakingly engineered publicity in Maurice Chevalier–style certainly raised his profile, but in the longer term it also insidiously narrowed what was generally taken by the average music lover to be his emotional and musical range.

THE MASKS AND MYTHS

"He left one with an undercurrent of panic, of suspected tragedy—of some man helplessly trapped behind a mask."[8]

Money

The myth was that Poulenc was rich and effortlessly generous. He was neither, although at his Noizay château he enjoyed playing the role of grandee and host; generosity and meanness seemed to alternate according to his state of mind.. From his family's business (which later became the Rhône-Poulenc chemical conglomerate) he had inherited a sufficient amount of money to buy that house and live comfortably during the 1920s, but the collapse of the Lyon-Allemand Bank in 1931 (in the wake of the Wall Street crash) lost Poulenc what remained of his paternal fortune.

Even before this catastrophe, Poulenc had acquired a reputation for being careful with money, while still maintaining "a well-to-do-air."[9] As early as 1923 the painter Jacques-Émile Blanche, embarrassed by the composer's tightness with money ("pingrerie"), complained about it in a letter to Cocteau.[10] By 1931 and the bank crash, the composer's stinginess had turned into an obsession. Poulenc went into a kind of overdrive with regard to performing activities as a pianist (both soloist and accompanist) and lecturer that lasted compulsively for the rest of his life. He traveled anywhere, often zigzagging the country in chaotic fashion, providing there was payment at the end of the day. He never learned to drive, but the number of trains he must have taken during his life defies calculation. He wrote a great deal of piano music in the early 1930s simply because there was a market for it then, and he was a canny negotiator with publishers, moving from one to the other in order to get the best price for his music. He avoided paying commission to agents whenever possible, and when abroad, he drew on funds owing to him from the publishers Chester in London and Ricordi in Milan (accounts were also held by friends in New York and Lausanne, among other places),[11] all of which suggests he was careful if not devious with his tax liabilities.

As the insecure younger composer of the 1930s gradually became the world-famous figure of the 1950s, money was less of a problem, but old habits died hard. Cocteau could scarcely believe that when Poulenc and Denise Duval were in Monte Carlo in 1959, he insisted that they both move from the Hôtel d'Angle-terre (1,800 francs a night) to the Plaza (1,700 francs).[12] In an interview given in

2004, Duval refers to the composer (whom she loved) as stingy ("radin"),[13] and Cocteau noted Poulenc's "agony at the idea of taking a taxi, of paying for a phone call, of using a box of matches."[14]

Patriotism

According to the myth, the composer was a member of the French Resistance, in receipt of secret communications (including Éluard's poem "Liberté") that may have put him in danger. This was not so. Poulenc was no collaborator, but neither was he a freedom fighter. Whatever his sympathies, and no one would deny that Poulenc was a patriot in spirit, he kept his head carefully beneath the parapet like millions of other Frenchmen. He was also wise enough to direct an eye to the future and keep his hands clean, realizing that collaborators would face severe penalties once the war was over.

For Poulenc, the Occupation years were particularly fruitful ones in terms of work and creativity (Paris was largely spared bombing). The lavish production of his ballet *Les Animaux modèles*, at the Opéra in 1942, inevitably required him to rub shoulders with collaborator colleagues, and be mindful of Germans sitting in the audience. His own resistance came in the form of concealed references to an old French patriotic song ("Non non, vous n'aurez pas notre Alsace Lorraine") in the orchestral score; nobody appears to have noticed them, least of all the Nazis, until the composer pointed them out after the war. Poulenc kept in touch with people like Alfred Cortot, who had efficacious links to the occupying government; the famous pianist intervened to save the life of the Jewish singer Marya Freund (see FP162)—though he failed to do the same for Max Jacob—and, responding to Poulenc's pleas, rescued Raymond Destouches from jail for black marketeering.

Notwithstanding a single recital performance of *C* FP122/i in a hall not far from Gestapo headquarters, Poulenc's handful of "resistant" works emerged as such only after the Occupation was over—though the timing does not, of course, make the sentiment behind these works any less sincere. There had been some risk in having scores of his choral cantata *Figure humaine* printed before the Germans were actually driven out of France, but the occupiers had more on their minds than scouring song texts by highbrow composers, and the risk-averse Poulenc knew it. Thousands of Frenchmen hinted they had been part of the Resistance, the secret nature of their work conveniently sparing them from offering any details. If Poulenc was guilty of anything, it was of occasionally giving the impression that he had played a more significant role than that of loyal Frenchman and canny survivor.

Work

The myth was that Poulenc was elegantly lazy and had to make himself work. The truth is that he worked madly and nonstop—although he devoted many more calendar days to performing, lecturing, and traveling back and forth across France, or to Britain and the United States, than to composing. He secluded himself to work at Noizay (particularly if deadlines were looming), but mostly for weeks rather than months at a time. He also composed as a house guest at Le Tremblay and Kerbastic, at the Hôtel Majestic in Cannes, at Brive, Autun, Lyon, Bagnols-en-Forêt—anywhere he could find or hire a piano. On all his multifarious travels he must have had with him a portfolio of manuscript paper containing various works at different stages of completion. Only rarely did Poulenc concentrate on any one piece at a time. We usually hear of a mooted work announced in a letter to a friend a long time (sometimes years) before it was completed.

The thing for him was getting started, the initial spark, and one might even say the Proustian madeleine dipped in tea. He might "find" two bars for a song (allied to a certain fragment of poetry that he found powerfully evocative), and that is when the inexplicable magic occurred. While waiting for that idea to progress, he turned his energies to one or more other works (behind the song's back, as it were), in a kind of promiscuity of attention that would have been fatal for most other composers. To make such a method of composition work, he needed to be, and was, a master at connecting fragments that had been composed separately into a seamless whole.

Matches between word and tone, between the composer's inner world and the poem's imagery, were noted down in the sketches (or "monstres," as he referred to them) he carried around with him, sometimes for years. On these sketches were planted the precious seeds that would grow into full-scale works. In real life at Noizay, Poulenc was an expert arranger of roses and gladioli (as witnessed by Audel), picked one by one, laid in a long basket and assembled with care, and so it was with his composing.[15] There was always a fragment that came first into bud and united with the words in a flash of genius (that moment of magic). The less spontaneous flowerings of inspiration that followed were painstakingly and patiently cultivated, as if in a greenhouse, and carefully placed in the gaps.[16] When complete, his musical bouquet has at its heart a color and texture (stemming from the initial inspiration) that suffuses the whole arrangement with vibrant life. Such assembling of a work from the ground up, as it were, is far removed from the myth of an easy and almost casual fecundity.

For his best compositions, Poulenc attaches music to fragments of memory: visual images, some of them from long ago, and also aural echoes, music by other composers that he was somehow able to turn into something entirely his own. A Proustian metamorphosis transforms a "stolen" passage (plagiarism if another composer were to do it) into the purest Poulenc, an act of transfiguration rather than theft. To set off the creative processes (either visual or aural), he often chose to "lie down where all the ladders start," as Yeats puts it. Recapturing past times meant revisiting memories of every kind, and among these were the hidden recesses of "the foul rag and bone shop of the heart."[17] Throwaway remarks made by the composer over the years implied that sexual memory had played a primal part in this magical process—and that certain parts of Paris and the Nogent of his adolescence remained powerfully evocative for him for that very reason.

Shame and Compulsion

Poulenc's own "foul rag and bone shop of the heart" was an enormous emporium revisited with artistic advantage and distressing personal cost. Although homosexuality was not criminalized in France in Poulenc's time,[18] this legislative anomaly should not be mistaken for any generalized toleration, particularly in circles of the *haute bourgeoisie* in the earlier part of the century. The myth has been that his sexual exploits, mere peccadilloes surely, were harmless and enjoyable. No doubt many of them were, but sex for Poulenc gradually became driven and joyless—and I believe this was the case much earlier in his life than has been realized. In a diary entry from 1964, Ned Rorem incidentally drew a convincing pen-portrait of a hobby that was becoming counterproductive for him as well: "Sex increasingly dominates sleep and waking hours, claims priority over friendship, work, ambition, repeats itself indistinguishably and has no issue, no construction."[19]

Compulsive sexual behavior often appears to be the result of an early history of overwhelming need. The person in its grip believes there is someone out there who will change his or her life: once this magical person is found, a primal longing will at last be satisfied. And this belief persists through repeated disappointments. Some writers and therapists relate such a pattern of feeling and thinking to "attachment theory," an attempt to satisfy childish needs.[20] Certainly the early loss of both parents may have contributed to a feeling of abandonment. "For gay men," notes Richard Goldstein, sex "is also an agent of communion, replacing an often hostile family and even shaping politics. It represents an ecstatic break with years of glances and guises, the furtive past we left behind."[21]

Repetitive patterns of sexual activity, in the current thinking, can constitute a "process" addiction, similar to gambling, obsessive shopping, and overworking—all related in turn to "substance" addictions like alcoholism and drug-taking. Whatever the background reason, the sexual addict leads an increasingly desperate life in a hunt for pleasure that is eventually meaningless and potentially dangerous, even if it remains within the boundaries of the law.[22] Sex without love is a kind of enforced chastity of the soul, but apart from the loneliness it can also be compulsively routine. In an unintentionally revealing moment, Poulenc compared the scenario he had invented for the supposedly chaste goddess Diana in his ballet *Aubade* to his own condition: *"Every day the goddess must reluctantly resume her hunting in the forest, carrying the bow that was as tedious to her as my piano was at that time to me."*[23] For "forest" read the boulevards of Paris, the fun-fairs of Nogent.

If he had longed for order in his life after the sexual hurly-burly of his twenties, proposing marriage to Raymonde Linossier in 1928 and falling in love with Chanlaire the following year might have seemed like solutions, but returning to his religious roots may have appeared as another means of escape. One of the most important events in Poulenc's life was his reconversion to Roman Catholicism in 1936, the result of what he later claimed had been a mystical experience during a visit to the shrine of the Black Virgin at Rocamadour. This change of direction would have extraordinary consequences for his music, but his conversion may have incidentally represented a call for help from someone battling sexual addiction (unidentified as such in those days). The stricter priests of the Catholic church, viewing homosexuality as a sin, would have counseled Poulenc to desist from his sexual adventures. Indeed, he would have expected them (and probably needed them) to insist on precisely that. Yet if the composer at first hoped his return to the church would create order from chaos, it is significant that in later life he sought out priests who were willing to overlook the sexual side of his life.[24]

Poulenc privately credited his lovers with some of his best music, but his gratitude sometimes seems fanciful. Usually his relationships came and went in quick succession, or lingered with complications. Ephemeral contacts were often made to fill a terrible void. To Father John Howard Griffin, of the Carmelite order in Dallas (see p. 385), he confessed: *"The loneliness is so hideous that I cannot stay in my room. I wander over to the hall, seeking contact with any human, talking with strangers. I have truly the impression that I am the devil's puppet."*[25] The only help available to him in times of distress was a doctor's medication and the sharing of his woes (or pleasures in the upbeat times) with an ad hoc counsel of gay friends, some more willing than others to listen to the details. Ned Rorem, for one, was made to feel distinctly uncomfortable by Poulenc's boasts concerning his sexual exploits.[26]

Pleasures experienced with the more extended liaisons were negated by Poulenc's anguish in attempting to micromanage those relationships. Since he almost always attached himself to younger men who could not match his level of intelligence and cultivation, his lovers were often as emotionally unavailable to him as he was to them. He made himself ill with jealous suspicions (sometimes justified, sometimes not), imperious demands alternating with self-abasement. In 1957, in a short-lived phase of feeling free of obsession, Poulenc wrote to Simone Girard: *"It is so good to be no longer ill, so pleasant no longer to be in love."*[27] (See also "The Sexual Milieu of Francis Poulenc," p. 194; and "The Crisis of 1954," p. 383.)

TWIN, COUNTERWEIGHT, AND GUARDIAN ANGEL: PIERRE BERNAC

Love comes in many forms. There was once a widespread belief, certainly in Britain, that Poulenc and Bernac were lovers; it was taken for granted that theirs was a gay relationship parallel to that of Benjamin Britten and Peter Pears. When correcting this misapprehension in others, I realized that insisting on the absence of a sexual or romantic element in a relationship can tend to downgrade its importance. *Pace* the ever-faithful Raymond Destouches, kept in the background in Noizay, neither composer nor singer had a "significant other" to influence and permeate his life and work; the advent of Bernac into Poulenc's life was quite simply an amazing piece of good luck for them both, almost as propitious as finding a partner with whom to build a life. Without Bernac, Poulenc, as both composer and human being, would have been entirely different, and arguably much less distinguished. Singer and composer never addressed each other with the familiar "tu," but Bernac played a role as friend, counselor, and inspiration (if not exactly muse) that far exceeded that of many a great composer's spouse. In return, it was Poulenc's music that brought joy and meaning into the singer's ascetic life, and a pathway to becoming a worldwide authority on mélodie.

Bernac was born on 12 January 1899, five days after Poulenc. If composer and singer were practically twins (they sometimes celebrated their birthdays together), they were so unlike that there could be no speculation about shared astrological attributes. Where Poulenc was ebullient and daring, Bernac was reserved and careful; if Poulenc was capable of inspired madness, Bernac represented the calm of reason. The composer's background was effortlessly well-heeled with inherited money, Bernac's a few rungs lower in the Parisian bourgeoisie—the difference between the glamour of the 8th arrondissement and the solid respectability of the 7th. Though they were not precisely on the same financial plane, Bernac's solid middle-class background ruled out any possibility that he could have appealed to Poulenc, who cared only for working-class lovers.

Bernac started off working for his stockbroker father while singing in a private theater, La Petite Scène, in his spare time.[28] Little by little he gained professional confidence. His mentors included the composer André Caplet, with whom the young Bernac established a duo shortly before Caplet's untimely death in 1925; the conductor Walter Straram (1876–1933); the great mélodie singer Claire Croiza, who worked with him on French song; and the baritone Reinhold von Warlich (1877–1939), with whom he studied lieder in Salzburg in the early 1930s.

Bernac at the height of his career, 1948.

Bernac and Poulenc gave the first performance of *Chansons gaillardes* FP42 in Paris in 1926, but they did not get on: Poulenc was too full of himself, the texts were too smutty for Bernac's liking, and the composer took him to be a hidebound prude. Bernac appeared twice as Pelléas in Debussy's opera, in Paris under Walter Straram (1933) and in Geneva under Ernest Ansermet (1936), but opera did not really interest him. Singer and composer found each other again in 1934 (see Outline, 1934–35) and remained steadfast musical partners for the next twenty-five years. For their numerous recitals (often planned by Bernac), Poulenc had to learn a great many songs from the mainstream repertoire he had never played before: by Schubert, Schumann, Liszt, Duparc, Chabrier, and Fauré. He later acknowledged the importance of this broadening of his horizons. As he got to know the standard classical song repertoire, his understanding of the voice, and how best to write for it, blossomed. (The same may be said about the development of Britten's duo with Pears. And like Pears, Bernac was far from a one-composer singer: he premiered works by Roussel, Milhaud, Honegger, Jean Françaix, André Jolivet, and Samuel Barber among others.)

Bernac's collaboration with Poulenc was his mainstay, and his career was dependent on that link. His honesty and integrity were legendary, but these were hardly popular qualities in Paris, where adroit political maneuvering in the arts is paramount; in that area Bernac was as little gifted as Poulenc was a master. The two men relied on each other to a remarkable extent. Few other artists would have been able to cope with the packed schedules, concerts back-to-back, insisted on by Poulenc; new songs were sometimes presented to Bernac in manuscript days before their first performances. But he always managed (one searches the documents in vain to find Bernac canceling a concert), and far from ever letting the composer down, he became his irreplaceable mouthpiece. Poulenc confided to Simone Girard, *"I need his voice, and I don't need any other voice"*[29] (of the composer's 145 songs, 90 were written for Bernac). In a strange way their relationship represented a reversal of traditional roles: a subtitle for an essay about Bernac could be "The Singer as Accompanist"—were it not for the fact that when he sings the songs in their many recorded performances, he owns them in magisterial fashion; and it is Poulenc, delighted and grateful for how his music has sprung into life, who accompanies, wonderfully.

For long periods in the 1940s and 50s, the composer abandoned songs in favor of his Apollinaire and Bernanos operas. And Bernac (without complaining that he had much less work as a result) had a huge role to play here too. The constant and detailed exchange of letters, with Bernac offering advice about prosody and about writing for the different kinds of operatic voices of which Poulenc had little experience, was invaluable to the composer. Without Bernac's recommendation of the text, there would have been no Poulenc *Gloria*. In private matters, the composer also received support in large and heroic measure from Bernac, who lived a single life and adopted with Poulenc the demeanor of a strict yet affectionate counselor.[30] In a 1954 letter to Poulenc of devastating clarity (p. 384), the singer asserts his right to work in conditions free from emotional upheaval, and he roundly calls the composer to account for what he sees as self-indulgent and self-destructive behavior: "Francis Poulenc, even on the human plane, is surely greater than this. Have no doubt that this feebleness will eventually make itself felt in your art."[31] Although he was devoutly Catholic, his exasperation did not stem from religious disapproval; Bernac never shrank from being completely frank, professionally and personally, while remaining essentially a loving friend.

The duo appeared for the last time at an all-Poulenc concert on 27 May 1959. Poulenc regretted the ending of this "*si fraternelle association*," but Bernac had a horror of singing at less than his best. For sixteen years after the composer's death, he was the guardian of the flame, coaching famous singers as well as much younger students and looking after Poulenc's best posthumous interests, both musically and personally. In 1970 he published *The Interpretation of French Song*, a still indispensable overview of the entire mélodie repertoire with helpful commentaries for performers, and followed this with a second book, *Francis Poulenc: The Man and His Songs*, toward the end of his life. Bernac died of heart disease on 17 October 1979, in the south of France, tenderly looked after by his (and Poulenc's) lifelong friend Simone Girard.

I once asked him why he had become a singer. His reply was telling: "It gave me the opportunity to recite the poems I loved with a heightened intensity." Without Bernac it is unlikely that we would now have in our possession songs by Poulenc with such emotional range and depth. The composer was challenged to write up to the singer's level of intelligence, refinement, and technical skill. Many of the greatest Poulenc songs (especially those Éluard settings in visionary mode, like *Tu vois le feu du soir*, and such Apollinaire songs as *Sanglots* and *Voyage*) should be regarded, at least in part, as the singer's enduring legacy.

THE APOTHEOSIS OF FRANCIS POULENC

Bernac, who died forty years ago, did his best to shield Poulenc from posthumous scrutiny; he was, of course, also a child of his time. But once the composer's flaws are revealed, they seem no worse than those of other great creators, who are self-centered almost to a man. (The title of Stéphane Audel's Poulenc book is *Moi et mes amis*, not *Mes Amis et moi*; Audel, although he loved Poulenc, meant that difference to be noticed.) At the center of his vulnerability stands the question of his sexuality, now common knowledge and certainly no stain on his reputation in the modern world. But it is crucial to remember that in the first decades of the twentieth century, in the wake of the Oscar Wilde scandal (even in France), there was huge opprobrium, both social and religious, attached to homosexuality. Poulenc's prosperous bourgeois background and an early religious education supervised by his deeply devout father added to the guilt.

It may seem almost unbelievable today that simply being gay should have been cause for such anguish. But Max Jacob's soul-destroying guilt (see p. 375) and Poulenc's plea to Father Griffin in 1954 ("*I have sinned so terribly, but how much I suffer for it. Pray that my soul be saved from eternal fire*"; see p. 385) derive entirely from an ingrained awareness of mortal sin. Possibly the most dislocating traumas of the composer's life were the result of the guilt and shame attached by others to sexual experiences, rather than the experiences themselves.

Secrecy and the invention of alternative realities are the tactics of survival assimilated early on in order to avoid becoming an outcast. Many a gay youngster, even today—and how much more so in the early twentieth century—has felt like a changeling, a traitor in the household, survival depending on disguising his or her true self. And it is also possible that those early-honed dissembling skills will make playing fast and loose with the truth a lifelong habit. Creating an alter-ego that is eminently lovable and blameless becomes a priority; the pay-off is a parallel life where secret contact with forbidden erotic pleasures remains possible, despite the ever-mounting guilt. Somewhere deep inside of himself Poulenc seems to have regarded his music, the reflection of his supposedly dark soul, as damaged goods that required vigilant protection, and the special pleading of his unique brand of salesmanship—a field in which he possessed an almost diabolical ability. Guilt can be joked about or even mined for musical purposes, but it can seldom be suppressed altogether.

Would Poulenc have lived and worked longer and more productively if he had been the inhabitant of an uncomplicated and untrammeled emotional landscape? Perhaps, and perhaps not. He would certainly have been better off without his lifelong and often debilitating hypochondria, which also very probably arose from some kind of guilt and expectation of punishment. He remained enmeshed in the prejudices of long ago, but, living in the sophisticated world of Paris, he found a way around the obstacles and managed to fulfill his considerable musical destiny by flipping some of the cards that had been stacked against him. His success came at a cost, of course. Toward the end of his life we sense the energy and the willpower draining out of him and his music, and this sad *decrescendo* is clearly not the result of declining physical health alone. His world of secrets and hidden compartments had damaged him as well as his lover Raymond, his niece Brigitte, and perhaps most of all his unacknowledged daughter, Marie-Ange. There were other victims as well. At his lowest moments he considered himself merely a man of straw, and feared the worst for his immortal soul. "*I am in terrible fear,*" he wrote to Father Griffin. "*Will God take into account my poor efforts—the Mass, the religious motets? Will he at least see them and me kindly, or as another bungler, a Jongleur de Notre Dame?*"[32]

On the morning of 30 January 1963, there was more than enough time between taking ill and dying for Poulenc to have experienced the fear of imminent death, a test faced at the scaffold by one of his greatest creations, Blanche de la Force in *Dialogues des Carmélites*. At the last possible moment, the usually terrified young woman finds herself able to confront her end at the guillotine with equanimity. The whole point of her story is that she surprises herself, and all who know her, with hidden reserves of grace and courage; *pace* Bernanos, and as fervently as he ascribes the outcome to a divine miracle, one can also see it as a victory for the human spirit and humanity in general. As she discovers within herself the calm and radiance to face death, the Carmelite nun experiences in death the kind of triumph that has always eluded her in life.

There is also such a thing as posthumous triumph for a composer, far more profound than any glamorous moment of success experienced during a career. In the fifty-seven years since his death, perceptions have greatly changed: the challenging aspects of Poulenc's output are no longer reserved for the cognoscenti, and his songs have long been accepted as an important part of the French mélodie tradition, to be mentioned in the same breath as those of Fauré, Debussy, and Ravel. The bounty of his music is now counted a blessing throughout the musical world. Perhaps Poulenc has never been taken seriously enough because the web of obfuscations spun around his life have made it impossible for us to see and celebrate, or even bemoan, who he really is. The recent researches of Carl Schmidt, Richard D. E. Burton, Hervé Lacombe, Nicolas Southon, and Pierre Miscevic have enabled a frank reappraisal of his biography. The composer made a terrible mess of certain aspects of his life, but of which of us is that not true? He was selfish and cowardly but scarcely ever malign, and intentional cruelty was not his style. He left song recitalists an incomparably enriched repertoire.

Even the religious among us who love this music would wish Poulenc to have been spared the divine retribution he so feared. I imagine hundreds of firefighting angels, Carmelites among them, welcoming the composer while singing the mélodies they had learned in a former life. I see them blocking his way to the scaffold and shielding him from the inferno while consigning to the flames the outer husks—the clown's costume, the caul of the phony monk and beret of the ragamuffin. The truth is that such lurid props are no longer needed by Poulenc or his music, whether in hell or heaven, and certainly not on this earth.

In defiance of all the laws of propriety into which he was born, Poulenc's musical achievements seem magnified, rather than diminished, by the uncensored details of his struggles, surely the only reason to discuss them now. Cap and bells cast aside, the great composer now stands unmasked, although other stories might unravel; and if they do, what does it really matter? Most of the masks were worn only because he learned early on to be ashamed of who he was. At a memorable party in his youth, "La belle Poulenka" had stripped naked in a madcap and drunken attempt to confront and overcome that shame. A century later, many of his secrets have come to light, and dividing walls of his psyche have been opened up to our gaze. His astounded friends got over the shock of seeing it all hang out in 1920, and so will we. In any case, the nakedness of Francis Poulenc has undergone several *Métamorphoses*, to revisit one of his song titles. His is a body of music that transcends the corporeal—out of shame's reach at last, and more cherished than he could ever have imagined.

ENVOI

At the end of this book, some questions and answers:

Q: Have we journeyed all this way merely to discover we have come full circle? Having been forgiven his various faults, can Poulenc simply return to being what he was before people began digging into his life? What is the point of examining problematical things if they end up shrugged off and not changing anything? Come to think of it, how important is it to know that Beethoven and Fauré were deaf (not their fault), or that Schubert and Schumann were syphilitic (more their fault)? These tragic afflictions have never affected us directly, and these men's works were triumphantly created despite their terrible setbacks.

A: Such details really do matter; biographies enabling us better to understand our heroes and heroines do bring about real change, if only slowly. Poulenc's position in the world is very different from where it was fifty years ago, and we could say that his works were also "triumphantly created." Most of us instinctively take background knowledge like deafness or syphilis into account when expressing our astonished admiration for great creators who lived in a time when surmounting such suffering was so much harder. Composers' biographies show us men and women just like us, but at the same time utterly unlike us, and this is surely the thrill of drawing closer to the otherwise inaccessible past.

Q: What about the music? How does all the contextual knowledge in the world actually affect a performance?

A: This is hard to say, and depends on imagination and empathy. A kind of awareness can enter the performing soul, sometimes in a flash and sometimes gradually and imperceptibly, often reaping rich dividends for singers, pianists, and listeners alike. Turning knowledge into sound and inflection is an imponderable process. It is a performer's mind, not a trick of technique, that unaccountably brings color and depth into music, like a door opening to reveal someone singing to us of something he or she deeply understands, where understanding is an adjunct to love and devotion. When someone sings of matters they truly know, we feel that connection, that authentic intimacy, instantly, and it is the performer's instincts backed up by knowledge that have made the miracle possible. As there is an infinite amount of color and depth in Poulenc's songs, performers benefit from all the help and stimulation they can get from outside sources.

Q (less friendly): What on earth is the point of exposing the peccadilloes of someone's sexual life to this kind of scrutiny and comment? Does it really help to reveal that Poulenc (and many of his friends) led an unhappy and turbulent private life that seems deeply at odds with the beauty of his music? Can anything good come out of this kind of examination of the gutter?

A: One of the most beautiful Schumann songs performed by Bernac and Poulenc was *Die Lotosblume*, the lotus flower prized by the Indians for a beauty that seems all the more poignant on account of the dirt and slime that nourish its roots. As Alexis de Tocqueville wrote of a big city in 1835: "It is in the middle of this putrid sewer that the greatest river of human industry springs up and carries fertility to the whole world."[33] The sewer as a talking point is generally best left to germaphobes and homophobes, but it has always been the case that unpalatable actions can translate into musical fertility ("from this foul drain pure gold flows forth," he continued). A less het-up questioner might prefer another kind of underground water imagery, linking subterranean streams with the regenerative powers of music: waters running still and deep, waters refreshing the soul and nourishing the imagination, waters irrigating the parched deserts of prejudice and bigotry.

Acknowledgments

THIS BOOK COULD NOT HAVE BEEN PREPARED OR WRITTEN WITHOUT THE HELP
of grants from the Leverhulme Trust, The Songmakers' Almanac, and Les Amis
de Francis Poulenc. Apart from the biographical and musical commentary, the
author of a book about a twentieth-century French composer who set to music
innumerable twentieth-century French poems finds himself faced with copyright obligations that are far heavier than one might imagine. Seeking out and
corresponding with the relevant rights holders connected with Poulenc's œuvre
was an epic task in itself. I am extremely grateful to Dr. Katy Hamilton and to the
Swiss baritone Joël Terrin for having undertaken it with charm and resilience. In
traversing this minefield, I have been generously supported by Guildhall School
of Music & Drama, London, and above all by the wise counsel of Professor
Cormac Newark, head of Research at my school. I am proud to be Professor in a
world-famous center of education that so generously encourages its staff to complement their teaching of student performers (the age-old task in any conservatoire) with the more modern challenge of contributing to the musical debate with
written material of lasting value. At an early stage, Professor Helena Gaunt was
most helpful in trying to find a publisher for this book; the failure of her attempt,
and my subsequent happy connection with Liveright, has turned out to be my
great good fortune.

For my entire career I have performed the songs of Poulenc with the dedicatee of this book and countless other singers, too numerous to mention by name. I
owe to all of them hundreds of insights born of their love for this music. I am further indebted to the memory of Pierre Bernac, an inspiration to me since I first
heard him on disc, and even more so when I got to know him; to that doyenne of
Poulenc scholars in London, Sidney Buckland, as well as to Myriam Chimènes,
of whom the same might be said in Paris; to my hostess in New York, Mimi Daitz,
herself a considerable maven of French song; to the distinguished psychiatrist Dr.
David Foreman; to Mike and Judy Hildesley, dearest of friends and supporters;
to my indefatigable colleague at Guildhall School Pamela Lidiard; to that closest

and most sympathetic of friends and translators, Uri Liebrecht; to the charming and helpful Pierre Miscevic; to the exquisitely dear memory of the late Winifred Radford; to my admired friend Tony Scotland, biographer of Lennox Berkeley; to Benoît Seringe, the composer's grand-nephew and now head of Les Amis de Francis Poulenc, whom I have known since he was a little boy; to the memory of the late Rosine and Jean Seringe, my hosts on visits to Paris, where I stayed in their unforgettable apartment in the rue d'Aumale (surrounded by precious Poulenciana); to my dear friends Paul and Jeanne Strang, who understand this composer so well; to my partner and best friend, Brandon Velarde; and to Susan Youens, who is a doyenne of song worldwide, and an unfailing inspiration. No praise can be too high for my editor at Liveright, the patient and marvelously efficient Susan Gaustad. Without her daily input, this book would have got nowhere.

The late Eric Sams was my trusted guide and mentor in the world of lieder, and by the early 1970s his son Jeremy was already the polished French mélodie expert; in his teens he knew many of the Poulenc songs, and their words, by heart. Although Jeremy inherited his father's brilliance ("Sams eyes, Sams teeth, Sams everything," as one of them quipped, I've forgotten which), French music was always more of the younger man's specialization. More than forty years later, Jeremy's name together with mine on the title page seems an appropriate acknowledgment of how close I was to Eric, and what an honor it is for me to continue my connection with the Sams family into another generation.

Notes

Preface

1. Poulenc to Simone Girard, March 1953, *Correspondance*, p. 751.
2. In Schumann's celebrated review ("Hats off gentlemen, a genius") of Chopin's Variations on Mozart's "Là ci darem la mano" (*Allgemeine musikalische Zeitung*, 7 December 1831); for Brahms, in the *Neue Zeitschrift für Musik* (October 1853).
3. This performance is available as part of the Hyperion edition of *The Complete Songs* (2013).

Part I

1. Poulenc/Audel, *Moi et mes amis*, p. 29.
2. Ibid.
3. Hell, p. 30.
4. Ibid.
5. Gilberte is the daughter of Charles Swann in Marcel Proust's *Swann's Way* (*À la recherche du temps perdu*).
6. Interview 1 with Claude Rostand, in Poulenc, *Notes from the Heart* (ed. Southon, trans. Nichols), p. 182.
7. Quoted in Schmidt, *Enchanting Muse*, p. 7.
8. Not to be confused with his namesake, the singing actor Pierre Bertin, the reason the younger Bertin had to find a new professional name.
9. L. Bertrand Dorléac, in P. Boucheron, ed., *Histoire mondiale de la France* (Paris: Seuil, 2017), p. 563. Dorléac identifies one of the five female figures in this seminal work (nominally depicting prostitutes from a bordello in Barcelona) as Apollinaire's partner, the painter and poet Marie Laurencin, later a good friend of Poulenc (see FP57).
10. Poulenc to an older composer's (almost) namesake, "Gabriel Faure" (he left out the accent on the final e), 11 June 1952, *Correspondance*, p. 730. Jeanne Raunay had been the first singer to perform Fauré's difficult late cycle *La Chanson d'Ève*.
11. Lacombe, p. 29.
12. Interview 1 with Rostand, in Poulenc, *Notes from the Heart*, p. 183.
13. "How I Composed *Dialogues des Carmélites*," open letter to Georges Hirsch, in Poulenc, *Notes from the Heart*, p. 55. Clément was a close friend of Poulenc's uncle, Marcel Royer.
14. Poulenc, *Notes from the Heart*, p. 105. FP refers to the Mallarmé poem that had been set by Debussy in 1884, music that only came to light in 1926.
15. Ibid. When FP's voice broke, *"there followed a nasty conversion into nasal braying."*

16. Lacombe, p. 15.
17. Ibid., p. 27.
18. Myriam Chimènes, *Mécènes et musiciens* (Paris: Fayard, 2004), p. 164.
19. Poulenc gives a further description of Debussy's piano playing in À *bâtons rompus*, p. 186.
20. Interview 2 with Rostand, in Poulenc, *Notes from the Heart*, p. 190.
21. Schmidt, *Entrancing Muse*, p. 15.
22. Poulenc, *Notes from the Heart*, p. 106.
23. Interview 3 with Rostand, ibid., p. 191.
24. Poulenc/Audel, *Moi et mes amis*, pp. 42–43.
25. Concluding sentence of Poulenc's monograph on Chabrier: reprinted in Poulenc, *J'écris* (Southon, ed.), p. 720.
26. Interview 8 with Rostand, in Poulenc, *Notes from the Heart*, p. 224.
27. Lacombe, p. 250.
28. This incident is recounted in Poulenc/Audel, *Moi et mes amis*, pp. 125–26.
29. Schmidt, *Entrancing Muse*, p. 48.
30. FP relates this incident to Viñes in a letter of 26 September 1917, *Correspondance*, p. 55.
31. Poulenc, *J'écris*, p. 374.
32. Interview 1 with Rostand, in Poulenc, *Notes from the Heart*, p. 185.
33. Poulenc claimed to have met the poet in 1917, and even in 1916, but that seems unlikely. His dating of events is often extremely approximate.
34. Poulenc to Viñes, 3 September 1918, *Correspondance*, p. 64.
35. Poulenc to Viñes, 31 December 1918, *Correspondance*, p. 80.
36. See Lacombe, p. 72.
37. The poem is best known in a duet setting by Saint-Saëns, although Poulenc may have been aware of the Caplet setting (1900) with flute.
38. Poulenc/Audel, *Moi et mes amis*, p. 50.
39. Cocteau to Poulenc, 13 September 1918, *Correspondance*, pp. 66–68.
40. Cocteau to Poulenc, 15 October 1918, *Correspondance*, pp. 71–72.
41. Poulenc to Cocteau, 9 February 1919, *Correspondance*, pp. 85–86.
42. Interview 12 with Rostand, in Poulenc, *Notes from the Heart*, p. 248.
43. *Journal*, pp. 63–65.
44. Poulenc, *Notes from the Heart*, p. 211.
45. Schmidt, *The First Poets: Lives of the Ancient Greek Poets* (New York: Knopf, 2005), p. 3. Schmidt makes the point that Orpheus's lyre was made from a tortoise shell, a gift from Apollo, and that Apollo also gifted the fatherless poet, French by adoption, with his own name—the "Apollinaris" in Wilhelm-Apollinaris de Kostrovitsky.
46. Poulenc, *Notes from the Heart*, p. 107. The comparison is with Jules Renard, poet of Ravel's cycle *Histoires naturelles*. In this same article Poulenc claims to have met Apollinaire only "*a dozen times or so*," which seems highly unlikely and contradicts the story, as told elsewhere, of the young man's admiration for the poet at a respectful distance.
47. Poulenc, *J'écris*, p. 646, conversation 1958.
48. Ibid., p. 477, lecture 1947.
49. Poulenc to Arthur Hoérée, 19 January 1925, *Correspondance*, pp. 248–49.
50. Poulenc, *Echo and Source*, p. 42.
51. See Lacombe, p. 244. Maria Olenina-d'Alheim (1869–1970) was the founder of the

influential Maison de Lied in Moscow. Her performances of Musorgsky inspired both Debussy and Ravel.

52. *Journal*, p. 21.
53. Bernac, p. 52.
54. Ibid., p. 53.
55. Interview 6 with Rostand, in Poulenc, *Notes from the Heart*, p. 211. If Poulenc is correct about the date of February 1919, and there is no guarantee that he is, the composition of this song preceded the others in the set, which were written a few months later.
56. *Journal*, p. 21.
57. Poulenc, *J'écris*, p. 646.
58. See Poulenc/Audel, *Moi et mes amis*, p. 108, where Angelica de Kostrowitsky is referred to as *"terrible"* by Poulenc and *"effrayante"* by Audel.
59. Poulenc, *Notes from the Heart*, pp. 106–7, talk 1947.
60. Ibid., p. 107.
61. Georges Auric, *Quand j'étais là* (Paris: Grasset, 1979), p. 158.
62. Quoted in Lacombe, p. 197.
63. Poulenc to Collaer, 21 January 1920, *Correspondance*, p. 103.
64. *Journal*, p. 23.
65. Milhaud, *Ma Vie heureuse* (*My Happy Life*), trans. Donald Evans (London: Calder and Boyars, 1952), pp. 83–84. Also quoted in Buckland and Chimènes, pp. 3–4.
66. See Interview 6 with Rostand in Poulenc, *Notes from the Heart*, p. 211.
67. Quoted in Lacombe, p. 175.
68. Poulenc to Cocteau, 30 August 1919, *Correspondance*, pp. 97–98.

Part II

1. Poulenc/Audel, *Moi et mes amis*, p. 129.
2. Lacombe, p. 212.
3. Poulenc to Cocteau, unpublished letter quoted in Schmidt, *Entrancing Muse*, p. 82.
4. Wiéner, *Allegro appassionato* (Paris: Belfond, 1978), pp. 44–45.
5. FP postcard to Valentine Hugo, 5 March 1921, *Correspondance*, p. 120, n. 1.
6. Poulenc/Audel, *Moi et mes amis*, p. 24.
7. Poulenc to Collær, 7 July 1922, *Correspondance*, p. 162.
8. Poulenc, *J'écris* (ed. Southon), p. 357.
9. *Satie Remembered*, ed. Robert Orledge (London: Faber and Faber, 1995), p. xxxvii.
10. Jacob to Poulenc, *Correspondance*, p. 211.
11. See Schmidt, *Entrancing Muse*, pp. 145–46.
12. Poulenc to Jeanne Manceaux, November 1927, *Correspondance*, pp. 281–82.
13. Poulenc to Alice Ardoin, 21 July 1928, *Correspondance*, pp. 287–89.
14. Poulenc to Charles de Noailles, 16 July 1928, *Correspondance*, pp. 284–86.
15. Tailleferre, "Mémoires à l'emporte-pièce," *in Revue internationale de musique française* 19 (1986).
16. Poulenc, *J'écris*, pp. 254–68.
17. Buckland and Chimènes, p. 120.
18. See Lacombe, p. 325.
19. The passage is taken from Burton, p. 36, but it was inspired by Mellers, *Poulenc*, pp. 24–25. "Deserts of vast eternity" is a quote from Andrew Marvell's poem "To His Coy Mistress."

20. Poulenc to Richard Chanlaire, 19 May 1929, *Correspondance,* p. 304.

21. Lacombe, p. 341.

22. Landowska to Poulenc, May 1929, *Correspondance,* p. 305.

23. Sachs, *Au temps du bœuf sur le toit* (Paris: Grasset, 1939; reprinted 1989), p. 233.

24. For programs, see Schmidt, *Entrancing Muse,* p. 175.

25. Poulenc to Paul Collær, 17 January 1925, *Correspondance,* p. 247.

26. Poulenc to Auric, 15 March 1925, *Correspondance,* p. 251.

27. Interview 6 with Rostand, in Poulenc, *Notes from the Heart,* pp. 211–12.

28. In Buckland and Chimènes, p. 47.

29. Interview with Lucien Chevallier, in Poulenc, *Notes from the Heart,* p. 119.

30. Even Poulenc himself did not think so, judging by the fact that he arranged these songs for large orchestra in 1934 for Suzanne Peignot (first performed 16 December 1934).

31. Bernac, p. 207.

32. Ibid., p. 211.

33. Poulenc to Wiéner, August 1922, *Correspondance,* pp. 173–74.

34. Letter from Poulenc to Milhaud, in the Milhaud archives and mentioned in *Correspondance,* p. 174, n. 5.

35. Poulenc, *J'écris,* p. 71, article 1929.

36. Poulenc to Collaer, 16 February 1927, *Correspondance,* pp. 276–77.

37. *Journal,* pp. 23–25.

38. Poulenc to Bernac, 17 August 1956, *Correspondance,* p. 848.

39. *Journal,* p. 25.

40. Bernac, p. 216.

41. Ibid., p. 217.

42. Quoted in Schmidt, *Poulenc Catalogue,* pp. 133–34.

43. Poulenc to Stravinsky, 11 May 1934, *Correspondance,* p. 394.

44. *Journal,* p. 25.

45. Poulenc to François Hepp, 3 May 1927, *Correspondance,* p. 277.

46. As recounted in interview 6 with Rostand, in Poulenc, *Notes from the Heart,* p. 212.

47. *Journal,* p. 25.

48. Bernac, p. 204.

49. *Journal,* p. 25. The same phrase is translated as "indefensible lack of originality" in Bernac, p. 205.

50. Bernac, p. 206.

Part III

1. A task undertaken by Carl Schmidt in *Entrancing Muse.*

2. Poulenc to Marie-Blanche de Polignac, August 1929, *Correspondance,* p. 48, n. 6.

3. Baker (1906–1975) was a famous Parisian music-hall star of American birth. Poulenc to Paul Rouart, 27 March 1931, *Correspondance,* p. 337.

4. Poulenc, *J'écris* (ed. Southon), p. 394, article 1953.

5. Schmidt, *Entrancing Muse,* pp. 190–91.

6. *Journal,* pp. 58–59.

7. The writer Violet Trefusis (née Kepel, 1894–1972), great-aunt of the present Duchess of Cornwall, is now best remembered for her extended liaison with Vita Sackville-

West. She had a great many other affairs, including one with Winnaretta Singer, Princesse de Polignac, and also probably with Colette.

8. André George, review in *Les Nouvelles Littéraires*, 23 December 1933.
9. Burton, p. 63.
10. Poulenc, *Notes from the Heart* (ed. Southon, trans. Nichols), pp. 4 and 67.
11. Poulenc, *J'écris*, p. 579, conversation 1957.
12. Schmidt, *Entrancing Muse*, p. 215.
13. The music, appreciated and praised at the time but long thought irretrievably lost, has recently resurfaced as part of a DVD of the animated films of Alexandre Alexeieff (1901–1982), with Poulenc at the harpsichord.
14. *Correspondance*, p. 1027.
15. Poulenc to Marie-Blanche de Polignac, 30 April 1936, *Correspondance*, p. 414.
16. Schmidt, *Entrancing Muse*, p. 228.
17. Poulenc to Marie-Blanche de Polignac, 15 August 1936, *Correspondance*, p. 420.
18. Gouverné, "Hommage à Francis Poulenc," in *Zodiac* (1974), p. 21.
19. Louise de Vilmorin to Poulenc, November 1936, *Correspondance*, p. 435.
20. Poulenc to the singer Madeleine Vhita, December 1936, unpublished letter.
21. Hell, p. 144.
22. Milhaud, *Notes Without Music*, trans. Donald Evans (London: Dobson, 1952), p. 255.
23. *Journal*, pp. 46–47.
24. Poulenc to Nora Auric, 17 August 1937, *Correspondance*, p. 447.
25. There is, sadly, no surviving trace of these recordings, or even a list of the exact repertoire. In a letter to Sauguet of August 1937, Poulenc refers to an "*intégrale*," but he must simply mean the complete songs that were suitable for Bernac's voice. The baritone could not possibly have sung the *Chansons de Bilitis*, for example, nor the many early Debussy songs, only four of which had been published at the time, and which were conceived for high soprano.
26. Bernac to Poulenc, 20 September 1939, *Correspondance*, p. 488, n.1.
27. Poulenc to Boulanger, 26 September 1939, *Correspondance*, p. 482.
28. This information is from an unpublished letter from FP to Simone Girard at the end of 1939; quoted in Lacombe, p. 490. Bernac's own incredulous reaction to the change of circumstances is quoted in Schmidt, *Entrancing Muse*, p. 265.
29. Bernac, p. 220.
30. *Journal*, p. 25.
31. Lacombe, p. 361.
32. Laurencin to Poulenc, quoted in Poulenc, *Echo and Source*, p. 211.
33. *Journal*, p. 27.
34. Ibid., p. 27.
35. Bernac, p. 55.
36. Ibid., p. 56.
37. Poulenc, *J'écris*, p. 581, conversation 1947.
38. Ibid, p. 579.
39. Poulenc, contribution to *Homage à Marie-Blanche Comtesse Jean de Polignac* (Monaco: Jaspar, Polus, 1965), p. 90.
40. *Correspondance*, pp. 420–41, n. 4. The Vuillard portrait of Marie-Blanche de Polignac (painted 1928–32) resides in the Musée d'Orsay.
41. *Journal*, p. 27.

42. Bernac, pp. 57–58.

43. Apollinaire, *Œuvres poétiques*, ed. André Adéma and Michel Décaudin (Paris: Gallimard, 1965), pp. 1110–1111.

44. Poulenc, *J'écris*, p. 602, conversation 1952.

45. Bernac, p. 59.

46. Apollinaire's weakness for redheads is shown in another poem set by Poulenc, *Dans le jardin d'Anna* FP94/i. In *Un poème* FP131/ii, even the matches are redheads.

47. Sophie Robert, "Raymonde Linossier: Lovely Soul Who Was My Flame," in Buckland and Chimènes, pp. 115–17.

48. Schmidt, in *Poulenc Catalogue*, p. 185, states that the poems were published posthumously in 1953; in fact this was a republication.

49. Jacob to Poulenc, in Poulenc, *Echo and Source*, p. 95.

50. *Journal*, p. 29.

51. Bernac, p. 153.

52. "*Surtout dans le genre Moussorgski français*": Poulenc to Jacques Lerolle, 16 December 1931, *Correspondance*, p. 358, n. 3.

53. *Journal*, p. 29.

54. Ibid., p. 28.

55. Ibid., p. 29.

56. Ibid., pp. 29–31.

57. Lacombe, p. 369.

58. *Journal*, p. 31.

59. Poulenc, *Notes from the Heart*, p. 100, lecture 1935.

60. Poulenc to Jacques Lerolle, *Correspondance*, p. 392.

61. Poulenc, *Notes from the Heart*, p. 99, lecture 1935.

62. Ibid.

63. Ibid.

64. Lacombe, p. 407.

65. Some of the Belloc poems, including "Henry King" and "Matilda," were memorably set to music by Liza Lehmann (1862–1918).

66. Saint-Marceaux, *Journal*, p. 1254.

67. *Journal*, p. 31.

68. Interview 8 with Claude Rostand, in Poulenc, *Notes from the Heart*, p. 224.

69. *Journal*, p. 31.

70. This illustration was for *Poésies de Stéphane Mallarmé*, published in 1932. The different stages of the drawing are illustrated in Carl Schmidt, "Distilling Essences," in Buckland and Chimènes, pp. 199–209.

71. Bernac, p. 94.

72. Lord, *Picasso and Dora: A Personal Memoir* (London: Orion, 1993).

73. Bernac, p. 95.

74. *Journal*, p. 33.

75. Compare the opening and closing songs of *Tel jour telle nuit* (FP86), and the opening song, *Pablo Picasso*, of *Le Travail du peintre* (FP161/i).

76. The marking in bar 6 is *Animer un peu*, but Bernac suggests the original tempo should be regained at bar 16 for "Ses yeux joueurs." Bernac, p. 96.

77. Ibid.

78. Interview 6 with Rostand, in Poulenc, *Notes from the Heart*, p. 213.
79. Bernac, p. 97.
80. *Journal*, p. 33.
81. *Wilhelm Meisters Lehrjahre* (1795).
82. Claude Roy, *La Conversation des poètes* (1993), pp. 150–51; quoted in Buckland and Chimènes, p. 153.
83. Quoted in Elizabeth Sharland, *A Theatrical Feast in Paris: From Molière to Deneuve* (New York: Antique Collectors Club, 2005), p. 5.
84. Poulenc, *J'écris*, p. 337.
85. Margot's appeal endures through the generations. She was played by Constance Talmadge in D. W. Griffith's 1916 film *Intolerance*; in 1994 Isabelle Adjani starred in *La Reine Margot*.
86. *Journal*, p. 33.
87. Bernac, p. 98.
88. Poulenc/Audel, *Moi et mes amis*, p. 136.
89. Buckland, "Éluard, Poulenc and *Tel jour telle nuit*," in Buckland and Chimènes, p. 161.
90. Quoted in Dominique Rabourdin's Afterword to the facsimile republication of *Facile* in *La Bibliothèque surréaliste* (2004).
91. Buckland, "Éluard, Poulenc," p. 162.
92. Ibid., p. 163.
93. *Journal*, p. 35.
94. Bernac, p. 99.
95. Ibid.
96. *Journal*, p. 35. This is the restored version of the paragraph that appears in the 1995 edition of the *Journal* (ed. Machart), p. 21.
97. Lacombe, p. 451, passage beginning: "Là, au coin d'une rue puis, pour ainsi dire, au coin d'un poème."
98. Letter to the author, 22 April 2016.
99. Buckland, "Éluard, Poulenc," p. 164.
100. Ibid., p. 165.
101. Luc Sante, *The Other Paris* (New York: Farrar, Straus and Giroux, 2015), pp. 53–70.
102. Blaise Cendrars, *L'Homme foudroyé* (Paris: Denoël, 1945), pp. 202–3.
103. *Journal*, p. 35.
104. Jean Burgos, "Éluard ou les rituels de regeneration," in *Pour une poétique de l'imaginaire* (Paris: Seuil, 1982), p. 362.
105. Bernac, p. 102.
106. Buckland, "Éluard, Poulenc," p. 166.
107. *Journal*, p. 35.
108. Buckland, "Éluard, Poulenc," pp. 167–68.
109. Bernac, p. 104.
110. *Journal*, p. 35.
111. Ibid.
112. Buckland, "Éluard, Poulenc," p. 169.
113. Bernac, p. 98.
114. Buckland, "Éluard, Poulenc," p. 160. Buckland quotes from Éluard's "Poésie interrompue," a poem beginning "Par toi je vais de la lumière a la lumière."

115. Bernac, p. 106.

116. From sleeve note to the RCA recording of Poulenc songs by Gérard Souzay and Dalton Baldwin, SB6782, issued in 1963. It is clear that Poulenc had given an interview to the writer, Robert Jacobson, in connection with this recording.

117. *Journal*, pp. 37–39.

118. Ibid., p. 37.

119. *Le Ménestrel*, owned by the publisher Heugel and published weekly, was a popular Parisian musical weekly. Bertrand's review appeared only a few months before the German occupation of France ended the journal's 107-year run.

120. Henri Hell, quoted in Bernac, p. 131.

121. Bernac, p. 133.

122. Patrick Mauriès, *Louise de Vilmorin: Un Album* (Paris: Gallimard, 2002), p. 34.

123. Author's conversation with Norwich, 2012.

124. Bernac, pp. 132–33.

125. Louise de Vilmorin to Poulenc, 15 July 1939, in Poulenc, *Echo and Source*, p. 119.

126. *Journal*, p. 39.

127. Ibid. The Swiss critic referred to here is Robert-Aloys Mooser (1876–1979), who wrote reviews for *La Suisse* that were almost always unfavorable to Poulenc's music.

128. Bernac, p. 136.

129. Schmidt, in *Poulenc Catalogue*, pp. 278–79, mistakenly claims that a copy of the poem was written down for Poulenc by Louise de Vilmorin. In that instance, the heading "Portrait" referred to the text for the Vilmorin setting *C'est ainsi que tu es* FP121/ii.

130. Colette to Poulenc, summer 1931, *Correspondance*, p. 342.

131. See Lacombe, p. 367.

132. *Journal*, pp. 44–45.

133. Lacombe, p. 469, and p. 947, n. 352.

134. *Journal*, pp. 41–43.

135. Bernac, p. 62.

136. *Journal*, pp. 41–43.

137. Lacombe, p. 67.

138. *Journal*, p. 43. The reference to a slipper may be explained by the close proximity of Poulenc's apartment (overlooking the Jardin de Luxembourg) to various famous Parisian gay cruising sites, including the park itself. On a May evening when it was not cold or raining, he could go in search of sex without even bothering to wear outdoor shoes. He is also reported to have enjoyed wearing slippers while playing the piano in recording sessions at the BBC.

139. Ibid., pp. 65–66. Poulenc used the home of Georges Salles in Montmartre as his pied-à-terre between 1931 and 1935.

140. Ibid., p. 43.

141. Poulenc to Boulanger, *Correspondance*, pp. 475–76.

142. Apart from its pianistic meaning of pedals, *pédales* is also slang for "queers"; the word's juxtaposition with *halo* (with its angelic inferences) was very possibly deliberate.

143. Poulenc to Alice Ardoin, 21 July 1928, *Correspondance*, p. 287.

144. For example, Linossier's reference to the homosexual element present at Satie's funeral—"chic, inoccupé et pédéraste"—seems hardly favorable: *Correspondance*, p. 256.

145. 10 May and 18 June 1929, *Correspondance*, pp. 304–5. Chanlaire was both an essential and, at the same time, strangely peripheral member of the Poulenc circle. The com-

poser stayed in touch with Chanlaire, who was a mainstay at certain times of crisis in the 1950s; but Chanlaire (a decorative artist, specializing in painting scarves) preserved a certain distance and anonymity as far as posterity is concerned.

146. Poulenc to Diaghilev, December 1923, *Correspondance*, p. 219.
147. Sauguet, *La Musique, ma vie* (Paris: Séguier, 1990), p. 229.
148. "*L'atmosphère érotique que je souhaitais: L'atmosphère de mes vingt ans*," in Poulenc, *Notes from the Heart*, p. 52.
149. Ibid., p. 204.
150. Poulenc to Audel, 27 July 1946, *Correspondance*, p. 626.
151. For a description of the sexual activity of older men and adolescents in the Paris of the time, see Burton, p. 24.
152. Poulenc, *À bâtons rompus*, p. 44. Mistinguett (Jeanne Florentine Bourgeois, 1873–1956) was a famous singer and dancer, often extravagantly costumed, in the music halls.
153. Moore, "Camp in Francis Poulenc's Early Ballets," in *The Musical Quarterly* 95, Nos. 2–3 (Summer–Fall 2012): 300.
154. There are letters from this Chanlaire period (May 1929) to Valentine Hugo and Wanda Landowska: *Correspondance*, pp. 304–5.
155. I am indebted to Sidney Buckland for this information.
156. In his *Journal*, pp. 48–49, Poulenc incorrectly cites this date as 28 September 1938.
157. See Bernac, p. 223. The error he mentions (a *subito forte* in b. 13 that should be *subito piano*) and that of the metronome marking have remained surprisingly uncorrected in modern reprintings of the song by Salabert.
158. *Journal*, p. 5.
159. Guy de Maupassant, *La Femme de Paul*, trans. Uri Liebrecht (the passage beginning "On sent là, à pleines narines"), Ollendorf edition of the illustrated *Œuvres completes* (Paris), pp. 11–12.
160. *Journal*, p. 51.
161. Interview 15 with Rostand, in Poulenc, *Notes from the Heart*, p. 270.
162. Ibid. The passage brings to mind one Musorgsky song in particular, *Sirotka* (*The Orphan*, 1858), where half-note and quarter-note chords underpin a vocal line of pleading vulnerability.
163. *Journal*, p. 45.
164. Ibid., p. 47.
165. Interview 14 with Rostand, in Poulenc, *Notes from the Heart*, pp. 259–60.
166. Poulenc to Bernac, 24 June 1944, in Poulenc, *Echo and Source*, p. 136; and *Correspondance*, p. 555.
167. *Journal*, p. 47. Poulenc was often described, when it came to the consumption of food, as "gourmet *et* gourmand"—fussy and refined in his judgment of food, but still liking it to be served in large quantities.
168. Ibid.
169. Ibid., p. 45.
170. Ibid., pp. 47–49.
171. Bernac, p. 111.
172. *Journal*, p. 51.
173. Poulenc to Simone Girard, October 1954, *Correspondance*, p. 809.
174. Bernac, p. 125.

175. *Journal*, pp. 52–55.
176. Vilmorin to Poulenc, 15 July 1939, *Correspondance*, p. 476.
177. These two poems together with "La Chale" were set as Auric's *Trois Poèmes de Louise de Vilmorin* (the same title used by Poulenc), a collection that was also dedicated to Marie-Blanche de Polignac.
178. *Journal*, ed. Renaud Machart (1995).
179. Ibid., pp. 30–31.
180. *Journal*, p. 111.
181. Bernac, p. 137.
182. Hell, p. 163.
183. André de Vilmorin, "Essai sur Louise de Vilmorin," in *Poètes d'aujourd'hui 91* (Paris: Éditions Seghers, 1962).
184. *Journal*, p. 55.
185. Ibid.
186. Ibid.
187. Some of Beydts's nearly 100 songs would repay examination by enterprising singers.
188. André de Vilmorin, "Louise de Vilmorin," p. 79; Lacombe, p. 509.
189. Burton, p. 81.
190. Lacombe, p. 509.
191. *Journal*, p. 55.
192. Bernac, p. 143.
193. *Journal*, p. 57.
194. Ibid.
195. Bernac, p. 145.
196. *Journal*, p. 57.
197. Ibid., pp. 57–58.

Part IV

1. Poulenc to Auric, c. March, *Correspondance*, p. 495.
2. Poulenc to Marie-Blanche de Polignac, *Correspondance*, p. 496.
3. Poulenc to Bernac, in Poulenc, *Echo and Source*, pp. 123–24.
4. See *Correspondance*, p. 508.
5. See *Correspondance*, p. 512, n. 1.
6. From a talk given in March 1947, published in Poulenc, *Notes from the Heart* (ed. Southon, trans. Nichols), p. 106.
7. Poulenc to Maurice Brianchon, *Correspondance*, p. 529.
8. Poulenc to André Schaeffner, October 1942, *Correspondance*, p. 532.
9. Poulenc, *J'écris* (ed. Southon), p. 103, article 1943.
10. This according to the composer's interview in *Ce soir* (25 November 1944), quoted in *Correspondance*, pp. 537–38, n. 2.
11. Of the various stories of how Poulenc obtained this text (some of them suggesting direct contact with the Resistance), this one, the first and least embroidered, seems the most plausible.
12. Lacombe, p. 541. Some of the most private, and sometimes salacious, incidents in the composer's life were published only in 2004, in Malou Haine's *Mon Irrésistible, Insupportable et Cher Poulenc*, taken from her readings of entries in the *Journal intime*

of Stéphane Audel. They are printed in *Les Cahiers du Cirem: In memoriam Francis Poulenc*, Nos. 49–51 (Rouen: University of Tours, 2004), pp. 157–227.

13. Lacombe, pp. 541–42.
14. Poulenc to Bernac, 24 June 1944, *Correspondance*, p. 556. The Messiaen works referred to are *Trois Petites Liturgies de la Présence divine*, for female chorus and orchestra; and *Visions de l'Amen*, for two pianos.
15. Lacombe, p. 554.
16. Poulenc to Marie-Blanche de Polignac, 27 July 1944, *Correspondance*, pp. 562–63.
17. Poulenc to Bernac, *Correspondance*, p. 570.
18. Ibid., p. 574. The stories casting Raymond as the unequivocal hero of the hour (perhaps exaggerated by his lover) are nevertheless credible from what we know of his character.
19. Cocteau, *Journal: 1942–1945*, ed. Jean Touzot (Paris: Gallimard, 1989), pp. 576–77.
20. Bernac, *Entretiens avec Gérard Michel*, France Culture (part of Radio France), 1970–71. Quoted in *Correspondance*, p. 579, n. 5.
21. Quoted in *Poulenc in London and Dreamland: His Letters to Felix Aprahamian, commentaries on songs and London concerts*, Mirage Press, 2000, p. 6.
22. Lacombe, p. 554.
23. Marc Pincherle, in *Les Nouvelles Littéraires*, 10 May 1945. Reprinted in Schmidt, *Entrancing Muse*, p. 309.
24. Poulenc to Bernac, *Correspondance*, p. 604.
25. Ibid., p. 609.
26. Poulenc to Stéphane Audel, 27 July 1946, *Correspondance*, p. 626.
27. Poulenc to Marthe Bosredon, 30 December 1945, *Correspondance*, p. 617.
28. Poulenc to Rose Lambiotte, unpublished letter of 2 November 1951.
29. Poulenc to Darius Milhaud, *Correspondance*, p. 624.
30. Schmidt, *Entrancing Muse*, p. 320.
31. Poulenc to Nadia Boulanger, 6 May 1946, *Correspondance*, pp. 621–22.
32. Bernac wrongly states in *Poulenc: The Man and His Songs* that the work dates from 1947, a mistake that results from the incorrect year being printed in the score.
33. Poulenc, *J'écris*, p. 133.
34. Interview 11 with Claude Rostand, in Poulenc, *Notes from the Heart*, pp. 242–43. Poulenc incorrectly remembered this incident as having happened in 1947.
35. The year of the first meeting between the composer and his future muse is often given as 1947, but FP is already writing to Duval in affectionate and intimate terms on January 16 of that year (*Correspondance*, p. 634).
36. Poulenc, *J'écris*, pp. 143–44, article 1947.
37. Poulenc, *Notes from the Heart*, p. 106, lecture 1947.
38. Poulenc to Milhaud, 11 June 1947, *Correspondance*, p. 638.
39. Poulenc to Edward Lockspeiser, April 1947, *Correspondance*, p. 643, n. 1.
40. Poulenc to Bernac, *Correspondance*, p. 640, n. 2.
41. Poulenc defines folklore as "*well-known songs of which one does not know the composer*" (*À bâtons rompus*, p. 50).
42. Poulenc to Bernac, *Correspondance*, pp. 646–47.
43. Arthur Gold and Robert Fizdale, *Misia: The Life of Misia Sert* (New York: Knopf, 1980), p. 306.
44. Poulenc to Thomson, *Correspondance*, p. 650.

45. Conrad, *Dodascalies*, p. 330.

46. Poulenc to Brigitte Manceaux, 10 November 1948, *Correspondance*, p. 654.

47. Gold and Fizdale, *Misia*, p. 308.

48. Ibid., pp. 308–9.

49. Poulenc, *J'écris*, p. 594, conversation 1947.

50. A discussion of the origins and influence of American popular music and jazz; see *À bâtons rompus*, p. 101, n. 35—the least well informed of any of Poulenc's sorties into musicology.

51. Poulenc to Marie-Blanche de Polignac, *Correspondance*, p. 660.

52. Stéphane Audel in *Moi et mes amis*, p. 13.

53. Copland, *Copland Since 1943* (New York: St. Martin's Press, 1989), p. 147.

54. Poulenc, *J'écris*, p. 337, extract from *L'Impromptu de Neuilly* (1953).

55. *Journal*, p. 67.

56. Lacombe, p. 500: "Sans être un cycle conçu . . . celle de souvenirs."

57. *Journal*, p. 67.

58. Poulenc to Bernac, 10 July 1940, *Correspondance*, pp. 497–98.

59. *Journal*, p. 67.

60. Ibid.

61. Ibid.

62. Bernac, p. 74.

63. Apollinaire, *Œuvres poétiques*, ed. André Adéma and Michel Décaudin (Paris: Gallimard, 1965), pp. 1118–19.

64. A variation of this music, in E-flat major, is to be heard again in the final section of a contemporary work: *L'Histoire de Babar*, at the spoken words "La nuit venue."

65. In his *Journal* (p. 95) Poulenc admits, in regard to *Sanglots*, that *"certain points will always trouble me"* and that he regards *Voyage*, the concluding song of *Calligrammes*, as *"greatly superior."*

66. Poulenc to Rose Lambiotte, 17 July 1947, *Correspondance*, p. 641.

67. Fombeure, *Poètes d'aujourd'hui*, No. 57 (Paris: Seghers, 1957), pp. 9–10.

68. Quoted in Hell, p. 178.

69. *Journal*, p. 71.

70. Bernac, p. 173.

71. For more on the role of Chevalier in Poulenc's life, see the commentaries on *Parisiana* FP157.

72. Poulenc, *Notes from the Heart*, p. 109.

73. *Journal*, p. 71.

74. Poulenc to Marie-Blanche de Polignac, in Poulenc, *Echo and Source*, p. 107; *Correspondance*, p. 420.

75. Poulenc, *J'écris*, p. 593, conversation 1947.

76. Poulenc, *Notes from the Heart*, p. 147, interview with Fernando Lopes-Graça.

77. *Journal*, p. 71; Bernac, p. 176.

78. Bernac, p. 178.

79. Poulenc, *Notes from the Heart*, p. 109.

80. Bernac, p. 146.

81. Ibid., p. 147.

82. Wordsworth, "Ode. Intimations of Immortality" (1807), stanza 10.

83. *Journal*, pp. 71–73.

84. Ibid.

85. Hell, p. 180.

86. *Journal*, ed. Renaud Machart (1995), p. 41.

87. Aragon, *Lettres à André Breton: 1918–1931*, ed. Lionel Follet (Paris: Gallimard, 2011), p. 96.

88. Ibid., pp. 101–2.

89. Despite Aragon's long manifesto, including a ringing quotation from the opening of Virgil's *Aeneid* ("I sing of arms and the man"), Poulenc considered Aragon a featherweight (*"poids-plume"*) poet. *Journal*, ed. Renaud Machart (1995), p. 42.

90. Poulenc, *Notes from the Heart*, p. 109, lecture 1947.

91. For the dedication, see Bernac, p. 187. The Swiss tenor Hugues Cuenod wrote an extremely risqué singing version of the poem (beginning "Je suis entré dans un W.C. / C'est là que tout a commencé" [I went into a public toilet / That's where it all began]), which, according to Cuenod, much delighted Poulenc.

92. Poulenc, *Notes from the Heart*, p. 101, lecture 1935.

93. Bernac, p. 188.

94. Ibid., p. 189.

95. Burton, p. 84.

96. Némirovsky's two 1940 novels (there were also plans for a third), undiscovered until 1998, were published only in 2004.

97. *Journal*, ed. Renaud Machart (1995), p. 40.

98. Poulenc/Audel, *Moi et mes amis*, p. 135.

99. *Journal*, p. 75.

100. Interview in Lisbon, 1947, with the Portuguese composer (and fellow Koechlin pupil) Fernando Lopes-Graça; reprinted in Poulenc, *Notes from the Heart*, p. 145.

101. *Journal*, pp. 75-77. The composer writes from memory, and sometimes inaccurately: his reference to finishing *Montparnasse* in February 1945 conflicts with the "January 1945" printed in the score.

102. Also recounted in Nigel Simeone, *Poulenc in London and Dreamland* (memoirs of Felix Aprahamian's friendship with the composer) (Cambridge: Mirage, 2000), p. 6.

103. The first invitation to Poulenc from Audrey (Margotine) to visit her in London was made in August 1922; *Correspondance*, pp. 172–73.

104. Peter Ackroyd, *Queer City* (London: Chatto & Windus, 2017), p. 164.

105. *Journal*, p. 81.

106. Ibid.

107. Dallapiccola to Poulenc, 24 November 1945, *Correspondance*, p. 612, also n. 1.

108. No. 4 of Barber's song cycle *Despite and Still*, Op. 41 (1968-69). The passage occurs in Chapter 17 of *Ulysses*.

109. *Journal*, p. 81.

110. Maurice Radiguet to Poulenc, 11 September 1924, *Correspondance*, p. 238.

111. Radiguet, *Les Joues en feu* (Paris: Grasset, 1925). Avant-propos signed by R. R.

112. Miscevic, *Poulenc et la mélodie*, p. 29.

113. *Journal*, pp. 89–91.

114. Poulenc/Audel, *Moi et mes amis*, p. 135.

115. *Journal*, ed. Renaud Machaut (1995), p. 50.

116. Published in Desnos's *Corps et biens* (Paris: Gallimard, 1930).

117. Édith Piaf (1915–1963)—called the "môme," the child or kid, because of her short

stature—was the greatest of the French *chansonnières* of the time. She was dedicatee of Poulenc's *Improvisation* 15 for piano (1959).

118. *Journal*, p. 85.

119. Hell, p. 211.

120. *Journal*, ed. Renaud Machaut (1995), p. 50. The marking in the score is *Baigné de pédales (les batteries à peine effleurées, les blanches pointées un peu en dehors)*. Poulenc was writing at a time when good pianists in France (of either sex) were seldom encouraged to take up accompaniment as a career. An established solo pianist might do so from time to time, as a favor to a distinguished colleague. It was undoubtedly sexist that male pianists, even if temperamentally suited to a life in accompanying, were led to believe that it was a job for women of limited talent; and so, at times, it inevitably appeared to be. Nevertheless, the greatest of French accompanists of the period, apart from Poulenc himself, was a woman: Jacqueline Robin Bonneau (1917–2007).

121. *Journal*, p. 87. Poulenc's diagram is taken from the unexpurgated *Journal*, ed. Renaud Machaut (1995), p. 51.

122. Bernac, p. 127.

123. Lacombe, p. 577.

124. Poulenc to Marie-Blanche de Polignac, 21 August 1946, *Correspondance*, p. 628, n. 1.

125. *Journal*, p. 91.

126. Poulenc to Bernac, 1 September 1947, *Correspondance*, p. 643, n. 1.

127. Ibid.

128. *Journal*, p. 91.

129. Poulenc to Bernac, 1 September 1947, *Correspondance*, p. 643. The reference to Souzay's lack of response is to be found in a later letter to Bernac (p. 644, n. 1).

130. Poulenc, *J'écris*, p. 159, American diary, December 1949.

131. *Journal*, p. 93.

132. Ibid., p. 95. Tremblay-en-France, about 19.5 kilometers from Paris, is not to be confused with Le Tremblay, the home of Poulenc's sister and brother-in-law in Normandy. Poulenc's grandparents had a house in Nogent-sur-Marne.

133. Ibid., p. 93.

134. Poulenc to Bernac, 18 July 1948, in Poulenc, *Echo and Source*, p. 171; *Correspondance*, pp. 646-47.

135. Bernac, p. 85.

136. *Journal*, p. 95.

137. In Debussy's *En sourdine* (*Fêtes galantes*, Book 1), the song of the nightingale is implied by a similarly tiny pianistic detail, sixteenth-note triplets rather than the grace notes of this song.

138. The second song of Debussy's set *Ariettes oubliées* (1888, rev. 1901).

139. Poulenc to Chanlaire, 10 May 1929, *Correspondance*, pp. 304–5.

140. *Journal*, p. 95.

141. Ibid. Poulenc goes on to compare *Sanglots*, the final song of *Banalités* FP107, unfavorably with *Voyage*.

142. Ibid., p. 97. The passage beginning *"Now added to that"* was expunged from the first edition of the *Journal* (it refers to Raymonde Linossier) and appears in the unexpurgated version edited by Renaud Machart (1995), p. 55.

143. *Journal*, p. 97.

144. Poulenc to Marie-Blanche de Polignac, 21 November 1948, *Correspondance*, p. 655.

145. *Journal*, p. 93.

146. Lacombe, p. 613.
147. Poulenc was perhaps unmoved to dedicate this song to Conrad formally, but acknowledged that it was written at his suggestion.
148. Poulenc's choice of C minor led Sauguet to select E-flat minor for his setting (No. 1), and Auric B-flat minor for No. 3.
149. Conrad, *Dodascalies*, p. 338.
150. Poulenc to Conrad, unpublished letter quoted in Schmidt, *Poulenc Catalogue*, p. 400.
151. *Journal*, p. 97.

Part V

1. Poulenc, *J'écris* (ed. Southon), p. 164, American diary 1950.
2. Poulenc to Maurice Brianchon, 12 January 1950, *Correspondance*, p. 671.
3. Poulenc to Brigitte Manceaux, 1 February 1950, Miscevic, *Lettres*, p. 81.
4. Quoted in Hell, pp. 217–18.
5. Poulenc to Hell, 16 February 1950, *Correspondance*, pp. 677–78.
6. Poulenc to Collaer, 2 March 1950, *Correspondance*, p. 689, n. 2.
7. Poulenc, *J'écris*, p. 291, article 1934.
8. Poulenc to Darius Milhaud, 28 February 1950, *Correspondance*, p. 682.
9. Poulenc to Simone Girard, 2 February 1950, *Correspondance*, p. 673.
10. Another version of the story gives Klemperer's remark as "Wie sagt man Scheisse auf französisch?" (How does one say "shit" in French?).
11. Rorem, *The Paris Diary of Ned Rorem* (New York: Braziller, 1966), p. 40.
12. Poulenc to Simone Girard, *Correspondance*, pp. 714–15, also n. 4.
13. Poulenc to Marie-Blanche de Polignac, 4 February 1952, in Poulenc, *Echo and Source*, p. 196.
14. Ibid.
15. Quoted in Schmidt, *Entrancing Muse*, pp. 370–71.
16. Poulenc to Conrad, *Correspondance*, p. 721.
17. Schmidt, *Entrancing Muse*, p. 371.
18. Poulenc to Brigitte Manceaux, 27 February 1952, Miscevic, *Lettres*, p. 120.
19. Poulenc to Yvonne de Casa Fuerte, *Correspondance*, p. 727.
20. Ibid., pp. 731–32.
21. Poulenc to Brigitte Manceaux, 5 June 1952, Miscevic, *Lettres*, p. 126.
22. Boulanger to Poulenc, *Correspondance*, p. 742.
23. Poulenc to Simone Girard, March 1953, *Correspondance*, p. 750. The composer refers to Bernac as "*my Pierre.*"
24. Poulenc, "Comment j'ai composé les *Dialogues des Carmélites,*" in *L'Opéra de Paris* 14 (1957):15–17.
25. Poulenc to Marie-Blanche de Polignac, 23 April 1952, *Correspondance*, p. 753, n. 2.
26. Poulenc to Barraud, *Correspondance*, p. 754.
27. Poulenc to Simone Girard, unpublished letter of November 1953, Bibliothèque Nationale.
28. Poulenc to Bernac, *Correspondance*, pp. 755–56.
29. A decade later Poulenc will begin a congratulatory birthday letter to Benjamin Britten with the words "*Here you are, as glorious as a young Verdi.*" Anthony Gishford, ed., *Tribute to Benjamin Britten on His Fiftieth Birthday* (London: Faber and Faber, 1963), p. 13.

30. Lacombe, p. 653.
31. Poulenc to Henri Hell, *Correspondance*, p. 775.
32. Miscevic, *Lettres*, p. 157, n. 526.
33. Poulenc to Honegger, *Correspondance*, p. 779.
34. See interview 17 with Claude Rostand, in Poulenc, *Notes from the Heart* (ed. Southon, trans. Nichols), p. 282.
35. Poulenc to Simone Girard, c. 28 March 1954, *Correspondance*, p. 790.
36. See interview 12 with Rostand, in Poulenc, *Notes from the Heart*, p. 247.
37. Honegger to Poulenc, *Correspondance*, p. 791.
38. This fascinating and moving document, Poulenc's only surviving will, is included as an "Annexe" to Miscevic, *Lettres*, pp. 361–66.
39. Poulenc to Marie-Ange Lebedeff, *Correspondance*, p. 807.
40. Poulenc to Girard, October 1954, *Correspondance*, p. 808.
41. Poulenc to Britten, December 1954, *Correspondance*, p. 814.
42. Poulenc to Brigitte Manceaux, 5 August 1955, Miscevic, *Lettres*, p. 183.
43. Poulenc to Rose Dercourt-Plaut, *Correspondance*, p. 825.
44. Poulenc to Bernac, *Correspondance*, p. 826.
45. Ibid., pp. 828–29.
46. Poulenc to Girard, *Correspondance*, p. 831.
47. Lacombe, p. 694.
48. Poulenc to Dallapiccola, *Correspondance*, p. 834.
49. Poulenc to Brigitte Manceaux, 28 March 1956, *Correspondance*, p. 835.
50. Ibid.
51. Britten to Poulenc, 12 July 1956, *Correspondance*, p. 844.
52. Poulenc to Leguerney, *Correspondance*, p. 841.
53. Poulenc to Landowska, *Correspondance*, p. 846.
54. Poulenc to Stravinsky, 7 September 1956, *Correspondance*, p. 851.
55. Poulenc to Milhaud, 15 May 1957, *Correspondance*, p. 871.
56. See Lacombe, p. 685.
57. See Poulenc to Bernac, 12 July 1957, *Correspondance*, p. 874.
58. Poulenc to Simone Girard, 13 July 1957, *Correspondance*, p. 864, n. 2.
59. See Poulenc to Bernac, 12 July 1957, *Correspondance*, p. 874.
60. Poulenc to Guido Valcarenghi, unpublished letter of 29 July 1957.
61. Poulenc to Brigitte Manceaux, 1 August 1957, Miscevic, *Lettres*, No. 238, n. 880.
62. Poulenc to Valcarenghi, unpublished letter of 25 September 1957.
63. Sackville-West, letter (in English) to Poulenc, 29 January 1958, in Poulenc, *Echo and Source*, pp. 249–50.
64. Poulenc to Nadia Boulanger, 18 February 1958, *Correspondance*, p. 887.
65. Poulenc to Dugardin, 30 March 1958, *Correspondance*, pp. 889–91.
66. Poulenc to Rose Dercourt-Plaut, 20 April 1958, *Correspondance*, p. 894.
67. Miscevic, *Lettres*, Annexe II, pp. 369–70.
68. Lacombe, p. 720.
69. See *Correspondance*, p. 892, n. 2.
70. Lacombe, pp. 721–22.
71. Poulenc to Rose Dercourt-Plaut, unpublished letter of 16 October 1958; see Lacombe, p. 722.
72. Lacombe, pp. 724–25. This information was taken from Audel's private journal, excerpts from which were published in 2004, after his death, by Malou Haine.

73. Ibid., pp. 725–26; see also p. 991, n. 73.

74. Ibid., p. 728.

75. Cocteau, *Le Passé défini* (Paris: Gallimard, 2011), vol. 6, p. 468.

76. Poulenc to Brigitte Manceaux, *Correspondance*, p. 908.

77. Bernac to Poulenc, *Correspondance*, p. 912.

78. Poulenc to Brigitte Manceaux, 27 April 1959, Miscevic, *Lettres*, p. 265.

79. *Journal*, pp. 108–9.

80. Poulenc to Claude Rostand, June 1959, *Correspondance*, p. 916.

81. Poulenc to Simone Girard, 13 June 1959, *Correspondance*, pp. 917–18.

82. The concluding movement of the choral cantata *Figure humaine* FP120.

83. *Journal*, pp. 97–99.

84. See Poulenc to Yvonne de Casa Fuerte, 26 February 1950, *Correspondance*, pp. 680–81.

85. Poulenc to Milhaud, 6 September 1950, *Correspondance*, p. 695.

86. Lacombe, p. 626.

87. Hell, p. 223.

88. Poulenc tells this story in *Hommage à Marie-Blanche de Polignac*, a beautiful boxed set of single-leaf reminiscences and pictures from her friends, published in Monaco (Jaspar, Polus) by the Polignac family in her memory in 1965; pp. 90–93. See also Bernac, p. 130.

89. Lacombe, p. 625.

90. Jacob to Poulenc, 29 September 1922, *Correspondance*, p. 181.

91. Auric, *Quand j'étais là* (Paris: Grasset, 1979), p. 80.

92. See Jacob's letter to Poulenc of 11 December 1931: "I authorize everything that pleases your precious fantasy, O master! It will be my only claim to glory that my name has appeared next to yours." *Correspondance*, p. 354.

93. Poulenc/Audel, *Moi et mes amis*, p. 94. The composer's memories of the poet are all taken from the Max Jacob chapter of this book of conversations.

94. Jacob, *La Défence de Tartuffe*, quoted in Burton, p. 54.

95. Poulenc/Audel, *Moi et mes amis*, p. 109.

96. Milhaud's copy surivived, and the work was published in 1995 (FP22).

97. Jacob to Poulenc, 12 May 1924, *Correspondance*, pp. 230–31.

98. Hell, p. 101.

99. Charles Dantzig, *Dictionnaire égoïste de la littérature française*, p. 406.

100. André Clavel, *Dictionnaire des littératures de la langue française*, p. 1181.

101. The original French was "moine et voyou," a coinage of Claude Rostand from 1944, the year of Jacob's death.

102. Poulenc to Marie-Blanche de Polignac, *Correspondance*, p. 562.

103. Interview 15 with Claude Rostand, in Poulenc, *Notes from the Heart*, p. 266.

104. Lacombe, p. 722.

105. Poulenc, *À bâtons rompus*, pp. 48–49. Poulenc would certainly not like to have undergone the enormous trials and scandals surrounding Chevalier's wartime collaboration with the Germans, for which the singer was eventually largely absolved by an adoring public.

106. Hell, p. 238.

107. Poulenc, *Echo and Source*, pp. 225–26; *Correspondance*, pp. 809–10.

108. *Correspondance*, p. 811, n. 1.

109. Griffin, "The Poulenc Behind the Mask," in *Ramparts* Magazine (October 1964), pp.

6–8; reprinted in *The John Howard Griffin Reader* (Boston: Houghton Mifflin, 1968), p. 568; and in Schmidt, *Enchanting Muse,* pp. 394–95.

110. Poulenc to Griffin, in Schmidt, *Entrancing Muse,* p. 395.

111. Poulenc to Griffin, 11 October 1954, in the *Griffin Reader,* p. 568.

112. Ibid. See also Paul Bailey's essay "Poulenc's Priest" in Bailey, *Censoring Sexuality* (Chicago: Seagull Books, 2007).

113. Hughes to Virgil Thomson, 8 January 1955, in Schmidt, *Enchanting Muse,* pp. 398–99.

114. Poulenc, *J'écris,* p. 481, lecture 1947.

115. Poulenc/Audel, *Moi et mes amis,* p. 74.

116. Poulenc, *J'écris,* p. 472, lecture 1935.

117. Ibid., p. 602, interview 1952.

118. Ibid., p. 462, lecture 1935.

119. Lacombe, p. 676. The last section of this paragraph quotes from a letter of Poulenc to Paul Collaer, 15 May 1920, *Correspondance,* p. 106.

120. Interview 15 with Rostand, in Poulenc, *Notes from the Heart,* p. 270.

121. Bernac, p. 34.

122. On 7 January 1950 Poulenc visited the Museum of Fine Arts in Boston; on 7 February the Metropolitan Museum in New York; and on 18 February the Art Institute of Chicago.

123. Extracts are from "'All My Pleasure Is in Making New Discoveries': Francis Poulenc Visits American Museums of Art," in Buckland and Chimènes, pp. 196–98.

124. *Journal,* ed. Renaud Machaut (1995), pp. 46–48.

125. The poem set as *Pablo Picasso* had appeared in Éluard's *Poésie ininterrompue* (1946), already with the title *Le Travail du peintre*—a pendant to another set of seven poems, *Le Travail du poète,* dedicated to the poet Eugène Guillevic (1907–1997).

126. *Journal,* p. 101.

127. See Carl Schmidt, "Distilling Essences: Poulenc and Matisse," in Buckland and Chimènes, pp. 199–209.

128. Poulenc to Bernac, unpublished letter of 1953, quoted in Poulenc, *Echo and Source,* p. 394.

129. Poulenc, *Echo and Source,* p. 394.

130. Auric to Poulenc, September 1955, *Correspondance,* p. 820, n. 4.

131. Esty began by commissioning Poulenc to compose French poems, but she went on to encourage many other composers to set French and English texts as well: Claude Arrieu (poems of Vilmorin), Lennox Berkeley (Apollinaire and W. H. Auden), Dutilleux (Paul Gibson), Darius Milhaud, Vittorio Rieti, Ned Rorem, Manuel Rosenthal, Henri Sauguet (Éluard), Germaine Tailleferre (Apollinaire), Virgil Thomson (Marianne Moore), and Ben Weber (Emily Dickinson) among them.

132. Éluard, *Picasso, dessins* (Paris: Braun, 1952), pp. 5–6.

133. Roy, *Nous* (Paris: Gallimard, 1972), p. 371.

134. Brassaï (Gyula Halàsz), *Conversations avec Picasso* (Paris: Gallimard, 1964), p. 188.

135. Laporte, *Si tard le soir* (Paris: Plon, 1973), p. 156.

136. Poulenc, *J'écris,* p. 634, conversation 1957.

137. John Richardson, *A Life of Picasso: The Triumphant Years, 1917–1932* (New York: Knopf, 2007), pp. 105–6.

138. Poulenc to Diaghilev, April 1919, *Correspondance,* p. 89.

139. Miscevic, *Lettres,* Annexe I, pp. 365–66.

140. Poulenc to Picasso, 16 December 1957, *Correspondance*, p. 884.

141. *Journal*, pp. 101–2.

142. Lacombe, p. 676.

143. Low, "Poulenc, Éluard and Art: *Le Travail du peintre*," in *Australian Voice* (2002), p. 30. The quote is from J.-C. Gateau, *Éluard, Picasso et la peinture* (Geneva: Droz, 1983), p. 158.

144. Chagall, *Marc Chagall on Art and Culture*, ed. Benjamin Harshav (Palo Alto: Stanford University Press, 2003).

145. Chagall to Poulenc, 3 October 1957, *Correspondance*, p. 882.

146. *Journal*, p. 103.

147. Lacombe, p. 676.

148. René Char was the poet of Boulez's most famous vocal work, *Le Marteau sans maître* (1955).

149. Poulenc, *J'écris*, p. 184, article 1952.

150. Ibid., p. 285.

151. Pierre Reverdy, in his review *Nord-Sud*, December 1917.

152. *Journal*, p. 103.

153. Robert Hughes, "World of Art and Fantasy," in *Time* Magazine, 7 November 1983.

154. Quoted in Frank Elgar, *Gris: Still Lifes* (London: Methuen, 1961).

155. Poulenc to Milhaud, 29 July 1923, *Correspondance*, pp. 198–99.

156. Daniel Henry Kahnweiler, *Juan Gris: His Life and Work*, trans. Douglas Cooper (London: Lund Humphries, 1947), pp. 28–29.

157. *Journal*, p. 101.

158. Gateau, *Éluard, Picasso et la peinture* (Geneva: Droz, 1983), p. 226.

159. See Poulenc, *Notes from the Heart*, p. 106, article 1943.

160. See "Le Musicien et le sorcier," in *Lettres françaises* (5 May 1945), reprinted in Poulenc, *Notes from the Heart*, pp. 113–17.

161. Ibid., p. 116.

162. *Journal*, p. 103.

163. Bernac, p. 122.

164. Richardson, *Sacred Monsters, Sacred Masters* (London: Cape, 2001), p. 184.

165. Miró, *Ceci est la couleur de mes rêves*, Entretiens avec Georges Raillard (Paris: Éditions du Seuil, 1977).

166. Richardson, *Sacred Monsters*, p. 183.

167. *Joan Miró: Instinct and Imagination*, exhibition catalogue, Denver Art Museum, 2015.

168. Richardson, *Sacred Monsters*, p. 183.

169. *Miró: Instinct and Imagination*.

170. *Journal*, p. 103.

171. Villon to Poulenc, 12 September 1957, *Correspondance*, p. 877.

172. *Journal*, p. 103.

173. Bernac, p. 124.

174. Low, *Poulenc, Éluard and Art*, p. 32. The quote is from Gateau, *Éluard, Picasso et la peinture*, p. 190.

175. Poulenc to Henri Hell, 16 September 1956, *Correspondance*, p. 852.

176. Poulenc to Simone Girard, 26 September 1956, *Correspondance*, p. 853, n. 2.

177. Poulenc, *J'écris*, p. 591.

178. Conrad, *Dodascalies*, pp. 386–88.

179. *Journal,* p. 105.

180. Quoted in Schmidt, *Poulenc Catalogue,* p. 454.

181. Ibid.

182. Beylié to Poulenc, *Correspondance,* p. 853, n. 3.

183. Poulenc to Rose Dercourt-Plaut, 12 August 1955, *Correspondance,* p. 825.

184. *Journal,* pp. 105–7.

185. Bernac, p. 196.

186. *Journal,* p. 107.

187. Bernac, p. 192.

188. *Journal,* p. 113.

189. Quoted in Schmidt, *Entrancing Muse,* p. 425.

190. Poulenc to Jean-Aubry, 8 June 1919, unpublished letter in the Beinecke Rare Book and Manuscript Library at Yale. The composer underlines the last five words of the second sentence.

191. Poulenc, *J'écris,* p. 222; and Schmidt, *Poulenc Catalogue,* pp. 81–82.

192. See *Correspondance,* pp. 474–75, n. 4.

193. Poulenc to Bernac, 4 August 1959, *Correspondance,* pp. 926–27.

194. Bernac to Poulenc, 11 August 1959, *Correspondance,* p. 928, n. 10.

195. Poulenc, *À bâtons rompus,* pp. 207–12.

196. Reed, "Poulenc, Britten, Aldeburgh: A Chronicle," in Buckland and Chimènes, pp. 349–62. This article gives an extended and rosy account of the friendship between Britten and Poulenc, with letters exchanged between them over the years.

197. Michel Ciry, in *Le Temps des promesses: Journal, 1942–1949* (Paris: Plon, 1979), pp. 162–64, describes an evening in 1944, chez Marie-Blanche de Polignac, when Ciry's songs were praised and performed by the hostess, to Poulenc's displeasure.

198. Poulenc, *J'écris,* p. 163, American diary, 27 January 1950.

199. Reed, "Poulenc, Britten, Aldeburgh," p. 353.

200. Poulenc to Britten, 1 August 1957, *Correspondance,* p. 876.

201. Poulenc to Britten, 13 June 1958, *Correspondance,* p. 895.

202. Britten to Poulenc, 12 July 1956, *Letters from a Life: The Selected Letters of Benjamin Britten,* vol. 4, *1952–57,* ed. Philip Reed, Mervyn Cooke, and Donald Mitchell (Suffolk: Boydell and Brewer, 2008), p. 529, n. 1.

203. See note 196.

204. This is amply confirmed by anecdotal incidents related to me by Felix Aprahamian and Hugues Cuenod, not to mention in the diaries of Ned Rorem.

205. Poulenc (from Aldeburgh) to Simone Girard, 24 June 1956, *Correspondance,* p. 842: "*Britten and Pears are sensational. They do everything here, and marvelously well.*"

206. Poulenc to Britten, 4 July 1956, *Correspondance,* p. 842.

207. Poulenc, *J'écris,* p. 214, article 1961.

208. Interview with Martine Cadieu, in Poulenc, *Notes from the Heart,* p. 164.

209. Poulenc to Yvonne de Casa Fuerte, 27 May and 8 July 1952, *Correspondance,* pp. 729 and 731–33.

210. Peter Pears, conversation with the author in 1978.

211. Poulenc speaking to Claire Brook (1961), in Schmidt, *Enchanted Muse,* p. 448.

212. I am indebted to Tony Scotland, Berkeley's biographer, for this information.

213. During a recording session for the BBC of *L'Histoire de Babar,* although the remark itself was not recorded.

Part VI

1. Poulenc to Thomson, *Correspondance*, p. 941.
2. Poulenc to Bernac, 26 February 1960, *Correspondance*, p. 942.
3. Poulenc to Bernac, quoted in Miscevic, *Lettres*, p. 300, n. 1133.
4. Poulenc to Stéphane Audel, March 1960, *Correspondance*, p. 943.
5. The phrase Poulenc uses is *"atteint de gérontisme."* Letter to Audel, 19 August 1960, *Correspondance*, p. 955.
6. Poulenc to Bernac, 19 January 1961, *Correspondance*, p. 971.
7. Ibid., p. 973.
8. Poulenc to Girard, 23 January 1961, *Correspondance*, p. 973.
9. Poulenc to Geneviève Sienkiewicz, 24 February 1961, in Myriam Chimènes, "Geneviève Sienkiewicz et Francis Poulenc," *Centenaire Georges Auric–Francis Poulenc* (Montpellier: Centre d'Étude du XX Siècle, 2001), p. 248.
10. Ibid. Also quoted in Lacombe, p. 764. The bistro owner is Mimi Martin.
11. Sienkiewicz to Poulenc, 9 March 1961, *Correspondance*, p. 976.
12. Poulenc, *J'écris* (ed. Southon), p. 660.
13. Ibid., p. 136.
14. See Schmidt, *Entrancing Muse*, p. 451.
15. Poulenc to Bernstein, 1 November 1961, *Correspondance*, p. 986.
16. From an article written by Peignot in February 1964, intended for the review *Adam*. Typescript in the possession of Sidney Buckland.
17. Poulenc to Bernac, in Poulenc, *Echo and Source*, p. 288.
18. Bernac to Poulenc, *Correspondance*, p. 997.
19. Lacombe, p. 779; information taken from Audel's private journal, excerpts from which were published in 2004 (after his death) by Malou Haine.
20. *Tribute to Benjamin Britten on His Fiftieth Birthday*, ed. Anthony Gishford (London: Faber and Faber, 1963).
21. Poulenc to Rose Dercourt-Plaut, 9 December 1962, *Correspondance*, p. 1005.
22. Poulenc/Audel, *My Friends and Myself*, p. 21. In *Sodome et Gomorrhe*, the fourth part (1921–22) of Proust's *À la récherche du temps perdu*, the suave and seductive Baron de Charlus is the major gay character.
23. Ibid., p. 25.
24. The use of the word *"dernière"* in *"dernière joie"* is ambiguous. *"Last"* may seem to credit the composer with premonitions of imminent mortality, but his words can also be translated as *"my most recent joy."*
25. Miscevic, *Lettres*, p. 18 and n. 12. Other sources state that the composer died of an embolism.
26. John Gruen, interview with the composer in *Musical America* 80/5 (April 1960).
27. *Journal*, p. 109.
28. Schmidt, *Entrancing Muse*, p. 442.
29. Carême to Poulenc, 20 January 1961, unpublished letter in the Bibliothèque Nationale.
30. Poulenc to Duval, 19 July 1960: *"When you see your impresario, try to be a little firmer with him . . . this does not make our work any easier."* Poulenc, *Echo and Source*, p. 274; *Correspondance*, pp. 947–48.
31. Bernac, p. 164.
32. Beethoven (Op. 75 No. 3, 1809) and Musorgsky (1879) were among many compos-

ers to have set Mephistopheles' flea song ("Es war einmal ein König") from Goethe's *Faust*.

33. Bernac (p. 165) points out two misprints in the score: there should be two sixteenth notes, not eighth notes, on "sa voi-."

34. There are two songs with texts by Baudelaire, both entitled *Le Chat*, in Sauguet's *Six Mélodies sur des poèmes symbolists* (Nos. V and VI); also *Le Chat* in the Éluard cycle *Les Animaux et leurs hommes*.

35. Bernac, p. 167.

36. The single Mozart work involving a harp is the Concerto for Flute, Harp, and Orchestra, K299/297c.

37. Bernac, p. 168.

38. Poulenc to Brigitte Manceaux, 14 October 1960, Miscevic, *Lettres,* p. 328.

39. Bernac, p. 169.

40. Poulenc to Mario Bois, 12 April 1960, *Correspondance,* p. 946.

41. *Journal,* p. 109. Dufy's *Canotiers aux bords de la Marne* is reproduced in Buckland and Chimènes, opposite p. 256.

42. Cocteau, "Deux Ballets actuels," in *Revue de Paris,* 15 June 1924, pp. 908–16.

43. Poulenc, *J'écris,* pp. 311–14.

44. *Journal,* p. 111.

45. Poulenc, *Notes from the Heart* (ed. Southon, trans. Nichols), p. 174.

46. Schmidt, *Entrancing Muse,* p. 451.

47. *Journal,* p. 113.

48. The embargo against piano performances of *La Voix humaine* (as printed in the vocal score) has been much flouted over the years, although when Felicity Lott and I recorded the "tragédie lyrique," we obtained permission from the Poulenc estate. Poulenc himself played piano for performances with Duval, which is one of the reasons the embargo has been difficult to enforce.

49. Sauguet to Poulenc, 6 December 1961, unpublished letter quoted in Lacombe, p. 768.

50. Auden, "Musée des Beaux Arts" (1938).

51. Lacombe, p. 770.

52. *Journal,* p. 113.

53. Arnaud, *Jean Cocteau,* trans. Lauren Elkin and Charlotte Mandell (London: Yale University Press, 2016), p. 51.

54. As a founder of Les Six, the poet felt he had to qualify as a musician by accompanying Auric and Poulenc on a drum that Stravinsky had lent him. "Given half a chance Cocteau would also perform on the castanets, drinking glasses, the mirliton and a klaxon": John Richardson, quoting Francis Steegmuller (*Cocteau: A Biography,* 1970), in *A Life of Picasso: The Triumphant Years, 1917–1932* (New York: Knopf, 2007), p. 208.

55. *Correspondance,* p. 61.

56. Cocteau, *Cock and Harlequin,* trans. Rollo Myers (London: Egoist Press, 1921), pp. 7 and 11.

57. *Correspondance,* p. 66.

58. Poulenc to Cocteau, 9 February 1919, *Correspondance,* p. 85.

59. Richardson, *Picasso,* p. 169.

60. Bernard Faÿ, *Les Précieux* (Paris: Perrin, 1966), p. 275.

61. Poulenc/Audel, *Moi et mes amis,* p. 52.

62. Poulenc, *Notes from the Heart,* p. 160.

63. Stillmann, "Cocteaux," a review of Arnaud's *Jean Cocteau* in the *London Review of Books*, 13 July 2017.

Poulenc's People: Patrons, Friends, Colleagues, Dedicatees, Publishers

1. Lacombe, p. 206.
2. Poulenc, *J'écris* (ed. Southon), pp. 213 and 432.
3. Unpublished letter from Poulenc to Duval, spring 1959, in Bruno Berenguer, *Denise Duval* (Lyon: Symétrie, 2005), p. 193.
4. Some of these letters have been seen by Sidney Buckland.
5. Poulenc, *J'écris*, pp. 624–27.
6. Ibid., pp. 548–49.
7. Poulenc to Darius Milhaud, 6 September 1950: *"J'aime certainement mieux cela* [Boulez's *Soleil des eaux*] *que la mi-figue mi-raisin de Messiaen"* (I much prefer the Boulez to the mixed bag of Messiaen). *Correspondance*, p. 696.
8. Poulenc to Messiaen, 1 August 1950, *Correspondance*, p. 690.
9. Messiaen to Poulenc, *Correspondance*, p. 983.
10. Poulenc/Audel, *My Friends and Myself*, p. 119.
11. Poulenc/Audel, *Moi et mes amis*, p. 115.
12. Poulenc to Thomson, *Correspondance*, pp. 650–51.
13. Burton, p. 42.
14. Poulenc, *J'écris*, p. 401.
15. Poulenc to Lerolle (regarding FP46), 9 February 1934, *Correspondance*, p. 392.
16. Poulenc to Milhaud, 28 December 1945, *Correspondance*, p. 615.
17. Poulenc, *J'écris*, p. 121.
18. Ibid, p. 455.

The Masks and Myths of Francis Poulenc, and His Eventual Triumph

1. Pierre Caizergues, *Jean Cocteau, la musique et les musiciens*, p. 11; in Lacombe, p. 246.
2. Poulenc, *Notes from the Heart* (ed. Southon, trans. Nichols), pp. 149–51.
3. Martine Cadieu, in Poulenc, *J'écris* (ed. Southon), p. 662.
4. Rorem, *Settling the Score: Essays on Music* (New York: Anchor Doubleday, 1989), p. 126.
5. Buckland and Chimènes, p. 6.
6. *Correspondance*, plate 18. The photograph was taken at Kerbastic (in Brittany) in 1939.
7. Poulenc, *J'écris*, p. 453.
8. John Howard Griffin, "The Poulenc Behind the Mask," in *Ramparts* Magazine (October 1964), pp. 6–8; reprinted in *The John Howard Griffin Reader* (Boston: Houghton Mifflin, 1968), p. 568; and in Schmidt, *Enchanting Muse*, pp. 394–95.
9. Maurice Sachs, *The Decade of Illusion: Paris, 1918–1928* (New York: Knopf, 1933), pp. 29–30.
10. Lacombe, p. 259.
11. Schmidt, *Entrancing Muse*, p. 427, n. 43.
12. Cocteau, *Le Passé défini* (Paris: Gallimard, 2011), 6:416. Quoted in Lacombe, p. 367.
13. Erica Dahan, conversation with Denise Duval in *Libération*, 6 November 2004. Quoted in Lacombe, p. 367.

14. Cocteau, *Le Passé défini*, 6:472; quoted in Lacombe, p. 730.

15. Poulenc/Audel, *My Friends and Myself*, p. 15.

16. See Poulenc's description of the composition of *Montparnasse* in *Journal*, pp. 75–77.

17. William Butler Yeats, "The Circus Animals' Desertion" (1937–38).

18. Burton, p. 9, provides a fascinating history of this anomaly, which goes back to the days of the French Revolution and Napoleonic code.

19. Rorem, *The Later Diaries: 1961–1972* (New York: North Point Press, 1983), p. 101.

20. I am grateful to Dr. David Foreman, Consultant and Visiting Professor in Child and Adolescent Psychiatry (Isle of Man), for discussions on this subject.

21. Goldstein, *Village Voice* (1983), quoted in the *London Review of Books*, 27 September 2018, p. 8.

22. I am taking the present-day laws of Europe and the United States as benchmarks here, not repressive sexual legislations in the Middle and Far East, and in many parts of Africa.

23. Article in *Ballet*, September 1946; in Poulenc, *Notes from the Heart*, p. 40.

24. See Paul Bailey's essay "Poulenc's Priest" in Bailey, *Censoring Sexuality* (Chicago: Seagull Books, 2007).

25. Griffin, "The Poulenc Behind the Mask," pp. 6–8.

26. Rorem, *The Paris Diary* (New York: Braziller, 1966), p. 211. Poulenc was in Cannes, recovered from his long illness but looking old and covered with pimples. "As he's always been le cher maître in my eyes, I was chilled by his talk of sexual success."

27. Poulenc to Girard, 6 March 1957, *Correspondance*, pp. 863–64.

28. Interview 8 with Claude Rostand, in Poulenc, *Notes from the Heart*, p. 221.

29. Myriam Chimènes, *Pierre Bernac, interprète et pedagogue*, quoted in *Correspondance*, p. 1012.

30. Bernac's single state is suggested perhaps by a line in a song from *Tel jour telle nuit* that is dedicated to him. The song is *Figure de force brûlante et farouche*, and the line is "Dans un lit jamais partagé" (In a bed never shared).

31. Poulenc to Bernac, August 1954, *Correspondance*, p. 803; translated in Poulenc, *Echo and Source*, p. 225. It is not certain that Bernac sent this letter.

32. Schmidt, *Entrancing Muse*, p. 395.

33. Alexis de Tocqueville (1805–1859), *Voyage en Angleterre et en Irlande de 1835*.

Bibliography

Bernac, Pierre. *Francis Poulenc: The Man and His Songs*. Foreword by Sir Lennox Berkeley. Translations of song texts by Winifred Radford. London: Victor Gollancz, 1977. London: Kahn and Averill, 2002. Footnotes citing "Bernac" refer to this book.

———. *The Interpretation of French Song*. Translations of song texts by Winifred Radford. London: Cassell, 1970. New York: Norton, 1978.

Buckland, Sidney, and Myriam Chimènes, eds. *Francis Poulenc: Music, Art and Literature*. Aldershot, UK: Ashgate, 1999. Fourteen chapters by different authors (including the editors) concerning various aspects of Poulenc's life and work.

Burton, Richard D. E. *Francis Poulenc*. London: Absolute Press, 2002.

Chimènes, Myriam. *La Vie musicale sous Vichy*. Brussels: Éditions Complexe, 2001.

———, and Yannick Simon, eds. *La Musique à Paris sous L'Occupation*. Paris: Fayard, 2013.

Conrad, Doda. *Dodascalies: Ma Chronique du XXe siècle*. Arles: Actes Sud, 1997.

Hell, Henri. *Francis Poulenc, musicien français*. Paris: Plon, 1958. 2nd rev. ed. Paris: Fayard, 1978. The first full-length biography.

Ivry, Benjamin. *Francis Poulenc*. London: Phaidon Press, 1996.

Johnson, Graham (with Richard Stokes). *A French Song Companion*. New York: Oxford University Press, 2000.

Jourdan-Morhange, Hélène. *Mes Amis musiciens*. Paris: Éditeurs Français Reunis, 1955.

Lacombe, Hervé. *Francis Poulenc*. Paris: Fayard, 2013. The most recent full-length biography.

———, and Nicolas Southon, eds. *Fortune de Francis Poulenc: Diffusion, interprétation, réception*. Presses Universitaires de Rennes, 2016.

Le Roux, François, and Roman Raynaldy. *Le Chant intime*. Paris: Fayard, 2004.

Machart, Renaud. *Poulenc*. Paris: Seuil, 1995.

Mellers, Willfred. *Francis Poulenc*. Oxford Studies of Composers. Oxford: Oxford University Press, 1993.

Miscevic, Pierre, ed. *Francis Poulenc et la mélodie*. Catalogue of exhibition, Musée des Beaux-Arts, Tours, 1 July to 31 August 2016.

———. *Lettres inédites à Brigitte Manceaux*. Paris: Éditions Orizons, 2019.

———, and Doriana Fournier. *Poulenc et l'Italie*, Catalogues d'exposition. Rome: Ambassade de France en Italie, 2006.

Poulenc, Francis. *À bâtons rompus*. Radio transcripts [in French]. Edited by Lucie Kayas. Arles: Actes Sud, 1999.

———. *Correspondance, 1915–1963*. Edited by Hélène de Wendel. Preface by Darius Milhaud. Paris: Seuil, 1967.

———. *Correspondance, 1910–1963*. Edited by Myriam Chimènes. Paris: Fayard, 1994. Footnote citations refer to this source.

———. *Echo and Source: Selected Correspondence, 1915–1963*. Translated and edited by Sidney Buckland. London: Victor Gollancz, 1991.

———. *Emmanuel Chabrier*. Paris: La Palatine, 1961.

———. *J'écris ce qui me chante* [I write what sings to me]. Edited by Nicolas Southon. Paris: Fayard, 2011. This comprehensive collection of 120 occasional texts includes not only articles and interviews but reprintings of entire books: Audel's *Moi et mes amis, Entretiens avec Claude Rostand*, and Poulenc's monograph *Emmanuel Chabrier*.

———. *Journal de mes mélodies*. Avant-propos by Henri Sauguet. Paris: Grasset, 1964.

———. *Journal de mes mélodies (Diary of My Songs)*. Bilingual edition, translated by Winifred Radford. Additional notes by Patrick Saul. Introduction by Graham Johnson. London: Gollancz, 1985. Unless otherwise noted, footnotes citing the *Journal* refer to this edition.

———. *Journal de mes mélodies*. Édition intégrale (unexpurgated edition). Edited by Renaud Machart. Paris: Cicero with Salabert, 1995.

———. *Moi et mes amis*. Confidences receuillies par Stéphane Audel. Paris: La Palatine, 1963.

———. *My Friends and Myself*. Conversations assembled by Stéphane Audel. Translated by James Harding. London: Dobson, 1978.

———. *Notes from the Heart*. Edited by Nicolas Southon. Translated by Roger Nichols. Farnham, UK: Ashgate, 2014. Selected items from the much larger Southon collection *J'écris ce qui me chante*. The 18 *Interviews with Claude Rostand* quoted throughout are from this source and in Nichols's translations.

Roy, Jean. *Francis Poulenc*. Paris: Seghers, 1964.

———. *Le Groupe des Six*. Paris: Seuil, 1994.

Saint-Marceaux, Marguerite de. *Journal, 1894–1927*. Edited by Myriam Chimènes. Paris: Fayard, 2007.

Schmidt, Carl B. *Enchanting Muse: A Documented Biography of Francis Poulenc*. Hillsdale, NY: Pendragon Press, 2001.

———. *The Music of Francis Poulenc: A Catalogue*. Oxford: Clarendon Press, 1991.

Woods, Vivian Lee Poates. *Poulenc's Songs: An Analysis of Style*. Jackson: University Press of Mississippi, 1979.

Credits

Illustrations

Poetry

Index of Song Titles

Titles in **bold** indicate song cycles. Page numbers in *italics* indicate illustrations.

Index of Names

Page numbers in *italics* indicate illustrations.

Snow, Carmel, 245

Soulé, Françoise, 247

Soulé, Jacques, as dedicatee, 320, 479

Soupault, Philippe, 145, 291

Southon, Nicolas, 494

Souvtchinsky, Pierre, 345
  as dedicatee, 298, 479

Souzay, Gérard, 62, 98, 233, 346, 360, 434,
      506n116
  as dedicatee, 314, 317, 478

Steegmuller, Francis, 520n54

Stein, Erwin, 422

Stein, Gertrude, 468

Stillman, Anne, 469

Stimer, David, 359

Stockhausen, Julius, 333

Stockhausen, Karlheinz, xiii

Straram, Walter, 490, 491

Straus, Oscar
  Les Trois Valses, 148
  Mariette, 148

Strauss, Richard
  Allerseelen, 111
  operas of, 84
  Der Rosenkavalier, 256–57
  Salome, 345

Stravinsky, Igor, 51, 55, 166–67, 251, 342
  Cantata, 350
  Canticum sacrum, 358
  Capriccio, 81
  as dedicatee, 368, 369, 370, 478
  Mavra, 41
  neoclassical works, 113, 115
  Les Noces, 41–42, 45, 210, 231, 240, 439
  Oedipus Rex, 68, 116, 468
  Pastorale, 68
  Perséphone, 83
  piano of, 210
  Poulenc and, 8, 44, 476, 480
  Pulcinella, 39, 62, 189
  The Rake's Progress, 344, 349, 363, 426
  Renard, 351

The Rite of Spring, 7, 349
  Serenade in A, 371, 408
  serial music of, 357
  Symphony of Psalms, 79
  Trois Histoires pour enfants, 241

Stravinsky, Soulima, 86, 231

Stravinsky, Vera, 251

Stuck, Franz von, 404

Stuna, Joseph, 417, 418

Suarès, André, 51

Suchodolski, Rajnold, 124–25

Sutherland, Joan, 149, 362

Szymanowski, Karol, 48

Tailleferre, Germaine, xv, 46, 51, 249, 347,
      476, 516n131
  Les Six and, 39
  Poulenc and, 9

Talmadge, Constance, 505n85

Tati, Jacques, 426

Tebaldi, Renata, 348, 367

Tesarova, Alena, 417

Teyte, Maggie, 7, 86, 241

Thomson, Virgil, 249, 250, 386, 433, 477,
      516n131
  Cello Concerto, 342
  Four Saints in Three Acts, 347, 427

Tilliard, Simone, as dedicatee, 320, 479

Tinan, "Dolly" de, 440

Torres, Manuel, 314

Toscanini, Arturo, 81, 250

Toulouse-Lautrec, Henri, 387

Toumanova, Tamara, 44

Touraine, Geneviève, 86, 233, 353
  as dedicatee, 314, 317, 478

Tragin, Lucienne, 237

Trefusis, Violet, 82, 183, 502–3n7

Triolet, Elsa, 291, 292, 297

Trutat, Jacqueline, 145, 147

Tully, Alice, 390

Tunnard, Viola, 363, 426

Tzara, Tristan, 29, 40, 310